The Poet
William Wordsworth

Volume III

Return, Content! for fondly I pursued,
Even when a child, the Streams—unheard, unseen;
Through tangled woods, impending rocks between;

Humanities-Ebooks

Humanities-Ebooks publishes primarily in electronic form and its Ebooks (with the facility of word and phrase search, and in some cases both internal and external hyperlinks) are available to private purchasers exclusively from http://www.humanities-ebooks.co.uk and to libraries from Ebrary, EBSCO and Ingram

Other Wordsworth Titles from Humanities-Ebooks

The Fenwick Notes of William Wordsworth, edited by Jared Curtis †

The Cornell Wordsworth: A Supplement, edited by Jared Curtis ††

The Prose Works of William Wordsworth, Volume 1, edited by W. J. B. Owen and Jane Worthington Smyser †

Wordsworth's Convention of Cintra, a Bicentennial Critical Edition, edited by W. J. B Owen, with a critical symposium by Simon Bainbridge, David Bromwich, Richard Gravil, Timothy Michael and Patrick Vincent

Wordsworth's Political Writings, edited by W. J. B. Owen and Jane Worthington Smyser. Reading texts of *A Letter to the Bishop of Llandaff*, *The Convention of Cintra*, *Two Addresses to the Freeholders of Westmorland*, and the 1835 *Postscript*. †

Richard Garvil, *Wordsworth's Bardic Vocation, 1787–1842* †

† ebook and paperback
†† ebook and hardback

The Poems of William Wordsworth

COLLECTED READING TEXTS
FROM
THE CORNELL WORDSWORTH SERIES

VOLUME III

EDITED BY JARED CURTIS

HEB ☼ Humanities-Ebooks, LLP

First published by *Humanities-Ebooks, LLP,*
Tirril Hall, Tirril, Penrith CA10 2JE.

4th printing, corrected, March 2014.

Cover image, from Great Dodd, © Richard Gravil.

The reading texts of Wordsworth's poems used in this volume are from the Cornell Wordsworth series, published by Cornell University Press, Sage House, 512 East State Street, Ithaca, NY 14850. Copyright © Cornell University. Volumes are available at: http://www.cornellpress.cornell.edu

ISBN 978-1-84760-087-5 EBOOK
ISBN 978-1-84760-091-2 PAPERBACK

Contents

Contents of volumes I and II

Preface

The Cornell Wordsworth series, under the general editorship of Stephen Parrish, began appearing in 1975. Through controversy and acclaim, the editions have steadily appeared over three decades, coming to completion in 2007 with the publication of the twenty-first volume—an edition of *The Excursion*—and a supplementary volume of indexes and guides for the series. The purpose of this edition is to collect all of the earliest complete reading texts garnered from the twenty-one volumes in the series.

The earliest records of Wordsworth's poetic composition date from 1785, when he was fifteen years old, and the latest date from 1847, when he was seventy-seven. In the interim he composed hundreds of poems, thousands of verses, not all of which reached—or survived in—a "completed" state. All of those that did are included here. If William Butler Yeats was remarkable for reinventing his poetic self, Wordsworth might be said to have constantly "revisited" his. Three of his lyrics bear the revealing sequential titles, "Yarrow Unvisited" (1803), "Yarrow Visited" (1814), and "Yarrow Revisited" (1831). In the first, the poet-traveler prefers his imagined Yarrow—the Yarrow of Scots balladeers Nicol Burne, John Logan, and William Hamilton—to the physical one. In the second, the "genuine" Yarrow engenders an image that

> Will dwell with me—to heighten joy,
> And cheer my mind in sorrow.

And the third pays tribute to his friend and fellow poet, Walter Scott, with whom he toured the Yarrow valley before the ailing Scott departed for Italy: in this time of "change and changing," he prays that the valley maintain its power to restore "brightness" to "the soul's deep valley." Significant threads of Wordsworth's development as a poet are embodied in these three elegiac tributes. They are all written in a ballad stanza that Wordsworth borrowed and adapted from the older Scots poets. A glance through the pages of this volume will illustrate the varied verse forms the poet adopted and transformed over his long career. Obvious favorites were his own meditative style of blank verse and the sonnet in its various guises. But he employed a variety of meters, stanzaic patterns, and rhyme schemes in producing poems ranging from ballads to autobiography, satirical squibs to verse romance, from epitaphs to royal tributes. The methods, too, of the three "Yarrows" are instructive. The primacy of the imagination is suggested in the poet's reluctance to visit the famed valley; upon visiting the place, the poet's response is to preserve it in memory as a "spot of time" to bind his days, "each to each" as a remedy for future sorrow; and on revisiting the valley he acknowledges that sorrow and attempts to recharge the healing power of memory.

Another example of "revisiting" can be found in the restless energy that Wordsworth displayed over his entire writing life in composing sonnets, both singly, as apparently instant responses to present scene, public event, or personal history, and in series, building both narrative and argument through this highly adaptive form. And, occupying the center of this metaphor are the several attempts to write the story of his inner life as a poet, here represented in the three versions of *The Prelude.*

Annotation is confined largely to reproducing the notes Wordsworth published with his poems. Editorial commentary has been kept to a minimum, given the rich resource in each of the Cornell Wordsworth volumes, leaving room instead for the poetry. For information about the source of the text, its compositional history, its textual and interpretive annotation, and its social and historical context, the reader is referred to the appropriate volumes in the series, cited in the editor's notes at the end of each volume.

Acknowledgments

For the impetus to prepare such an edition and for his continuing and enthusiastic support for its completion I owe thanks to Stephen Parrish. I have gained from fruitful discussions with James Butler, Stephen Gill, and Mark Reed from the beginning stages, and for making my task easier by helping with proofreading and other tasks, I especially thank James and Mark. I owe thanks, too, to the editors who prepared each of the editions from which the reading texts making up this edition were drawn. All of them are acknowledged by name, and their work cited, in the editor's notes. None of these generous scholars can be held responsible for any flaws in detail or judgment. I am pleased to acknowledge the Wordsworth Trust for graciously permitting the use of materials from their collections and Cornell University Press for both the permission and the assistance needed to prepare this gathering of reading texts from their landmark series of Wordsworth editions. And for wise counsel and technical assistance in the enterprize of producing an electronic text of these volumes, I am grateful to Richard Gravil of Humanities-Ebooks.

Note on the Text

The source for each poem is the earliest and most complete reading text presented in the volume in the Cornell Wordsworth series that contains that poem. With the few exceptions noted below, no attempt has been made to include the many alternate readings and revisions that these volumes provide. Early evidence of Wordsworth revisiting his own work is found in the two versions of *Pity* ("Now too while o'er the heart we feel") and in the "extracts" from *The Vale of Esthwaite*; both the original poems and their later development are included. In the case of *The Prelude*, each of the three versions that stood as complete is represented. In 1799 Wordsworth revised the ending to *The Ruined Cottage*, within a year of composing the first ending, and in 1803–1804 incorporated much of the earlier poem in an expanded portrait of the Pedlar in *The Pedlar*. Wordsworth then incorporated large parts of both poems into *The Excursion* in 1814. These three distinct poems are included. Wordsworth occasionally folded a free-standing sonnet into a subsequent sonnet series or sequence, in which case the free-standing sonnet is repeated in its later context.

The aim throughout has been to present clean reading texts of Wordsworth's poems. In most cases the poet's and his earliest printers' orthography has not been altered, though some exceptions have been made for consistency. To distinguish a poem originally published without a title from poems that immediately precede or follow it, I have used the familiar anthologist's convention of quoting the first line of the poem as its "title," even though neither Wordsworth nor his publishers did so.

A few editorial devices have proven necessary, especially where the source for the reading text is a manuscript. For further comment on the gaps and irregularities in the manuscript sources, see the original Cornell editions.

[   ]   A gap in the source, either left by the poet, or caused by a dam-
           aged manuscript.

[word]   Within the brackets are missing letters or words, supplied from
           a different authorial source, or by the editor; in a few instances,
           brackets enclose lines that Wordsworth apparently canceled,
           but without indicating a substitute.

** —   Asterisks and solid lines, employed by Wordsworth to indicate
           omissions or breaks in the text.

═══   A double solid line, used by the editor to indicate an interrup-
           tion in the text.

Wordsworth's long notes, prose dedications, and other prose writings con-nected to the poems, are gathered in the "Notes" section at the end of the volume, and their presence is indicated in the on-page notes.

Jared Curtis
Seattle, Washington

Shorter Poems (1807–1820)[1]

"Mark the concentred Hazels that enclose"

Mark the concentred Hazels that enclose
Yon old grey Stone, protected from the ray
Of noontide suns:—and even the beams that play
And glance, while wantonly the rough wind blows,
Are seldom free to touch the moss that grows   5
Upon that roof—amid embowering gloom
The very image framing of a Tomb,
In which some ancient Chieftain finds repose
Among the lonely mountains.—Live, ye Trees!
And Thou, grey Stone, the pensive likeness keep   10
Of a dark chamber where the Mighty sleep:
For more than Fancy to the influence bends
When solitary Nature condescends
To mimic Time's forlorn humanities.

"The Shepherd, looking eastward, softly said"

The Shepherd, looking eastward, softly said,
"Bright is thy veil, O Moon, as thou art bright!"
Forthwith, that little Cloud, in ether spread,
And penetrated all with tender light,
She cast away, and shewed her fulgent head   5
Uncover'd;—dazzling the Beholder's sight
As if to vindicate her beauty's right,
Her beauty thoughtlessly disparaged.
Meanwhile that Veil, removed or thrown aside,
Went, floating from her, darkening as it went;   10
And a huge Mass, to bury or to hide,
Approached this glory of the firmament;
Who meekly yields, and is obscur'd;—content
With one calm triumph of a modest pride.

---

1 For the sources of the reading texts and the editor's commentary see *Shorter Poems, 1807–1820*, ed. Carl H. Ketcham (1989).

"Eve's lingering clouds extend in solid bars"

Eve's lingering clouds extend in solid bars
Through the grey west; and lo! these waters, steeled
By breezeless air to smoothest polish, yield
A vivid repetition of the stars;
Jove—Venus—and the ruddy crest of Mars,   5
Amid his fellows, beauteously revealed
At happy distance from earth's groaning field,
Where ruthless mortals wage incessant wars.
Is it a mirror?—or the nether sphere
Opening its vast abyss, while fancy feeds   10
On the rich show!—But list! a voice is near;
Great Pan himself low-whispering through the reeds,
"Be thankful thou; for, if unholy deeds
Ravage the world, tranquillity is here!"

Sonnet on Milton[1]

Amid the dark control of lawless sway,
Ambitions, rivalry, fanatic hate
And various ills that shook the unsettled State,
The dauntless Bard pursued his studious way,
Not more his lofty genius to display,   5
Than raise and dignify our mortal date,
And sing the blessings which the Just await,
That Man might hence in humble hope obey.
Thus on a rock in Norway's bleak domain,
Nature impels the stately Pine to grow;   10
[   ]
And restless Ocean dashes all below:
Still he preserves his firm majestic reign
While added strength his spreading branches shew.

---

1   "The subject from Symonds's *Life*." WW's MS. note. DW left a gap in the manuscript
    at l. 11.

Elegiac Stanzas,

COMPOSED IN THE CHURCHYARD OF GRASMERE, WESTMORLAND,
A FEW DAYS AFTER THE INTERMENT THERE, OF A MAN AND
HIS WIFE, INHABITANTS OF THE VALE, WHO WERE LOST
UPON THE NEIGHBOURING MOUNTAINS, ON THE NIGHT
OF THE NINETEENTH OF MARCH LAST

Who weeps for Strangers?—Many wept
For George and Sarah Green;
Wept for that Pair's unhappy end,
Whose Grave may here be seen.

By night, upon these stormy Heights   5
Did Wife and Husband roam:
Six little-Ones the Pair had left
And could not find their Home.

 For any Dwelling-place of men
As vainly did they seek.—   10
He perish'd, and a voice was heard,
The Widow's lonely shriek.

Down the dark precipice he fell,
And she was left alone,
Not long to think of her Children dear,   15
Not long to pray or groan!

A few wild steps—she too was left,
A Body without life!
The chain of but a few wild steps
To the Husband bound the Wife.   20

Now lodge they in one Grave, this Grave,
A House with two-fold Roof,
Two Hillocks but one Grave, their own,
A covert tempest-proof.

And from all agony of mind   25
It keeps them safe and far,

From fear, and from all need of hope,
From sun, or guiding Star.

Our peace is of the immortal Soul,
Our anguish is of clay;   30
Such bounty is in Heaven, so pass
The bitterest pangs away.

———

Three days did teach the Mother's Babe
Forgetfully to rest
In reconcilement how serene!   35
Upon another's breast.

———

The trouble of the elder Brood
I know not that it stay'd
So long—they seiz'd their joy, and They
Have sung, and danc'd, and play'd.   40

———

Now do the sternly-featur'd Hills
Look gently on this Grave,
And quiet now is the depth of air
As a sea without a wave.

———

But deeper lies the heart of peace,   45
In shelter more profound;
The heart of quietness is here,
Within this Church-yard ground.

———

O Darkness of the Grave! how calm
After that living night,   50
That last and dreary living one
Of sorrow and affright!

O sacred Marriage-bed of Death
That holds them side by side,
In bond of love, in bond of God,   55
Which may not be untied!

"A few bold Patriots, Reliques of the Fight"[1]

A few bold Patriots, Reliques of the Fight
That crush'd the Gothic sovereignty of Spain,
Beneath Pelayo's banner did unite;
In hope they from the Arabian crescent fled,
And when their steps had measured [   ] Plain,   5
Cross'd Deva's [   ] flood and [   ] snow-clad Height,
And wound through depth of many a sunless Vale
On which the noontide dew lay wet and pale,
And now had reach'd Auseva's rugged breast,
The Leader turn'd, and from a jutting rock,   10
Calm as a Shepherd beck'ning to his flock,
    The little band addrest.

"Stop, Christian Warriors, faithful and undaunted!
This Hill shall be our Fortress and the gloom
Of yon wide Cave our harbour or our tomb.   15
Yet if the Saints and pitying Angels bless
The efforts of the brave in their distress,
Not vainly shall your Standard here be planted!
With swords to guard our Virtue are we come
To these Asturian Wilds, a proud retreat   20
Where Friends surround us in their antient seat,
An inextinguishable people's home.
Aloft while here we hover, night and day
Shall multiply our host and strengthen our array.

—What earthly power can check the gathering clouds   25
When from afar, along the craggy chain
Of these huge mountains they appear in crowds?
What mortal enmity the work restrain?
Which an impenetrable darkness shrouds
While steadfastly embodied they remain,   30
Feeding a silent force of thunder, wind, and rain,
Which at the sovereign word
Of their almighty Lord
Breaks forth and spreads in ravage o'er the plain—

---

1 This version is the earliest recoverable beneath later revisions. The poem was left
   incomplete.

No otherwise shall we descend and quell   35
The astounded Infidel.

"Meanwhile till Heav'n, O patient Warriors, call
Our Valor to the onset, yon wide Cave
Which opens like a ready grave
For *desperate* Fugitives, to us shall be   40
A Legislative Hall
Chear'd by the gladsome voice of Liberty;
   And to that Sanctuary dark
   Will we entrust the holy Ark,
   The Covenant of the faith   45
   That saves the soul from death,
And shall uphold our frail and mortal hands
Till we, or men as brave, the favored bands
Of our exalted Countrymen, regain
For Lordship without end the fields of Universal Spain."   50

Thus spake Pelayo on his chosen Hill;
And shall at this late [   ] the Heavens belie
The heroic prophecy
And put to shame the great Diviner's skill?
The Power which, issuing like a slender rill   55
From those high places, waxed by slow degrees,
Swoln with access of many sovereignties,
And gained a River's strength and rolled a mighty wave—
   The Stream which in Pelayo's Cave
Upon the illustrious Mountain took its birth—   60
Has disappeared from earth:
A foreign Tyrant speaks his impious will,
And Spain hath own'd the Monarch which he gave.

Most horrible attempt! unthought-of hour
Of human shame and black indignity!   65
Alas, not unprovoked those Tempests low'r,
Not uninvited this malignity.
Full long relinquishing a precious dower
By Gothic Virtue won, secured by oath
Of king and people pledged in mutual troth,   70
The Spaniard hath approached on servile knee
The native Ruler; all too willingly

Full many an age in that degenerate Land
The rightful Master hath betrayed his trust.
Earthward the Imperial flower was bent   75
   In mortal languishment;
This knew the Spoiler whose victorious hand
Hath snapp'd th'enfeebled Stalk and laid its head in dust.

"Say, what is Honour?—Tis the finest sense"

Say, what is Honour?—Tis the finest sense
Of *justice* which the human mind can frame,
Intent each lurking frailty to disclaim,
And guard the way of life from all offence
Suffered or done. When lawless violence   5
A Kingdom doth assault, and in the scale
Of perilous war her weightiest Armies fail,
Honour is hopeful elevation—whence
Glory—and Triumph. Yet with politic skill
Endangered States may yield to terms unjust,   10
Stoop their proud heads;—but not unto the dust,—
A Foe's most favourite purpose to fulfil!
Happy occasions oft by self-mistrust
Are forfeited; but infamy doth kill.

Composed while the Author was Engaged in Writing a Tract, Occasioned by the Convention of Cintra, 1808

Not 'mid the World's vain objects that enslave
The free-born Soul,—that world whose vaunted skill
In selfish interest perverts the will,
Whose factions lead astray the wise and brave;
Not there! but in dark wood and rocky cave,   5
And hollow vale which foaming torrents fill
With omnipresent murmur as they rave
Down their steep beds that never shall be still:
Here, mighty Nature!—in this school sublime
I weigh the hopes and fears of suffering Spain: 10
For her consult the auguries of time,
And through the human heart explore my way,
And look and listen,—gathering where I may
Triumph, and thoughts no bondage can restrain.

Composed at the Same Time, and on the Same Occasion

I dropped my pen;—and listened to the wind
That sang of trees up-torn and vessels tost;
—A midnight harmony, and wholly lost
To the general sense of men by chains confined
Of business, care, or pleasure,—or resigned   5
To timely sleep.— Thought I, the impassioned strain,
Which, without aid of numbers, I sustain,
Like acceptation from the World will find.
Yet some with apprehensive ear shall drink
A dirge devoutly breathed o'er sorrows past,   10
And to the attendant promise will give heed,
The prophecy,—like that of this wild blast,
Which, while it makes the heart with sadness shrink,
Tells also of bright calms that shall succeed.

"Hail, Zaragoza! If with unwet eye"

Hail, Zaragoza! If with unwet eye
We can approach, thy sorrow to behold,
Yet is the heart not pitiless nor cold;
Such spectacle demands not tear or sigh.
These desolate Remains are trophies high   5
Of more than martial courage in the breast
Of peaceful civic virtue: they attest
Thy matchless worth to all posterity.
Blood flowed before thy sight without remorse;
Disease consumed thy vitals; War upheaved   10
The ground beneath thee with volcanic force;
Dread trials! yet encountered and sustained
Till not a wreck of help or hope remained,
And Law was from *necessity* received.

1810

Ah! where is Palafox? Nor tongue nor pen
Reports of him, his dwelling or his grave!
Does yet the unheard-of Vessel ride the wave?
Or is she swallowed up—remote from ken
Of pitying human nature? Once again   5

Methinks that we shall hail thee, Champion brave,
Redeemed to baffle that imperial Slave;
And through all Europe cheer desponding men
With new-born hope. Unbounded is the might
Of martyrdom, and fortitude, and right.   10
Hark, how thy Country triumphs!—Smilingly
The Eternal looks upon her sword that gleams,
Like his own lightning, over mountains high,
On rampart, and the banks of all her streams.

"Call not the royal Swede unfortunate"

Call not the royal Swede unfortunate
Who never did to Fortune bend the knee;
Who slighted fear,—rejected steadfastly
Temptation; and whose kingly name and state
Have "perished by his choice, and not his fate!"   5
Hence lives He, to his inner self endeared;
And hence, wherever virtue is revered,
He sits a more exalted Potentate,
Throned in the hearts of men. Should Heaven ordain
That this great Servant of a righteous cause   10
Must still have sad or vexing thoughts to endure,
Yet may a sympathizing spirit pause,
Admonished by these truths, and quench all pain
In thankful joy and gratulation pure.

"Look now on that Adventurer who hath paid"

Look now on that Adventurer who hath paid
His vows to Fortune; who, in cruel slight
Of virtuous hope, of liberty, and right,
Hath followed wheresoe'er a way was made
By the blind Goddess;—ruthless, undismayed;   5
And so hath gained at length a prosperous Height,
Round which the Elements of worldly might
Beneath his haughty feet, like clouds, are laid.
O joyless power that stands by lawless force!
Curses are *his* dire portion, scorn, and hate,   10
Internal darkness and unquiet breath;
And, if old judgments keep their sacred course,

Him from that Height shall Heaven precipitate
By violent and ignominious death.

"Is there a Power that can sustain and cheer"

Is there a Power that can sustain and cheer
The captive Chieftain—by a Tyrant's doom
Forced to descend alive into his tomb,
A dungeon dark!—where he must waste the year,
And lie cut off from all his heart holds dear;   5
What time his injured Country is a stage
Whereon deliberate Yalour and the Rage
Of righteous Vengeance side by side appear,—
Filling from morn to night the heroic scene
With deeds of hope and everlasting praise: 10
Say can he think of this with mind serene
And silent fetters?— Yes, if visions bright
Shine on his soul, reflected from the days
When he himself was tried in open light.

"Brave Schill! by death delivered, take thy flight"

Brave Schill! by death delivered, take thy flight
From Prussia's timid region. Go, and rest
With Heroes 'mid the Islands of the Blest,
Or in the Fields of empyrean light.
A Meteor wert thou in a darksome night;   5
Yet shall thy name, conspicuous and sublime,
Stand in the spacious firmament of time,
Fixed as a star: such glory is thy right.
Alas! it may not be: for earthly fame
Is Fortune's frail dependant; yet there lives   10
A Judge, who, as man claims by merit, gives;
To whose all-pondering mind a noble aim,
Faithfully kept, is as a noble deed;
In whose pure sight all virtue doth succeed.

Feelings of the Tyrolese

The Land we from our Fathers had in trust,
And to our Children will transmit, or die:
This is our maxim, this our piety;

And God and Nature say that it is just.
That which we *would* perform in arms—we must!   5
We read the dictate in the Infant's eye;
In the Wife's smile; and in the placid sky;
And, at our feet, amid the silent dust
Of them that were before us.—Sing aloud
Old Songs, the precious music of the heart!   10
Give, Herds and Flocks! your voices to the wind!
While we go forth, a self-devoted crowd,
With weapons in the fearless hand, to assert
Our virtue, and to vindicate mankind.

"Alas! what boots the long, laborious quest"

Alas! what boots the long, laborious quest
Of moral prudence, sought through good and ill,
Or pains abstruse, to elevate the will,
And lead us on to that transcend-ant rest
Where every passion shall the sway attest   5
Of Reason seated on her sovereign hill;—
What is it but a vain and curious skill,
If sapient Germany must lie deprest,
Beneath the brutal sword?—Her haughty Schools
Shall blush; and may not we with sorrow say,   10
A few strong instincts and a few plain rules,
Among the herdsmen of the Alps, have wrought
More for mankind at this unhappy day
Than all the pride of intellect and thought.

"And is it among rude untutored Dales"

And is it among rude untutored Dales,
There, and there only, that the heart is true?
And, rising to repel or to subdue,
Is it by rocks and woods that man prevails?
Ah, no!—though Nature's dread protection fails   5
There is a bulwark in the *soul*.— This knew
Iberian Burghers when the sword they drew
In Zaragoza, naked to the gales
Of fiercely-breathing war. The truth was felt
By Palafox, and many a brave Compeer,   10

Like him of noble birth and noble mind;
By Ladies, meek-eyed Women without fear;
And Wanderers of the street, to whom is dealt
The bread which without industry they find.

"O'er the wide earth, on mountain and on plain"

O'er the wide earth, on mountain and on plain,
Dwells in the affections and the soul of man
A Godhead, like the universal PAN,
But more exalted, with a brighter train.
And shall his bounty be dispensed in vain,   5
Showered equally on City and on Field,
And neither hope nor steadfast promise yield
In these usurping times of fear and pain?
Such doom awaits us.—Nay, forbid it Heaven!
We know the arduous strife, the eternal laws   10
To which the triumph of all good is given,
High sacrifice, and labour without pause,
Even to the death:—else wherefore should the eye
Of man converse with immortality?

"Advance—come forth from thy Tyrolean ground"

Advance—come forth from thy Tyrolean ground
Dear Liberty!—stern Nymph of soul untamed,
Sweet Nymph, Oh! rightly of the mountains named!
Through the long chain of Alps from mound to mound
And o'er the eternal snows, like Echo, bound,—   5
Like Echo, when the Hunter-train at dawn
Have rouzed her from her sleep: and forest-lawn,
Cliffs, woods, and caves her viewless steps resound
And babble of her pastime!—On, dread Power,
With such invisible motion speed thy flight,   10
Through hanging clouds, from craggy height to height,
Through the green vales and through the Herdsman's bower,
That all the Alps may gladden in thy might,
Here, there, and in all places at one hour.

Hôffer

Of mortal Parents is the Hero born

By whom the undaunted Tyrolese are led?
Or is it Tell's great Spirit, from the dead
Returned to animate an age forlorn?
He comes like Phœbus through the gates of morn   5
When dreary darkness is discomfited:
Yet mark his modest state!—upon his head,
That simple crest—a heron's plume—is worn.
O Liberty! they stagger at the shock;
The Murderers are aghast; they strive to flee   10
And half their Host is buried:—rock on rock
Descends:—beneath this godlike Warrior, see!
Hills, Torrents, Woods, embodied to bemock
The Tyrant, and confound his cruelty.

On the Final Submission of the Tyrolese

It was a *moral* end for which they fought;
Else how, when mighty Thrones were put to shame,
Could they, poor Shepherds, have preserved an aim,
A resolution, or enlivening thought?
Nor hath that moral good been *vainly* sought;   5
For in their magnanimity and fame
Powers have they left—an impulse—and a claim
Which neither can be overturned nor bought.
Sleep, Warriors, sleep! among your hills repose!
We know that ye, beneath the stern controul   10
Of awful prudence, keep the unvanquished soul.
And when, impatient of her guilt and woes
Europe breaks forth; then, Shepherds! shall ye rise
For perfect triumph o'er your Enemies.

[Epitaphs Translated from Chiabrera][1]

"True is it that Ambrosio Salinero"

True is it that Ambrosio Salinero
With an untoward fate was long involved
In odious litigation; and full long,
Fate harder still! had he to endure assaults

---

1 Gabriello Chiabrera (1552–1638).

Of racking malady. And true it is   5
That not the less a frank courageous heart
And buoyant spirit triumphed over pain;
And he was strong to follow in the steps
Of the fair Muses. Not a covert path
Leads to the dear Parnassian forest's shade,   10
That might from him be hidden; not a track
Mounts to pellucid Hippocrene, but he
Had traced its windings.— This Savona knows,
Yet no sepulchral honors to her Son
She paid, for in our age the heart is ruled   15
Only by gold. And now a simple stone
Inscribed with this memorial here is raised
By his bereft, his lonely, Chiabrera.
Think not, O Passenger! who read'st the lines
That an exceeding love hath dazzled me;   20
No—he was One whose memory ought to spread
Where'er Permessus bears an honoured name,
And live as long as its pure stream shall flow.

"Not without heavy grief of heart did He"

Not without heavy grief of heart did He,
On whom the duty fell, (for at that time
The Father sojourned in a distant Land)
Deposit in the hollow of this Tomb
A Brother's Child, most tenderly beloved!   5
FRANCESCO was the name the Youth had borne,
POZZOBONNELLI his illustrious House;
And when beneath this stone the Corse was laid
The eyes of all Savona streamed with tears.
Alas! the twentieth April of his life   10
Had scarcely flowered: and at this early time,
By genuine virtue he inspired a hope
That greatly cheered his Country: to his Kin
He promised comfort; and the flattering thoughts
His Friends had in their fondness entertained,[1]   15
He suffered not to languish or decay.

---

1   "In justice to the Author I subjoin the original.
            ———e degli amici
    Non lasciava languire i bei pensieri." WW

Now is there not good reason to break forth
Into a passionate lament?—O Soul!
Short while a Pilgrim in our nether world,
Do thou enjoy the calm empyreal air;   20
And round this earthly tomb let roses rise,
An everlasting spring! in memory
Of that delightful fragrance which was once,
From thy mild manners, quietly exhaled.

"Pause, courteous Spirit!—Balbi supplicates"

Pause, courteous Spirit!—Balbi supplicates
That Thou, with no reluctant voice, for him
Here laid in mortal darkness, wouldst prefer
A prayer to the Redeemer of the world.
This to the Dead by sacred right belongs;   5
All else is nothing.—Did occasion suit
To tell his worth, the marble of this tomb
Would ill suffice: for Plato's lore sublime
And all the wisdom of the Stagyrite
Enriched and beautified his studious mind: 10
With Archimedes also he conversed
As with a chosen Friend, nor did he leave
Those laureat wreaths ungathered which the Nymphs
Twine on the top of Pindus.—Finally,
Himself above each lower thought uplifting,   15
His ears he closed to listen to the Song
Which Sion's Kings did consecrate of old;
And fixed his Pindus upon Lebanon.
A blessed Man! who of protracted days
Made not, as thousands do, a vulgar sleep;   20
But truly did *He* live his life.—Urbino
Take pride in him;—O Passenger farewell!

"There never breathed a man who when his life"

There never breathed a man who when his life
Was closing might not of that life relate
Toils long and hard.— The Warrior will report
Of wounds, and bright swords flashing in the field,
And blast of trumpets. He, who hath been doomed   5

To bow his forehead in the courts of kings,
Will tell of fraud and never-ceasing hate,
Envy, and heart-inquietude, derived
From intricate cabals of treacherous friends.
I, who on ship-board lived from earliest Youth,   10
Could represent the countenance horrible
Of the vexed waters, and the indignant rage
Of Auster and Boötes. Forty years
Over the well-steered Gallies did I rule:—
From huge Pelorus to the Atlantic pillars,   15
Rises no mountain to mine eyes unknown;
And the broad gulfs I traversed oft—and—oft:
Of every cloud which in the heavens might stir
I knew the force; and hence the rough sea's pride
Availed not to my Vessel's overthrow.   20
What noble pomp and frequent have not I
On regal decks beheld! yet in the end
I learn that one poor moment can suffice
To equalize the lofty and the low.
We sail the sea of life—a *Calm* One finds,   25
And One a *Tempest*—and, the voyage o'er,
Death is the quiet haven of us all.
If more of my condition ye would know,
Savona was my birth-place, and I sprang
Of noble Parents: sixty years and three   30
Lived I—then yielded to a slow disease.

"Destined to war from very infancy"

Destined to war from very infancy
Was I, Roberto Dati, and I took
In Malta the white symbol of the Cross.
Nor in life's vigorous season did I shun
Hazard or toil; among the Sands was seen   5
Of Lybia, and not seldom on the Banks
Of wide Hungarian Danube, 'twas my lot
To hear the sanguinary trumpet sounded.
So lived I, and repined not at such fate;
This only grieves me, for it seems a wrong,   10
That stripped of arms I to my end am brought

On the soft down of my paternal home.
Yet haply Arno shall be spared all cause
To blush for me. Thou, loiter not nor halt
In thy appointed way, and bear in mind   15
How fleeting and how frail is human life.

"Weep not, beloved Friends! nor let the air"

Weep not, beloved Friends! nor let the air
For me with sighs be troubled. Not from life
Have I been taken; this is genuine life
And this alone—the life which now I live
In peace eternal; where desire and joy   5
Together move in fellowship without end.—
Francesco Ceni after death enjoined
That thus his tomb should speak for him. And surely
Small cause there is for that fond wish of ours
Long to continue in this world; a world   10
That keeps not faith, nor yet can point a hope
To good, whereof itself is destitute.

"Perhaps some needful service of the State"

Perhaps some needful service of the State
Drew Titus from the depth of studious bowers,
And doomed him to contend in faithless courts,
Where gold determines between right and wrong.
Yet did at length his loyalty of heart   5
And his pure native genius lead him back
To wait upon the bright and gracious Muses
Whom he had early loved. And not in vain
Such course he held! Bologna's learned schools
Were gladdened by the Sage's voice, and hung   10
With fondness on those sweet Nestorian strains.
There pleasure crowned his days; and all his thoughts[1]
A roseate fragrance breathed.—O human life,
That never art secure from dolorous change!
Behold a high injunction suddenly   15

---

1   "I vi vivea giocondo e i suoi pensieri
       Erano tutti rose.
     The Translator had not skill to come nearer to his original." WW

To Arno's side conducts him, and he charmed
A Tuscan audience: but full soon was called
To the perpetual silence of the grave.
Mourn, Italy, the loss of him who stood
A Champion steadfast and invincible,   20
To quell the rage of literary War!

"O Thou who movest onward with a mind"

O Thou who movest onward with a mind
Intent upon thy way, pause though in haste!
'Twill be no fruitless moment. I was born
Within Savona's walls of gentle blood.
On Tiber's banks my youth was dedicate   5
To sacred studies; and the Roman Shepherd
Gave to my charge Urbino's numerous Flock.
Much did I watch, much laboured; nor had power
To escape from many and strange indignities;
Was smitten by the great ones of the World   10
But did not fall, for virtue braves all shocks,
Upon herself resting immoveably.
Me did a kindlier fortune then invite
To serve the glorious Henry, King of France,
And in his hands I saw a high reward   15
Stretched out for my acceptance—but Death came.—
Now, Reader, learn from this my fate—how false,
How treacherous to her promise is the World,
And trust in God—to whose eternal doom
Must bend the sceptred Potentates of Earth.   20

"O Lelius, beauteous flower of gentleness"

O Lelius, beauteous flower of gentleness,
The fair Aglaia's friend above all friends,
O darling of the fascinating Loves,
By what dire envy moved did De[a]th uproot
Thy days e'er yet full blown and what ill chance   5
Hath robbed Savona of her noblest grace?
She weeps for thee and shall for ever weep,
And if the fountain of her tears should fail
She would implore Sabete to supply

Her need—Sabete, sympathizing stream   10
Who on his margin saw thee close thine eyes
On the chaste bosom of thy Lady dear.
Oh what do riches, what does youth avail?
Dust are our hopes; I weeping did inscribe
In bitterness thy monument and pray   15
Of every gentle Spirit bitterly
To read the record with as copious tears.

"Torquato Tasso rests within this Tomb"

Torquato Tasso rests within this Tomb;
This Figure weeping from her inmost heart
Is Poesy; from such impassioned grief
Let everyone conclude what this Man was.

"O flower of all that springs from gentle blood"

O flower of all that springs from gentle blood,
And all that generous nurture breeds, to make
Youth amiable; O friend so true of soul
To fair Aglaia; by what envy moved,
Lelius! has death cut short thy brilliant day   5
In its sweet opening? and what dire mishap
Has from Savona torn her best delight?
For thee she mourns, nor e'er will cease to mourn;
And, should the out-pourings of her eyes suffice not
For her heart's grief, she will entreat Sebeto   10
Not to withhold his bounteous aid, Sebeto
Who saw thee, on his margin, yield to death,
In the chaste arms of thy belovéd Love!
What profit riches? what does youth avail?
Dust are our hopes;—I, weeping bitterly,   15
Penned these sad lines, nor can forbear to pray
That every gentle Spirit hither led
May read them not without some bitter tears.

————————

The Oak of Guernica

The ancient Oak of Guernica, says Laborde in his account of Biscay, is a most venerable natural Monument. Ferdinand and Isabella, in the year 1476, after hearing mass in the Church of Santa Maria de la Antigua, repaired to this tree, under which they swore to the Biscayans to maintain their *fueros* (privileges). What other interest belongs to it in the minds of this People will appear from the following

Supposed Address to the Same

1810

Oak of Guernica! Tree of holier power
Than that which in Dodona did enshrine
(So faith too fondly deemed) a voice divine
Heard from the depths of its aerial bower,
How canst thou flourish at this blighting hour?   5
What hope, what joy can sunshine bring to thee,
Or the soft breezes from the Atlantic sea,
The dews of morn, or April's tender shower?
——Stroke merciful and welcome would that be
Which should extend thy branches on the ground,   10
If never more within their shady round
Those lofty-minded Lawgivers shall meet,
Peasant and Lord, in their appointed seat,
Guardians of Biscay's ancient liberty.

"In due observance of an ancient rite"

In due observance of an ancient rite,
The rude Biscayans, when their Children lie
Dead in the sinless time of infancy,
Attire the peaceful Corse in vestments white;
And, in like sign of cloudless triumph bright,   5
They bind the unoffending Creature's brows
With happy garlands of the pure white rose:
This done, a festal Company unite
In choral song; and, while the uplifted Cross
Of Jesus goes before, the Child is borne   10
Uncovered to his grave.—Her piteous loss
The lonesome Mother cannot chuse but mourn;

Yet soon by Christian faith is grief subdued,
And joy attends upon her fortitude.

Feelings of a Noble Biscayan

AT ONE OF THESE FUNERALS
1810

Yet, yet, Biscayans, we must meet our Foes
With firmer soul,—yet labour to regain
Our ancient freedom; else 'twere worse than vain
To gather round the Bier these festal shows!
A garland fashioned of the pure white rose   5
Becomes not one whose Father is a Slave:
Oh! bear the Infant covered to his Grave!
These venerable mountains now enclose
A People sunk in apathy and fear.
If this endure, farewell, for us, all good!   10
The awful light of heavenly Innocence
Will fail to illuminate the Infant's bier;
And guilt and shame, from which is no defence,
Descend on all that issues from our blood.

1810

O'erweening Statesmen have full long relied
On fleets and armies, and external wealth:
But from *within* proceeds a Nation's health;
Which shall not fail, though poor men cleave with pride
To the paternal floor; or turn aside,   5
In the thronged City, from the walks of gain,
As being all unworthy to detain
A Soul by contemplation sanctified.
There are who cannot languish in this strife,
Spaniards of every rank, by whom the good   10
Of such high course was felt and understood;
Who to their Country's cause have bound a life,
Ere while by solemn consecration given
To labour, and to prayer, to nature, and to heaven.[1]

---

1   "See Laborde's Character of the Spanish People; from him the sentiment of these two
    last lines is taken." WW; he cites from Alexander De Laborde, *A View of Spain* (5 vols.,
    London, 1809).

"Avaunt all specious pliancy of mind"

Avaunt all specious pliancy of mind
In men of low degree, all smooth pretence!
I better like a blunt indifference
And self-respecting slowness, disinclined
To win me at first sight:—and be there joined   5
Patience and temperance with this high reserve,—
Honour that knows the path and will not swerve;
Affections, which, if put to proof, are kind;
And piety tow'rds God.—Such Men of old
Were England's native growth; and, throughout Spain,   10
Forests of such do at this day remain;
Then for that Country let our hopes be bold;
For matched with these shall Policy prove vain,
Her arts, her strength, her iron, and her gold.

Indignation of a High-minded Spaniard. 1810

We can endure that He should waste our lands,
Despoil our temples,—and by sword and flame
Return us to the dust from which we came;
Such food a Tyrant's appetite demands:
And we can brook the thought that by his hands   5
Spain may be overpowered, and he possess,
For his delight, a solemn wilderness,
Where all the Brave lie dead. But when of bands,
Which he will break for us, he dares to speak,—
Of benefits, and of a future day   10
When our enlightened minds shall bless his sway,
Then, the strained heart of fortitude proves weak:
Our groans, our blushes, our pale cheeks declare
That he has power to inflict what we lack strength to bear.

The French, and the Spanish Guerillas

Hunger, and sultry heat, and nipping blast
From bleak hill-top, and length of march by night
Through heavy swamp, or over snow-clad height,
These hardships ill sustained, these dangers past,
The roving Spanish Bands are reached at last,   5

Charged, and dispersed like foam:—but as a flight
Of scattered quails by signs do reunite
So these,—and, heard of once again, are chased
With combinations of long practised art
And newly-kindled hope;—but they are fled,   10
Gone are they, viewless as the buried dead;
Where now?— Their sword is at the Foeman's heart!
And thus from year to year his walk they thwart,
And hang like dreams around his guilty bed.

Spanish Guerillas. 1811

They seek, are sought; to daily battle led,
Shrink not, though far out-numbered by their Foes:
For they have learnt to open and to close
The ridges of grim War; and at their head
Are Captains such as erst their Country bred   5
Or fostered, self-supported Chiefs,—like those
Whom hardy Rome was fearful to oppose,
Whose desperate shock the Carthaginian fled.
In one who lived unknown a Shepherd's life
Redoubted Viriatus breathes again;   10
And Mina, nourished in the studious shade,
With that great Leader vies, who, sick of strife
And bloodshed, longed in quiet to be laid
In some green Island of the western main.

"The martial courage of a day is vain—"

The martial courage of a day is vain—
An empty noise of death the battle's roar—
If vital hope be wanting to restore,
Or fortitude be wanting to sustain,
Armies or Kingdoms. We have heard a strain   5
Of triumph, how the labouring Danube bore
A weight of hostile corses: drenched with gore
Were the wide fields, the hamlets heaped with slain.
Yet see, the mighty tumult overpast,
Austria a Daughter of her Throne hath sold!   10
And her Tyrolean Champion we behold
Murdered like one ashore by shipwreck cast,

Murdered without relief. Oh! blind as bold,
To think that such assurance can stand fast!

Conclusion. 1811

Here pause: the Poet claims at least this praise
That virtuous Liberty hath been the scope
Of his pure song, which did not shrink from hope
In the worst moment of these evil days;
From hope, the paramount *duty* that Heaven lays,   5
For its own honour, on man's suffering heart.
Never may from our souls one truth depart,
That an *accursed* thing it is to gaze
On prosperous Tyrants with a dazzled eye;
Nor, touched with due abhorrence of *their* guilt   10
For whose dire ends tears flow, and blood is spilt,
And justice labours in extremity,
Forget thy weakness, upon which is built,
O wretched Man, the throne of Tyranny!

1811

The power of Armies is a visible thing,
Formal, and circumscribed in time and place;
But who the limits of that power can trace
Which a brave People into light can bring,
Or hide, at will,—for Freedom combating,   5
By just revenge enflamed? No foot can chase,
No eye can follow to a *fatal* place
That power, that spirit, whether on the wing
Like the strong wind, or sleeping like the wind
Within its awful caves.—From year to year   10
Springs this indigenous produce far and near;
No craft this subtle element can bind,
Rising like water from the soil, to find
In every nook a lip that it may cheer.

On a Celebrated Event in Ancient History

A Roman Master stands on Grecian ground,
And to the Concourse of the Isthmian Games
He, by his Herald's voice, aloud proclaims

THE LIBERTY OF GREECE:—the words rebound
Until all voices in one voice are drowned;   5
Glad acclamation by which air was rent!
And birds, high-flying in the element,
Dropped to the earth, astonished at the sound!
—A melancholy Echo of that noise
Doth sometimes hang on musing Fancy's ear: 10
Ah! that a *Conqueror's* words should be so dear;
Ah! that a *boon* could shed such rapturous joys!
A gift of that which is not to be given
By all the blended powers of Earth and Heaven.

Upon the Same Event

When, far and wide, swift as the beams of morn
The tidings passed of servitude repealed,
And of that joy which shook the Isthmian Field,
The rough Ætolians smiled with bitter scorn.
"'Tis known," cried they, "that He, who would adorn   5
His envied temples with the Isthmian Crown,
Must either win, through effort of his own,
The prize, or be content to see it worn
By more deserving brows.— Yet so ye prop,
Sons of the Brave who fought at Marathon,   10
Your feeble Spirits. Greece her head hath bowed,
As if the wreath of Liberty thereon
Would fix itself as smoothly as a cloud,
Which, at Jove's will, descends on Pelion's top!"

Upon the Sight of a Beautiful Picture

Praised be the Art whose subtle power could stay
Yon Cloud, and fix it in that glorious shape;
Nor would permit the thin smoke to escape,
Nor those bright sunbeams to forsake the day;
Which stopped that Band of Travellers on their way   5
Ere they were lost within the shady wood;
And shewed the Bark upon the glassy flood
For ever anchored in her sheltering Bay.
Soul-soothing Art! which Morning, Noon-tide, Even
Do serve with all their changeful pageantry!   10

Thou, with ambition modest yet sublime,
Here, for the sight of mortal man, hast given
To one brief moment caught from fleeting time
The appropriate calm of blest eternity.

Departure

FROM THE VALE OF GRASMERE. AUGUST 1803

The gentlest Shade that walked Elysian Plains
Might sometimes covet dissoluble chains;
Even for the Tenants of the Zone that lies
Beyond the stars, celestial Paradise,
Methinks 'twould heighten joy, to overleap   5
At will the crystal battlements, and peep
Into some other region, though less fair,
To see how things are made and managed there:
Change for the worse might please, incursion bold
Into the tracts of darkness and of cold;   10
O'er Limbo lake with aëry flight to steer,
And on the verge of Chaos hang in fear.
Such animation often do I find,
Power in my breast, wings growing in my mind,
Then, when some rock or hill is overpast,   15
Perchance without one look behind me cast,
Some barrier with which Nature, from the birth
Of things, has fenced this fairest spot on earth.
O pleasant transit, Grasmere! to resign
Such happy fields, abodes so calm as thine;   20
Not like an outcast with himself at strife;
The slave of business, time, or care for life,
But moved by choice; or, if constrained in part,
Yet still with Nature's freedom at the heart;
To cull contentment upon wildest shores,   25
And luxuries extract from bleakest moors;
With prompt embrace all beauty to enfold,
And having rights in all that we behold.
—Then why these lingering steps? A bright adieu,
For a brief absence, proves that love is true;   30
Ne'er can the way be irksome or forlorn,
That winds into itself, for sweet return.

[*Epistle to Sir George Howland Beaumont, Bart. From the
South-west Coast of Cumberland.—1811*][1]

Far from [   ] Grasmere's lake serene,
Her Vale profound and mountains ever green,
Fixed within hearing of loud Ocean's roar
Where daily, on a bleak and lonesome shore,
Even at this summer season, huge Black Comb   5
Frowns, deep'ning *visibly* his native gloom.
Unless perchance, rejecting in despite
What on the Plain *we* have of warmth and light,
In his own Tempests hide himself from Sight.
Here am I, Friend, where neither sheltered road   10
Nor hedgerow screen, invite my steps abroad,
Where one poor Plane-tree, having as it can
Attained a stature twice the height of Man,
Hopeless of further growth, and brown and sere,
Thro' half the summer stands with top cut sheer   15
Like an unshifting weathercock that proves
How cold the Quarter that the wind best loves,
Or Centinel, that placed in front before
Darkens the window, not defends the door
Of this unfinished House; a Fortress bare,   20
Where strength has been the Builder's only care,
Whose rugged walls may still for years demand
The finer polish of the Plaisterer's hand;
This Dwelling's Inmate more than three weeks' space
And oft a Prisoner in the cheerless place   25
I, of whose touch the fiddle would complain,
Whose breath would labour at the flute in vain,
In music all unversed—and without skill
A bridge to copy, or to paint a mill;
Tired of my books, a scanty company,   30
And tired of listening to the boisterous Sea,
Pace between door and window murmuring rhyme,
An old resource to cheat the froward time!
And it would well content me to disclaim

---

1 The reading text is drawn from the earliest complete version, which is untitled. WW's notes
   are those he published with the poem in *Poems*, 1815. The first line in 1815 is "Far from
   our home by Grasmere's quiet Lake."

In these dull hours a more ambitious aim.   35
But if there be a Muse, who, free to take
Her Seat upon Olymphus, doth forsake
Those Heights (like Phœbus when his golden locks
He veiled, attendant on Thessalian Flocks)
And in disguise, a Milkmaid with her pail   40
Trips on the pathways of some winding dale;
Or like a Mermaid warbles on the shores
To Fishers, mending nets beside their doors;
Or like a tired Way-farer faint in mind,
Gives plaintive Ballads to the heedless wind—   45
If such a visitant of Earth there be
And she would deign this day to smile on me
And aid my Verse content with narrow bounds,
Life's beaten road and Nature's daily rounds,
Thoughts, chances, sights or doings, which we tell   50
Without reserve to those whom we love well,
Then haply Beaumont, for my pen is near,
The unlaboured lines to your indulgent ear
May be transmitted, else will perish here.
What shall I treat of? News from Mona's Isle?   55
Such have I, but unvaried in its style;
No tales of Runnagates fresh landed, whence
And wherefore fugitive, or on what pretence—
Of feasts or scandal eddying like the wind
Most restlessly alive, when most confined.   60
Ask not of me whose tongue can best appease
The mighty tumults of the *House of Keys*,
The last Year's Cup whose Ram or Heifer gained,
What slopes are planted, and what mosses drained?
An eye of Fancy only can I cast   65
On that proud pageant, now at hand or past,
When full five hundred boats in trim array
With nets and Sails outspread, and streamers gay
And chaunted hymns and stiller voice of prayer
For the old Manx harvest to the Deep repair,   70
Soon as the Herring-shoals at distance shine
Like beds of moonlight shifting on the brine.
Mona from my Abode is daily seen

But with a wilderness of waves between,
And by conjecture only can I speak   75
Of aught transacted there, in bay or creek;
No tidings reach me thence from town or field;
Only faint news the mountain sun-beams yield,
And some I gather from the misty air,
And some the hovering clouds, my telegraph, declare.   80
But these poetic mysteries I withhold,
For Fancy hath her fits both hot and cold
And should the colder fit with you be on
When you must read, my credit would be gone.
   Let more substantial themes our care engage   85
And humbler business occupy the Stage
—First, for our journey hither. Ere the dawn
Had from the east her silver star withdrawn
The Wain stood ready at our Cottage door
Thoughtfully freighted with a various store   90
And long before the uprising of the Sun,
O'er dew-damp'd dust our travel was begun,
A needful journey, under summer skies
Thro' peopled Vales, yet something in the guise
Of those old Patriarchs, when from Well to Well   95
They roamed, where now the tented Arabs dwell.
   Say then, to whom this charge did we confide,
Who promptly undertook the Wain to guide
Up many a sharply-twining road, and down,
And over many a wide hill's craggy crown,   100
Thro' the quick turns of many a hollow nook
And the rough bed of many an unbridged brook?
A blooming Lass, who in her better hand
Bore a light switch, her sceptre of command
When yet a slender Girl, she often led,   105
Skilful and bold, the Horse and burdened Sled[1]
From the peat-yielding Moss on Gowdar's head.
What could we dread with such a Charioteer!
For goods and chattels, or those Infants dear
Escaped not long from malady severe,   110
A Pair who smilingly sate side by side

---

1   "A local word for Sledge." WW

Our hope confirming, that the salt-sea tide
Whose free embraces we were bound to seek
Would their lost strength restore, and freshen the pale cheek:
Such hope did either Parent entertain   115
Pacing behind, along the silent Lane.
   Advancing Summer, Nature's tasks fulfilled,
The Choristers in Copse and grove had stilled,
But we, we lacked not music of our own,
For lightsome Fanny had thus early thrown   120
Mid the gay prattle of those busy tongues
Some notes prelusive from that round of Songs
With which, more zealous than the liveliest bird
That in wide Arden's brakes was ever heard,
Her work and her work's partners she can cheer   125
The whole day long, and all days of the year.
Thus gladdened, soon we saw, and could not pass
Without a pause, Diana's looking glass!
To Loughrigg's pool,[1] round, clear and bright as heaven
Such name Italian fancy would have given—   130
Ere on its banks those few grey Cabins rose
That yet molest not its concealed repose
More than the ruffling wind that idly blows.
   Ah Beaumont, when an opening in the road
Stopped me at once by charm of what it showed   135
And I beheld (how vividly impressed!)
The encircling landscape on its peaceful breast—
Woods intermingling with a rocky bield,[2]
And the smooth green of many a pendent field,

---

1   "LOUGHRIGG TARN, alluded to in the foregoing Epistle, resembles, though much smaller in compass, the Lake Nemi, or *Speculum Diana*, as it is often called, not only in its clear waters and circular form, and the beauty immediately surrounding it, but also as being overlooked by the eminence of Langdale Pikes as Lake Nemi is by that of Monte Calvo. Since this Epistle was written Loughrigg Tarn has lost much of its beauty by the felling of many natural clumps of wood, relics of the old forest, particularly upon the farm called 'The Oaks," from the abundance of that tree which grew there.
   It is to be regretted, upon public grounds, that Sir George Beaumont did not carry into effect his intention of constructing here a Summer Retreat in the style I have described; as his Taste would have set an example how buildings, with all the accommodations modern society requires, might be introduced even into the most secluded parts of this country without injuring their native character. The design was not abandoned from failure of inclination on his part, but in consequence of local untowardnesses which need not be particularised." WW
2   "A word common in the country, signifying shelter, as in Scotland." WW

One chimney smoking and its azure wreath—   140
All, all reflected in the Pool beneath,
With here and there a faint imperfect gleam
Of water lilies, veiled in misty steam.
What wonder, at this hour of stillness deep,
A shadowy link 'twixt wakefulness and sleep   145
When Nature's self amid these watery gleams
Is rendering visible her own soft dreams,
If mixed with what appeared of rock, lawn, wood
Truly repeated in the tranquil flood,
A glimpse I caught of that Abode by Thee   150
Designed to rise in humble privacy,
A lowly Dwelling, here to be outspread
Like a small hamlet with its bashful head
Half hid in native trees. Alas, 'tis not
Nor ever was; I sighed and left the spot   155
Repining at its own untoward lot.
I thought in silence with regret most keen
Of intermingled joys that *might* have been,
Of neighbourhood, and intermingling Arts
And golden summer days uniting peaceful hearts.   160
But Time, irrecoverable Time is flown
And let us utter thanks for blessings sown
And reaped—what *hath* been, and what is our own.

To the Poet, Dyer

Bard of the Fleece, whose skilful Genius made
That Work a living landscape fair and bright;
Nor hallowed less with musical delight
Than those soft scenes through which thy Childhood stray'd,
Those southern Tracts of Cambria, "deep embayed,   5
By green hills fenced, by Ocean's murmur lulled;"
Though hasty Fame hath many a chaplet culled
For worthless brows, while in the pensive shade
Of cold neglect she leaves thy head ungraced,
Yet pure and powerful minds, hearts meek and still,   10
A grateful few, shall love thy modest Lay
Long as the Shepherd's bleating flock shall stray
O'er naked Snowdon's wide aerial waste;

Long as the thrush shall pipe on Grongar Hill.

Written with a Slate-pencil, on a Stone, on the
Side of the Mountain of Black Comb[1]

Stay, bold Adventurer; rest awhile thy limbs
On this commodious Seat! for much remains
Of hard ascent before thou reach the top
Of this huge Eminence,—from blackness named,
And, to far-travelled storms of sea and land,   5
A favourite spot of tournament and war!
But thee may no such boisterous visitants
Molest; may gentle breezes fan thy brow;
And neither cloud conceal, nor misty air
Bedim, the grand terraqueous spectacle,   10
From centre to circumference, unveiled!
Know, if thou grudge not to prolong thy rest,
That, on the summit whither thou art bound,
A geographic Labourer pitched his tent,
With books supplied and instruments of art,   15
To measure height and distance; lonely task,
Week after week pursued!— To him was given
Full many a glimpse (but sparingly bestowed
On timid man) of Nature's processes
Upon the exalted hills. He made report   20
That once, while there he plied his studious work
Within that canvass Dwelling, suddenly
The many-coloured map before his eyes
Became invisible: for all around
Had darkness fallen—unthreatened, unproclaimed—   25
As if the golden day itself had been
Extinguished in a moment; total gloom,
In which he sate alone with unclosed eyes
Upon the blinded mountain's silent top!

View from the Top of Black Comb

This Height a ministering Angel might select:

---

1   "Black Comb stands at the southern extremity of Cumberland; its base covers a much
    greater extent of ground than any other Mountain in these parts; and, from its situation,.
    the summit commands a more extensive view than any other point in Britain." WW

For from the summit of BLACK COMB (dread name
Derived from clouds and storms!) the amplest range
Of unobstructed prospect may be seen
That British ground commands:—low dusky tracts,   5
Where Trent is nursed, far southward! Cambrian Hills
To the south-west, a multitudinous show;
And, in a line of eye-sight linked with these,
The hoary Peaks of Scotland that give birth
To Tiviot's Stream, to Annan, Tweed, and Clyde;—   10
Crowding the quarter whence the sun comes forth
Gigantic Mountains rough with crags; beneath,
Right at the imperial Station's western base,
Main Ocean, breaking audibly, and stretched
Far into silent regions blue and pale;—   15
And visibly engirding Mona's Isle
That, as we left the Plain, before our sight
Stood like a lofty Mount, uplifting slowly,
(Above the convex of the watery globe)
Into clear view the cultured fields that streak   20
Its habitable shores; but now appears
A dwindled object, and submits to lie
At the Spectator's feet.— Yon azure Ridge,
Is it a perishable cloud? Or there
Do we behold the frame of Erin's Coast?   25
Land sometimes by the roving shepherd swain,
Like the bright confines of another world
Not doubtfully perceived.—Look homeward now!
In depth, in height, in circuit, how serene
The spectacle, how pure!—Of Nature's works,   30
In earth, and air, and earth-embracing sea,
A Revelation infinite it seems;
Display august of man's inheritance,
Of Britain's calm felicity and power.

In the Grounds of Coleorton, the Seat of Sir George Beaumont, Bart. Leicestershire

The embowering Rose, the Acacia, and the Pine
Will not unwillingly their place resign;
If but the Cedar thrive that near them stands,

Planted by Beaumont's and by Wordsworth's hands.
One wooed the silent Art with studious pains,—   5
These Groves have heard the Other's pensive strains;
Devoted thus, their spirits did unite
By interchange of knowledge and delight.
May Nature's kindliest powers sustain the Tree,
And Love protect it from all injury!   10
And when its potent branches, wide out-thrown,
Darken the brow of this memorial Stone,
And to a favourite resting-place invite,
For coolness grateful and a sober light;
Here may some Painter sit in future days,   15
Some future Poet meditate his lays;
Not mindless of that distant age renowned
When Inspiration hovered o'er this ground,
The haunt of Him who sang how spear and shield
In civil conflict met on Bosworth Field;   20
And of that famous Youth, full soon removed
From earth, perhaps by Shakespear's self approved,
Fletcher's Associate, Jonson's Friend beloved.

Written at the Request of Sir George Beaumont, Bart. and in his Name, for
an Urn, placed by him at the Termination of a newly-planted Avenue, in
the same Grounds

Ye Lime-trees, ranged before this hallowed Urn,
Shoot forth with lively power at Spring's return;
And be not slow a stately growth to rear
Of Pillars, branching off from year to year
Till they at length have framed a darksome Aisle;—   5
Like a recess within that awful Pile
Where Reynolds, mid our Country's noblest Dead,
In the last sanctity of Fame is laid.

—There, though by right the excelling Painter sleep
Where Death and Glory a joint sabbath keep,   10
Yet not the less his Spirit would hold dear
Self-hidden praise and Friendship's private tear:
Hence on my patrimonial Grounds have I
Raised this frail tribute to his memory,
From youth a zealous follower of the Art   15

That he professed, attached to him in heart;
Admiring, loving, and with grief and pride
Feeling what England lost when Reynolds died.

In a Garden of the same

Oft is the Medal faithful to its trust
When Temples, Columns, Towers are laid in dust;
And 'tis a common ordinance of fate
That things obscure and small outlive the great:
Hence, when yon Mansion and the flowery trim   5
Of this fair Garden, and its alleys dim,
And all its stately trees, are passed away,
This little Niche, unconscious of decay,
Perchance may still survive.—And be it known
That it was scooped within the living stone,—   10
Not by the sluggish and ungrateful pains
Of labourer plodding for his daily gains;
But by an industry that wrought in love,
With help from female hands, that proudly strove
To shape the work, what time these walks and bowers   15
Were framed to cheer dark winter's lonely hours.

Inscription for a Seat in the Groves of Coleorton

Beneath yon eastern Ridge, the craggy Bound,
Rugged and high, of Charnwood's forest ground,
Stand yet, but, Stranger! hidden from thy view,
The ivied Ruins of forlorn GRACE DIEU;
Erst a religious House, that day and night   5
With hymns resounded, and the chaunted rite:
And when those rites had ceased, the Spot gave birth
To honourable Men of various worth:
There, on the margin of a Streamlet wild,
Did Francis Beaumont sport, an eager Child;   10
There, under shadow of the neighbouring rocks,
Sang youthful tales of shepherds and their flocks;
Unconscious prelude to heroic themes,
Heart-breaking tears, and melancholy dreams
Of slighted love, and scorn, and jealous rage,   15
With which his genius shook the buskined Stage.

Communities are lost, and Empires die,—
And things of holy use unhallowed lie;
They perish;—but the Intellect can raise,
From airy words alone, a Pile that ne'er decays.   20

Song for the Spinning Wheel

FOUNDED UPON A BELIEF PREVALENT AMONG THE PASTORAL VALES OF
WESTMORLAND

Swiftly turn the murmuring wheel!
Night has brought the welcome hour,
When the weary fingers feel
Help, as if from fairy power;
Dewy night o'ershades the ground;   5
Turn the swift wheel round and round!

Now, beneath the starry sky,
Rest the widely-scatter'd sheep;—
Ply, the pleasant labour, ply!—
For the spindle, while they sleep,   10
With a motion smooth and fine
Gathers up a trustier line.

Short-liv'd likings may be bred
By a glance from fickle eyes;
But true love is like the thread   15
Which the kindly wool supplies,
When the flocks are all at rest,
Sleeping on the mountain's breast.

"Grief, thou hast lost an ever ready Friend"

Grief, thou hast lost an ever ready Friend
Now that the cottage spinning-wheel is mute;
And Care—a Comforter that best could suit
Her froward mood, and softliest reprehend;
And Love—a Charmer's voice, that used to lend,   5
More efficaciously than aught that flows
From harp or lute, kind influence to compose
The throbbing pulse,—else troubled without end:
Ev'n Joy could tell, Joy craving truce and rest

From her own overflow, what power sedate   10
On those revolving motions did await
Assiduously, to sooth her aching breast;
And—to a point of just relief—abate
The mantling triumphs of a day too blest.

"The fairest, brightest hues of ether fade"

The fairest, brightest hues of ether fade;
The sweetest notes must terminate and die;
O Friend! thy flute has breathed a harmony
Softly resounded through this rocky glade;
Such strains of rapture as[1] the Genius played   5
In his still haunt on Bagdad's summit high;
He who stood visible to Mirzah's eye,
Never before to human sight betrayed.
Lo, in the vale the mists of evening spread!
The visionary Arches are not there,   10
Nor the green Islands, nor the shining Seas;
Yet sacred is to me this Mountain's head,
From which I have been lifted on the breeze
Of harmony, above all earthly care.

"Even as a dragon's eye that feels the stress"

Even as a dragon's eye that feels the stress
Of a bedimming sleep, or as a lamp
Sullenly glaring through sepulchral damp,
So burns yon Taper mid its black recess
Of mountains, silent, dreary, motionless: 5
The Lake below reflects it not; the sky
Muffled in clouds affords no company
To mitigate and cheer its loneliness.
Yet round the body of that joyless Thing,
Which sends so far its melancholy light,   10
Perhaps are seated in domestic ring
A gay society with faces bright,
Conversing, reading, laughing;—or they sing,
While hearts and voices in the song unite.

---

1   "See the vision of Mirzah in the Spectator." WW; he cites Joseph Addison in *The Spectator*,
    no. 159, Saturday, September 1, 1711.

"Hail Twilight,—sovereign of one peaceful hour!"

Hail Twilight,—sovereign of one peaceful hour!
Not dull art Thou as undiscerning Night;
But studious only to remove from sight
Day's mutable distinctions.—Ancient Power!
Thus did the waters gleam, the mountains lower   5
To the rude Briton, when, in wolf-skin vest
Here roving wild, he laid him down to rest
On the bare rock, or through a leafy bower
Looked ere his eyes were closed. By him was seen
The self-same Vision which we now behold,   10
At thy meek bidding, shadowy Power, brought forth;—
These mighty barriers, and the gulph between;
The floods,—the stars,—a spectacle as old
As the beginning of the heavens and earth!

Composed on the Eve of the Marriage of a Friend, in the Vale of Grasmere

What need of clamorous bells, or ribbands gay,
These humble Nuptials to proclaim or grace?
Angels of Love, look down upon the place,
Shed on the chosen Vale a sun-bright day!
Even for such omen would the Bride display   5
No mirthful gladness:—serious is her face,
Modest her mien; and she, whose thoughts keep pace
With gentleness, in that becoming way
Will thank you. Faultless does the Maid appear,
No disproportion in her soul, no strife: 10
But, when the closer view of wedded life
Hath shewn that nothing human can be clear
From frailty, for that insight may the Wife
To her indulgent Lord become more dear.

"Surprized by joy—impatient as the Wind"

Surprized by joy—impatient as the Wind
I wished to share the transport—Oh! with whom
But thee, long buried in the silent Tomb,
That spot which no vicissitude can find?   except death.

Love, faithful love recalled thee to my mind— 5
But how could I forget thee?— Through what power,
Even for the least division of an hour,
Have I been so beguiled as to be blind
To my most grievous loss?— That thought's return *Cur.?*
Was the worst pang that sorrow ever bore, 10
Save one, one only, when I stood forlorn,
Knowing my heart's best treasure was no more;
That neither present time, nor years unborn
Could to my sight that heavenly face restore.

Characteristics
Of a Child three Years old

Loving she is, and tractable, though wild; *from the heart*
And Innocence hath privilege in her
To dignify arch looks and laughing eyes;
And feats of cunning; and the pretty round
Of trespasses, affected to provoke 5
Mock-chastisement and partnership in play.
And, as a faggot sparkles on the hearth,
Not less if unattended and alone
Than when both young and old sit gathered round
And take delight in its activity, 10
Even so this happy Creature of herself
Is all sufficient: solitude to her
Is blithe society, who fills the air
With gladness and involuntary songs.
Light are her sallies as the tripping Fawn's 15
Forth-startled from the fern where she lay couched;
Unthought-of, unexpected as the stir
Of the soft breeze ruffling the meadow flowers;
Or from before it chasing wantonly
The many-coloured images impressed 20
Upon the bosom of a placid lake.

Maternal Grief

Departed Child! I could forget thee once
Though at my bosom nursed; this woeful gain
Thy dissolution brings, that in my soul

Is present and perpetually abides
A shadow, never, never to be displaced,   5
By the returning substance, seen or touched,
Seen by mine eyes, or clasped in my embrace.
Absence and death how differ they! and how
Shall I admit that nothing can restore
What one short sigh so easily removed?—   10
Death, life, and sleep, reality and thought,
Assist me God their boundaries to know,
O teach me calm submission to thy Will!

The Child she mourned had overstepped the pale
Of Infancy, but still did breathe the air   15
That sanctifies its confines, and partook
Reflected beams of that celestial light
To all the Little-ones on sinful earth
Not unvouchsafed—a light that warmed and cheered
Those several qualities of heart and mind   20
Which, in her own blest nature, rooted deep
Daily before the Mother's watchful eye,
And not hers only, their peculiar charms
Unfolded,—beauty, for its present self
And for its promises to future years,   25
With not unfrequent rapture fondly hailed.

Have you espied upon a dewy lawn
A pair of Leverets each provoking each
To a continuance of their fearless sport,
Two separate Creatures in their several gifts   30
Abounding, but so fashioned that, in all
That Nature prompts them to display, their looks
Their starts of motion and their fits of rest,
An undistinguishable style appears
And character of gladness, as if Spring   35
Lodged in their innocent bosoms, and the spirit
Of the rejoicing morning were their own.

Such union, in the lovely Girl maintained
And her twin Brother, had the parent seen,
Ere, pouncing like a ravenous bird of prey,   40

Death in a moment parted them, and left
The Mother, in her turns of anguish, worse
Than desolate; for oft-times from the sound
Of the survivor's sweetest voice (dear child,
He knew it not) and from his happiest looks,   45
Did she extract the food of self-reproach,
As one that lived ungrateful for the stay,
By Heaven afforded to uphold her maimed
And tottering spirit. And full oft the Boy,
Now first acquainted with distress and grief,   50
Shrunk from his Mother's presence, shunned with fear
Her sad approach, and stole away to find,
In his known haunts of joy where'er he might,
A more congenial object. But, as time
Softened her pangs and reconciled the child   55
To what he saw, he gradually returned,
Like a scared Bird encouraged to renew
A broken intercourse; and, while his eyes
Were yet with pensive fear and gentle awe
Turned upon her who bore him, she would stoop   60
To imprint a kiss that lacked not power to spread
Faint colour over both their pallid cheeks,
And stilled his tremulous lip. Thus they were calmed
And cheered; and now together breathe fresh air
In open fields; and when the glare of day   65
Is gone, and twilight to the Mother's wish
Befriends the observance, readily they join
In walks whose boundary is the lost One's grave,
Which he with flowers hath planted, finding there
Amusement, where the Mother does not miss   70
Dear consolation, kneeling on the turf
In prayer, yet blending with that solemn rite
Of pious faith the vanities of grief;
For such, by pitying Angels and by Spirits
Transferred to regions upon which the clouds   75
Of our weak nature rest not, must be deemed
Those willing tears, and unforbidden sighs,
And all those tokens of a cherished sorrow,
Which, soothed and sweetened by the grace of Heaven

As now it is, seems to her own fond heart,   80
Immortal as the love that gave it being.

"If Thou indeed derive thy light from Heaven"

If Thou indeed derive thy light from Heaven,
Shine, Poet, in thy place, and be content!
The Star that from the zenith darts its beams,
Visible though it be to half the Earth,
Though half a sphere be conscious of its brightness,   5
Is yet of no diviner origin,
No purer essence, than the One that burns,
Like an untended watch-fire, on the ridge
Of some dark mountain; or than those which seem
Humbly to hang, like twinkling winter lamps,   10
Among the branches of the leafless trees.

"Six months to six years added, He remain'd"

Six months to six years added, He remain'd
Upon this sinful earth, by sin unstain'd.
O blessed Lord, whose mercy then remov'd
A Child whom every eye that look'd on lov'd,
Support us, teach us calmly to resign   5
What we possess'd and now is wholly thine.

November, 1813[1]

Now that all hearts are glad, all faces bright,
Our aged Sovereign sits;—to the ebb and flow
Of states and kingdoms, to their joy or woe
Insensible;—he sits deprived of sight,
And lamentably wrapped in twofold night,   5
Whom no weak hopes deceived,—whose mind ensued,
Through perilous war, with regal fortitude,
Peace that should claim respect from lawless Might.
Dread King of Kings, vouchsafe a ray divine
To his forlorn condition! let thy grace   10
Upon his inner soul in mercy shine;

---

1   The sonnet appeared first in the *Courier*, January 1, 1814, about a month after the defeat of
    Napoleon at Leipzig was announced in London. Published in 1815 as "Added, November
    1813"—that is, added to the sonnet series "Liberty."

Permit his heart to kindle, and embrace,
(Though were it only for a moment's space)
The triumphs of this hour; for they are THINE!

Composed in one of the Valleys of Westmoreland, on Easter Sunday

With each recurrence of this glorious morn
That saw the Saviour in his human frame
Rise from the dead, erewhile the Cottage-dame
Put on fresh raiment—till that hour unworn:
Domestic hands the home-bred wool had shorn,   5
And she who span it culled the daintiest fleece,
In thoughtful reverence to the Prince of Peace
Whose temples bled beneath the platted thorn.
A blest estate when piety sublime
These humble props disdain'd not! O green dales!   10
Sad may *I* be who heard your sabbath chime
When Art's abused inventions were unknown;
Kind Nature's various wealth was all your own;
And benefits were weighed in Reason's scales!

"Weak is the will of Man, his judgment blind"

"Weak is the will of Man, his judgment blind;
Remembrance persecutes, and Hope betrays;
Heavy is woe;—and joy, for human-kind,
A mournful thing,—so transient is the blaze!"
Thus might *he* paint our lot of mortal days   5
Who wants the glorious faculty assigned
To elevate the more-than-reasoning Mind,
And colour life's dark cloud with orient rays.
Imagination is that sacred power,
Imagination lofty and refined: 10
'Tis hers to pluck the amaranthine Flower
Of Faith, and round the Sufferer's temples bind
Wreaths that endure affliction's heaviest shower,
And do not shrink from sorrow's keenest wind.

Composed at Cora Linn,

IN SIGHT OF WALLACE'S TOWER

> "—How Wallace fought for Scotland, left the name
> Of Wallace to be found, like a wild flower,
> All over his dear Country; left the deeds
> Of Wallace, like a family of ghosts,
> To people the steep rocks and river banks
> Her natural sanctuaries, with a local soul
> Of independence and stern liberty."   *MS.*

Lord of the Vale! astounding Flood!
The dullest leaf, in this thick wood,
Quakes—conscious of thy power;
The caves reply with hollow moan;
And vibrates, to its central stone,   5
Yon time-cemented Tower!

And yet how fair the rural scene!
For thou, O Clyde, hast ever been
Beneficent as strong;
Pleased in refreshing dews to steep   10
The little trembling flowers that peep
Thy shelving rocks among.

Hence all who love their country, love
To look on thee—delight to rove
Where they thy voice can hear;   15
And, to the patriot-warrior's Shade,
Lord of the vale! to Heroes laid
In dust, that voice is dear!

Along thy banks, at dead of night,
Sweeps visibly the Wallace Wight;   20
Or stands, in warlike vest,
Aloft, beneath the moon's pale beam,
A Champion worthy of the Stream,
Yon grey tower's living crest!

But clouds and envious darkness hide   25
A Form not doubtfully descried:—
Their transient mission o'er,

O say to what blind regions flee
These Shapes of awful phantasy?
To what untrodden shore?   30

Less than divine command they spurn;
But this we from the mountains learn,
And this the valleys show,
That never will they deign to hold
Communion where the heart is cold   35
To human weal and woe.

The man of abject soul in vain
Shall walk the Marathonian Plain;
Or thrid the shadowy gloom,
That still invests the guardian Pass,   40
Where stood sublime Leonidas,
Devoted to the tomb.

Nor deem that it can aught avail
For such to glide with oar or sail
Beneath the piny wood,   45
Where Tell once drew, by Uri's lake,
His vengeful shafts—prepared to slake
Their thirst in Tyrants' blood!

Suggested by a beautiful ruin
upon one of the islands of Loch Lomond,
a place chosen for the retreat of a solitary individual,
from whom this habitation acquired the name of
The Brownie's Cell

To barren heath, and quaking fen,
Or depth of labyrinthine glen;
Or into trackless forest set
With trees, whose lofty umbrage met;
World-wearied Men withdrew of yore,—   5
(Penance their trust, and Prayer their store;)
And in the wilderness were bound
To such apartments as they found;
Or with a new ambition raised;
That God might suitably be praised.   10

High lodged the Warrior, like a bird of prey;
Or where broad waters round him lay:
But this wild Ruin is no ghost
Of his devices—buried, lost!
Within this little lonely Isle   15
There stood a consecrated Pile;
Where tapers burn'd, and mass was sung,
For them whose timid spirits clung
To mortal succour, though the tomb
Had fixed, for ever fixed, their doom!   20

Upon those servants of another world
When madding Power her bolts had hurled,
Their habitation shook;—it fell,
And perish'd—save one narrow Cell;
Whither, at length, a Wretch retir'd   25
Who neither grovell'd nor aspir'd:
He, struggling in the net of pride,
The future scorned, the past defied;
Still tempering, from the unguilty forge
Of vain conceit, an iron scourge!   30

Proud Remnant was he of a fearless Race,
Who stood and flourished face to face
With their perennial hills;—but Crime
Hastening the stern decrees of Time,
Brought low a Power, which from its home   35
Burst, when repose grew wearisome;
And, taking impulse from the sword,
And mocking its own plighted word,
Had found, in ravage widely dealt,
Its warfare's bourn, its travel's belt!   40

All, all were dispossess'd, save Him whose smile
Shot lightning through this lonely Isle!
No right had he but what he made
To this small spot, his leafy shade;
But the ground lay within that ring   45
To which he only dared to cling;
Renouncing here, as worse than dead,
The craven few who bowed the head

Beneath the change, who heard a claim
How loud! yet liv'd in peace with shame.   50

From year to year this shaggy Mortal went
(So seem'd it) down a strange descent:
Till they, who saw his outward frame,
Fix'd on him an unhallow'd name;
Him—free from all malicious taint,   55
And guiding, like the Patmos Saint,
A pen unwearied—to indite,
In his lone Isle, the dreams of night;
Impassion'd dreams, that strove to span
The faded glories of his Clan!   60

Suns that through blood their western harbour sought,
And stars that in their courses fought,—
Towers rent, winds combating with woods—
Lands delug'd by unbridled floods,—
And beast and bird that from the spell   65
Of sleep took import terrible,—
These types mysterious (if the show
Of battle and the routed foe
Had failed) would furnish an array
Of matter for the dawning day!   70

How disappeared He?—ask the Newt and Toad,
Inheritors of his abode;
The Otter crouching undisturb'd,
In her dank cleft;—but be thou curb'd
O froward Fancy! mid a scene   75
Of aspect winning and serene;
For those offensive creatures shun
The inquisition of the sun!
And in this region flowers delight,
And all is lovely to the sight.   80

Spring finds not here a melancholy breast,
When she applies her annual test
To dead and living; when her breath
Quickens, as now, the wither'd heath;—
Nor flaunting Summer—when he throws   85

His soul into the briar-rose;
Or calls the lily from her sleep
Prolong'd beneath the bordering deep;
Nor Autumn, when the viewless wren
Is warbling near the Brownie's Den.   90

Wild Relique! beauteous as the chosen spot
In Nysa's isle, the embellish'd Grot;
Whither, by care of Lybian Jove,
(High Servant of paternal Love)
Young Bacchus was conveyed—to lie   95
Safe from his step-dame Rhea's eye;
Where bud, and bloom, and fruitage, glowed,
Close-crowding round the Infant God;
All colours, and the liveliest streak
A foil to his celestial cheek!   100

Effusion,

IN THE PLEASURE-GROUND ON THE BANKS OF THE BRAN, NEAR DUNKELD

"The water fall, by a loud roaring, warned us when we must expect it. We were first, however, conducted into a small apartment where the Gardener desired us to look at the picture of Ossian, which, while he was telling the history of the young Artist who executed the work, disappeared, parting in the middle—flying asunder as by the touch of magic—and lo! we are at the entrance of a splendid apartment, which was almost dizzy and alive with waterfalls, that tumbled in all directions; the great cascade, opposite the window, which faced us, being reflected in innumerable mirrors upon the ceilings and against the walls."

Extract from the Journal of my Fellow-Traveller.

What! He—who, mid the kindred throng
Of Heroes that inspired his song,
Doth yet frequent the hill of storms,
The Stars dim-twinkling through their: forms!
What! Ossian here?—a painted Thrall,   5
Mute fixture on a stuccoed wall;
To serve—an unsuspected screen
For show that must not yet be seen;
And, when the moment comes, to part
And vanish, by mysterious art;   10

Head, Harp, and, Body, split asunder,
For ingress to a world of wonder;
A gay Saloon, with waters dancing
Upon the sight wherever glancing;
One loud Cascade in front, and lo!   15
A thousand like it, white as snow—
Streams on the walls, and torrent foam
As active round the hollow dome,
Illusive cataracts! of their terrors
Not stripped, nor voiceless in the Mirrors,   20
That catch the pageant from the Flood
Thundering adown a rocky wood!
Strange scene, fantastic and uneasy
As ever made a Maniac dizzy,
When disenchanted from the mood   25
That loves on sullen thoughts to brood!

   O Nature, in thy changeful visions,
Through all thy most abrupt transitions,
Smooth, graceful, tender, or sublime,
Ever averse to Pantomime,   30
Thee neither do they know nor us
Thy Servants, who can trifle thus;
Else surely had the sober powers
Of rock that frowns, and stream that roars,
Exalted by congenial sway   35
Of Spirits, and the undying Lay,
And names that moulder not away,
Awakened some redeeming thought
More worthy of this favoured Spot;
Recalled some feeling—to set free   40
The Bard from such indignity!

   The Effigies of a valiant Wight[1]
I once beheld, a Templar Knight;
Not postrate, not like those that rest
On Tombs, with palms together prest,   45
But sculptured out of living stone,
And standing upright and alone,

---

1 "On the banks of the River Nid, near Knaresborough." WW

Both hands with rival energy
Employed in setting his sword free
From its dull sheath—stern Sentinel   50
Intent to guard St. Robert's Cell;
As if with memory of the affray
Far distant, when, as legends say,
The Monks of Fountain's thronged to force
From its dear home the Hermit's corse,   55
That in their keeping it might lie,
To crown their Abbey's sanctity.
So had they rushed into the Grot
Of sense despised, a world forgot,
And torn him from his loved Retreat,   60
Where Altar-stone and rock-hewn seat
Still hint that quiet best is found,
Even by the *Living*, under ground;
But a bold Knight, the selfish aim
Defeating, put the Monks to shame,   65
There where you see his Image stand
Bare to the sky, with threatening brand
Which lingering Nid is proud to show
Reflected in the pool below.

　　Thus, like the Men of earliest days,   70
Our Sires set forth their grateful praise;
Uncouth the workmanship, and rude!
But, nursed in mountain solitude,
Might some aspiring Artist dare
To seize whate'er, through misty air,   75
A Ghost, by glimpses, may present
Of imitable lineament,
And give the Phantom such array
As less should scorn the abandoned clay;
Then let him hew with patient stroke   80
An Ossian out of mural rock,
And leave the figurative Man
Upon thy Margin, roaring Bran!
Fixed, like the Templar of the steep,
An everlasting watch to keep;   85
With local sanctities in trust,

More precious than a Hermit's dust;
And virtues through the mass infused,
Which old Idolatry abused.

 What though the Granite would deny   90
All fervour to the sightless eye;
And touch from rising Suns in vain
Solicit a Memnonian strain;
Yet, in some fit of anger sharp,
The Wind might force the deep-grooved harp   95
To utter melancholy moans
Not unconnected with the tones
Of soul-sick flesh and weary bones;
While grove and river notes would lend,
Less deeply sad, with these to blend!   100

 Vain Pleasures of luxurious life,
For ever with yourselves at strife;
Through town and country both deranged
By affectations interchanged,
And all the perishable gauds   105
That heaven-deserted Man applauds;
When will your hapless Patrons learn
To watch and ponder—to discern
The freshness, the eternal youth,
Of admiration sprung from truth;   110
From beauty infinitely growing
Upon a mind with love o'erflowing;
To sound the depths of every Art
That seeks its wisdom through the heart?

 Thus (where the intrusive Pile, ill-graced   115
With baubles of Theatric taste,
O'erlooks the Torrent breathing showers
On motley bands of alien flowers,
In stiff confusion set or sown,
Till Nature cannot find her own,   120
Or keep a remnant of the sod
Which Caledonian Heroes trod)
I mused; and, thirsting for redress,
Recoiled into the wilderness.

Yarrow Visited,

SEPTEMBER, 1814[1]

And is this—Yarrow?—*This* the Stream
Of which my fancy cherish'd,
So faithfully, a waking dream?
An image that hath perish'd!
O that some Minstrel's harp were near,   5
To utter notes of gladness,
And chase this silence from the air,
That fills my heart with sadness!

Yet why?—a silvery current flows
With uncontrolled meanderings;   10
Nor have these eyes by greener hills
Been soothed, in all my wanderings.
And, through her depths, Saint Mary's Lake
Is visibly delighted;
For not a feature of those hills   15
Is in the mirror slighted.

A blue sky bends o'er Yarrow vale,
Save where that pearly whiteness
Is round the rising sun diffused,
A tender, hazy brightness;   20
Mild dawn of promise! that excludes
All profitless dejection;
Though not unwilling here to admit
A pensive recollection.

Where was it that the famous Flower   25
Of Yarrow Vale lay bleeding?
His bed perchance was yon smooth mound
On which the herd is feeding:
And haply from this crystal pool,
Now peaceful as the morning,   30
The Water-wraith ascended thrice—
And gave his doleful warning.

---

1   In a note published with the poem in 1836, WW refers his reader to *Yarrow Unvisited* (c.
1803). See vol. 1 of this edition, and a third Yarrow poem, *Yarrow Revisited*, below.

Delicious is the Lay that sings
The haunts of happy Lovers,
The path that leads them to the grove,   35
The leafy grove that covers:
And Pity sanctifies the verse
That paints, by strength of sorrow,
The unconquerable strength of love;
Bear witness, rueful Yarrow!   40

But thou, that didst appear so fair
To fond imagination,
Dost rival in the light of day
Her delicate creation:
Meek loveliness is round thee spread,   45
A softness still and holy;
The grace of forest charms decayed,
And pastoral melancholy.

That Region left, the Vale unfolds
Rich groves of lofty stature,   50
With Yarrow winding through the pomp
Of cultivated nature;
And, rising from those lofty groves,
Behold a Ruin hoary!
The shattered front of Newark's Towers,   55
Renowned in Border story.

Fair scenes for childhood's opening bloom,
For sportive youth to stray in;
For manhood to enjoy his strength;
And age to wear away in!   60
Yon Cottage seems a bower of bliss;
It promises protection
To studious ease, and generous cares,
And every chaste affection!

How sweet, on this autumnal day,   65
The wild wood's fruits to gather,
And on my True-love's forehead plant
A crest of blooming heather!
And what if I enwreathed my own!

'Twere no offence to reason;   70
The sober Hills thus deck their brows
To meet the wintry season.

I see—but not by sight alone,
Lov'd Yarrow, have I won thee;
A ray of Fancy still survives—   75
Her sunshine plays upon thee!
Thy ever-youthful waters keep
A course of lively pleasure;
And gladsome notes my lips can breathe,
Accordant to the measure.   80

The vapours linger round the Heights,
They melt—and soon must vanish;
One hour is theirs, nor more is mine—
Sad thought, which I would banish,
But that I know, where'er I go,   85
Thy genuine image, Yarrow,
Will dwell with me—to heighten joy,
And cheer my mind in sorrow.

To ———

From the dark chambers of dejection freed,
Spurning the unprofitable yoke of care
Rise, * * * * rise:[1] the gales of youth shall bear
Thy genius forward like a winged steed.
Though bold Bellerophon (so Jove decreed   5
In wrath) fell headlong from the fields of air,
Yet a high guerdon waits on minds that dare,
If aught be in them of immortal seed,
And reason govern that audacious flight
Which heav'n-ward they direct.— Then droop not thou,   10
Erroneously renewing a sad vow
In the low dell mid Roslin's fading grove:
A cheerful life is what the Muses love,
A soaring spirit is their prime delight.

---

1   In 1820 WW replaced the asterisks with the surname of his Scottish friend, R. P. Gillies
    (1778–1858).

Extract

FROM THE CONCLUSION OF A POEM, COMPOSED UPON LEAVING SCHOOL[1]

Dear native Regions, I foretell
From what I feel at this farewell,
That, wheresoe'er my steps shall tend,
And whensoe'er my course shall end,
If in that hour a single tie   5
Survive of local sympathy,
My soul will cast the backward view,
The longing look alone on you.

Thus, when the Sun, prepared for rest,
Hath gained the precincts of the West,   10
Though his departing radiance fail
To illuminate the hollow Vale,
A lingering light he fondly throws
On the dear Hills where first he rose.

Laodamìa

"With sacrifice, before the rising morn
Performed, my slaughtered Lord have I required;
And in thick darkness, amid shades forlorn,
Him of the infernal Gods have I desired:
Celestial pity I again implore;—   5
Restore him to my sight—great Jove, restore!"

So speaking, and by fervent love endowed
With faith, the suppliant heav'n-ward lifts her hands;
While, like the Sun emerging from a Cloud,
Her countenance brightens,—and her eye expands,   10
Her bosom heaves and spreads, her stature grows,
And she expects the issue in repose.

O terror! what hath she perceived?—O joy!
What doth she look on?—whom doth she behold?
Her hero slain upon the beach of Troy?   15
His vital presence—his corporeal mold?

---

1   The reading text is that of *Poems*, 1815. For the early poem mentioned in the title, see ll.
354–365 of *The Vale of Esthwaite* in vol. 1 of this edition.

It is—if sense deceive her not—'tis He!
And a God leads him—winged Mercury!

Mild Hermes spake—and touched her with his wand
That calms all fear, "Such grace hath crowned thy prayer,   20
Laodamia, that at Jove's command
Thy Husband walks the paths of upper air:
He comes to tarry with thee three hours' space;
Accept the gift, behold him face to face."

Forth sprang the impassion'd Queen her Lord to clasp;   25
Again that consummation she essayed;
But unsubstantial Form eludes her grasp
As often as that eager grasp was made.
The Phantom parts—but parts to re-unite,
And re-assume his place before her sight.   30

"Protesilaus, lo! thy guide is gone!
Confirm, I pray, the Vision with thy voice:
This is our Palace,—yonder is thy throne;
Speak, and the floor thou tread'st on will rejoice.
Not to appal me have the Gods bestowed   35
This precious boon,—and blest a sad Abode."

"Great Jove, Laodamia, doth not leave
His gifts imperfect:—Spectre though I be,
I am not sent to scare thee or deceive;
But in reward of thy fidelity.   40
And something also did my worth obtain;
For fearless virtue bringeth boundless gain.

Thou know'st, the Delphic oracle foretold
That the first Greek who touch'd the Trojan strand
Should die; but me the threat did not withhold: 45
A generous cause a Victim did demand;
And forth I leapt upon the sandy plain;
A self-devoted Chief—by Hector slain."

"Supreme of Heroes—bravest, noblest, best!
Thy matchless courage I bewail no more,   50
That then, when tens of thousands were deprest
By doubt, propelled thee to the fatal shore:

Thou found'st—and I forgive thee—here thou art—
A nobler counsellor than my poor heart.

But thou, though capable of sternest deed,   55
Wert kind as resolute, and good as brave;
And he, whose power restores thee, hath decreed
That thou shouldst cheat the malice of the grave;
Redundant are thy locks, thy lips as fair
As when their breath enriched Thessalian air.   60

No Spectre greets me,—no vain Shadow this:
Come, blooming Hero, place thee by my side!
Give, on this well-known couch, one nuptial kiss
To me, this day, a second time thy bride!"
Jove frowned in heaven; the conscious Parcæ threw   65
Upon those roseate lips a Stygian hue.

"This visage tells thee that my doom is past:
Know, virtue were not virtue if the joys
Of sense were able to return as fast
And surely as they vanish.—Earth destroys   70
Those raptures duly—Erebus disdains:
Calm pleasures there abide—majestic pains.

Be taught, O faithful Consort, to control
Rebellious passion: for the Gods approve
The depth, and not the tumult of the soul;   75
The fervor—not the impotence of love.
Thy transports moderate; and meekly mourn
When I depart, for brief is my sojourn—"

"Ah, wherefore?—Did not Hercules by force
Wrest from the guardian Monster of the tomb   80
Alcestis, a reanimated Corse,
Given back to dwell on earth in beauty's bloom?
Medea's spells dispersed the weight of years,
And Æson stood a Youth mid youthful peers.

The Gods to us are merciful—and they   85
Yet further may relent: for mightier far
Than strength of nerve and sinew, or the sway
Of magic potent over sun and star

Is love, though oft to agony distrest,
And though his favorite seat be feeble Woman's breast.　　　90

But if thou go'st, I follow—" "Peace!" he said—
She looked upon him and was calmed and cheered;
The ghastly colour from his lips had fled;
In his deportment, shape, and mien, appeared
Elysian beauty—melancholy grace—　　　　　　　95
Brought from a pensive though a happy place.

He spake of love, such love as Spirits feel
In worlds whose course is equable and pure;
No fears to beat away—no strife to heal—
The past unsighed for, and the future sure;　　　100
Spake, as a witness, of a second birth
For all that is most perfect upon earth:

Of all that is most beauteous—imaged there
In happier beauty; more pellucid streams,
An ampler ether, a diviner air,　　　　　　　105
And fields invested with purpureal gleams;
Climes which the Sun, who sheds the brightest day
Earth knows, is all unworthy to survey.

Yet there the Soul shall enter which hath earned
That privilege by virtue.— "Ill," said he,　　　110
"The end of man's existence I discerned,
Who from ignoble games and revelry[1]
Could draw, when we had parted, vain delight
While tears were thy best pastime,—day and night:

And while my youthful peers, before my eyes,　　　115
(Each Hero following his peculiar bent)
Prepared themselves for glorious enterprize
By martial sports,—or, seated in the tent,
Chieftains and kings in council were detained;
What time the Fleet at Aulis lay enchained.　　　120

The wish'd-for wind was given:—I then revolved

1　"For this feature in the character of Protesilaus, see the Iphigenia in Aulis of Euripides."
　WW

Our future course, upon the silent sea;
And, if no worthier led the way, resolved
That, of a thousand vessels, mine should be
The foremost prow in pressing to the strand,— 125
Mine the first blood that tinged the Trojan sand.

Yet bitter, oft-times bitter, was the pang
When of thy loss I thought, beloved Wife;
On thee too fondly did my memory hang,
And on the joys we shared in mortal life,— 130
The paths which we had trod—these fountains—flowers;
My new-planned Cities, and unfinished Towers.

But should suspense permit the Foe to cry,
"Behold they tremble!—haughty their array,
Yet of their number no one dares to die?"— 135
In soul I swept the indignity away:
Old frailties then recurred:—but lofty thought,
In act embodied, my deliverance wrought.

And thou, though strong in love, art all too weak
In reason, in self-government too slow; 140
I counsel thee by fortitude to seek
Our blest re-union in the shades below.
The invisible world with thee hath sympathized;
Be thy affections raised and solemnized.

Learn by a mortal yearning to ascend 145
Towards a higher object:—Love was given,
Encouraged, sanctioned, chiefly for this end.
For this the passion to excess was driven—
That self might be annulled; her bondage prove
The fetters of a dream, opposed to love." 150

Aloud she shrieked! for Hermes re-appears!
Round the dear Shade she would have clung—'tis vain:
The hours are past, too brief had they been years;
And him no mortal effort can detain:
Swift tow'rd the realms that know not earthly day, 155
He through the portal takes his silent way—
And on the palace-floor a lifeless corse she lay.

Ah, judge her gently who so deeply loved!
Her, who, in reason's spite, yet without crime,
Was in a trance of passion thus removed;   160
Delivered from the galling yoke of time
And these frail elements to gather flowers
Of blissful quiet mid unfading bowers.

Yet tears to human suffering are due;
And mortal hopes defeated and o'erthrown   165
Are mourned by man, and not by man alone,
As fondly he believes.—Upon the side
Of Hellespont (such faith was entertained)
A knot of spiry trees for ages grew
From out the tomb of him for whom she died;   170
And ever, when such stature they had gained
That Ilium's walls were subject to their view,
The trees' tall summits wither'd at the sight;
A constant interchange of growth and blight![1]

"Through Cumbrian wilds, in many a mountain cove"

Through Cumbrian wilds, in many a mountain cove,
The pastoral Muse laments the Wheel—no more
Engaged, near blazing hearth on clean-swept floor,
In tasks which guardian Angels might approve;
Friendly the weight of leisure to remove,   5
And to beguile the lassitude of ease;
Gracious to all the dear dependences
Of house and field,—to plenty, peace, and love.
There, too, did *Fancy* prize the murmuring wheel;
For sympathies, inexplicably fine,   10
Instilled a confidence—how sweet to feel!
That ever in the night calm, when the Sheep
Upon their grassy beds lay couch'd in sleep,
The quickening spindle drew a trustier line.

"Emperors and Kings, how oft have Temples rung"

Emperors and Kings, how oft have Temples rung
With impious thanksgiving, the Almighty's scorn!

---

1   "For the account of these long-lived trees, see Pliny's Natural History, Lib. 16. Cap. 44." WW

How oft above their altars have been hung
Trophies that led the Good and Wise to mourn
Triumphant wrong, battle of battle born,   5
And sorrow that to fruitless sorrow clung!
Now, from Heaven-sanctioned Victory, Peace is sprung;
In this firm hour Salvation lifts her horn.
Glory to arms! but, conscious that the nerve
Of popular Reason, long mistrusted, freed   10
Your Thrones, from duty, Princes! fear to swerve;
Be just, be grateful; nor, the Oppressor's creed
Reviving, heavier chastisement deserve
Than ever forced unpitied hearts to bleed.

*Written, November 13,1814, on a blank leaf in a Copy of the Author's
Poem* THE EXCURSION, *upon hearing of the death of the late
Vicar of Kendal*

To public notice, with reluctance strong,
Did I deliver this unfinished Song;
Yet for one happy issue;—and I look
With self-congratulation on the Book
Which pious, learned MURFITT saw and read;—   5
Upon my thoughts his saintly Spirit fed;
He conn'd the new-born Lay with grateful heart;
Foreboding not how soon he must depart,
Unweeting that to him the joy was given
Which good Men take with them from Earth to Heaven.   10

Artegal and Elidure—

Where be the Temples which in Britain's Isle
To his paternal Gods the Trojan reared?
Gone like a morning dream or like a Pile
Of gorgeous clouds that in the west appeared!
Ere Julius landed on her white-cliff'd shore   5
They sank—deliver'd o'er
To fatal dissolution, and I ween
No vestige then was left that such had ever been.

A British Record that had lain concealed
Mid fairy-haunted woods and sainted springs,   10

In old Armorica the course revealed,
The wondrous course of long-forgotten things,
How Brutus came by oracles impelled
And Albion's Giants quelled,
A brood whom no civility could melt,   15
Who never tasted grace and goodness ne'er had felt.

By brave Corineus aided he subdued
And rooted out the intolerable kind;
And this too-long-polluted Land imbued
With gentle arts and usages refined;   20
Whence golden harvests, cities, warlike towers,
And pleasure's peaceful bowers;
Whence all the fix'd delights of house and home,
Friendship that will not break and love that cannot roam.

O, happy Britain!—Region all too fair   25
For self-delighting fancy to endure
That Silence only should inhabit there,
Wild Beasts, or uncouth Savages impure!
But intermingled with the generous seed
Grew many [a] poisonous weed;   30
Thus fares it still with all that takes its birth
From human care, or grows upon the breast of earth.

Hence, and how soon! that uncouth warfare waged
By Guendolen against her faithless Lord,
Till She, in jealous fury unassuaged,   35
Had slain the Paramours with ruthless sword.
Then, into Severn hideously defiled
She cast their blameless Child,
Sabrina, vowing that the Stream should bear
That name through every age, her hatred to declare.   40

Thus speaks the Chronicle, and tells of Lear,
By his ungrateful Daughters turn'd adrift.
Hear him ye Elements.— They cannot hear,
Nor can the winds restore his simple gift.
But one there is, a Child of Nature meek   45
Who comes her sire to seek,

And he, recovering sense, upon her breast
Leans smilingly, and sinks into a perfect rest.

There, too, we read of Spenser's faery themes,
And those that Milton loved in youthful years,   50
The sage enchanter Merlin's subtle schemes,
The marvellous feats of Arthur and his peers,
That British Hero, who, to light restored
With that terrific sword
Which now he wields in subterraneous war,   55
Shall spread his country's name in conquest wide and far.

What wonder then if [in] the ample field
Of that rich Volume one particular Flower,
Doth seemingly in vain its sweetness yield
And blooms unnoticed even till this late hour?   60
Yet Gentle Muses your assistance grant
While I this Flower transplant
Into that Garden of pure poesy
Which I have tended long in all humility.

———

A King more worthy of respect and love   65
Than wise Gorbonean ruled not in his day;
And Britain rose in happiness above
All neighboring Countries through his righteous sway;
He poured rewards and favours on the good,
The Oppressor he withstood,   70
And while he served the Gods with reverence due
Fields smiled, and Cities rose and Towns and Temples grew.

Him Artegal succeeds—but oft the Son
Degenerates from the Sire and so did he.
A hopeful reign auspiciously begun   75
Was darkened soon by vilest tyranny.
From bad to worse he sank until at length
The Nobles leagued their strength
With the vex'd people and the Tyrant chased
From out the realm whose throne his vices had disgraced.   80

From land to land, the royal Exile went

Suppliant for aid his sceptre to regain;
To many a court, and many a Warrior's tent
He urg'd his persevering suit in vain;
Him, in whose wretched heart ambition failed   85
Dire poverty assailed
And tired of slights which he no more could brook
Towards his native Land he cast a longing look.

The winds and waves have aided him to reach
That coast the object of his heart's desire;   90
But as the crownless Sovereign trod the beach
His eye balls kindle with resentful ire
As if incensed with all that he beholds—
The woods, the naked wolds,
And with the remnant of that faithful band   95
That to his fortunes cleave and wait on his command.

"Forgive this passion!—" Artegal exclaimed
And as he spake they drew into a wood,
And from its shady boughs protection claimed,
For light they feared and busy neighbourhood.   100
How changed from him who, born to highest place,
Had swayed the royal mace
Flattered and feared, despiséd and defied,
In Troynovant, his seat by silver Thames's side!

Oft by imaginary terrors scared   105
And sometimes into real danger brought
To Calaterium's forest he repaired
And in its depth securer refuge sought.
Thence to a few whom he esteemed his Friends
A Messenger he sends,   110
And from their secret loyalty requires
Shelter and daily bread—the amount of his desires.

With his Attendants, there, at break of morn
Wandering by stealth abroad, he chanced to hear
A startling outcry made by hound and horn;   115
He would escape but sees the flying deer
And scouring toward him o'er the grassy plain,
Behold the hunter train;

And bids his Friends advance and meet the Chase
With seeming unconcern and with unaltered pace.   120

The royal Elidure who leads the chase
Hath checked his foaming Courser—"Can it be!
Methinks that I should recognize that face
Though much disguised by long adversity!"
He gazed rejoicing—and again he gazed   125
Confounded and amazed—
"It is the King my Brother"—and by sound
Of his own voice confirmed he leaps upon the ground.

Long, strait, and tender was the embrace he gave,
Feebly returned by trembling Artegal,   130
Whose natural affection doubts enslave
And apprehensions dark and criminal.
Loth to disturb the moving interview
The attendant Lords withdrew,
And while they stood upon the plain apart   135
Thus Elidure by words relieved his struggling heart.

"Gorbonian's heir, dear Brother, gladly met;
Whence comest thou, to my knowledge lost so long?—
But neither lost to love nor to regret—
Nor to my wishes lost,—Forgive the wrong   140
(Such it may seem) if I thy crown have borne,
Thy regal mantle worn;
I was their natural guardian, and 'tis just
That now I should restore what hath been held in trust."

"To me the wretched, helpless, destitute,   145
To me a Kingdom? Mock me not, I pray,"
Said Artegal; "thy love bears bitter fruit,
Ah let not Insult move me on my way!
Had justice rul'd in breasts of foreign kings
Then, then, upon the wings   150
Of war had I returned to claim my right;
This will I here avow not dreading thy despite."

"I do not blame thee," Elidure replied,
"But if my looks did with my words agree

At once I should be trusted—not defied—   155
And thou from all unwelcome thoughts be free.
May spotless Dian, Goddess of the chase,
Who to this blessed place
At this blest moment led me, if I speak
With insincere intent, on me her vengeance wreak!   160

"If this same spear which in my hand I grasp
Were Britain's Sceptre here would I [to] Thee
The symbol yield and would undo this clasp
If it confined the robe of sovereignty.
Joyless to me [the] pomp of regal court   165
And joyless sylvan sport
While thou art roving wretched and forlorn,
Thy couch the dewy earth, thy roof the forest thorn!"

Then Artegal thus spake—"I only sought
Within this realm a place of safe retreat;   170
Beware of rouzing an ambitious thought,
Beware of kindling hopes for me unmeet!
Thou bearst the name of wise; but in my mind
Art pitiably blind.
Full soon this generous impulse thou may'st rue   175
When that which has been done no wishes can undo.

"The greedy thirst of sovereignty, 'tis said,
Allows no kindred and regards no right;
But thou, I know not whence inspired, how led,
Wouldst change the course of things in all men's sight!   180
And this for one that cannot imitate
Thy virtue—who may hate;
For if by such strange sacrifice restored
He reign, thou still must be his king and sovereign Lord.

"Lifted in magnanimity above   185
Aught that my feeble nature could perform
Or even conceive—surpassing me in Love
Far as in power the eagle doth the worm—
I only, brother, should be king in name
And govern to my shame;   190
A Shadow in an odious Land where all

Of prompt and willing service to thy share would fall."

"Believe it not," said Elidure; "respect
Awaits on virtuous life, and ever most
Attends on goodness with dominion decked   195
That stands the universal empire's boast;
This can thy own experience testify,
Nor shall thy foes deny
That in the opening of thy gracious reign
Our Father's Spirit seem'd, in thee, to rule again.   200

"And what if o'er this bright unbosoming
Clouds of disgrace and envious fortune past!
Have we not seen the glories of the Spring
By noontide darkness veiled and overcast?
The lake that glitter'd like a sun-bright shield,   205
The sky, the gay green field,
Are vanished—gladness ceases in the [groves]
And trepidation strikes the blackened mountain coves.

"Once more the Sun victorious glimmers forth
And the wide world is brighter than before!   210
Such power is granted to thy latent worth
To spread the light and joy from shore to shore;
For past misdeeds how [?grateful] to atone!
—Reseated on thy throne
Give proof that long adversity and pain   215
And sorrow have confirmed thy inborn right to reign!—

"Yet not to overlook what thou mayst know
Thy enemies are neither weak nor few;
And circumspect must be our course and slow
Or ruin from my purpose may ensue.   220
Dismiss thy followers—Let them calmly wait
Such change in thy estate,
As I already have in thought devised
And which with caution due may soon be realiz'd."

The Story tells that Artegal straitway   225
Was by his Brother privily convey'd
To a far distant city, at that day

Alclwyd named, whose fortress, undismayed
By the hostility of mortals, stood
In sight of land and flood,   230
Obnoxious only on its lofty rock
To the careering storms, and perilous lightning's stroke.

When this impregnable retreat was gain'd,
In prudent furth'rance of his first intent
King Elidure a mortal sickness feign'd   235
And to his mightiest Lords a summons sent.
—Softly and one by one into such gloom
As suits a sick man's room
The Attendants introduce each potent peer
That he his Sovereign's will in singleness may hear.   240

Said Elidure, "Behold thy rightful king;
The banished Artegal before thee stands;
Kneel and renew to him the offering
Of thy allegiance: Justice this demands,
Immortal justice speaking through thy voice;   245
Receive him and rejoice!
His guilt is expiated; he will prove
Worthier than I have been of universal love."

If firm command and mild persuasion failed
To change the temper of an adverse mind   250
With such by other engines he prevail'd,
Threatening to fling their bodies to the wind
From the dread summit of a [?lonely] rock,
Alclwyd, lofty rock,
Alclwyd then but now Dumbarton named,   255
A memorable crag through widest Albion famed.

Departing thence to York their way they bent
While the glad people flowers before them strewed
And there King Elidure with glad consent
Of all who saw, a mighty multitude,   260
Upon his Brother's head replaced the crown,
Relinquished by his own,
Triumph of justice and affection pure

Whence he the title gained of pious Elidure.

A Brother thus a Brother did reclaim: 265
Through admiration of the heroic deed
The reelected Artegal became
"A true converted man," from bondage freed
Of Vice,—from that day forward, on his Soul
Possessing no controul;   270
And when he died the worthy and the brave
Shed tears of fond regret upon his honored grave.

Inscription for a National Monument

IN COMMEMORATION OF THE BATTLE OF WATERLOO

Intrepid sons of Albion!—not by you
Is life despised!—Ah no—the spacious earth
Ne'er saw a race who held, by right of birth,
So many objects to which love is due:
Ye slight not life—to God and Nature true;   5
But death, becoming death, is dearer far,
When duty bids you bleed in open war:
Hence hath your prowess quelled that impious crew.
Heroes, for instant sacrifice prepared,
Yet filled with ardour, and on triumph bent,   10
Mid direst shocks of mortal accident,
To you who fell, and you whom slaughter spared,
To guard the fallen, and consummate the event,
Your Country rears this sacred Monument!

Occasioned by the Same Battle.

FEBRUARY 1816

The Bard, whose soul is meek as dawning day,
Yet trained to judgments righteously severe;
Fervid, yet conversant with holy fear,
As recognizing one Almighty sway:
He whose experienced eye can pierce the array   5
Of past events,—to whom, in vision clear,
The aspiring heads of future things appear,
Like mountain-tops whence mists have rolled away:

Assoiled from all incumbrance of our time,[1]
He only, if such breathe, in strains devout   10
Shall comprehend this victory sublime;
And worthily rehearse the hideous rout,
Which the blest Angels, from their peaceful clime
Beholding, welcomed with a choral shout.

February 1816

O, for a kindling touch of that pure flame
Which taught the offering of song to rise
From thy lone bower, beneath Italian skies,
Great FILICAIA!— With celestial aim
It rose,—thy saintly rapture to proclaim,   5
Then, when the imperial city stood released
From bondage threatened by the embattled East,
And Christendom respired; from guilt and shame
Redeemed,—from miserable fear set free
By one day's feat—one mighty victory.   10
—Chaunt the Deliverer's praise in every tongue!
The cross shall spread,—the crescent hath waxed dim,—
He conquering—as in Earth and Heaven was sung—
HE CONQUERING THROUGH GOD, AND GOD BY HIM.[2]

To R. B. Haydon, Esq.

High is our calling, Friend!—Creative Art
(Whether the instrument of words she use,
Or pencil pregnant with etherial hues,)
Demands the service of a mind and heart,
Though sensitive, yet, in their weakest part,   5
Heroically fashioned—to infuse
Faith in the whispers of the lonely Muse,

---

1   "'From all this world's encumbrance did himself assoil.' *Spenser*." WW quotes from
    Edmund Spenser's *Faerie Queen*, VI, v.
2   "Ond'è ch'lo grido e griderò: giugnesti,
            Guerregiasti, è vincesti;
            Si, si, vincesti, O Campion forte e pio,
            Per Dio vinasti, e per te vinse Iddio. (1816)
    See Filicaia's Canzone, addressed to John Sobieski, king of Poland, upon his raising the
    siege of Vienna. This, and his other poems on the same occasion, are superior perhaps to
    any lyrical pieces that contemporary events have ever given birth to, those of the Hebrew
    Scriptures only excepted." WW refers to Vincenzo da Filicaia (1642-1707).

While the whole world seems adverse to desert:
And, oh! when Nature sinks, as oft she may,
Through long-lived pressure of obscure distress,   10
Still to be strenuous for the bright reward,
And in the soul admit of no decay,—
Brook no continuance of weak-mindedness:—
Great is the glory, for the strife is hard!

November 1, 1815

How clear, how keen, how marvellously bright
The effluence from yon distant mountain's head,
Which, strewn with snow as smooth as Heaven can shed,
Shines like another Sun—on mortal sight
Uprisen, as if to check approaching night,   5
And all her twinkling stars. Who now would tread,
If so he might, yon mountain's glittering head—
Terrestrial—but a surface, by the flight
Of sad mortality's earth-sullying wing,
Unswept, unstained? Nor shall the aerial Powers   10
Dissolve that beauty—destined to endure
White, radiant, spotless, exquisitely pure,
Through all vicissitudes—till genial spring
Have filled the laughing vales with welcome flowers.

September 1815

While not a leaf seems faded,—while the fields,
With ripening harvests prodigally fair,
In brightest sunshine bask,—this nipping air,
Sent from some distant clime where Winter wields
His icy scymetar, a foretaste yields   5
Of bitter change—and bids the Flowers beware;
And whispers to the silent Birds, "Prepare
Against the threatening Foe your trustiest shields."
For me, who under kindlier laws belong
To Nature's tuneful quire, this rustling dry   10
Through the green leaves, and yon crystalline sky,
Announce a season potent to renew,
Mid frost and snow, the instinctive joys of song,—
And nobler cares than listless summer knew.

"I watch, and long have watch'd, with calm regret"

I watch, and long have watch'd, with calm regret
Yon slowly-sinking Star,—immortal Sire
(So might he seem) of all the glittering quire!
Blue ether still surrounds him—yet—and yet;
But now the horizon's rocky parapet   5
Is reach'd; where, forfeiting his bright attire,
He burns—transmuted to a sullen fire,
That droops and dwindles; and, the appointed debt
To the flying moments paid, is seen no more.
Angels and Gods! we struggle with our fate,   10
While health, power, glory, pitiably decline,
Depress'd and then extinguish'd: and our state,
In this, how different, lost Star, from thine,
That no to-morrow shall our beams restore!

"Aerial Rock—whose solitary brow"

Aerial Rock—whose solitary brow
From this low threshold daily meets my sight;
When I look forth to hail the morning light,
Or quit the stars with lingering farewell—how
Shall I discharge to thee a grateful vow?—   5
By planting on thy head (in verse, at least,
As I have often done in thought) the crest
Of an imperial Castle, which the plough
Of ruin shall not touch. Innocent scheme!
That doth presume no more than to supply
A grace the sinuous vale and roaring stream
Want, through neglect of hoar Antiquity.
Rise, then, ye votive Towers, and catch a gleam
Of golden sun-set—ere it fade and die!

Ode

THE MORNING OF THE DAY APPOINTED FOR A GENERAL THANKSGIVING.

JANUARY 18, 1816[1]

Hail, universal Source of pure delight!

---

1   For the Advertisement to the volume in which this poem appeared see the notes at the end
of this volume.

Thou that canst shed the bliss of gratitude
On hearts howe'er insensible or rude,
Whether thy orient visitations smite
The haughty towers where monarchs dwell;   5
Or thou, impartial Sun, with presence bright
Cheer'st the low threshold of the Peasant's cell!
—Not unrejoiced I see thee climb the sky
In naked splendour, clear from mist or haze,
Or cloud approaching to divert the rays,   10
Which even in deepest winter testify
         Thy power and majesty,
Dazzling the vision that presumes to gaze.
—Well does thine aspect usher in this Day;
As aptly suits therewith that timid pace,   15
Framed in subjection to the chains
That bind thee to the path which God ordains
         That thou shalt trace,
Till, with the heavens and earth, thou pass away!
Nor less the stillness of these frosty plains,   20
Their utter stillness,—and the silent grace
Of yon etherial summits white with snow,
Whose tranquil pomp, and spotless purity,
         Report of storms gone by
         To us who tread below,   25
Do with the service of this Day accord.
—Divinest object, which the uplifted eye
Of mortal man is suffered to behold;
Thou, who upon yon snow-clad Heights hast poured
Meek splendour, nor forget'st the humble Vale,   30
Thou who dost warm Earth's universal mould,—
And for thy bounty wert not unadored
         By pious men of old;
Once more, heart-cheering Sun, I bid thee hail!
Bright be thy course to-day, let not this promise fail!   35

   Mid the deep quiet of this morning hour,
All nature seems to hear me while I speak,—
By feelings urged, that do not vainly seek
Apt language, ready as the tuneful notes
That stream in blithe succession from the throats   40

Of birds in leafy bower,
Warbling a farewell to a vernal shower.
—There is a radiant but a short-lived flame,
That burns for Poets in the dawning East;—
And oft my soul hath kindled at the same,   45
When the captivity of sleep had ceased;
But he who fixed immovably the frame
Of the round world, and built, by laws as strong,
     A solid refuge for distress,
          The towers of righteousness;   50
He knows that from a holier altar came
The quickening spark of this day's sacrifice;
Knows that the source is nobler whence doth rise
     The current of this matin song;
          That deeper far it lies   55
Than aught dependant on the fickle skies.

     Have we not conquered?—By the vengeful sword?
Ah no, by dint of Magnanimity;
That curbed the baser passions, and left free
A loyal band to follow their liege Lord,   60
Clear-sighted Honour—and his staid Compeers,
Along a track of most unnatural years,
In execution of heroic deeds;
Whose memory, spotless as the crystal beads
Of morning dew upon the untrodden meads,   65
Shall live enrolled above the starry spheres.
— Who to the murmurs of an earthly string
          Of Britain's acts would sing,
     He with enraptured voice will tell
Of One whose spirit no reverse could quell;   70
Of one that mid the failing never failed:
Who paints how Britain struggled and prevailed,
Shall represent her labouring with an eye
          Of circumspect humanity;
          Shall shew her clothed with strength and skill,   75
     All martial duties to fulfil;
Firm as a rock in stationary fight;
In motion rapid as the lightning's gleam;
Fierce as a flood-gate bursting in the night

To rouse the wicked from their giddy dream—   80
Woe, woe to all that face her in the field!
Appalled she may not be, and cannot yield.

    And thus is missed the sole true glory
    That can belong to human story!
    At which *they* only shall arrive   85
    Who through the abyss of weakness dive:
The very humblest are too proud of heart:
And one brief day is rightly set apart
To Him who lifteth up and layeth low;
For that Almighty God to whom we owe,   90
Say not that we have vanquished—but that we survive.

How dreadful the dominion of the impure!
Why should the song be tardy to proclaim
That less than power unbounded could not tame
That Soul of Evil—which, from Hell let loose,   95
Had filled the astonished world with such abuse,
As boundless patience only could endure?
— Wide-wasted regions—cities wrapped in flame—
Who sees, and feels, may lift a streaming eye
To Heaven,—who never saw may heave a sigh;   100
But the foundation of our nature shakes,
And with an infinite pain the spirit aches,
When desolated countries, towns on fire,
    Are but the avowed attire
Of warfare waged with desperate mind   105
Against the life of virtue in mankind;
    Assaulting without ruth
    The citadels of truth;
While the old forest of civility
Is doomed to perish, to the last fair tree.   110

A crouching purpose—a distracted will—
Opposed to hopes that battened upon scorn,
And to desires whose ever-waxing horn
Not all the light of earthly power could fill;
Opposed to dark, deep plots of patient skill,   115
And the celerities of lawless force
Which, spurning God, had flung away remorse—

What could they gain but shadows of redress?
—So bad proceeded propagating worse;
And discipline was passion's dire excess.[1]   120
Widens the fatal web—its lines extend,
And deadlier poisons in the chalice blend—
When will your trials teach you to be wise?
—O prostrate Lands, consult your agonies!

    No more—the guilt is banished,   125
      And with the Guilt the Shame is fled,
And with the Guilt and Shame the Woe hath vanished,
Shaking the dust and ashes from her head!
—No more, these lingerings of distress
Sully the limpid stream of thankfulness.   130
What robe can Gratitude employ
So seemly as the radiant vest of Joy?
What steps so suitable as those that move
In prompt obedience to spontaneous measures
Of glory—and felicity—and love,   135
    Surrendering the whole heart to sacred pleasures?

    Land of our fathers! precious unto me
Since the first joys of thinking infancy;
When of thy gallant chivalry I read,
And hugged the volume on my sleepless bed!   140
O England!—dearer far than life is dear,
If I forget thy prowess, never more
Be thy ungrateful son allowed to hear
Thy green leaves rustle, or thy torrents roar!
But how can *He* be faithless to the past,   145
Whose soul, intolerant of base decline,
Saw in thy virtue a celestial sign,
That bade him hope, and to his hope cleave fast!
The nations strove with puissance;—at length
Wide Europe heaved, impatient to be cast,   150
      With *all* her living strength,
      With *all* her armed powers,
      Upon the offensive shores.

---

1   " 'A discipline the rule whereof is passion.'—LORD BROOK." WW quotes a phrase from Fulke
   Greville, 1st Baron Brooke (1554– 1628), poet and biographer of Sir Philip Sidney.

The trumpet blew a universal blast!
But Thou art foremost in the field;—there stand: 155
Receive the triumph destined to thy Hand!
All States have glorified themselves;—their claims
Are weighed by Providence, in balance even;
And now, in preference to the mightiest names,
To Thee the *exterminating sword* is given.   160
Dread mark of approbation, justly gained!
Exalted office, worthily sustained!

   Imagination, ne'er before content,
   But aye ascending, restless in her pride,
   From all that man's performance could present,   165
   Stoops to that closing deed magnificent,
      And with the embrace is satisfied.
      —Fly, ministers of Fame,
Whate'er your means, whatever help ye claim,
Bear through the world these tidings of delight!   170
—Hours, Days, and Months, have borne them in the sight
Of mortals, travelling faster than the shower,
   That land-ward stretches from the sea,
   The morning's splendors to devour;
But this appearance scattered extacy,—   175
And heart-sick Europe blessed the healing power.
   — *The shock is given—The Adversaries bleed—*
   Lo, Justice triumphs! Earth is freed!
Such glad assurance suddenly went forth—
It pierced the caverns of the sluggish North—   180
   It found no barrier on the ridge
Of Andes—frozen gulphs became its bridge—
The vast Pacific gladdens with the freight—
Upon the Lakes of Asia 'tis bestowed—
The Arabian desart shapes a willing road   185
      Across her burning breast,
For this refreshing incense from the West!
      —Where snakes and lions breed,
Where towns and cities thick as stars appear,
Wherever fruits are gathered, and where'er   190
The upturned soil receives the hopeful seed—
While the Sun rules, and cross the shades of night—

The unwearied arrow hath pursued its flight!
The eyes of good men thankfully give heed,
    And in its sparkling progress read   195
How Virtue triumphs, from her bondage freed!
Tyrants exult to hear of kingdoms won,
And slaves are pleased to learn that mighty feats are done;
Even the proud Realm, from whose distracted borders
This messenger of good was launched in air,   200
France, conquered France, amid her wild disorders,
Feels, and hereafter shall the truth declare,
That she too lacks not reason to rejoice,
And utter England's name with sadly-plausive voice.

      Preserve, O Lord! within our hearts   205
      The memory of thy favour,
      That else insensibly departs,
      And loses its sweet savour!
Lodge it within us!—As the power of light
Lives inexhaustibly in precious gems,   210
Fixed on the front of Eastern diadems,
So shine our thankfulness for ever bright!
What offering, what transcendant monument
Shall our sincerity to Thee present?
—Not work of hands; but trophies that may reach   215
To highest Heaven—the labour of the soul;
That builds, as thy unerring precepts teach,
Upon the inward victories of each,
Her hope of lasting glory for the whole.
—Yet might it well become that City now,   220
Into whose breast the tides of grandeur flow,
To whom all persecuted men retreat;
If a new temple lift its votive brow
Upon the shore of silver Thames—to greet
The peaceful guest advancing from afar?   225
Bright be the distant fabric, as a star
Fresh risen—and beautiful within!—there meet
Dependance infinite, proportion just;
—A pile that grace approves, and time can trust.

      But if the valiant of this land   230

In reverential modesty demand,
That all observance, due to them, be paid
Where their serene progenitors are laid;
Kings, warriors, high-souled poets, saint-like sages,
England's illustrious sons of long, long ages;   235
Be it not unordained that solemn rites,
Within the circuit of those gothic walls,
Shall be performed at pregnant intervals;
Commemoration holy that unites
The living generations with the dead;   240
     By the deep soul-moving sense
     Of religious eloquence,—
     By visual pomp, and by the tie
     Of sweet and threatening harmony;
     Soft notes, awful as the omen   245
     Of destructive tempests coming,
     And escaping from that sadness
     Into elevated gladness;
     While the white-rob'd choir attendant,
     Under mouldering banners pendant,   250
Provoke all potent symphonies to raise
     Songs of victory and praise,
For them who bravely stood unhurt—or bled
With medicable wounds, or found their graves
Upon the battle field—or under ocean's waves;   255
Or were conducted home in single state,
And long procession—there to lie,
Where their sons' sons, and all posterity,
Unheard by them, their deeds shall celebrate!

     Nor will the God of peace and love   260
     Such martial service disapprove.
     He guides the Pestilence—the cloud
     Of locusts travels on his breath;
     The region that in hope was ploughed
His drought consumes, his mildew taints with death;   265
  He springs the hushed Volcano's mine,
He puts the Earthquake on her still design,
Darkens the sun, hath bade the forest sink,
And, drinking towns and cities, still can drink

Cities and towns—'tis Thou—the work is Thine!   270
— The fierce Tornado sleeps within thy courts—
   He hears the word—he flies—
   And navies perish in their ports;
For Thou art angry with thine enemies!
   For these, and for our errors,   275
   And sins that point their terrors,
We bow our heads before Thee, and we laud
And magnify thy name, Almighty God!
   But thy most dreaded instrument,
   In working out a pure intent,   280
   Is Man—arrayed for mutual slaughter,—
   Yea, Carnage is thy daughter!
Thou cloth'st the wicked in their dazzling mail,
And by thy just permission they prevail;
   Thine arm from peril guards the coasts   285
   Of them who in thy laws delight:
Thy presence turns the scale of doubtful fight,
Tremendous God of battles, Lord of Hosts!

   To THEE—TO THEE—
On this appointed Day shall thanks ascend,   290
That Thou hast brought our warfare to an end,
And that we need no further victory!
Ha! what a ghastly sight for man to see;
And to the heavenly saints in peace who dwell,
   For a brief moment, terrible;   295
But to thy sovereign penetration fair,
Before whom all things are, that were,
All judgments that have been, or e'er shall be,
Links in the chain of thy tranquillity!
Along the bosom of this favoured nation,   300
Breathe thou, this day, a vital undulation!
   Let all who do this land inherit
   Be conscious of Thy moving spirit!
Oh, 'tis a goodly Ordinance,—the sight,
Though sprung from bleeding war, is one of pure delight;   305
Bless thou the hour, or ere the hour arrive,
When a whole people shall kneel down in prayer,
And, at one moment, in one spirit, strive

With lip and heart to tell their gratitude
  For thy protecting care,   310
Their solemn joy—praising the Eternal Lord
  For tyranny subdued,
And for the sway of equity renewed,
For liberty confirmed, and peace restored!

 But hark—the summons!—down the placid Lake 315
Floats the soft cadence of the Church-tower bells;
Bright shines the Sun, as if his beams might wake
The tender insects sleeping in their cells;
Bright shines the Sun—and not a breeze to shake
The drops that point the melting icicles:—   320
  O, enter now his temple gate!
Inviting words—perchance already flung,
(As the crowd press devoutly down the aisle
Of some old minster's venerable pile)
From voices into zealous passion stung,   325
While the tubed engine feels the inspiring blast, = organ !
And has begun—its clouds of sound to cast
  Towards the empyreal Heaven,
  As if the fretted roof were riven.
Us, humbler ceremonies now await;   330
But in the bosom with devout respect,
The banner of our joy we will erect,
And strength of love our souls shall elevate:
For to a few collected in his name,
Their heavenly Father will incline his ear,   335
Hallowing himself the service which they frame;—
Awake! the majesty of God revere!
 Go—and with foreheads meekly bowed
Present your prayers—go—and rejoice aloud—
  The Holy One will hear!   340
And what mid silence deep, with faith sincere,
Ye, in your low and undisturbed estate,
Shall simply feel and purely meditate
Of warnings—from the unprecedented might,
Which, in our time, the impious have disclosed; 345
And of more arduous duties thence imposed
Upon the future advocates of right;

Of mysteries revealed,
And judgments unrepealed,—
Of earthly revolution,   350
And final retribution,—
To his omniscience will appear
An offering not unworthy to find place,
On this high DAY OF THANKS, before the Throne of Grace!

Elegiac Verses

FEBRUARY 1816

"Rest, rest, perturbèd Earth!
O rest, thou doleful Mother of Mankind!"
A Spirit sang in tones more plaintive than the wind;
"From regions where no evil thing has birth
    I come—thy stains to wash away,   5
    Thy cherished fetters to unbind,
To open thy sad eyes upon a milder day!
— The Heavens are thronged with martyrs that have risen
    From out thy noisome prison;
    The penal caverns groan   10
With tens of thousands rent from off the tree
Of hopeful life,—by Battle's whirlwind blown
    Into the desarts of Eternity.
    Unpitied havoc! Victims unlamented!
But not on high, where madness is resented,   15
And murder causes some sad tears to flow,
Though, from the widely-sweeping blow,
The choirs of Angels spread, triumphantly augmented.

    "False Parent of Mankind!
    Obdurate, proud, and blind,   20
I sprinkle thee with soft celestial dews,
Thy lost maternal heart to reinfuse!
Scattering this far-fetched moisture from my wings,
Upon the act a blessing I implore,
Of which the rivers in their secret springs,   25
The rivers stained so oft with human gore,
Are conscious;—may the like return no more!
May Discord—for a Seraph's care

Shall be attended with a bolder prayer—
May she, who once disturbed the seats of bliss,   30
    These mortal spheres above,
Be chained for ever to the black abyss!
And thou, O rescued Earth, by peace and love,
And merciful desires, thy sanctity approve!"

    The Spirit ended his mysterious rite,   35
And the pure vision closed in darkness infinite.

Ode,

COMPOSED IN JANUARY 1816

————Carmina possumus
Donare, et pretium dicere muneri.
Non incisa notis marmora publicis,
Per quæ spiritus et vita redit bonis
Post mortem ducibus————
————————clarius indicant
Laudes, quam————Pierides; neque,
Si charæ sileant quod bene feceris,
Mercedem tuleris.——Hor. Car. 8. Lib. 4.[1]

When the soft hand of sleep had closed the latch
On the tired household of corporeal sense,
And Fancy in her airy bower kept watch,
Free to exert some kindly influence;
I saw—but little boots it that my verse   5
A shadowy visitation should rehearse,
For to our Shores such glory hath been brought,
That dreams no brighter are than waking thought—
I saw, in wondrous perspective displayed,
A landscape richer than the happiest skill   10
Of pencil ever clothed with light and shade;
An intermingled pomp of vale and hill,
Tower, town, and city—and suburban grove,

---

1 The epigraph is from Horace's ode to Censorinus, which opens with the poet saying that if he could, he would give his friends works of art, and Censorinus does not care for such things: he takes pleasure in poems. Horace continues, in the passage WW quotes, "We can give verses, and declare the worth of the gift. Marbles inscribed with public notices, through which spirit and life return after death to good leaders, do not set forth praises more clearly than the Muses; nor will you receive a reward if writings are silent about your achievements."

And stately forest where the wild deer rove;
And, in a clouded quarter of the sky,   15
Through such a portal as with chearful eye
The traveller greets in time of threatened storm,
Issued, to sudden view, a radiant Form!
Earthward it glided with a swift descent:
Saint George himself this Visitant may be;   20
And ere a thought could ask on what intent
He sought the regions of humanity,
A thrilling voice was heard, that vivified
My patriotic heart;—aloud it cried,

    "I, the Guardian of this Land,   25
    Speak not now of toilsome duty—
    Well obeyed was that command,
    Days are come of festive beauty;
Haste, Virgins, haste!—the flowers which summer gave
    Have perished in the field;   30
But the green thickets plenteously will yield
    Fit garlands for the Brave,
That will be welcome, if by you entwined!
Haste, Virgins, haste;—and you, ye Matrons grave,

Go forth with rival youthfulness of mind,   35
    And gather what ye find
Of hardy laurel and wild holly boughs,
To deck your stern defenders' modest brows!
    Such simple gifts prepare,
Though they have gained a worthier meed;   40
    And in due time shall share
Those palms and amaranthine wreaths,
Unto their martyred Countrymen decreed,
In realms where everlasting freshness breathes!"

    And lo! with crimson banners proudly streaming,   45
And upright weapons innocently gleaming,
Along the surface of a spacious plain,
Advance in order the redoubted bands,
And there receive green chaplets from the hands
    Of a fair female train,   50
    Maids and Matrons—dight

In robes of purest white,—
While from the crowd burst forth a rapturous noise
    By the cloud-capt hills retorted,—
    And a throng of rosy boys 55
    In loose fashion told their joys,—
And grey-haired Sires, on staffs supported,
Looked round—and by their smiling seemed to say,
Thus strives a grateful Country to display
The mighty debt which nothing can repay! 60

   Anon, I saw, beneath a dome of state,
The feast dealt forth with bounty unconfined;
And while the vaulted roof did emulate
The starry heavens through splendour of the show,
It rang with music,—and methought the wind 65
Scattered the tuneful largess far and near,
That they who asked not might partake the cheer,
    Who listened not could hear,
Where'er the wild winds were allowed to blow!
—That work reposing, on the verge 70
Of busiest exultation hung a dirge,
Breathed from a soft and lonely instrument,
    That kindled recollections
    Of agonized affections;
And, though some tears the strain attended, 75
    The mournful passion ended
In peace of spirit, and sublime content!

   —But garlands wither,—festal shows depart,
Like dreams themselves, and sweetest sound,
    Albeit of effect profound, 80
    It was—and it is gone!
Victorious England! bid the silent art
Reflect, in glowing hues that shall not fade,
These high achievements,—even as she arrayed
With second life the deed of Marathon 85
    Upon Athenian walls:
So may she labour for thy civic halls;
    And be the guardian spaces
    Of consecrated places,

Graced with such gifts as Sculpture can bestow,   90
When inspiration guides her patient toil;
And let imperishable trophies grow
Fixed in the depths of this courageous soil;
Expressive records of a glorious strife,
And competent to shed a spark divine   95
Into the torpid breast of daily life;
Trophies on which the morning sun may shine,
    As changeful ages flow,
With gratulation thoroughly benign!

And ye, Pierian sisters, sprung from Jove   100
And sage Mnemosyne,—full long debarred
From your first mansions,—exiled all too long
From many a consecrated stream and grove,
Dear native regions where ye wont to rove,
Chaunting for patriot heroes the reward   105
    Of never-dying song!
Now, (for, though truth descending from above
The Olympian summit hath destroyed for aye
Your kindred deities, *ye* live and move,
And exercise unblamed a generous sway,)   110
Now, on the margin of some spotless fountain,
Or top serene of unmolested mountain,
Strike audibly the noblest of your lyres,
And for a moment meet my soul's desires!
That I, or some more favoured Bard, may hear   115
What ye, celestial maids! have often sung
Of Britain's acts,—may catch it with rapt ear,
And give the treasure to our British tongue!
So shall the characters of that proud page
Support their mighty theme from age to age;   120
And, in the desart places of the earth,
When they to future empires have given birth,
So shall the people gather and believe
The bold report, transferred to every clime;
And the whole world, not envious but admiring,   125
    And to the like aspiring,
Own that the progeny of this fair Isle
Had power as lofty actions to achieve

As were performed in Man's heroic prime;
Nor wanted, when their fortitude had held 130
Its even tenour and the foe was quelled,
A corresponding virtue to beguile
The hostile purpose of wide-wasting Time;
That not in vain they laboured to secure
For their great deeds perpetual memory, 135
And Fame as largely spread as Land and Sea,
By works of spirit high and passion pure!

Again empty rhetoric, only
137 lines (this poem!)

Composed in Recollection of the Expedition of the French into Russia

FEBRUARY 1816

Humanity, delighting to behold
A fond reflexion of her own decay,
Hath painted Winter like a shrunken, old,
And close-wrapt Traveller—through the weary day—
Propped on a staff, and limping o'er the Plain, 5
As though his weakness were disturbed by pain;
Or, if a juster fancy should allow
An undisputed symbol of command,
The chosen sceptre is a withered bough,
Infirmly grasped within a palsied hand. 10
These emblems suit the helpless and forlorn;
But mighty Winter the device shall scorn.

For he it was—dread Winter!—who beset,
Flinging round van and rear his ghastly net,
That host,—when from the regions of the Pole 15
They shrunk, insane ambition's barren goal,
That host,—as huge and strong as e'er defied
Their God, and placed their trust in human pride!
As Fathers persecute rebellious sons,
He smote the blossoms of their warrior youth; 20
He called on Frost's inexorable tooth
Life to consume in manhood's firmest hold;
Nor spared the reverend blood that feebly runs,—
For why, unless for liberty enrolled
And sacred home, ah! why should hoary age be bold? 25

Fleet the Tartar's reinless steed,—
But fleeter far the pinions of the Wind,
Which from Siberian caves the monarch freed,
And sent him forth, with squadrons of his kind,
And bade the Snow their ample backs bestride,   30
    And to the battle ride;—
No pitying voice commands a halt—
No courage can repel the dire assault,—
Distracted, spiritless, benumbed and blind,
Whole legions sink—and, in one instant, find   35
Burial and death: look for them—and descry,
When morn returns, beneath the clear blue sky,
A soundless waste, a trackless vacancy!

Sonnet,

ON THE SAME OCCASION.
FEBRUARY 1816

Ye Storms, resound the praises of your King!
And ye mild Seasons—in a sunny clime,
Midway on some high hill, while Father Time
Looks on delighted—meet in festal ring,
And loud and long of Winter's triumph sing!   5
Sing ye, with blossoms crowned, and fruits, and flowers,
Of Winter's breath surcharged with sleety showers,
And the dire flapping of his hoary wing!
Knit the blithe dance upon the soft green grass;
With feet, hands, eyes, looks, lips, report your gain;   10
Whisper it to the billows of the main,
And to the aerial zephyrs as they pass,
That old decrepit Winter—*He* hath slain
That Host, which rendered all your bounties vain!

Ode

Who rises on the banks of Seine,
And binds her temples with the civic wreath?
What joy to read the promise of her mien!
How sweet to rest her wide-spread wings beneath!
    But they are ever playing,   5

And twinkling in the light,—
And if a breeze be straying,
That breeze she will invite;
And stands on tiptoe, conscious she is fair,
And calls a look of love into her face—   10
And spreads her arms—as if the general air
Alone could satisfy her wide embrace.
—Melt, Principalities, before her melt!
Her love ye hailed—her wrath have felt!
But She through many a change of form hath gone,   15
And stands amidst you now, an armed Creature,
Whose panoply is not a thing put on,
But the live scales of a portentous nature;
That, having wrought its way from birth to birth,
Stalks round—abhorred by Heaven, a terror to the Earth!   20

I marked the breathings of her dragon crest;
My soul in many a midnight vision bowed
Before the meanings which her spear expressed;
Whether the mighty Beam, in scorn upheld,
Threatened her foes,—or, pompously at rest,   25
Seemed to bisect the orbit of her shield,
Like to a long blue bar of solid cloud
At evening stretched across the fiery West.

So did she daunt the Earth, and God defy!
And, wheresoe'er she spread her sovereignty,   30
Pollution tainted all that was most pure.
—Have we not known—and live we not to tell
That Justice seemed to hear her final knell?
Faith buried deeper in her own deep breast
Her stores—and sighed to find them insecure!   35
And Hope was maddened by the drops that fell
From shades—her chosen place of short-lived rest,
Which, when they first received her, she had blest:
Shame followed shame—and woe supplanted woe—
In this the only change that time can show?   40
How long shall vengeance sleep? Ye patient Heavens, how long?
—Infirm ejaculation—from the tongue
Of Nations wanting virtue to be strong

Up to the measure of accorded might,—
And daring not to feel the majesty of right!   45

    Weak spirits are there—who would ask,
Upon the pressure of a painful thing,
The Lion's sinews, or the Eagle's wing;
Or let their wishes loose, in forest glade,
        Among the lurking powers   50
        Of herbs and lowly flowers,
Or seek, from Saints above, miraculous aid;
That Man may be accomplished for a task
Which his own Nature hath enjoined—and why?
If, when that interference hath relieved him,   55
        He must sink down to languish
In worse than former helplessness—and lie
        Till the caves roar,—and, imbecility
        Again engendering anguish,
The same weak wish returns—that had before deceived him.   60

    But Thou, Supreme Disposer! might'st not speed
The course of things, and change the creed,
Which hath been held aloft before Men's sight
Since the first framing of societies;
Whether, as Bards have told in ancient song,   65
Built up by soft seducing harmonies,—
Or pressed together by the appetite,
        And by the power of wrong!

A Fact, and an Imagination;
Or, Canute and Alfred

The Danish Conqueror, on his royal chair
Mustering a face of haughtiest sovereignty,
To aid a covert purpose, cried—"O ye
Approaching waters of the deep, that share
With this green isle my fortunes, come not where   5
Your Master's throne is set!"—Absurd decree!
A mandate, uttered to the foaming sea,
Is to its motions less than wanton air.

—Then Canute, rising from the invaded Throne,

Said to his servile courtiers, "Poor the reach,   10
The undisguised extent, of mortal sway!
He only is a king, and he alone
Deserves the name, (this truth the billows preach)
Whose everlasting laws, sea, earth, and heaven obey."

This just reproof the prosperous Dane   15
Drew, from the impulse of the Main,
For some whose rugged northern mouths would strain
At oriental flattery;
And Canute (truth more worthy to be known)
From that time forth did for his brows disown   20
The ostentatious symbol of a Crown;
Esteeming earthly royalty
Contemptible and vain.

   Now hear what one of elder days,
Rich theme of England's fondest praise,   25
Her darling Alfred, *might* have spoken;
To cheer the remnant of his host
When he was driven from coast to coast,
Distress'd and harass'd, but with mind unbroken;
"My faithful Followers, lo! the tide is spent;   30
That rose, and steadily advanced to fill
The shores and channels, working Nature's will
Among the mazy streams that backward went, ,
And in the sluggish pools where ships are pent.
And now, its task perform'd, the Flood stands still   35
At the green base of many an inland hill,
In placid beauty and sublime content!
Such the repose that Sage and Hero find;
Such measured rest the sedulous and good
Of humbler name; whose souls do, like the flood   40
Of Ocean, press right on; or gently wind,
Neither to be diverted nor withstood,
Until they reach the bounds by Heaven assigned."

   On the Disinterment of the Remains of the Duke D'enghien

Dear Reliques! from a pit of vilest mold
Uprisen—to lodge among ancestral kings;

And to inflict shame's salutary stings
On the remorseless hearts of men grown old
In a blind worship; men perversely bold   5
Even to this hour; yet at this hour they quake;
And some their monstrous Idol shall forsake,
If to the living truth was ever told
By aught surrendered from the hollow grave:
O murdered Prince! meek, loyal, pious, brave!   10
The power of retribution once was given;
But 'tis a rueful thought that willow bands
So often tie the thunder-wielding hands
Of Justice, sent to earth from highest Heaven!

Dion

Fair is the Swan, whose majesty—prevailing
O'er breezeless water on Loccarno's Lake—
Bears him on while, proudly sailing,
He leaves behind a moon-illumin'd wake:
Behold, the mantling Spirit of reserve   5
Fashions his neck into a goodly curve,
An arch thrown back between luxuriant wings
Of whitest garniture, like firtree boughs
To which on some unruffled morning clings
A flaky weight of winter's purest snows!   10
—Behold—as with a gushing impulse heaves
That downy prow, and softly cleaves
The mirror of the crystal flood,
Vanish the dusky Hill and shadowy wood
And pendent rocks where'er in gliding state   15
Winds the mute creature without visible Mate
Or Rival, save the Queen of night
Showering down a silver light
From heaven, upon her chosen Favorite.

2

So pure—so bright—so fitted to embrace,   20
Where'er he turned, a natural grace
Of haughtiness without pretence,
And to unfold a still magnificence

Was princely Dion, in the power
And beauty of his happier hour.   25
Nor less the homage that was seen to wait
On Dion's virtue when the lunar beam
Of Plato's genius from its lofty sphere
Fell round him in the grove of Academe,
Softening his inbred dignity austere.   30

3

If on thy faith the World delight to gaze,
Pride of the World—beware! for thou mayst live,
Like Dion, to behold the torch of Praise
Inverted in thy presence, and to give
Proof, for the historian's page and poet's lays,   35
That Peace, even Peace herself, is fugitive.

4

Five thousand Warriors (O the joyful day!)
Each crown'd with flowers and arm'd with spear and Shield
Or ruder weapon such as chance might yield,
To Syracuse advanc'd in bright array.   40
Who leads them on?— The anxious People see
Long-exil'd Dion marching at their head,
He also crown'd with flowers of Sicily
And in a white far-beaming corselet clad.
Pure transport undisturb'd by doubt or fear   45
The Gazers feel, and, rushing to the Plain,
Salute those Strangers as a holy train
Or blest Procession (to the Immortals dear)
That brought their precious liberty again.
Lo! when the gates are entered, on each hand   50
Down the long street rich Goblets fill'd with wine
        In seemly order stand
On tables set as if for rites divine—
And wheresoe'er the great Deliverer pass'd
        Fruits were strewn before his eye   55
And flowers upon his person cast
        In boundless prodigality;
Nor did the general Voice abstain from prayer,
Invoking Dion's tutelary care

As if a very Deity he were.   60

5

Mourn, olive bowers of Attica—and Thou,
Partake the sadness of the groves,
Famed Hill Hymettus, round whose fragrant brow,
Industrious Bees each seeking what she loves
Or fraught with treasure which she best approves   65
Their murmurs blend,—in choral elevation,
Not wholly lost upon the abstracted ear
Of unambitious men who wander near
Immersed in lonely contemplation,—
Mourn, sunny Hill, and shady Grove!—and mourn,   70
Ilyssus, bending o'er thy classic urn!
For He, who to divinity aspired
Not on the wings of popular applause
But through dependance on the Sacred laws
Framed in the Schools where Wisdom dwelt retired,   75
Hath stained the robes of civil power with blood,
Unjustly shed though for the public good—
Droops the Slave of fear and Sorrow,
Depress'd today and unrelieved tomorrow,
And oft his cogitations sank as low   80
As through the abysses of a joyless heart
The heaviest Plummet of despair can go—
But whence that sudden check—that fearful start?
      He hears an uncouth Sound—
            Anon his lifted eyes   85
Saw, at a long-drawn gallery's dusky bound,
A Shape of more than mortal size
And hideous aspect, stalking round and round!
            A Woman's garb the Phantom wore
            And fiercely swept the marble floor—   90
            Like winged Auster stooping low
            His force on Caspian foam to try,
Or Boreas when he scow'rs the snow
That skins the plains of Thessaly,
Or when aloft on Mænalus he stops   95
His flight, mid eddying pine-tree tops.

6

So, but from toil less sign of profit reaping,
The sullen Spectre to her purpose bowed,
   Sweeping—vehemently sweeping—
Long gazed the Chieftain—ere he spake—aloud—   100
With even voice, and stern composure wrought
Into his brow by self-supporting thought:
"Avaunt, inexplicable Guest—avaunt,
Intrusive Phantom!—let me rather see
What they behold whom vengeful Furies haunt   105
Who, while they struggle from the Scourge to flee,
Move where the wretched Soil is not unworn
And in their anguish bear what other minds have borne!"—

7

But Shapes that come not at an earthly call
Will not depart when mortal Voices bid—   110
Lords of the visionary Eye whose lid
Once raised, remains aghast, and will not fall—

"Ye Gods, that servile Implement
Obeys a mystical intent!
Your Minister would brush away   115
The spots that to my Soul adhere;
But should She labour, night and day,
They will not, cannot disappear—
Whence angry perturbations,—and a look
Which no Philosophy can brook."—   120

8

Away—for hark! a rushing sound
A Conflict—and a groan profound!
O matchless perfidy!—portentous lust
Of monstrous crime—that horror—striking blade,
Drawn in defiance of the Gods, hath laid   125
The noble Syracusan low in dust!

— Thus were the hopeless troubles that involved
The soul of Dion instantly dissolved.—
Released from life and cares of princely state,

He left this moral grafted on his Fate: 130

"Him only pleasure leads and peace attends,
Him, only him, the Shield of Jove defends
Whose Means are fair and spotless as his ends."

To ———,

ON HER FIRST ASCENT TO THE
SUMMIT OF HELVELLYN

Inmate of a mountain Dwelling,
Thou hast clomb aloft, and gaz'd,
From the watch-towers of Helvellyn;
Awed, delighted, and amazed!

Potent was the spell that bound thee   5
In the moment of dismay,
While blue Ether's arms, flung round thee,
Still'd the pantings of dismay.

Lo! the dwindled woods and meadows!
What a vast abyss is there!   10
Lo! the clouds, the solemn shadows,
And the glistenings—heavenly fair!

And a record of commotion
Which a thousand ridges yield;
Ridge, and gulph, and distant ocean   15
Gleaming like a silver shield!

—Take thy flight;—possess, inherit
Alps or Andes—they are thine!
With the morning's roseate spirit,
Sweep their length of snowy line;   20

Or survey the bright dominions
In the gorgeous colours drest,
Flung from off the purple pinions,
Evening spreads throughout the west!

Thine are all the choral fountains   25
Warbling in each sparry vault

Of the untrodden lunar mountains;
Listen to their songs!—or halt,

To Niphate's top invited,
Whither spiteful Satan steer'd;   30
Or descend where the ark alighted
When the green earth re-appeared;

For the power of hills is on thee,
As was witnessed through thine eye
Then, when old Helvellyn won thee   35
To confess their majesty!

"A little onward lend thy guiding hand"

"A little onward lend thy guiding hand
To these dark steps, a little further on!"
— What trick of memory to *my* voice hath brought,
This mournful iteration? For though Time,
The Conqueror, crowns the Conquer'd, on this brow   5
Planting his favourite silver diadem,
Nor he, nor minister of his intent
To run before him, hath enrolled me yet,
Though not unmenaced, among those who lean
Upon a living staff, with borrowed sight.   10
—O my Antigone, beloved child!
Should that day come—but hark! the birds salute
The cheerful dawn brightening for me the east;
For me, thy natural Leader, once again
Impatient to conduct thee, not as erst   15
A tottering Infant, with compliant stoop
From flower to flower supported; but to curb
Thy nymph-like step swift-bounding o'er the lawn,
Along the loose rocks, or the slippery verge
Of foaming torrents.—From thy orisons   20
Come forth; and, while the morning air is yet
Transparent as the soul of innocent youth,
Let me, thy happy Guide, now point thy way,
And now precede thee, winding to and fro,
Till we by perseverance gain the top   25
Of some smooth ridge, whose brink precipitous

Kindles intense desire for powers withheld
From this corporeal frame; whereon who stands,
Is seized with strong incitement to push forth
His arms, as swimmers use, and plunge—dread thought!   30
For pastime plunge—into the "abrupt abyss,"
Where Ravens spread their plumy vans, at ease!
    And yet more gladly thee would I conduct
Through woods and spacious forests,—to behold
There, how the Original of human art,   35
Heaven-prompted Nature, measures and erects
Her temples, fearless for the stately work,
Though waves in every breeze its high-arched roof,
And storms the pillars rock. But we such schools
Of reverential awe will chiefly seek   40
In the still summer noon, while beams of light;
Reposing here, and in the aisles beyond
Traceably gliding through the dusk, recall
To mind the living presences of nuns;
A gentle, pensive, white-robed sisterhood,   45
Whose saintly radiance mitigates the gloom
Of those terrestrial fabrics, where they serve,
To Christ, the Sun of Righteousness, espoused.
    Re-open now thy everlasting gates,
Thou Fane of holy writ! Ye classic Domes,   50
To these glad orbs from darksome bondage freed,
Unfold again your portals! Passage lies
Through you to heights more glorious still, and shades
More awful, where this Darling of my care,
Advancing with me hand in hand, may learn   55
Without forsaking a too earnest world,
To calm the affections, elevate the soul,
And consecrate her life to truth and love.

"I heard (alas, 'twas only in a dream)"

I heard (alas, 'twas only in a dream)
Strains—which, as sage Antiquity believed,
By waking ears have sometimes been received,
Wafted adown the wind from lake or stream;
A most melodious requiem,—a supreme   5

And perfect harmony of notes, achieved
By a fair Swan on drowsy billows heaved,
O'er which her pinions shed a silver gleam:—
For is she not the votary of Apollo?
And knows she not, singing as he inspires,   10
That bliss awaits her which the ungenial hollow[1]
Of the dull earth partakes not, nor desires?
Mount, tuneful Bird, and join the immortal quires!
She soared—and I awoke,—struggling in vain to follow.

[*Lament of Mary Queen of Scots, on the Eve of a New Year*][2]

"Smile of the Moon—for so I name
That silent greeting from above,
A gentle flash of light that came
From her whom drooping Captives love;
Or art thou of still higher birth,   5
Thou that did'st part the clouds of earth
My torpor to reprove!

"Bright boon of pitying Heaven—alas,
I may not trust thy placid cheer,
Pondering that Time to-night will pass   10
The threshold of another Year;
For years to me are sad and dull;
My very moments are too full
Of hopelessness and fear.

"And yet the soul-awakening gleam   15
That struck perchance the farthest cone
Of Scotland's rocky wilds did seem
To visit me, and me alone;
Me unapproached by any Friend
But those who to my sorrows lend   20
Tears due unto their own.

"Meek effluence—that while I trod
With downcast eye, in narrow space

---

1 "See the Phedo of Plato, by which this Sonnet was suggested." WW refers to to a passage
   in Plato's *Phaedo* in which Socrates relates the legend of the swans, who are sacred to
   Apollo and through him have the gift of prophecy at their death, their "swan song."
2 Untitled in this early version, but so titled in print in 1820.

Did'st vivify the wintry sod
As if an Angel filled the place   25
With softened light—thou wert a touch
Even to my heart of hearts—and such
Is every gift of grace.

"Yet wherefore did it leave the sky,
And wherefore did it seem to speak   30
Of something bordering all too nigh
On what full oft I dare to seek?
A happier order for my doom,
A favoured æra when the gloom
At length will cleave and break.   35

"To-night the church-tower bells shall ring
Through these wide realms a festive peal;
To the new year a welcoming,
A tuneful offering for the weal
Of happy millions lulled in sleep,   40
While I am forced lone watch to keep
By wounds that may not heal.

"Born all too high—by wedlock raised
Still higher—to be cast thus low!
Would that mine eyes had never gazed   45
On aught of more ambitious show
Than the sweet flowerets of the fields!
—It is my royal State that yields
The bitterness of woe.

"A woman rules my prison's key;   50
A Sister Queen against the bent
Of law and holiest sympathy
Detains me doubtful of the event;
Great God who feel'st for my distress,
My thoughts are all that I possess;   55
O keep them innocent!

"Farewell for ever human aid
Which abject Mortals blindly court!
By friends deceived, by foes betrayed,

Of fears the prey, of hopes the sport,   60
Nought but the world-redeeming Cross
Is able to supply my loss,
My burthen to support.

"Hark! the death-note of the year,
Sounded by the Castle clock!"   65
From her sunk eyes a stagnant Tear
Stole forth, unsettled by the shock;
But oft the woods renewed their green
Ere the tired head of Scotland's Queen
Reposed upon the block.   70

Captivity

"As the cold aspect of a sunless way
Strikes through the Traveller's frame with deadlier chill,
Oft as appears a grove, or obvious hill,
Glistening with unparticipated ray,
Or shining slope where he must never stray;   5
So joys, remembered without wish or will,
Sharpen the keenest edge of present ill,—
On the crush'd heart a heavier burthen lay.
Just Heaven, contract the compass of my mind
To fit proportion with my altered state!   10
Quench those felicities whose light I find
Burning within my bosom all too late!—
O be my spirit, like my thraldom, strait;
And like mine eyes, that stream with sorrow, blind!"

Sequel to the Foregoing [Beggars]

COMPOSED MANY YEARS AFTER[1]

Where are they now, those wanton Boys?
For whose free range the daedal earth
Was filled with animated toys.
And implements of frolic mirth;
With tools for ready wit to guide;   5
And ornaments of seemlier pride,

---

1 WW's *Beggars*, first published in 1807 in *Poems, in Two Volumes*, preceded *Sequel* in
  Poetical Works, 1827. For the text of *Beggars*, see vol. 1 of this edition.

More fresh, more bright, than Princes wear;
For what one moment flung aside,
Another could repair;
What good or evil have they seen   10
Since I their pastime witnessed here,
Their daring wiles, their sportive cheer?
I ask—but all is dark between!

Spirits of beauty and of grace!
Associates in that eager chase;   15
Ye, by a course to nature true,
The sterner judgment can subdue;
And waken a relenting smile
When she encounters fraud or guile;
And sometimes ye can charm away   20
The inward mischief, or allay,
Ye, who within the blameless mind
Your favourite seat of empire find!

They met me in a genial hour,
When universal nature breathed   25
As with the breath of one sweet flower,—
A time to overrule the power
Of discontent, and check the birth
Of thoughts with better thoughts at strife,
The most familiar bane of life   30
Since parting Innocence bequeathed
Mortality to Earth!
Soft clouds, the whitest of the year,
Sailed through the sky—the brooks ran clear;
The lambs from rock to rock were bounding;   35
With songs the budded groves resounding;
And to my heart is still endeared
The faith with which it then was cheered;
The faith which saw that gladsome pair
Walk through the fire with unsinged hair.   40
Or, if such thoughts must needs deceive,
Kind Spirits! may we not believe
That they, so happy and so fair,
Through your sweet influence, and the care

Of pitying Heaven, at least were free   45
From touch of *deadly* injury?
Destined, whate'er their earthly doom,
For mercy and immortal bloom!

Long after the event of their encounter, he still wishes them well

[*Ode.—1817*][1]

Forsake me not, Urania, but when Ev'n
Fades into night, resume the enraptur'd song
That shadowed forth the immensity of Heavn
In music—uttered surely without wrong
(For 'twas thy work,) though here the Listener lay   5
Couch'd on green herbage mid the warmth of May
—A parting promise makes a bright farewell:
　　Empow'rd to wait for thy return,
　　Voice of the Heavn's, I will not mourn;
Content that holy peace and mute remembrance dwell   10
　　Within the bosom of the chorded shell
　　Tuned mid those seats of love and joy concealed
　　　　By day;
By Night imperfectly revealed;
Thy native mansions that endure—   15
Beyond their purest seeming—pure
From taint of dissolution or decay.
—No blights, no wintry desolations
Affect those blissful habitations
Built such as hope might gather from the hue   20
Profound of the celestial blue
And from the aspect of each radiant orb
Some fix'd, some wandering with no timid curb
Yet both permitted to proclaim
Their Maker's Glory with unaltered frame.   25

2

And what if his presiding breath
Impart a sympathetic motion
Unto the gates of life and death
Throughout the bounds of earth and ocean;

1　In 1820 WW titled the poem thus in *The River Duddon, a Series of Sonnets*; *Vaudracour and Julia: and Other Poems*; the poem is untitled in this early manuscript version. After considerable revision it became *Vernal Ode* in 1827...

Though all that feeds on nether air   30
Howe'er magnificent or fair,
Grows but to perish and entrust
Its ruins to their kindred dust,
Yet by her ever-during care,
Her procreant cradle Nature keeps   35
Amid the unfathomable deeps
And saves the changeful fields of earth
From fear of emptiness or dearth.
Thus, in their stations, lifting towards the sky
The foliag'd head in cloud-like majesty,   40
The shadow-casting race of trees survive;
    Thus in the train of Spring arrive
      Sweet Flowers;—what living eye hath viewed
    Their numbers—endlessly renewed,
    Wherever strikes the Sun's glad ray,   45
    Where'er the joyous waters stray;
    Wherever sportive Zephyrs bend
    Their course, or genial showers descend.

3

O nurs'd at happy distance from the cares
Of a too anxious World, mild, pastoral Muse   50
That to the sparkling crown Urania wears
And to her Sister Clio's laurel wreath
Preferr'st a garland cull'd from purple heath
Or blooming thicket moist with morning dews;
Oft side by side with some lov'd Votary   55
Wrapp'd like Thyself in pleasing indolence
While thy tired Lute hung on the hawthorn tree
Hast thou sate listening till oer-drowsed sense
Sank, hardly conscious of the influence
To the soft murmur of the vagrant Bee.   60
—A slender sound!—yet hoary Time
Doth, to *the Soul*, exalt it—with the Chime
Of all his years—a company
Of ages coming, ages gone;
Yet each and all in unison   65
With that faint Utterance which tells

Of treasure suck'd from buds and bells
And stored with frugal [?care] in waxen cells.

4

And is she brought within the power
Of vision by this tempting flower,   70
Observe each wing—a tiny van—
The structure of her laden thigh
How fragile—yet of ancestry
Mysteriously remote and high;
High as the imperial front of Man,   75
The roseate bloom on woman's cheek,
The soaring Eagle's curved beak,
The white plumes of the floating swan—
Old as the tyger's paws, the lion's mane
Ere shaken by that mood of stern disdain   80
At which the Desart trembles.—Humming Bee,
Thy sting was needless then, perchance unknown;
The seeds of malice were not sown;
All Creatures met in peace from fierceness free
And no pride blended with their majesty.   85

Sonnet

The Stars are Mansions built by Nature's hand;
And, haply, there the spirits of the blest
Live, clothed in radiance, their immortal vest;
Huge Ocean frames, within his yellow strand,
A Habitation marvellously planned,   5
For life to occupy in love and rest;
All that we see—is dome, or vault, or nest,
Or fort, erected at her sage command.
Is this a vernal thought? Even so, the Spring
Gave it while cares were weighing on my heart,   10
Mid song of birds, and insects murmuring;
And while the youthful year's prolific art—
Of bud, leaf, blade, and flower—was fashioning
Abodes, where self-disturbance hath no part.

Ode

TO LYCORIS,
MAY, 1817

An age hath been when Earth was proud
Of lustre too intense
To be sustain'd; and Mortals bowed
The front in self-defence.
Who *then*, if Dian's crescent gleamed,   5
Or Cupid's sparkling arrow streamed
While on the wing the Urchin play'd,
Could fearlessly approach the shade?
—Enough for one soft vernal day,
If I, a Bard of ebbing time   10
And nurtur'd in a fickle clime,
May haunt this horned bay;
Whose amorous water multiplies
The flitting halcyon's vivid dyes;
And smoothes its liquid breast—to show   15
These swan-like specks of mountain snow,
White, as the pair that slid along the plains
Of Heaven, when Venus held the reins!

II

In youth we love the darksome lawn
Brush'd by the owlet's wing;   20
Then, Twilight is preferred to Dawn,
And Autumn to the Spring.
Sad fancies do we then affect,
In luxury of disrespect
To our own prodigal excess   25
Of too familiar happiness.
Lycoris (if such name befit
Thee, thee my life's celestial sign!)
When Nature marks the year's decline
Be ours to welcome it;   30
Pleased with the soil's requited cares;
Pleased with the blue that ether wears;
Pleased while the sylvan world displays
Its ripeness to the feeding gaze;

Pleased when the sullen winds resound the knell   35
Of the resplendent miracle.

III

But something whispers to my heart
That, as we downward tend,
Lycoris! life requires an *art*
To which our sôuls must bend;   40
A skill—to balance and supply;
And, ere the flowing fount be dry,
As soon it must, a sense to sip,
Or drink, with no fastidious lip.
Frank greetings, then, to that blithe Guest   45
Diffusing smiles o'er land and sea,
To aid the vernal Deity
Whose home is in the breast!
May pensive Autumn ne'er present
A claim to her disparagement!   50
While blossoms and the budding spray
Inspire us in our own decay;
Still, as we nearer draw to life's dark goal,
Be hopeful Spring the favourite of the Soul!

Addressed to ———,

ON THE LONGEST DAY

Let us quit the leafy Arbour,
And the torrent murmuring by;
Sol has dropped into his harbour,
Weary of the open sky.

Evening now unbinds the fetters   5
Fashioned by the glowing light;
All that breathe are thankful debtors
To the harbinger of night.

Yet by some grave thoughts attended
Eve renews her calm career;   10
For the day that now is ended,
Is the Longest of the Year.

Laura! sport, as now thou sportest,
On this platform, light and free;
Take thy bliss, while longest, shortest   15
Are indifferent to thee!

Who would check the happy feeling
That inspires the linnet's song?
Who would stop the swallow wheeling
On her pinions swift and strong?   20

Yet, at this impressive season,
Words, which tenderness can speak
From the truths of homely reason,
Might exalt the loveliest cheek;

And, while shades to shades succeeding   25
Steal the landscape from the sight,
I would urge this moral pleading,
Last forerunner of "Good night!"

Summer ebbs;—each day that follows
Is a reflux from on high,   30
Tending to the darksome hollows
Where the frosts of winter lie.

He who governs the creation,
In his providence assigned
Such a gradual declination   35
To the life of human kind.

Yet we mark it not;—fruits redden,
Fresh flowers blow as flowers have blown,
And the heart is loth to deaden
Hopes that she so long hath known.   40

Be thou wiser, youthful Maiden!
And, when thy decline shall come,
Let not flowers, or boughs fruit-laden,
Hide the knowledge of thy doom.

Now, even now, ere wrapped in slumber,   45
Fix thine eyes upon the sea

That absorbs time, space, and number,
Look towards Eternity!

Follow thou the flowing River
On whose breast are thither borne   50
All Deceiv'd, and each Deceiver,
Through the gates of night and morn;

Through the years' successive portals;
Through the bounds which many a star
Marks, not mindless of frail mortals   55
When his light returns from far.

Thus, when Thou with Time hast travell'd
Tow'rds the mighty gulph of things,
And the mazy Stream unravell'd
With thy best imaginings;   60

Think, if thou on beauty leanest,
Think how pitiful that stay,
Did not virtue give the meanest
Charms superior to decay.

Duty, like a strict preceptor,   65
Sometimes frowns, or seems to frown;
Choose her thistle for thy sceptre,
While thy brow youth's roses crown.

Grasp it,—if thou shrink and tremble,
Fairest Damsel of the green!   70
Thou wilt lack the only symbol
That proclaims a genuine Queen;

And ensures those palms of honour
Which selected spirits wear,
Bending low before the Donor,   75
Lord of Heaven's unchanging Year!

Ode.

THE PASS OF KIRKSTONE

I

Within the mind strong fancies work,
A deep delight the bosom thrills,
Oft as I pass along the fork
Of these fraternal hills:
Where, save the rugged road, we find   5
No appanage of human kind;
Nor hint of man, if stone or rock
Seem not his handy-work to mock
By something cognizably shaped;
Mockery—or model—roughly hewn,   10
And left as if by earthquake strewn,
Or from the Flood escaped:—
Altars for Druid service fit;
(But where no fire was ever lit
Unless the glow-worm to the skies   15
Thence offer nightly sacrifice;)
Wrinkled Egyptian monument;
Green moss-grown tower; or hoary tent;
Tents of a camp that never shall be raised;
On which four thousand years have gazed!   20

II

Ye plowshares sparkling on the slopes!
Ye snow-white lambs that trip
Imprison'd mid the formal props
Of restless ownership!
Ye trees that may to-morrow fall,   25
To feed the insatiate Prodigal!
Lawns, houses, chattels, groves, and fields,
All that the fertile valley shields;
Wages of folly—baits of crime,—
Of life's uneasy game the stake,—   30
Playthings that keep the eyes awake
Of drowsy, dotard Time;—
O care! O guilt!—O vales and plains,

Here, mid his own unvexed domains,
A Genius dwells, that can subdue   35
At once all memory of You,—
Most potent when mists veil the sky,
Mists that distort and magnify;
While the coarse rushes, to the sweeping breeze,
Sigh forth their ancient melodies!   40

III

List to those shriller notes!—*that* march
Perchance was on the blast,
When through this Height's inverted arch
Rome's earliest legion passed!
— They saw, adventurously impell'd,   45
And older eyes than theirs beheld,
This block—and yon whose Church-like frame
Gives to the savage Pass its name.
Aspiring Road! that lov'st to hide
Thy daring in a vapoury bourn,   50
Not seldom may the hour return
When thou shalt be my Guide;
And I (as often we find cause,
When life is at a weary pause,
And we have panted up the hill   55
Of duty with reluctant will)
Be thankful, even though tired and faint,
For the rich bounties of Constraint;
Whence oft invigorating transports flow
That Choice lacked courage to bestow!   60

IV

My soul was grateful for delight
That wore a threatening brow;
A veil is lifted—can she slight
The scene that opens now?
Though habitation none appear,   65
The greenness tells, man must be there;
The shelter—that the perspective
Is of the clime in which we live;
Where Toil pursues his daily round;

Where Pity sheds sweet tears, and Love,   70
In woodbine bower or birchen grove,
Inflicts his tender wound.
—Who comes not hither ne'er shall know
How beautiful the world below;
Nor can he guess how lightly leaps   75
The brook adown the rocky steeps.
Farewell thou desolate Domain!
Hope, pointing to the cultur'd Plain,
Carols like a shepherd boy;
And who is she?—can that be Joy?   80
Who, with a sun-beam for her guide,
Smoothly skims the meadows wide;
While Faith, from yonder opening cloud,
To hill and vale proclaims aloud,
"Whate'er the weak may dread the wicked dare,   85
Thy lot, O man, is good, thy portion fair!"

[*To the Same*]¹

Here let us rest—here, where the gentle beams
Of noontide stealing in between the boughs
Illuminate their faded leaves;—the air
In the habitual silence of this wood
Is more than silent; and this tuft of heath   5
Deck'd with the fullness of its flowers presents
As beautiful a couch as e'er was framed.
Come—let us venture to exchange the pomp
Of widespread landscape for the internal wealth
Of quiet thought—protracted till thine eye   10
Be calm as water when the winds are gone
And no one can tell whither. Dearest Friend!
We two have had such blissful hours together
That were power granted to replace them (fetched
From out the pensive shadows where they lie)   15
In the first warmth of their original sunshine,
Loth should I be to use it. Passing sweet
Are the domains of tender memory!

---

1   This poem and the later version that follows refer back to *Ode. To Lycoris, May, 1817,*
    included above.

To the Same

Enough of climbing toil!—Ambition treads
Here, as mid busier scenes, ground steep and rough,
Or slippery even to peril! and each step,
As we for most uncertain recompense
Mount tow'rd the empire of the fickle clouds,   5
Each weary step, dwarfing the world below,
Induces, for its old familiar sights,
Unacceptable feelings of contempt,
With wonder mixed—that Man could e'er be tied,
In anxious bondage, to such nice array   10
And formal fellowship of petty things!
—Oh! 'tis the *heart* that magnifies this life,
Making a truth and beauty of her own;
And moss-grown alleys, circumscribing shades,
And gurgling rills, assist her in the work   15
More efficaciously than realms outspread,
As in a map, before the adventurer's gaze—
Ocean and Earth contending for regard.

    The umbrageous woods are left—how far beneath!
But lo! where darkness seems to guard the mouth   20
Of yon wild cave, whose jagged brows are fringed
With flaccid threads of ivy, in the still
And sultry air, depending motionless.
Yet cool the space within, and not uncheered
(As whoso enters shall ere long perceive)   25
By stealthy influx of the timid day
Mingling with night, such twilight to compose
As Numa loved; when, in the Egerian Grot,
From the sage Nymph appearing at his wish,
He gained whate'er a regal mind might ask,   30
Or need, of council breathed through lips divine.

Long as the heat shall rage, let that dim cave
Protect us, there deciphering as we may
Diluvian records; or the sighs of Earth
Interpreting; or counting for old Time   35
His minutes, by reiterated drops,
Audible tears, from some invisible source

That deepens upon fancy—more and more
Drawn tow'rd the centre whence those sighs creep forth
To awe the lightness of humanity.   40
Or, shutting up thyself within thyself,
There let me see thee sink into a mood
Of gentler thought, protracted till thine eye
Be calm as water when the winds are gone,
And no one can tell whither. Dearest Friend!   45
We two have known such happy hours together,
That, were power granted to replace them (fetched
From out the pensive shadows where they lie)
In the first warmth of their original sunshine,
Loth should I be to use it: passing sweet   50
Are the domains of tender memory!

Ode,

COMPOSED UPON AN EVENING OF EXTRAORDINARY SPLENDOR AND BEAUTY

1

Had this effulgence disappeared
With flying haste, I might have sent
Among the speechless clouds a look
Of blank astonishment;
But 'tis endued with power to stay   5
And solemnize one closing day
That frail Mortality may see
What is? ah no—but what *can* be.
Time was when field and watry cove
With modulated echoes rang   10
Of harp and voice while Angels sang
Amid the umbrageous grove;
Or ranged like stars along some sovereign Height
Warbled for heaven above and earth below
Strains suitable to both. Ye Sons of light,   15
If such communion were repeated now
Nor harp nor Seraph's voice could move
Sublimer rapture, holier love,
Than doth this silent spectacle—the gleam,
The shadow—and the peace supreme.   20

2

What though no sound be heard? A deep
And solemn harmony pervades
The hollow vale from steep to steep
And penetrates the glades.
Far-distant images draw nigh   25
Call'd forth by wondrous potency
Of beamy radiance that imbues
Whate'er it strikes with gem-like hues.
In vision exquisitely clear
Herds graze along the mountain-side   30
And glistening antlers are descried
And gilded flocks appear.
Thine is the tranquil hour, purpureal Eve!
But long as god-like wish or hope divine
Informs my spirit, ne'er I can believe   35
That this magnificence is wholly thine!
From worlds unquicken'd by the Sun
A portion of the gift is won,
An intermingling of heav'n's pomp is spread
On ground which British Shepherds tread.   40

3

Whence but from some celestial urn
These colours—wont to meet my eye
Where'er I wandered in the morn
Of blissful infancy?
This glimpse of glory, why renewed?   45
Nay, rather speak in gratitude!
For, if a vestige of those gleams
Survived, 'twas only in my dreams.
Dread Power! whom peace and calmness serve
No less than Nature's threatening voice,   50
If aught unworthy be my choice,
From Thee if I would swerve,
O let thy grace remind me of the light,
Full early lost and fruitlessly deplored,
Which, at this moment, on my waking sight   55
Appears to shine, by miracle restored.

My Soul though yet confined to earth
Rejoices in a second birth!
—Tis past—the visionary splendor fades
And Night approaches with her shades.   60

"Indulgent Muse, if Thou the labour share"

Indulgent Muse, if Thou the labour share
This Object of my care
Shall grow a garden stock'd with poesy—
Bright Weeds and flowers of song
Which have been tended long
In all humility.   5

Hint from the Mountains

FOR CERTAIN POLITICAL ASPIRANTS

Stranger, 'tis a sight of pleasure
When the wings of genius rise,
Their ability to measure
    With great enterprise;
But in man was ne'er such daring   5
As yon Hawk exhibits, pairing
His brave spirit with the war in
    The stormy skies!

Mark him, how his power he uses,
Lays it by, at will resumes!   10
Mark, ere for his haunt he chooses
    Clouds and utter glooms!
There, he wheels in downward mazes;
Sunward now his flight he raises,
Catches fire, as seems, and blazes   15
    With uninjur'd plumes!—

ANSWER

Traveller, 'tis no act of courage
Which aloft thou dost discern;
No bold bird gone forth to forage
    Mid the tempest stern;   20
But such mockery as the Nations

See, when Commonwealth-vexations
Lift men from their native stations,
   Like yon tuft of fern;

Such it is, and not a Haggard   25
Soaring on undaunted wing;
'Tis by nature dull and laggard,
   A poor helpless Thing,
Dry, and withered, light and yellow;—
That to be the tempest's fellow!   30
Wait—and you shall see how hollow
   Its endeavouring!

Inscriptions,

SUPPOSED TO BE FOUND IN, AND NEAR, A HERMIT'S CELL

I

Hast thou seen, with train incessant,
Bubbles gliding under ice,
Bodied forth and evanescent,
No one knows by what device?

Such are thoughts!—a wind-swept meadow   5
Mimicking a troubled sea—
Such is life;—and death a shadow
From the rock eternity!

II

INSCRIBED UPON A ROCK

Pause, Traveller! whosoe'er thou be
Whom chance may lead to this retreat,
Where silence yields reluctantly
Even to the fleecy straggler's bleat;

Give voice to what my hand shall trace,   5
And fear not lest an idle sound
Of words unsuited to the place,
Disturb its solitude profound.

I saw this Rock, while vernal air

Blew softly o'er the russet heath,   10
Uphold a Monument as fair
As Church or Abbey furnisheth.

Unsullied did it meet the day,
Like marble white, like ether pure;
As if beneath some hero lay,   15
Honour'd with costliest sepulture.

My fancy kindled as I gazed;
And, ever as the sun shone forth,
The flatter'd structure glisten'd, blazed,
And seemed the proudest thing on earth.   20

But Frost had reared the gorgeous Pile
Unsound as those which fortune builds;
To undermine with secret guile,
Sapp'd by the very beam that gilds.

And, while I gazed, with sudden shock   25
Fell the whole Fabric to the ground;
And naked left this dripping Rock,
With shapeless ruin spread around!

III

Hopes what are they?—Beads of morning
Strung on slender blades of grass;
Or a spider's web adorning
In a strait and treacherous pass.

What are fears but voices airy?   5
Whispering harm where harm is not,
And deluding the unwary
Till the fatal bolt is shot!

What is glory?—in the socket
See how dying Tapers fare!   10
What is pride?—a whizzing rocket
That would emulate a star.

What is friendship?—do not trust her,
Nor the vows which she has made;

Diamonds dart their brightest lustre   15
From a palsy-shaken head.

What is truth?—a staff rejected;
Duty?—an unwelcome clog;
Joy?—a dazzling moon reflected
In a swamp or watery bog;   20

Bright, as if through ether steering,
To the Traveller's eye it shone:
He hath hailed it re-appearing—
And as quickly it is gone;

Gone, as if for ever hidden,   25
Or misshapen to the sight;
And by sullen weeds forbidden
To resume its native light.

What is youth?—a dancing billow,
Winds behind, and rocks before!   30
Age?—a drooping, tottering willow
On a flat and lazy shore.

What is peace?—when pain is over,
And love ceases to rebel,
Let the last faint sigh discover   35
That precedes the passing knell!

IV

NEAR THE SPRING OF THE HERMITAGE

Troubled long with warring notions,
Long impatient of thy rod,
I resign my soul's emotions
Unto Thee, mysterious God!

What avails the kindly shelter   5
Yielded by this craggy rent,
If my spirit toss and welter
On the waves of discontent?

Parching Summer hath no warrant

To consume this crystal well;   10
Rains, that make each rill a torrent,
Neither sully it nor swell.

Thus dishonouring not her station,
Would my Life present to Thee,
Gracious God, the pure oblation   15
Of divine Tranquillity!

V

Not seldom, clad in radiant vest,
Deceitfully goes forth the Morn;
Not seldom Evening in the west
Sinks smilingly forsworn.

The smoothest seas will sometimes prove,   5
To the confiding Bark, untrue;
And, if she trust the stars above,
They can be treacherous too.

The umbrageous Oak, in pomp outspread,
Full oft, when storms the welkin rend,   10
Draws lightning down upon the head
It promis'd to defend.

But Thou art true, incarnate Lord!
Who didst vouchsafe for man to die;
Thy smile is sure, thy plighted word   15
No change can falsify!

I bent before thy gracious throne,
And asked for peace with suppliant knee;
And peace was given,—nor peace alone,
But faith, and hope, and extacy!   20

Placard for a Poll bearing an Old Shirt

If money I lack
The shirt on my back
Shall off—and go to the hammer;

For though with bare skin[1]
By G— I'll be in,   5
   And raise up a radical clamor!

"The Scottish Broom on Bird-nest brae"

The Scottish Broom on Bird-nest brae
Twelve tedious years ago,
When many plants strange blossoms bore
That puzzled high and low,
A not unnatural longing felt,   5
What longing, would ye know?
Why, Friend, to deck her supple twigs
With *yellow* in full blow.

To Lowther Castle she addressed
A prayer both bold and sly,   10
(For all the Brooms on Bird-nest Brae
Can talk and speechify)
That flattering breezes blowing thence
Their succour would supply;
Then she would instantly put forth   15
A flag of *Yellow* die.

But from the Castle turret blew
A chill forbidding blast,
Which the poor Broom no sooner felt
Than she shrank up as fast: 20
Her *wished*-for yellow she foreswore,
And since that time has cast
Fond looks on colours three or four,
And put forth *Blue* at last.

But now my Lads, the Election comes   25
In June's sunshiny hours
When every field, and bank, and brae
Is clad with yellow flowers;
While factious Blue from Shops and Booths
Tricks out her blustering powers,   30

---

1   WW suggested an improvement on this line, "Though I sell shirt, and skin," to his corre-
    spondent, Lord Lonsdale, February 25, 1818.

Lo! smiling Nature's lavish hand
Has furnished wreathes for ours.

The Pilgrim's Dream

OR, THE STAR AND THE GLOW-WORM

A Pilgrim, when the summer day
Had closed upon his weary way,
A lodging begg'd beneath a castle's roof;
But him the haughty Warder spurn'd;
And from the gate the Pilgrim turn'd,   5
To seek such covert as the field
Or heath-besprinkled copse might yield,
Or lofty wood, shower-proof.

He paced along; and, pensively
Halting beneath a shady tree,   10
Whose moss-grown root might serve for couch or seat,
Fixed on a Star his upward eye;
Then, from the tenant of the sky
He turned, and watch'd with kindred look,
A glow-worm, in a dusky nook,   15
Apparent at his feet.

The murmur of a neighbouring stream
Induced a soft and slumb'rous dream,
A pregnant dream within whose shadowy bounds
He recognised the earth-born Star,   20
And *That* whose radiance gleam'd from far;
And (strange to witness!) from the frame
Of the ethereal Orb there came
Intelligible sounds.

Much did it taunt the humbler Light   25
That now, when day was fled, and night
Hushed the dark earth—fast closing weary eyes,
A very Reptile could presume
To show her taper in the gloom,
As if in rivalship with One   30
Who sate a Ruler on his throne
Erected in the skies.

"Exalted Star!" the Worm replied,
"Abate this unbecoming pride,
Or with a less uneasy lustre shine;   35
Thou shrink'st as momently thy rays
Are master'd by the breathing haze;
While neither mist, nor thickest cloud
That shapes in heaven its murky shroud,
Hath power to injure mine.   40

Yet not for this do I aspire
To match the spark of local fire,
That at my will burns on the dewy lawn,
With thy acknowledged glories;—No!
But it behoves that thou shouldst know   45
What favours do attend me here,
Till, like thyself, I disappear
Before the purple dawn."

When this in modest guise was said,
Across the welkin seem'd to spread   50
A boding sound—for aught but sleep unfit!
Hills quaked—the rivers backward ran—
That Star, so proud of late, looked wan;
And reeled with visionary stir
In the blue depth, like Lucifer   55
Cast headlong to the pit!

Fire raged,—and when the spangled floor
Of ancient ether was no more,
New heavens succeeded, by the dream brought forth:
And all the happy souls that rode   60
Transfigured through that fresh abode,
Had heretofore, in humble trust,
Shone meekly mid their native dust,
The Glow-worms of the earth!

This knowledge, from an Angel's voice   65
Proceeding, made the heart rejoice
Of Him who slept upon the open lea:
Waking at morn he murmur'd not;
And, till life's journey closed, the spot

Was to the Pilgrim's soul endeared,   70
Where by that dream he had been cheered
Beneath the shady tree.

Sonnets

SUGGESTED BY MR. W. WESTALL'S VIEWS OF THE CAVES, &C.

IN YORKSHIRE

"Pure element of waters! wheresoe'er"

Pure element of waters! wheresoe'er
Thou dost forsake thy subterranean haunts,
Green herbs, bright flowers, and berry-bearing plants,
— Rise into life and in thy train appear:
And, through the sunny portion of the year,   5
Swift insects shine, thy hovering pursuivants:
And, if thy bounty fail, the forest pants;
And hart and hind and hunter with his spear,
Languish and droop together. Nor unfelt
In man's perturbed soul thy sway benign;   10
And, haply, far within the marble belt
Of central earth, where tortured Spirits pine
For grace and goodness lost, thy murmurs melt
Their anguish,—and they blend sweet songs with thine![1]

Malham Cove

Was the aim frustrated by force or guile,
When giants scoop'd from out the rocky ground
— Tier under tier—this semicirque profound?
(Giants—the same who built in Erin's isle
That Causeway with incomparable toil!)   5
O, had this vast theatric structure wound
With finish'd sweep into a perfect round,
No mightier work had gain'd the plausive smile
Of all-beholding Phœbus! But, alas,
Vain earth!—false world! Foundations must be laid   10
In Heav'n; for, mid the wreck of IS and WAS,

---

1   "Waters (as Mr. Westall informs us in the letter-press prefixed to his admirable views) are
    invariably found to flow through these caverns." WW

Things incomplete and purposes betrayed
Make sadder transits o'er truth's mystic glass
Than noblest objects utterly decayed.

Gordale

At early dawn,—or rather when the air
Glimmers with fading light, and shadowy eve
Is busiest to confer and to bereave,—
Then, pensive votary, let thy feet repair
To Gordale-chasm, terrific as the lair   5
Where the young lions couch;—for so, by leave
Of the propitious hour, thou may'st perceive
The local Deity, with oozy hair
And mineral crown, beside his jagged urn
Recumbent:—Him thou may'st behold, who hides   10
His lineaments by day, and there presides,
Teaching the docile waters how to turn;
Or, if need be, impediment to spurn,
And force their passage to the salt-sea tides!

Composed on the Banks of a Rocky Stream

Dogmatic Teachers, of the snow-white fur!
Ye wrangling Schoolmen, of the scarlet hood!
Who, with a keenness not to be withstood,
Press the point home,—or falter and demur,
Checked in your course by many a teazing burr;   5
These natural council-seats your acrid blood
Might cool;—and, as the Genius of the flood
Stoops willingly to animate and spur
Each lighter function slumbering in the brain,
Yon eddying balls of foam—these arrowy gleams,   10
That o'er the pavement of the surging streams
Welter and flash—a synod might detain
With subtile speculations, haply vain,
But surely less so than your far-fetched themes!

To a Snow-drop, appearing very early in the Season.

Lone Flower, hemmed in with snows and white as they
But hardier far, though modestly thou bend

Thy front—as if *such* presence could offend!
Who guards thy slender stalk while, day by day,
Storms, sallying from the mountain-tops, way-lay   5
The rising sun, and on the plains descend?
Accept the greeting that befits a friend
Whose zeal outruns his promise! Blue-eyed May
Shall soon behold this border thickly set
With bright jonquils, their odours lavishing   10
On the soft west-wind and his frolic peers;
Yet will I not thy gentle grace forget
Chaste Snow-drop, vent'rous harbinger of Spring,
And pensive monitor of fleeting years!

Sonnet

ON SEEING A TUFT OF SNOWDROPS IN A STORM

When haughty expectations prostrate lie,
And grandeur crouches like a guilty thing,
Oft shall the lowly weak, till nature bring
Mature release, in fair society
Survive, and Fortune's utmost anger try;   5
Like these frail snow-drops that together cling,
And nod their helmets smitten by the wing
Of many a furious whirlblast sweeping by.
Observe the faithful flowers! if small to great
May lead the thoughts, thus struggling used to stand   10
The Emathian phalanx, nobly obstinate;
And so the bright immortal Theban band,
Whom onset, fiercely urged at Jove's command,
Might overwhelm, but could not separate!

Composed during one of the most awful of the late Storms, *Feb. 1819*

One who was suffering tumult in his soul
Yet fail'd to seek the sure relief of prayer—
Went forth—his course surrendering to the care
Of the fierce wind, while mid-day lightnings prowl
Insidiously,—untimely thunders growl,—   5
While trees, dim-seen, in frenzied numbers tear

The lingering remnant of their yellow hair,—
And shivering wolves, surpris'd with darkness, howl
As if the sun were not;—he lifted high
His head—and in a moment did appear   10
Large space, mid dreadful clouds, of purest sky,
An' azure orb—shield of Tranquillity,
Invisible unlook'd-for minister
Of providential goodness ever nigh!

To ——————

Those silver clouds collected round the sun
His mid-day warmth abate not, seeming less
To overshade than multiply his beams
By soft reflection—grateful to the sky,
To rocks, fields, woods. Nor doth our human sense   5
Ask, for its pleasure, screen or canopy
More ample than that time-dismantled Oak
Spreads o'er this tuft of heath: which now, attired
In the whole fulness of its bloom, affords
As beautiful a couch as e'er on earth   10
Was fashioned; whether by the hand of art
That Eastern Sultan, amid flowers enwrought
On silken tissue, might diffuse his limbs
In languor; or, by Nature, for repose
Of panting Wood-nymph weary of the chace.   15
O Lady! fairer in thy Poet's sight
Than fairest spiritual Creature of the groves,
Approach—and, thus invited, crown with rest
The noon-tide hour:—though truly some there are
Whose footsteps superstitiously avoid   20
This venerable Tree; for, when the wind
Blows keenly, it sends forth a creaking sound,
Above the general roar of woods and crags;
Distinctly heard from far—a doleful note
As if (so Grecian shepherds would have deem'd)   25
The Hamadryad, pent within, bewailed
Some bitter wrong. Nor is it unbelieved,
By ruder fancy, that a troubled Ghost
Haunts this old Trunk; lamenting deeds of which

The flowery ground is conscious. But no wind   30
Sweeps now along this elevated ridge;
Not even a zephyr stirs;—the obnoxious Tree
Is mute,—and, in his silence, would look down
On thy reclining form with more delight
Than his Coevals in the sheltered vale   35
Seem to participate, the whilst they view
Their own far-stretching arms and leafy heads
Vividly pictured in some glassy pool,
That, for a brief space, checks the hurrying stream!

Sonnet

ON THE DETRACTION WHICH FOLLOWED
THE PUBLICATION OF A CERTAIN POEM

See Milton's Sonnet, beginning
"A Book was writ of late called 'Tetrachordon.'"[1]

A Book came forth of late called, "Peter Bell;"
Not negligent the style;—the matter?—good .
As aught that song records of Robin Hood;
Or Roy, renowned through many a Scottish dell;
But some (who brook these hacknied themes full well,   5
Nor heat, at Tam o' Shanter's name, their blood)
Wax'd wrath, and with foul claws, a harpy brood—
On Bard and Hero clamorously fell.
Heed not, wild Rover once through heath and glen
Who mad'st at length the better life thy choice,   10
Heed not such onset! nay, if praise of men
To thee appear not an unmeaning voice,
Lift up that grey-haired forehead, and rejoice
In the just tribute of thy Poet's pen!

September, 1819

The sylvan slopes with corn-clad fields
Are hung, as if with golden shields,
Bright trophies of the sun!
Like a fair sister of the sky,
Unruffled doth the blue Lake lie,   5

---

1   WW's first three lines are patterned after Milton's sonnet.11.

The Mountains looking on.

And, sooth to say, yon vocal Grove
Albeit uninspired by love,
By love untaught to ring,
May well afford to mortal ear   10
An impulse more profoundly dear
Than music of the Spring.

For *that* from turbulence and heat
Proceeds, from some uneasy seat
In Nature's struggling frame,   15
Some region of impatient life;
And jealousy, and quivering strife,
Therein a portion claim.

This, this is holy;—while I hear
These vespers of another year,   20
This hymn of thanks and praise,
My spirit seems to mount above
The anxieties of human love,
And earth's precarious days.

But list!—though winter storms be nigh,   25
Unchecked is that soft harmony:
There lives Who can provide
For all his creatures; and in Him,
Even like the radiant Seraphim,
These Choristers confide.   30

Upon the Same Occasion

Departing Summer hath assumed
An aspect tenderly illumed,
The gentlest look of Spring:
That calls from yonder leafy shade
Unfaded, yet prepared to fade,   5
A timely caroling.

No faint and hesitating trill,
Such tribute as to Winter chill
The lonely red-breast pays!

Clear, loud, and lively is the din,   10
From social Warblers gathering in
Their harvest of sweet lays.

Nor doth the example fail to cheer
Me conscious that my leaf is sear,
And yellow on the bough:—   15
Fall, rosy garlands, from my head!
Ye myrtle wreaths, your fragrance shed
Around a younger brow!

Yet will I temperately rejoice;
Wide is the range, and free the choice   20
Of undiscordant themes;
Which, haply, kindred souls may prize
Not less than vernal extacies,
And passion's feverish dreams.

For deathless powers to verse belong,   25
And they like Demi-gods are strong
On whom the Muses smile;
But some their function have disclaimed,
Best pleased with what is aptliest framed
To enervate and defile.   30

Not such the initiatory strains
Committed to the silent plains
In Britain's earliest dawn;
Trembled the groves, the stars grew pale,
While all-too-daringly the veil   35
Of Nature was withdrawn!

Nor, such the spirit-stirring note
When the live chords Alcæus smote,
Inflamed by sense of wrong;
Woe! woe to Tyrants! from the lyre   40
Broke threateningly, in sparkles dire
Of fierce vindictive song.

And not unhallow'd was the page
By winged Love inscrib'd, to assuage
The pangs of vain pursuit;   45

Love listening while the Lesbian Maid
With passion's finest finger swayed
Her own Æolian lute.

O ye who patiently explore
The wreck of Herculanean lore,   50
What rapture could ye seize
Some Theban fragment, or unroll
One precious, tender-hearted scroll
Of pure Simonides!

That were, indeed, a genuine birth   55
Of poesy; a bursting forth
Of Genius from the dust:
What Horace boasted to behold,
What Maro loved, shall we enfold?
Can haughty Time be just!   60

To ———

WITH A SELECTION FROM THE POEMS OF ANNE, COUNTESS OF WINCHELSEA; AND
EXTRACTS OF SIMILAR CHARACTER FROM OTHER WRITERS;
THE WHOLE TRANSCRIBED BY A FEMALE FRIEND

Lady! I rifled a Parnassian Cave
(But seldom trod) of mildly-gleaming ore;
And cull'd, from sundry beds, a lucid store
Of genuine crystals, pure as those that pave
The azure brooks where Dian joys to lave   5
Her spotless limbs; and ventur'd to explore
Dim shades—for reliques, upon Lethe's shore,
Cast up at random by the sullen wave.
To female hands the treasures were resign'd;
And lo this work!—a grotto bright and clear   10
From stain or taint; in which thy blameless mind
May feed on thoughts though pensive not austere;
Or if thy deeper spirit be inclin'd
To holy musing it may enter here.

On the Death of His Late Majesty

Ward of the Law!—dread Shadow of a King!

Whose Realm had dwindled to one stately room;
Whose universe was gloom immers'd in gloom,
Darkness as thick as Life o'er Life could fling,
Yet haply cheered with some faint glimmering   5
Of Faith and Hope; if thou by nature's doom
Gently hast sunk into the quiet tomb,
Why should we bend in grief, to sorrow cling,
When thankfulness were best?—Fresh-flowing tears,
Or, where tears flow not, sigh succeeding sigh,   10
Yield to such after-thought the sole reply
Which justly it can claim. The Nation hears
In this deep knell—silent for threescore years,
An unexampled voice of awful memory!

Oxford, May 30, 1820

Ye sacred Nurseries of blooming Youth!
In whose collegiate shelter England's Flowers
Expand—enjoying through their vernal hours
The air of liberty, the light of truth;
Much have ye suffered from Time's gnawing tooth,   5
Yet, O ye Spires of Oxford! Domes and Towers!
Gardens and Groves! your presence overpowers
The soberness of Reason; 'till, in sooth,
Transformed, and rushing on a bold exchange,
I slight my own beloved Cam, to range   10
Where silver Isis leads my stripling feet;
Pace the long avenue, or glide adown
The stream-like windings of that glorious street,
—An eager Novice robed in fluttering gown!

Oxford, May 30, 1820

Shame on this faithless heart! that could allow
Such transport—though but for a moment's space:
Not while—to aid the spirit of the place—
The crescent moon cleaves with its glittering prow
The clouds, or night-bird sings from shady bough;   5
But in plain day-light:—She, too, at my side,
Who, with her heart's experience satisfied,
Maintains inviolate its slightest vow.

Sweet Fancy! other gifts must I receive;
Proofs of a higher sovereignty I claim;   10
Take from *her* brow the withering flowers of Eve,
And to that brow Life's morning wreath restore;
Let *her* be comprehended in the frame
Of these illusions, or they please no more.

June, 1820

Fame tells of Groves—from England far away—
Groves that inspire the Nightingale to trill[1]
And modulate, with subtle reach of skill
Elsewhere unmatched, her ever-varying lay;
Such bold report I venture to gainsay: 5
For I have heard the choir of Richmond hill
Chaunting with indefatigable bill;
While I bethought me of a distant day;
When, haply under shade of that same wood,
And scarcely conscious of the dashing oars   10
Plied steadily between those willowy shores,
The sweet-souled Poet of the Seasons stood—
Listening, and listening long, in rapturous mood,
Ye heavenly Birds! to your Progenitors.

---

1   "Wallachia is the country alluded to." WW

The Prelude (1824–1839)[1]

BOOK FIRST
INTRODUCTION, CHILDHOOD, AND SCHOOL-TIME

O there is blessing in this gentle Breeze,
A visitant that, while he fans my cheek,
Doth seem half-conscious of the joy he brings
From the green fields, and from yon azure sky.
Whate'er his mission, the soft breeze can come   5
To none more grateful than to me; escaped
From the vast City, where I long have pined
A discontented Sojourner—Now free,
Free as a bird to settle where I will.
What dwelling shall receive me? in what vale   10
Shall be my harbour? underneath what grove
Shall I take up my home? and what clear stream
Shall with its murmur lull me into rest?
The earth is all before me: with a heart
Joyous, nor scared at its own liberty,   15
I look about; and should the chosen guide
Be nothing better than a wandering cloud,
I cannot miss my way. I breathe again;
Trances of thought and mountings of the heart
Come fast upon me: it is shaken off,   20
That burthen of my own unnatural self,
The heavy weight of many a weary day
Not mine, and such as were not made for me.
Long months of peace (if such bold word accord
With any promises of human life),   25
Long months of ease and undisturbed delight
Are mine in prospect; whither shall I turn,
By road or pathway, or through trackless field,
Up hill or down, or shall some floating thing
Upon the River point me out my course?   30
Dear Liberty! Yet what would it avail,

---

1   During the years 1824–1839, WW prepared his fourteen-book version of *The Prelude* for
    publication after his death. For the source of the reading text and the editor's commentary,
    see *The Fourteen-Book "Prelude,"* ed. W. J. B. Owen (1985).

But for a gift that consecrates the joy?
For I, methought, while the sweet breath of heaven
Was blowing on my body, felt, within,
A correspondent breeze, that gently moved   35
With quickening virtue, but is now become
A tempest, a redundant energy,
Vexing its own creation. Thanks to both,
And their congenial powers that, while they join
In breaking up a long continued frost,   40
Bring with them vernal promises, the hope
Of active days urged on by flying hours;
Days of sweet leisure taxed with patient thought
Abstruse, nor wanting punctual service high,
Matins and vespers, of harmonious verse!   45
  Thus far, O Friend! did I, not used to make
A present joy the matter of a Song,
Pour forth, that day, my soul in measured strains,
That would not be forgotten, and are here
Recorded:—to the open fields I told   50
A prophecy:—poetic numbers came
Spontaneously, to clothe in priestly robe
A renovated Spirit singled out,
Such hope was mine, for holy services:
My own voice cheered me, and, far more, the mind's   55
Internal echo of the imperfect sound;
To both I listened, drawing from them both
A chearful confidence in things to come.
  Content, and not unwilling now to give
A respite to this passion, I paced on   60
With brisk and eager steps; and came at length
To a green shady place where down I sate
Beneath a tree, slackening my thoughts by choice,
And settling into gentler happiness.
'Twas Autumn, and a clear and placid day,   65
With warmth, as much as needed, from a sun
Two hours declined towards the west, a day
With silver clouds, and sunshine on the grass,
And, in the sheltered and the sheltering grove,
A perfect stillness. Many were the thoughts   70

Encouraged and dismissed, till choice was made
Of a known Vale whither my feet should turn,
Nor rest till they had reached the very door
Of the one Cottage which methought I saw.
No picture of mere memory ever looked   75
So fair; and while upon the fancied scene
I gazed with growing love, a higher power
Than Fancy gave assurance of some work
Of glory, there forthwith to be begun,
Perhaps too there performed. Thus long I mused,   80
Nor e'er lost sight of what I mused upon,
Save where, amid the stately grove of Oaks,
Now here—now there—an acorn, from its cup
Dislodged, through sere leaves rustled, or at once
To the bare earth dropped with a startling sound.   85
    From that soft couch I rose not, till the sun
Had almost touched the horizon; casting then
A backward glance upon the curling cloud
Of city smoke, by distance ruralized,
Keen as a Truant or a Fugitive,   90
But as a Pilgrim resolute, I took,
Even with the chance equipment of that hour,
The road that pointed tow'rd the chosen Vale.
    It was a splendid evening: and my Soul
Once more made trial of her strength, nor lacked   95
Eolian visitations; but the harp
Was soon defrauded, and the banded host
Of harmony dispersed in straggling sounds;
And lastly utter silence! "Be it so;
Why think of any thing but present good?"   100
So, like a Home-bound Labourer, I pursued
My way, beneath the mellowing sun, that shed
Mild influence; nor left in me one wish
Again to bend the sabbath of that time
To a servile yoke. What need of many words?   105
A pleasant loitering journey, through three days
Continued, brought me to my hermitage.
I spare to tell of what ensued, the life
In common things,—the endless store of things

Rare, or at least so seeming, every day   110
Found all about me in one neighbourhood;
The self-congratulation, and from morn
To night unbroken cheerfulness serene.
But speedily an earnest longing rose
To brace myself to some determined aim,   115
Reading or thinking; either to lay up
New stores, or rescue from decay the old
By timely interference: and therewith
Came hopes still higher, that with outward life
I might endue some airy phantasies   120
That had been floating loose about for years;
And to such Beings temperately deal forth
The many feelings that oppressed my heart.
That hope hath been discouraged; welcome light
Dawns from the East, but dawns—to disappear   125
And mock me with a sky that ripens not
Into a steady morning: if my mind,
Remembering the bold promise of the past,
Would gladly grapple with some noble theme,
Vain is her wish: where'er she turns, she finds   130
Impediments from day to day renewed.
      And now it would content me to yield up
Those lofty hopes awhile for present gifts
Of humbler industry. But, O dear Friend!
The Poet, gentle Creature as he is,   135
Hath, like the Lover, his unruly times,
His fits when he is neither sick nor well,
Though no distress be near him but his own
Unmanageable thoughts: his mind, best pleas'd
While she, as duteous as the Mother Dove,   140
Sits brooding, lives not always to that end,
But, like the innocent Bird, hath goadings on
That drive her, as in trouble, through the groves:
With me is now such passion, to be blamed
No otherwise than as it lasts too long.   145
      When, as becomes a Man who would prepare
For such an arduous Work, I through myself
Make rigorous inquisition, the report

Is often chearing; for I neither seem
To lack that first great gift, the vital Soul,   150
Nor general Truths, which are themselves a sort
Of Elements and Agents, Under-powers,
Subordinate helpers of the living Mind:
Nor am I naked of external things,
Forms, images, nor numerous other aids   155
Of less regard, though won perhaps with toil,
And needful to build up a Poet's praise.
Time, place, and manners do I seek, and these
Are found in plenteous store, but no where such
As may be singled out with steady choice: 160
No little band of yet remembered names
Whom I in perfect confidence might hope
To summon back from lonesome banishment,
And make them dwellers in the hearts of men
Now living, or to live in future years.   165
Sometimes the ambitious Power of choice, mistaking
Proud spring-tide swellings for a regular sea,
Will settle on some British theme, some old
Romantic Tale by Milton left unsung:
More often turning to some gentle place   170
Within the groves of Chivalry, I pipe
To Shepherd Swains, or seated, harp in hand,
Amid reposing knights by a River side
Or fountain, listen to the grave reports
Of dire enchantments faced, and overcome   175
By the strong mind, and Tales of warlike feats
Where spear encountered spear, and sword with sword
Fought, as if conscious of the blazonry
That the shield bore, so glorious was the strife;
Whence inspiration for a song that winds   180
Through ever changing scenes of votive quest,
Wrongs to redress, harmonious tribute paid
To patient courage and unblemished truth,
To firm devotion, zeal unquenchable,
And Christian meekness hallowing faithful loves.   185
Sometimes, more sternly moved, I would relate
How vanquished Mithridates northward passed,

And, hidden in the cloud of years, became
Odin, the Father of a Race by whom
Perished the Roman Empire; how the friends   190
And followers of Sertorius, out of Spain
Flying, found shelter in the Fortunate Isles;
And left their usages, their arts, and laws
To disappear by a slow gradual death;
To dwindle and to perish, one by one,   195
Starved in those narrow bounds: but not the soul
Of Liberty, which fifteen hundred years
Survived, and, when the European came
With skill and power that might not be withstood,
Did, like a pestilence, maintain its hold,   200
And wasted down by glorious death that Race
Of natural Heroes;—or I would record
How, in tyrannic times, some high-souled Man,
Unnamed among the chronicles of Kings,
Suffered in silence for truth's sake: or tell   205
How that one Frenchman, through continued force
Of meditation on the inhuman deeds
Of those who conquered first the Indian isles,
Went, single in his ministry, across
The Ocean;—not to comfort the Oppressed,   210
But, like a thirsty wind, to roam about,
Withering the Oppressor:—how Gustavus sought
Help at his need in Dalecarlia's mines:
How Wallace fought for Scotland, left the name
Of Wallace to be found, like a wild flower,   215
All over his dear Country, left the deeds
Of Wallace, like a family of Ghosts,
To people the steep rocks and river banks,
Her natural sanctuaries, with a local soul
Of independence and stern liberty.   220
Sometimes it suits me better to invent
A Tale from my own heart, more near akin
To my own passions, and habitual thoughts,
Some variegated Story, in the main
Lofty, but the unsubstantial Structure melts   225
Before the very sun that brightens it,

Mist into air dissolving! Then, a wish,
My last and favourite aspiration, mounts,
With yearning, tow'rds some philosophic Song
Of Truth that cherishes our daily life;   230
With meditations passionate, from deep
Recesses in man's heart, immortal verse
Thoughtfully fitted to the Orphean lyre;
But from this awful burthen I full soon
Take refuge, and beguile myself with trust   235
That mellower years will bring a riper mind
And clearer insight. Thus my days are passed
In contradiction; with no skill to part
Vague longing, haply bred by want of power,
From paramount impulse—not to be withstood;   240
A timorous capacity from prudence;
From circumspection, infinite delay.
Humility and modest awe themselves
Betray me, serving often for a cloke
To a more subtile selfishness; that now   245
Locks every function up in blank reserve,
Now dupes me, trusting to an anxious eye
That with intrusive restlessness beats off
Simplicity, and self-presented truth.
     Ah! better far than this, to stray about   250
Voluptuously, through fields and rural walks,
And ask no record of the hours, resigned
To vacant musing, unreproved neglect
Of all things, and deliberate holiday:
Far better never to have heard the name   255
Of zeal and just ambition, than to live
Baffled and plagued by a mind that every hour
Turns recreant to her task, takes heart again,
Then feels immediately some hollow thought
Hang like an interdict upon her hopes.   260
This is my lot; for either still I find
Some imperfection in the chosen theme;
Or see of absolute accomplishment
Much wanting, so much wanting, in myself
That I recoil and droop, and seek repose   265

In listlessness from vain perplexity;
Unprofitably travelling toward the grave,
Like a false Steward who hath much received,
And renders nothing back.
                    Was it for this
That one, the fairest of all rivers, loved   270
To blend his murmurs with my Nurse's song;
And, from his alder shades and rocky falls,
And from his fords and shallows, sent a voice
That flowed along my dreams? For this didst Thou,
O Derwent! winding among grassy holms   275
Where I was looking on, a Babe in arms,
Make ceaseless music, that composed my thoughts
To more than infant softness, giving me,
Amid the fretful dwellings of mankind,
A foretaste, a dim earnest, of the calm   280
That Nature breathes among the hills and groves?
      When he had left the mountains, and received
On his smooth breast the shadow of those Towers
That yet survive, a shattered Monument
Of feudal sway, the bright blue River passed   285
Along the margin of our Terrace Walk;
A tempting Playmate whom we dearly loved.
O many a time have I, a five years' Child,
In a small mill-race severed from his stream,
Made one long bathing of a summer's day;   290
Basked in the sun, and plunged, and basked again,
Alternate all a summer's day, or scoured
The sandy fields, leaping through flow'ry groves
Of yellow ragwort; or when rock and hill,
The woods and distant Skiddaw's lofty height,   295
Were bronzed with deepest radiance, stood alone
Beneath the sky, as if I had been born
On Indian plains, and from my Mother's hut
Had run abroad in wantonness, to sport,
A naked Savage, in the thunder shower.   300
      Fair seed-time had my soul, and I grew up
Fostered alike by beauty and by fear;
Much favoured in my birth-place, and no less'

In that beloved Vale to which erelong
We were transplanted—there were we let loose   305
For sports of wider range. Ere I had told
Ten birth-days, when among the mountain slopes
Frost, and the breath of frosty wind, had snapped
The last autumnal Crocus, 'twas my joy,
With store of Springes o'er my Shoulder slung,   310
To range the open heights where woodcocks ran
Along the smooth green turf. Through half the night,
Scudding away from snare to snare, I plied
That anxious visitation;—moon and stars
Were shining o'er my head; I was alone,   315
And seemed to be a trouble to the peace
That dwelt among them. Sometimes it befel,
In these night-wanderings, that a strong desire
O'erpowered my better reason, and the Bird
Which was the Captive of another's toil   320
Became my prey; and when the deed was done
I heard, among the solitary hills,
Low breathings coming after me, and sounds
Of undistinguishable motion, steps
Almost as silent as the turf they trod.   325
    Nor less, when Spring had warmed the cultured Vale,
Roved we as plunderers where the Mother-bird
Had in high places built her lodge; though mean
Our object, and inglorious, yet the end
Was not ignoble. Oh! when I have hung   330
Above the Raven's nest, by knots of grass
And half-inch fissures in the slippery rock
But ill-sustained; and almost (so it seemed)
Suspended by the blast that blew amain,
Shouldering the naked crag; Oh, at that time,   335
While on the perilous ridge I hung alone,
With what strange utterance did the loud dry wind
Blow through my ears! the sky seemed not a sky
Of earth, and with what motion moved the clouds!
    Dust as we are, the immortal Spirit grows   340
Like harmony in music; there is a dark
Inscrutable workmanship that reconciles

Discordant elements, makes them cling together
In one society. How strange that all
The terrors, pains, and early miseries,   345
Regrets, vexations, lassitudes, interfused
Within my mind, should e'er have borne a part,
And that a needful part, in making up
The calm existence that is mine when I
Am worthy of myself! Praise to the end!   350
Thanks to the means which Nature deigned to employ!
Whether her fearless visitings or those
That came with soft alarm like hurtless lightning
Opening the peaceful clouds, or she would use
Severer interventions, ministry   355
More palpable, as best might suit her aim.
    One summer evening (led by her) I found
A little Boat tied to a Willow-tree
Within a rocky cave, its usual home.
Strait I unloosed her chain, and, stepping in,   360
Pushed from the shore. It was an act of stealth
And troubled pleasure, nor without the voice
Of mountain-echoes did my Boat move on,
Leaving behind her still, on either side,
Small circles glittering idly in the moon,   365
Until they melted all into one track
Of sparkling light. But now, like one who rows
(Proud of his skill) to reach a chosen point
With an unswerving line, I fixed my view
Upon the summit of a craggy ridge,   370
The horizon's utmost boundary; for above
Was nothing but the stars and the grey sky.
She was an elfin Pinnace; lustily
I dipped my oars into the silent Lake;
And, as I rose upon the stroke, my boat   375
Went heaving through the Water like a swan:
When, from behind that craggy Steep, till then
The horizon's bound, a huge peak, black and huge,
As if with voluntary power instinct,
Upreared its head.—I struck, and struck again,   380
And, growing still in stature, the grim Shape

Towered up between me and the stars, and still,
For so it seemed, with purpose of its own
And measured motion, like a living Thing
Strode after me. With trembling oars I turned,   385
And through the silent water stole my way
Back to the Covert of the Willow-tree;
There, in her mooring-place, I left my Bark,—
And through the meadows homeward went, in grave
And serious mood; but after I had seen   390
That spectacle, for many days, my brain
Worked with a dim and undetermined sense
Of unknown modes of being; o'er my thoughts
There hung a darkness, call it solitude
Or blank desertion. No familiar Shapes   395
Remained, no pleasant images of trees,
Of sea or Sky, no colours of green fields,
But huge and mighty Forms, that do not live
Like living men, moved slowly through the mind
By day, and were a trouble to my dreams.   400
    Wisdom and Spirit of the Universe!
Thou Soul that art the eternity of thought,
That giv'st to forms and images a breath
And everlasting Motion! not in vain,
By day or star-light, thus from my first dawn   405
Of Childhood didst thou intertwine for me
The passions that build up our human Soul,
Not with the mean and vulgar works of man,
But with high objects, with enduring things,
With life and nature, purifying thus   410
The elements of feeling and of thought,
And sanctifying, by such discipline,
Both pain and fear; until we recognize
A grandeur in the beatings of the heart.
    Nor was this fellowship vouchsafed to me   415
With stinted kindness. In November days
When vapours, rolling down the valley, made
A lonely scene more lonesome; among woods
At noon, and 'mid the calm of summer nights,
When, by the margin of the trembling Lake,   420

Beneath the gloomy hills homeward I went
In solitude, such intercourse was mine:
Mine was it, in the fields both day and night,
And by the waters, all the summer long.
   —And in the frosty season, when the sun   425
Was set, and visible for many a mile,
The cottage windows blazed through twilight gloom,
I heeded not their summons;—happy time
It was indeed for all of us; for me
It was a time of rapture!—Clear and loud   430
The village Clock toll'd six—I wheeled about,
Proud and exulting like an untired horse
That cares not for his home.—All shod with steel,
We hissed along the polished ice, in games
Confederate, imitative of the chase   435
And woodland pleasures,—the resounding horn,
The Pack loud-chiming and the hunted hare.
So through the darkness and the cold we flew,
And not a voice was idle: with the din
Smitten, the precipices rang aloud;   440
The leafless trees and every icy crag
Tinkled like iron; while far distant hills
Into the tumult sent an alien sound
Of melancholy, not unnoticed while the stars,
Eastward, were sparkling clear, and in the west   445
The orange sky of evening died away.
Not seldom from the uproar I retired
Into a silent bay,—or sportively
Glanced sideway, leaving the tumultuous throng
To cut across the reflex of a star   450
That fled, and, flying still before me, gleamed
Upon the glassy plain: and oftentimes,
When we had given our bodies to the wind,
And all the shadowy banks on either side
Came sweeping through the darkness, spinning still   455
The rapid line of motion, then at once
Have I, reclining back upon my heels,
Stopped short; yet still the solitary cliffs
Wheeled by me—even as if the earth had rolled

With visible motion her diurnal round!   460
Behind me did they stretch in solemn train,
Feebler and feebler, and I stood and watched
Till all was tranquil as a dreamless sleep.
    Ye presences of Nature, in the sky,
And on the earth! Ye visions of the hills!   465
And Souls of lonely places! can I think
A vulgar hope was yours when ye employed
Such ministry, when ye, through many a year,
Haunting me thus among my boyish sports,
On caves and trees, upon the woods and hills,   470
Impressed upon all forms the characters
Of danger or desire; and thus did make
The surface of the universal earth
With triumph and delight, with hope and fear,
Work like a sea?
                Not uselessly employed,   475
Might I pursue this theme through every change
Of exercise and play, to which the year
Did summon us in his delightful round.
    —We were a noisy crew; the sun in heaven
Beheld not vales more beautiful than ours,   480
Nor saw a Band in happiness and joy
Richer, or worthier of the ground they trod.
I could record with no reluctant voice
The woods of Autumn, and their hazel bowers
With milk-white clusters hung; the rod and line,   485
True symbol of hope's foolishness, whose strong
And unreproved enchantment led us on,
By rocks and pools shut out from every star
All the green summer, to forlorn cascades
Among the windings hid of mountain brooks.   490
—Unfading recollections! at this hour
The heart is almost mine with which I felt,
From some hill-top on sunny afternoons,
The paper-Kite, high among fleecy clouds,
Pull at her rein, like an impatient Courser;   495
Or, from the meadows sent on gusty days,
Beheld her breast the wind, then suddenly

Dashed headlong, and rejected by the storm.
    Ye lowly Cottages in which we dwelt,
A ministration of your own was yours!   500
Can I forget you, being as ye were
So beautiful among the pleasant fields
In which ye stood? or can I here forget
The plain and seemly countenance with which
Ye dealt out your plain Comforts? Yet had ye   505
Delights and exultations of your own.
Eager and never weary, we pursued
Our home-amusements by the warm peat-fire
At evening, when with pencil, and smooth slate
In square divisions parcelled out, and all   510
With crosses and with cyphers scribbled o'er,
We schemed and puzzled, head opposed to head,
In strife too humble to be named in verse;
Or round the naked table, snow-white deal,
Cherry, or maple, sate in close array,   515
And to the Combat, Lu or Whist, led on
A thick-ribbed Army, not as in the world
Neglected and ungratefully thrown by
Even for the very service they had wrought,
But husbanded through many a long campaign.   520
Uncouth assemblage was it, where no few
Had changed their functions; some, plebeian cards
Which Fate, beyond the promise of their birth,
Had dignified, and called to represent
The Persons of departed Pontentates.   525
Oh, with what echoes on the board they fell!
Ironic diamonds; Clubs, Hearts, Diamonds, Spades,
A congregation piteously akin!
Cheap matter offered they to boyish wit,
Those sooty Knaves, precipitated down   530
With scoffs and taunts like Vulcan out of heaven;
The paramount Ace, a moon in her eclipse,
Queens gleaming through their Splendor's last decay,
And Monarchs surly at the wrongs sustained
By royal visages. Meanwhile abroad   535
Incessant rain was falling, or the frost

Raged bitterly, with keen and silent tooth;
And, interrupting oft that eager game,
From under Esthwaite's splitting fields of ice
The pent-up air, struggling to free itself,   540
Gave out to meadow-grounds and hills, a loud
Protracted yelling, like the noise of wolves
Howling in Troops along the Bothnic Main.
    Nor, sedulous as I have been to trace
How Nature by extrinsic passion first   545
Peopled the mind with forms sublime or fair
And made me love them, may I here omit
How other pleasures have been mine, and joys
Of subtler origin; how I have felt,
Not seldom even in that tempestuous time,   550
Those hallowed and pure motions of the sense
Which seem, in their simplicity, to own
An intellectual charm;—that calm delight
Which, if I err not, surely must belong
To those first-born affinities that fit   555
Our new existence to existing things,
And, in our dawn of being, constitute
The bond of union between life and joy.
    Yes, I remember when the changeful earth
And twice five summers on my mind had stamped   560
The faces of the moving year, even then
I held unconscious intercourse with beauty
Old as creation, drinking in a pure
Organic pleasure from the silver wreaths
Of curling mist, or from the level plain   565
Of waters, colored by impending clouds.
    The sands of Westmorland, the creeks and bays
Of Cumbria's rocky limits, they can tell
How, when the Sea threw off his evening shade,
And to the Shepherd's hut on distant hills   570
Sent welcome notice of the rising moon,
How I have stood, to fancies such as these
A Stranger, linking with the Spectacle
No conscious memory of a kindred sight,
And bringing with me no peculiar sense   575

Of quietness or peace, yet have I stood,
Even while mine eye hath moved o'er many a league
Of shining water, gathering, as it seemed,
Through every hair-breadth in that field of light,
New pleasure, like a bee among the flowers.   580
    Thus oft amid those fits of vulgar joy
Which, through all seasons, on a Child's pursuits
Are prompt Attendants; 'mid that giddy bliss
Which like a tempest works along the blood
And is forgotten: even then I felt   585
Gleams like the flashing of a shield,—the earth
And common face of Nature spake to me
Rememberable things; sometimes, 'tis true,
By chance collisions and quaint accidents
(Like those ill-sorted unions, work supposed   590
Of evil-minded fairies), yet not vain
Nor profitless, if haply they impressed
Collateral objects and appearances,
Albeit lifeless then, and doomed to sleep
Until maturer seasons called them forth   595
To impregnate and to elevate the mind.
—And, if the vulgar joy by its own weight
Wearied itself out of the memory,
The scenes which were a witness of that joy
Remained, in their substantial lineaments   600
Depicted on the brain, and to the eye
Were visible, a daily sight: and thus
By the impressive discipline of fear,
By pleasure and repeated happiness,
So frequently repeated, and by force   605
Of obscure feelings representative
Of things forgotten; these same scenes so bright,
So beautiful, so majestic in themselves,
Though yet the day was distant, did become
Habitually dear; and all their forms   610
And changeful colours by invisible links
Were fastened to the affections.
                          I began
My Story early, not misled, I trust,

By an infirmity of love for days
Disowned by memory, fancying flowers where none,   615
Not even the sweetest, do or can survive
For him at least whose dawning day they cheered;
Nor will it seem to Thee, O Friend! so prompt
In sympathy, that I have lengthened out,
With fond and feeble tongue, a tedious tale.   620
Meanwhile, my hope has been, that I might fetch
Invigorating thoughts from former years;
Might fix the wavering balance of my mind,
And haply meet reproaches too, whose power
May spur me on, in manhood now mature,   625
To honorable toil. Yet should these hopes
Prove vain, and thus should neither I be taught
To understand myself, nor thou to know
With better knowledge how the heart was framed
Of him thou lovest, need I dread from thee   630
Harsh judgments, if the Song be loth to quit
Those recollected hours that have the charm
Of visionary things, those lovely forms
And sweet sensations that throw back our life,
And almost make remotest infancy   635
A visible scene, on which the sun is shining?
    One end at least hath been attained—my mind
Hath been revived; and, if this genial mood
Desert me not, forthwith shall be brought down
Through later years the story of my life: 640
The road lies plain before me,—'tis a theme
Single, and of determined bounds; and hence
I chuse it rather, at this time, than work
Of ampler or more varied argument,
Where I might be discomfited and lost;   645
And certain hopes are with me that to thee
This labour will be welcome, honoured Friend!

BOOK SECOND
SCHOOL-TIME CONTINUED

Thus far, O Friend! have we, though leaving much
Unvisited, endeavoured to retrace

The simple ways in which my childhood walked,
Those chiefly, that first led me to the love
Of rivers, woods, and fields. The passion yet   5
Was in its birth, sustained, as might befal,
By nourishment that came unsought; for still,
From week to week, from month to month, we lived
A round of tumult. Duly were our games
Prolonged in summer till the day-light failed;   10
No chair remained before the doors, the bench
And threshold steps were empty; fast asleep
The Labourer, and the old Man who had sate,
A later Lingerer, yet the revelry
Continued, and the loud uproar; at last,   15
When all the ground was dark, and twinkling stars
Edged the black clouds, home and to bed we went,
Feverish, with weary joints and beating minds.
Ah! is there One who ever has been young
Nor needs a warning voice to tame the pride   20
Of intellect, and virtue's self-esteem?
One is there, though the wisest and the best
Of all mankind, who covets not at times
Union that cannot be; who would not give,
If so he might, to duty and to truth   25
The eagerness of infantine desire?
A tranquillizing spirit presses now
On my corporeal frame, so wide appears
The vacancy between me and those days,
Which yet have such self-presence in my mind,   30
That, musing on them, often do I seem
Two consciousnesses, conscious of myself
And of some other Being. A rude mass
Of native rock, left midway in the Square
Of our small market Village, was the goal   35
Or centre of these sports; and, when, returned
After long absence, thither I repaired,
Gone was the old grey stone, and in its place
A smart Assembly-room usurped the ground
That had been ours. There let the fiddle scream,   40
And be ye happy! Yet, my Friends, I know

That more than one of you will think with me
Of those soft starry nights, and that old Dame
From whom the Stone was named, who there had sate
And watched her table with its huckster's wares   45
Assiduous, through the length of sixty years.
—We ran a boisterous course, the year span round
With giddy motion. But the time approached
That brought with it a regular desire
For calmer pleasures, when the winning forms   50
Of Nature were collaterally attached
To every scheme of holiday delight,
And every boyish sport, less grateful else
And languidly pursued.
                              When summer came,
Our pastime was, on bright half-holidays,   55
To sweep along the plain of Windermere
With rival oars; and the selected bourne
Was now an Island musical with birds
That sang and ceased not; now a sister isle,
Beneath the oaks' umbrageous covert, sown   60
With lilies of the valley like a field;
And now a third small island, where survived,
In solitude, the ruins of a shrine
Once to our Lady dedicate, and served
Daily with chaunted rites. In such a race,   65
So ended, disappointment could be none,
Uneasiness, or pain, or jealousy;
We rested in the Shade, all pleased alike,
Conquered and Conqueror. Thus the pride of strength,
And the vain-glory of superior skill,   70
Were tempered, thus was gradually produced
A quiet independence of the heart:
And, to my Friend who knows me, I may add,
Fearless of blame, that hence, for future days,
Ensued a diffidence and modesty;   75
And I was taught to feel, perhaps too much,
The self-sufficing power of solitude.
    Our daily meals were frugal, Sabine fare!
More than we wished we knew the blessing then

Of vigorous hunger—hence corporeal strength 80
Unsapped by delicate viands; for, exclude
A little weekly stipend, and we lived
Through three divisions of the quartered year
In pennyless poverty. But now, to school
From the half-yearly holidays returned, 85
We came with weightier purses, that sufficed
To furnish treats more costly than the Dame
Of the old grey stone, from her scanty board, supplied.
Hence rustic dinners on the cool green ground,
Or in the woods, or by a river side, 90
Or shady fountains, while among the leaves
Soft airs were stirring, and the mid-day sun
Unfelt shone brightly round us in our joy.
    Nor is my aim neglected if I tell
How sometimes, in the length of those half years, 95
We from our funds drew largely—proud to curb,
And eager to spur on, the galloping Steed:
And with the cautious Inn-keeper, whose Stud
Supplied our want, we haply might employ
Sly subterfuges, if the Adventure's bound 100
Were distant, some famed Temple where of yore
The Druids worshipped, or the antique Walls
Of that large Abbey which within the Vale
Of Nightshade, to St Mary's honour built,
Stands yet, a mouldering Pile, with fractured arch, 105
Belfry, and Images, and living Trees;
A holy Scene!—Along the smooth green Turf
Our Horses grazed:—to more than inland peace
Left by the west wind sweeping overhead
From a tumultuous ocean, trees and towers 110
In that sequestered Valley may be seen
Both silent and both motionless alike;
Such the deep shelter that is there, and such
The safeguard for repose and quietness.
    Our Steeds remounted, and the summons given, 115
With whip and spur we through the Chauntry flew
In uncouth race, and left the cross-legged Knight
And the Stone-abbot, and that single Wren

Which one day sang so sweetly in the Nave
Of the old Church, that, though from recent Showers   120
The earth was comfortless, and, touched by faint
Internal breezes, sobbings of the place
And respirations, from the roofless walls
The shuddering ivy dripped large drops, yet still
So sweetly 'mid the gloom the invisible Bird   125
Sang to herself, that there I could have made
My dwelling-place, and lived for ever there
To hear such music. Through the Walls we flew,
And down the Valley, and, a circuit made
In wantonness of heart, through rough and smooth   130
We scampered homewards. Oh, ye rocks and streams,
And that still Spirit shed from evening air!
Even in this joyous time I sometimes felt
Your presence, when with slackened step we breathed
Along the sides of the steep hills, or when,   135
Lighted by gleams of moonlight from the sea,
We beat with thundering hoofs the level sand.
　　Midway on long Winander's Eastern shore,
Within the crescent of a pleasant Bay,
A Tavern stood, no homely-featured House,   140
Primeval like its neighbouring Cottages;
But 'twas a splendid place, the door beset
With Chaises, Grooms, and Liveries,—and within
Decanters, Glasses, and the blood-red Wine.
In ancient times, or ere the Hall was built   145
On the large Island, had this Dwelling been
More worthy of a Poet's love, a Hut
Proud of its one bright fire and sycamore shade.
But, though the rhymes were gone that once inscribed
The threshold, and large golden characters   150
Spread o'er the spangled sign-board had dislodged
The old Lion, and usurped his place in slight
And mockery of the rustic Painter's hand,
Yet to this hour the spot to me is dear
With all its foolish pomp. The garden lay   155
Upon a slope surmounted by the plain
Of a small Bowling-green: beneath us stood

A grove, with gleams of water through the trees
And over the tree-tops; nor did we want
Refreshment, strawberries, and mellow cream.   160
There, while through half an afternoon we played
On the smooth platform, whether skill prevailed
Or happy blunder triumphed, bursts of glee
Made all the mountains ring. But ere night-fall,
When in our pinnace we returned, at leisure   165
Over the shadowy Lake, and to the beach
Of some small Island steered our course with one,
The Minstrel of our Troop, and left him there,
And rowed off gently, while he blew his flute
Alone upon the rock,—Oh then the calm   170
And dead still water lay upon my mind
Even with a weight of pleasure, and the sky,
Never before so beautiful, sank down
Into my heart, and held me like a dream!
    Thus were my sympathies enlarged, and thus   175
Daily the common range of visible things
Grew dear to me: already I began
To love the sun; a boy I loved the sun,
Not as I since have loved him, as a pledge
And surety of our earthly life, a light   180
Which we behold, and feel we are alive;
Nor for his bounty to so many worlds,
But for this cause, that I had seen him lay
His beauty on the morning hills, had seen
The western mountain touch his setting orb,   185
In many a thoughtless hour, when, from excess
Of happiness, my blood appear'd to flow
For its own pleasure, and I breathed with joy;
And from like feelings, humble though intense,
To patriotic and domestic love   190
Analogous, the moon to me was dear;
For I would dream away my purposes,
Standing to gaze upon her while she hung
Midway between the hills, as if she knew
No other region; but belonged to thee,   195
Yea, appertained by a peculiar right

To thee, and thy grey huts, thou one dear Vale!
   Those incidental charms which first attached
My heart to rural objects, day by day
Grew weaker, and I hasten on to tell   200
How Nature, intervenient till this time
And secondary, now at length was sought
For her own sake. But who shall parcel out
His intellect, by geometric rules,
Split like a province into round and square?   205
Who knows the individual hour in which
His habits were first sown, even as a seed?
Who that shall point, as with a wand, and say,
"This portion of the river of my mind
Came from yon fountain"? Thou, my friend! art one   210
More deeply read in thy own thoughts; to thee
Science appears but what in truth she is,
Not as our glory and our absolute boast,
But as a succedaneum, and a prop
To our infirmity. No officious slave   215
Art thou of that false secondary power
By which we multiply distinctions, then
Deem that our puny boundaries are things
That we perceive, and not that we have made.
To thee, unblinded by these formal arts,   220
The unity of all hath been revealed;
And thou wilt doubt with me, less aptly skilled
Than many are to range the faculties
In scale and order, class the cabinet
Of their sensations, and in voluble phrase   225
Run through the history and birth of each
As of a single independent thing.
Hard task, vain hope, to analyse the mind,
If each most obvious and particular thought,
Not in a mystical and idle sense,   230
But in the words of reason deeply weighed,
Hath no beginning.
                        Blest the infant Babe,
(For with my best conjecture I would trace
Our Being's earthly progress) blest the Babe,

Nursed in his Mother's arms, who sinks to sleep   235
Rocked on his Mother's breast; who, when his soul
Claims manifest kindred with a human soul,
Drinks in the feelings of his Mother's eye!
For him, in one dear Presence, there exists
A virtue which irradiates and exalts   240
Objects through widest intercourse of sense.
No outcast he, bewildered and depressed;
Along his infant veins are interfused
The gravitation and the filial bond
Of nature that connect him with the world.   245
Is there a flower to which he points with hand
Too weak to gather it, already love
Drawn from love's purest earthly fount for him
Hath beautified that flower; already shades
Of pity cast from inward tenderness   250
Do fall around him upon aught that bears
Unsightly marks of violence or harm.
Emphatically such a Being lives,
Frail Creature as he is, helpless as frail,
An inmate of this active universe.   255
For feeling has to him imparted power
That through the growing faculties of sense
Doth, like an Agent of the one great Mind,
Create, creator and receiver both,
Working but in alliance with the works   260
Which it beholds.—Such, verily, is the first
Poetic spirit of our human life,
By uniform control of after years
In most abated or suppressed, in some,
Through every change of growth and of decay,   265
Preeminent till death.
               From early days,
Beginning not long after that first time
In which, a Babe, by intercourse of touch,
I held mute dialogues with my Mother's heart,
I have endeavoured to display the means   270
Whereby this infant sensibility,
Great birth-right of our being, was in me

Augmented and sustained. Yet is a path
More difficult before me, and I fear
That, in its broken windings, we shall need   275
The chamois' sinews, and the eagle's wing:
For now a trouble came into my mind
From unknown causes. I was left alone,
Seeking the visible world, nor knowing why.
The props of my affections were removed,   280
And yet the building stood, as if sustained
By its own spirit! All that I beheld
Was dear, and hence to finer influxes
The mind lay open, to a more exact
And close communion. Many are our joys   285
In youth, but Oh! what happiness to live
When every hour brings palpable access
Of knowledge, when all knowledge is delight,
And sorrow is not there! The seasons came,
And every season, wheresoe'er I moved,   290
Unfolded transitory qualities
Which, but for this most watchful power of love,
Had been neglected, left a register
Of permanent relations, else unknown.
Hence life, and change, and beauty; solitude   295
More active even than "best society,"
Society made sweet as solitude
By inward concords, silent, inobtrusive;
And gentle agitations of the mind
From manifold distinctions, difference   300
Perceived in things where, to the unwatchful eye,
No difference is, and hence, from the same source,
Sublimer joy: for I would walk alone
Under the quiet stars, and at that time
Have felt whate'er there is of power in sound   305
To breathe an elevated mood, by form
Or Image unprofaned: and I would stand,
If the night blackened with a coming storm,
Beneath some rock, listening to notes that are
The ghostly language of the ancient earth,   310
Or make their dim abode in distant winds.

Thence did I drink the visionary power;
And deem not profitless those fleeting moods
Of shadowy exultation: not for this,
That they are kindred to our purer mind   315
And intellectual life; but that the soul,
Remembering how she felt, but what she felt
Remembering not, retains an obscure sense
Of possible sublimity, whereto
With growing faculties she doth aspire,   320
With faculties still growing, feeling still
That, whatsoever point they gain, they yet
Have something to pursue.
                             And not alone
'Mid gloom and tumult, but no less 'mid fair
And tranquil scenes, that universal power   325
And fitness in the latent qualities
And essences of things, by which the mind
Is moved with feelings of delight, to me
Came strengthened with a superadded soul,
A virtue not its own.—My morning walks   330
Were early;—oft before the hours of School
I travelled round our little Lake, five miles
Of pleasant wandering; happy time! more dear
For this, that One was by my side, a Friend
Then passionately loved; with heart how full   335
Would he peruse these lines! for many years
Have since flowed in between us, and, our minds
Both silent to each other, at this time
We live as if those hours had never been.
Nor seldom did I lift our Cottage latch   340
Far earlier, and ere one smoke-wreath had risen
From human dwelling, or the thrush, high perched,
Piped to the woods his shrill *reveillè*, sate
Alone upon some jutting eminence
At the first gleam of dawn-light, when the Vale,   345
Yet slumbering, lay in utter solitude.
How shall I seek the origin, where find
Faith in the marvellous things which then I felt?
Oft in those moments such a holy calm

Would overspread my soul, that bodily eyes   350
Were utterly forgotten, and what I saw
Appeared like something in myself, a dream,
A prospect in the mind.
                                'Twere long to tell
What spring and autumn, what the winter snows,
And what the summer shade, what day and night,   355
Evening and morning, sleep and waking thought,
From sources inexhaustible, poured forth
To feed the spirit of religious love,
In which I walked with Nature. But let this
Be not forgotten, that I still retained   360
My first creative sensibility,
That by the regular action of the world
My soul was unsubdued. A plastic power
Abode with me, a forming hand, at times
Rebellious, acting in a devious mood,   365
A local Spirit of his own, at war
With general tendency, but, for the most,
Subservient strictly to external things
With which it communed. An auxiliar light
Came from my mind which on the setting sun   370
Bestowed new splendor; the melodious birds,
The fluttering breezes, fountains that ran on
Murmuring so sweetly in themselves, obeyed
A like dominion; and the midnight storm
Grew darker in the presence of my eye;   375
Hence my obeisance, my devotion hence,
And hence my transport.
                                Nor should this, perchance,
Pass unrecorded, that I still had loved
The exercise and produce of a toil
Than analytic industry to me   380
More pleasing, and whose character I deem
Is more poetic, as resembling more
Creative agency. The Song would speak
Of that interminable building reared
By observation of affinities   385
In objects where no brotherhood exists

To passive minds. My seventeenth year was come;
And, whether from this habit rooted now
So deeply in my mind, or from excess
Of the great social principle of life   390
Coercing all things into sympathy,
To unorganic Natures were transferred
My own enjoyments; or the Power of truth,
Coming in revelation, did converse
With things that really are; I, at this time,   395
Saw blessings spread around me like a sea.
Thus while the days flew by and years passed on,
From Nature overflowing on my soul
I had received so much, that every thought
Was steeped in feeling; I was only then   400
Contented when with bliss ineffable
I felt the sentiment of Being spread
O'er all that moves, and all that seemeth still;   √
O'er all that, lost beyond the reach of thought
And human knowledge, to the human eye   405
Invisible, yet liveth to the heart;
O'er all that leaps, and runs, and shouts, and sings,
Or beats the gladsome air; o'er all that glides
Beneath the wave, yea, in the wave itself,
And mighty depth of waters. Wonder not   410
If high the transport, great the joy I felt,
Communing in this sort through earth and Heaven
With every form of Creature, as it looked
Towards the Uncreated with a countenance
Of adoration, with an eye of love.   415
One song they sang, and it was audible,
Most audible, then, when the fleshly ear,
O'ercome by humblest prelude of that strain,
Forgot her functions and slept undisturbed.
    If this be error, and another faith   420
Find easier access to the pious mind,
Yet were I grossly destitute of all
Those human sentiments that make this earth
So dear, if I should fail with grateful voice
To speak of you, Ye Mountains, and Ye Lakes,   425

And sounding Cataracts, Ye Mists and Winds
That dwell among the Hills where I was born.
If in my Youth I have been pure in heart,
If, mingling with the world, I am content
With my own modest pleasures, and have lived,   430
With God and Nature communing, removed
From little enmities and low desires,
The gift is yours: if in these times of fear,
This melancholy waste of hopes o'erthrown,
If, 'mid indifference and apathy   435
And wicked exultation, when good men,
On every side, fall off, we know not how,
To selfishness, disguised in gentle names
Of peace and quiet and domestic love,
Yet mingled, not unwillingly, with sneers   440
On visionary minds; if, in this time
Of dereliction and dismay, I yet
Despair not of our Nature, but retain
A more than Roman confidence, a faith
That fails not, in all sorrow my support,   445
The blessing of my life, the gift is yours,
Ye Winds and sounding Cataracts, 'tis yours,
Ye Mountains! thine, O Nature! Thou hast fed
My lofty speculations; and in thee,
For this uneasy heart of ours, I find   450
A never-failing principle of joy
And purest passion.
                    Thou, my Friend! wert reared
In the great City, 'mid far other scenes;
But we, by different roads, at length have gained
The self-same bourne. And for this cause to Thee   455
I speak, unapprehensive of contempt,
The insinuated scoff of coward tongues,
And all that silent language which so oft,
In conversation between Man and Man,
Blots from the human countenance all trace   460
Of beauty and of love. For Thou hast sought
The truth in solitude, and, since the days
That gave thee liberty, full long desired,

To serve in Nature's Temple, thou hast been
The most assiduous of her Ministers,   465
In many things my Brother, chiefly here
In this our deep devotion.
                            Fare Thee well!
Health, and the quiet of a healthful mind,
Attend Thee! seeking oft the haunts of Men,
And yet more often living with thyself   470
And for thyself, so haply shall thy days
Be many, and a blessing to mankind.

BOOK THIRD
RESIDENCE AT CAMBRIDGE

It was a dreary Morning when the Wheels
Rolled over a wide plain o'erhung with clouds,
And nothing cheered our way till first we saw
The long-roof'd Chapel of King's College lift
Turrets, and pinnacles in answering files   5
Extended high above a dusky grove.
    Advancing, we espied upon the road
A Student, clothed in Gown and tasselled Cap,
Striding along, as if o'ertasked by Time
Or covetous of exercise and air.   10
He passed—nor was I Master of my eyes
Till he was left an arrow's flight behind.
As near and nearer to the Spot we drew,
It seemed to suck us in with an eddy's force;
Onward we drove beneath the Castle, caught,   15
While crossing Magdalene Bridge, a glimpse of Cam,
And at the *Hoop* alighted, famous Inn!
    My Spirit was up, my thoughts were full of hope;
Some friends I had, acquaintances who there
Seemed friends, poor simple School-boys! now hung round   20
With honor and importance: in a world
Of welcome faces up and down I roved;
Questions, directions, warnings, and advice
Flowed in upon me, from all sides; fresh day
Of pride and pleasure! to myself I seemed   25
A man of business and expence, and went

From shop to shop, about my own affairs,
To Tutor or to Tailor, as befel,
From street to street, with loose and careless mind.
    I was the Dreamer, they the dream: I roamed   30
Delighted through the motley spectacle;
Gowns grave or gaudy, Doctors, Students, Streets,
Courts, Cloisters, flocks of Churches, gateways, towers.
Migration strange for a Stripling of the Hills,
A Northern Villager! As if the change   35
Had waited on some Fairy's wand, at once
Behold me rich in monies; and attired
In splendid garb, with hose of silk, and hair
Powdered like rimy trees, when frost is keen.
My lordly dressing-gown, I pass it by,   40
With other signs of manhood that supplied
The lack of beard.— The weeks went roundly on
With invitations, suppers, wine and fruit,
Smooth housekeeping within, and all without
Liberal, and suiting Gentleman's array!   45
    The Evangelist St. John my Patron was;
Three gothic Courts are his, and in the first
Was my abiding-place, a nook obscure!
Right underneath, the College Kitchens made
A humming sound, less tuneable than bees,   50
But hardly less industrious; with shrill notes
Of sharp command and scolding intermixed.
Near me hung Trinity's loquacious Clock,
Who never let the quarters, night or day,
Slip by him unproclaimed, and told the hours   55
Twice over, with a male and female voice.
Her pealing Organ was my neighbour too;
And from my pillow, looking forth by light
Of moon or favoring stars, I could behold
The Antechapel, where the Statue stood   60
Of Newton, with his prism, and silent face:
The marble index of a Mind for ever
Voyaging through strange seas of Thought, alone.
    Of College labors, of the Lecturer's room
All studded round, as thick as chairs could stand,   65

With loyal Students faithful to their books,
Half-and-half Idlers, hardy Recusants,
And honest Dunces—of important days,
Examinations when the man was weighed
As in a balance! of excessive hopes,   70
Tremblings withal, and commendable fears;
Small jealousies, and triumphs good or bad,
Let others, that know more, speak as they know.
Such glory was but little sought by me
And little won. Yet, from the first crude days   75
Of settling time in this untried abode,
I was disturbed at times by prudent thoughts,
Wishing to hope, without a hope; some fears
About my future worldly maintenance;
And, more than all, a strangeness in the mind,   80
A feeling that I was not for that hour,
Nor for that place. But wherefore be cast down?
For (not to speak of Reason and her pure
Reflective acts to fix the moral law
Deep in the conscience; nor of Christian Hope   85
Bowing her head before her Sister Faith
As one far mightier), hither I had come,
Bear witness, Truth, endowed with holy powers
And faculties, whether to work or feel.
Oft when the dazzling shew no longer new   90
Had ceased to dazzle, ofttimes did I quit
My Comrades, leave the Crowd, buildings and groves,
And as I paced alone the level fields
Far from those lovely sights and sounds sublime
With which I had been conversant, the mind   95
Drooped not, but there into herself returning
With prompt rebound, seemed fresh as heretofore.
At least I more distinctly recognized
Her native instincts; let me dare to speak
A higher language, say that now I felt   100
What independent solaces were mine
To mitigate the injurious sway of place
Or circumstance, how far soever changed
In youth, or *to* be changed in manhood's prime;

Or, for the few who shall be called to look   105
On the long shadows, in our evening years,
Ordained Precursors to the night of death.
As if awakened, summoned, roused, constrained,
I looked for universal things, perused
The common countenance of earth and sky;   110
Earth no where unembellished by some trace
Of that first paradise whence man was driven;
And sky whose beauty and bounty are expressed
By the proud name she bears, the name of heaven.
I called on both to teach me what they might;   115
Or, turning the mind in upon herself,
Pored, watched, expected, listened, spread my thoughts
And spread them with a wider creeping; felt
Incumbencies more awful, visitings
Of the Upholder, of the tranquil Soul   120
That tolerates the indignities of Time;
And, from his centre of eternity
All finite motions overruling, lives
In glory immutable. But peace!—enough
Here to record I had ascended now   125
To such community with highest truth.
—A track pursuing, not untrod before,
From strict analogies by thought supplied,
Or consciousnesses not to be subdued,
To every natural form, rock, fruit or flower,   130
Even the loose stones that cover the high-way,
I gave a moral life; I saw them feel,
Or linked them to some feeling: the great mass
Lay bedded in a quickening soul, and all
That I beheld respired with inward meaning.   135
Add, that whate'er of Terror or of Love
Or Beauty, Nature's daily face put on
From transitory passion, unto this
I was as sensitive as waters are
To the sky's influence: in a kindred mood   140
Of passion, was obedient as a lute
That waits upon the touches of the wind.
Unknown, unthought of, yet I was most rich;

I had a world about me; 'twas my own,
I made it; for it only lived to me,   145
And to the God who sees into the heart.
Such sympathies, though rarely, were betrayed
By outward gestures and by visible looks:
Some called it madness—so, indeed, it was,
If child-like fruitfulness in passing joy,   150
If steady moods of thoughtfulness, matured
To inspiration, sort with such a name;
If prophecy be madness; if things viewed
By Poets in old time, and higher up
By the first men, earth's first inhabitants,   155
May in these tutored days no more be seen
With undisordered sight. But, leaving this,
It was no madness: for the bodily eye
Amid my strongest workings evermore
Was searching out the lines of difference   160
As they lie hid in all external forms,
Near or remote; minute or vast, an eye
Which from a tree, a stone, a withered leaf,
To the broad ocean, and the azure heavens
Spangled with kindred multitudes of Stars,   165
Could find no surface where its power might sleep;
Which spake perpetual logic to my Soul,
And by an unrelenting agency
Did bind my feelings, even as in a chain.

    And here, O friend! have I retraced my life   170
Up to an eminence, and told a tale
Of matters which not falsely may be called
The glory of my Youth. Of genius, power,
Creation, and Divinity itself,
I have been speaking, for my theme has been   175
What passed within me. Not of outward things
Done visibly for other minds; words, signs,
Symbols, or actions, but of my own heart
Have I been speaking, and my youthful mind.
O Heavens! how awful is the might of Souls   180
And what they do within themselves, while yet
The yoke of earth is new to them, the world

Nothing but a wild field where they were sown.
This is, in truth, heroic argument,
This genuine prowess, which I wished to touch   185
With hand however weak, but in the main
It lies far hidden from the reach of words.
Points have we, all of us, within our Souls,
Where all stand single: this I feel, and make
Breathings for incommunicable powers.   190
But is not each a memory to himself?
And, therefore, now that we must quit this theme,
I am not heartless; for there's not a man
That lives who hath not known his god-like hours,
And feels not what an empire we inherit,   195
As natural Beings, in the strength of Nature.
    No more:—for now into a populous plain
We must descend.—A Traveller I am
Whose tale is only of himself; even so,
So be it, if the pure of heart be prompt   200
To follow, and if Thou, O honored Friend!
Who in these thoughts art ever at my side,
Support, as heretofore, my fainting steps.
    It hath been told, that when the first delight
That flashed upon me from this novel shew   205
Had failed, the mind returned into herself.
Yet true it is, that I had made a change
In climate, and my nature's outward coat
Changed also slowly and insensibly.
Full oft the quiet and exalted thoughts   210
Of loneliness gave way to empty noise,
And superficial pastimes; now and then
Forced labor, and more frequently forced hopes;
And, worst of all, a treasonable growth
Of indecisive judgments, that impaired   215
And shook the mind's simplicity.—And yet
This was a gladsome time. Could I behold—
Who, less insensible than sodden clay
In a sea-river's bed at ebb of tide,
Could have beheld—with undelighted heart,   220
So many happy Youths, so wide and fair

A congregation in its budding-time
Of health and hope and beauty; all at once
So many divers samples from the growth
Of life's sweet season; could have seen unmoved   225
That miscellaneous garland of wild flowers
Decking the matron temples of a Place
So famous through the world? To me at least
It was a goodly prospect: for, in sooth,
Though I had learnt betimes to stand unpropped,   230
And independent musings pleased me so,
That spells seemed on me when I was alone;
Yet could I only cleave to Solitude
In lonely places; if a throng was near,
That way I leaned by nature; for my heart   235
Was social, and loved idleness and joy.
     Not seeking those who might participate
My deeper pleasures (nay, I had not once,
Though not unused to mutter lonesome songs,
Even with myself divided such delight,   240
Or looked that way for aught that might be clothed
In human language), easily I passed
From the remembrances of better things,
And slipped into the ordinary works
Of careless youth, unburdened, unalarmed.   245
Caverns there were within my mind, which sun
Could never penetrate, yet did there not
Want store of leafy *arbours* where the light
Might enter in at will. Companionships,
Friendships, acquaintances, were welcome all;   250
We sauntered, played, or rioted, we talked
Unprofitable talk at morning hours,
Drifted about along the streets and walks,
Read lazily in trivial books, went forth
To gallop through the Country in blind zeal   255
Of senseless horsemanship, or on the breast
Of Cam sailed boisterously, and let the stars
Come forth, perhaps without one quiet thought.
     Such was the tenor of the second act
In this new life. Imagination slept,   260

And yet not utterly: I could not print
Ground where the grass had yielded to the steps
Of generations of illustrious men,
Unmoved; I could not always lightly pass
Through the same gateways, sleep where they had slept,   265
Wake where they waked, range that inclosure old,
That garden of great intellects, undisturbed.
Place also by the side of this dark sense
Of nobler feeling, that those spiritual men,
Even the great Newton's own etherial Self,   270
Seemed humbled in these precincts, thence to be
The more endeared. Their several Memories here
(Even like their Persons in their portraits, clothed
With the accustomed garb of daily life)
Put on a lowly and a touching grace   275
Of more distinct humanity, that left
All genuine admiration unimpaired.
—Beside the pleasant Mill of Trompington
I laughed with Chaucer, in the hawthorn shade
Heard him, while birds were warbling, tell his tales   280
Of amorous passion. And that gentle Bard,
Chosen by the Muses for their Page of State,
Sweet Spenser, moving through his clouded Heaven
With the Moon's beauty and the Moon's soft pace,
I called him Brother, Englishman, and Friend!   285
Yea, our blind Poet, who, in his later day,
Stood almost single, uttering odious truth,
Darkness before and danger's voice behind;
Soul awful—if the earth hath ever lodged
An awful Soul, I seemed to see him here   290
Familiarly, and in his Scholar's dress
Bounding before me, yet a Stripling Youth,
A Boy, no better, with his rosy cheeks
Angelical, keen eye, courageous look,
And conscious step of purity and pride.   295
    Among the Band of my Compeers was One
Whom Chance had stationed in the very Room
Honored by Milton's Name. O temperate Bard!
Be it confest that, for the first time, seated

Within thy innocent Lodge and Oratory,   300
One of a festive Circle, I poured out
Libations, to thy memory drank, till pride
And gratitude grew dizzy in a brain
Never excited by the fumes of wine
Before that hour, or since. Forth I ran,   305
From that assembly through a length of streets
Ran, Ostrich-like, to reach our Chapel door
In not a desperate or opprobrious time,
Albeit long after the importunate bell
Had stopped, with wearisome Cassandra voice   310
No longer haunting the dark winter night.
    Call back, O Friend! a moment to thy mind
The place itself, and fashion of the Rites.
With careless ostentation shouldering up
My Surplice, through the inferior throng I clove   315
Of the plain Burghers, who in audience stood
On the last skirts of their permitted ground
Under the pealing Organ. Empty thoughts!
I am ashamed of them: and that great Bard
And Thou, O friend! who in thy ample mind   320
Hast placed me high above my best deserts,
Ye will forgive the weakness of that hour,
In some of its unworthy vanities
Brother to many more.
                  In this mixed sort
The months passed on, remissly, not given up   325
To wilful alienation from the right,
Or walks of open scandal, but in vague
And loose indifference, easy likings, aims
Of a low pitch,—duty and zeal dismissed,
Yet Nature, or a happy course of things,   330
Not doing, in their stead, the needful work.
The memory languidly revolved, the heart
Reposed in noontide rest; the inner pulse
Of contemplation almost failed to beat.
Such life might not inaptly be compared   335
To a floating island, an amphibious Spot
Unsound, of spungy texture, yet withal

Not wanting a fair face of water weeds
And pleasant flowers.— The thirst of living praise,
Fit reverence for the glorious Dead, the Sight   340
Of those long Vistos, sacred Catacombs
Where mighty *minds* lie visibly entombed,
Have often stirred the heart of Youth, and bred
A fervent love of rigorous discipline.
Alas! such high emotion touched not me;   345
Look was there none within these walls to shame
My easy spirits, and discountenance
Their light composure, far less to instil
A calm resolve of mind, firmly addressed
To puissant efforts. Nor was this the blame   350
Of others, but my own: I should, in truth,
As far as doth concern my single self,
Misdeem most widely, lodging it elsewhere.—
For I, bred up 'mid Nature's luxuries,
Was a spoiled Child; and rambling like the wind,   355
As I had done in daily intercourse
With those crystalline Rivers, solemn heights
And mountains;—ranging like a fowl of the air,
I was ill-tutored for captivity,
To quit my pleasure, and from month to month   360
Take up a station calmly on the perch
Of sedentary peace. Those lovely forms
Had also left less space within my mind,
Which, wrought upon instinctively, had found
A freshness in those objects of her love,   365
A winning power, beyond all other power.
Not that I slighted Books—that were to lack
All sense—but other passions in me ruled,
Passions more fervent, making me less prompt
To in-door study than was wise or well,   370
Or suited to those years. Yet I, though used
In magisterial liberty to rove—
Culling such flowers of Learning as might tempt
A random choice—could shadow forth a Place
(If now I yield not to a flattering dream)   375
Whose studious aspect should have bent me down

To instantaneous service, should at once
Have made me pay to science and to arts,
And written lore, acknowledged my liege lord,
A homage frankly offered up, like that   380
Which I had paid to Nature. Toil and pains,
In this Recess by thoughtful Fancy built,
Should spread from heart to heart; and stately groves,
Majestic edifices, should not want
A corresponding dignity within.   385
The congregating temper, that pervades
Our unripe years, not wasted, should be taught
To minister to works of high attempt,
Works which the enthusiast would perform with love.
Youth should be awed, religiously possessed   390
With a conviction of the power that waits
On knowledge, when sincerely sought and prized
For its own sake, on glory and on praise
If but by labor won, and fit to endure.
The passing day should learn to put aside   395
Her trappings here, should strip them off abashed
Before antiquity and stedfast truth
And strong book-mindedness; and over all
A healthy sound simplicity should reign,
A seemly plainness, name it what you will,   400
Republican or pious.
                          If these thoughts
Are a gratuitous emblazonry
That mocks the recreant age *we* live in, then
Be Folly and False-seeming free to affect
Whatever formal gait of discipline   405
Shall raise them highest in their own esteem;
Let them parade among the Schools at will;
But spare the house of God. Was ever known
The witless Shepherd who persists to drive
A flock that thirsts not to a pool disliked?   410
A weight must surely hang on days begun
And ended with such mockery. Be wise,
Ye Presidents, and Deans, and till the spirit
Of ancient Times revive, and Youth be trained

At home in pious service, to your bells   415
Give seasonable rest, for 'tis a sound
Hollow as ever vexed the tranquil air;
And your officious doings bring disgrace
On the plain Steeples of our English Church,
Whose worship, 'mid remotest Village trees,   420
Suffers for this. Even Science, too, at hand,
In daily sight of this irreverence,
Is smitten thence with an unnatural taint,
Loses her just authority, falls beneath
Collateral suspicion, else unknown.   425
This truth escaped me not, and I confess
That, having 'mid my native hills given loose
To a school-boy's vision, I had raised a pile
Upon the basis of the coming time,
That fell in ruins round me. Oh! what joy   430
To see a Sanctuary for our Country's Youth,
Informed with such a spirit as might be
Its own protection; a primeval grove
Where, though the shades with chearfulness were filled,
Nor indigent of songs warbled from crowds   435
In under-coverts, yet the countenance
Of the whole Place should wear a stamp of awe:
A habitation sober and demure
For ruminating Creatures; a domain
For quiet things to wander in; a haunt   440
In which the heron should delight to feed
By the shy rivers, and the Pelican
Upon the Cypress spire in lonely thought
Might sit and sun himself. Alas! Alas!
In vain for such solemnity I looked;   445
Mine eyes were crossed by butterflies, ears vexed
By chattering Popinjays; the inner heart
Seemed trivial, and the impresses without
Of a too gaudy region.
                       Different sight
Those venerable Doctors saw of old,   450
When all who dwelt within these famous Walls
Led in abstemiousness a studious life:

When, in forlorn and naked chambers, cooped
And crowded, o'er their ponderous books they hung,
Like catterpillers eating out their way   455
In silence, or with keen devouring noise
Not to be tracked or fathered. Princes then
At matins froze, and couched at curfew-time,
Trained up through piety and zeal to prize
Spare diet, patient labor, and plain weeds.   460
O Seat of Arts! renowned throughout the world!
Far different service in those homely days
The Muses' modest Nurslings underwent
From their first childhood: in that glorious time
When Learning, like a Stranger come from far,   465
Sounding through Christian lands her Trumpet, roused
Peasant and King, when Boys and Youths, the growth
Of ragged villages and crazy huts,
Forsook their homes; and, errant in the quest
Of Patron, famous School, or friendly nook,   470
Where, pensioned, they in shelter might sit down,
From town to town, and through wide-scattered realms,
Journeyed with ponderous folios in their hands;
And often, starting from some covert place,
Saluted the chance Comer in the road,   475
Crying, "an obolus, a penny give
To a poor Scholar": when illustrious Men,
Lovers of truth, by penury constrained,
Bucer, Erasmus, or Melancthon, read
Before the doors or windows of their cells   480
By moonshine, through mere lack of taper light.
    But peace to vain regrets! we see but darkly
Even when we look behind us; and best things
Are not so pure by nature that they needs
Must keep to all, as fondly all believe,   485
Their highest promise. If the Mariner,
When at reluctant distance he hath passed
Some tempting Island, could but know the ills
That must have fallen upon him, had he brought
His bark to land upon the wished-for shore,   490
Good cause would oft be his to thank the surf

Whose white belt scared him thence, or wind that blew
Inexorably adverse! for myself
I grieve not; happy is the gowned Youth
Who only misses what I missed, who falls   495
No lower than I fell.
              I did not love,
Judging not ill perhaps, the timid course
Of our scholastic studies, could have wished
To see the river flow with ampler range
And freer pace; but more, far more, I grieved   500
To see displayed, among an eager few
Who in the field of contest persevered,
Passions unworthy of Youth's generous heart
And mounting spirit, pitiably repaid,
When so disturbed, whatever palms are won.   505
From these I turned to travel with the shoal
Of more unthinking Natures—easy Minds
And pillowy, yet not wanting love that makes
The day pass lightly on, when foresight sleeps
And wisdom, and the pledges interchanged   510
With our own inner being are forgot.
   Yet was this deep vacation not given up
To utter waste. Hitherto I had stood
In my own mind remote from social life,
At least from what we commonly so name,   515
Like a lone shepherd on a promontory,
Who, lacking occupation, looks far forth
Into the boundless sea, and rather makes
Than finds what he beholds. And sure it is
That this first transit from the smooth delights   520
And wild outlandish walks of simple Youth
To something that resembled an approach
Towards human business; to a privileged world
Within a world, a midway residence
With all its intervenient imagery,   525
Did better suit my visionary mind,
Far better, than to have been bolted forth,
Thrust out abruptly into Fortune's way,
Among the conflicts of substantial life;

By a more just gradation did lead on   530
To higher things, more naturally matured,
For permanent possession, better fruits,
Whether of truth or virtue, to ensue.
    In serious mood, but oftener, I confess,
With playful zest of fancy, did we note   535
(How could we less?) the manners and the ways
Of those who lived distinguished by the badge
Of good or ill report; or those with whom,
By frame of academic discipline,
We were perforce connected, men whose sway   540
And known authority of office served
To set our minds on edge, and did no more.
Nor wanted we rich pastime of this kind,
Found every where; but chiefly in the ring
Of the grave Elders—Men unscoured, grotesque   545
In character; tricked out like aged trees
Which, through the lapse of their infirmity,
Give ready place to any random seed
That chuses to be reared upon their trunks.
    Here, on my view, confronting vividly   550
Those shepherd swains whom I had lately left,
Appeared a different aspect of old age;
How different! yet both distinctly marked,
Objects embossed, to catch the general eye,
Or portraitures for special use designed,   555
As some might seem, so aptly do they serve
To illustrate Nature's book of rudiments,
That book upheld as with maternal care
When she would enter on her tender scheme
Of teaching comprehension with delight   560
And mingling playful with pathetic thoughts.
    The surfaces of artificial life
And manners finely wrought, the delicate race
Of colours, lurking, gleaming up and down
Through that state arras woven with silk and gold;   565
This wily interchange of snaky hues,
Willingly or unwillingly revealed,
I neither knew nor cared for; and, as such

Were wanting here, I took what might be found
Of less elaborate fabric. At this day   570
I smile in many a mountain Solitude,
Conjuring up scenes as obsolete in freaks
Of character, in points of wit as broad,
As aught by wooden Images performed
For entertainment of the gaping crowd   575
At Wake or fair. And oftentimes do flit
Remembrances before me of Old Men,
Old Humorists who have been long in their graves,
And, having almost in my mind put off
Their human names, have into Phantoms passed   580
Of texture midway between life and books.
        I play the Loiterer; 'tis enough to note
That here, in dwarf proportions, were expressed
The limbs of the great world, its eager strifes
Collaterally pourtrayed, as in mock fight;   585
A Tournament of blows, some hardly dealt
Though short of mortal combat; and whate'er
Might in this pageant be supposed to hit
An artless rustic's notice, this way less,
More that way, was not wasted upon me.   590
—And yet the spectacle may well demand
A more substantial name, no mimic shew,
Itself a living part of a live whole,
A creek in the vast sea;—for all degrees
And shapes of spurious fame and short-lived praise   595
Here sate in state, and fed with daily alms
Retainers won away from solid good;
And here was Labor his own bondslave—Hope
That never set the pains against the prize;
Idleness, halting with his weary clog;   600
And poor misguided Shame, and witless Fear,
And simple Pleasure foraging for Death;
Honor misplaced, and Dignity astray;
Feuds, factions, flatteries, enmity, and guile;
Murmuring Submission, and bald Government;   605
The Idol weak as the Idolater;
And Decency and Custom starving Truth;

And blind Authority beating with his staff
The Child that might have led him; Emptiness
Followed as of good omen; and meek Worth   610
Left to Herself, unheard of and unknown.
    Of these and other kindred notices
I cannot say what portion is in truth
The naked recollection of that time,
And what may rather have been called to life   615
By after-meditation. But delight,
That, in an easy temper lulled asleep,
Is still with innocence its own reward,
This was not wanting. Carelessly I roamed
As through a wide Museum, from whose stores   620
A casual rarity is singled out,
And has its brief perusal, then gives way
To others, all supplanted in their turn;
Till 'mid this crowded neighbourhood of things
That are, by nature, most unneighbourly,   625
The head turns round—and cannot right itself;
And though an aching and a barren sense
Of gay confusion still be uppermost,
With few wise longings and but little love,
Yet to the memory something cleaves at last,   630
Whence profit may be drawn in times to come.
    Thus in submissive idleness, my Friend,
The laboring time of Autumn, Winter, Spring,
Eight months! rolled pleasingly away,—the ninth
Came and returned me to my native hills.   635

BOOK FOURTH
SUMMER VACATION

Bright was the summer's noon when quick'ning steps
Followed each other till a dreary moor
Was crossed, a bare ridge clomb, upon whose top
Standing alone, as from a rampart's edge
I overlooked the bed of Windermere   5
Like a vast river stretching in the sun!
With exultation at my feet I saw
Lake, islands, promontories, gleaming bays,

A universe of Nature's fairest forms
Proudly revealed with instantaneous burst,   10
Magnificent and beautiful and gay.
I bounded down the hill, shouting amain
For the old Ferryman—to the shout the rocks
Replied, and when the Charon of the flood
Had staid his oars and touched the jutting pier   15
I did not step into the well-known boat
Without a cordial greeting. Thence, with speed
Up the familiar hill I took my way
Towards that sweet valley where I had been reared.
'Twas but a short hour's walk ere, veering round,   20
I saw the snow-white Church upon her hill
Sit like a thronèd Lady, sending out
A gracious look all over her domain.
Yon azure smoke betrays the lurking Town;
With eager footsteps I advance, and reach   25
The Cottage threshold where my journey closed.
Glad welcome had I, with some tears, perhaps,
From my old Dame, so kind, and motherly!
While she perused me with a Parent's pride.
The thoughts of gratitude shall fall like dew   30
Upon thy grave, good Creature! while my heart
Can beat, never will I forget thy name.
Heaven's blessing be upon thee where thou liest,
After thy innocent and busy stir
In narrow cares, thy little daily growth   35
Of calm enjoyments; after eighty years,
And more than eighty, of untroubled life,
Childless, yet by the strangers to thy blood
Honored with little less than filial love.
What joy was mine to see thee once again,   40
Thee and thy dwelling; and a crowd of things
About its narrow precincts, all beloved,
And many of them seeming yet my own!
Why should I speak of what a thousand hearts
Have felt, and every man alive can guess?   45
The rooms, the court, the garden were not left
Long unsaluted, nor the sunny seat

Round the stone table, under the dark Pine,
Friendly to studious or to festive hours;
Nor that unruly Child, of mountain birth,   50
The froward Brook—who, soon as he was boxed
Within our Garden, found himself at once,
As if by trick insidious and unkind,
Stripped of his voice, and left to dimple down
(Without an effort, and without a will)   55
A channel pav'd by Man's officious care.
I looked at him and smiled, and smiled again,
And, in the press of twenty thousand thoughts,
"Ha!" quoth I, "pretty Prisoner, are you there?"
Well might sarcastic Fancy then have whispered,   60
"An emblem here behold of thy own life
In its late course of even days, with all
Their smooth enthralment"—but the heart was full,
Too full for that reproach. My aged Dame
Walked proudly at my side; She guided me,   65
I willing, nay—nay—wishing to be led.
—The face of every neighbour whom I met
Was like a volume to me; some were hailed
Upon the road—some, busy at their work;
Unceremonious greetings, interchanged   70
With half the length of a long field between.
Among my Schoolfellows I scattered round
Like recognitions, but with some constraint
Attended, doubtless from a little pride,
But with more shame, for my habiliments,   75
The transformation wrought by gay attire.
    Not less delighted did I take my place
At our domestic table; and, dear Friend!
In this endeavour simply to relate
A Poet's history, may I leave untold   80
The thankfulness with which I laid me down
In my accustomed bed, more welcome now,
Perhaps, than if it had been more desired,
Or been more often thought of with regret?—
That lowly bed, whence I had heard the wind   85
Roar, and the rain beat hard; where I so oft

Had lain awake, on summer nights, to watch
The moon in splendor couched among the leaves
Of a tall Ash, that near our Cottage stood;
Had watched her with fixed eyes while to and fro,   90
In the dark summit of the waving tree,
She rocked, with every impulse of the breeze.
    Among the favorites whom it pleased me well
To see again, was one, by ancient right
Our Inmate, a rough terrier of the hills,   95
By birth and call of nature pre-ordained
To hunt the badger, and unearth the fox,
Among the impervious crags; but having been
From youth our own adopted, he had passed
Into a gentler service. And when first   100
The boyish spirit flagged, and day by day
Along my veins I kindled with the stir,
The fermentation and the vernal heat
Of poesy, affecting private shades
Like a sick lover, then this Dog was used   105
To watch me, an attendant and a friend
Obsequious to my steps, early and late,
Though often of such dilatory walk
Tired, and uneasy at the halts I made.
A hundred times when, roving high and low,   110
I have been harrassed with the toil of verse,
Much pains and little progress, and at once
Some lovely Image in the Song rose up
Full-formed, like Venus rising from the Sea;
Then have I darted forwards and let loose   115
My hand upon his back, with stormy joy;
Caressing him again, and yet again.
And when at evening on the public Way
I sauntered, like a river murmuring
And talking to itself, when all things else   120
Are still, the Creature trotted on before—
Such was his custom; but whene'er he met
A passenger approaching, he would turn
To give me timely notice; and, straitway,
Grateful for that admonishment, I hushed   125

My voice, composed my gait, and with the air
And mien of one whose thoughts are free, advanced
To give and take a greeting, that might save
My name from piteous rumours, such as wait
On men suspected to be crazed in brain.   130
    Those walks, well worthy to be prized and loved,
Regretted! that word too was on my tongue,
But they were richly laden with all good,
And cannot be remembered but with thanks
And gratitude, and perfect joy of heart;   135
Those walks, in all their freshness, now came back,
Like a returning Spring. When first I made
Once more the circuit of our little Lake,
If ever happiness hath lodged with man,
That day consummate happiness was mine,   140
Wide-spreading, steady, calm, contemplative.
The sun was set, or setting, when I left
Our cottage door, and evening soon brought on
A sober hour,—not winning or serene,
For cold and raw the air was, and untuned: 145
But as a face we love is sweetest then
When sorrow damps it; or, whatever look
It chance to wear, is sweetest if the heart
Have fulness in herself, even so with me
It fared that evening. Gently did my Soul   150
Put off her veil, and, self-transmuted, stood
Naked, as in the presence of her God.
While on I walked, a comfort seemed to touch
A heart that had not been disconsolate;
Strength came where weakness was not known to be,   155
At least not felt; and restoration came,
Like an intruder, knocking at the door
Of unacknowledged weariness. I took
The balance, and with firm hand weighed myself.
—Of that external scene which round me lay   160
Little, in this abstraction, did I see,
Remembered less; but I had inward hopes
And swellings of the Spirit: was rapt and soothed,
Conversed with promises; had glimmering views

How life pervades the undecaying mind,   165
How the immortal Soul with God-like power
Informs, creates, and thaws the deepest sleep
That time can lay upon her; how on earth,
Man, if he do but live within the light
Of high endeavours, daily spreads abroad   170
His being armed with strength that cannot fail.
Nor was there want of milder thoughts, of love,
Of innocence, and holiday repose;
And more than pastoral quiet 'mid the stir
Of boldest projects; and a peaceful end   175
At last, or glorious, by endurance won.
Thus musing, in a wood I sate me down,
Alone, continuing there to muse; the slopes
And heights, meanwhile, were slowly overspread
With darkness; and before a rippling breeze   180
The long lake lengthened out its hoary line:
And in the sheltered coppice where I sate,
Around me from among the hazel leaves,
Now here, now there, moved by the straggling wind,
Came ever and anon a breath-like sound,   185
Quick as the pantings of the faithful Dog,
The off and on Companion of my walk;
And such, at times, believing them to be,
I turned my head, to look if he were there;
Then into solemn thought I passed once more.   190
     A freshness also found I at this time
In human Life, the daily life of those
Whose occupations really I loved.
The peaceful scene oft filled me with surprize,
Changed like a garden in the heat of Spring   195
After an eight-days' absence. For (to omit
The things which were the same, and yet appeared
Far otherwise) amid this rural Solitude,
(A narrow Vale where each was known to all)
'Twas not indifferent, to a youthful mind,   200
To mark some sheltering bower or sunny nook,
Where an old Man had used to sit alone,
Now vacant,—pale-faced Babes, whom I had left

In arms, now rosy Prattlers, at the feet
Of a pleased Grandame, tottering up and down: 205
And growing girls, whose beauty, filched away
With all its pleasant promises, was gone
To deck some slighted Playmate's homely cheek.
—Yes, I had something of a subtler sense,
And often, looking round, was moved to smiles,   210
Such as a delicate Work of humor breeds.
I read, without design, the opinions, thoughts,
Of those plain-living people, now observed
With clearer knowledge; with another eye
I saw the quiet Woodman in the woods,   215
The Shepherd roam the hills. With new delight,
This chiefly, did I note my gray-haired Dame,
Saw her go forth to Church, or other work
Of state, equipped in monumental trim,
Short velvet cloak (her bonnet of the like),   220
A mantle such as Spanish Cavaliers
Wore in old time. Her smooth domestic life,
Affectionate without disquietude,
Her talk, her business, pleased me; and no less
Her clear, though shallow, stream of piety,   225
That ran on Sabbath days a fresher course.
With thoughts, unfelt till now, I saw her read
Her Bible, on hot Sunday afternoons;
And loved the book, when she had dropped asleep
And made of it a pillow for her head.   230
     Nor less do I remember to have felt,
Distinctly manifested at this time,
A human-heartedness about my love
For objects, hitherto the absolute wealth
Of my own private being, and no more;   235
Which I had loved, even as a blessed Spirit,
Or Angel, if he were to dwell on earth,
Might love, in individual happiness.
But now there opened on me other thoughts,
Of change, congratulation, or regret—   240
A pensive feeling! It spread far and wide;
The trees, the mountains shared it, and the brooks;

The stars of heaven, now seen in their old haunts,
White Sirius, glittering o'er the southern crags,
Orion with his belt, and those fair Seven,   245
Acquaintances of every little Child,
And Jupiter, my own beloved Star!
Whatever shadings of mortality,
Whatever imports from the world of death
Had come among these objects heretofore,   250
Were, in the main, of mood less tender:—strong,
Deep, gloomy were they, and severe; the scatterings
Of awe, or tremulous dread, that had given way,
In later youth, to yearnings of a love
Enthusiastic, to delight and hope.   255
    As one who hangs down-bending from the side
Of a slow-moving boat, upon the breast
Of a still water, solacing himself
With such discoveries as his eye can make,
Beneath him, in the bottom of the deep,   260
Sees many beauteous sights, weeds, fishes, flowers,
Grots, pebbles, roots of trees, and fancies more;
Yet often is perplexed, and cannot part
The shadow from the substance, rocks and sky,
Mountains and clouds reflected in the depth   265
Of the clear flood, from things which there abide
In their true Dwelling: now is crossed by gleam
Of his own image, by a sun-beam now,
And wavering motions, sent he knows not whence,
Impediments that make his task more sweet—   270
Such pleasant office have we long pursued,
Incumbent o'er the surface of past time,
With like success, nor often have appeared
Shapes fairer, or less doubtfully discerned
Than these to which the Tale, indulgent Friend!   275
Would now direct thy notice. Yet in spite
Of pleasure won and knowledge not withheld,
There was an inner falling-off. I loved,
Loved deeply, all that had been loved before,
More deeply even than ever: but a swarm   280
Of heady schemes, jostling each other, gawds,

And feast, and dance, and public revelry;
And sports, and games (too grateful in themselves,
Yet in themselves less grateful, I believe,
Than as they were a badge, glossy and fresh,   285
Of manliness and freedom) all conspired
To lure my mind from firm habitual quest
Of feeding pleasures; to depress the zeal
And damp those daily yearnings which had once been mine—
A wild unworldly-minded youth, given up   290
To his own eager thoughts. It would demand
Some skill, and longer time than may be spared,
To paint these vanities, and how they wrought
In haunts where they, till now, had been unknown.
It seemed the very garments that I wore   295
Preyed on my strength, and stopped the quiet stream
Of self-forgetfulness.
                          Yes, that heartless chase
Of trivial pleasures was a poor exchange
For books and nature at that early age.
'Tis true some casual knowledge might be gained   300
Of character or life; but at that time,
Of manners put to School I took small note;
And all my deeper passions lay elsewhere.
Far better had it been to exalt the mind
By solitary Study; to uphold   305
Intense desire through meditative peace.
And yet, for chastisement of these regrets,
The memory of one particular hour
Doth here rise up against me.—'Mid a throng
Of Maids and Youths, old Men and Matrons staid,   310
A medley of all tempers, I had passed
The night in dancing, gaiety, and mirth;
With din of instruments, and shuffling feet,
And glancing forms, and tapers glittering,
And unaimed prattle flying up and down—   315
Spirits upon the stretch, and here and there
Slight shocks of young love-liking interspersed,
Whose transient pleasure mounted to the head,
And tingled through the veins. Ere we retired

The cock had crowed; and now the eastern sky   320
Was kindling, not unseen from humble copse
And open field through which the pathway wound
That homeward led my steps. Magnificent
The Morning rose, in memorable pomp,
Glorious as e'er I had beheld; in front   325
The Sea lay laughing at a distance;—near,
The solid mountains shone bright as the clouds,
Grain-tinctured, drenched in empyrean light:
And, in the meadows and the lower grounds,
Was all the sweetness of a common dawn;   330
Dews, vapours, and the melody of birds;
And Labourers going forth to till the fields.
    Ah! need I say, dear Friend, that to the brim
My heart was full: I made no vows, but vows
Were then made for me; bond unknown to me   335
Was given, that I should be, else sinning greatly,
A dedicated Spirit. On I walked
In thankful blessedness which yet survives.
    Strange rendezvous my mind was at that time,
A party-colored shew of grave and gay,   340
Solid and light, short-sighted and profound;
Of inconsiderate habits and sedate,
Consorting in one mansion, unreproved.
The worth I knew of powers that I possessed,
Though slighted and too oft misused. Besides,   345
That summer, swarming as it did with thoughts
Transient and idle, lacked not intervals
When Folly from the frown of fleeting Time
Shrunk, and the Mind experienced in herself
Conformity as just as that of old   350
To the end and written spirit of God's works,
Whether held forth in Nature or in Man,
Through pregnant vision, separate or conjoined.
    When from our better selves we have too long
Been parted by the hurrying world, and droop,   355
Sick of its business, of its pleasures tired,
How gracious, how benign is Solitude!
How potent a mere image of her sway!

Most potent when impressed upon the mind
With an appropriate human centre—Hermit   360
Deep in the bosom of the Wilderness;
Votary (in vast Cathedral, where no foot
Is treading and no other face is seen)
Kneeling at prayer; or Watchman on the top
Of Lighthouse beaten by Atlantic Waves;   365
Or as the soul of that great Power is met
Sometimes embodied on a public road,
When, for the night deserted, it assumes
A character of quiet more profound
Than pathless Wastes.
          Once, when those summer Months   370
Were flown, and Autumn brought its annual shew
Of oars with oars contending, sails with sails,
Upon Winander's spacious breast, it chanced
That—after I had left a flower-decked room
(Whose in-door pastime, lighted-up, survived   375
To a late hour) and spirits overwrought
Were making night do penance for a day
Spent in a round of strenuous idleness—
My homeward course led up a long ascent
Where the road's watery surface, to the top   380
Of that sharp rising, glittered to the moon
And bore the semblance of another stream
Stealing with silent lapse to join the brook
That murmured in the Vale. All else was still;
No living thing appeared in earth or air,   385
And, save the flowing Water's peaceful voice,
Sound was there none: but lo! an uncouth shape
Shewn by a sudden turning of the road,
So near, that, slipping back into the shade
Of a thick hawthorn, I could mark him well,   390
Myself unseen. He was of stature tall,
A span above man's *common* measure tall,
Stiff, lank, and upright;—a more meagre man
Was never seen before by night or day.
Long were his arms, pallid his hands;—his mouth   395
Looked ghastly in the moonlight. From behind,

A mile-stone propped him; I could also ken
That he was clothed in military garb,
Though faded, yet entire. Companionless,
No dog attending, by no staff sustained   400
He stood; and in his very dress appeared
A desolation, a simplicity
To which the trappings of a gaudy world
Make a strange background. From his lips erelong
Issued low muttered sounds, as if of pain   405
Or some uneasy thought; yet still his form
Kept the same awful steadiness;—at his feet
His shadow lay and moved not. From self-blame
Not wholly free, I watched him thus; at length
Subduing my heart's specious cowardice,   410
I left the shady nook where I had stood,
And hailed him. Slowly, from his resting-place
He rose; and, with a lean and wasted arm
In measured gesture lifted to his head,
Returned my salutation: then resumed   415
His station as before; and when I asked
His history, the Veteran, in reply,
Was neither slow nor eager; but, unmoved,
And with a quiet uncomplaining voice,
A stately air of mild indifference,   420
He told, in few plain words, a Soldier's tale—
That in the Tropic Islands he had served,
Whence he had landed, scarcely three weeks past,
That on his landing he had been dismissed,
And now was travelling towards his native home.   425
This heard, I said in pity, "Come with me."
He stooped, and straightway from the ground took up
An oaken staff, by me yet unobserved—
A staff which must have dropped from his slack hand
And lay till now neglected in the grass.   430
    Though weak his step and cautious, he appeared
To travel without pain, and I beheld,
With an astonishment but ill suppressed,
His ghastly figure moving at my side;
Nor could I, while we journeyed thus, forbear   435

To turn from present hardships to the past,
And speak of war, battle, and pestilence,
Sprinkling this talk with questions, better spared,
On what he might himself have seen or felt.
He all the while was in demeanour calm,   440
Concise in answer; solemn and sublime
He might have seemed, but that in all he said
There was a strange half-absence, as of one
Knowing too well the importance of his theme,
But feeling it no longer. Our discourse   445
Soon ended, and together on we passed,
In silence, through a wood, gloomy and still.
Up-turning then along an open field,
We reached a Cottage. At the door I knocked,
And earnestly to charitable care   450
Commended him, as a poor friendless Man
Belated, and by sickness overcome.
Assured that now the Traveller would repose
In comfort, I entreated, that henceforth
He would not linger in the public ways,   455
But ask for timely furtherance and help,
Such as his state required.—At this reproof,
With the same ghastly mildness in his look,
He said, "My trust is in the God of Heaven,
And in the eye of him who passes me."   460
     The Cottage door was speedily unbarred,
And now the Soldier touched his hat once more
With his lean hand; and, in a faltering voice
Whose tone bespake reviving interests
Till then unfelt, he thanked me; I returned   465
The farewell blessing of the patient Man,
And so we parted. Back I cast a look,
And lingered near the door a little space;
Then sought with quiet heart my distant home.
     This passed, and He who deigns to mark with care   470
By what rules governed, with what end in view
This Work proceeds, *he* will not wish for more.[1]

---

1   Lines 470–2, queried for deletion in MSS D and E, were omitted in the 1850 text.

BOOK FIFTH
BOOKS

When Contemplation, like the night-calm felt
Through earth and sky, spreads widely, and sends deep
Into the Soul its tranquillizing power,
Even then I sometimes grieve for thee, O Man,
Earth's paramount Creature! not so much for woes   5
That thou endurest; heavy though that weight be,
Cloud-like it mounts, or touched with light divine
Doth melt away; but for those palms achieved
Through length of time, by patient exercise
Of study and hard thought—there, there it is   10
That sadness finds its fuel. Hitherto,
In progress through this Work, my mind hath looked
Upon the speaking face of earth and heaven
As her prime Teacher, intercourse with man
Established by the sovereign Intellect   15
Who through that bodily Image hath diffused,
As might appear to the eye of fleeting Time,
A deathless Spirit. Thou also, Man! hast wrought,
For commerce of thy nature with herself,
Things that aspire to unconquerable life: 20
And yet we feel, we cannot chuse but feel
That they must perish. Tremblings of the heart
It gives, to think that our immortal being
No more shall need such garments; and yet Man,
As long as he shall be the Child of earth,   25
Might almost "weep to have" what he may lose,
Nor be himself extinguished; but survive
Abject, depressed, forlorn, disconsolate.
A thought is with me sometimes, and I say—
Should the whole frame of earth by inward throes   30
Be wrenched, or fire come down from far to scorch
Her pleasant habitations, and dry up
Old Ocean in his bed, left singed and bare,
Yet would the living Presence still subsist
Victorious; and composure would ensue,   35
And kindlings like the morning—presage sure
Of day returning, and of life revived.

But all the meditations of mankind,
Yea, all the adamantine holds of truth,
By reason built, or passion, which itself   40
Is highest reason in a soul sublime;
The consecrated works of Bard and Sage,
Sensuous or intellectual, wrought by men,
Twin labourers, and heirs of the same hopes;
Where would they be? Oh! why hath not the Mind   45
Some element to stamp her image on
In nature somewhat nearer to her own?
Why, gifted with such powers to send abroad
Her spirit, must it lodge in shrines so frail?
    One day, when from my lips a like complaint   50
Had fallen in presence of a studious friend,
He with a smile made answer that in truth
'Twas going far to seek disquietude,
But, on the front of his reproof, confessed
That he himself had oftentimes given way   55
To kindred hauntings. Whereupon I told
That once in the stillness of a summer's noon,
While I was seated in a rocky cave
By the sea-side, perusing, so it chanced,
The famous history of the errant Knight   60
Recorded by Cervantes, these same thoughts
Beset me, and to height unusual rose,
While listlessly I sate, and, having closed
The Book, had turned my eyes tow'rd the wide Sea.
On Poetry, and geometric truth,   65
And their high privilege of lasting life,
From all internal injury exempt,
I mused; upon these chiefly: and, at length,
My senses yielding to the sultry air,
Sleep seized me, and I passed into a dream.   70
I saw before me stretched a boundless plain,
Of sandy wilderness, all blank and void;
And as I looked around, distress and fear
Came creeping over me, when at my side,
Close at my side, an uncouth Shape appeared   75
Upon a Dromedary, mounted high.

He seemed an Arab of the Bedouin Tribes:
A Lance he bore, and underneath one arm
A Stone; and, in the opposite hand, a Shell
Of a surpassing brightness. At the sight   80
Much I rejoiced, not doubting but a Guide
Was present, one who with unerring skill
Would through the desert lead me; and while yet
I looked, and looked, self-questioned what this freight
Which the New-comer carried through the Waste   85
Could mean, the Arab told me that the Stone
(To give it in the language of the Dream)
Was Euclid's Elements; "and this," said he,
"This other," pointing to the Shell, "this book
Is something of more worth"; and, at the word,   90
Stretched forth the Shell, so beautiful in shape,
In color so resplendent, with command
That I should hold it to my ear. I did so,—
And heard, that instant, in an unknown tongue,
Which yet I understood, articulate sounds,   95
A loud prophetic blast of harmony—
An Ode, in passion uttered, which foretold
Destruction to the Children of the Earth,
By Deluge now at hand. No sooner ceased
The Song than the Arab with calm look declared   100
That all would come to pass, of which the voice
Had given forewarning, and that he himself
Was going then to bury those two Books:
The One that held acquaintance with the stars,
And wedded Soul to Soul in purest bond   105
Of Reason, undisturbed by space or time:
Th'other, that was a God, yea many Gods,
Had voices more than all the winds, with power
To exhilarate the Spirit, and to soothe,
Through every clime, the heart of human kind.   110
While this was uttering, strange as it may seem,
I wondered not, although I plainly saw
The One to be a Stone, the Other a Shell,
Nor doubted once but that they both were Books;
Having a perfect faith in all that passed.   115

Far stronger now grew the desire I felt
To cleave unto this Man; but when I prayed
To share his enterprize, he hurried on,
Reckless of me: I followed, not unseen,
For oftentimes he cast a backward look,   120
Grasping his twofold treasure. Lance in rest,
He rode, I keeping pace with him; and now
He to my fancy had become the Knight
Whose tale Cervantes tells; yet not the Knight,
But was an Arab of the desert, too,   125
Of these was neither, and was both at once.
His countenance, meanwhile, grew more disturbed,
And looking backwards when he looked, mine eyes
Saw, over half the wilderness diffused,
A bed of glittering light: I asked the cause.   130
"It is," said he, "the waters of the Deep
Gathering upon us"; quickening then the pace
Of the unwieldy Creature he bestrode,
He left me; I called after him aloud,—
He heeded not; but with his twofold charge   135
Still in his grasp, before me, full in view,
Went hurrying o'er the illimitable Waste
With the fleet waters of a drowning World
In chase of him; whereat I waked in terror;
And saw the Sea before me, and the Book,   140
In which I had been reading, at my side.

    Full often, taking from the world of Sleep
This Arab Phantom, which I thus beheld,
This semi-Quixote, I to him have given
A substance, fancied him a living man,   145
A gentle Dweller in the desert, crazed
By love and feeling, and internal thought
Protracted among endless solitudes;
Have shaped him, in the oppression of his brain,
And so equipped, wandering upon this quest!   150
Nor have I pitied him; but rather felt
Reverence was due to a Being thus employed;
And thought that, in the blind and awful lair
Of such a madness, reason did lie couched.

Enow there are on earth to take in charge   155
Their Wives, their Children, and their virgin Loves,
Or whatsoever else the heart holds dear;
Enow to stir for these;—yea, will I say,
Contemplating in soberness the approach
Of an event so dire, by signs, in earth   160
Or heaven, made manifest,—that I could share
That maniac's fond anxiety, and go
Upon like errand. Oftentimes, at least,
Me hath such strong entrancement overcome,
When I have held a volume in my hand,   165
Poor earthly casket of immortal Verse,
Shakespear, or Milton, Labourers divine!
       Great and benign, indeed, must be the power
Of living Nature, which could thus so long
Detain me from the best of other Guides   170
And dearest Helpers left unthanked, unpraised.
Even in the time of lisping Infancy,
And later down, in prattling Childhood, even,
While I was travelling back among those days,
How could I ever play an Ingrate's part?   175
Once more should I have made those bowers resound,
By intermingling strains of thankfulness
With their own thoughtless melodies; at least,
It might have well beseemed me to repeat
Some simply fashioned tale, to tell again,   180
In slender accents of sweet Verse, some tale
That did bewitch me then, and soothes me now.
O Friend! O Poet! Brother of my soul,
Think not that I could pass along untouched
By these remembrances. Yet wherefore speak?   185
Why call upon a few weak words to say
What is already written in the hearts
Of all that breathe? what in the path of all
Drops daily from the tongue of every Child,
Wherever Man is found? The trickling tear   190
Upon the cheek of listening Infancy
Proclaims it, and the insuperable look
That drinks as if it never could be full.

That portion of my Story I shall leave
There registered; whatever else of power   195
Or pleasure, sown or fostered thus, may be
Peculiar to myself, let that remain
Where still it works, though hidden from all search,
Among the depths of time. Yet is it just
That here, in memory of all books which lay   200
Their sure foundations in the heart of man,
Whether by native prose, or numerous verse;
That in the name of all inspired Souls,
From Homer the great Thunderer, from the voice
That roars along the bed of Jewish Song: 205
And that more varied and elaborate,
Those trumpet-tones of harmony that shake
Our shores in England; from those loftiest notes
Down to the low and wren-like warblings, made
For Cottagers, and Spinners at the wheel,   210
And sun-burnt Travellers resting their tired limbs,
Stretched under way-side hedgerows, ballad tunes,
Food for the hungry ears of little ones,
And of old Men who have survived their joy;
'Tis just that in behalf of these, the Works,   215
And of the men that framed them, whether known,
Or sleeping nameless in their scattered graves,
That I should here assert their rights, attest
Their honours, and should, once for all, pronounce
Their benediction: speak of them as Powers   220
For ever to be hallowed; only less,
For what we are and what we may become,
Than Nature's self, which is the breath of God;
Or His pure Word by miracle revealed.
      Rarely, and with reluctance, would I stoop   225
To transitory themes; yet I rejoice,
And, by these thoughts admonished, will pour out
Thanks with uplifted heart, that I was reared
Safe from an evil which these days have laid
Upon the Children of the Land, a pest   230
That might have dried me up, body and soul.
This Verse is dedicate to Nature's self

And things that teach as Nature teaches: then
Oh! where had been the Man, the Poet where,
Where had we been, we two, beloved Friend?   235
If in the season of unperilous choice,
In lieu of wandering, as we did, through Tales
Rich with indigenous produce, open ground
Of Fancy, happy pastures ranged at will,
We had been followed, hourly watched,—and noosed   240
Each in his several melancholy walk,
Stringed like a poor-man's heifer, at its feed
Led through the lanes in forlorn servitude;
Or rather like a stallèd Ox debarred
From touch of growing grass, that may not taste   245
A flower, till it have yielded up its sweets
A prelibation to the mower's scythe.
     Behold the Parent Hen amid her Brood,
Though fledged and feathered and well-pleased to part
And straggle from her presence, still a Brood,—   250
And she herself from the maternal bond
Still undischarged; yet doth she little more
Than move with them in tenderness and love,
A centre to the circle which they make;
And, now and then, alike from need of theirs,   255
And call of her own natural appetites,
She scratches, ransacks up the earth for food
Which they partake at pleasure. Early died
My honored Mother, she who was the heart
And hinge of all our learnings and our loves;   260
She left us destitute, and as we might
Trooping together. Little suits it me
To break upon the sabbath of her rest
With any thought that looks at others' blame;
Nor would I praise her but in perfect love;   265
Hence am I checked; but let me boldly say,
In gratitude, and for the sake of truth,
Unheard by her, that she, not falsely taught,
Fetching her goodness rather from times past
Than shaping novelties for times to come,   270
Had no presumption, no such jealousy;

Nor did by habit of her thoughts mistrust
Our Nature, but had virtual faith that He
Who fills the Mother's breast with innocent milk,
Doth also for our nobler part provide,   275
Under His great correction and controul,
As innocent instincts and as innocent food;
Or draws for minds that are left free to trust
In the simplicities of opening life
Sweet honey out of spurned or dreaded weeds.   280
This was her creed; and therefore she was pure
From anxious fear of error or mishap,
And evil,—overweeningly so called;
Was not puffed up by false unnatural hopes;
Nor selfish with unnecessary cares;   285
Nor with impatience from the season asked
More than its timely produce—rather loved
The hours for what they are than from regards
Glanced on their promises, in restless pride.
Such was she—not from faculties more strong   290
Than others have, but from the times, perhaps,
And spot in which she lived, and through a grace
Of modest meekness, simple-mindedness,
A heart that found benignity and hope,
Being itself benign.
           My drift, I fear,   295
Is scarcely obvious; but, that Common sense
May try this modern system by its fruits,
Leave let me take to place before her sight
A specimen pourtrayed with faithful hand.
Full early trained to worship seemliness,   300
This model of a Child is never known
To mix in quarrels—that were far beneath
His dignity; with gifts he bubbles o'er
As generous as a fountain; selfishness
May not come near him, nor the little throng   305
Of flitting pleasures tempt him from his path;
The wandering beggars propagate his name,
Dumb creatures find him tender as a Nun;
And natural or supernatural fear,

Unless it leap upon him in a dream,   310
Touches him not. To enhance the wonder, see
How arch his notices, how nice his sense
Of the ridiculous; not blind is he
To the broad follies of the licenced world;
Yet innocent himself withal, though shrewd,   315
And can read Lectures upon innocence.
A miracle of scientific lore,
Ships he can guide across the pathless sea,
And tell you all their cunning;—he can read
The inside of the earth, and spell the stars;   320
He knows the policies of foreign Lands;
Can string you names of districts, cities, towns,
The whole world over, tight as beads of dew
Upon a gossamer thread; he sifts, he weighs;
All things are put to question; he must live   325
Knowing that he grows wiser every day
Or else not live at all, and seeing, too,
Each little drop of wisdom as it falls
Into the dimpling Cistern of his heart.
    For this unnatural growth the Trainer blame,   330
Pity the Tree.—Poor human Vanity!
Wert thou extinguished, little would be left
Which he could truly love; but how escape?
For, ever as a thought of purer birth
Rises to lead him toward a better clime,   335
Some Intermedler still is on the watch
To drive him back, and pound him like a Stray
Within the pinfold of his own conceit.
Meanwhile old Grandame Earth is grieved to find
The play-things which her love designed for him   340
Unthought of: in their woodland beds the flowers
Weep, and the river sides are all forlorn.
Oh! give us once again the wishing-Cap
Of Fortunatus, and the invisible Coat
Of Jack the Giant-killer, Robin Hood,   345
And Sabra in the Forest with St George!
The Child, whose love is here, at least doth reap
One precious gain, that he forgets himself.

These mighty Workmen of our later age
Who with a broad highway have overbridged   350
The froward chaos of futurity,
Tamed to their bidding; they who have the skill
To manage books and things, and make them act
On Infant minds as surely as the sun
Deals with a flower; the Keepers of our Time,   355
The Guides and Wardens of our faculties,
Sages who in their prescience would control
All accidents, and to the very road
Which they have fashioned would confine us down
Like engines; when will their presumption learn   360
That in the unreasoning progress of the world
A wiser Spirit is at work for us,
A better eye than theirs, most prodigal
Of blessings and most studious of our good,
Even in what seem our most unfruitful hours?   365
    There was a Boy;—ye knew him well, Ye Cliffs
And Islands of Winander!—many a time
At evening, when the earliest stars began
To move along the edges of the hills,
Rising or setting, would he stand alone,   370
Beneath the trees, or by the glimmering lake;
And there, with fingers interwoven, both hands
Pressed closely palm to palm and to his mouth
Uplifted, he, as through an instrument,
Blew mimic hootings to the silent owls   375
That they might answer him.—And they would shout
Across the watery Vale, and shout again,
Responsive to his call,—with quivering peals,
And long halloos, and screams, and echoes loud
Redoubled and redoubled; concourse wild   380
Of jocund din! and when a lengthened pause
Of silence came, and baffled his best skill,
Then, sometimes, in that silence, while he hung
Listening, a gentle shock of mild surprize
Has carried far into his heart the voice   385
Of mountain torrents; or the visible scene
Would enter unawares into his mind

With all its solemn imagery, its rocks,
Its woods, and that uncertain heaven, received
Into the bosom of the steady lake.   390
    This Boy was taken from his Mates, and died
In childhood, ere he was full twelve years old.
Fair is the Spot, most beautiful the Vale
Where he was born: the grassy Church-yard hangs
Upon a slope above the Village School;   395
And through that Church-yard when my way has led
On summer evenings, I believe that there
A long half-hour together I have stood
Mute—looking at the grave in which he lies!
    Even now appears before the mind's clear eye   400
That self-same Village Church; I see her sit
(The throned Lady whom erewhile we hailed)
On her green hill, forgetful of this Boy
Who slumbers at her feet, forgetful, too,
Of all her silent neighbourhood of graves,   405
And listening only to the gladsome sounds
That, from the rural School ascending, play
Beneath her, and about her. May she long
Behold a race of Young Ones like to those
With whom I herded! (easily, indeed,   410
We might have fed upon a fatter soil
Of Arts and Letters, but be that forgiven)
A race of *real* children; not too wise,
Too learned, or too good: but wanton, fresh,
And bandied up and down by love and hate;   415
Not unresentful where self-justified;
Fierce, moody, patient, venturous, modest, shy;
Mad at their sports like withered leaves in winds:
Though doing wrong and suffering, and full oft
Bending beneath our life's mysterious weight   420
Of pain, and doubt, and fear; yet yielding not
In happiness to the happiest upon earth.
Simplicity in habit, truth in speech,
Be these the daily strengtheners of their minds!
May books and nature be their early joy!   425
And knowledge, rightly honored with that name,

Knowledge not purchased by the loss of power!
   Well do I call to mind the very week
When I was first entrusted to the care
Of that sweet Valley; when its paths, its shores,   430
And brooks were like a dream of novelty
To my half-infant thoughts,—that very week,
While I was roving up and down alone,
Seeking I knew not what, I chanced to cross
One of those open fields, which, shaped like ears,   435
Make green peninsulas on Esthwaite's lake.
Twilight was coming on, yet, through the gloom,
Appeared distinctly on the opposite shore
A heap of garments, as if left by One
Who might have there been bathing. Long I watched,   440
But no one owned them; meanwhile, the calm Lake
Grew dark, with all the shadows on its breast,
And, now and then, a fish upleaping snapped
The breathless stillness. The succeeding day,
Those unclaimed garments, telling a plain tale,   445
Drew to the spot an anxious Crowd; some looked
In passive expectation from the shore,
While from a boat others hung o'er the deep,
Sounding with grappling irons and long poles.
At last, the dead Man, 'mid that beauteous scene   450
Of trees and hills and water, bolt upright
Rose with his ghastly face: a spectre shape
Of terror, yet no soul-debasing fear,
Young as I was, a Child not nine years old,
Possessed me; for my inner eye had seen   455
Such sights before, among the shining streams
Of fairey land, the forests of romance;
Their spirit hallowed the sad spectacle
With decoration and ideal grace;
A dignity, a smoothness, like the works   460
Of Grecian Art, and purest Poesy.
   A precious treasure I had long possessed,
A little, yellow, canvas-covered book,
A slender abstract of the Arabian tales;
And, from companions in a new abode,   465

When first I learnt that this dear prize of mine
Was but a block hewn from a mighty quarry—
That there were four large Volumes, laden all
With kindred matter, 'twas to me, in truth,
A promise scarcely earthly. Instantly,   470
With one not richer than myself, I made
A covenant that each should lay aside
The monies he possessed, and hoard up more,
Till our joint savings had amassed enough
To make this Book our own. Through several months,   475
In spite of all temptation, we preserved
Religiously that vow, but firmness failed;
Nor were we ever Masters of our wish.
    And when thereafter to my Father's house
The holidays returned me, there to find   480
That golden store of books which I had left,
What joy was mine! How often, in the course
Of those glad respites, though a soft west wind
Ruffled the waters to the Angler's wish
For a whole day together, have I lain   485
Down by thy side, O Derwent, murmuring stream!
On the hot stones, and in the glaring sun,
And there have read, devouring as I read,
Defrauding the day's glory, desperate!
Till, with a sudden bound of smart reproach,   490
Such as an Idler deals with in his shame,
I to the sport betook myself again.
    A gracious Spirit o'er this earth presides,
And o'er the heart of man: invisibly
It comes, to works of unreproved delight,   495
And tendency benign, directing those
Who care not, know not, think not what they do.
The Tales that charm away the wakeful night
In Araby,—romances, legends, penned
For solace, by dim light of monkish lamps;   500
Fictions, for Ladies of their Love, devised
By youthful Squires; adventures endless, spun
By the dismantled Warrior in old age
Out of the bowels of those very schemes

In which his youth did first extravagate;   505
These spread like day, and something in the shape
Of these will live till man shall be no more.
Dumb yearnings, hidden appetites are ours,
And *they* MUST *have their food*; our childhood sits,
Our simple childhood sits upon a throne   510
That hath more power than all the elements.
I guess not what this tells of Being past,
Nor what it augurs of the life to come,
But so it is; and, in that dubious hour,
That twilight when we first begin to see   515
This dawning earth, to recognize, expect;
And, in the long probation that ensues,
The time of trial, ere we learn to live
In reconcilement with our stinted powers,
To endure this state of meagre vassalage;   520
Unwilling to forego, confess, submit,
Uneasy and unsettled; yoke-fellows
To custom, mettlesome, and not yet tamed
And humbled down—Oh! then we feel, we feel,
We know where we have friends.—Ye dreamers, then,   525
Forgers of daring Tales! we bless you then,
Impostors, drivellers, dotards, as the Ape
Philosophy will call you; *then* we feel
With what, and how great might ye are in league,
Who make our wish our power, our thought a deed,   530
An empire, a possession; ye whom time
And seasons serve; all faculties,—to whom
Earth crouches, the elements are potter's clay,
Space like a heaven filled up with Northern lights,
Here, no where, there, and every where at once.   535
     Relinquishing this lofty eminence
For ground, though humbler, not the less a tract
Of the same isthmus which our Spirits cross
In progress from their native Continent
To earth and human life, the Song might dwell   540
On that delightful time of growing Youth
When craving for the marvellous gives way
To strengthening love for things that we have seen;

When sober truth and steady sympathies
Offered to notice by less daring pens   545
Take firmer hold of us; and words themselves
Move us with conscious pleasure.
                               I am sad
At thought of raptures now for ever flown;
Almost to tears I sometimes could be sad
To think of, to read over, many a page,   550
Poems withal of name, which at that time
Did never fail to entrance me, and are now
Dead in my eyes, dead as a Theatre
Fresh emptied of Spectators. Twice five years,
Or less, I might have seen, when first my mind   555
With conscious pleasure opened to the charm
Of words in tuneful order, found them sweet
For *their own sakes*, a passion and a power;
And phrases pleased me, chosen for delight,
For pomp, or love. Oft in the public roads   560
Yet unfrequented, while the morning light
Was yellowing the hill-tops, I went abroad
With a dear Friend, and for the better part
Of two delightful hours we strolled along
By the still borders of the misty Lake,   565
Repeating favourite Verses with one voice,
Or conning more,—as happy as the birds
That round us chaunted. Well might we be glad,
Lifted above the ground by airy fancies
More bright than madness or the dreams of wine;   570
And, though full oft the objects of our love
Were false, and in their splendour overwrought,
Yet was there, surely, then no vulgar power
Working within us, nothing less, in truth,
Than that most noble attribute of Man,   575
Though yet untutored and inordinate,
That wish for something loftier, more adorned,
Than is the common aspect, daily garb
Of human life. What wonder then, if sounds
Of exultation echoed through the groves!   580
For images, and sentiments, and words,

And every thing encountered or pursued
In that delicious world of poesy,
Kept holiday; a never-ending shew,
With music, incense, festival, and flowers!   585
    Here must we pause; this only let me add,
From heart-experience, and in humblest sense
Of modesty, that he, who, in his youth,
A daily Wanderer among woods and fields,
With living Nature hath been intimate,   590
Not only in that raw unpractised time
Is stirred to extasy, as others are,
By glittering verse; but, further, doth receive,
In measure only dealt out to himself,
Knowledge and increase of enduring joy   595
From the great Nature that exists in works
Of mighty Poets. Visionary Power
Attends the motions of the viewless winds
Embodied in the mystery of words:
There darkness makes abode, and all the host   600
Of shadowy things work endless changes there,
As in a mansion like their proper home.
Even forms and substances are circumfused
By that transparent veil with light divine;
And, through the turnings intricate of verse,   605
Present themselves as objects recognized,
In flashes, and with glory not their own.
    Thus far a scanty record is deduced
Of what I owed to Books in early life;
Their later influence yet remains untold;   610
But as this work was taking in my mind
Proportions that seemed larger than had first
Been meditated, I was indisposed
To any further progress, at a time
When these acknowledgments were left unpaid.   615

BOOK SIXTH
CAMBRIDGE, AND THE ALPS

The leaves were fading, when to Esthwaite's banks
And the simplicities of Cottage life

I bade farewell; and, one among the Youth
Who, summoned by that season, reunite
As scattered birds troop to the Fowler's lure,   5
Went back to Granta's cloisters; not so prompt
Or eager, though as gay and undepressed
In mind, as when I thence had taken flight,
A few short months before. I turned my face,
Without repining, from the coves and heights   10
Clothed in the sunshine of their withering fern;
Quitted, not loth, the mild magnificence
Of calmer Lakes, and louder streams;—and you,
Frank-hearted Maids of rocky Cumberland,
You, and your not unwelcome days of mirth,   15
Relinquished, and your nights of revelry;
And in my own unlovely Cell sate down
In lightsome mood,—such privilege has youth
That cannot take long-leave of pleasant thoughts.
    The bonds of indolent society   20
Relaxing in their hold, henceforth I lived
More to myself. Two winters may be passed
Without a separate notice: many books
Were skimmed, devoured, or studiously perused,
But with no settled plan. I was detached   25
Internally from academic cares;
Yet independent study seemed a course
Of hardy disobedience toward friends
And kindred, proud rebellion and unkind.
This spurious virtue,—rather let it bear   30
A name it more deserves,—this cowardise
Gave treacherous sanction to that over-love
Of freedom, which encouraged me to turn
From regulations even of my own,
As from restraints and bonds. Yet who can tell,   35
Who knows, what thus may have been gained both then
And at a later season, or preserved;
What love of Nature, what original strength
Of contemplation, what intuitive truths,
The deepest and the best, what keen research   40
Unbiassed, unbewildered, and unawed?

The Poet's soul was with me at that time,
Sweet meditations, the still overflow
Of present happiness, while future years
Lacked not anticipations, tender dreams   45
No few of which have since been realized;
And some remain hopes for my future life.
Four years and thirty, told this very week,   *X* = 1804
Have I been now a Sojourner on earth,
By sorrow not unsmitten, yet for me   50
Life's morning radiance hath not left the hills,
Her dew is on the flowers. Those were the days
Which also first emboldened me to trust
With firmness, hitherto but lightly touched
By such a daring thought, that I might leave   55
Some monument behind me which pure hearts
Should reverence. The instinctive humbleness,
Maintained even by the very name and thought
Of printed books and authorship, began
To melt away: and further, the dread awe   60
Of mighty names was softened down, and seemed
Approachable, admitting fellowship
Of modest sympathy. Such aspect now,
Though not familiarly, my mind put on,
Content to observe, to admire, and to enjoy.   65
    All winter long, whenever free to chuse,
Did I by night frequent the College Groves
And tributary Walks; the last and oft
The only One who had been lingering there
Through hours of silence; till the Porter's bell,   70
A punctual follower on the stroke of nine,
Rang with its blunt unceremonious voice,
Inexorable summons! Lofty Elms,
Inviting shades of opportune recess,
Bestowed composure on a neighbourhood   75
Unpeaceful in itself. A single Tree,
With sinuous trunk, boughs exquisitely wreathed,
Grew there—an Ash which Winter for himself
Decked as in pride, and with outlandish grace.
Up from the ground, and almost to the top,   80

parasitic

The trunk and every master branch were green
With clustering ivy, and the lightsome twigs
And outer spray profusely tipped with seeds
That hung in yellow tassels, while the air
Stirred them, not voiceless. Often have I stood   85
Foot-bound, uplooking at this lovely Tree
Beneath a frosty moon. The hemisphere
Of magic fiction, verse of mine perchance
May never tread, but scarcely Spenser's Self
Could have more tranquil visions in his Youth,   90
Nor could more bright appearances create
Of human Forms with superhuman powers,
Than I beheld loitering on calm clear nights,
Alone, beneath this fairy work of earth.
    On the vague Reading of a truant Youth   95
'Twere idle to descant. My inner judgment
Not seldom differed from my taste in books
As if it appertained to another mind.
And yet the books which then I valued most
Are dearest to me *now*; for, having scanned,   100
Not heedlessly, the laws, and watched the forms
Of nature, in that knowledge I possessed
A standard, often usefully applied,
Even when unconsciously, to things removed
From a familiar sympathy.—In fine,   105
I was a better judge of thoughts than words;
Misled, in estimating words, not only
By common inexperience of youth,
But by the trade in classic niceties,
The dangerous craft of culling term and phrase   110
From languages that want the living voice
To carry meaning to the natural heart;
To tell us what is passion, what is truth,
What reason, what simplicity and sense.
    Yet may we not entirely overlook   115
The pleasure gathered from the rudiments
Of geometric science. Though advanced
In these enquiries, with regret I speak,
No farther than the threshold, there I found

Both elevation and composed delight.   120
With Indian awe and wonder, Ignorance pleased
With its own struggles, did I meditate
On the relation those abstractions bear
To Nature's laws, and by what process led
Those immaterial Agents bowed their heads   125
Duly to serve the mind of earth-born Man
From star to star, from kindred sphere to sphere,
From system on to system without end.
More frequently from the same source I drew
A pleasure quiet and profound, a sense   130
Of permanent and universal sway
And paramount belief: there recognized
A type, for finite natures, of the one
Supreme Existence, the surpassing life
Which, to the boundaries of space and time,   135
Of melancholy space and doleful time,
Superior, and incapable of change,
Nor touched by welterings of passion, *is*,
And hath the name of God. Transcendent peace
And silence did await upon these thoughts   140
That were a frequent comfort to my youth.
    'Tis told by One whom stormy waters threw
With Fellow-sufferers, by the Shipwreck spared,
Upon a desert Coast, that, having brought
To land a single volume, saved by chance,   145
A treatise of Geometry, he wont,
Although of food and clothing destitute
And beyond common wretchedness depressed,
To part from Company, and take this Book
(Then first a self-taught Pupil in its truths)   150
To spots remote, and draw his diagrams
With a long staff upon the sand, and thus
Did oft beguile his sorrow, and almost
Forget his feeling: so (if like effect
From the same cause produced, 'mid outward things   155
So different, may rightly be compared),
So was it then with me, and so will be
With Poets, ever. Mighty is the charm

Of those abstractions to a mind beset
With images, and haunted by herself;   160
And specially delightful unto me
Was that clear Synthesis, built up aloft
So gracefully! even then when it appeared
Not more than a mere play-thing, or a toy
To sense embodied; not the thing it is   165
In verity, an independent world
Created out of pure Intelligence.
        Such dispositions then were mine, unearned
By aught, I fear, of genuine desert,
Mine, through heaven's grace, and inborn aptitudes.   170
And, not to leave the story of that time
Imperfect, with these habits must be joined
Moods melancholy, fits of spleen, that loved
A pensive sky, sad days, and piping winds,
The twilight more than dawn, autumn than Spring,   175
A treasured and luxurious gloom, of choice
And inclination mainly, and the mere
Redundancy of Youth's contentedness.
— To time thus spent, add multitudes of hours
Pilfered away, by what the Bard, who sang   180
Of the Enchanter Indolence, hath called
"Good-natured lounging," and behold a map
Of my Collegiate life,—far less intense
Than Duty called for, or, without regard
To Duty, *might* have sprung up of itself   185
By change of accidents,—or even, to speak
Without unkindness, in another place;
Yet why take refuge in that plea?—the fault,
This I repeat, was mine, mine be the blame.
        In summer, making quest for works of Art   190
Or scenes renowned for beauty, I explored
That Streamlet whose blue current works its way
Between romantic Dovedale's spiry rocks,
Pryed into Yorkshire dales, or hidden tracts
Of my own native region, and was blest   195
Between these sundry wanderings with a joy
Above all joys, that seemed another morn

Risen on mid noon; blest with the presence, Friend!
Of that sole Sister, she who hath been long
Dear to Thee also, thy true Friend, and mine,   200
Now after separation desolate
Restored to me, such absence that she seemed
A gift then first bestowed. The varied banks
Of Emont, hitherto unnamed in Song,
And that monastic Castle 'mid tall trees   205
Low-standing by the margin of the Stream,
A mansion visited (as fame reports)
By Sidney; where, in sight of our Helvellyn
Or stormy Cross-fell, snatches he might pen
Of his Arcadia, by fraternal love   210
Inspired;—that River and those mouldering Towers
Have seen us side by side when, having clomb
The darksome windings of a broken stair,
And crept along a ridge of fractured wall,
Not without trembling, we in safety looked   215
Forth through some gothic window's open space,
And gathered with one mind a rich reward
From the far-stretching landscape, by the light
Of morning beautified, or purple eve:
Or, not less pleased, lay on some turret's head,   220
Catching from tufts of grass and hare-bell flowers
Their faintest whisper, to the passing breeze
Given out while mid-day heat oppressed the plains.
—Another Maid there was, who also shed
A gladness o'er that season, then to me,   225
By her exulting outside look of Youth,
And placid under countenance, first endeared;
That other Spirit, Coleridge! who is now
So near to us, that meek confiding Heart
So reverenced by us both. O'er paths and fields   230
In all that neighbourhood, through narrow lanes
Of eglantine, and through the shady woods,
And o'er the Border Beacon, and the Waste
Of naked pools, and common crags that lay
Exposed on the bare Fell, were scattered love,   235
The spirit of pleasure, and Youth's golden gleam.

O Friend! we had not seen thee at that time;
And yet a power is on me, and a strong
Confusion, and I seem to plant thee there.——
Far art Thou wandered now in search of health,   240
And milder breezes, melancholy lot!
But Thou art with us, with us in the past,
The present, with us in the times to come:
There is no grief, no sorrow, no despair,
No languor, no dejection, no dismay,   245
No absence scarcely can there be, for those
Who love as we do. Speed thee well! divide
With us thy pleasure; thy returning strength,
Receive it daily as a joy of ours;
Share with us thy fresh spirits, whether gift   250
Of gales Etesian, or of tender thoughts.
    I too have been a Wanderer; but, alas!
How different the fate of different Men!
Though mutually unknown, yea nursed and reared
As if in several elements, we were framed   255
To bend at last to the same discipline,
Predestined, if two Beings ever were,
To seek the same delights, and have one health,
One happiness. Throughout this Narrative,
Else sooner ended, I have borne in mind   260
For whom it registers the birth, and marks the growth,
Of gentleness, simplicity, and truth,
And joyous loves that hallow innocent days
Of peace and self-command. Of rivers, fields,
And groves, I speak to thee, my Friend: to thee   265
Who, yet a liveried School-boy, in the depths
Of the huge City, on the leaded roof
Of that wide Edifice, thy School and home,
Wert used to lie, and gaze upon the clouds
Moving in heaven; or, of that pleasure tired,   270
To shut thine eyes, and by internal light
See trees, and meadows, and thy native Stream
Far distant, thus beheld from year to year
Of a long exile. Nor could I forget,
In this late portion of my argument,   275

That scarcely, as my term of pupilage
Ceased, had I left those academic Bowers
When Thou wert thither guided. From the heart
Of London, and from cloisters there, thou cam'st,
And didst sit down in temperance and peace,   280
A rigorous Student. What a stormy course
Then followed! Oh! it is a pang that calls
For utterance, to think what easy change
Of circumstances might to thee have spared
A world of pain, ripened a thousand hopes   285
For ever withered. Through this retrospect
Of my Collegiate life, I still have had
Thy after-sojourn in the self-same place
Present before my eyes; have played with times
And accidents as Children do with cards,   290
Or as a Man, who, when his house is built,
A frame locked up in wood and stone, doth still,
As impotent fancy prompts, by his fire-side
Rebuild it to his liking. I have thought
Of Thee, thy learning, gorgeous eloquence,   295
And all the strength and plumage of thy youth,
Thy subtile speculations, toils abstruse
Among the Schoolmen, and platonic forms
Of wild ideal pageantry, shaped out
From things well-matched or ill, and words for things,   300
The self-created sustenance of a Mind
Debarred from Nature's living images,
Compelled to be a life unto herself,
And unrelentingly possessed by thirst
Of greatness, love, and beauty. Not alone,   305
Ah! surely not in singleness of heart,
Should I have seen the light of evening fade
From smooth Cam's silent waters, had we met
Even at that early time: needs must I trust
In the belief that my maturer age,   310
My calmer habits, and more steady voice,
Would with an influence benign have soothed
Or chased away the airy wretchedness
That battened on thy youth. But thou hast trod,

In watchful meditation thou hast trod,   315
A march of glory, which doth put to shame
These vain regrets: health suffers in thee, else
Such grief for Thee would be the weakest thought
That ever harboured in the breast of man.
    A passing word erewhile did lightly touch   320
On wanderings of my own, that now embraced,
With livelier hope, a region wider far.
When the third summer freed us from restraint,
A youthful Friend, he too a Mountaineer,
Not slow to share my wishes, took his staff,   325
And, sallying forth, we journeyed, side by side,
Bound to the distant Alps. A hardy slight
Did this unprecedented course imply
Of College studies and their set rewards;
Nor had, in truth, the scheme been formed by me   330
Without uneasy forethought of the pain,
The censures, and ill-omening of those
To whom my worldly interests were dear.
But Nature then was Sovereign in my mind,
And mighty Forms, seizing a youthful fancy,   335
Had given a charter to irregular hopes.
In any age of uneventful calm
Among the Nations, surely would my heart
Have been possessed by similar desire;
But Europe at that time was thrilled with joy,   340
France standing on the top of golden hours,
And human nature seeming born again.
    Lightly equipped, and but a few brief looks
Cast on the white cliffs of our native shore
From the receding Vessel's deck, we chanced   345
To land at Calais on the very Eve
Of that great federal Day; and there we saw,
In a mean City, and among a few,
How bright a face is worn when joy of one
Is joy for tens of millions. Southward thence   350
We held our way direct, through Hamlets, Towns,
Gaudy with reliques of that Festival,
Flowers left to wither on triumphal Arcs,

And window-garlands. On the public roads,
And, once, three days successively, through paths   355
By which our toilsome journey was abridged,
Among sequestered villages we walked,
And found benevolence and blessedness
Spread like a fragrance every where, when Spring
Hath left no corner of the land untouched.   360
Where Elms for many and many a league in files
With their thin umbrage, on the stately roads
Of that great Kingdom, rustled o'er our heads,
For ever near us as we paced along;
How sweet at such a time, with such delights   365
On every side, in prime of youthful strength,
To feed a Poet's tender melancholy
And fond conceit of sadness, with the sound
Of undulations varying as might please
The wind that swayed them! once, and more than once,   370
Unhoused beneath the evening star we saw
Dances of liberty, and, in late hours
Of darkness, dances in the open air
Deftly prolonged, though grey-haired lookers-on
Might waste their breath in chiding.   375
                          Under hills,
The vine-clad hills and slopes of Burgundy,
Upon the bosom of the gentle Saone
We glided forward with the flowing Stream;
Swift Rhone! thou wert the *wings* on which we cut
A winding passage with majestic ease   380
Between thy lofty rocks. Enchanting shew
Those woods, and farms, and orchards did present,
And single cottages, and lurking towns,
Reach after reach, succession without end
Of deep and stately Vales! A lonely Pair   385
Of Strangers, till day closed, we sailed along,
Clustered together with a merry crowd
Of those emancipated; a blithe Host
Of Travellers, chiefly Delegates, returning
From the great Spousals newly solemnized   390
At their chief City, in the sight of heaven.

Like bees they swarmed, gaudy and gay as bees;
Some vapoured in the unruliness of joy
And, with their swords, flourished, as if to fight
The saucy air. In this proud Company   395
We landed, took with them our evening meal,
Guests welcome almost as the Angels were
To Abraham of old. The supper done,
With flowing cups elate and happy thoughts,
We rose at signal given, and formed a ring   400
And, hand in hand, danced round and round the Board:
All hearts were open, every tongue was loud
With amity and glee; we bore a name
Honored in France, the name of Englishmen,
And hospitably did they give us hail!   405
As their forerunners in a glorious course;
And round and round the board we danced again.
With these blithe Friends our voyage we renewed
At early dawn. The Monastery bells
Made a sweet jingling in our youthful ears;   410
The rapid River flowing without noise,
And each uprising or receding Spire
Spake with a sense of peace, at intervals
Touching the heart, amid the boisterous crew
By whom we were encompassed. Taking leave   415
Of this glad Throng, foot-Travellers side by side,
Measuring our steps in quiet we pursued
Our journey, and, ere twice the sun had set,
Beheld the Convent of Chartreuse, and there
Rested within an awful *Solitude*.   420
Yes, for even then no other than a Place
Of soul-affecting *Solitude* appeared
That far-famed region, though our eyes had seen,
As toward the sacred Mansion we advanced,
Arms flashing, and a military glare   425
Of riotous men commissioned to expel
The blameless Inmates; and belike subvert
That frame of social being, which so long
Had bodied forth the ghostliness of things
In silence visible, and perpetual calm.   430

—"Stay, stay your sacrilegious hands!"—the voice
Was Nature's, uttered from her Alpine throne;
I heard it then, and seem to hear it now:
"Your impious work forbear; perish what may,
Let this one Temple last, be this one spot   435
Of earth devoted to Eternity!"
She ceased to speak; but while St Bruno's pines
Waved their dark tops, not silent as they waved;
And while below, along their several beds,
Murmured the Sister Streams of Life and Death,   440
Thus by conflicting passions pressed, my Heart
Responded, "Honor to the Patriot's zeal!
Glory and hope to new-born Liberty!
Hail to the mighty projects of the Time!
Discerning Sword that Justice wields, do thou   445
Go forth and prosper; and ye purging fires
Up to the loftiest Towers of Pride ascend,
Fanned by the breath of angry Providence;
But Oh! if past and future be the wings
On whose support harmoniously conjoined   450
Moves the great Spirit of human Knowledge, spare
These courts mysterious, where a step advanced
Between the portals of the shadowy rocks
Leaves far behind life's treacherous vanities,
For penitential tears and trembling hopes   455
Exchanged—to equalize in God's pure sight
Monarch and Peasant: be the house redeemed
With its unworldly Votaries, for the sake
Of conquest over sense hourly atchieved
Through faith and meditative reason, resting   460
Upon the word of heaven-imparted Truth
Calmly triumphant; and for humbler claim
Of that imaginative impulse sent
From these majestic floods, yon shining cliffs,
The untransmuted Shapes of many worlds,   465
Cerulean Ether's pure inhabitants;
These forests unapproachable by death,
That shall endure as long as man endures
To think, to hope, to worship, and to feel,

To struggle, to be lost within himself   470
In trepidation; from the blank abyss
To look with bodily eyes, and be consoled."
Not seldom since that moment have I wished
That thou, O Friend! the trouble or the calm
Hadst shared, when, from profane regards apart,   475
In sympathetic reverence we trod
The floor of those dim cloisters, till that hour,
From their foundation, strangers to the presence
Of unrestricted and unthinking Man.
Abroad, how chearingly the sunshine lay   480
Upon the open lawns! Vallombre's groves
Entering, we fed the Soul with darkness, thence
Issued, and with uplifted eyes beheld,
In different quarters of the bending sky,
The Cross of Jesus stand erect, as if   485
Hands of angelic Powers had fixed it there,
Memorial reverenced by a thousand Storms;
Yet then, from the undiscriminating sweep
And rage of one State-whirlwind, insecure.
    'Tis not my present purpose to retrace   490
That variegated journey step by step;
A march it was of military speed,
And earth did change her images and forms
Before us, fast as clouds are changed in heaven.
Day after day, up early and down late,   495
From hill to vale we dropped—from vale to hill
Mounted,—from province on to province swept—
Keen hunters in a chase of fourteen weeks,
Eager as birds of prey, or as a Ship
Upon the stretch when winds are blowing fair.   500
Sweet coverts did we cross of pastoral life,
Enticing Vallies, greeted them and left
Too soon, while yet the very flash and gleam
Of salutation were not passed away.
Oh! sorrow for the Youth who could have seen   505
Unchastened, unsubdued, unawed, unraised
To patriarchal dignity of mind
And pure simplicity of wish and will,

Those sanctified Abodes of peaceful Man;
Pleased (though to hardship born, and compassed round   510
With danger, varying as the seasons change),
Pleased with his daily tasks, or, if not pleased,
Contented, from the moment that the Dawn,
Ah! surely not without attendant gleams
Of soul-illumination, calls him forth   515
To industry, by glistenings flung on rocks
Whose evening shadows lead him to repose.
     Well might a Stranger look with bounding heart
Down on a green Recess, the first I saw
Of those deep haunts, an aboriginal Vale,   520
Quiet, and lorded over, and possessed
By naked huts, wood-built and sown like tents,
Or Indian Cabins over the fresh lawns
And by the river side. That very day,
From a bare ridge we also first beheld   525
Unveiled the summit of Mont Blanc, and grieved
To have a soulless image on the eye
Which had usurped upon a living thought
That never more could be. The wondrous Vale
Of Chamouny stretched far below, and soon   530
With its dumb cataracts, and streams of ice,
A motionless array of mighty waves,
Five rivers broad and vast, made rich amends,
And reconciled us to realities.
There small birds warble from the leafy trees,   535
The eagle soars high in the element;
There doth the Reaper bind the yellow sheaf,
The Maiden spread the hay-cock in the sun,
While Winter like a well-tamed lion walks,
Descending from the Mountain to make sport   540
Among the Cottages by beds of flowers.
     Whate'er in this wide circuit we beheld,
Or heard, was fitted to our unripe state
Of intellect and heart. With such a book
Before our eyes we could not chuse but read   545
Lessons of genuine brotherhood, the plain
And universal reason of mankind,

The truths of Young and Old. Nor, side by side
Pacing, two social Pilgrims, or alone
Each with his humour, could we fail to abound   550
In dreams and fictions pensively composed,
Dejection taken up for pleasure's sake,
And gilded sympathies; the willow wreath,
And sober posies of funereal flowers
Gathered, among those solitudes sublime,   555
From formal gardens of the Lady Sorrow,
Did sweeten many a meditative hour.
      Yet still in me with those soft luxuries
Mixed something of stern mood, an under thirst
Of vigor seldom utterly allayed.   560
And from that source how different a sadness
Would issue, let one incident make known.
When from the Vallais we had turned, and clomb
Along the Simplon's steep and rugged road,
Following a band of Muleteers, we reached   565
A halting-place where all together took
Their noon-tide meal. Hastily rose our Guide,
Leaving *us* at the Board; awhile we lingered,
Then paced the beaten downward way that led
Right to a rough stream's edge and there broke off.   570
The only track now visible was one
That from the torrent's further brink held forth
Conspicuous invitation to ascend
A lofty mountain. After brief delay
Crossing the unbridged stream, that road we took   575
And clomb with eagerness, till anxious fears
Intruded, for we failed to overtake
Our Comrades gone before. By fortunate chance,
While every moment added doubt to doubt,
A Peasant met us, from whose mouth we learned   580
That to the Spot which had perplexed us first
We must descend, and there should find the road,
Which in the stony channel of the Stream
Lay a few steps, and then along its banks,
And that our future course, all plain to sight,   585
Was downwards, with the current of that Stream.

Loth to believe what we so grieved to hear,
For still we had hopes that pointed to the clouds,
We questioned him again, and yet again;
But every word that from the Peasant's lips   590
Came in reply, translated by our feelings,
Ended in this, *that we had crossed the Alps.*
    Imagination—here the Power so called
Through sad incompetence of human speech—
That awful Power rose from the Mind's abyss   595
Like an unfathered vapour that enwraps
At once some lonely Traveller. I was lost,
Halted without an effort to break through;
But to my conscious soul I now can say,
"I recognize thy glory"; in such strength   600
Of usurpation, when the light of sense
Goes out, but with a flash that has revealed
The invisible world, doth Greatness make abode,
There harbours, whether we be young or old;
Our destiny, our being's heart and home,   605
Is with infinitude, and only there;
With hope it is, hope that can never die,
Effort, and expectation, and desire,
And something evermore about to be.
Under such banners militant the Soul   610
Seeks for no trophies, struggles for no spoils,
That may attest her prowess, blest in thoughts
That are their own perfection and reward,
Strong in herself, and in beatitude
That hides her like the mighty flood of Nile   615
Poured from his fount of Abyssinian clouds
To fertilize the whole Egyptian plain.
    The melancholy slackening that ensued
Upon those tidings by the Peasant given
Was soon dislodged; downwards we hurried fast   620
And, with the half-shaped road, which we had missed,
Entered a narrow chasm. The brook and road
Were fellow-Travellers in this gloomy Strait,
And with them did we journey several hours
At a slow pace. The immeasurable height   625

Of woods decaying, never to be decayed,
The stationary blasts of waterfalls,
And in the narrow rent at every turn
Winds thwarting winds, bewildered and forlorn,
The torrents shooting from the clear blue sky,   630
The rocks that muttered close upon our ears,
Black drizzling crags that spake by the way-side
As if a voice were in them, the sick sight
And giddy prospect of the raving stream,
The unfettered clouds, and region of the Heavens,   635
Tumult and peace, the darkness and the light—
Were all like workings of one mind, the features
Of the same face, blossoms upon one tree,
Characters of the great Apocalypse,
The types and symbols of Eternity,   640
Of first and last, and midst, and without end.
    That night our lodging was a House that stood
Alone within the valley, at a point
Where tumbling from aloft a torrent swelled
The rapid stream whose margin we had trod;   645
A dreary Mansion large beyond all need,
With high and spacious rooms, deafened and stunned
By noise of waters, making innocent sleep
Lie melancholy among weary bones.
    Uprisen betimes, our journey we renewed,   650
Led by the stream, ere noon-day magnified
Into a lordly river, broad and deep,
Dimpling along in silent majesty;
With mountains for its neighbours, and in view
Of distant mountains and their snowy tops;   655
And thus proceeding to Locarna's Lake,
Fit resting-place for such a Visitant.
—Locarna, spreading out in width like Heaven,
How dost Thou cleave to the poetic Heart,
Bask in the sunshine of the memory!   660
And Como, thou a treasure whom the earth
Keeps to herself, confined as in a depth
Of Abyssinian privacy! I spake
Of thee, thy chestnut woods, and garden plots

Of Indian corn tended by dark-eyed Maids,   665
Thy lofty steeps, and pathways roofed with vines
Winding from house to house, from town to town,
Sole link that binds them to each other, walks
League after league, and cloistral avenues
Where silence dwells, if music be not there;   670
While yet a Youth undisciplined in verse,
Through fond ambition of that hour, I strove
To chaunt your praise, nor can approach you now
Ungreeted by a more melodious Song
Where tones of Nature smoothed by learned Art   675
May flow in lasting current. Like a breeze
Or sunbeam, over your domain I passed
In motion without pause, but Ye have left
Your beauty with me, a serene accord
Of forms and colors, passive, yet endowed   680
In their submissiveness with power as sweet
And gracious, almost might I dare to say,
As virtue is, or goodness; sweet as love
Or the remembrance of a generous deed,
Or mildest visitations of pure thought   685
When God, the giver of all joy, is thanked
Religiously, in silent blessedness,
Sweet as this last herself, for such it is.
    With those delightful pathways we advanced
For two days' space in presence of the Lake,   690
That, stretching far among the Alps, assumed
A character more stern. The second night,
From sleep awakened, and misled by sound
Of the Church clock telling the hours with strokes
Whose import then we had not learned, we rose   695
By moon-light, doubting not that day was nigh,
And that, meanwhile, by no uncertain path
Along the winding margin of the lake
Led as before, we should behold the scene
Hushed in profound repose. We left the Town   700
Of Gravedona with this hope; but soon
Were lost, bewildered among woods immense,
And on a rock sate down, to wait for day.

An open place it was, and overlooked,
From high, the sullen water far beneath,   705
On which a dull red image of the moon
Lay bedded, changing oftentimes its form
Like an uneasy snake. From hour to hour
We sate, and sate, wondering, as if the Night
Had been ensnared by witchcraft. On the rock   710
At last we stretched our weary limbs for sleep,
But *could not* sleep,—tormented by the stings
Of Insects, which with noise like that of noon
Filled all the woods. The cry of unknown birds;
The mountains, more by blackness visible   715
And their own size, than any outward light;
The breathless wilderness of clouds; the clock
That told with unintelligible voice
The widely-parted hours; the noise of streams;
And sometimes rustling motions nigh at hand   720
That did not leave us free from personal fear;
And lastly the withdrawing moon, that set
Before us while she still was high in heaven;
These were our food; and such a summer night
Followed that pair of golden days, that shed   725
On Como's Lake and all that round it lay
Their fairest, softest, happiest influence.
     But here I must break off, and bid farewell
To days each offering some new sight, or fraught
With some untried adventure, in a course   730
Prolonged till sprinklings of autumnal snow
Checked our unwearied steps. Let this alone
Be mentioned as a parting word, that not
In hollow exultation, dealing out
Hyperboles of praise comparative,   735
Not rich one moment to be poor for ever,
Not prostrate, overborne, as if the mind
Herself were nothing, a mere pensioner
On outward forms, did we in presence stand
Of that magnificent region. On the front   740
Of this whole Song is written, that my heart
Must in such Temple needs have offered up

A different worship. Finally, whate'er
I saw, or heard, or felt, was but a stream
That flowed into a kindred Stream; a gale   745
Confederate with the current of the Soul
To speed my voyage; every sound or sight,
In its degree of power, administered
To grandeur or to tenderness, to the one
Directly, but to tender thoughts, by means   750
Less often instantaneous in effect:
Led me to these by paths that in the main
Were more circuitous, but not less sure
Duly to reach the point marked out by heaven.
    Oh! most beloved Friend, a glorious time,   755
A happy time that was; triumphant looks
Were then the common language of all eyes:
As if awaked from sleep, the Nations hailed
Their great expectancy: the fife of War
Was then a spirit-stirring sound indeed,   760
A black-bird's whistle in a budding grove.
We left the Swiss exulting in the fate
Of their near Neighbours: and, when shortening fast
Our pilgrimage, nor distant far from home,
We crossed the Brabant Armies, on the fret   765
For battle in the cause of Liberty.
A Stripling, scarcely of the household then
Of social life, I looked upon these things
As from a distance; heard, and saw, and felt,
Was touched, but with no intimate concern;   770
I seemed to move among them, as a bird
Moves through the air, or as a fish pursues
Its sport or feeds in its proper element;
I wanted not that joy, I did not need
Such help; the ever-living Universe,   775
Turn where I might, was opening out its glories;
And the independent Spirit of pure Youth
Called forth, at every season, new delights
Spread round my steps like sunshine o'er green fields.

BOOK SEVENTH
RESIDENCE IN LONDON

Six changeful years have vanished since I first
Poured out (saluted by that quickening breeze
Which met me issuing from the City's Walls)
A glad preamble to this verse: I sang
Aloud with fervour irresistible   5
Of short-lived transport,—like a torrent bursting
From a black thunder cloud, down Scafell's side
To rush and disappear. But soon broke forth
(So willed the Muse) a less impetuous Stream
That flowed awhile with unabating strength,   10
Then stopped for years; not audible again
Before last primrose-time. Beloved Friend!
The assurance which then cheared some heavy thoughts
On thy departure to a foreign Land
Has failed,—too slowly moves the promised Work;   15
Through the whole Summer have I been at rest,
Partly from voluntary holiday
And part through outward hinderance. But I heard,
After the hour of sunset yestereven,
Sitting within doors between light and dark,   20
A choir of redbreasts, gathered somewhere near
My threshold, Minstrels from the distant woods
Sent in on Winter's service, to announce,
With preparation artful and benign,
That the rough Lord had left the surly north   25
On his accustomed journey. The delight
Due to this timely notice unawares
Smote me, and, listening, I in whispers said,
"Ye heartsome Choristers, ye and I will be
Associates, and unscared by blustering winds   30
Will chaunt together." Thereafter, as the shades
Of twilight deepened, going forth I spied
A glow-worm underneath a dusky plume
Or canopy of yet unwithered fern
Clear-shining, like a Hermit's taper seen   35
Through a thick forest. Silence touched me here
No less than sound had done before; the Child

Of Summer, lingering, shining by herself,
The voiceless worm on the unfrequented hills,
Seemed sent on the same errand with the Choir   40
Of Winter that had warbled at my door;
And the whole year breathed tenderness and love.
        The last night's genial feeling overflowed
Upon this morning, and my favourite Grove,
Tossing in sunshine its dark boughs aloft   45
As if to make the strong wind visible,
Wakes in me agitations like its own,
A spirit friendly to the Poet's task,
Which we will now resume with lively hope,
Nor checked by aught of tamer argument   50
That lies before us, needful to be told.
        Returned from that excursion, soon I bade
Farewell for ever to the sheltered seats
Of gowned Students, quitted Hall and Bower
And every comfort of that privileged ground,   55
Well pleased to pitch a vagrant Tent among
The unfenced regions of society.
        Yet undetermined to what course of life
I should adhere, and seeming to possess
A little space of intermediate time   60
At full command, to London first I turned,
In no disturbance of excessive hope,
By personal ambition unenslaved,
Frugal as there was need, and, though self-willed,
From dangerous passions free. Three years had flown   65
Since I had felt in heart and soul the shock
Of the huge Town's first presence, and had paced
Her endless streets, a transient visitant.
Now, fixed amid that concourse of mankind
Where Pleasure whirls about incessantly,   70
Or life and labour seem but one, I filled
An Idler's place—an Idler well content
To have a house (what matter for a home?)
That owned him; living chearfully abroad,
With unchecked fancy ever on the stir,   75
And all my young affections out of doors.

There was a time, when whatsoe'er is feigned
Of airy palaces and gardens built
By Genii of Romance; or hath in grave
Authentic history been set forth of Rome,   80
Alcairo, Babylon, or Persepolis,
Or given upon report by Pilgrim Friars
Of golden Cities ten months' journey deep
Among Tartarean Wilds, fell short, far short,
Of what my fond simplicity believed   85
And thought of London; held me by a chain
Less strong of wonder and obscure delight.
Whether the bolt of childhood's Fancy shot
For me beyond its ordinary mark,
'Twere vain to ask, but in our flock of Boys   90
Was one, a Cripple from his birth, whom Chance
Summoned from School to London; fortunate
And envied Traveller! When the Boy returned
After short absence, curiously I scanned
His mien and person, nor was free, in sooth,   95
From disappointment, not to find some change
In look and air, from that new region brought
As if from fairy land. Much I questioned him,
And every word he uttered, on my ears
Fell flatter than a caged Parrot's note,   100
That answers unexpectedly awry,
And mocks the Prompter's listening. Marvellous things
Had Vanity (quick Spirit that appears
Almost as deeply seated and as strong
In a Child's heart as Fear itself) conceived   105
For my enjoyment. Would that I could now
Recal what then I pictured to myself
Of mitred Prelates, Lords in ermine clad,
The King and the King's Palace, and, not last
Nor least, heaven bless him! the renowned Lord Mayor;   110
Dreams not unlike to those which once begot
A change of purpose in young Whittington
When he, a friendless and a drooping Boy,
Sate on a Stone, and heard the bells speak out
Articulate music. Above all, one thought   115

Baffled my understanding, how men lived
Even next-door neighbours, as we say, yet still
Strangers, nor knowing each the other's name.
—Oh wondrous power of words, by simple faith
Licenced to take the meaning that we love!   120
Vauxhall and Ranelagh, I then had heard
Of your green groves, and wilderness of lamps
Dimming the stars, fire-works magical,
And gorgeous Ladies under splendid Domes
Floating in dance, or warbling high in air   125
The Songs of Spirits! Nor had Fancy fed
With less delight upon that other class
Of marvels, broad-day wonders permanent;
The River proudly bridged; the dizzy top
And Whispering Gallery of St Paul's; the Tombs   130
Of Westminster; the Giants of Guildhall;
Bedlam, and those carved Maniacs at her gates
Perpetually recumbent; Statues, Man
And the horse under him, in gilded pomp,
Adorning flowery Gardens 'mid vast squares;   135
The Monument, and that chamber of the Tower
Where England's Sovereigns sit in long array
Their Steeds bestriding, every mimic Shape
Cased in the gleaming mail the Monarch wore,
Whether for gorgeous tournament addressed   140
Or life, or death, upon the battle field.
Those bold Imaginations in due time
Had vanished, leaving others in their stead;
And now I looked upon the living scene,
Familiarly perused it, oftentimes,   145
In spite of strongest disappointment, pleased
Through courteous self-submission, as a tax
Paid to the object by prescriptive right.
    Rise up, thou monstrous Ant-hill on the plain
Of a too busy world! Before me flow,   150
Thou endless stream of men and moving things!
Thy every day appearance as it strikes—
With wonder heightened or sublimed by awe—
On Strangers, of all ages,—the quick dance

Of colors, lights, and forms; the deafening din;   155
The comers and the goers face to face,
Face after face; the String of dazzling wares,
Shop after Shop, with Symbols, blazoned Names,
And all the Tradesman's honors overhead;
Here, fronts of houses, like a title-page,   160
With letters huge inscribed from top to toe:
Stationed above the door, like guardian Saints,
There, allegoric shapes, female or male;
Or physiognomies of real men,
Land-Warriors, Kings, or Admirals of the Sea,   165
Boyle, Shakespeare, Newton; or the attractive head
Of some Quack-Doctor, famous in his day.
    Meanwhile the roar continues, till at length,
Escaped as from an enemy, we turn
Abruptly into some sequestered nook,   170
Still as a sheltered place when winds blow loud!
At leisure thence through tracts of thin resort,
And sights and sounds that come at intervals,
We take our way: a raree-shew is here,
With Children gathered round; another street   175
Presents a Company of dancing-dogs;
Or Dromedary, with an antic pair
Of Monkies on his back,—a minstrel band
Of Savoyards,—or, single and alone,
An English ballad-singer. Private Courts,   180
Gloomy as coffins; and unsightly lanes
Thrilled by some female vendor's scream, belike
The very shrillest of all London Cries,
May then entangle our impatient steps
Conducted through those labyrinths unawares   185
To priviledged Regions and inviolate,
Where, from their airy lodges, studious Lawyers
Look out on waters, walks, and gardens green.
    Thence back into the throng, until we reach,
Following the tide that slackens by degrees,   190
Some half-frequented scene where wider streets
Bring straggling breezes of suburban air.
Here files of ballads dangle from dead walls;

Advertisements of giant size from high
Press forward in all colors on the sight;   195
These bold in conscious merit, lower down
That, fronted with a most imposing word,
Is, peradventure, one in masquerade.
As on the broadening Causeway we advance,
Behold, turned upwards, a face hard and strong   200
In lineaments, and red with overtoil;
'Tis one encountered here and every-where,
A travelling Cripple by the trunk cut short,
And stumping on his arms. In Sailor's garb,
Another lies at length beside a range   205
Of well-formed characters, with chalk inscribed
Upon the smooth flat stones: the Nurse is here,
The Bachelor that loves to sun himself,
The military Idler, and the Dame
That fieldward takes her walk, with decent steps.   210
  Now homeward through the thickening hubbub, where
See, among less distinguishable shapes,
The begging Scavenger, with hat in hand;
The Italian, as he thrids his way with care,
Steadying, far-seen, a frame of Images   215
Upon his head; with basket at his waist
The Jew; the stately and slow-moving Turk
With freight of slippers piled beneath his arm!
  —Enough—the mighty concourse I surveyed
With no unthinking mind, well pleased to note   220
Among the crowd, all specimens of man,
Through all the colors which the sun bestows
And every character of form and face;
The Swede, the Russian; from the genial South,
The Frenchman and the Spaniard; from remote   225
America, the Hunter-indian; Moors,
Malays, Lascars, the Tartar, the Chinese,
And Negro Ladies in white muslin Gowns.
  At leisure then I viewed from day to day
The Spectacles within doors—birds and beasts   230
Of every nature, and strange Plants convened
From every clime; and next, those sights that ape

The absolute presence of reality,
Expressing, as in mirror, sea and land,
And what earth is, and what she hath to shew.   235
I do not here allude to subtlest craft
By means refined attaining purest ends,
But imitations fondly made in plain
Confession of Man's weakness and his loves;
Whether the Painter, whose ambitious skill   240
Submits to nothing less than taking in
A whole horizon's circuit, do, with power
Like that of angels or commissioned Spirits,
Fix us upon some lofty Pinnacle,
Or in a Ship on Waters, with a World   245
Of Life, and life-like mockery, beneath,
Above, behind, far-stretching, and before;
Or more mechanic Artist represent
By scale exact, in model, wood or clay,
From blended colors also borrowing help,   250
Some miniature of famous Spots or Things,
St Peter's Church, or, more aspiring aim,
In microscopic vision Rome herself;
Or haply some choice rural haunt, the Falls
Of Tivoli, and high upon that Steep   255
The Sybil's mouldering Temple! every Tree,
Villa—or Cottage lurking among rocks
Throughout the landscape, tuft, stone, scratch minute—
All that the Traveller sees when he is there.
    Add to these exhibitions, mute and still,   260
Others of wider scope, where living men,
Music, and shifting pantomimic scenes
Diversified the allurement. Need I fear
To mention by its name, as in degree
Lowest of these, and humblest in attempt,   265
Yet richly graced with honors of her own,
Half-rural Sadler's Wells? Though at that time
Intolerant, as is the way of Youth,
Unless itself be pleased, here more than once
Taking my seat, I saw (nor blush to add,   270
With ample recompense) Giants and Dwarfs,

Clowns, Conjurers, Posture-masters, Harlequins,
Amid the uproar of the rabblement,
Perform their feats. Nor was it mean delight
To watch crude Nature work in untaught minds;   275
To note the laws and progress of belief;
Though obstinate on this way, yet on that
How willingly we travel, and how far!
To have, for instance, brought upon the scene
The Champion Jack the Giant-Killer—Lo!   280
He dons his Coat of darkness; on the Stage
Walks, and achieves his wonders, from the eye
Of living mortal covert, as the moon
"Hid in her vacant interlunar Cave."
Delusion bold! and how can it be wrought?   285
The garb he wears is black as death, the word
Invisible flames forth upon his chest!
    Here too were "forms and pressures of the time,"
Rough, bold, as Grecian Comedy displayed
When Art was young, dramas of living Men;   290
And recent things yet warm with life—a Sea-fight,
Ship-wreck, or some domestic incident
Divulged by Truth, and magnified by Fame,
Such as the daring Brotherhood, of late,
Set forth, too serious theme for that light place!   295
I mean, O distant Friend! a story drawn
From our own ground, the Maid of Buttermere,
And how, unfaithful to a virtuous Wife
Deserted and deceived, the Spoiler came,
And wooed the artless Daughter of the Hills,   300
And wedded her, in cruel mockery
Of love and marriage bonds. These words to thee
Must needs bring back the moment when we first,
Ere the broad world rang with the Maiden's name,
Beheld her serving at the Cottage Inn,   305
Both stricken, as she entered or withdrew,
With admiration of her modest mien
And carriage, marked by unexampled grace.
Not unfamiliarly we since that time
Have seen her; her discretion have observed,   310

Her just opinions, delicate reserve,
Her patience, and humility of mind
Unspoiled by commendation, and the excess
Of public notice—an offensive light
To a meek spirit, suffering inwardly.   315
    From this memorial Tribute, to my Theme
I was returning, when with sundry Forms
Commingled, Shapes which meet me in the way
That we must tread, thy Image rose again,
Maiden of Buttermere! She lives in peace,   320
Upon the Spot where she was born and reared;
Without contamination doth she live
In quietness, without anxiety.
Beside the mountain Chapel sleeps in earth
Her new-born Infant, fearless as a Lamb   325
That, thither driven from some unsheltered place,
Rests underneath the little rock-like Pile
When storms are raging. Happy are they both—
Mother and Child! These feelings, in themselves
Trite, do yet scarcely seem so when I think   330
On those ingenuous moments of our youth
Ere we have learnt by use to slight the crimes
And sorrows of the world. Those simple days
Are now my theme, and, foremost of the scenes
Which yet survive in memory, appears   335
One at whose centre sate a lovely boy,
A sportive Infant, who, for six months' space,
Not more, had been of age to deal about
Articulate prattle; Child as beautiful
As ever clung around a Mother's neck,   340
Or Father fondly gazed upon with pride!
There too, conspicuous for stature tall
And large dark eyes, beside her infant stood
The Mother—but, upon her cheeks diffused,
False tints too well accorded with the glare   345
From Play-house lustres thrown without reserve
On every Object near. The Boy had been
The pride and pleasure of all lookers-on
In whatsoever place; but seemed in this

A sort of Alien scattered from the clouds.   350
Of lusty vigour, more than Infantine,
He was in limb, in cheek a summer rose
Just three parts blown—a Cottage Child, if e'er
By Cottage-door on breezy mountain side,
Or in some sheltering Vale, was seen a Babe   355
By Nature's gifts so favored. Upon a Board
Decked with refreshments had this Child been placed,
His little Stage in the vast Theatre,
And there he sate, surrounded with a Throng
Of chance Spectators, chiefly dissolute Men   360
And shameless women; treated and caressed,
Ate, drank, and with the fruit and glasses played,
While oaths and laughter and indecent speech
Were rife about him as the songs of birds
Contending after showers. The Mother now   365
Is fading out of memory, but I see
The lovely Boy as I beheld him then,
Among the wretched and the falsely gay,
Like one of those who walked with hair unsinged
Amid the fiery furnace. Charms and spells   370
Muttered on black and spiteful instigation
Have stopped, as some believe, the kindliest growths;
Ah, with how different spirit might a prayer
Have been preferred, that this fair Creature, checked
By special privilege of Nature's love,   375
Should in his Childhood be detained for ever!
But with its universal freight the tide
Hath rolled along, and this bright Innocent,
Mary! may now have lived till he could look
With envy on thy nameless Babe, that sleeps,   380
Beside the mountain Chapel, undisturbed!
    Four rapid years had scarcely then been told
Since, travelling southward from our pastoral hills,
I heard, and for the first time in my life,
The voice of Woman utter blasphemy;   385
Saw Woman as she is to open shame
Abandoned, and the pride of public vice.
I shuddered, for a barrier seemed at once

Thrown in, that from humanity divorced
Humanity, splitting the race of Man   390
In twain, yet leaving the same outward Form.
Distress of mind ensued upon the sight,
And ardent meditation. Later years
Brought to such spectacle a milder sadness,
Feelings of pure commiseration, grief   395
For the individual, and the overthrow
Of her Soul's beauty; farther I was then
But seldom led, or wished to go; in truth
The sorrow of the passion stopped me there.
     But let me now, less moved, in order take   400
Our argument. Enough is said to shew
How casual incidents of real life,
Observed where pastime only had been sought,
Outweighed, or put to flight, the set Events
And measured Passions of the Stage, albeit   405
By Siddons trod in the fullness of her power.
Yet was the Theatre my dear delight;
The very gilding, lamps and painted scrolls,
And all the mean upholstery of the place
Wanted not animation when the tide   410
Of pleasure ebbed but to return as fast
With the ever shifting Figures of the scene,
Solemn or gay: whether some beauteous Dame
Advanced in radiance through a deep recess
Of thick entangled forest, like the Moon   415
Opening the clouds; or sovereign King, announced
With flourishing Trumpet, came in full-blown State
Of the World's greatness, winding round with Train
Of Courtiers, Banners, and a length of Guards;
Or Captive led in abject weeds, and jingling   420
His slender manacles; or romping Girl
Bounced, leapt, and pawed the air; or mumbling Sire,
A scare-crow pattern of old Age, dressed up
In all the tatters of infirmity
All loosely put together, hobbled in   425
Stumping upon a Cane, with which he smites,
From time to time, the solid boards, and makes them

Prate somewhat loudly of the whereabout
Of one so overloaded with his years.
But what of this? the laugh, the grin, grimace,   430
The antics striving to outstrip each other,
Were all received, the least of them not lost,
With an unmeasured welcome. Through the night,
Between the shew, and many-headed mass
Of the Spectators, and each several nook   435
Filled with its fray or brawl, how eagerly,
And with what flashes, as it were, the mind
Turned this way, that way! Sportive and alert,
And watchful, as a kitten when at play
While winds are eddying round her, among straws   440
And rustling leaves. Enchanting age and sweet!
Romantic almost, looked at through a space
How small of intervening years! For then,
Though surely no mean progress had been made
In meditations holy and sublime,   445
Yet something of a girlish child-like gloss
Of novelty survived for scenes like these;
Enjoyment haply handed down from times
When at a Country-playhouse, some rude Barn
Tricked out for that proud use, if I perchance   450
Caught on a summer evening, through a chink
In the old wall, an unexpected glimpse
Of daylight, the bare thought of where I was
Gladdened me more than if I had been led
Into a dazzling Cavern of Romance,   455
Crowded with Genii busy among works
Not to be looked at by the common sun.
　　The matter that detains us now may seem
To many neither dignified enough
Nor arduous; yet will *not* be scorned by them   460
Who, looking inward, have observed the ties
That bind the perishable hours of life
Each to the other, and the curious props
By which the world of memory and thought
Exists, and is sustained. More lofty themes,   465
Such as at least do wear a prouder face,

Solicit our regard; but when I think
Of these I feel the imaginative Power
Languish within me; even then it slept
When, pressed by tragic sufferings, the heart   470
Was more than full;—amid my sobs and tears
It slept, even in the pregnant season of Youth:
For though I was most passionately moved,
And yielded to all changes of the scene
With an obsequious promptness, yet the storm   475
Passed not beyond the suburbs of the mind;
Save when realities of act and mien,
The incarnation of the Spirits that move
In harmony amid the Poet's world,
Rose to ideal grandeur, or, called forth   480
By power of contrast, made me recognize,
As at a glance, the things which I had shaped,
And yet not shaped, had seen, and scarcely seen,
When, having closed the mighty Shakespeare's page,
I mused, and thought, and felt in solitude.   485
　　　　Pass we from entertainments that are such
Professedly, to others titled higher,
Yet, in the estimate of Youth at least,
More near akin to those than names imply;
I mean the brawls of Lawyers in their Courts   490
Before the ermined Judge; or that great Stage
Where Senators, tongue-favored men, perform,
Admired and envied. Oh! the beating heart,
When one among the prime of these rose up,
One, of whose name from Childhood we had heard   495
Familiarly, a household term, like those,
The Bedfords, Glo'sters, Salisburys of old
Whom the fifth Harry talks of. Silence! hush!
This is no trifler, no short-flighted wit,
No stammerer of a minute, painfully   500
Delivered, No! the Orator hath yoked
The Hours, like young Aurora, to his Car:
Thrice welcome Presence! how can patience e'er
Grow weary of attending on a track
That kindles with such glory! All are charmed,   505

Astonished; like a Hero in Romance,
He winds away his never-ending horn;
Words follow words, sense seems to follow sense;
What memory and what logic! till the Strain
Transcendent, superhuman as it seemed,   510
Grows tedious even in a young Man's ear.
    —Genius of Burke! forgive the pen seduced
By specious wonders, and too slow to tell
Of what the ingenuous, what bewildered Men
Beginning to mistrust their boastful guides,   515
And wise men, willing to grow wiser, caught,
Rapt auditors! from thy most eloquent tongue—
Now mute, for ever mute, in the cold grave.
I see him, old but vigorous in age,
Stand, like an Oak whose stag-horn branches start   520
Out of its leafy brow, the more to awe
The younger brethren of the grove. But some—
While he forewarns, denounces, launches forth,
Against all systems built on abstract rights,
Keen ridicule; the majesty proclaims   525
Of Institutes and Laws hallowed by Time;
Declares the vital power of social ties
Endeared by Custom; and with high disdain
Exploding upstart Theory, insists
Upon the Allegiance to which Men are born—   530
Some—say at once a froward multitude—
Murmur (for truth is hated, where not loved)
As the winds fret within the Eolian cave,
Galled by their Monarch's chain. The times were big
With ominous change which, night by night, provoked   535
Keen struggles, and black clouds of passion raised;
But memorable moments intervened
When Wisdom, like the Goddess from Jove's brain,
Broke forth in armour of resplendent words,
Startling the Synod. Could a Youth, and one   540
In ancient story versed, whose breast had heaved
Under the weight of classic eloquence,
Sit, see, and hear, unthankful, uninspired?
    Nor did the Pulpit's oratory fail

To achieve its higher triumph. Not unfelt   545
Were its admonishments, nor lightly heard
The awful truths delivered thence by tongues
Endowed with various power to search the soul;
Yet ostentation, domineering, oft
Poured forth harangues, how sadly out of place!   550
There have I seen a comely Bachelor,
Fresh from a toilette of two hours, ascend
His Rostrum, with seraphic glance look up;
And, in a tone elaborately low
Beginning, lead his voice through many a maze,   555
A minuet course; and, winding up his mouth,
From time to time, into an orifice
Most delicate, a lurking eyelet, small
And only not invisible, again
Open it out, diffusing thence a smile   560
Of rapt irradiation, exquisite.
Meanwhile the Evangelists, Isaiah, Job,
Moses, and he who penned, the other day,
The Death of Abel, Shakespear, and the Bard
Whose genius spangled o'er a gloomy theme   565
With fancies thick as his inspiring stars;
And Ossian (doubt not, 'tis the naked truth)
Summoned from streamy Morven, each and all
Would in their turn lend ornaments and flowers
To entwine the crook of eloquence that helped   570
This pretty Shepherd, pride of all the plains,
To rule, and guide his captivated Flock.
    I glance but at a few conspicuous marks;
Leaving a thousand others that in hall,
Court, Theatre, Conventicle, or Shop,   575
In public Room or Private, Park or Street,
Each fondly reared on his own Pedestal,
Looked out for admiration. Folly, vice,
Extravagance in gesture, mien, and dress,
And all the strife of singularity; .   580
Lies to the ear, and lies to every sense,
Of these, and of the living shapes they wear,
There is no end. Such Candidates for regard,

Although well pleased to be where they were found,
I did not hunt after, nor greatly prize,   585
Nor made unto myself a secret boast
Of reading them with quick and curious eye;
But as a common produce, things that are
Today—tomorrow will be, took of them
Such willing note as, on some errand bound   590
That asks not speed, a Traveller might bestow
On sea-shells that bestrew the sandy beach,
Or daisies swarming through the fields of June.
　　But foolishness and madness in parade,
Though most at home in this their dear domain,   595
Are scattered every where; no rarities
Even to the rudest novice of the Schools.
Me rather it employed to note, and keep
In memory, those individual sights
Of courage, or integrity, or truth,   600
Or tenderness, which, there set off by foil,
Appeared more touching. One will I select,
A Father—for he bore that sacred name!
Him saw I sitting in an open Square,
Upon a corner-stone of that low wall   605
Wherein were fixed the iron pales that fenced
A spacious Grass-plot: there in silence sate
This one Man, with a sickly Babe outstretched
Upon his knee, whom he had thither brought
For sunshine, and to breathe the fresher air.   610
Of those who passed, and me who looked at him,
He took no heed; but in his brawny arms
(The Artificer was to the elbow bare,
And from his work this moment had been stolen)
He held the Child, and, bending over it,   615
As if he were afraid both of the sun
And of the air which he had come to seek,
Eyed the poor Babe with love unutterable.
　　As the black storm upon the mountain top
Sets off the sunbeam in the Valley, so   620
That huge fermenting Mass of human-kind
Serves as a solemn background or relief

To single forms and objects, whence they draw,
For feeling and contemplative regard,
More than inherent liveliness and power.   625
How oft amid those overflowing streets
Have I gone forward with the Crowd, and said
Unto myself, "The face of every one
That passes by me is a mystery!"
Thus have I looked, nor ceased to look, oppressed   630
By thoughts of what and whither, when and how,
Until the Shapes before my eyes became
A second-sight procession, such as glides
Over still mountains, or appears in dreams.
And once, far-travelled in such mood, beyond   635
The reach of common indication, lost
Amid the moving pageant, I was smitten
Abruptly with the view (a sight not rare)
Of a blind Beggar who, with upright face,
Stood propped against a Wall; upon his chest   640
Wearing a written paper to explain
His Story, whence he came, and who he was.
Caught by the spectacle, my mind turned round
As with the might of waters; an apt type
This Label seemed, of the utmost we can know   645
Both of ourselves and of the universe;
And on the Shape of that unmoving Man,
His steadfast face, and sightless eyes, I gazed
As if admonished from another world.
    Though reared upon the base of outward things,   650
Structures like these the excited Spirit mainly
Builds for herself. Scenes different there are,
Full-formed, that take, with small internal help,
Possession of the faculties—the peace
That comes with night; the deep solemnity   655
Of Nature's intermediate hours of rest,
When the great tide of human life stands still,
The business of the day to come—unborn,
Of that gone by—locked up as in the grave;
The blended calmness of the heavens and earth,   660
Moonlight, and stars, and empty streets, and sounds

Unfrequent as in deserts: at late hours
Of winter evenings when unwholesome rains
Are falling hard, with people yet astir,
The feeble salutation from the voice   665
Of some unhappy woman, now and then
Heard as we pass; when no one looks about,
Nothing is listened to. But these, I fear,
Are falsely catalogued; things that are, are not,
As the mind answers to them, or the heart   670
Is prompt or slow to feel. What say you, then,
To times when half the City shall break out
Full of one passion, vengeance, rage, or fear?
To executions, to a Street on fire,
Mobs, riots, or rejoicings? From these sights   675
Take one, that annual Festival, the Fair
Holden where Martyrs suffered in past time,
And named of St Bartholomew; there see
A work completed to our hands, that lays,
If any spectacle on earth can do,   680
The whole creative powers of Man asleep!
For once the Muse's help will we implore,
And she shall lodge us, wafted on her wings,
Above the press and danger of the Crowd,
Upon some Shewman's platform. What a shock   685
For eyes and ears! what anarchy and din
Barbarian and infernal—a phantasma
Monstrous in color, motion, shape, sight, sound!
Below, the open space, through every nook
Of the wide area, twinkles, is alive   690
With heads; the midway region and above
Is thronged with staring pictures, and huge scrolls,
Dumb proclamations of the Prodigies!
With chattering monkeys dangling from their poles,
And children whirling in their roundabouts;   695
With those that stretch the neck, and strain the eyes;
And crack the voice in rivalship, the crowd
Inviting; with buffoons against buffoons
Grimacing, writhing, screaming, him who grinds
The hurdy-gurdy, at the fiddle weaves,   700

Rattles the salt-box, thumps the Kettle-drum;
And him who at the trumpet puffs his cheeks;
The silver-collared Negro with his timbrel;
Equestrians, tumblers, women, girls, and boys,
Blue-breeched, pink-vested, with high-towering plumes.   705
—All moveables of wonder from all parts
Are here, Albinos, painted-Indians, Dwarfs,
The Horse of Knowledge, and the learned Pig,
The Stone-eater, the Man that swallows fire—
Giants; Ventriloquists, the Invisible-girl,   710
The Bust that speaks, and moves its goggling eyes,
The Wax-work, Clock-work, all the marvellous craft
Of modern Merlins, Wild-beasts, Puppet-shews,
All out-o'th'-way, far-fetched, perverted things,
All freaks of Nature, all Promethean thoughts   715
Of man; his dullness, madness, and their feats,
All jumbled up together, to compose
A Parliament of Monsters. Tents and Booths,
Meanwhile, as if the whole were one vast mill,
Are vomiting, receiving, on all sides,   720
Men, Women, three-years' Children, Babes in arms.
    Oh blank confusion! true epitome
Of what the mighty City is herself
To thousands upon thousands of her Sons,
Living amid the same perpetual whirl   725
Of trivial objects, melted and reduced
To one identity, by differences
That have no law, no meaning, and no end;
Oppression under which even highest minds
Must labour, whence the strongest are not free!   730
But though the picture weary out the eye,
By nature an unmanageable sight,
It is not wholly so to him who looks
In steadiness, who hath among least things
An undersense of greatest; sees the parts   735
As parts, but with a feeling of the whole.
This, of all acquisitions first, awaits
On sundry and most widely different modes
Of education; nor with least delight

On that through which I passed. Attention springs,   740
And comprehensiveness and memory flow,
From early converse with the works of God,
Among all regions; chiefly where appear
Most obviously simplicity and power.
Think, how the everlasting streams and woods,   745
Stretched and still stretching far and wide, exalt
The roving Indian: on his desart sands
What grandeur not unfelt, what pregnant show
Of beauty meets the sun-burnt Arab's eye!
And as the Sea propels from Zone to Zone   750
Its currents, magnifies its Shoals of life
Beyond all compass spread, and sends aloft
Armies of Clouds, even so, its powers and aspects
Shape for Mankind, by principles as fixed,
The views and aspirations of the Soul   755
To majesty. Like Virtue have the forms
Perennial of the ancient hills; nor less
The changeful language of their countenances
Quickens the slumbering mind, and aids the thoughts,
However multitudinous, to move   760
With order and relation. This, if still,
As hitherto, in freedom I may speak,
And the same perfect *openness of mind*,
Not violating any just restraint,
As may be hoped, of real modesty,   765
This did I feel in London's vast Domain;
The Spirit of Nature was upon me there;
The Soul of Beauty and enduring life
Vouchsafed her inspiration; and diffused,
Through meagre lines and colours, and the press   770
Of self-destroying transitory things,
Composure, and ennobling harmony.

BOOK EIGHTH
RETROSPECT, LOVE OF NATURE LEADING TO LOVE OF MAN

What sounds are those, Helvellyn, that are heard
Up to thy summit? Through the depth of air
Ascending, as if distance had the power

To make the sounds more audible; what Crowd
Covers, or sprinkles o'er, yon Village green?   5
Crowd seems it, solitary hill! to thee,
Though but a little Family of Men,
Shepherds and Tillers of the ground—betimes
Assembled with their Children and their Wives,
And here and there a Stranger interspersed.   10
They hold a rustic Fair:—a festival
Such as, on this side now and now on that,
Repeated through his tributary Vales,
Helvellyn, in the silence of his rest,
Sees annually, if clouds towards either ocean   15
Blown from their favorite resting-place, or mists
Dissolved have left him an unshrouded head.
Delightful day it is for all who dwell
In this secluded Glen, and eagerly
They give it welcome. Long ere heat of noon,   20
From *Byre* or field the Kine were brought; the sheep
Are penned in Cotes, the chaffering is begun.
The Heifer lows, uneasy at the voice
Of a new Master; bleat the Flocks aloud;
Booths are there none; a Stall or two is here;   25
A lame Man, or a blind, the one to beg,
The other to make music; hither, too,
From far, with Basket slung upon her arm
Of Hawker's wares, books, pictures, combs, and pins,
Some aged Woman finds her way again,   30
Year after year, a punctual Visitant!
There also stands a Speech-maker by rote,
Pulling the strings of his boxed raree-shew;
And in the lapse of many years may come
Prouder Itinerant, Mountebank, or He   35
Whose wonders in a covered Wain lie hid.
But One there is, the loveliest of them all,
Some sweet Lass of the Valley, looking out
For gains, and who that sees her would not buy?
Fruits of her Father's Orchard are her wares,   40
And with the ruddy produce she walks round
Among the crowd, half-pleased with, half-ashamed

Of her new office, blushing restlessly.
The Children now are rich, for the old today
Are generous as the young, and if, content   45
With looking on, some ancient wedded Pair
Sit in the shade together, while they gaze,
"A cheerful smile unbends the wrinkled brow,
The days departed start again to life,
And all the scenes of Childhood reappear,   50
Faint, but more tranquil, like the changing sun
To him who slept at noon and wakes at eve."[1]
Thus gaiety and cheerfulness prevail,
Spreading from young to old, from old to young,
And no one seems to want his part.—Immense   55
Is the Recess, the circumambient World
Magnificent by which they are embraced.
They move about upon the soft green turf:
How little they, they and their doings seem,
And all that they can further or obstruct!   60
Through utter weakness pitiably dear,
As tender Infants are: and yet how great!
For all things serve them: them the morning light
Loves as it glistens on the silent rocks,
And them the silent rocks, which now from high   65
Look down upon them: the reposing Clouds,
The wild Brooks prattling from invisible haunts,
And old Helvellyn, conscious of the stir
Which animates this day their calm abode.
    With deep devotion, Nature, did I feel,   70
In that enormous City's turbulent world
Of men and things, what benefit lowed
To Thee and those Domains of rural peace
Where to the sense of beauty first my heart
Was opened; tract more exquisitely fair   75
Than that famed Paradise of ten thousand trees,
Or Gehol's matchless Gardens, for delight
Of the Tartarian Dynasty, composed
(Beyond that mighty Wall, not fabulous,

---

1   "These lines are from a descriptive Poem—'Malvern Hills'—by one of Mr. Wordsworth's oldest friends, Mr. Joseph Cottle." This note appears in the first edition of *The Prelude*, 1850, prepared for the press by his nephew Christopher Wordsworth, Jr.

China's stupendous mound) by patient toil   80
Of myriads and boon Nature's lavish help;
There, in a clime from widest empire chosen,
Fulfilling (could enchantment have done more?)
A sumptuous dream of flowery lawns, with Domes
Of pleasure sprinkled over, shady dells   85
For Eastern Monasteries, sunny Mounts
With temples crested, bridges, gondolas,
Rocks, dens;—and groves of foliage taught to melt
Into each other their obsequious hues,
Vanished and vanishing in subtile chase,   90
Too fine to be pursued; or standing forth
In no discordant opposition, strong
And gorgeous as the colors side by side
Bedded among rich plumes of Tropic birds;
And mountains over all, embracing all;   95
And all the Landscape endlessly enriched
With waters running, falling, or asleep.
       But lovelier far than this the Paradise
Where I was reared; in Nature's primitive gifts
Favoured no less, and more to every sense   100
Delicious, seeing that the sun and sky,
The elements, and seasons as they change,
Do find a worthy fellow-labourer there;
Man free, man working for himself, with choice
Of time, and place, and object; by his wants,   105
His comforts, native occupations, cares,
Chearfully led to individual ends
Or social, and still followed by a train
Unwooed, unthought-of even, simplicity
And beauty, and inevitable grace.   110
       Yea, when a glimpse of those imperial bowers
Would to a Child be transport over-great,
When but a half-hour's roam through such a place
Would leave behind a dance of images
That shall break in upon his sleep for weeks;   115
Even then the common haunts of the green earth
And ordinary interests of man
Which they embosom, all without regard

As both may seem, are fastening on the heart
Insensibly, each with the other's help.   120
    For me, when my affections first were led
From kindred, friends, and playmates, to partake
Love for the human creature's absolute self,
That noticeable kindliness of heart
Sprang out of fountains, there abounding most,   125
Where sovereign Nature dictated the tasks
And occupations which her beauty adorned;
And Shepherds were the Men that pleased me first.
Not such as Saturn ruled 'mid Latian wilds,
With laws and arts so tempered, that their lives   130
Left, even to us toiling in this late day,
A bright tradition of the golden age;
Not such as, 'mid Arcadian fastnesses
Sequestered, handed down among themselves
Felicity in Grecian song renowned;—   135
Nor such as, when an adverse fate had driven
From house and home the courtly Band, whose fortunes
Entered, with Shakespeare's genius, the wild woods
Of Arden, amid sunshine or in shade,
Culled the best fruits of Time's uncounted hours,   140
Ere Phœbe sighed for the false Ganymede;
Or there, where Perdita and Florizel
Together danced, Queen of the feast and King;
Nor such as Spenser fabled.— True it is
That I had heard (what he perhaps had seen)   145
Of Maids at sunrise, bringing in from far
Their May-bush, and along the street in flocks
Parading with a Song of taunting rhymes
Aimed at the Laggards slumbering within doors;
Had also heard, from those who yet remembered,   150
Tales of the May-pole dance, and wreaths that decked
Porch, door-way, or Kirk-pillar; and of Youths,
Each with his Maid, before the sun was up,
By annual custom issuing forth in troops
To drink the Waters of some sainted Well   155
And hang it round with garlands. Love survives,
But for such purpose flowers no longer grow.

The times too sage, perhaps too proud, have dropped
These lighter graces; and the rural ways
And manners which my childhood looked upon   160
Were the unluxuriant produce of a life
Intent on little but substantial needs,
Yet rich in beauty, beauty that was felt.
But images of danger and distress,
Man suffering among awful Powers and Forms;   165
Of this I heard and saw enough to make
Imagination restless; nor was free
Myself from frequent perils, nor were tales
Wanting, the tragedies of former times,
Hazards and strange escapes, of which the rocks   170
Immutable, and everflowing streams,
Where'er I roamed, were speaking monuments.
    Smooth life had Flock and Shepherd in old time,
Long springs and tepid winters, on the banks
Of delicate Galesus; and no less   175
Those scattered along Adria's myrtle shores;
Smooth life had Herdsman, and his snow-white Herd,
To triumphs and to sacrificial Rites
Devoted, on the inviolable Stream
Of rich Clitumnus; and the Goatherd lived   180
As calmly, underneath the pleasant brows
Of cool Lucretilis, where the pipe was heard
Of Pan, invisible God, thrilling the rocks
With tutelary music, from all harm
The Fold protecting. I myself, mature   185
In manhood then, have seen a pastoral Tract
Like one of these, where Fancy might run wild,
Though under skies less generous, less serene.
There, for her own delight, had Nature framed
A Pleasure-ground, diffused a fair expanse   190
Of level pasture, islanded with groves
And banked with woody risings; but the plain
Endless; here opening widely out, and there
Shut up in lesser lakes or beds of lawn
And intricate recesses, creek, or bay   195
Sheltered within a shelter, where at large

The Shepherd strays, a rolling hut his home.
Thither he comes with spring-time, there abides
All summer, and at sunrise ye may hear
His flagelet to liquid notes of love   200
Attuned, or spritely fife resounding far.
Nook is there none, nor strait of that vast space
Where passage opens, but the same shall have
In turn its Visitant, telling there his hours
In unlaborious pleasure, with no task   205
More toilsome than to carve a beechen bowl
For Spring or Fountain, which the Traveller finds
When through the region he pursues at will
His devious course. A glimpse of such sweet life
I saw when, from the melancholy walls   210
Of Goslar, once Imperial! I renewed
My daily walk along that wide Champaign,
That, reaching to her Gates, spreads east and west,
And northwards, from beneath the mountainous verge
Of the Hercynian forest. Yet hail to You,   215
Moors, mountains, headlands, and Ye hollow Vales,
Ye long deep channels for the Atlantic's voice,
Powers of my native region.— Ye that seize
The heart with firmer grasp! Your snows and streams
Ungovernable, and your terrifying winds   220
That howl so dismally for him who treads,
Companionless, your awful Solitudes!
There 'tis the Shepherd's task, the winter long,
To wait upon the Storms: of their approach
Sagacious, into sheltering coves he drives   225
His flock, and thither from the homestead bears
A toilsome burden up the craggy ways,
And deals it out, their regular nourishment
Strewn on the frozen snow. And when the Spring
Looks out, and all the pastures dance with lambs,   230
And when the Flock, with warmer weather, climbs
Higher and higher, him his office leads
To watch their goings, whatsoever track
The wanderers chuse. For this he quits his home
At day-spring, and no sooner doth the sun   235

Begin to strike him with a fire-like heat
Than he lies down upon some shining rock
And breakfasts with his Dog. When they have stolen,
As is their wont, a pittance from strict time,
For rest, not needed, or exchange of love,   240
Then from his couch he starts; and now his feet
Crush out a livelier fragrance from the flowers
Of lowly thyme, by Nature's skill enwrought
In the wild turf: the lingering dews of morn
Smoke round him, as from hill to hill he hies,   245
His staff portending like a Hunter's Spear,
Or by its aid leaping from crag to crag
And o'er the brawling beds of unbridged streams.
Philosophy, methinks, at Fancy's call
Might deign to follow him through what he does   250
Or sees in his day's march; himself he feels,
In those vast regions where his service lies,
A Freeman; wedded to his life of hope
And hazard, and hard labour interchanged
With that majestic indolence so dear   255
To native Man. A rambling School-boy, thus
I felt his presence in his own domain
As of a Lord and Master; or a Power
Or Genius, under Nature, under God
Presiding; and severest solitude   260
Had more commanding looks when he was there.
When up the lonely brooks on rainy days
Angling I went, or trod the trackless hills
By mists bewildered, suddenly mine eyes
Have glanced upon him distant a few steps,   265
In size a Giant, stalking through thick fog,
His sheep like Greenland bears; or, as he stepped
Beyond the boundary line of some hill-shadow,
His form hath flashed upon me, glorified
By the deep radiance of the setting sun: 270
Or him have I descried in distant sky,
A solitary object and sublime,
Above all height! like an aerial cross
Stationed alone upon a spiry rock

Of the Chartreuse, for worship. Thus was Man   275
Ennobled outwardly before my sight,
And thus my heart was early introduced
To an unconscious love and reverence
Of human nature; hence the human Form
To me became an index of delight,   280
Of grace, and honor, power, and worthiness.
Meanwhile this Creature, spiritual almost
As those of Books, but more exalted far;
Far more of an imaginative Form
Than the gay Corin of the groves, who lives   285
For his own fancies, or to dance by the hour
In coronal, with Phillis in the midst—
Was, for the purposes of Kind, a Man
With the most common; husband, father; learned,
Could teach, admonish, suffered with the rest   290
From vice and folly, wretchedness and fear;
Of this I little saw, cared less for it;
But something must have felt.
                        Call ye these appearances
Which I beheld of Shepherds in my youth,
This sanctity of Nature given to man—   295
A shadow, a delusion, ye who pore
On the dead letter, miss the spirit of things;
Whose truth is not a motion or a shape
Instinct with vital functions, but a Block
Or waxen image which yourselves have made,   300
And ye adore. But blessed be the God
Of Nature and of Man, that this was so,
That men before my inexperienced eyes
Did first present themselves thus purified,
Removed, and to a distance that was fit.   305
And so we all of us in some degree
Are led to knowledge, whencesoever led
And howsoever; were it otherwise,
And we found evil fast as we find good
In our first years, or think that it is found,   310
How could the innocent heart bear up and live?
But doubly fortunate my lot; not here

Alone, that something of a better life
Perhaps was round me than it is the privilege
Of most to move in, but that first I looked   315
At Man through objects that were great or fair,
First communed with him by their help. And thus
Was founded a sure safeguard and defence
Against the weight of meanness, selfish cares,
Coarse manners, vulgar passions, that beat in   320
On all sides from the ordinary world
In which we traffic. Starting from this point,
I had my face turned tow'rd the truth, began
With an advantage furnished by that kind
Of prepossession without which the soul   325
Receives no knowledge that can bring forth good,
No genuine insight ever comes to her.
From the restraint of over-watchful eyes
Preserved, I moved about, year after year
Happy, and now most thankful, that my walk   330
Was guarded from too early intercourse
With the deformities of crowded life,
And those ensuing laughters and contempts
Self-pleasing, which, if we would wish to think
With a due reverence on earth's rightful Lord,   335
Here placed to be the Inheritor of heaven,
Will not permit us; but pursue the mind
That to devotion willingly would rise,
Into the Temple, and the Temple's heart.
        Yet deem not, Friend, that human-kind with me   340
Thus early took a place preeminent;
Nature herself was at this unripe time
But secondary to my own pursuits
And animal activities, and all
Their trivial pleasures: and when these had drooped   345
And gradually expired, and Nature, prized
For her own sake, became my joy, even then—
And upwards through late youth, until not less
Than two and twenty summers had been told—
Was Man in my affections and regards   350
Subordinate to her; her visible Forms

And viewless agencies: a passion she,
A rapture often, and immediate love
Ever at hand; *he* only a delight
Occasional, an accidental grace,   355
His hour being not yet come. Far less had then
The inferior Creatures, beast or bird, attuned
(Though they had long been carefully observed)
My Spirit to that gentleness of love,
Won from me those minute obeisances   360
Of tenderness, which I may number now
With my first blessings. Nevertheless on these
The light of beauty did not fall in vain,
Or grandeur circumfuse them to no end.
    But when that first poetic Faculty   365
Of plain imagination and severe,
No longer a mute influence of the soul,
Ventured at some rash Muse's earnest call
To try her strength among harmonious words,
And to book-notions and the rules of art   370
Did knowingly conform itself; there came
Among the simple shapes of human life
A wilfulness of fancy and conceit;
And Nature and her objects beautified
These fictions, as in some sort, in their turn,   375
They burnished her. From touch of this new Power
Nothing was safe: the Elder tree that grew
Beside the well known charnel-house had then
A dismal look: the yew-tree had its ghost
That took his Station there, for ornament;   380
The dignities of plain occurrence then
Were tasteless, and truth's golden mean, a point
Where no sufficient pleasure could be found.
Then if a Widow, staggering with the blow
Of her distress, was known to have turned her steps   385
To the cold grave in which her Husband slept,
One night, or haply more than one, through pain
Or half insensate impotence of mind,
The fact was caught at greedily, and there
She must be visitant the whole year through,   390

Wetting the turf with never-ending tears.
　　Through quaint obliquities I might pursue
These cravings: when the Fox-glove, one by one,
Upwards through every Stage of the tall stem
Had shed beside the public way its bells,　　　　　　　　395
And stood of all dismantled, save the last
Left at the tapering ladder's top, that seemed
To bend as doth a slender blade of grass
Tipped with a rain drop; Fancy loved to seat
Beneath the plant, despoiled but crested still　　　　　400
With this last relic, soon itself to fall,
Some Vagrant Mother, whose arch Little-ones,
All unconcerned by her dejected plight,
Laughed, as with rival eagerness their hands
Gathered the purple cups that round them lay　　　　　405
Strewing the turf's green slope.
　　　　　　　　　　　　　　A diamond light
(Whene'er the summer sun, declining, smote
A smooth rock wet with constant springs) was seen
Sparkling from out a copse-clad bank that rose
Fronting our Cottage. Oft beside the hearth　　　　　410
Seated with open door, often and long
Upon this restless lustre have I gazed
That made my fancy restless as itself.
'Twas now for me a burnished silver shield
Suspended over a Knight's tomb, who lay　　　　　　415
Inglorious, buried in the dusky wood:
An entrance now into some magic cave
Or Palace built by Fairies of the Rock.
Nor could I have been bribed to disenchant
The Spectacle, by visiting the Spot.　　　　　　　　420
　　Thus wilful fancy, in no hurtful mood,
Engrafted far-fetched Shapes on feelings bred
By pure imagination: busy Power
She was, and with her ready Pupil turned
Instinctively to human passions, then　　　　　　　425
Least understood. Yet, 'mid the fervent swarm
Of these vagaries, with an eye so rich
As mine was through the bounty of a grand

And lovely region, I had forms distinct
To steady me: each airy thought revolved   430
Round a substantial centre which at once
Incited it to motion, and controlled.
I did not pine like One in cities bred,
As was thy melancholy lot, dear Friend!
Great Spirit as thou art, in endless dreams   435
Of sickliness, disjoining, joining things
Without the light of knowledge. Where the harm
If, when the Woodman languished with disease
Induced by sleeping nightly on the ground
Within his sod-built Cabin, Indian-wise,   440
I called the pangs of disappointed love
And all the sad etcetera of the wrong
To help him to his grave? Meanwhile the Man,
If not already from the woods retired
To die at home, was haply, as I knew,   445
Withering by slow degrees, 'mid gentle airs,
Birds, running Streams, and hills so beautiful
On golden evenings, while the charcoal Pile
Breathed up its smoke, an image of his ghost
Or spirit that full soon must take her flight.   450
Nor shall we not be tending towards that point
Of sound humanity to which our Tale
Leads, though by sinuous ways, if here I shew
How Fancy, in a season when she wove
Those slender cords, to guide the unconscious Boy   455
For the Man's sake, could feed at Nature's call
Some pensive musings which might well beseem
Maturer years.
                    A grove there is whose boughs
Stretch from the western marge of Thurston-mere,
With length of shade so thick that whoso glides   460
Along the line of low-roofed water moves
As in a cloister. Once, while in that shade
Loitering, I watched the golden beams of light
Flung from the setting sun, as they reposed
In silent beauty on the naked ridge   465
Of a high eastern hill. Thus flowed my thoughts

In a pure stream of words fresh from the heart:
"Dear native Region, wheresoe'er shall close
My mortal course, there will I think on you:
Dying, will cast on you a backward look,   470
Even as this setting sun (albeit the Vale
Is no where touched by one memorial gleam)
Doth with the fond remains of his last power
Still linger, and a farewell lustre sheds
On the dear mountain-tops where first he rose."   475
    Enough of humble arguments! recal,
My Song, those high emotions which thy voice
Has heretofore made known, that bursting forth
Of sympathy, inspiring and inspired,
When every where a vital pulse was felt,   480
And all the several frames of things, like stars
Through every magnitude distinguishable,
Shone mutually indebted, or half lost
Each in the other's blaze, a galaxy
Of life and glory. In the midst stood Man,   485
Outwardly, inwardly contemplated,
As of all visible natures crown, though born
Of dust and Kindred to the worm, a Being,
Both in perception and discernment, first
In every capability of rapture,   490
Through the divine effect of power and love,
As, more than any thing we know, instinct
With Godhead, and by reason and by will
Acknowledging dependency sublime.
    Erelong, the lonely Mountains left, I moved   495
Begirt from day to day with temporal shapes
Of vice and folly thrust upon my view,
Objects of sport, and ridicule, and scorn,
Manners and characters discriminate,
And little bustling passions that eclipsed,   500
As well they might, the impersonated thought,
The Idea or abstraction of the Kind.
    An Idler among academic Bowers,
Such was my new condition, as at large
Has been set forth; yet here the vulgar light   505

Of present, actual, superficial life,
Gleaming through coloring of other times,
Old usages, and local privilege,
Was welcome, softened, if not solemnized;
This notwithstanding, being brought more near   510
To vice and guilt, forerunning wretchedness,
I trembled—thought at times of human life
With an indefinite terror and dismay,
Such as the storms and angry elements
Had bred in me, but gloomier far, a dim   515
Analogy to uproar and misrule,
Disquiet, danger, and obscurity.
—It might be told (but wherefore speak of things
Common to all?) that, seeing, I was led
Gravely to ponder, judging between good   520
And evil, not as for the mind's delight
But for her guidance, one who was to *act*,
As sometimes to the best of feeble means
I did, by human sympathy impelled: .
And through dislike and most offensive pain   525
Was to the truth conducted; of this faith
Never forsaken, that by acting well
And understanding, I should learn to love,
The end of life, and every thing we know.
      Grave Teacher! stern Preceptress! for at times   530
Thou canst put on an aspect most severe;
London, to thee I willingly return.
Erewhile my verse played idly with the flowers
Enwrought upon thy mantle, satisfied
With that amusement, and a simple look   535
Of child-like inquisition now and then
Cast upwards on thy countenance, to detect
Some inner meanings which might harbour there.
But how could I in mood so light indulge,
Keeping such fresh remembrance of the day   540
When, having thridded the long labyrinth
Of the suburban villages, I first
Entered thy vast Dominion? On the roof
Of an itinerant Vehicle I sate,

With vulgar men about me, trivial forms   545
Of houses, pavement, streets, of men and things;
Mean shapes on every side: but at the instant
When to myself it fairly might be said,
The threshold now is overpassed,—(how strange
That aught external to the living mind   550
Should have such mighty sway! Yet so it was)
A weight of ages did at once descend
Upon my heart, no thought embodied, no
Distinct remembrances; but weight and power,—
Power growing under weight: alas! I feel   555
That I am trifling: 'twas a moment's pause—
All that took place within me came and went
As in a moment, yet with Time it dwells
And grateful memory, as a thing divine.
    The curious Traveller who from open day   560
Hath passed with torches into some huge cave,
The Grotto of Antiparos, or the Den
In old time haunted by that Danish Witch
Yordas, he looks around and sees the Vault
Widening on all sides; sees, or thinks he sees,   565
Erelong the massy roof above his head,
That instantly unsettles and recedes,—
Substance and shadow, light and darkness, all
Commingled, making up a Canopy
Of shapes and forms, and tendencies to shape   570
That shift and vanish, change and interchange
Like Spectres, ferment silent and sublime!
That, after a short space, works less and less
Till, every effort, every motion gone,
The scene before him stands in perfect view   575
Exposed, and lifeless as a written book!
—But let him pause awhile, and look again,
And a new quickening shall succeed, at first
Beginning timidly, then creeping fast,
Till the whole Cave, so late a senseless mass,   580
Busies the eye with images and forms
Boldly assembled,—here is shadowed forth
From the projections, wrinkles, cavities,

A variegated landscape, there the shape
Of some gigantic Warrior clad in mail,   585
The ghostly Semblance of a hooded Monk,
Veiled Nun, or Pilgrim resting on his staff,—
Strange congregation! yet not slow to meet
Eyes that perceive through Minds that can inspire.
    Even in such sort had I at first been moved,   590
Nor otherwise continued to be moved,
As I explored the vast metropolis,
Fount of my Country's destiny and the World's;
That great Emporium, Chronicle at once
And burial-place of passions, and their home   595
Imperial, their chief living residence.
    With strong sensations teeming as it did
Of past and present, such a place must needs
Have pleased me, seeking knowledge at that time
Far less than craving power, yet knowledge came,   600
Sought or unsought, and influxes of power
Came of themselves, or at her call derived
In fits of kindliest apprehensiveness
From all sides, when whate'er was in itself
Capacious found, or seemed to find, in me   605
A correspondent amplitude of mind;
Such is the strength and glory of our Youth.
The human nature unto which I felt
That I belonged, and reverenced with love,
Was not a punctual Presence, but a spirit   610
Diffused through time and space, with aid derived
Of evidence from monuments, erect,
Prostrate, or leaning towards their common rest
In earth, the widely scattered wreck sublime
Of vanished Nations, or more clearly drawn   615
From Books, and what they picture and record.
    'Tis true the History of our native Land,
With those of Greece compared and popular Rome,
And in our high-wrought modern Narratives
Stript of their harmonizing soul, the life   620
Of manners and familiar incidents,
Had never much delighted me. And less

Than other Intellects had mine been used
To lean upon extrinsic circumstance
Of record or tradition: but a sense   625
Of what in the great City had been done
And suffered, and was doing, suffering still,
Weighed with me, could support the test of thought,
And, in despite of all that had gone by,
Or was departing never to return,   630
There I conversed with majesty and power
Like independent Nature's. Hence the place
Was thronged with Impregnations, like the *Wilds*,
In which my early feelings had been nursed,
Bare hills and vallies—full of caverns, rocks,   635
And audible seclusions, dashing lakes,
Echoes and waterfalls, and pointed crags
That into music touch the passing wind.
     Here then a young Imagination found
No uncongenial element, could here   640
Among new objects serve or give command
Even as the heart's occasions might require
To forward Reason's else too scrupulous march.
The effect was still more elevated views
Of human nature. Neither vice nor guilt,   645
Debasement undergone by body or mind,
Nor all the misery forced upon my sight,
Misery not lightly passed, but sometimes scanned
Most feelingly, could overthrow my trust
In what we *may* become, induce belief   650
That I was ignorant, had been falsely taught,
A Solitary, who with vain conceits
Had been inspired, and walked about in dreams.
From those sad scenes when meditation turned,
Lo! every thing that was indeed divine   655
Retained its purity inviolate,
Nay brighter shone, by this portentous gloom
Set off; such opposition as aroused
The mind of Adam, yet in Paradise,
Though fallen from bliss, when in the East he saw   660
Darkness ere day's mid course, and morning light

More orient in the western cloud, that drew
O'er the blue firmament a radiant white,
Descending slow, with something heavenly fraught.
    Add also that among the multitudes   665
Of that huge City, oftentimes was seen
Affectingly set forth, more than elsewhere
Is possible, the unity of man,
One spirit over ignorance and vice
Predominant, in good and evil hearts   670
One sense for moral judgments, as one eye
For the sun's light. The soul, when smitten thus
By a sublime *idea*, whencesoe'er
Vouchsafed for union or communion, feeds
On the pure bliss, and takes her rest with God.   675
    Thus, from a very early age, O Friend!
My thoughts, by slow gradations, had been drawn
To human-kind, and to the good and ill
Of human life; Nature had led me on,
And oft amid the "busy hum" I seemed   680
To travel independent of her help,
As if I had forgotten her; but no,
The world of human-kind outweighed not hers
In my habitual thoughts; the scale of love,
Though filling daily, still was light compared   685
With that in which *her* mighty objects lay.

BOOK NINTH
RESIDENCE IN FRANCE

Even as a River—partly (it might seem)
Yielding to old remembrances, and swayed
In part by fear to shape a way direct
That would engulph him soon in the ravenous Sea—
Turns, and will measure back his course, far back,   5
Seeking the very regions which he crossed
In his first outset; so have we, my Friend!
Turned and returned with intricate delay.
Or as a Traveller, who has gained the brow
Of some aerial Down, while there he halts   10
For breathing-time, is tempted to review

The region left behind him; and if aught
Deserving notice have escaped regard,
Or been regarded with too careless eye,
Strives, from that height, with one, and yet one more   15
Last look, to make the best amends he may,
So have we lingered. Now we start afresh
With courage, and new hope risen on our toil.
Fair greetings to this shapeless eagerness,
Whene'er it comes! needful in work so long,   20
Thrice needful to the argument which now
Awaits us! Oh, how much unlike the past!
    Free as a Colt, at pasture on the hill,
I ranged at large through London's wide Domain
Month after Month. Obscurely did I live,   25
Not seeking frequent intercourse with men
By literature, or elegance, or rank
Distinguished. Scarcely was a year thus spent
Ere I forsook the crowded Solitude;
With less regret for its luxurious pomp   30
And all the nicely-guarded shews of Art,
Than for the humble Bookstalls in the Streets,
Exposed to eye and hand where'er I turned.
—France lured me forth, the realm that I had crossed
So lately, journeying toward the snow-clad Alps.   35
But now relinquishing the scrip and staff
And all enjoyment which the summer sun
Sheds round the steps of those who meet the day
With motion constant as his own, I went
Prepared to sojourn in a pleasant Town   40
Washed by the current of the stately Loire.
    Through Paris lay my readiest course, and there
Sojourning a few days, I visited
In haste each spot, of old or recent fame,
The latter chiefly; from the field of Mars   45
Down to the suburbs of St Anthony;
And from Mont Martyr southward to the Dome
Of Genevieve. In both her clamorous Halls,
The National Synod and the Jacobins,
I saw the Revolutionary Power   50

Toss like a Ship at anchor, rocked by storms;
The Arcades I traversed, in the Palace huge
Of Orleans, coasted round and round the line
Of Tavern, Brothel, Gaming-house, and Shop,
Great rendezvous of worst and best, the walk   55
Of all who had a purpose, or had not;
I stared, and listened with a Stranger's ears
To Hawkers and Haranguers, hubbub wild!
And hissing Factionists, with ardent eyes,
In knots, or pairs, or single. Not a look   60
Hope takes, or Doubt or Fear are forced to wear,
But seemed there present, and I scanned them all,
Watched every gesture uncontrollable
Of anger, and vexation, and despite,
All side by side, and struggling face to face   65
With Gaiety and dissolute Idleness.
— Where silent zephyrs sported with the dust
Of the Bastille, I sate in the open sun,
And from the rubbish gathered up a stone
And pocketed the Relic in the guise   70
Of an Enthusiast; yet, in honest truth,
I looked for Something that I could not find,
Affecting more emotion than I felt;
For 'tis most certain that these various sights,
However potent their first shock, with me   75
Appeared to recompence the Traveller's pains
Less than the painted Magdalene of Le Brun,
A Beauty exquisitely wrought, with hair
Dishevelled, gleaming eyes, and rueful cheek
Pale, and bedropp'd with everflowing tears.   80
    But hence to my more permanent Abode
I hasten; there by novelties in speech,
Domestic manners, customs, gestures, looks,
And all the attire of ordinary life,
Attention was engrossed; and, thus amused,   85
I stood 'mid those concussions unconcerned,
Tranquil almost, and careless as a flower
Glassed in a green-house, or a Parlour shrub
That spreads its leaves in unmolested peace

While every bush and tree, the country through,   90
Is shaking to the roots; indifference this
Which may seem strange; but I was unprepared
With needful knowledge, had abruptly passed
Into a theatre whose stage was filled,
And busy with an action far advanced.   95
Like Others I had skimmed, and sometimes read
With care, the master pamphlets of the day;
Nor wanted such half-insight as grew wild
Upon that meagre soil, helped out by talk
And public news; but having never seen   100
A Chronicle that might suffice to shew
Whence the main Organs of the public Power
Had sprung, their transmigrations when and how
Accomplished, giving thus unto events
A form and body; all things were to me   105
Loose and disjointed, and the affections left
Without a vital interest. At that time,
Moreover, the first storm was overblown,
And the strong hand of outward violence
Locked up in quiet. For myself, I fear   110
Now, in connection with so great a Theme,
To speak (as I must be compelled to do)
Of one so unimportant; night by night
Did I frequent the formal haunts of men
Whom, in the City, privilege of birth   115
Sequestered from the rest: societies
Polished in Arts, and in punctilio versed;
Whence, and from deeper causes, all discourse
Of good and evil of the time was shunned
With scrupulous care: but these restrictions soon   120
Proved tedious, and I gradually withdrew
Into a noisier world, and thus erelong
Became a Patriot; and my heart was all
Given to the People, and my love was theirs.
    A Band of military Officers   125
Then stationed in the City were the chief
Of my associates: some of these wore swords
That had been seasoned in the Wars, and all

Were men well born; the Chivalry of France.
In age and temper differing, they had yet   130
One spirit ruling in each heart, alike
(Save only one, hereafter to be named)
Were bent upon undoing what was done:
This was their rest and only hope, therewith
No fear had they of bad becoming worse;   135
For worst to them was come; nor would have stirred,
Or deemed it worth a moment's thought to stir,
In any thing, save only as the act
Looked thitherward. One, reckoning by years,
Was in the prime of manhood, and erewhile   140
He had sate Lord in many tender hearts,
Though heedless of such honors now, and changed:
His temper was quite mastered by the times,
And they had blighted him, had eat away
The beauty of his person, doing wrong   145
Alike to body and to mind: his port,
Which once had been erect and open, now
Was stooping and contracted, and a face
Endowed by Nature with her fairest gifts
Of symmetry, and light, and bloom, expressed   150
As much as any that was ever seen
A ravage out of season, made by thoughts
Unhealthy and vexatious. With the hour
That from the Press of Paris duly brought
Its freight of public news, the fever came,   155
A punctual Visitant, to shake this Man,
Disarmed his voice and fanned his yellow cheek
Into a thousand colours: while he read
Or mused, his sword was haunted by his touch
Continually, like an uneasy place   160
In his own body. 'Twas in truth an hour
Of universal ferment; mildest men
Were agitated; and commotions, strife
Of passion and opinion, filled the walls
Of peaceful houses with unquiet sounds.   165
The soil of common life was at that time
Too hot to tread upon. Oft said I then,

And not then only, "What a mockery this
Of history, the past and that to come!
Now do I feel how all men are deceived,   170
Reading of Nations and their works, in faith,
Faith given to vanity and emptiness;
Oh! laughter for the Page that would reflect
To future times the face of what now is!"
The Land all swarmed with passion, like a Plain   175
Devoured by locusts;—Carra, Gorcas; add
A hundred other names, forgotten now,
Nor to be heard of more, yet they were Powers
Like earthquakes, shocks repeated day by day,
And felt through every nook of town and field.   180
    Such was the state of things. Meanwhile the chief
Of my Associates stood prepared for flight
To augment the band of Emigrants in Arms
Upon the Borders of the Rhine, and leagued
With foreign foes mustered for instant War.   185
This was their undisguised intent, and they
Were waiting with the whole of their desires
The moment to depart.
                An Englishman,
Born in a land whose very name appeared
To licence some unruliness of mind,   190
A Stranger, with Youth's further privilege,
And the indulgence that a half-learnt speech
Wins from the Courteous; I, who had been else
Shunned and not tolerated, freely lived
With these Defenders of the Crown, and talked,   195
And heard their notions, nor did they disdain
The wish to bring me over to their cause.
    But though untaught by thinking or by books
To reason well of polity or law,
And nice distinctions, then on every tongue,   200
Of natural rights and civil; and to acts
Of Nations and their passing interests
(If with unworldly ends and aims compared)
Almost indifferent, even the Historian's Tale
Prizing but little otherwise than I prized   205

Tales of the Poets, as it made the heart
Beat high and filled the fancy with fair forms,
Old Heroes and their sufferings and their deeds;
Yet in the regal Sceptre, and the pomp
Of Orders and Degrees, I nothing found   210
Then, or had ever, even in crudest Youth,
That dazzled me: but rather what I mourned
And ill could brook, beholding that the best
Ruled not, and feeling that they ought to rule.
    For, born in a poor District, and which yet   215
Retaineth more of ancient homeliness
Than any other nook of English ground,
It was my fortune scarcely to have seen
Through the whole tenor of my School-day time
The face of One, who, whether boy or man,   220
Was vested with attention or respect
Through claims of wealth or blood; nor was it least
Of many benefits, in later years
Derived from academic institutes
And rules, that they held something up to view   225
Of a Republic, where all stood thus far
Upon equal ground, that we were brothers all
In honor, as in one community,
Scholars and Gentlemen; where, furthermore,
Distinction lay open to all that came,   230
And wealth and titles were in less esteem
Than talents, worth, and prosperous industry.
Add unto this, subservience from the first
To Presences of God's mysterious power
Made manifest in Nature's sovereignty,   235
And fellowship with venerable books,
To sanction the proud workings of the Soul
And mountain liberty. It could not be
But that one tutored thus should look with awe
Upon the faculties of man, receive   240
Gladly the highest promises, and hail
As best the government of equal rights
And individual worth. And hence, O Friend,
If at the first great outbreak I rejoiced

Less than might well befit my Youth, the cause   245
In part lay here, that unto me the events
Seemed nothing out of Nature's certain course,
A gift that rather was come late than soon.
No wonder then if Advocates like these,
Inflamed by passion, blind with prejudice,   250
And stung with injury, at this riper day,
Were impotent to make my hopes put on
The shape of theirs, my understanding bend
In honor to their honor,—zeal which yet
Had slumbered, now in opposition burst   255
Forth like a polar summer: every word
They uttered was a dart, by counter-winds
Blown back upon themselves; their reason seemed
Confusion-stricken by a higher Power
Than human understanding, their discourse   260
Maimed, spiritless; and, in their weakness strong,
I triumphed.
                    Meantime, day by day, the roads
Were crowded with the bravest Youth of France
And all the promptest of her spirits, linked
In gallant Soldiership, and posting on   265
To meet the War, upon her Frontier Bounds.
Yet at this very moment do tears start
Into mine eyes: I do not say I weep—
I wept not then,—but tears have dimmed my sight
In memory of the farewells of that time,   270
Domestic severings, female fortitude
At dearest separation, patriot love
And self-devotion, and terrestrial hope
Encouraged with a martyr's confidence;
Even files of Strangers merely, seen but once   275
And for a moment, men from far with sound
Of music, martial tunes, and banners spread,
Entering the City, here and there a face
Or person singled out among the rest,
Yet still a Stranger and beloved as such;   280
Even by these passing spectacles my heart
Was oftentimes uplifted, and they seemed

Arguments sent from heaven, to prove the cause
Good, pure, which no one could stand up against
Who was not lost, abandoned, selfish, proud,   285
Mean, miserable, wilfully depraved,
Hater perverse of equity and truth.
    Among that Band of Officers, was One,
Already hinted at, of other mold,
A Patriot, thence rejected by the rest,   290
And with an oriental loathing spurned,
As of a different Cast. A meeker Man
Than this lived never, nor a more benign,
Meek, though enthusiastic. Injuries
Made *Him* more gracious, and his nature then   295
Did breathe its sweetness out most sensibly
As aromatic flowers on Alpine turf
When foot hath crushed them. He through the events
Of that great change wandered in perfect faith,
As through a Book, an old Romance or Tale   300
Of Fairy, or some dream of actions wrought
Behind the summer clouds. By birth he ranked
With the most noble, but unto the Poor
Among mankind he was in service bound
As by some tie invisible, oaths professed   305
To a religious order. Man he loved
As Man; and, to the mean and the obscure
And all the homely in their homely works,
Transferred a courtesy which had no air
Of condescension; but did rather seem   310
A passion and a gallantry, like that
Which he, a Soldier, in his idler day
Had paid to Woman: somewhat vain he was,
Or seemed so, yet it was not vanity,
But fondness, and a kind of radiant joy   315
Diffused around him while he was intent
On works of love or freedom, or revolved
Complacently the progress of a Cause
Whereof he was a part; yet this was meek
And placid, and took nothing from the man   320
That was delightful: oft in solitude

With him did I discourse about the end
Of civil government, and its wisest forms,
Of ancient loyalty, and chartered rights,
Custom and habit, novelty and change,   325
Of self-respect, and virtue in the Few
For patrimonial honor set apart,
And ignorance in the labouring Multitude.
For he, to all intolerance indisposed,
Balanced these contemplations in his mind;   330
And I, who at that time was scarcely dipped
Into the turmoil, bore a sounder judgement
Than later days allowed; carried about me,
With less alloy to its integrity,
The experience of past ages, as through help   335
Of Books and common life it makes sure way
To youthful minds, by objects over near
Not pressed upon, nor dazzled or misled
By struggling with the Crowd for present ends.
     But though not deaf, nor obstinate to find   340
Error without excuse upon the side
Of them who strove against us, more delight
We took, and let this freely be confessed,
In painting to ourselves the miseries
Of royal Courts, and that voluptuous life   345
Unfeeling, where the Man who is of Soul
The meanest, thrives the most, where dignity,
True personal dignity, abideth not;
A light, a cruel, and vain world, cut off
From the natural inlets of just sentiment,   350
From lowly sympathy, and chastening truth;
Where Good and Evil interchange their names,
And thirst for bloody spoils abroad is paired
With vice at home. We added dearest themes,
Man and his noble nature, as it is   355
The gift which God has placed within his power,
His blind desires and steady faculties
Capable of clear truth, the one to break
Bondage, the other to build liberty
On firm foundations, making social life,   360

Through knowledge spreading and imperishable,
As just in regulation, and as pure
As individual in the wise and good.
—We summoned up the honorable deeds
Of ancient Story, thought of each bright spot   365
That could be found in all recorded time,
Of truth preserved, and error passed away,
Of single Spirits that catch the flame from Heaven,
And how the multitudes of men will feed
And fan each other, thought of Sects, how keen   370
They are to put the appropriate nature on,
Triumphant over every obstacle
Of custom, language, Country, love, and hate,
And what they do and suffer for their creed,
How far they travel, and how long endure,   375
How quickly mighty Nations have been formed
From least beginnings, how, together locked
By new opinions, scattered tribes have made
One body, spreading wide as clouds in heaven.
To aspirations then of our own minds   380
Did we appeal; and finally beheld
A living confirmation of the whole
Before us, in a People from the depth
Of shameful imbecility upris'n,
Fresh as the morning star: elate we looked   385
Upon their virtues, saw in rudest men
Self-sacrifice the firmest, generous love
And continence of mind, and sense of right
Uppermost in the midst of fiercest strife.
      Oh! sweet it is, in academic Groves   390
Or such retirement, Friend! as we have known
In the green dales beside our Rotha's Stream,
Greta, or Derwent, or some nameless Rill,
To ruminate with interchange of talk
On rational Liberty, and hope in Man,   395
Justice and peace; but far more sweet such toil—
Toil say I, for it leads to thoughts abstruse—
If nature then be standing on the brink
Of some great trial, and we hear the voice

Of One devoted, One whom circumstance   400
Hath called upon to embody his deep sense
In action, give it outwardly a shape,
And that of benediction to the world;
Then doubt is not, and truth is more than truth,—
A hope it is and a desire, a creed   405
Of zeal, by an Authority divine
Sanctioned, of danger, difficulty, or death.
Such conversation under Attic Shades
Did Dion hold with Plato, ripened thus
For a Deliverer's glorious Task, and such   410
He, on that ministry already bound,
Held with Eudemus and Timonides,
Surrounded by Adventurers in Arms,
When those two vessels with their daring Freight,
For the Sicilian Tyrant's overthrow   415
Sailed from Zacynthus, philosophic War
Led by Philosophers. With harder fate
Though like ambition, such was he, O Friend!
Of whom I speak, so Beaupuis (let the name
Stand near the worthiest of Antiquity)   420
Fashioned his life, and many a long discourse
With like persuasion honored, we maintained;
He, on his part, accoutred for the worst.
He perished fighting in supreme command
Upon the borders of the unhappy Loire,   425
For Liberty, against deluded men,
His fellow-countrymen, and yet most blessed
In this, that he the Fate of later times
Lived not to see, nor what we now behold
Who have as ardent hearts as he had then.   430
      Along that very Loire, with festal mirth
Resounding at all hours, and innocent yet
Of civil slaughter, was our frequent walk;
Or in wide Forests of continuous shade,
Lofty and overarched, with open space   435
Beneath the trees, clear footing many a mile—
A solemn region. Oft, amid those haunts,
From earnest dialogues I slipped in thought,

And let remembrance steal to other times,
When o'er those interwoven roots, moss-clad,   440
And smooth as marble, or a waveless sea,
Some Hermit, from his Cell forth-strayed, might pace
In sylvan meditation, undisturbed;
As on the pavement of a gothic Church
Walks a lone Monk, when service hath expired,   445
In peace and silence. But if e'er was heard,
Heard though unseen, a devious Traveller
Retiring, or approaching from afar,
With speed, and echoes loud of trampling hoofs
From the hard floor reverberated, then   450
It was Angelica thundering through the woods
Upon her Palfrey, or that gentle maid
Erminia, fugitive as fair as She.
Sometimes I saw, methought, a pair of Knights
Joust underneath the trees, that as in storm   455
Rocked high above their heads; anon, the din
Of boisterous merriment, and music's roar,
In sudden proclamation! burst from haunt
Of Satyrs in some viewless glade, with dance
Rejoicing o'er a Female in the midst,   460
A mortal Beauty, their unhappy Thrall;
The width of those huge Forests, unto me
A novel scene, did often in this way
Master my fancy, while I wandered on
With that revered Companion. And sometimes—   465
When to a Convent in a meadow green,
By a brook-side, we came, a roofless Pile,
And not by reverential touch of Time
Dismantled, but by violence abrupt,
In spite of those heart-bracing colloquies,   470
In spite of real fervor, and of that
Less genuine and wrought up within myself—
I could not but bewail a wrong so harsh,
And for the matin bell to sound no more
Grieved, and the twilight taper, and the Cross   475
High on the topmost pinnacle, a sign
(How welcome to the weary Traveller's eyes!)

Of hospitality and peaceful rest.
And when the Partner of those varied walks
Pointed upon occasion to the Site   480
Of Romorentin, home of ancient Kings,
To the imperial Edifice of Blois,
Or to that rural Castle, name now slipped
From my remembrance, where a Lady lodged
By the first Francis wooed, and bound to him   485
In chains of mutual passion; from the Tower,
As a tradition of the Country tells,
Practised to commune with her royal Knight
By cressets and love-beacons, intercourse
'Twixt her high-seated Residence and his   490
Far off at Chambord on the Plain beneath;
Even here, though less than with the peaceful House
Religious, 'mid those frequent monuments
Of Kings, their vices, and their better deeds,
Imagination, potent to inflame,   495
At times, with virtuous wrath, and noble scorn,
Did also often mitigate the force
Of civic prejudice, the bigotry,
So call it, of a youthful Patriot's mind,
And on these spots with many gleams I looked   500
Of chivalrous delight. Yet not the less
Hatred of absolute rule, where will of One
Is law for all, and of that barren pride
In them who, by immunities unjust,
Between the Sovereign and the People stand,   505
His helper and not theirs, laid stronger hold
Daily upon me, mixed with pity too
And love; for where hope is, there love will be
For the abject multitude. And when we chanced
One day to meet a hunger-bitten Girl   510
Who crept along fitting her languid gait
Unto a heifer's motion, by a cord
Tied to her arm, and picking thus from the lane
Its sustenance, while the Girl with pallid hands
Was busy knitting in a heartless mood   515
Of solitude, and at the sight my Friend

In agitation said, "'Tis against *that*,
That we are fighting," I with him believed
That a benignant Spirit was abroad
Which might not be withstood, that poverty,   520
Abject as this, would in a little time
Be found no more, that we should see the earth
Unthwarted in her wish to recompence
The meek, the lowly, patient Child of Toil,
All institutes for ever blotted out   525
That legalized exclusion, empty pomp
Abolished, sensual State and cruel Power,
Whether by edict of the One or few;
And finally, as sum and crown of all,
Should see the People having a strong hand   530
In framing their own Laws, whence better days
To all mankind. But, these things set apart,
Was not this single confidence enough
To animate the mind that ever turned
A thought to human welfare, that henceforth   535
Captivity by mandate without law
Should cease, and open accusation lead
To sentence in the hearing of the world,
And open punishment, if not the air
Be free to breathe in, and the heart of Man   540
Dread nothing? From this height I shall not stoop
To humbler matter that detained us oft
In thought or conversation, public acts
And public persons, and emotions wrought
Within the breast, as ever varying winds   545
Of record or report swept over us;
But I will here, instead, repeat a Tale
Told by my Patriot friend of sad events
That prove to what low depth had struck the roots,
How widely spread the boughs, of that old tree   550
Which, as a deadly mischief, and a foul
And black dishonour, France was weary of.
    "Oh! happy time of youthful Lovers! (thus
My Story may begin) O balmy time
In which a Love-Knot on a Lady's brow   555

Is fairer than the fairest star in Heaven!"
So might—and with that prelude *did* begin
The Record; and in faithful Verse was given
The doleful sequel. But our little Bark
On a strong River boldly hath been launched,   560
And from the driving current should we turn
To loiter wilfully within a Creek,
Howe'er attractive, Fellow Voyager!
Wouldst thou not chide? Yet deem not my pains lost;
For Vaudracour and Julia (so were named   565
The ill-fated pair) in that plain Tale will draw
Tears from the hearts of others when their own
Shall beat no more. Thou also there may'st read
At leisure, how the enamoured Youth was driven,
By public Power abused, to fatal crime,   570
Nature's rebellion against monstrous law;
How between heart and heart oppression thrust
Her mandates, severing whom true love had joined,
Harrassing both; until he sank and pressed
The couch his fate had made for him—supine,   575
Save when the stings of viperous remorse,
Trying their strength, forced him to start up,
Aghast and prayerless. Into a deep wood
He fled to shun the haunts of human kind;
There dwelt, weakened in spirit more and more.   580
Nor could the voice of Freedom, which through France
Full speedily resounded, public hope,
Or personal memory of his own worst wrongs,
Rouse him, but, hidden in those gloomy shades,
His days he wasted, an imbecile mind.   585

BOOK TENTH
FRANCE CONTINUED

It was a beautiful and silent day
That overspread the countenance of earth,
Then fading with unusual quietness—
A day as beautiful as e'er was given
To soothe regret, though deepening what it soothed,   5
When by the gliding Loire I paused, and cast

Upon his rich domains, vineyard and tilth,
Green meadow-ground and many-colored woods,
Again, and yet again, a farewell look;
Then from the quiet of that scene passed on,   10
Bound to the fierce Metropolis. From his throne
The King had fallen; and that invading Host,
Presumptuous cloud on whose black front was written
The tender mercies of the dismal wind
That bore it, on the plains of Liberty   15
Had burst innocuous. Say in bolder words,
They who had come elate as eastern Hunters
Banded beneath the great Mogul, when He
Ere while went forth from Agra or Lahor,
Rajas and Omras in his train, intent   20
To drive their prey enclosed within a ring
Wide as a Province, but, the signal given,
Before the point of the life-threatening spear
Narrowing itself by moments—they, rash Men,
Had seen the anticipated Quarry turned   25
Into Avengers, from whose wrath they fled
In terror. Disappointment and dismay
Remained for all whose fancies had run wild
With evil expectations; confidence
And perfect triumph for the better cause.   30
— The State, as if to stamp the final seal
On her security, and to the world
Show what she was, a high and fearless Soul
Exulting in defiance, or heart-stung
By sharp resentment, or belike to taunt   35
With spiteful gratitude the baffled League
That had stirred up her slackening faculties
To a new transition, when the King was crushed,
Spared not the empty Throne, and in proud haste
Assumed the body and venerable name   40
Of a Republic. Lamentable crimes,
'Tis true, had gone before this hour, dire work
Of massacre, in which the senseless sword
Was prayed to as a Judge; but these were past,
Earth free from them for ever, as was thought;   45

Ephemeral Monsters to be seen but once!
Things that could only shew themselves and die.
    Cheared with this hope, to Paris I returned;
And ranged, with ardor heretofore unfelt,
The spacious City, and in progress passed   50
The Prison where the unhappy Monarch lay,
Associate with his Children and his Wife,
In Bondage; and the Palace lately stormed,
With roar of Cannon, by a furious Host.
I crossed the Square (an empty Area then!)   55
Of the Carousel, where so late had lain
The Dead, upon the Dying heaped; and gazed
On this and other Spots, as doth a Man
Upon a Volume whose contents he knows
Are memorable, but from him locked up,   60
Being written in a tongue he cannot read;
So that he questions the mute leaves with pain,
And half-upbraids their silence. But, that night,
I felt most deeply in what world I was,
What ground I trod on, and what air I breathed.   65
High was my Room and lonely, near the roof
Of a large Mansion or Hotel, a Lodge
That would have pleased me in more quiet times,
Nor was it wholly without pleasure, then.
With unextinguished taper I kept watch,   70
Reading at intervals; the fear gone by
Pressed on me almost like a fear to come.
I thought of those September massacres,
Divided from me by one little month,
Saw them and touched; the rest was conjured up   75
From tragic fictions, or true history,
Remembrances and dim admonishments.
The Horse is taught his manage, and no Star
Of wildest course but treads back his own steps;
For the spent hurricane the air provides   80
As fierce a Successor; the tide retreats
But to return out of its hiding place
In the great Deep; all things have second birth;
The earthquake is not satisfied at once;

And in this way I wrought upon myself   85
Until I seemed to hear a voice that cried
To the whole City, "Sleep no more." The Trance
Fled with the Voice to which it had given birth,
But vainly comments of a calmer mind
Promised soft peace and sweet forgetfulness.   90
The place, all hushed and silent as it was,
Appeared unfit for the repose of Night,
Defenceless as a wood where Tygers roam.
    With early morning towards the Palace walk
Of Orleans eagerly I turned; as yet   95
The streets were still; not so those long Arcades;
There—'mid a peal of ill-matched Sounds and cries
That greeted me on entering—I could hear
Shrill voices from the Hawkers in the throng
Bawling, "Denunciation of the crimes   100
Of Maximilian Robespierre;" the hand,
Prompt as the voice, held forth a printed Speech,
The same that had been recently pronounced
When Robespierre, not ignorant for what mark
Some words of indirect reproof had been   105
Intended, rose in hardihood and dared
The Man who had an ill-surmise of him
To bring his charge in openness; whereat,
When a dead pause ensued and no one stirred,
In silence of all present, from his seat   110
Louvet walked single through the Avenue
And took his station in the Tribune, saying,
"I, Robespierre, accuse thee!" Well is known
The inglorious issue of that charge, and how
He who had launched the startling thunderbolt,   115
The one bold Man whose voice the attack had sounded,
Was left without a Follower to discharge
His perilous duty and retire, lamenting
That Heaven's best aid is wasted upon Men
Who to themselves are false.
                  But these are things   120
Of which I speak only as they were storm
Or sunshine to my individual mind,

No further. Let me then relate that now,
In some sort seeing with my proper eyes
That Liberty, and Life, and Death would soon   125
To the remotest corners of the Land
Lie in the arbitriment of those who ruled
The capital City, what was struggled for,
And by what Combatants victory must be won,
The indecision on their part whose aim   130
Seemed best, and the strait-forward path of those
Who in attack or in defence were strong
Through their impiety; my inmost soul
Was agitated; yea, I could almost
Have prayed that throughout earth upon all men,   135
By patient exercise of reason made
Worthy of Liberty, all Spirits filled
With zeal expanding in Truth's holy light,
The gift of tongues might fall, and Power arrive
From the four quarters of the winds to do   140
For France what without help she could not do,
A work of honor; think not that to this
I added work of safety: from all doubt
Or trepidation for the end of things
Far was I, far as Angels are from guilt.   145
      Yet did I grieve, nor only grieved, but thought
Of opposition and of remedies;
An insignificant Stranger and obscure,
And one, moreover, little graced with power
Of eloquence even in my native speech,   150
And all unfit for tumult or intrigue,
Yet would I at this time with willing heart
Have undertaken for a cause so great
Service however dangerous. I revolved
How much the destiny of Man had still   155
Hung upon single Persons, that there was,
Transcendant to all local patrimony,
One Nature as there is one Sun in Heaven,
That Objects, even as they are great, thereby
Do come within the reach of humblest eyes,   160
That Man is only weak through his mistrust

And want of hope, where evidence divine
Proclaims to him that hope should be most sure.
Nor did the inexperience of my youth
Preclude conviction that a spirit, strong   165
In hope and trained to noble aspirations,
A spirit thoroughly faithful to itself,
Is for Society's unreasoning herd
A domineering instinct, serves at once
For way and guide, a fluent receptacle   170
That gathers up each petty straggling rill
And vein of Water, glad to be rolled on
In safe obedience; that a mind whose rest
Is where it ought to be, in self-restraint,
In circumspection and simplicity,   175
Falls rarely in entire discomfiture
Below its aim, or meets with from without
A treachery that foils it or defeats;
And lastly, if the means on human will,
Frail human will, dependent should betray   180
Him who too boldly trusted them, I felt
That 'mid the loud distractions of the world
A sovereign voice subsists within the soul,
Arbiter undisturbed of right and wrong,
Of life and death, in majesty severe   185
Enjoining, as may best promote the aims
Of Truth and justice, either sacrifice,
From whatsoever region of our cares
Or our infirm affections nature pleads,
Earnest and blind, against the stern decree.   190
—On the other side I called to mind those truths
That are the common-places of the Schools,
A theme for Boys, too hackneyed for their Sires,
Yet, with a revelation's liveliness,
In all their comprehensive bearings known   195
And visible to Philosophers of old,
Men who, to business of the world untrained,
Lived in the shade; and to Harmodius known
And his Compeer Aristogiton, known
To Brutus, that tyrannic Power is weak,   200

Hath neither gratitude, nor faith, nor love,
Nor the support of good or evil men
To trust in, that the Godhead which is ours
Can never utterly be charmed or stilled,
That nothing hath a natural right to last   205
But equity and reason, that all else
Meets foes irreconcilable, and at best
Lives only by variety of disease.
   Well might my wishes be intense, my thoughts
Strong and perturbed, not doubting at that time   210
But that the virtue of one paramount mind
Would have abashed those impious crests, have quelled
Outrage and bloody power, and, in despite
Of what the People long had been and were
Through ignorance and false teaching, sadder proof   215
Of immaturity, and in the teeth
Of desperate opposition from without,
Have cleared a passage for just government,
And left a solid birthright to the State,
Redeemed according to example given   220
By ancient Lawgivers.
               In this frame of mind,
Dragged by a chain of harsh necessity,
So seemed it,—now I thankfully acknowledge,
Forced by the gracious providence of Heaven—
To England I returned, else (though assured   225
That I both was, and must be, of small weight,
No better than a Landsman on the deck
Of a ship struggling with a hideous storm)
Doubtless I should have then made common cause
With some who perished, haply perished too,   230
A poor mistaken and bewildered offering,
Should to the breast of Nature have gone back
With all my resolutions, all my hopes,
A Poet only to myself, to Men
Useless, and even, belovéd Friend, a Soul   235
To thee unknown!
             Twice had the trees let fall
Their leaves, as often Winter had put on

His hoary crown, since I had seen the surge
Beat against Albion's shore, since ear of mine
Had caught the accents of my native speech   240
Upon our native Country's sacred ground.
A Patriot of the World, how could I glide
Into communion with her sylvan shades,
Erewhile my tuneful haunt?—it pleased me more
To abide in the great City, where I found   245
The general Air still busy with the stir
Of that first memorable onset made
By a strong levy of Humanity
Upon the Traffickers in Negro blood:
Effort which, though defeated, had recalled   250
To notice old forgotten principles
And through the Nation spread a novel heat,
Of virtuous feeling. For myself, I own
That this particular strife had wanted power
To rivet my affections, nor did now   255
Its unsuccessful issue much excite
My sorrow, for I brought with me the faith
That, if France prospered, good men would not long
Pay fruitless worship to humanity,
And this most rotten branch of human shame,   260
Object, so seemed it, of superfluous pains,
Would fall together with its parent tree.
What then were my emotions, when in Arms
Britain put forth her free-born strength in league,
O pity and shame! with those confederate Powers?   265
Not in my single self alone I found,
But in the minds of all ingenuous Youth,
Change and subversion from that hour. No shock
Given to my moral nature had I known
Down to that very moment; neither lapse   270
Nor turn of sentiment that might be named
A revolution, save at this one time;
All else was progress on the self-same path
On which, with a diversity of pace,
I had been travelling: this a stride at once   275
Into another region.—As a light

And pliant hare-bell swinging in the breeze
On some gray rock, its birth-place, so had I
Wantoned, fast rooted on the ancient tower
Of my beloved Country, wishing not   280
A happier fortune than to wither there.
Now was I from that pleasant station torn
And tossed about in whirlwind. I rejoiced,
Yea, afterwards, truth most painful to record!
Exulted, in the triumph of my Soul,   285
When Englishmen by thousands were o'erthrown,
Left without glory on the field, or driven,
Brave hearts, to shameful flight. It was a grief,—
Grief call it not, 'twas any thing but that,—
A conflict of sensations without name,   290
Of which *he* only who may love the sight
Of a Village Steeple as I do can judge,
When, in the Congregation bending all
To their great Father, prayers were offered up,
Or praises, for our Country's victories,   295
And, 'mid the simple Worshippers, perchance
I only, like an uninvited Guest,
Whom no one owned, sate silent, shall I add,
Fed on the day of vengeance yet to come?
    Oh! much have they to account for, who could tear   300
By violence, at one decisive rent,
From the best Youth in England, their dear pride,
Their joy in England: this too at a time
In which worst losses easily might wear
The best of names, when patriotic love   305
Did of itself in modesty give way,
Like the Precursor when the Deity
Is come whose Harbinger he was, a time
In which apostasy from ancient faith
Seemed but conversion to a higher creed;   310
Withal a season dangerous and wild,
A time when sage Experience would have snatched
Flowers out of any hedge-row to compose
A chaplet in contempt of his grey locks.
    When the proud Fleet that bears the red-cross Flag   315

In that unworthy service were prepared
To mingle, I beheld the Vessels lie,
A brood of gallant Creatures, on the Deep,
I saw them in their rest, a Sojourner
Through a whole month of calm and glassy days,   320
In that delightful Island which protects
Their place of convocation—there I heard,
Each evening, pacing by the still sea-shore,
A monitory sound that never failed,—
The sunset Cannon. While the orb went down   325
In the tranquillity of Nature, came
That voice, ill requiem! seldom heard by me
Without a spirit overcast by dark
Imaginations, sense of woes to come,
Sorrow for human kind, and pain of heart.   330
    In France the men who, for their desperate ends,
Had plucked up mercy by the roots, were glad
Of this new enemy. Tyrants, strong before
In wicked pleas, were strong as Demons now;
And thus, on every side beset with foes,   335
The goaded land waxed mad; the crimes of few
Spread into madness of the many, blasts
From hell came sanctified like airs from heaven;
The sternness of the Just, the faith of those
Who doubted not that Providence had times   340
Of vengeful retribution;—theirs who throned
The human understanding paramount
And made of that their God, the hopes of men
Who were content to barter short-lived pangs
For a paradise of ages, the blind rage   345
Of insolent tempers, the light vanity
Of intermeddlers, steady purposes
Of the suspicious, slips of the indiscreet,
And all the accidents of life were pressed
Into one service, busy with one work.   350
The Senate stood aghast, her prudence quenched,
Her wisdom stifled, and her justice scared,
Her frenzy only active to extol
Past outrages, and shape the way for new,

Which no one dared to oppose or mitigate.   355
—Domestic carnage now filled the whole year
With Feast-days; old Men from the Chimney-nook,
The Maiden from the bosom of her Love,
The Mother from the Cradle of her Babe,
The Warrior from the Field, all perished, all,   360
Friends, enemies, of all parties, ages, ranks,
Head after head, and never heads enough
For those that bade them fall. They found their joy,
They made it, proudly eager as a Child
(If like desires of innocent little ones   365
May with such heinous appetites be compared),
Pleased in some open field to exercise
A toy that mimics with revolving wings
The motion of a windmill, though the air
Do of itself blow fresh and make the Vanes   370
Spin in his eyesight, *that* contents him not,
But, with the play-thing at arm's length, he sets
His front against the blast, and runs amain
That it may whirl the faster.
                              'Mid the depth
Of those enormities, even thinking minds   375
Forgot at seasons whence they had their being,
Forgot that such a sound was ever heard
As Liberty upon earth; yet all beneath
Her innocent authority was wrought,
Nor could have been without her blessed name.   380
The illustrious wife of Roland, in the hour
Of her composure, felt that agony
And gave it vent in her last words. O Friend!
It was a lamentable time for man,
Whether a hope had e'er been his or not,   385
A woeful time for them whose hopes survived
The shock—most woeful for those few who still
Were flattered and had trust in human-kind:
They had the deepest feeling of the grief.
Meanwhile the Invaders fared as they deserved: 390
The Herculean Commonwealth had put forth her arms
And throttled with an infant Godhead's might

The snakes about her cradle: that was well
And as it should be, yet no cure for them
Whose souls were sick with pain of what would be   395
Hereafter brought in charge against mankind.
Most melancholy at that time, O Friend!
Were my day-thoughts, my nights were miserable;
Through months, through years, long after the last beat
Of those atrocities, the hour of sleep   400
To me came rarely charged with natural gifts,
Such ghastly Visions had I of despair
And tyranny, and implements of death,
And innocent victims sinking under fear,
And momentary hope, and worn-out prayer,   405
Each in his separate cell, or penned in crowds
For sacrifice, and struggling with forced mirth
And levity in dungeons where the dust
Was laid with tears. Then suddenly the scene
Changed, and the unbroken dream entangled me   410
In long orations which I strove to plead
Before unjust tribunals—with a voice
Labouring, a brain confounded, and a sense
Death-like of treacherous desertion, felt
In the last place of refuge, my own soul.   415
    When I began in Youth's delightful prime
To yield myself to Nature, when that strong
And holy passion overcame me first,
Nor day nor night, evening or morn, were free
From its oppression. But, O Power supreme!   420
Without whose care this world would cease to breathe,
Who from the fountain of thy grace dost fill
The veins that branch through every frame of life,
Making man what he is, Creature divine,
In single or in social eminence   425
Above the rest raised infinite ascents
When reason that enables him to be
Is not sequestered, what a change is here!
How different ritual for this after-worship!
What countenance to promote this second love!   430
The first was service paid to things which lie

Guarded within the bosom of thy will.
Therefore to serve was high beatitude;
Tumult was therefore gladness, and the fear
Ennobling, venerable; sleep secure,   435
And waking thoughts more rich than happiest dreams.
      But as the ancient Prophets, borne aloft
In vision, yet constrained by natural laws
With them to take a troubled human heart,
Wanted not consolations nor a creed   440
Of reconcilement, then when they denounced
On Towns and Cities wallowing in the abyss
Of their offences punishment to come;
Or saw, like other men, with bodily eyes,
Before them, in some desolated place,   445
The wrath consummate and the threat fulfilled;
So, with devout humility be it said,
So did a portion of that spirit fall
On me, uplifted from the vantage ground
Of pity and sorrow to a state of being   450
That through the time's exceeding fierceness saw
Glimpses of retribution, terrible
And in the order of sublime behests;
But even if that were not, amid the awe
Of unintelligible chastisement,   455
Not only acquiescences of faith
Survived, but daring sympathies with power,
Motions not treacherous or profane, else why
Within the folds of no ungentle breast
Their dread vibration to this hour prolonged?   460
Wild blasts of music thus could find their way
Into the midst of turbulent events,
So that worst tempests might be listened to.
Then was the truth received into my heart,
That, under heaviest sorrow earth can bring,   465
If from the affliction somewhere do not grow
Honor which could not else have been, a faith,
An elevation, and a sanctity,
If new strength be not given nor old restored,
The blame is ours, not Nature's. When a taunt   470

Was taken up by scoffers in their pride,
Saying, "Behold the harvest that we reap
From popular Government and Equality,"
Clearly I saw that neither these, nor aught
Of wild belief engrafted on their names   475
By false philosophy, had caused the woe,
But a terrific reservoir of guilt
And ignorance, filled up from age to age,
That could no longer hold its loathsome charge,
But burst and spread in deluge through the Land.   480
    And, as the desert hath green spots, the sea
Small islands scattered amid stormy waves,
So *that* disastrous period did not want
Bright sprinklings of all human excellence
To which the silver wands of Saints in heaven   485
Might point with rapturous joy. Yet not the less,
For those examples in no age surpassed
Of fortitude and energy and love;
And human nature faithful to herself
Under worst trials, was I driven to think   490
Of the glad times when first I traversed France,
A youthful Pilgrim; above all reviewed
That even-tide, when under windows bright
With happy faces, and with garlands hung,
And through a rainbow arch that spanned the street,   495
Triumphal pomp for Liberty confirmed,
I paced, a dear Companion at my side,
The Town of Arras, whence with promise high
Issued, on Delegation to sustain
Humanity and right, *that* Robespierre,   500
He who thereafter, and in how short time!
Wielded the sceptre of the Atheist Crew.
When the calamity spread far and wide,
And this same City, that did then appear
To outrun the rest in exultation, groaned   505
Under the vengeance of her cruel Son
As Lear reproached the winds, I could almost
Have quarrelled with that blameless Spectacle
For lingering yet an Image in my mind

To mock me under such a strange reverse.   510
    O Friend! few happier moments have been mine,
Than that which told the downfall of this Tribe
So dreaded, so abhorr'd.— The day deserves
A separate Record. Over the smooth Sands
Of Leven's ample Æstuary lay   515
My journey, and beneath a genial Sun,
With distant prospect among gleams of sky,
And clouds, and intermingling mountain tops,
In one inseparable glory clad,
Creatures of one etherial substance met   520
In Consistory, like a diadem
Or crown of burning Seraphs, as they sit
In the Empyrean. Underneath that pomp
Celestial, lay unseen the pastoral Vales
Among whose happy fields I had grown up   525
From Childhood. On the fulgent Spectacle,
That neither passed away nor changed, I gazed
Enrapt; but brightest things are wont to draw
Sad opposites out of the inner heart,
As soon their pensive influence drew from mine.   530
How could it otherwise? for not in vain
That very morning had I turned aside
To seek the ground where, 'mid a throng of Graves,
An honored Teacher of my Youth was laid.
While we were School-boys, he had died among us,   535
And was borne thither, as I knew, to rest
With his own Family. A plain stone inscribed
With name, date, office, pointed out the Spot,
And on the Stone were graven, by his desire,
Lines from the Churchyard Elegy of Gray.   540
This faithful Guide, speaking from his death-bed,
Added no farewell to his parting counsel,
But said to me, "My head will soon lie low;"
And when I saw the turf that covered him,
After the lapse of full eight years, those words,   545
With sound of voice, and countenance of the Man,
Came back upon me, so that some few tears
Fell from me in my own despite. But now

I thought, still traversing that wide-spread plain,
With tender pleasure of the Verses graven   550
Upon his Tomb-stone, whispering to myself:
He loved the Poets, and if now alive
Would have loved me, as One not destitute
Of promise, nor belying the kind hope
That he had formed, when I, at his command,   555
Began to spin with toil my earliest Songs.
—As I advanced, all that I saw or felt
Was gentleness and peace. Upon a small
And rocky Island near, a fragment stood
(Itself like a sea-rock), the low remains   560
(With shells encrusted, dark with briny weeds)
Of a dilapidated Structure, once
A Romish Chapel, where the vested Priest
Said matins at the hour that suited those
Who crossed the Sands with ebb of morning-tide;   565
Not far from that still Ruin all the Plain
Lay spotted with a variegated Crowd
Of Vehicles, and Travellers, horse and foot,
Wading beneath the Conduct of their Guide
In loose Procession through the shallow Stream   570
Of Inland Waters: the Great Sea, meanwhile,
Heaved at safe distance, far retired. I paused,
Longing for skill to paint a scene so bright
And chearful—but the foremost of the Band
As he approached, no salutation given,   575
In the familiar language of the day
Cried, "Robespierre is dead!"—nor was a doubt,
After strict question, left within my mind
That He and his Supporters all were fallen.
      Great was my transport, deep my gratitude   580
To everlasting justice, by this fiat
Made manifest. "Come now, Ye golden times,"
Said I, forth-pouring on those open Sands
A Hymn of triumph, "as the morning comes
From out the bosom of the night, come Ye: 585
Thus far our trust is verified; behold!
They who with clumsy desperation brought

A river of blood, and preached that nothing else
Could cleanse the Augean Stable, by the might
Of their own Helper have been swept away;   590
Their madness stands declared and visible;
Elsewhere will safety now be sought, and Earth
March firmly towards righteousness and peace."
— Then schemes I framed more calmly, when, and how,
The madding Factions might be tranquillized,   595
And how through hardships manifold and long
The glorious renovation would proceed.
Thus interrupted by uneasy bursts
Of exultation, I pursued my way
Along that very Shore which I had skimmed   600
In former days, when, spurring from the Vale
Of Nightshade, and St Mary's mouldering Fane,
And the Stone Abbot, after circuit made
In wantonness of heart, a joyous Band
Of School-boys, hastening to their distant home,   605
Along the margin of the moon-light Sea
We beat with thundering hoofs the level Sand.

BOOK ELEVENTH
FRANCE, CONCLUDED

From that time forth Authority in France
Put on a milder face; terror had ceased,
Yet every thing was wanting that might give
Courage to them who looked for good by light
Of rational experience, for the shoots   5
And hopeful blossoms of a second spring:
Yet in me confidence was unimpaired;
The Senate's language and the public acts
And measures of the Government, though both
Weak, and of heartless omen, had not power   10
To daunt me; in the People was my trust
And in the virtues which mine eyes had seen.
I knew that wound external could not take
Life from the young Republic, that new foes
Would only follow in the path of shame   15
Their brethren, and her triumphs be in the end

Great, universal, irresistible.
This intuition led me to confound
One victory with another, higher far,
Triumphs of unambitious peace at home   20
And noiseless fortitude. Beholding still
Resistance strong as heretofore, I thought
That what was in degree the same was likewise
The same in quality, that as the worse
Of the two Spirits then at strife remained   25
Untired, the better surely would preserve
The heart that first had roused him. Youth maintains,
In all conditions of society,
Communion more direct and intimate
With Nature—hence, ofttimes, with Reason too—   30
Than Age or Manhood, even. To Nature then
Power had reverted: habit, custom, law,
Had left an interregnum's open space
For her to move about in, uncontrolled.
Hence could I see how Babel-like their task   35
Who, by the recent deluge stupified,
With their whole souls went culling from the day
Its petty promises, to build a tower
For their own safety; laughed with my Compeers
At gravest heads, by enmity to France   40
Distempered, till they found, in every blast
Forced from the Street-disturbing Newsman's horn,
For her great cause Record or Prophesy
Of utter ruin. How might we believe
That wisdom could in any shape come near   45
Men clinging to delusions so insane?
And thus, experience proving that no few
Of our opinions had been just, We took
Like credit to ourselves where less was due,
And thought that other notions were as sound,   50
Yea, could not but be right, because we saw
That foolish men opposed them.
                                        To a strain
More animated I might here give way,
And tell, since juvenile errors are my theme,

What in those days through Britain was performed   55
To turn *all* judgments out of their right course;
But this is passion overnear ourselves,
Reality too close, and too intense,
And intermixed with something in my mind
Of scorn and condemnation personal   60
That would profane the sanctity of Verse.
—Our Shepherds, this say merely, at that time
Acted, or seemed at least to act, like Men
Thirsting to make the guardian crook of Law
A tool of murder; they who ruled the State,   65
Though with such awful proof before their eyes
That he who would sow death, reaps death, or worse,
And can reap nothing better, child-like, longed
To imitate, not wise enough to avoid;
Or left (by mere timidity betrayed)   70
The plain straight road for one no better chosen
Than if their wish had been to undermine
Justice, and make an end of Liberty.
    But from these bitter truths I must return
To my own History. It hath been told   75
That I was led to take an eager part
In arguments of civil polity
Abruptly, and indeed before my time:
I had approached, like other Youth, the Shield
Of human nature from the golden side,   80
And would have fought, even to the death, to attest
The quality of the metal which I saw.
What there is best in individual man,
Of wise in passion, and sublime in power,
Benevolent in small societies,   85
And great in large ones, I had oft revolved,
Felt deeply, but not thoroughly understood
By Reason: nay, far from it, they were yet,
As cause was given me afterwards to learn,
Not proof against the injuries of the day,   90
Lodged only at the Sanctuary's door,
Not safe within its bosom. Thus prepared,
And with such general insight into evil,

And of the bounds which sever it from good,
As books and common intercourse with life   95
Must needs have given—to the inexperienced mind,
When the World travels in a beaten road,
Guide faithful as is needed—I began
To meditate with ardour on the Rule
And management of Nations, what it is   100
And ought to be, and strove to learn how far
Their power or weakness, wealth or poverty,
Their happiness or misery, depend
Upon their laws, and fashion of the State.
    O pleasant exercise of hope and joy!   105
For mighty were the Auxiliars which then stood
Upon our side, we who were strong in Love!
Bliss was it in that dawn to be alive,
But to be young was very Heaven! O times,
In which the meagre, stale, forbidding ways   110
Of custom, law, and statute, took at once
The attraction of a Country in Romance!
When Reason seemed the most to assert her rights,
When most intent on making of herself
A prime Enchantress—to assist the work   115
Which then was going forward in her name!
Not favored spots alone, but the whole earth
The beauty wore of promise—that which sets
(As at some moments might not be unfelt
Among the bowers of Paradise itself)   120
The budding rose above the rose full blown.
What Temper at the prospect did not wake
To happiness unthought of? The inert
Were roused, and lively natures rapt away!
They who had fed their Childhood upon dreams,   125
The play-fellows of Fancy, who had made
All powers of swiftness, subtilty, and strength
Their ministers,—who in lordly wise had stirred
Among the grandest objects of the Sense,
And dealt with whatsoever they found there   130
As if they had within some lurking right
To wield it;—they, too, who of gentle mood

Had watched all gentle motions, and to these
Had fitted their own thoughts, schemers more mild,
And in the region of their peaceful selves;—   135
Now was it that *both* found, the Meek and Lofty
Did both find helpers to their hearts' desire,
And stuff at hand, plastic as they could wish,—
Were called upon to exercise their skill,
Not in Utopia,—subterranean Fields,—   140
Or some secreted Island, Heaven knows where!
But in the very world, which is the world
Of all of us,—the place where in the end
We find our happiness, or not at all!
　　Why should I not confess that Earth was then   145
To me what an Inheritance new-fallen
Seems, when the first time visited, to one
Who thither comes to find in it his home?
He walks about and looks upon the spot
With cordial transport, moulds it and remoulds,   150
And is half-pleased with things that are amiss,
'Twill be such joy to see them disappear.
　　An active partisan, I thus convoked
From every object pleasant circumstance
To suit my ends; I moved among mankind   155
With genial feelings still predominant;
When erring, erring on the better part,
And in the kinder spirit; placable,
Indulgent, as not uninformed that men
See as they have been taught, and that Antiquity   160
Gives rights to error; and aware no less
That throwing off oppression must be work
As well of licence as of liberty;
And above all, for this was more than all,
Not caring if the wind did now and then   165
Blow keen upon an eminence that gave
Prospect so large into futurity;
In brief, a Child of Nature, as at first,
Diffusing only those affections wider
That from the cradle had grown up with me,   170
And losing, in no other way than light

Is lost in light, the weak in the more strong.
　In the main outline, such, it might be said,
Was my condition, till with open war
Britain opposed the Liberties of France;　　　　　　　175
This threw me first out of the pale of love,
Soured, and corrupted, upwards to the source,
My sentiments; was not, as hitherto,
A swallowing up of lesser things in great;
But change of them into their contraries;　　　　　　180
And thus a way was opened for mistakes
And false conclusions, in degree as gross,
In kind more dangerous. What had been a pride
Was now a shame; my likings and my loves
Ran in new channels, leaving old ones dry,　　　　　185
And hence a blow that in maturer age
Would but have touched the judgement, struck more deep
Into sensations near the heart; meantime,
As from the first, wild theories were afloat
To whose pretensions sedulously urged　　　　　　190
I had but lent a careless ear, assured
That time was ready to set all things right,
And that the multitude so long oppressed
Would be oppressed no more.
　　　　　　　　But when events
Brought less encouragement, and unto these　　　　195
The immediate proof of principles no more
Could be entrusted, while the events themselves,
Worn out in greatness, stripped of novelty,
Less occupied the mind; and sentiments
Could through my understanding's natural growth　　200
No longer keep their ground, by faith maintained
Of inward consciousness, and hope that laid
Her hand upon her object; evidence
Safer, of universal application, such
As could not be impeached, was sought elsewhere.　　205
　But now, become Oppressors in their turn,
Frenchmen had changed a war of self-defence
For one of Conquest, losing sight of all
Which they had struggled for: and mounted up,

Openly in the eye of Earth and Heaven,   210
The scale of Liberty. I read her doom
With anger vexed, with disappointment sore,
But not dismayed, nor taking to the shame
Of a false Prophet. While resentment rose,
Striving to hide, what nought could heal, the wounds   215
Of mortified presumption, I adhered
More firmly to old tenets, and, to prove
Their temper, strained them more; and thus, in heat
Of contest, did opinions every day
Grow into consequence, till round my mind   220
They clung, as if they were its life, nay more,
The very being of the immortal Soul.
      This was the time when, all things tending fast
To depravation, speculative schemes
That promised to abstract the hopes of Man   225
Out of his feelings, to be fixed thenceforth
For ever in a purer element,
Found ready welcome. Tempting region *that*
For Zeal to enter and refresh herself,
Where passions had the privilege to work,   230
And never hear the sound of their own names:
But, speaking more in charity, the dream
Flattered the young, pleased with extremes, nor least
With that which makes our Reason's naked self
The object of its fervour: What delight!   235
How glorious! in self-knowledge and self-rule
To look through all the frailties of the world,
And, with a resolute mastery shaking off
Infirmities of Nature, time, and place,
Build social upon personal Liberty,   240
Which, to the blind restraints of general Laws
Superior, magisterially adopts
One guide, the light of circumstances, flashed
Upon an independent intellect.
Thus expectation rose again; thus hope,   245
From her first ground expelled, grew proud once more.
Oft, as my thoughts were turned to human kind,
I scorned indifference; but, inflamed with thirst

Of a secure intelligence, and sick
Of other longing, I pursued what seemed   250
A more exalted nature, wished that Man
Should start out of his earthy worm-like state
And spread abroad the wings of liberty,
Lord of himself in undisturbed delight;
A noble aspiration! *yet* I feel   255
(Sustained by worthier as by wiser thoughts)
The aspiration, nor shall ever cease
To feel it; but return we to our course.
        Enough, 'tis true, could such a plea excuse
Those aberrations, had the clamorous friends   260
Of ancient Institutions said and done
To bring disgrace upon their very names;
Disgrace of which custom and written law,
And sundry moral sentiments as props
Or emanations of those institutes,   265
Too justly bore a part. A veil had been
Uplifted; why deceive ourselves? in sooth,
'Twas even so; and sorrow for the Man
Who either had not eyes wherewith to see,
Or, seeing, had forgotten; a strong shock   270
Was given to old opinions; all Men's minds
Had felt its power, and mine was both let loose,
Let loose and goaded. After what hath been
Already said of patriotic love,
Suffice it here to add, that, somewhat stern   275
In temperament, withal a happy man,
And therefore bold to look on painful things,
Free likewise of the world, and thence more bold,
I summoned my best skill, and toiled, intent
To anatomize the frame of social life,   280
Yea, the whole body of society
Searched to its heart. Share with me, Friend! the wish
That some dramatic tale indued with shapes
Livelier, and flinging out less guarded words
Than suit the Work we fashion, might set forth   285
What then I learned, or think I learned, of truth,
And the errors into which I fell, betrayed

By present objects, and by reasonings false
From their beginnings, inasmuch as drawn
Out of a heart that had been turned aside   290
From Nature's way by outward accidents,
And which was thus confounded more and more,
Misguided and misguiding. So I fared,
Dragging all precepts, judgments, maxims, creeds,
Like culprits to the bar; calling the mind,   295
Suspiciously, to establish in plain day
Her titles and her honors, now believing,
Now disbelieving, endlessly perplexed
With impulse, motive, right and wrong, the ground
Of obligation, what the rule and whence   300
The sanction, till, demanding formal *proof*
And seeking it in every thing, I lost
All feeling of conviction, and, in fine,
Sick, wearied out with contrarieties,
Yielded up moral questions in despair.   305
    This was the crisis of that strong disease,
This the soul's last and lowest ebb; I drooped,
Deeming our blessed Reason of least use
Where wanted most: the lordly attributes
Of will and choice (I bitterly exclaimed),   310
What are they but a mockery of a Being
Who hath in no concerns of his a test
Of good and evil? knows not what to fear
Or hope for, what to covet or to shun?
And who, if those could be discerned, would yet   315
Be little profited, would see, and ask
Where is the obligation to enforce?
And, to acknowledged law rebellious, still
As selfish passion urged would act amiss:
The dupe of folly, or the slave of crime?   320
    Depressed, bewildered thus, I did not walk
With scoffers, seeking light and gay revenge
From indiscriminate laughter, nor sate down
In reconcilement with an utter waste
Of Intellect; such sloth I could not brook.   325
(Too well I loved, in that my spring of life,

Pains-taking thoughts and truth, their dear reward),
But turned to abstract science, and there sought
Work for the reasoning faculty, enthroned
Where the disturbances of space and time—   330
Whether in matter's various properties
Inherent, or from human will and power
Derived—find no admission.— Then it was,
Thanks to the bounteous Giver of all good!
That the beloved Woman in whose sight   335
Those days were passed, now speaking in a voice
Of sudden admonition—like a brook
That does but *cross* a lonely road, and now
Seen, heard, and felt, and caught at every turn,
Companion never lost through many a league—   340
Maintained for me a saving intercourse
With my true self: for, though bedimmed and changed
Both as a clouded and a waning moon,
She whispered still that brightness would return,
She in the midst of all preserved me still   345
A Poet, made me seek beneath that name,
And that alone, my office upon earth.
And lastly, as hereafter will be shewn,
If willing audience fail not, Nature's self,
By all varieties of human love   350
Assisted, led me back through opening day
To those sweet counsels between head and heart
Whence grew that genuine knowledge fraught with peace
Which, through the later sinkings of this cause,
Hath still upheld me, and upholds me now   355
In the catastrophe (for so they dream,
And nothing less), when, finally to close
And rivet down the gains of France, a Pope
Is summoned in, to crown an Emperor:
This last opprobrium, when we see a people   360
That once looked up in faith, as if to Heaven
For manna, take a lesson from the Dog
Returning to his vomit; when the Sun
That rose in splendour, was alive, and moved
In exultation with a living pomp   365

Of clouds—his glory's natural retinue—
Hath dropped all functions by the Gods bestowed,
And, turned into a gewgaw, a machine,
Sets like an Opera phantom.
                              Thus through times
Of honor and through times of bitter shame   370
Descending, have I faithfully retraced
The perturbations of a youthful mind
Under a long-lived storm of great events—
A Story destined for thy ear, who now
Among the fallen of Nations dost abide   375
Where Ætna over hill and valley casts
His shadow, stretching towards Syracuse,
The City of Timoleon. Righteous Heaven!
How are the mighty prostrated! they first,
They first of all that breathe should have awaked   380
When the great voice was heard from out the Tombs
Of ancient Heroes. If I suffered grief
For ill-requited France, by many deemed
A trifler only in her proudest day;
Have been distressed to think of what she once   385
Promised, now is; a far more sober cause
Thine eyes must see of sorrow in a Land,
Though with the wreck of loftier years bestrewn,
To the reanimating influence lost
Of Memory, to virtue lost and hope.   390
    But indignation works where hope is not,
And thou, O Friend! wilt be refreshed. There is
One great Society alone on Earth,
The noble Living, and the noble Dead.
    Thine be such converse strong and sanative,   395
A ladder for thy Spirit to reascend
To health and joy and pure contentedness:
To me the grief confined that Thou art gone
From this last spot of earth where Freedom now
Stands single in her only Sanctuary;   400
A lonely Wanderer art gone, by pain
Compelled and sickness, at this latter day,
This sorrowful reverse for all mankind.

I feel for thee, must utter what I feel:
The sympathies erewhile in part discharged   405
Gather afresh, and will have vent again;
My own delights do scarcely seem to me
My own delights; the lordly Alps themselves,
Those rosy peaks, from which the morning looks
Abroad on many Nations, for my mind   410
Are not that image of pure gladsomeness
Which they were wont to be: through kindred scenes,
For purpose, at a time how different!
Thou tak'st thy way, carrying the heart and soul
That Nature gives to Poets, now by thought   415
Matured, and in the summer of their strength.
Oh! wrap him in your Shades, Ye Giant woods
On Etna's side, and thou, O flowery Field
Of Enna! is there not some nook of thine
From the first play-time of the infant world   420
Kept sacred to restorative delight
When from afar invoked by anxious love?
    Child of the Mountains, among Shepherds reared,
Ere yet familiar with the Classic page,
I learnt to dream of Sicily; and lo!   425
The gloom that, but a moment past, was deepened
At her command, at her command gives way;
Sensations changing as thoughts shift their ground,
A pleasant promise, wafted from her shores,
Comes o'er my heart: in fancy I behold   430
Her seas yet smiling, her once happy Vales,
Nor can my tongue give utterance to a name
Of note belonging to that honored Isle,
Philosopher or Bard, Empedocles,
Or Archimedes, pure abstracted Soul!   435
That doth not yield a solace to my grief;
And O Theocritus, so far have some
Prevailed among the powers of heaven and earth
By their endowments good or great, that they
Have had, as thou reportest, miracles   440
Wrought for them in old time: yea, not unmoved
When thinking on my own beloved Friend,

I hear thee tell how bees with honey fed
Divine Comates, by his impious Lord
Within a Chest imprisoned, how they came   445
Laden from blooming grove or flowery field,
And fed him there, alive month after month,
Because the Goatherd, blessed Man! had lips
Wet with the Muses' Nectar.
                              Thus I soothe
The pensive moments by this calm fire side,   450
And find a thousand bounteous images
To chear the thoughts of those I love, and mine;
Our prayers have been accepted, thou wilt stand
On Etna's summit above earth and sea
Triumphant, winning from the invaded heavens   455
Thoughts without bound, magnificent designs
Worthy of Poets who attuned the Harp
In wood or echoing cave, for discipline
Of Heroes; or, in reverence to the Gods,
'Mid Temples served by sapient Priests and choirs   460
Of Virgins crowned with roses. Not in vain
Those temples, where they in their ruins yet
Survive for inspiration, shall attract
Thy solitary steps. And on the brink
Thou wilt recline of pastoral Arethuse;   465
Or, if that fountain be in truth no more,
Then near some other Spring which by the name
Thou gratulatest, willingly deceived,
I see Thee linger, a glad Votary,
And not a Captive pining for his home.   470

BOOK TWELFTH
IMAGINATION AND TASTE, HOW IMPAIRED AND RESTORED

Long time have human ignorance and guilt
Detained us, on what spectacles of woe
Compelled to look, and inwardly oppressed
With sorrow, disappointment, vexing thoughts,
Confusion of the judgment, zeal decayed,   5
And, lastly, utter loss of hope itself
And things to hope for! Not with these began

Our Song, and not with these our Song must end.
Ye motions of delight, that haunt the sides
Of the green hills; ye breezes and soft airs,   10
Whose subtile intercourse with breathing flowers,
Feelingly watched, might teach Man's haughty race
How without injury to take, to give
Without offence; ye who, as if to shew
The wondrous influence of power gently used,   15
Bend the complying heads of lordly pines,
And with a touch shift the stupendous clouds
Through the whole compass of the sky; ye brooks
Muttering along the stones, a busy noise
By day, a quiet sound in silent night;   20
Ye waves that out of the great deep steal forth
In a calm hour to kiss the pebbly shore,
Not mute, and then retire, fearing no storm;
And you, ye Groves, whose ministry it is
To interpose the covert of your shades,   25
Even as a sleep, between the heart of man
And outward troubles, between man himself,
Not seldom, and his own uneasy heart!
Oh that I had a music and a voice
Harmonious as your own, that I might tell   30
What Ye have done for me! The morning shines,
Nor heedeth Man's perverseness; Spring returns,
I saw the Spring return and could rejoice,
In common with the Children of her love
Piping on boughs, or sporting on fresh fields,   35
Or boldly seeking pleasure nearer heaven
On wings that navigate cerulean skies.
So neither were complacency nor peace
Nor tender yearnings wanting for my good
Through those distracted times; in Nature still   40
Glorying, I found a counterpoise in her,
Which, when the Spirit of evil reached its height,
Maintained for me a secret happiness.
    This Narrative, my Friend, hath chiefly told
Of intellectual power, fostering love,   45
Dispensing truth, and over men and things,

Where reason yet might hesitate, diffusing
Prophetic sympathies of genial faith.
So was I favored, such my happy lot,
Until that natural graciousness of mind   50
Gave way to overpressure from the times
And their disastrous issues. What availed,
When spells forbade the Voyager to land,
That fragrant notice of a pleasant shore
Wafted at intervals from many a bower   55
Of blissful gratitude and fearless peace?
Dare I avow that wish was mine to see,
And hope that future times *would* surely see,
The man to come parted as by a gulph
From him who had been, that I could no more   60
Trust the elevation which had made me one
With the great Family that still survives
To illuminate the abyss of ages past,
Sage, Warrior, Patriot, Hero?—for it seemed
That their best virtues were not free from taint   65
Of something false and weak, that could not stand
The open eye of Reason. Then I said,
"Go to the Poets; they will speak to thee
More perfectly of purer Creatures; yet
If Reason be nobility in Man,   70
Can aught be more ignoble than the Man
Whom they delight in, blinded as he is
By prejudice, the miserable slave
Of low ambition, or distempered love?"
    In such strange passion (if I may once more   75
Review the past) I warred against myself,
A Bigot to a New Idolatry;
Like a cowled Monk who hath forsworn the world,
Zealously labour'd to cut off my heart
From all the sources of her former strength;   80
And as by simple waving of a Wand
The wizard instantaneously dissolves
Palace or grove, even so could I unsoul
As readily by syllogistic words
Those mysteries of being which have made,   85

And shall continue evermore to make,
Of the whole human race one brotherhood.
   What wonder, then, if to a mind so far
Perverted, even the visible Universe
Fell under the dominion of a taste   90
Less Spiritual, with microscopic view
Was scanned, as I had scanned the moral world?
   Oh Soul of Nature, excellent and fair!
That didst rejoice with me, with whom I too
Rejoiced, through early Youth, before the winds   95
And roaring waters, and in lights and shades
That marched and countermarched about the hills
In glorious apparition, powers on whom
I daily waited, now all eye and now
All ear; but never long without the heart   100
Employed, and Man's unfolding intellect!
Oh Soul of Nature! that, by laws divine
Sustained and governed, still dost overflow
With an impassioned life, what feeble ones
Walk on this earth! how feeble have I been   105
When thou wert in thy strength! Nor this through stroke
Of human suffering, such as justifies
Remissness and inaptitude of mind,
But through presumption; even in pleasure pleased
Unworthily, disliking here, and there   110
Liking; by rules of mimic Art transferred
To things above all Art, but more,—for this,
Although a strong infection of the age,
Was never much my habit—giving way
To a comparison of scene with scene,   115
Bent overmuch on superficial things,
Pampering myself with meagre novelties
Of colour and proportion, to the moods
Of time and season, to the moral power,
The affections and the spirit of the Place,   120
Insensible. Nor only did the love
Of sitting thus in judgment interrupt
My deeper feelings, but another cause,
More subtile and less easily explained,

That almost seems inherent in the Creature,   125
A twofold frame of body and of mind.
I speak in recollection of a time
When the bodily eye, in every stage of life
The most despotic of our senses, gained
Such strength in *me* as often held my mind   130
In absolute dominion. Gladly here,
Entering upon abstruser Argument,
Could I endeavour to unfold the means
Which Nature studiously employs to thwart
This tyranny, summons all the senses each   135
To counteract the other, and themselves,
And makes them all, and the Objects with which all
Are conversant, subservient in their turn
To the great ends of Liberty and Power.
But leave we this: enough that my delights   140
(Such as they were) were sought insatiably.
Vivid the transport, vivid, though not profound;
I roamed from hill to hill, from rock to rock,
Still craving combinations of new forms,
New pleasure, wider empire for the sight,   145
Proud of her own endowments, and rejoiced
To lay the inner faculties asleep.
Amid the turns and counterturns, the strife
And various trials of our complex being,
As we grow up, such thraldom of that sense   150
Seems hard to shun. And yet I knew a Maid,
A young Enthusiast, who escaped these bonds;
Her eye was not the Mistress of her heart;
Far less did rules prescribed by passive taste
Or barren intermeddling subtleties   155
Perplex her mind; but, wise as women are
When genial circumstance hath favoured them,
She welcomed what was given and craved no more;
Whate'er the scene presented to her view,
That was the best, to that she was attuned   160
By her benign simplicity of life
And through a perfect happiness of Soul
Whose variegated feelings were in this

Sisters, that they were each some new delight.
Birds in the bower, and lambs in the green field,   165
Could they have known her, would have loved; methought
Her very presence such a sweetness breathed
That flowers, and trees, and even the silent hills,
And every thing she looked on should have had
An intimation how she bore herself   170
Towards them and to all creatures. God delights
In such a being; for her common thoughts
Are piety, her life is gratitude.
      Even like this Maid, before I was called forth
From the retirement of my native hills,   175
I loved whate'er I saw: nor lightly loved,
But most intensely; never dreamt of aught
More grand, more fair, more exquisitely framed
Than those few nooks to which my happy feet
Were limited. I had not at that time   180
Lived long enough, nor in the least survived
The first diviner influence of this world
As it appears to unaccustomed eyes.
Worshipping then among the depth of things
As piety ordained, could I submit   185
To measured admiration, or to aught
That should preclude humility and love?
I felt, observed, and pondered; did not judge,
Yea, never thought of judging; with the gift
Of all this glory filled and satisfied.   190
And afterwards, when through the gorgeous Alps
Roaming, I carried with me the same heart:
In truth, the degradation, howsoe'er
Induced, effect in whatsoe'er degree
Of custom that prepares a partial scale   195
In which the little oft outweighs the great,
Or any other cause that hath been named;
Or lastly, aggravated by the times,
And their empassioned sounds, which well might make
The milder minstrelsies of rural scenes   200
Inaudible, was transient; I had known
Too forcibly, too early in my life,

Visitings of imaginative power
For this to last: I shook the habit off
Entirely and for ever, and again.   205
In Nature's presence stood, as now I stand,
A sensitive Being, a *creative* Soul.
    There are in our existence spots of time,
That with distinct pre-eminence retain
A renovating virtue, whence, depressed   210
By false opinion and contentious thought,
Or aught of heavier or more deadly weight,
In trivial occupations, and the round
Of ordinary intercourse, our minds
Are nourished and invisibly repaired;   215
A virtue by which pleasure is inhanced,
That penetrates, enables us to mount,
When high, more high, and lifts us up when fallen.
This efficacious Spirit chiefly lurks
Among those passages of life that give   220
Profoundest knowledge how and to what point
The mind is lord and master—outward sense
The obedient Servant of her will. Such moments
Are scattered every where, taking their date
From our first Childhood. I remember well   225
That once, while yet my inexperienced hand
Could scarcely hold a bridle, with proud hopes
I mounted, and we journied towards the hills:
An ancient Servant of my Father's house
Was with me, my encourager and Guide.   230
We had not travelled long ere some mischance
Disjoined me from my Comrade, and, through fear
Dismounting, down the rough and stony Moor
I led my horse, and, stumbling on, at length
Came to a bottom, where in former times   235
A Murderer had been hung in iron chains.
The Gibbet mast had mouldered down, the bones
And iron case were gone, but on the turf
Hard by, soon after that fell deed was wrought,
Some unknown hand had carved the Murderer's name.   240
The monumental Letters were inscribed

In times long past, but still from year to year,
By superstition of the neighbourhood,
The grass is cleared away, and to that hour
The characters were fresh and visible.   245
A casual glance had shewn them, and I fled,
Faultering and faint and ignorant of the road:
Then, reascending the bare common, saw
A naked Pool that lay beneath the hills,
The Beacon on its summit, and, more near,   250
A Girl who bore a Pitcher on her head,
And seemed with difficult steps to force her way
Against the blowing wind. It was in truth
An ordinary sight; but I should need
Colors and words that are unknown to man   255
To paint the visionary dreariness
Which, while I looked all round for my lost Guide,
Invested Moorland waste and naked Pool,
The Beacon crowning the lone eminence,
The Female and her garments vexed and tossed   260
By the strong wind.—When, in the blessed hours
Of early love, the loved One at my side,
I roamed, in daily presence of this scene,
Upon the naked Pool and dreary Crags,
And on the melancholy Beacon, fell   265
A spirit of pleasure, and Youth's golden gleam;
And think ye not with radiance more sublime
For these remembrances, and for the power
They had left behind? So feeling comes in aid
Of feeling, and diversity of strength   270
Attends us, if but once we have been strong.
Oh! mystery of Man, from what a depth
Proceed thy honors! I am lost, but see
In simple child-hood something of the base
On which thy greatness stands; but this I feel,   275
That from thyself it comes, that thou must give,
Else never canst receive. The days gone by
Return upon me almost from the dawn
Of life: the hiding-places of Man's power
Open; I would approach them, but they close.   280

I see by glimpses now; when age comes on
May scarcely see at all, and I would give,
While yet we may, as far as words can give,
Substance and life to what I feel, enshrining,
Such is my hope, the spirit of the past   285
For future restoration.— Yet another
Of these memorials.
                          One Christmas-time,
On the glad Eve of its dear holidays,
Feverish, and tired, and restless, I went forth
Into the fields, impatient for the sight   290
Of those led Palfreys that should bear us home,
My Brothers and myself. There rose a Crag
That, from the meeting point of two highways
Ascending, overlooked them both, far stretched;
Thither, uncertain on which road to fix   295
My expectation, thither I repaired,
Scout-like, and gained the summit; 'twas a day
Tempestuous, dark, and wild, and on the grass
I sate, half-sheltered by a naked wall;
Upon my right hand couched a single sheep,   300
Upon my left a blasted hawthorn stood:
With those Companions at my side, I sate,
Straining my eyes intensely, as the mist
Gave intermitting prospect of the copse
And plain beneath. Ere we to School returned   305
That dreary time, ere we had been ten days
Sojourners in my Father's House, he died,
And I and my three Brothers, Orphans then,
Followed his Body to the Grave. The Event,
With all the sorrow that it brought, appeared   310
A chastisement; and when I called to mind
That day so lately passed, when from the Crag
I looked in such anxiety of hope,
With trite reflections of morality,
Yet in the deepest passion, I bowed low   315
To God, who thus corrected my desires;
And afterwards, the wind and sleety rain
And all the business of the Elements,

The single Sheep, and the one blasted tree,
And the bleak music of that old stone wall,   320
The noise of wood and water, and the mist
That on the line of each of those two Roads
Advanced in such indisputable shapes;
All these were kindred spectacles and sounds
To which I oft repaired, and thence would drink   325
As at a fountain; and on winter nights,
Down to this *very* time, when storm and rain
Beat on my roof, or haply at noon-day,
While in a grove I walk whose lofty trees,
Laden with summer's thickest foliage, rock   330
In a strong wind, some working of the spirit,
Some inward agitations, thence are brought,
Whate'er their office, whether to beguile
Thoughts over-busy in the course they took,
Or animate an hour of vacant ease.   335

BOOK THIRTEENTH
SUBJECT CONCLUDED

From Nature doth emotion come, and moods
Of calmness equally are Nature's gift:
This is her glory; these two attributes
Are sister horns that constitute her strength.
Hence Genius, born to thrive by interchange   5
Of peace and excitation, finds in her
His best and purest friend, from her receives
That energy by which he seeks the truth,
From her that happy stillness of the mind
Which fits him to receive it, when unsought.   10
     Such benefit the humblest intellects
Partake of, each in their degree: 'tis mine
To speak of what myself have known and felt.
Smooth task! for words find easy way, inspired
By gratitude and confidence in truth.   15
Long time in search of knowledge did I range
The field of human life, in heart and mind
Benighted, but the dawn beginning now
To reappear, 'twas proved that not in vain

I had been taught to reverence a Power   20
That is the visible quality and shape
And image of right reason, that matures
Her processes by steadfast laws, gives birth
To no impatient or fallacious hopes,
No heat of passion or excessive zeal,   25
No vain conceits,—provokes to no quick turns
Of self-applauding intellect,—but trains
To meekness, and exalts by humble faith;
Holds up before the mind, intoxicate
With present objects, and the busy dance   30
Of things that pass away, a temperate shew
Of objects that endure; and by this course
Disposes her, when over-fondly set
On throwing off incumbrances, to seek
In Man, and in the frame of social life,   35
Whate'er there is desireable and good
Of kindred permanence, unchanged in form
And function, or through strict vicissitude
Of life and death revolving. Above all
Were re-established now those watchful thoughts   40
Which (seeing little worthy or sublime
In what the Historian's pen so much delights
To blazon, Power and Energy detached
From moral purpose) early tutored me
To look with feelings of fraternal love   45
Upon the unassuming things that hold
A silent station in this beauteous world.
    Thus moderated, thus composed, I found
Once more in Man an object of delight,
Of pure imagination, and of love;   50
And, as the horizon of my mind enlarged,
Again I took the intellectual eye
For my Instructor, studious more to see
Great Truths, than touch and handle little ones.
Knowledge was given accordingly; my trust   55
Became more firm in feelings that had stood
The test of such a trial; clearer far
My sense of excellence—of right and wrong:

The promise of the present time retired
Into its true proportion; sanguine schemes,   60
Ambitious projects, pleased me less; I sought
For present good in life's familiar face,
And built thereon my hopes of good to come.
     With settling judgments now of what would last
And what must disappear, prepared to find   65
Presumption, folly, madness, in the Men
Who thrust themselves upon the passive world
As Rulers of the world, to see in these,
Even when the public welfare is their aim,
Plans without thought, or built on theories   70
Vague and unsound, and having brought the Books
Of modern Statists to their proper test,
Life, human life with all its sacred claims
Of sex and age, and heaven-descended rights
Mortal, or those beyond the reach of death;   75
And having thus discerned how dire a thing
Is worshipped in that Idol proudly named
"The Wealth of Nations," where alone that wealth
Is lodged, and how encreased; and having gained
A more judicious knowledge of the worth   80
And dignity of individual Man,
No composition of the brain, but Man
Of whom we read, the Man whom we behold
With our own eyes—I could not but enquire,
Not with less interest than heretofore,   85
But greater, though in Spirit more subdued,
Why is this glorious Creature to be found
One only in ten thousand? What one is,
Why may not millions be? What bars are thrown
By Nature in the way of such a hope?   90
Our animal appetites, and daily wants,
Are these obstructions insurmountable?
If not, then others vanish into air.
"Inspect the basis of the social Pile:
Enquire," said I, "how much of mental Power   95
And genuine virtue they possess who live
By bodily toil, labour exceeding far

Their due proportion, under all the weight
Of that injustice which upon ourselves
Ourselves entail." Such estimate to frame   100
I chiefly looked (what need to look beyond?)
Among the natural Abodes of men,
Fields with their rural works, recalled to mind
My earliest notices, with these compared
The observations made in later youth,   105
And to that day continued.—For the time
Had never been when throes of mightiest Nations
And the world's tumult unto me could yield,
How far soe'er transported and possessed,
Full measure of content; but still I craved   110
An intermingling of distinct regards
And truths of individual sympathy
Nearer ourselves. Such often might be gleaned
From the great City, else it must have proved
To me a heart-depressing wilderness;   115
But much was wanting; therefore did I turn
To you, ye pathways, and ye lonely roads;
Sought you enriched with every thing I prized,
With human kindnesses and simple joys.
　　Oh! next to one dear State of bliss, vouchsafed   120
Alas! to few in this untoward world,
The bliss of walking daily in Life's prime
Through field or forest with the Maid we love,
While yet our hearts are young, while yet we breathe
Nothing but happiness; in some lone nook,   125
Deep vale, or any where, the home of both,
From which it would be misery to stir;
Oh! next to such enjoyment of our youth,
In my esteem, next to such dear delight
Was that of wandering on from day to day   130
Where I could meditate in peace, and cull
Knowledge that step by step might lead me on
To wisdom; or, as lightsome as a Bird
Wafted upon the wind from distant lands,
Sing notes of greeting to strange fields or groves,   135
Which lacked not voice to welcome me in turn;

And when that pleasant toil had ceased to please,
Converse with men, where if we meet a face
We almost meet a friend: on naked heaths
With long long ways before, by Cottage bench   140
Or well-spring, where the weary Traveller rests.
    Who doth not love to follow with his eye
The windings of a public way? the sight
Hath wrought on my imagination since the morn
Of childhood, when a disappearing line,   145
One daily present to my eyes, that crossed
The naked summit of a far-off hill
Beyond the limits that my feet had trod,
Was like an invitation into space
Boundless, or guide into eternity!   150
Yes, something of the grandeur which invests
The Mariner who sails the roaring sea
Through storm and darkness, early in my mind
Surrounded, too, the Wanderers of the Earth—
Grandeur as much, and loveliness far more.   155
Awed have I been by strolling Bedlamites,
From many other uncouth Vagrants (passed
In fear) have walked with quicker step; but why
Take note of this? When I began to enquire,
To watch and question those I met, and speak   160
Without reserve to them, the lonely roads
Were open Schools in which I daily read
With most delight the passions of mankind,
Whether by words, looks, sighs, or tears revealed;
There saw into the depth of human souls—   165
Souls that appear to have no depth at all
To careless eyes. And now—convinced at heart
How little those formalities, to which
With overweening trust alone we give
The name of Education, have to do   170
With real feeling and just sense, how vain
A correspondence with the talking world
Proves to the most, and called to make good search
If man's estate, by doom of Nature yoked
With toil, is therefore yoked with ignorance,   175

If virtue be indeed so hard to rear,
And intellectual strength so rare a boon—
I prized such walks still more, for there I found
Hope to my hope, and to my pleasure peace
And steadiness; and healing and repose   180
To every angry passion. There I heard,
From mouths of men obscure and lowly, truths
Replete with honour; sounds in unison
With loftiest promises of good and fair.
  There are who think that strong affections, love   185
Known by whatever name, is falsely deemed
A gift, to use a term which they would use,
Of vulgar nature, that its growth requires
Retirement, leisure, language purified
By manners studied and elaborate;   190
That whoso feels such passion in its strength
Must live within the very light and air
Of courteous usages refined by Art.
True is it where oppression worse than death
Salutes the Being at his birth, where grace   195
Of culture hath been utterly unknown,
And poverty and labour in excess
From day to day preoccupy the ground
Of the affections, and to Nature's self
Oppose a deeper Nature; there indeed   200
Love cannot be, nor does it thrive with ease
Among the close and overcrowded haunts
Of cities, where the human heart is sick
And the eye feeds it not, and cannot feed.
—Yes, in those wanderings deeply did I feel   205
How we mislead each other; above all,
How Books mislead us, seeking their reward
From judgments of the wealthy Few, who see
By artificial lights; how they debase
The Many for the pleasure of those Few;   210
Effeminately level down the truth
To certain general notions for the sake
Of being understood at once, or else
Through want of better knowledge in the heads

That framed them, flattering self-conceit with words   215
That, while they most ambitiously set forth
Extrinsic differences, the outward marks
Whereby Society has parted man
From man, neglect the universal heart.
    Here, calling up to mind what then I saw,   220
A youthful Traveller, and see daily now
In the familiar circuit of my home,
Here might I pause and bend in reverence
To Nature, and the power of human minds,
To Men as they are Men within themselves.   225
How oft high service is performed within,
When all the external Man is rude in shew!
Not like a Temple rich with pomp and gold,
But a mere mountain Chapel that protects
Its simple Worshippers from sun and shower.   230
Of these, said I, shall be my song, of these,
If future years mature me for the task,
Will I record the praises, making Verse
Deal boldly with substantial things; in truth
And sanctity of passion speak of these,   235
That justice may be done, obeisance paid
Where it is due: thus haply shall I teach, —   *dream on!*
Inspire, through unadulterated ears
Pour rapture, tenderness, and hope, my theme
No other than the very heart of Man   240
As found among the best of those who live
Not unexalted by religious faith,
Nor uninformed by Books, good books, though few,
In Nature's presence: thence may I select
Sorrow, that is not sorrow, but delight,   245
And miserable love that is not pain
To hear of, for the glory that redounds
Therefrom to human kind and what we are.
Be mine to follow with no timid step
Where knowledge leads me; it shall be my pride   250
That I have dared to tread this holy ground,
Speaking no dream, but things oracular,
Matter not lightly to be heard by those

Who to the letter of the outward promise
Do read the invisible Soul, by Men adroit   255
In speech, and for communion with the world
Accomplished, minds whose faculties are then
Most active when they are most eloquent,
And elevated most, when most admired.
Men may be found of other mold than these,   260
Who are their own Upholders, to themselves
Encouragement, and energy, and will,
Expressing liveliest thoughts in lively words
As native passion dictates. Others, too,
There are, among the walks of homely life,   265
Still higher, men for contemplation framed,
Shy, and unpractised in the strife of phrase,
Meek men, whose very souls perhaps would sink
Beneath them, summoned to such intercourse:
Theirs is the language of the heavens, the power,   270
The thought, the image, and the silent joy;
Words are but under-agents in their Souls;
When they are grasping with their greatest strength
They do not breathe among them; this I speak
In gratitude to God, who feeds our hearts   275
For his own service; knoweth, loveth us
When we are unregarded by the world.
     Also, about this time did I receive
Convictions still more strong than heretofore
Not only that the inner frame is good,   280
And graciously composed, but that, no less,
Nature for all conditions wants not power
To consecrate, if we have eyes to see,
The outside of her Creatures, and to breathe
Grandeur upon the very humblest face   285
Of human life. I felt that the array
Of act and circumstance, and visible form,
Is mainly, to the pleasure of the mind,
What passion makes them, that meanwhile the forms
Of Nature have a passion in themselves   290
That intermingles with those works of man
To which she summons him; although the works

Be mean, have nothing lofty of their own;
And that the Genius of the Poet hence
May boldly take his way among mankind   295
Wherever Nature leads, that he hath stood
By Nature's side among the Men of old,
And so shall stand for ever. Dearest Friend,
If thou partake the animating faith
That Poets, even as Prophets, each with each   300
Connected in a mighty scheme of truth,
Have each his own peculiar faculty,
Heaven's gift, a sense that fits him to perceive
Objects unseen before, thou wilt not blame
The humblest of this band who dares to hope   305
That unto him hath also been vouchsafed
An insight, that in some sort he possesses
A Privilege, whereby a Work of his,
Proceeding from a source of untaught things,
Creative and enduring, may become   310
A Power like one of Nature's. To a hope
Not less ambitious once among the Wilds
Of Sarum's Plain my youthful Spirit was raised;
There, as I ranged at will the pastoral downs
Trackless and smooth, or paced the bare white roads   315
Lengthening in solitude their dreary line,
Time with his retinue of ages fled
Backwards, nor checked his flight until I saw
Our dim Ancestral Past in Vision clear;
Saw multitudes of men, and here and there   320
A single Briton clothed in Wolf-skin vest,
With shield and stone-axe, stride across the wold;
The voice of Spears was heard, the rattling spear
Shaken by arms of mighty bone, in strength,
Long mouldered, of barbaric majesty.   325
I called on Darkness—but before the word
Was uttered, midnight darkness seemed to take
All objects from my sight; and lo! again
The Desart visible by dismal flames;
It is the Sacrificial Altar, fed   330
With living Men—how deep the groans! the voice

Of those that crowd the giant wicker thrills
The monumental hillocks, and the pomp
Is for both worlds, the living and the dead.
At other moments (for through that wide waste   335
Three summer days I roamed) where'er the Plain
Was figured o'er with circles, lines, or mounds,
That yet survive, a work, as some divine,
Shaped by the Druids, so to represent
Their knowledge of the heavens, and image forth   340
The constellations; gently was I charmed
Into a waking dream, a reverie
That with believing eyes, where'er I turned,
Beheld long-bearded Teachers with white wands
Uplifted, pointing to the starry sky   345
Alternately, and Plain below, while breath
Of music swayed their motions, and the Waste
Rejoiced with them and me in those sweet Sounds.
      This for the past, and things that may be viewed
Or fancied, in the obscurity of years   350
From monumental hints: and thou, O Friend!
Pleased with some unpremeditated strains
That served those wanderings to beguile, hast said
That then and there my mind had exercised
Upon the vulgar forms of present things,   355
The actual world of our familiar days,
Yet higher power, had caught from them a tone,
An image, and a character, by books
Not hitherto reflected. Call we this
A partial judgement—and yet why? for *then*   360
We were as Strangers; and I may not speak
Thus wrongfully of verse, however rude,
Which on thy young imagination, trained
In the great City, broke like light from far.
Moreover, each man's mind is to herself   365
Witness and judge; and I remember well
That in Life's every-day appearances
I seemed about this time to gain clear sight
Of a new world, a world, too, that was fit
To be transmitted and to other eyes   370
Made visible, as ruled by those fixed laws

Whence spiritual dignity originates,
Which do both give it being and maintain
A balance, an ennobling interchange
Of action from without, and from within;   375
The excellence, pure function, and best power
Both of the object seen, and eye that sees.

BOOK FOURTEENTH
CONCLUSION

In one of those Excursions (may they ne'er
Fade from remembrance!), through the Northern tracts
Of Cambria ranging with a youthful Friend,
I left Bethgellert's huts at couching-time,
And westward took my way, to see the sun   5
Rise from the top of Snowdon. To the door
Of a rude Cottage at the Mountain's base
We came, and rouzed the Shepherd who attends
The adventurous Stranger's steps, a trusty Guide;
Then, cheered by short refreshment, sallied forth.   10
—It was a close, warm, breezeless summer night,
Wan, dull, and glaring, with a dripping fog
Low-hung and thick, that covered all the sky.
But, undiscouraged, we began to climb
The mountain-side. The mist soon girt us round,   15
And, after ordinary Travellers' talk
With our Conductor, pensively we sank
Each into commerce with his private thoughts:
Thus did we breast the ascent, and by myself
Was nothing either seen or heard that checked   20
Those musings or diverted, save that once
The Shepherd's Lurcher, who, among the crags,
Had to his joy unearthed a Hedgehog, teased
His coiled-up Prey with barkings turbulent.
This small adventure, for even such it seemed   25
In that wild place, and at the dead of night,
Being over and forgotten, on we wound
In silence as before. With forehead bent
Earthward, as if in opposition set
Against an enemy, I panted up   30

With eager pace, and no less eager thoughts.
Thus might we wear a midnight hour away,
Ascending at loose distance each from each
And I, as chanced, the foremost of the Bard:
When at my feet the ground appeared to brighten,   35
And with a step or two seemed brighter still;
Nor was time given to ask, or learn, the cause;
For instantly a light upon the turf
Fell like a flash; and lo! as I looked up,
The Moon hung naked in a firmament   40
Of azure without cloud, and at my feet
Rested a silent sea of hoary mist.
A hundred hills their dusky backs upheavd
All over this still Ocean; and beyond,
Far, far beyond, the solid vapours stretched,   45
In Headlands, tongues, and promontory shapes,
Into the main Atlantic, that appeared
To dwindle, and give up his majesty,
Usurped upon far as the sight could reach
Not so the ethereal Vault; encroachment none   50
Was there, nor loss; only the inferior stars
Had disappeared, or shed a fainter light
In the clear presence of the full-orbed Moon;
Who, from her sovereign elevation, gazed
Upon the billowy ocean, as it lay   55
All meek and silent, save that through a rift
Not distant from the shore whereon we stood,
A fixed, abysmal, gloomy breathing-place,
Mounted the roar of waters—torrents—streams
Innumerable, roaring with one voice!   60
Heard over earth and sea, and in that hour,
For so it seemed, felt by the starry heavens.
    When into air had partially dissolved
That Vision, given to Spirits of the night,
And three chance human Wanderers, in calm thought   65
Reflected, it appeared to me the type
Of a majestic Intellect, its acts
And its possessions, what it has and craves,
What in itself it is, and would become.

There I beheld the emblem of a Mind 70
That feeds upon infinity, that broods
Over the dark abyss, intent to hear
Its voices issuing forth to silent light
In one continuous stream; a mind sustained
By recognitions of transcendent power 75
In sense, conducting to ideal form;
In soul, of more than mortal privilege.
One function, above all, of such a mind
Had Nature shadowed there, by putting forth,
'Mid circumstances awful and sublime, 80
That mutual domination which she loves
To exert upon the face of outward things,
So moulded, joined, abstracted; so endowed
With interchangeable supremacy,
That Men least sensitive see, hear, perceive, 85
And cannot chuse but feel. The power which all
Acknowledge when thus moved, which Nature thus
To bodily sense exhibits, is the express
Resemblance of that glorious faculty
That higher minds bear with them as their own. 90
This is the very spirit in which they deal
With the whole compass of the universe:
They, from their native selves, can send abroad
Kindred mutations; for themselves create
A like existence; and whene'er it dawns 95
Created for them, catch it;—or are caught
By its inevitable mastery,
Like angels stopped upon the wing by sound
Of harmony from heaven's remotest spheres.
Them the enduring and the transient both 100
Serve to exalt; they build up greatest things
From least suggestions; ever on the watch,
Willing to work and to be wrought upon,
They need not extraordinary calls
To rouse them, in a world of life they live; 105
By sensible impressions not enthralled,
But, by their quickening impulse, made more prompt
To hold fit converse with the spiritual world,

And with the generations of mankind
Spread over time, past, present, and to come,   110
Age after age, till Time shall be no more.
Such minds are truly from the Deity,
For they are powers; and hence the highest bliss
That flesh can know is theirs,—the consciousness
Of whom they are, habitually infused   115
Through every image, and through every thought,
And all affections by communion raised
From earth to heaven, from human to divine.
Hence endless occupation for the Soul,
Whether discursive or intuitive;   120
Hence chearfulness for acts of daily life,
Emotions which best foresight need not fear,
Most worthy then of trust when most intense:
Hence, amid ills that vex, and wrongs that crush
Our hearts, if here the words of holy Writ   125
May with fit reverence be applied, that peace
Which passeth understanding,—that repose
In moral judgements which from this pure source
Must come, or will by Man be sought in vain.
    Oh! who is he that hath his whole life long   130
Preserved, enlarged, this freedom in himself?
For this alone is genuine Liberty.
Where is the favoured Being who hath held
That course, unchecked, unerring, and untired,
In one perpetual progress smooth and bright?   135
—A humbler destiny have we retraced,
And told of lapse and hesitating choice,
And backward wanderings along thorny ways:
Yet, compassed round by Mountain Solitudes
Within whose solemn temple I received   140
My earliest visitations, careless then
Of what was given me; and which now I range
A meditative, oft a suffering Man,
Do I declare, in accents which, from truth
Deriving chearful confidence, shall blend   145
Their modulation with these vocal streams,
That, whatsoever falls my better mind

Revolving with the accidents of life
May have sustained, that, howsoe'er misled,
Never did I, in quest of right and wrong,   150
Tamper with conscience from a private aim;
Nor was in any public hope the dupe
Of selfish passions; nor did ever yield,
Wilfully, to mean cares or low pursuits;
But shrunk with apprehensive jealousy   155
From every combination which might aid
The tendency, too potent in itself,
Of use and custom to bow down the Soul
Under a growing weight of vulgar sense,
And substitute a universe of death   160
For that which moves with light and life informed,
Actual, divine, and true. To fear and love,
To love as prime and chief, for there fear ends,
Be this ascribed; to early intercourse
In presence of sublime or beautiful forms   165
With the adverse principles of pain and joy—
Evil, as one is rashly named by men
Who know not what they speak. By love subsists
All lasting grandeur, by pervading love;
That gone, we are as dust.—Behold the fields   170
In balmy spring-time full of rising flowers
And joyous Creatures; see that Pair, the lamb
And the lamb's Mother, and their tender ways
Shall touch thee to the heart; thou callest this love,
And not inaptly so, for love it is,   175
Far as it carries thee. In some green Bower
Rest, and be not alone, but have thou there
The One who is thy choice of all the world:
There linger, listening, gazing with delight
Impassioned, but delight how pitiable!   180
Unless this love by a still higher love
Be hallowed, love that breathes not without awe;
Love that adores, but on the knees of prayer,
By heaven inspired; that frees from chains the soul,
Bearing in union with the purest, best   185
Of earth-born passions, on the wings of praise,

A mutual tribute to the Almighty's Throne.
    This spiritual love acts not, nor can exist
Without Imagination, which in truth
Is but another name for absolute power   190
And clearest insight, amplitude of mind,
And reason, in her most exalted mood.
This faculty hath been the feeding source
Of our long labor: we have traced the stream
From the blind cavern whence is faintly heard   195
Its natal murmur; followed it to light
And open day; accompanied its course
Among the ways of Nature; for a time
Lost sight of it, bewildered and engulphed;
Then given it greeting as it rose once more   200
In strength, reflecting from its placid breast
The works of man, and face of human life;
And lastly, from its progress have we drawn
Faith in life endless, the sustaining thought
Of human being, Eternity, and God.   205
—Imagination having been our theme,
So also hath that intellectual love,
For they are each in each, and cannot stand
Dividually.—Here must thou be, O Man!
Power to thyself; no Helper hast thou here;   210
Here keepest thou in singleness thy state;
No other can divide with thee this work;
No secondary hand can intervene
To fashion this ability; 'tis thine,
The prime and vital principle is thine   215
In the recesses of thy nature, far
From any reach of outward fellowship,
Else is not thine at all. But joy to him,
Oh, joy to him who here hath sown, hath laid
Here the foundation of his future years!   220
For all that friendship, all that love can do,
All that a darling countenance can look
Or dear voice utter to complete the man,
Perfect him, made imperfect in himself,
All shall be his: and he whose soul hath risen   225

Up to the height of feeling intellect
Shall want no humbler tenderness, his heart
Be tender as a nursing Mother's heart;
Of female softness shall his life be full,
Of humble cares, and delicate desires,   230
Mild interests and gentlest sympathies.
    Child of my Parents! Sister of my Soul!
Thanks in sincerest Verse have been elsewhere
Poured out for all the early tenderness
Which I from thee imbibed: and 'tis most true   235
That later seasons owed to thee no less;
For spite of thy sweet influence and the touch
Of kindred hands that opened out the springs
Of genial thought in childhood, and in spite
Of all that, unassisted, I had marked,   240
In life or nature, of dose charms minute
That win their way into the heart by stealth,
Still, to the very going out of Youth,
I too exclusively esteemed *that* love,
And sought that beauty, which, as Milton sings,   245
Hath terror in it. Thou didst soften down
This over-sternness: rut for thee, dear Friend,
My soul, too reckless of mild grace, had stood
In her original self too confident,
Retained too long a countenance severe,   250
A rock with torrents roaring, with the clouds
Familiar, and a favorite of the Stars:
But thou didst plant its crevices with flowers,
Hang it with shrubs that twinkle in the breeze,
And teach the little birds to build their nests   255
And warble in its chambers. At a time
When Nature, destined to remain so long
Foremost in my affections, had fallen back
Into a second place, pleased to become
A handmaid to a nobler than herself,   260
When every day brought with it some new sense
Of exquisite regard for common things,
And all the earth was budding with these gifts
Of more refined humanity, thy breath,

Dear Sister, was a kind of gentler spring   265
That went before my steps. Thereafter came
One, whom with thee friendship had early paired;
She came, no more a Phantom to adorn
A moment, but an inmate of the heart,
And yet a Spirit, there for me enshrined   270
To penetrate the lofty and the low;
Even as one essence of pervading light
Shines in the brightest of ten thousand stars,
And the meek worm that feeds her lonely lamp
Couched in the dewy grass.
                 With such a theme,   275
Coleridge! with this my argument, of thee
Shall I be silent? O capacious Soul!
Placed on this earth to love and understand,
And from thy presence shed the light of love,
Shall I be mute ere thou be spoken of?   280
Thy kindred influence to my heart of hearts
Did also find its way. Thus fear relaxed
Her overweening grasp, thus thoughts and things
In the self-haunting spirit learned to take
More rational proportions; mystery,   285
The incumbent mystery of sense and soul,
Of Life and death, time and eternity,
Admitted more habitually a mild
Interposition—a serene delight
In closelier gathering cares, such as become   290
A human creature, howsoe'er endowed,
Poet, or destined for a humbler name;
And so the deep enthusiastic joy,
The rapture of the hallelujah sent
From all that breathes and is, was chastened, stemmed,   295
And balanced by pathetic truth, by trust
In hopeful reason, leaning on the stay
Of Providence;—and in reverence for duty,
Here, if need be, struggling with storms, and there
Strewing in peace Life's humblest ground with herbs   300
At every season green, sweet at all hours.
    And now, O Friend! this History is brought

To its appointed close: the discipline
And consummation of a Poet's mind
In every thing that stood most prominent   305
Have faithfully been pictured; we have reached
The time (our guiding object from the first)
When we may, not presumptuously, I hope,
Suppose my powers so far confirmed, and such
My knowledge, as to make me capable   310
Of building up a Work that shall endure;
Yet much hath been omitted, as need was,
Of books how much! and even of the other wealth
That is collected among woods and fields
Far more: for Nature's secondary grace   315
Hath hitherto been barely touched upon:
The charm more superficial that attends
Her works, as they present to Fancy's choice
Apt illustrations of the moral world
Caught at a glance or traced with curious pains.   320
    Finally, and above all, O Friend (I speak
With due regret), how much is overlooked
In human nature and her subtile ways
As studied first in our own hearts, and then
In life among the passions of mankind,   325
Varying their composition and their hue,
Where'er we move, under the diverse shapes
That individual character presents
To an attentive eye! For progress meet
Along this intricate and difficult path,   330
Whate'er was wanting, something had I gained
As One of many School-fellows, compelled
In hardy independance to stand up
Amid conflicting interests, and the shock
Of various tempers, to endure and note   335
What was not understood though known to be:
Among the mysteries of love and hate,
Honour and shame, looking to right and left,
Unchecked by innocence too delicate,
And moral notions too intolerant,   340
Sympathies too contracted. Hence when called

To take a station among Men, the step
Was easier, the transition more secure,
More profitable also; for the mind
Learns from such timely exercise to keep   345
In wholesome separation the two natures,
The one that feels, the other that observes.
   Yet one word more of personal concern—
Since I withdrew unwillingly from France
I led an undomestic Wanderer's life,   350
In London chiefly harboured; whence I roamed,
Tarrying at will in many a pleasant spot
Of rural England's cultivated Vales
Or Cambrian solitudes.—
               A Youth (he bore
The name of Calvert, it shall live if words   355
Of mine can give it life) in firm belief
That by endowments not from me withheld
Good might be furthered, in his last decay
Withdrawing, and from kindred whom he loved,
A part of no redundant Patrimony,   360
By a bequest sufficient for my needs
Enabled me to pause for choice, and walk
At large and unrestrained, nor damped too soon
By mortal cares. Himself no Poet, yet
Far less a common Follower of the world,   365
He deemed that my pursuits and labors lay
Apart from all that leads to wealth, or even
A necessary maintenance ensures
Without some hazard to the finer sense;
—He cleared a passage for me, and the stream   370
Flowed in the bent of Nature.
                  Having now
Told what best merits mention, further pains
Our present purpose seems not to require,
And I have other tasks. Recall to mind
The mood in which this labour was begun.   375
O Friend! the termination of my course
Is nearer now, much nearer; yet even then,
In that distraction, and intense desire,

I said unto the life which I had lived,
Where art thou? Hear I not a voice from thee   380
Which 'tis reproach to hear? Anon I rose
As if on wings, and saw beneath me stretched
Vast prospect of the world which I had been
And was; and hence this Song, which like a Lark
I have protracted, in the unwearied heavens   385
Singing, and often with more plaintive voice
To Earth attempered and her deep-drawn sighs,
Yet centering all in love, and in the end
All gratulant, if rightly understood.
    Whether to me shall be allotted life,   390
And with life, power, to accomplish aught of worth
That will be deemed no insufficient plea
For having given this Story of myself,
Is all uncertain: but, beloved Friend!
When, looking back, thou seest, in clearer view   395
Than any liveliest sight of yesterday,
That summer under whose indulgent skies
Upon smooth Quantock's airy ridge we roved
Unchecked, or loitered 'mid her sylvan Combs,
Thou in bewitching words with happy heart   400
Didst chaunt the Vision of that Ancient Man,
The bright-eyed Mariner, and rueful woes
Didst utter of the Lady Christabel;
And I, Associate with such labor, steeped
In soft forgetfulness the live-long hours,   405
Murmuring of Him who, joyous hap, was found,
After the perils of his moonlight ride,
Near the loud Waterfall; or her who sate
In misery near the miserable Thorn;
When Thou dost to that Summer turn thy thoughts,   410
And hast before thee all which then we were,
To thee, in memory of that happiness,
It will be known, by thee at least, my Friend,
Felt, that the History of a Poet's mind
Is labour not unworthy of regard.   415
To thee the Work shall justify itself.
    The last and later portions of this Gift

Have been prepared, not with the buoyant spirits
That were our daily portion when we first
Together wantoned in wild Poesy,   420
But under pressure of a private grief
Keen and enduring, which the mind and heart
That in this meditative History
Have been laid open needs must make me feel
More deeply, yet enable me to bear   425
More firmly; and a comfort now hath risen
From hope that Thou art near, and wilt be soon
Restored to us, in renovated health:
When, after the first mingling of our tears,
'Mong other consolations, we may draw   430
Some pleasure from this Offering of my love.
     Oh! yet a few short years of useful life,
And all will be complete, thy race be run,
Thy monument of glory will be raised;
Then, though, too weak to tread the ways of truth,   435
This Age fall back to old idolatry,
Though Men return to servitude as fast
As the tide ebbs, to ignominy and shame
By Nations sink together, we shall still
Find solace—knowing what we have learnt to know,   440
Rich in true happiness if allowed to be
Faithful alike in forwarding a day
Of firmer trust, joint laborers in the Work
(Should Providence such grace to us vouchsafe)
Of their deliverance, surely yet to come.   445
Prophets of Nature, we to them will speak
A lasting inspiration, sanctified
By reason, blest by faith: what we have loved
Others will love, and we will teach them how,
Instruct them how the mind of Man becomes   450
A thousand times more beautiful than the earth
On which he dwells, above this Frame of things
(Which 'mid all revolutions in the hopes
And fears of Men doth still remain unchanged)
In beauty exalted, as it is itself   455
Of quality and fabric more divine.

Sonnet Series and Itinerary Poems, (1820–1845)

The River Duddon

A SERIES OF

SONNETS[1]

The River Duddon rises upon Wrynose Fell, on the confines of Westmorland, Cumberland, and Lancashire; and, serving as a boundary to the two latter counties, for the space of about twenty-five miles, enters the Irish sea, between the isle of Walney and the lordship of Millum.

I

Not envying shades which haply yet may throw
A grateful coolness round that rocky spring,
Bandusia, once responsive to the string
Of the Horatian lyre with babbling flow;
Careless of flowers that in perennial blow   5
Round the moist marge of Persian fountains cling;
Heedless of Alpine torrents thundering
Through icy portals radiant as heaven's bow;
I seek the birth-place of a native Stream.—
All hail ye mountains, hail thou morning light!   10
Better to breathe upon this aëry height
Than pass in needless sleep from dream to dream;
Pure flow the verse, pure, vigorous, free, and bright,
For Duddon, long-lov'd Duddon, is my theme!

II

Child of the clouds! remote from every taint
Of sordid industry thy lot is cast;
Thine are the honors of the lofty waste;
Not seldom, when with heat the valleys faint,
Thy hand-maid Frost with spangled tissue quaint   5
Thy cradle decks;—to chaunt thy birth, thou hast

---

1   WW's notes all appeared in the first edition of the series in 1820. For the sources of the reading text and the editor's commentary, see *Sonnet Series and Itinerary Poems, 1820–1845*, ed. Geoffrey Jackson (2004), pp. 49–53, and 99–111.

No meaner Poet than the whistling Blast,
And Desolation is thy Patron-saint!
She guards thee, ruthless Power! who would not spare
Those mighty forests, once the bison's screen,   10
Where stalk'd the huge deer to his shaggy lair[1]
Through paths and alleys roofed with sombre green,
Thousands of years before the silent air
Was pierced by whizzing shaft of hunter keen!

III

How shall I paint thee?—Be this naked stone
My seat while I give way to such intent;
Pleased could my verse, a speaking monument,
Make to the eyes of men thy features known.
But as of all those tripping lambs not one   5
Outruns his fellows, so hath nature lent
To thy beginning nought that doth present
Peculiar grounds for hope to build upon.
To dignify the spot that gives thee birth,
No sign of hoar Antiquity's esteem   10
Appears, and none of modern Fortune's care;
Yet thou thyself hast round thee shed a gleam
Of brilliant moss, instinct with freshness rare;
Prompt offering to thy Foster-mother, Earth!

IV

Take, cradled Nursling of the mountain, take
This parting glance, no negligent adieu!
A Protean change seems wrought while I pursue
The curves, a loosely-scattered chain doth make;
Or rather thou appear'st a glistering snake,   5
Silent, and to the gazer's eye untrue,
Thridding with sinuous lapse the rushes, through
Dwarf willows gliding, and by ferny brake.
Starts from a dizzy steep the undaunted Rill
Rob'd instantly in garb of snow-white foam;   10
And laughing dares the Adventurer, who hath clomb
So high, a rival purpose to fulfil;

---

1   "The deer alluded to is the Leigh, a gigantic species long since extinct." WW

Else let the Dastard backward wend, and roam,
Seeking less bold achievement, where he will!

V

Sole listener, Duddon! to the breeze that play'd
With thy clear voice, I caught the fitful sound
Wafted o'er sullen moss and craggy mound,
Unfruitful solitudes, that seem'd to upbraid
The sun in heaven!—but now, to form a shade   5
For Thee, green alders have together wound
Their foliage; ashes flung their arms around;
And birch-trees risen in silver colonnade.
And thou hast also tempted here to rise,
'Mid sheltering pines, this Cottage rude and grey;   10
Whose ruddy children, by the mother's eyes
Carelessly watch'd, sport through the summer day,
Thy pleas'd associates:—light as endless May
On infant bosoms lonely Nature lies.

VI
Flowers

Ere yet our course was graced with social trees
It lacked not old remains of hawthorn bowers,
Where small birds warbled to their paramours;
And, earlier still, was heard the hum of bees;
I saw them ply their harmless robberies,   5
And caught the fragrance which the sundry flowers,
Fed by the stream with soft perpetual showers,
Plenteously yielded to the vagrant breeze.
There bloomed the strawberry of the wilderness;
The trembling eye-bright showed her sapphire blue,   10
The thyme her purple like the blush of even;[1]
And, if the breath of some to no caress
Invited, forth they peeped so fair to view,
All kinds alike seemed favourites of Heaven.

---

1   For WW's note to ll. 10–11, see the notes at the end of this volume.

VII

"Change me, some God, into that breathing rose!"
The love-sick Stripling fancifully sighs,
The envied flower beholding, as it lies
On Laura's breast, in exquisite repose;
Or he would pass into her Bird, that throws   5
The darts of song from out its wiry cage;
Enraptured,—could he for himself engage
The thousandth part of what the Nymph bestows,
And what the little careless Innocent
Ungraciously receives. Too daring choice!   10
There are whose calmer mind it would content
To be an unculled flow'ret of the glen,
Fearless of plough and scythe; or darkling wren,
That tunes on Duddon's banks her slender voice.

VIII

What aspect bore the Man who roved or fled,
First of his tribe, to this dark dell—who first
In this pellucid Current slaked his thirst?
What hopes came with him? what designs were spread
Along his path? His unprotected bed   5
What dreams encompass'd? Was the Intruder nurs'd
In hideous usages, and rites accurs'd,
That thinned the living and disturbed the dead?
No voice replies;—the earth, the air is mute;
And Thou, blue Streamlet, murmuring yield'st no more   10
Than a soft record that whatever fruit
Of ignorance thou might'st witness heretofore,
Thy function was to heal and to restore,
To soothe and cleanse, not madden and pollute!

IX
The Stepping-stones

The struggling Rill insensibly is grown
Into a Brook of loud and stately march,
Cross'd ever and anon by plank and arch;
And, for like use, lo! what might seem a zone

Chosen for ornament; stone match'd with stone   5
In studied symmetry, with interspace
For the clear waters to pursue their race
Without restraint.—How swiftly have they flown!
Succeeding—still succeeding! Here the Child
Puts, when the high-swoln Flood runs fierce and wild,   10
His budding courage to the proof;—and here
Declining Manhood learns to note the sly
And sure encroachments of infirmity,
Thinking how fast time runs, life's end how near!

X
The Same Subject

Not so that Pair whose youthful spirits dance
With prompt emotion, urging them to pass;
A sweet confusion checks the Shepherd-lass;
Blushing she eyes the dizzy flood askance,—
To stop ashamed—too timid to advance;   5
She ventures once again—another pause!
His outstretch'd hand He tauntingly withdraws—
She sues for help with piteous utterance!
Chidden she chides again; the thrilling touch
Both feel when he renews the wish'd-for aid: 10
Ah! if their fluttering hearts should stir too much,
Should beat too strongly, both may be betrayed.
The frolic Loves who, from yon high rock, see
The struggle, clap their wings for victory!

XI
The Faëry Chasm

No fiction was it of the antique age:
A sky-blue stone, within this sunless cleft,
Is of the very foot-marks unbereft
Which tiny Elves impress'd;—on that smooth stage
Dancing with all their brilliant equipage   5
In secret revels—haply after theft
Of some sweet babe, flower stolen, and coarse weed left,
For the distracted mother to assuage
Her grief with, as she might!—But, where, oh where

Is traceable a vestige of the notes   10
That ruled those dances, wild in character?
—Deep underground?—Or in the upper air,
On the shrill wind of midnight? or where floats
O'er twilight fields the autumnal gossamer?

XII
Hints for the Fancy

On, loitering Muse!—The swift Stream chides us—on!
Albeit his deep-worn channel doth immure
Objects immense, pourtray'd in miniature,
Wild shapes for many a strange comparison!
Niagaras, Alpine passes, and anon   5
Abodes of Naïads, calm abysses pure,
Bright liquid mansions, fashion'd to endure
When the broad Oak drops, a leafless skeleton,
And the solidities of mortal pride,
Palace and Tower, are crumbled into dust!   10
—The Bard who walks with Duddon for his guide,
Shall find such toys of Fancy thickly set:—
Turn from the sight, enamour'd Muse—we must;
Leave them—and, if thou canst, without regret!

XIII
Open Prospect

Hail to the fields—with Dwellings sprinkled o'er,
And one small Hamlet, under a green hill,
Cluster'd with barn and byer, and spouting mill!
A glance suffices,—should we wish for more,
Gay June would scorn us;—but when bleak winds roar   5
Through the stiff lance-like shoots of pollard ash,
Dread swell of sound! loud as the gusts that lash
The matted forests of Ontario's shore
By wasteful steel unsmitten, then would I
Turn into port,—and, reckless of the gale,   10
Reckless of angry Duddon sweeping by,
While the warm hearth exalts the mantling ale,
Laugh with the generous household heartily,
At all the merry pranks of Donnerdale!

XIV

O Mountain Stream! the Shepherd and his Cot
Are privileged Inmates of deep solitude;
Nor would the nicest Anchorite exclude
A field or two of brighter green, or plot
Of tillage-ground, that seemeth like a spot   5
Of stationary sunshine:—thou hast view'd
These only, Duddon! with their paths renew'd
By fits and starts, yet this contents thee not.
Thee hath some awful Spirit impelled to leave,
Utterly to desert, the haunts of men,   10
Though simple thy companions were and few;
And through this wilderness a passage cleave
Attended but by thy own voice, save when
The Clouds and Fowls of the air thy way pursue!

XV

From this deep chasm—where quivering sun-beams play
Upon its loftiest crags—mine eyes behold
A gloomy NICHE, capacious, blank, and cold;
A concave free from shrubs and mosses grey;
In semblance fresh, as if, with dire affray,   5
Some Statue, placed amid these regions old
For tutelary service, thence had rolled,
Startling the flight of timid Yesterday!
Was it by mortals sculptur'd?—weary slaves
Of slow endeavour! or abruptly cast   10
Into rude shape by fire, with roaring blast
Tempestuously let loose from central caves?
Or fashioned by the turbulence of waves,
Then, when o'er highest hills the Deluge past?

XVI
American Tradition

Such fruitless questions may not long beguile
Or plague the fancy, 'mid the sculptured shows
Conspicuous yet where Oroonoko flows;
There would the Indian answer with a smile

Aim'd at the White Man's ignorance, the while   5
Of the Great Waters telling, how they rose,
Covered the plains, and wandering where they chose,
Mounted through every intricate defile,
Triumphant.—Inundation wide and deep,
O'er which his Fathers urged, to ridge and steep   10
Else unapproachable, their buoyant way;
And carved, on mural cliff's undreaded side,
Sun, moon, and stars, and beast of chase or prey;
Whate'er they sought, shunn'd, loved, or deified![1]

XVII
Return[2]

A dark plume fetch me from yon blasted Yew
Perched on whose top the Danish Raven croaks;
Aloft, the imperial Bird of Rome invokes
Departed ages, shedding where he flew
Loose fragments of wild wailing that bestrew   5
The clouds, and thrill the chambers of the rocks,
And into silence hush the timorous flocks,
That slept so calmly while the nightly dew
Moisten'd each fleece, beneath the twinkling stars:
These couch'd 'mid that lone Camp on Hardknot's height,   10
Whose Guardians bent the knee to Jove and Mars:
These near that mystic Round of Druid frame,
Tardily sinking by its proper weight
Deep into patient Earth, from whose smooth breast it came!

XVIII
Seathwaite Chapel[3]

Sacred Religion, "mother of form and fear,"
Dread Arbitress of mutable respect,
New rites ordaining when the old are wreck'd,

---

1   "See Humboldt's Personal Narrative." WW; he cites *A Personal Narrative of Travels to the Equinoctial Regions of the New Continent during the Years 1788–1804* (tr. H. M. Williams, 4 vols.; London, 1819) by Alexander von Humboldt and Aimé Bonpland.
2   WW's lengthy note to this and the following sonnet is reproduced at the end of this volume.
3   For the literary allusions in this sonnet see Jackson, *Sonnet Series and Itinerary Poems*, pp. 106–107.

Or cease to please the fickle worshipper;
If one strong wish may be embosomed here,   5
Mother of LOVE! for this deep vale, protect
Truth's holy lamp, pure source of bright effect,
Gifted to purge the vapoury atmosphere
That seeks to stifle it;—as in those days
When this low Pile a Gospel Teacher knew,   10
Whose good works formed an endless retinue:
Such Priest as Chaucer sang in fervent lays;
Such as the heaven-taught skill of Herbert drew;
And tender Goldsmith crown'd with deathless praise!

XIX
Tributary Stream

My frame hath often trembled with delight
When hope presented some far-distant good,
That seemed from heaven descending, like the flood
Of yon pure waters, from their aëry height,
Hurrying with lordly Duddon to unite;   5
Who, 'mid a world of images imprest
On the calm depth of his transparent breast,
Appears to cherish most that Torrent white,
The fairest, softest, liveliest of them all!
And seldom hath ear listen'd to a tune   10
More lulling than the busy hum of Noon,
Swoln by that voice—whose murmur musical
Announces to the thirsty fields a boon
Dewy and fresh, till showers again shall fall.

XX
The Plain of Donnerdale

The old inventive Poets, had they seen,
Or rather felt, the entrancement that detains
Thy waters, Duddon! 'mid these flow'ry plains,
The still repose, the liquid lapse serene,
Transferr'd to bowers imperishably green,   5
Had beautified Elysium! But these chains
Will soon be broken;—a rough course remains,
Rough as the past; where Thou, of placid mien,

Innocuous as a firstling of a flock,
And countenanced like a soft cerulean sky,   10
Shalt change thy temper; and, with many a shock
Given and received in mutual jeopardy,
Dance like a Bacchanal from rock to rock,
Tossing her frantic thyrsus wide and high!

XXI

Whence that low voice?—A whisper from the heart,
That told of days long past when here I roved
With friends and kindred tenderly beloved;
Some who had early mandates to depart,
Yet are allowed to steal my path athwart   5
By Duddon's side; once more do we unite,
Once more beneath the kind Earth's tranquil light;
And smother'd joys into new being start.
From her unworthy seat, the cloudy stall
Of Time, breaks forth triumphant Memory;   10
Her glistening tresses bound, yet light and free
As golden locks of birch, that rise and fall
On gales that breathe too gently to recal
Aught of the fading year's inclemency!

XXII
Tradition

A love-lorn Maid, at some far-distant time,
Came to this hidden pool, whose depths surpass
In crystal clearness Dian's looking-glass;
And, gazing, saw that rose, which from the prime
Derives its name, reflected as the chime   5
Of echo doth reverberate some sweet sound:
The starry treasure from the blue profound
She long'd to ravish;—shall she plunge, or climb
The humid precipice, and seize the guest
Of April, smiling high in upper air?   10
Desperate alternative! what field could dare
To prompt the thought?—Upon the steep rock's breast
The lonely Primrose yet renews its bloom,
Untouched memento of her hapless doom!

XXIII
Sheep-washing

Sad thoughts, avaunt!—the fervour of the year,
Poured on the fleece-encumbered flock, invites
To laving currents, for prelusive rites
Duly performed before the Dales-men shear
Their panting charge. The distant Mountains hear,   5
Hear and repeat, the turmoil that unites
Clamour of boys with innocent despites
Of barking dogs, and bleatings from strange fear.
Meanwhile, if Duddon's spotless breast receive
Unwelcome mixtures as the uncouth noise   10
Thickens, the pastoral River will forgive
Such wrong; nor need *we* blame the licensed joys
Though false to Nature's quiet equipoise:
Frank are the sports, the stains are fugitive.

XXIV
The Resting-place

Mid-noon is past;—upon the sultry mead
No zephyr breathes, no cloud its shadow throws:
If we advance unstrengthen'd by repose,
Farewell the solace of the vagrant reed.
This Nook, with woodbine hung and straggling weed,   5
Tempting recess as ever pilgrim chose,
Half grot, half arbour, proffers to enclose
Body and mind, from molestation freed,
In narrow compass—narrow as itself:
Or if the Fancy, too industrious Elf,   10
Be loth that we should breathe awhile exempt
From new incitements friendly to our task,
There wants not stealthy prospect, that may tempt
Loose Idless to forego her wily mask.

XXV

Methinks 'twere no unprecedented feat
Should some benignant Minister of air
Lift, and encircle with a cloudy chair,

The One for whom my heart shall ever beat
With tenderest love;—or, if a safer seat   5
Atween his downy wings be furnished, there
Would lodge her, and the cherish'd burden bear
O'er hill and valley to this dim retreat!
Rough ways my steps have trod; too rough and long
For her companionship; here dwells soft ease: 10
With sweets which she partakes not some distaste
Mingles, and lurking consciousness of wrong;
Languish the flowers; the waters seem to waste
Their vocal charm; their sparklings cease to please.

XXVI

Return, Content! for fondly I pursued,
Even when a child, the Streams—unheard, unseen;
Through tangled woods, impending rocks between;
Or, free as air, with flying inquest viewed
The sullen reservoirs whence their bold brood,   5
Pure as the morning, fretful, boisterous, keen,
Green as the salt-sea billows, white and green,
Poured down the hills, a choral multitude!
Nor have I tracked their course for scanty gains,
They taught me random cares and truant joys,   10
That shield from mischief and preserve from stains
Vague minds, while men are growing out of boys;
Maturer Fancy owes to their rough noise
Impetuous thoughts that brook not servile reins.

XXVII
Journey Renewed.

I rose while yet the cattle, heat-opprest,
Crowded together under rustling trees,
Brushed by the current of the water-breeze;
And for *their* sakes, and love of all that rest,
On Duddon's margin, in the sheltering nest;   5
For all the startled scaly tribes that slink
Into his coverts, and each fearless link
Of dancing insects forged upon his breast;
For these, and hopes and recollections worn

Close to the vital seat of human clay;   10
Glad meetings—tender partings—that upstay
The drooping mind of absence, by vows sworn
In his pure presence near the trysting thorn;
I thanked the Leader of my onward way.

XXVIII

No record tells of lance opposed to lance,
Horse charging horse, 'mid these retired domains;
Nor that their turf drank purple from the veins
Of heroes fall'n, or struggling to advance,
Till doubtful combat issued in a trance   5
Of victory, that struck through heart and reins,
Even to the inmost seat of mortal pains,
And lightened o'er the pallid countenance.
Yet, to the loyal and the brave, who lie
In the blank earth, neglected and forlorn,   10
The passing Winds memorial tribute pay;
The Torrents chaunt their praise, inspiring scorn
Of power usurp'd,—with proclamation high,
And glad acknowledgment of lawful sway.

XXIX

Who swerves from innocence, who makes divorce
Of that serene companion—a good name,
Recovers not his loss; but walks with shame,
With doubt, with fear, and haply with remorse.
And oft-times he, who, yielding to the force   5
Of chance-temptation, ere his journey end,
From chosen comrade turns, or faithful friend,
In vain shall rue the broken intercourse.
Not so with such as loosely wear the chain
That binds them, pleasant River! to thy side:—   10
Through the rough copse wheel Thou with hasty stride,
I choose to saunter o'er the grassy plain,
Sure, when the separation has been tried,
That we, who part in love, shall meet again.

XXX

The Kirk of Ulpha to the Pilgrim's eye
Is welcome as a Star, that doth present
Its shining forehead through the peaceful rent
Of a black cloud diffused o'er half the sky;
Or as a fruitful palm-tree towering high   5
O'er the parched waste beside an Arab's tent;
Or the Indian tree whose branches, downward bent,
Take root again, a boundless canopy.
How sweet were leisure! could it yield no more
Than 'mid that wave-washed Church-yard to recline,   10
From pastoral graves extracting thoughts divine;
Or there to pace, and mark the summits hoar
Of distant moon-lit mountains faintly shine,
Sooth'd by the unseen River's gentle roar.

XXXI

Not hurled precipitous from steep to steep;
Lingering no more 'mid flower-enamelled lands
And blooming thickets; nor by rocky bands
Held;—but in radiant progress tow'rd the Deep
Where mightiest rivers into powerless sleep   5
Sink, and forget their nature;—*now* expands
Majestic Duddon, over smooth flat sands,
Gliding in silence with unfettered sweep!
Beneath an ampler sky a region wide
Is opened round him;—hamlets, towers, and towns,   10
And blue-topp'd hills, behold him from afar;
In stately mien to sovereign Thames allied,
Spreading his bosom under Kentish downs,
With Commerce freighted or triumphant War.

XXXII

But here no cannon thunders to the gale;
Upon the wave no haughty pendants cast
A crimson splendour; lowly is the mast
That rises here, and humbly spread the sail;
While less disturbed than in the narrow Vale   5

Through which with strange vicissitudes he pass'd,
The Wanderer seeks that receptacle vast
Where all his unambitious functions fail.
And may thy Poet, cloud-born Stream! be free,
The sweets of earth contentedly resigned,   10
And each tumultuous working left behind
At seemly distance, to advance like Thee,
Prepared, in peace of heart, in calm of mind
And soul, to mingle with Eternity!

XXXIII
Conclusion.

I thought of Thee, my partner and my guide,
As being past away.—Vain sympathies!
For, *backward*, Duddon! as I cast my eyes,
I see what was, and is, and will abide;
Still glides the Stream, and shall for ever glide;   5
The Form remains, the Function never dies;
While *we*, the brave, the mighty, and the wise,
We Men, who in our morn of youth defied
The elements, must vanish;—be it so!
Enough, if something from our hands have power   10
To live, and act, and serve the future hour;
And if, as tow'rd the silent tomb we go,
Thro' love, thro' hope, and faith's transcendant dower,
We feel that we are greater than we know.[1]

[Poems not included in series as first published]

To the Rev. Dr. W——

(WITH THE SONNETS TO THE RIVER DUDDON, AND OTHER
POEMS IN THIS COLLECTION)

The Minstrels played their Christmas tune
To-night beneath my cottage eaves;
While, smitten by a lofty moon,

---

1   "'And feel that I am happier than I know.'—Milton.
       The allusion to the Greek Poet will be obvious to the classical reader." WW cites
    Paradise Lost, VIII, l. 282.
       For WW's "Postscript" to *The River Duddon* see the notes at the end of this volume.

The encircling Laurels, thick with leaves,
Gave back a rich and dazzling sheen,   5
That overpowered their natural green.

Through hill and valley every breeze
Had sunk to rest with folded wings;
Keen was the air, but could not freeze
Nor check the music of the strings;   10
So stout and hardy were the band
That scrap'd the chords with strenuous hand.

And who but listen'd?—till was paid
Respect to every Inmate's claim;
The greeting given, the music played   15
In honour of each household name,
Duly pronounc'd with lusty call,
And "merry Christmas" wish'd to all!

O Brother! I revere the choice
That took thee from thy native hills;   20
And it is given thee to rejoice:
Though public care full often tills
(Heaven only witness of the toil)
A barren and ungrateful soil.

Yet, would that Thou, with me and mine,   25
Hadst heard this never-failing rite;
And seen on other faces shine
A true revival of the light;
Which Nature, and these rustic Powers,
In simple childhood, spread through ours!   30

For pleasure hath not ceased to wait
On these expected annual rounds,
Whether the rich man's sumptuous gate
Call forth the unelaborate sounds,
Or they are offered at the door   35
That guards the lowliest of the poor.

How touching, when, at midnight, sweep
Snow-muffled winds, and all is dark,
To hear—and sink again to sleep!
Or, at an earlier call, to mark,   40

By blazing fire, the still suspense
Of self-complacent innocence;

The mutual nod,—the grave disguise
Of hearts with gladness brimming o'er;
And some unbidden tears that rise   45
For names once heard, and heard no more;
Tears brighten'd by the serenade
For infant in the cradle laid!

Ah! not for emerald fields alone,
With ambient streams more pure and bright   50
Than fabled Cytherea's zone
Glittering before the Thunderer's sight,
Is to my heart of hearts endeared,
The ground where we were born and rear'd!

Hail, ancient Manners! sure defence,   55
Where they survive, of wholesome laws;
Remnants of love whose modest sense
Thus into narrow room withdraws;
Hail, Usages of pristine mould,
And ye, that guard them, Mountains old!   60

Bear with me, Brother! quench the thought
That slights this passion, or condemns;
If thee fond Fancy ever brought
From the proud margin of the Thames,
And Lambeth's venerable towers,   65
To humbler streams, and greener bowers.

Yes, they can make, who fail to find,
Short leisure even in busiest days;
Moments—to cast a look behind,
And profit by those kindly rays   70
That through the clouds do sometimes steal,
And all the far-off past reveal.

Hence, while the imperial City's din
Beats frequent on thy satiate ear,
A pleas'd attention I may win   75
To agitations less severe,
That neither overwhelm nor cloy,

But fill the hollow vale with joy!

Written upon a Blank Leaf in "The Complete Angler."

While flowing Rivers yield a blameless sport,
Shall live the name of Walton;—Sage benign!
Whose pen, the mysteries of the rod and line
Unfolding, did not fruitlessly exhort
To reverent watching of each still report   5
That Nature utters from her rural shrine.—
O nobly versed in simple discipline,
Meek, thankful soul, the vernal day how short
To thy lov'd pastime given by sedgy Lee,
Or down the tempting maze of Shawford brook!   10
Fairer than life itself, in thy sweet Book,
The cowslip bank and shady willow-tree,
And the fresh meads; where flow'd, from every nook
Of thy full bosom, gladsome Piety!

The Wild Duck's Nest.

The Imperial Consort of the Fairy King
Owns not a sylvan bower; or gorgeous cell
With emerald floor'd, and with purpureal shell
Ceiling'd and roof'd; that is so fair a thing
As this low structure—for the tasks of Spring   5
Prepared by one who loves the buoyant swell
Of the brisk waves, yet here consents to dwell;
And spreads in stedfast peace her brooding wing.
Words cannot paint the o'ershadowing yew-tree bough,
And dimly-gleaming Nest,—a hollow crown   10
Of golden leaves inlaid with silver down,
Fine as the Mother's softest plumes allow:
I gaze—and almost wish to lay aside
Humanity, weak slave of cumbrous pride!

"Fallen, and diffus'd into a shapeless heap"

Fallen, and diffus'd into a shapeless heap,
Or quietly self-buried in earth's mold,
Is that embattled House, whose massy Keep
Flung from yon cliff a shadow large and cold.—

There dwelt the gay, the bountiful, the bold,   5
Till nightly lamentations, like the sweep
Of winds—when winds were silent, struck a deep
And lasting terror through that ancient Hold.
Its line of Warriors fled;—they shrunk when tried
By ghostly power:—but Time's unsparing hand   10
Hath pluck'd such foes, like weeds, from out the land;
And now, if men with men in peace abide,
All other strength the weakest may withstand,
All worse assaults may safely be defied.

Ecclesiastical Sketches (1822)[1]

Ecclesiastical Sketches
Part I

FROM THE INTRODUCTION OF CHRISTIANITY INTO BRITAIN,
TO THE CONSUMMATION OF THE PAPAL DOMINION

I. Introduction

I, who descended with glad step to chase
Cerulean Duddon from his cloud-fed spring,
And of my wild Companion dared to sing,
In verse that moved with strictly-measured pace;
I, who essayed the nobler Stream to trace   5
Of Liberty, and smote the plausive string
Till the checked Torrent, fiercely combating,
In victory found her natural resting-place;
Now seek upon the heights of Time the source
Of a holy River, on whose banks are found   10
Sweet pastoral flowers, and laurels that have crowned
Full oft the unworthy brow of lawless force;
Where, for delight of him who tracks its course,
Immortal amaranth and palms abound.

II. Conjectures

If there be Prophets on whose spirits rest
Past things, revealed like future, they can tell
What Powers, presiding o'er the sacred Well
Of Christian Faith, this savage Island bless'd
With its first bounty. Wandering through the West,   5
Did holy Paul a while in Britain dwell,[2]

---

1   WW's notes all appeared in the first edition of the poem in 1822. For the sources of the reading text and the editor's commentary, see *Sonnet Series and Itinerary Poems, 1820–1845*, ed. Geoffrey Jackson (2004), pp. 127–136, and 235–282. For WW's "Advertisement" see the notes at the end of this volume.
2   "Stillingfleet adduces many arguments in support of this opinion, but they are unconvincing. The latter part of this Sonnet alludes to a favourite notion of Catholic Writers, that Joseph of Arimathea and his Companions brought Christianity into Britain, and built a rude Church at Glastonbury alluded to hereafter in the passage upon the dissolution of Monasteries." WW's many references to the works of historians, naturalists, and other

And call the Fountain forth by miracle,
And with dread signs the nascent Stream invest?
Or He, whose bonds dropp'd off, whose prison doors
Flew open, by an Angel's voice unbarred?   10
Or some, of humbler name, to these wild shores
Storm-driven, who having seen the cup of woe
Pass from their Master, sojourned here to guard
The precious current they had taught to flow?

III. Trepidation of the Druids

Screams round the Arch-druid's brow the Seamew[1]—white
As Menai's foam; and towards the mystic ring
Where Augurs stand, the future questioning,
Slowly the Cormorant aims her heavy flight,
Portending ruin to each baleful rite,   5
That, in the lapse of seasons, hath crept o'er
Diluvian truths, and patriarchal lore:
Haughty the Bard;—can these meek doctrines blight
His transports? wither his heroic strains?
But all shall be fulfilled;—the Julian spear   10
A way first open'd; and, with Roman chains,
The tidings come of Jesus crucified;
They come—they spread—the weak, the suffering, hear;
Receive the faith, and in the hope abide.

IV. Druidical Excommunication

Mercy and Love have met thee on thy road,
Thou wretched Outcast, from the gift of fire
And food cut off by sacerdotal ire,
From every sympathy that Man bestowed!
Yet shall it claim our reverence, that to God,   5
Ancient of days! that to the eternal Sire
These jealous Ministers of Law aspire,
As to the one sole fount whence Wisdom flowed,

---

scholars throughout *Ecclesiastical Sketches* reflect his wide reading in preparation for composing it, as he himself explains in his note to *Saxon Conquest* (I.i), below. For information on these sources, consult the edition by Geoffrey Jackson cited above.

1   "This water-fowl was, among the Druids, an emblem of those traditions connected with the deluge that made an important part of their mysteries. The Cormorant was a bird of bad omen." WW

Justice, and Order. Tremblingly escaped,
As if with prescience of the coming storm,   10
That intimation when the stars were shaped;
And yon thick woods maintain the primal truth,
Debased by many a superstitious form,
That fills the Soul with unavailing ruth.

V. Uncertainty

Darkness surrounds us; seeking, we are lost
On Snowdon's wilds, amid Brigantian coves,
Or where the solitary Shepherd roves
Along the Plain of Sarum, by the Ghost
Of silently departed ages crossed;   5
And where the boatman of the Western Isles
Slackens his course—to mark those holy piles
Which yet survive on bleak Iona's coast.
Nor these, nor monuments of eldest name,
Nor Taliesin's unforgotten lays,   10
Nor Characters of Greek or Roman fame,
To an unquestionable Source have led;
Enough—if eyes that sought the fountain-head,
In vain, upon the growing Rill may gaze.

VI. Persecution

Lament! for Dioclesian's fiery sword
Works busy as the lightning; but instinct
With malice ne'er to deadliest weapon linked,
Which God's ethereal storehouses afford:
Against the Followers of the incarnate Lord   5
It rages;—some are smitten in the field—
Some pierced beneath the unavailing shield
Of sacred home;—with pomp are others gor'd
And dreadful respite. Thus was Alban tried,
England's first Martyr! whom no threats could shake;   10
Self-offered Victim, for his friend he died,
And for the faith—nor shall his name forsake
That Hill,[1]whose flowery platform seems to rise

---

1   "'This hill at St. Alban's must have been an object of great interest to the imagination of
    the venerable Bede, who thus describes it with a delicate feeling delightful to meet with in

By Nature decked for holiest sacrifice.

VII. Recovery

As, when a storm hath ceased, the birds regain
Their cheerfulness, and busily retrim
Their nests, or chaunt a gratulating hymn
To the blue ether and bespangled plain;
Even so, in many a re-constructed fane,   5
Have the Survivors of this Storm renewed
Their holy rites with vocal gratitude;
And solemn ceremonials they ordain
To celebrate their great deliverance;
Most feelingly instructed 'mid their fear,   10
That persecution, blind with rage extreme,
May not the less, thro' Heaven's mild countenance,
Even in her own despite, both feed and cheer;
For all things are less dreadful than they seem.

VIII. Temptations from Roman Refinements

Watch, and be firm! for soul-subduing vice,
Heart-killing luxury, on your steps await.
Fair houses, baths, and banquets delicate,
And temples flashing, bright as polar ice,
Their radiance through the woods, may yet suffice   5
To sap your hardy virtue, and abate
Your love of him upon whose forehead sate
The crown of thorns; whose life-blood flowed, the price
Of your redemption. Shun the insidious arts
That Rome provides, less dreading from her frown   10
Than from her wily praise, her peaceful gown,
Language, and letters;—these, tho' fondly viewed
As humanizing graces, are but parts
And instruments of deadliest servitude!

---

that rude age, traces of which are frequent in his works: "Variis herbarum floribus depic-
tus imò usquequaque vestitus in quo nihil repentè arduum nihil præceps, nihil abruptum,
quem lateribus longè latèque deductum in modum æquoris natura complanat, dignum
videlicet eum pro insita sibi specie venustatis jam olim reddens, qui beati martyris cruore
dicaretur.'" WW

IX. Dissensions

That heresies should strike (if truth be scanned
Presumptuously) their roots both wide and deep,
Is natural as dreams to feverish sleep.
Lo! Discord at the Altar dares to stand,
Lifting towards high Heaven her fiery brand,   5
A cherished Priestess of the new baptized!
But chastisement shall follow peace despised.
The Pictish cloud darkens the enervate land
By Rome abandoned; vain are suppliant cries,
And prayers that would undo her forced farewell,   10
For she returns not.—Awed by her own knell,
She casts the Britons upon strange Allies,
Soon to become more dreaded enemies,
Than heartless misery called them to repel.

X. Struggle of the Britons against the Barbarians

Rise!—they *have* risen: of brave Aneurin ask
How they have scourged old foes, perfidious friends:
The spirit of Caractacus defends
The Patriots, animates their glorious task:—
Amazement runs before the towering casque   5
Of Arthur, bearing thro' the stormy field
The Virgin sculptured on his Christian shield:—
Stretched in the sunny light of victory bask
The Host that followed Urien as he strode
O'er heaps of slain;—from Cambrian wood and moss   10
Druids descend, auxiliars of the Cross;
Bards, nursed on blue Plinlimmon's still abode,
Rush on the fight, to harps preferring swords,
And everlasting deeds to burning words!

XI. Saxon Conquest

Nor wants the cause the panic-striking aid
Of hallelujahs[1] tossed from hill to hill—
For instant victory. But Heaven's high will
Permits a second and a darker shade

---

[1]   "Alluding to the victory gained under Germanus.—See Bede." WW

Of Pagan night. Afflicted and dismayed, 5
The Relics of the sword flee to the mountains:
O wretched Land, whose tears have flowed like fountains!
Whose arts and honours in the dust are laid,
By men yet scarcely conscious of a care
For other monuments than those of Earth;[1] 10
Intent, as fields and woods have given them birth,
To build their savage fortunes only there;
Witness the foss, the barrow, and the girth
Of many a long-drawn rampart, green and bare!

XII. Monastery of Old Bangor[2]

The oppression of the tumult—wrath and scorn—
The tribulation—and the gleaming blades—
Such is the impetuous spirit that pervades
The song of Taliesin[3];—Ours shall mourn
The *unarmed* Host who by their prayers would turn 5
The sword from Bangor's walls, and guard the store
Of Aboriginal and Roman lore,
And Christian monuments, that now must burn
To senseless ashes. Mark! how all things swerve
From their known course, or pass away like steam; 10
Another language spreads from coast to coast;

---

1 "The last six lines of this Sonnet are chiefly from the prose of Daniel; and here I will state (though to the Readers whom this Poem will chiefly interest it is unnecessary), that my obligations to other Prose Writers are frequent,—obligations, which even if I had not a pleasure in courting, it would have been presumptuous to shun, in treating an historical subject. I must, however, particularize Fuller, to whom I am indebted in the Sonnet upon Wicliffe and in other instances. And upon the Acquittal of the Seven Bishops I have done little more than versify a lively description of that Event in the Memoirs of the first Lord Lonsdale." WW

2 "'Ethelforth reached the Convent of Bangor, he perceived the Monks, twelve hundred in number, offering prayers for the success of their Countrymen: 'if they are praying against us,' he exclaimed, 'they are fighting against us,' and he ordered them to be first attacked: they were destroyed; and appalled by their fate, the courage of Brocmail wavered, and he fled from the field in dismay. Thus abandoned by their leader, his army soon gave way, and Ethelforth obtained a decisive conquest. Ancient Bangor itself soon fell into his hands and was demolished; the noble monastery was levelled to the ground; its library, which is mentioned as a large one, the collection of ages, the repository of the most precious monuments of the ancient Britons, was consumed; half-ruined walls, gates, and rubbish, were all that remained of the magnificent edifice.'—See Turner's valuable History of the Anglo-Saxons.
    The account Bede gives of this remarkable event, suggests a most striking warning against National and Religious prejudices." WW

3 "Taliesin was present at the battle which preceded this desolation." WW

Only perchance some melancholy Stream
And some indignant Hills old names preserve,
When laws, and creeds, and people, all are lost!

XIII. Casual Incitement

A bright-haired company of youthful Slaves,
Beautiful Strangers, stand within the pale
Of a sad market, ranged for public sale,
Where Tiber's stream the glorious City laves:
Angli by name; and not an Angel waves   5
His wing who seemeth lovelier in Heaven's eye
Than they appear to holy Gregory,
Who, having learnt that name, salvation craves
For Them, and for their Land. The earnest Sire,
His questions urging, feels in slender ties   10
Of chiming sound commanding sympathies;
De-irians—he would save them from God's ire;
Subjects of Saxon Ælla—they shall sing
Sweet Hallelujahs to the eternal King!

XIV. Glad Tidings

For ever hallowed be this morning fair,
Blest be the unconscious shore on which ye tread,
And blest the silver Cross, which ye, instead
Of martial banner, in procession bear;
The Cross preceding Him who floats in air,   5
The pictured Saviour!—By Augustin led
They come—and onward travel without dread,
Chaunting in barbarous ears a tuneful prayer,
Sung for themselves, and those whom they would free!
Rich conquest waits them:—the tempestuous sea   10
Of Ignorance, that ran so rough and high,
And heeded not the voice of clashing swords,
These good men humble by a few bare words,
And calm with fear of God's divinity.

XV. Paulinus

But, to remote Northumbria's royal Hall,
Where thoughtful Edwin, tutored in the School

Of Sorrow, still maintains a Heathen rule,
Who comes with functions Apostolical?
Mark him, of shoulders curved, and stature tall,[1]   5
Black hair, and vivid eye, and meagre cheek,
His prominent feature like an eagle's beak;
A Man whose aspect doth at once appal,
And strike with reverence. The Monarch leans
Towards the Truths this Delegate propounds,—   10
Repeatedly his own deep mind he sounds
With careful hesitation,—then convenes
A synod of his Counsellors,—give ear,
And what a pensive Sage doth utter, hear!

XVI. Persuasion[2]

"Man's life is like a Sparrow, mighty King!
"That, stealing in while by the fire you sit
"Housed with rejoicing Friends, is seen to flit
"Safe from the storm, in comfort tarrying.
"Here did it enter—there, on hasty wing   5
"Flies out, and passes on from cold to cold;
"But whence it came we know not, nor behold
"Whither it goes. Even such that transient Thing,
"The Human Soul; not utterly unknown
"While in the Body lodged, her warm abode;   10

---

1 "The person of Paulinus is thus described by Bede, from the memory of an eye-witness: 'Longæ staturæ, paululum incurvus, nigro capillo, facie macilentâ, naso adunco, pertenui, venerabilis simul et terribilis aspectu.'" WW; "Of tall stature, slightly stooping, with black hair, a lean face, a nose hooked and slender; and in his appearance boh venerable and awe-inspiring." (See Bede, II.xvi.)

2 "See the original of this speech in Bede.—The Conversion of Edwin as related by him is highly interesting—and the breaking up of this Council accompanied with an event so striking and characteristic, that I am tempted to give it at length in a translation. 'Who, exclaimed the King, when the Council was ended, shall first desecrate the Altars and the Temples? I, answered the Chief Priest, for who more fit than myself, through the wisdom which the true God hath given me to destroy, for the good example of others, what in foolishness I worshipped. Immediately, casting away vain superstition, he besought the King to grant him, what the laws did not allow to a priest, arms and a courser; which mounting, and furnished with a sword and lance, he proceeded to destroy the Idols. The crowd, seeing this, thought him mad—he however halted not, but, approaching, he profaned the Temple, casting against it the lance which he had held in his hand, and, exulting in acknowledgment of the worship of the true God, he ordered his companions to pull down the Temple, with all its enclosures. The place is shown where those idols formerly stood, not far from York, at the source of the river Derwent, and is at this day called Gormund Gaham.'" WW

"But from what world She came, what woe or weal
"On her departure waits, no tongue hath shewn;
"This mystery if the Stranger can reveal,
"His be a welcome cordially bestowed!"

XVII. Conversion

Prompt transformation works the novel lore;
The Council closed, the Priest in full career
Rides forth, an armed Man, and hurls a spear
To desecrate the Fane which heretofore
He served in folly.—Woden falls—and Thor   5
Is overturned; the Mace, in battle heaved
(So might they dream) till Victory was achieved,
Drops—and the God himself is seen no more.
Temple and Altar sink—to hide their shame
Amid oblivious weeds. "O come to me   10
Ye heavy laden!" such the inviting voice
Heard near fresh streams,—and thousands, who rejoice[1]
In the new Rite—the pledge of sanctity,
Shall, by regenerate life, the promise claim.

XVIII. Apology

Nor scorn the aid which Fancy oft doth lend
The soul's eternal interests to promote:
Death, darkness, danger, are our natural lot;
And evil Spirits *may* our walk attend
For aught the wisest know or comprehend;   5
Then let the *good* be free to breathe a note
Of elevation—let their odours float
Around these Converts, and their glories blend,
Outshining nightly tapers, or the blaze
Of the noon-day. Nor doubt that golden cords   10
Of good works, mingling with the visions, raise
The soul to purer worlds: and *who* the line
Shall draw, the limits of the power define,
That even imperfect faith to Man affords?

---

1   "The early propagators of Christianity were accustomed to preach near rivers for the con-
    venience of baptism." WW.

XIX. Primitive Saxon Clergy [1]

How beautiful your presence, how benign,
Servants of God! who not a thought will share
With the vain world; who, outwardly as bare
As winter trees, yield no fallacious sign
That the firm soul is clothed with fruit divine!   5
Such Priest, when service worthy of his care
Has called him forth to breathe the common air,
Might seem a saintly Image from its shrine
Descended; happy are the eyes that meet
The Apparition; evil thoughts are stayed
At his approach, and low-bowed necks entreat   10
A benediction from his voice or hand;
Whence grace, thro' which the heart can understand,
And vows, that bind the will, in silence made.

XX. Other Influences

Ah, when the Frame, round which in love we clung,
Is chilled by death, does mutual service fail?
Is tender pity then of no avail?
Are intercessions of the fervent tongue
A waste of hope?—From this sad source have sprung   5
Rites that console the spirit, under grief
Which ill can brook more rational relief;
Hence, prayers are shaped amiss, and dirges sung
For those whose doom is fix'd! The way is smooth
For Power that travels with the human heart:—   10
Confession ministers, the pang to soothe
In him who at the ghost of guilt doth start.
Ye holy Men, so earnest in your care,

---

1 "Having spoken of the zeal, disinterestedness, and temperance of the clergy of those times, Bede thus proceeds: 'Unde et in magna erat veneratione tempore illo religionis habitus, ita ut ubicunque clericus aliquis, aut monachus adveniret, gaudenter ab omnibus tanquam Dei famulus exciperetur. Etiam si in itinere pergens inveniretur, accurrebant, et flexâ cervice, vel manu signari, vel ore illius se benedici, gaudebant. Verbis quoque horum exhortatoriis diligenter auditum præbebant.' Lib. iii. cap. 26." WW. "Therefore, the religious garb was greatly revered at that time, so that wherever some priest or monk arrived, he was received joyfully by everyone as a servant of God. And if he was discovered proceeding on his way, they would run up to him and, with necks bowed rejoiced to receive the sign [of the cross] from his hand or to be blessed by his mouth. Also, the exhortations of these men were listened to attentively."

Of your own mighty instruments beware!

XXI. Seclusion

Lance, shield, and sword relinquished—at his side
A Bead-roll, in his hand a clasped Book,
Or staff more harmless than a Shepherd's crook,
The war-worn Chieftain quits the world—to hide
His thin autumnal locks where Monks abide   5
In cloistered privacy. But not to dwell
In soft repose he comes. Within his cell,
Round the decaying trunk of human pride,
At morn, and eve, and midnight's silent hour,
Do penitential cogitations cling:
Like ivy, round some ancient elm, they twine   10
In grisly folds and strictures serpentine;
Yet, while they strangle without mercy, bring
For recompense their own perennial bower.

XXII. Continued

Methinks that to some vacant Hermitage
My feet would rather turn—to some dry nook
Scoop'd out of living rock, and near a brook
Hurl'd down a mountain-cove from stage to stage,
Yet tempering, for my sight, its bustling rage   5
In the soft heaven of a translucent pool;
Thence creeping under forest arches cool,
Fit haunt of shapes whose glorious equipage
Perchance would throng my dreams. A beechen bowl,
A maple dish, my furniture should be;   10
Crisp, yellow leaves my bed; the hooting Owl
My night-watch: nor should e'er the crested Fowl
From thorp or vill his matins sound for me,
Tired of the world and all its industry.

XXIII. Reproof

But what if One, thro' grove or flowery mead,
Indulging thus at will the creeping feet
Of a voluptuous indolence, should meet
The hovering Shade of venerable Bede;

The Saint, the Scholar, from a circle freed   5
Of toil stupendous, in a hallowed seat
Of Learning, where he heard the billows beat
On a wild coast—rough monitors to feed
Perpetual industry. Sublime Recluse!
The recreant soul, that dares to shun the debt   10
Imposed on human kind, must first forget
Thy diligence, thy unrelaxing use
Of a long life; and, in the hour of death,
The last dear service of thy passing breath![1]

XXIV. Saxon Monasteries, and Lights and Shades of the Religion[2]

By such examples moved to unbought pains,
The people work like congregated bees;
Eager to build the quiet Fortresses
Where Piety, as they believe, obtains
From Heaven a *general* blessing; timely rains   5
Or needful sunshine; prosperous enterprize,
And peace, and equity.—Bold faith! yet rise
The sacred Towers for universal gains.
The Sensual think with reverence of the palms
Which the chaste Votaries seek, beyond the grave;   10
If penance be redeemable, thence alms
Flow to the Poor, and freedom to the Slave;
And, if full oft the Sanctuary save
Lives black with guilt, ferocity it calms.

XXV. Missions and Travels

Not sedentary all: there are who roam
To scatter seeds of Life on barbarous shores;
Or quit with zealous step their knee-worn floors
To seek the general Mart of Christendom;
Whence they, like richly laden Merchants, come   5
To their beloved Cells:—or shall we say
That, like the Red-cross Knight, they urge their way,

---

1 "He expired in the act of concluding a translation of St. John's Gospel." WW
2 "See in Turner's History, vol. iii. p. 528, the account of the erection of Ramsey Monastery.
   Penances were removable by the performances of acts of charity and benevolence." WW.
   WW cites Sharon Turner, *History of the Anglo-Saxons* (3d ed., 3 vols.; London, 1820).

To lead in memorable triumph home
Truth—their immortal Una? Babylon,
Learned and wise, hath perished utterly,   10
Nor leaves her speech wherewith to clothe a sigh
That would lament her;—Memphis, Tyre, are gone
With all their Arts—while classic Lore glides on
By these Religious saved for all posterity.

XXVI. Alfred

Behold a Pupil of the Monkish gown,
The pious Alfred, King to Justice dear;
Lord of the harp and liberating spear;
Mirror of Princes! Indigent Renown
Might range the starry ether for a crown   5
Equal to *his* deserts, who, like the year,
Pours forth his bounty, like the day doth cheer,
And awes like night with mercy-tempered frown.
Ease from this noble Miser of his time
No moment steals; pain narrows not his cares.[1]   10
Though small his kingdom as a spark or gem,
Of Alfred boasts remote Jerusalem,
And Christian India gifts with Alfred shares
By sacred converse link'd with India's clime.

XXVII. His Descendants

Can aught survive to linger in the veins
Of kindred bodies—an essential power
That may not vanish in one fatal hour,
And wholly cast away terrestrial chains?
The race of Alfred covets glorious pains   5
When dangers threaten—dangers ever new!
Black tempests bursting—blacker still in view!
But manly sovereignty its hold retains;
The root sincere—the branches bold to strive
With the fierce storm; meanwhile, within the round   10
Of their protection, gentle virtues thrive;
As oft, 'mid some green plot of open ground,
Wide as the oak extends its dewy gloom,

---

1   "Through the whole of his life, Alfred was subject to grievous maladies." WW

The fostered hyacinths spread their purple bloom.

XXVIII. Influence Abused

Urged by Ambition, who with subtlest skill
Changes her means,—the Enthusiast as a dupe
Shall soar, and as a hypocrite can stoop,
And turn the instruments of good to ill,
Moulding the credulous People to his will.   5
Such DUNSTAN:—from its Benedictine coop
Issues the master Mind, at whose fell swoop
The chaste affections tremble to fulfil
Their purposes. Behold, pre-signified
The might of spiritual sway! his thoughts—his dreams   10
Do in the supernatural world abide:
So vaunt a throng of Followers, filled with pride
In shows of virtue pushed to its extremes,
And sorceries of talent misapplied.

XXIX. Danish Conquests

Woe to the Crown that doth the Cowl obey!
Dissension checks the arms that would restrain
The incessant Rovers of the Northern Main,
And widely spreads once more a Pagan sway;
But Gospel-Truth is potent to allay   5
Fierceness and rage; and soon the cruel Dane
Feels, thro' the influence of her gentle reign,
His native superstitions melt away.
Thus, often, when thick gloom the east o'ershrouds,
The full-robed Moon, slow-climbing, doth appear   10
Silently to consume the heavy clouds;
How no one can resolve; but every eye
Around her sees, while air is hushed, a clear
And widening circuit of etherial sky.[1]

XXX. Canute

A pleasant music floats along the Mere,

---

1 "The violent measures, carried on under the influence of Dunstan, for strengthening the
   Benedictine Order, were a leading cause of the second series of Danish Invasions. See
   TURNER." WW

From Monks in Ely chaunting service high,
Whileas Canùte the King is rowing by:
"My Oarsmen," quoth the mighty King, "draw near,
"That we the sweet song of the Monks may hear!"   5
He listen'd (all past conquests and all schemes
Of future vanishing like empty dreams)
Heart-touch'd, and haply not without a tear.
The Royal Minstrel, ere the choir was still,
While his free Barge skims the smooth flood along,   10
Gives to that rapture a memorial Rhyme.[1]
O suffering Earth! be thankful; sternest clime
And rudest age are subject to the thrill
Of heaven-descended Piety and Song.

XXXI. The Norman Conquest

The woman-hearted Confessor prepares
The evanescence of the Saxon line.
Hark! 'tis the Curfew's knell! the stars may shine;
But of the lights that cherish household cares
And festive gladness, burns not one that dares   5
To twinkle after that dull stroke of thine,
Emblem and instrument, from Thames to Tyne,
Of force that daunts, and cunning that ensnares!
Yet, as the terrors of the lordly bell,
That quench from hut to palace lamps and fires,   10
Touch not the tapers of the sacred quires,
Even so a thraldom studious to expel
Old laws, and ancient customs to derange,
Brings to Religion no injurious change.

XXXII. The Council of Clermont

"And shall," the Pontiff asks, "profaneness flow
"From Nazareth—source of Christian Piety,
"From Bethlehem, from the Mounts of Agony
"And glorified Ascension? Warriors go,
"With prayers and blessings we your path will sow;   5
"Like Moses hold our hands erect, till ye

---

1   "Which is still extant." WW. The Latin "song" dates from the twelfth century and was often
    translated into English.

"Have chased far off by righteous victory
"These sons of Amalec, or laid them low!"
"GOD WILLETH IT," the whole assembly cry;
Shout which the enraptured multitude astounded.   10
The Council-roof and Clermont's towers reply:
"God willeth it," from hill to hill rebounded;
Sacred resolve, in countries far and nigh,
Through "Nature's hollow arch," that night, resounded![1]

XXXIII. Crusades

The Turban'd Race are poured in thickening swarms
Along the West; though driven from Aquitaine,
The Crescent glitters on the towers of Spain;
And soft Italia feels renewed alarms;
The scimitar, that yields not to the charms   5
Of ease, the narrow Bosphorus will disdain;
Nor long (that crossed) would Grecian hills detain
Their tents, and check the current of their arms.
Then blame not those who, by the mightiest lever
Known to the moral world, Imagination,   10
Upheave (so seems it) from her natural station
All Christendom:—they sweep along—(was never
So huge a host!)—to tear from the Unbeliever
The precious Tomb, their haven of salvation.

XXXIV. Richard I

Redoubted King, of courage leonine,
I mark thee, Richard! urgent to equip
Thy warlike person with the staff and scrip;
I watch thee sailing o'er the midland brine;
In conquered Cyprus see thy Bride decline   5
Her blushing cheek, Love's vow upon her lip,
And see love-emblems streaming from thy ship,
As thence she holds her way to Palestine.
My Song (a fearless Homager) would attend
Thy thundering battle-axe as it cleaves the press   10
Of war, but duty summons her away

---

1   "The decision of this council was believed to be instantly known in remote parts of Europe."
    WW

To tell, how finding in the rash distress
Of those enthusiast powers a constant Friend,
Through giddier heights hath clomb the Papal sway.

XXXV. An Interdict

Realms quake by turns: proud Arbitress of grace,
The Church, by mandate shadowing forth the power
She arrogates o'er heaven's eternal door,
Closes the gates of every sacred place;—
Straight from the sun and tainted air's embrace   5
All sacred things are covered: cheerful morn
Grows sad as night—no seemly garb is worn,
Nor is a face allowed to meet a face
With natural smile of greeting.—Bells are dumb;
Ditches are graves—funereal rights denied;   10
And in the Church-yard he must take his Bride
Who dares be wedded! Fancies thickly come
Into the pensive heart ill fortified,
And comfortless despairs the soul benumb.

XXXVI. Papal Abuses

As with the stream our voyage we pursue
The gross materials of this world present
A marvellous study of wild accident;
Uncouth proximities of old and new;
And bold transfigurations, more untrue   5
(As might be deemed) to disciplined intent
Than aught the sky's fantastic element,
When most fantastic, offers to the view.
Saw we not Henry scourged at Becket's shrine?
Lo! John self-stripped of his insignia—crown,   10
Sceptre and mantle, sword and ring, laid down
At a proud Legate's feet! The spears that line
Baronial Halls, the opprobrious insult feel;
And angry Ocean roars a vain appeal.

XXXVII. Scene in Venice

Black Demons hovering o'er his mitred head,
To Cæsar's Successor the Pontiff spake;

"Ere I absolve thee, stoop! that on thy neck
"Levelled with Earth this foot of mine may tread."
Then, he who to the Altar had been led,   5
He, whose strong arm the Orient could not check,
He, who had held the Soldan at his beck,
Stooped, of all glory disinherited,
And even the common dignity of man!
Amazement strikes the crowd;—while many turn   10
Their eyes away in sorrow, others burn
With scorn, invoking a vindictive ban
From outraged Nature; but the sense of most
In abject sympathy with power is lost.

XXXVIII. Papal Dominion

Unless to Peter's Chair the viewless wind
Must come and ask permission when to blow,
What further empire would it have? for now
A ghostly Domination, unconfined
As that by dreaming Bards to Love assigned,   5
Sits there in sober truth—to raise the low—
Perplex the wise—the strong to overthrow—
Through earth and heaven to bind and to unbind!
Resist—the thunder quails thee!—crouch—rebuff
Shall be thy recompence! from land to land   10
The ancient thrones of Christendom are stuff
For occupation of a magic wand,
And 'tis the Pope that wields it,—whether rough
Or smooth his front, our world is in his hand!

Ecclesiastical Sketches.
Part II

TO THE CLOSE OF THE TROUBLES IN THE REIGN OF CHARLES I

I. Cistertian Monastery

"Here Man more purely lives, less oft doth fall,
"More promptly rises, walks with nicer heed,
"More safely rests, dies happier, is freed
"Earlier from cleansing fires, and gains withal

"A brighter crown."—On yon Cistertian wall   5
That confident assurance may be read;[1]
And, to like shelter, from the world have fled
Encreasing multitudes. The potent call
Doubtless shall cheat full oft the heart's desires;
Yet, while the rugged age on pliant knee   10
Vows to rapt Fancy humble fealty,
A gentler life spreads round the holy spires;
Where'er they rise the sylvan waste retires,
And aëry harvests crown the fertile lea.

II. Monks, and Schoolmen

Record we too, with just and faithful pen,
That many hooded Cenobites there are,
Who in their private Cells have yet a care
Of public quiet: unambitious Men,
Counsellors for the world, of piercing ken;   5
Whose fervent exhortations from afar
Move Princes to their duty, peace or war;
And oft-times in the most forbidding den
Of solitude, with love of science strong,
How patiently the yoke of thought they bear!   10
How subtly glide its finest threads along!
Spirits that crowd the intellectual sphere
With mazy boundaries, as the Astronomer
With orb and cycle girds the starry throng.

III. Other Benefits

And not in vain embodied to the sight
Religion finds even in the stern Retreat
Of feudal Sway her own appropriate Seat;
From the Collegiate pomps on Windsor's height,
Down to the humble Altar, which the Knight   5
And his Retainers of the embattled hall
Seek in domestic oratory small,
For prayer in stillness, or the chaunted rite;

---

1   "'Bonum est nos hic esse, quia homo vivit purius, cadit rarius, surgit velocius, incedit cautius, quiescit securius, moritur felicius, purgatur citius, præmiatur copiosius.' Bernard. 'This sentence,' says Dr. Whitaker, 'is usually inscribed on some conspicuous part of the Cistertian houses.'" WW

Then chiefly dear, when foes are planted round,
Who teach the intrepid guardians of the place,   10
Hourly exposed to death, with famine worn,
And suffering under many a doubtful wound,
How sad would be their durance, if forlorn
Of offices dispensing heavenly grace!

IV. Continued

And what melodious sounds at times prevail!
And, ever and anon, how bright a gleam
Pours on the surface of the turbid Stream!
What heartfelt fragrance mingles with the gale
That swells the bosom of our passing sail!   5
For where, but on *this* River's margin, blow
Those flowers of Chivalry, to bind the brow
Of hardihood with wreaths that shall not fail?
Fair Court of Edward! wonder of the world!
I see a matchless blazonry unfurled   10
Of wisdom, magnanimity, and love;
And meekness tempering honourable pride;
The Lamb is couching by the Lion's side,
And near the flame-eyed Eagle sits the Dove.

V. Crusaders

Nor can Imagination quit the shores
Of these bright scenes without a farewell glance
Given to those dream-like Issues—that Romance
Of many-coloured life which Fortune pours
Round the Crusaders, till on distant shores   5
Their labours end; or they return to lie,
The vow performed, in cross-legged effigy,
Devoutly stretched upon their chancel floors.
Am I deceived? Or is their Requiem chaunted
By voices never mute when Heaven unties   10
Her inmost, softest, tenderest harmonies;
Requiem which Earth takes up with voice undaunted,
When she would tell how Good, and Brave, and Wise,
For their high guerdon not in vain have panted!

VI. *Transubstantiation*

Enough! for see, with dim association
The tapers burn; the odorous incense feeds
A greedy flame; the pompous mass proceeds;
The Priest bestows the appointed consecration;
And, while the Host is raised, its elevation   5
An awe and supernatural horror breeds,
And all the People bow their heads like reeds,
To a soft breeze, in lowly adoration.
This Valdo brook'd not. On the banks of Rhone
He taught, till persecution chased him thence,   10
To adore the Invisible, and Him alone.
Nor were his Followers loth to seek defence,
'Mid woods and wilds, on Nature's craggy throne,
From rites that trample upon soul and sense.

VII. *Waldenses*

These who gave earliest notice, as the Lark
Springs from the ground the morn to gratulate;
Who rather rose the day to antedate,
By striking out a solitary spark,
When all the world with midnight gloom was dark—   5
These Harbingers of good, whom bitter hate
In vain endeavoured to exterminate,
Fell Obloquy pursues with hideous bark?[1]
Meanwhile the unextinguishable fire,
Rekindled thus, from dens and savage woods   10
Moves, handed on with never-ceasing care,
Through Courts, through Camps, o'er limitary Floods;
Nor lacks this sea-girt Isle a timely share

---

1   "The list of foul names bestowed upon those poor creatures is long and curious;—and, as
    is, alas! too natural, most of the opprobrious appellations are drawn from circumstances
    into which they were forced by their persecutors, who even consolidated their miseries into
    one reproachful term, calling them Patarenians or Paturins, from pati, to suffer.
        Dwellers with wolves she names them, for the Pine
        And green Oak are their covert; as the gloom
        Of night oft foils their Enemy's design,
        She calls them Riders on the flying broom;
        Sorcerers, whose frame and aspect have become
        One and the same through practices malign." In his note WW quotes the sestet from
    an earlier version of the sonnet.

Of the new Flame, not suffered to expire.

VIII. Archbishop Chicheley to Henry V

"What Beast in wilderness or cultured field
"The lively beauty of the Leopard shews?
"What Flower in meadow-ground or garden grows
"That to the towering Lily doth not yield?
"Let both meet only on thy royal shield!   5
"Go forth, great King! claim what thy birth bestows;
"Conquer the Gallic Lily which thy foes
"Dare to usurp;—thou hast a sword to wield,
"And Heaven will crown the right."—The mitred Sire
Thus spake—and lo! a Fleet, for Gaul addressed, 10
Ploughs her bold course across the wondering seas;
For, sooth to say, ambition, in the breast
Of youthful Heroes, is no sullen fire,
But one that leaps to meet the fanning breeze.

IX. Wars of York and Lancaster

Thus is the storm abated by the craft
Of a shrewd Counsellor, eager to protect
The Church, whose power hath recently been check'd,
Whose monstrous riches threatened. So the shaft
Of victory mounts high, and blood is quaff'd   5
In fields that rival Cressy and Poictiers.
But mark the dire effect in coming years!
Deep, deep as hell itself, the future draught
Of civil slaughter. Yet, while Temporal power
Is by these shocks exhausted, Spiritual truth 10
Maintains the else endangered gift of life;
Proceeds from infancy to lusty youth;
And, under cover of that woeful strife,
Gathers unblighted strength from hour to hour.

X. Wicliffe

Once more the Church is seized with sudden fear,
And at her call is Wicliffe disinhumed:
Yea, his dry bones to ashes are consumed,
And flung into the brook that travels near;

Forthwith, that ancient Voice which Streams can hear   5
Thus speaks, (that voice which walks upon the wind,
Though seldom heard by busy human kind,)
"As thou these ashes, little Brook! wilt bear
"Into the Avon, Avon to the tide
"Of Severn, Severn to the narrow seas,   10
"Into main Ocean they, this Deed accurst
"An emblem yields to friends and enemies
"How the bold Teacher's Doctrine, sanctified
"By Truth, shall spread throughout the world dispersed."

XI. Corruptions of the Higher Clergy

"Woe to you, Prelates! rioting in ease
"And cumbrous wealth—the shame of your estate;
"You on whose progress dazzling trains await
"Of pompous horses; whom vain titles please,
"Who will be served by others on their knees,   5
"Yet will yourselves to God no service pay;
"Pastors who neither take nor point the way
"To Heaven; for either lost in vanities
"Ye have no skill to teach, or if ye know
"And speak the word——" Alas! of fearful things   10
'Tis the most fearful when the People's eye
Abuse hath cleared from vain imaginings;
And taught the general voice to prophesy
Of Justice armed, and Pride to be laid low.

XII. Abuse of Monastic Power

And what is Penance with her knotted thong,
Mortification with the shirt of hair,
Wan cheek, and knees indùrated with prayer,
Vigils, and fastings rigorous as long,
If cloistered Avarice scruple not to wrong   5
The pious, humble, useful Secular,
And robs the People of his daily care,
Scorning their wants because her arm is strong?
Inversion strange! that to a Monk, who lives
For self, and struggles with himself alone,   10
The amplest share of heavenly favour gives;

And hath allotted, in the world's esteem,
To such a higher station than to him
Who on the good of others builds his own.

XIII. Monastic Voluptuousness

Yet more,—round many a Convent's blazing fire
Unhallowed threads of revelry are spun;
There Venus sits disguisèd like a Nun,—
While Bacchus, clothed in semblance of a Friar,
Pours out his choicest beverage high and higher   5
Sparkling, until it cannot chuse but run
Over the bowl, whose silver lip hath won
An instant kiss of masterful desire—
To stay the precious waste. In every brain
Spreads the dominion of the sprightly juice,   10
Through the wide world to madding Fancy dear,
Till the arch'd roof, with resolute abuse
Of its grave echoes, swells a choral strain,
Whose votive burthen is—"OUR KINGDOM'S HERE!"

XIV. Dissolution of the Monasteries

Threats come which no submission may assuage;
No sacrifice avert, no power dispute;
The tapers shall be quenched, the belfries mute,
And, 'mid their choirs unroofed by selfish rage,
The warbling wren shall find a leafy cage;   5
The gadding bramble hang her purple fruit;
And the green lizard and the gilded newt
Lead unmolested lives, and die of age.[1]
The Owl of evening, and the woodland Fox
For their abode the shrines of Waltham chuse: 10
Proud Glastonbury can no more refuse
To stoop her head before these desperate shocks—

---

1   "These two lines are adopted from a MS. written about the year 1770, which accidentally
    fell into my possession. The close of the preceding Sonnet on monastic voluptuousness is
    taken from the same source as is the verse, "Where Venus sits, &c."
        WW refers to ll. 3ff. ("There Venus sits . . . ") of *II.vii. Monastic Voluptuousness*, above.
    The manuscript poem has been identified as *The Ruins of St. Mary's Abby, near Dalton,
    in Furness, Lancashire* by William Robinson (See *Sonnet Series and Itinerary Poems*, p.
    259).

She whose high pomp displaced, as story tells,
Arimathean Joseph's wattled cells.

XV. The Same Subject

The lovely Nun (submissive but more meek
Through saintly habit, than from effort due
To unrelenting mandates that pursue
With equal wrath the steps of strong and weak)
Goes forth—unveiling timidly her cheek   5
Suffused with blushes of celestial hue,
While through the Convent gate to open view
Softly she glides, another home to seek.
Not Iris, issuing from her cloudy shrine,
An Apparition more divinely bright!   10
Not more attractive to the dazzled sight
Those wat'ry glories, on the stormy brine
Pour'd forth, while summer suns at distance shine,
And the green vales lie hush'd in sober light!

XVI. Continued

Yet some, Noviciates of the cloistral shade,
Or chained by vows, with undissembled glee
The warrant hail—exulting to be free;
Like ships before whose keels, full long embayed
In polar ice, propitious winds have made   5
Unlook'd-for outlet to an open sea,
Their liquid world, for bold discovery,
In all her quarters temptingly displayed!
Hope guides the young; but when the old must pass
The threshold, whither shall they turn to find   10
The hospitality—the alms (alas!
Alms may be needed) which that House bestowed?
Can they, in faith and worship, train the mind
To keep this new and questionable road?

XVII. Saints

Ye, too, must fly before a chasing hand,
Angels and Saints, in every hamlet mourned!
Ah! if the old idolatry be spurned,

Let not your radiant Shapes desert the Land:
Her adoration was not your demand,
The fond heart proffered it—the servile heart;   5
And therefore are ye summoned to depart,
Michael, and thou St. George whose flaming brand
The Dragon quelled; and valiant Margaret
Whose rival sword a like Opponent slew: 10
And rapt Cecilia, seraph-haunted Queen
Of harmony; and weeping Magdalene,
Who in the penitential desart met
Gales sweet as those that over Eden blew!

XVIII. The Virgin

Mother! whose virgin bosom was uncrost
With the least shade of thought to sin allied;
Woman! above all women glorified,
Our tainted nature's solitary boast;
Purer than foam on central Ocean tost;   5
Brighter than eastern skies at day-break strewn
With fancied roses, than the unblemished moon
Before her wane begins on heaven's blue coast;
Thy Image falls to earth. Yet some, I ween,
Not unforgiven the suppliant knee might bend,   10
As to a visible Power, in which did blend
All that was mixed and reconciled in Thee
Of mother's love with maiden purity,
Of high with low, celestial with terrene!

XIX. Apology

Not utterly unworthy to endure
Was the supremacy of crafty Rome;
Age after age to the arch of Christendom
Aërial keystone haughtily secure;
Supremacy from Heaven transmitted pure,   5
As many hold; and, therefore, to the tomb
Pass, some through fire—and by the scaffold some—
Like saintly Fisher, and unbending More.
"Lightly for both the bosom's lord did sit
"Upon his throne;" unsoftened, undismayed   10

By aught that mingled with the tragic scene
Of pity or fear; and More's gay genius played
With the inoffensive sword of native wit,
Than the bare axe more luminous and keen.

XX. Imaginative Regrets

Deep is the lamentation! Not alone
From Sages justly honoured by mankind,
But from the ghostly Tenants of the wind,
Demons and Spirits, many a dolorous groan
Issues for that dominion overthrown: 5
Proud Tiber grieves, and far-off Ganges, blind
As his own worshippers;—and Nile, reclined
Upon his monstrous urn, the farewell moan
Renews.—Through every forest, cave, and den,
Where frauds were hatch'd of old, hath sorrow past—   10
Hangs o'er the Arabian Prophet's native Waste
Where once his airy helpers schemed and planned,
'Mid phantom lakes bemocking thirsty men,
And stalking pillars built of fiery sand.

XXI. Reflections

Grant, that by this unsparing Hurricane
Green leaves with yellow mixed are torn away,
And goodly fruitage with the mother spray,
'Twere madness—wished we, therefore, to detain,
With farewell sighs of mollified disdain,   5
The "trumpery" that ascends in bare display,—
Bulls, pardons, relics, cowls black, white, and grey,
Upwhirl'd—and flying o'er the ethereal plain
Fast bound for Limbo Lake.—And yet not choice
But habit rules the unreflecting herd,   10
And airy bonds are hardest to disown;
Hence, with the spiritual sovereignty transferred
Unto itself, the Crown assumes a voice
Of reckless mastery, hitherto unknown.

XXII. Translation of the Bible

But, to outweigh all harm, the sacred Book,

In dusty sequestration wrapp'd too long,
Assumes the accents of our native tongue;
And he who guides the plough, or wields the crook,
With understanding spirit now may look   5
Upon her records, listen to her song,
And sift her laws—much wondering that the wrong,
Which Faith has suffered, Heaven could calmly brook.
Transcendant Boon! noblest that earthly King
Ever bestowed to equalize and bless   10
Under the weight of mortal wretchedness!
But passions spread like plagues, and thousands wild
With bigotry shall tread the Offering
Beneath their feet—detested and defiled.

XXIII. Edward VI

"Sweet is the holiness of Youth"—so felt
Time-honoured Chaucer when he framed the lay
By which the Prioress beguiled the way,
And many a Pilgrim's rugged heart did melt.
Hadst thou, loved Bard! whose spirit often dwelt   5
In the clear land of vision, but foreseen
King, Child, and Seraph, blended in the mien
Of pious Edward kneeling as he knelt
In meek and simple Infancy, what joy
For universal Christendom had thrilled   10
Thy heart! what hopes inspired thy genius, skilled
(O great Precursor, genuine morning star)
The lucid shafts of reason to employ,
Piercing the Papal darkness from afar!

XXIV. Edward Signing the Warrant for the Execution of Joan of Kent

The tears of man in various measure gush
From various sources; gently overflow
From blissful transport some—from clefts of woe
Some with ungovernable impulse rush;
And some, coëval with the earliest blush   5
Of infant passion, scarcely dare to show
Their pearly lustre—coming but to go;

And some break forth when others' sorrows crush
The sympathizing heart. Nor these, nor yet
The noblest drops to admiration known,   10
To gratitude, to injuries forgiv'n,
Claim Heaven's regard like waters that have wet
The innocent eyes of youthful monarchs driven
To pen the mandates, nature doth disown.

XXV. Cranmer

Outstretching flame-ward his upbraided hand
(O God of mercy, may no earthly Seat
Of judgment such presumptuous doom repeat!)
Amid the shuddering throng doth Cranmer stand;
Firm as the stake to which with iron band   5
His Frame is tied; firm from the naked feet
To the bare head, the victory complete;
The shrouded Body, to the Soul's command,
Answering with more than Indian fortitude,
Through all her nerves with finer sense endued;   10
Now wrapt in flames—and now in smoke embowered—
Till self-reproach and panting aspirations
Are, with the heart that held them, all devoured;
The Spirit set free, and crown'd with joyful acclamations!

XXVI. General View of the Troubles of the Reformation

Aid, glorious Martyrs, from your fields of light
Our mortal ken! Inspire a perfect trust
(While we look round) that Heaven's decrees are just;
Which few can hold committed to a fight
That shews, ev'n on its better side, the might   5
Of proud Self-will, Rapacity, and Lust,
'Mid clouds envelop'd of polemic dust,
Which showers of blood seem rather to incite
Than to allay.—Anathemas are hurled
From both sides; veteran thunders (the brute test   10
Of Truth) are met by fulminations new—
Tartarean flags are caught at, and unfurled—
Friends strike at Friends—the flying shall pursue—

And Victory sickens, ignorant where to rest!

XXVII. English Reformers in Exile

Scattering, like Birds escaped the Fowler's net,
Some seek with timely flight a foreign strand,
Most happy, re-assembled in a land
By dauntless Luther freed, could they forget
Their Country's woes. But scarcely have they met,   5
Partners in faith, and Brothers in distress,
Free to pour forth their common thankfulness,
Ere hope declines; their union is beset
With prurient speculations rashly sown,
Whence thickly-sprouting growth of poisonous weeds;   10
Their forms are broken staves; their passions steeds
That master them. How enviably blest
Is he who can, by help of grace, enthrone
The peace of God within his single breast!

XXVIII. Elizabeth

Hail, Virgin Queen! o'er many an envious bar
Triumphant—snatched from many a treacherous wile!
All hail, Sage Lady, whom a grateful Isle
Hath blest, respiring from that dismal war
Stilled by thy voice! But quickly from afar   5
Defiance breathes with more malignant aim;
And alien storms with home-bred ferments claim
Portentous fellowship. Her silver car
Meanwhile, by prudence ruled, glides slowly on;
Unhurt by violence, from menaced taint   10
Emerging pure, and seemingly more bright!
For, wheresoe'er she moves, the clouds anon
Disperse; or—under a Divine constraint—
Reflect some portion of her glorious light!

XXIX. Eminent Reformers

Methinks that I could trip o'er heaviest soil,
Light as a buoyant Bark from wave to wave,
Were mine the trusty Staff that Jewel gave
To youthful Hooker, in familiar style

The gift exalting, and with playful smile:[1]   5
For, thus equipped, and bearing on his head
The Donor's farewell blessing, could he dread
Tempest, or length of way, or weight of toil?
More sweet than odours caught by him who sails
Near spicy shores of Araby the blest,   10
A thousand times more exquisitely sweet,
The freight of holy feeling which we meet,
In thoughtful moments, wafted by the gales
From fields where good men walk, or bowers wherein they rest.

XXX. The Same

Holy and heavenly Spirits as they were,
Spotless in life, and eloquent as wise,
With what entire affection did they prize
Their new-born Church! labouring with earnest care
To baffle all that might her strength impair;   5
That Church—the unperverted Gospel's seat;
In their afflictions a divine retreat;
Source of their liveliest hope, and tenderest prayer!
The Truth exploring with an equal mind,
In polity and discipline they sought   10
Firmly between the two extremes to steer;
But theirs the wise man's ordinary lot,
To trace right courses for the stubborn blind,
And prophesy to ears that will not hear.

XXXI. Distractions [2]

Men, who have ceased to reverence, soon defy
Their Forefathers;—lo! Sects are formed—and split
With morbid restlessness—the ecstatic fit
Spreads wide; though special mysteries multiply,
The Saints must govern, is their common cry;   5
And so they labour; deeming Holy Writ
Disgraced by aught that seems content to sit
Beneath the roof of settled Modesty.

---

1   See WW's note at the end of this volume.
2   "A common device in religious and political conflicts. See Strype in support of this instance."
    WW

The Romanist exults; fresh hope he draws
From the confusion—craftily incites   10
The overweening—personates the mad—
To heap disgust upon the worthier Cause:
The Throne is plagued; the New-born Church is sad,
For every wave against her peace unites.

XXXII. Gunpowder Plot

— for Rock

Fear hath a hundred eyes that all agree
To plague her beating heart; and there is one
(Nor idlest that!) which holds communion
With things that were not, yet were *meant* to be.
Aghast within its gloomy cavity   5
That eye (which sees as if fulfilled and done
Crimes that might stop the motion of the sun)
Beholds the horrible catastrophe
Of an assembled Senate unredeemed
From subterraneous Treason's darkling power: 10
Merciless act of sorrow infinite!
Worse than the product of that dismal night,
When gushing, copious as a thunder shower,
The blood of Huguenots through Paris stream'd.

XXXIII. Illustration

The Virgin Mountain,[1] wearing like a Queen
A brilliant crown of everlasting Snow,
Sheds ruin from her sides; and men below

not to be 2021!

Wonder that aught of aspect so serene
Can link with desolation. Smooth and green,   5
And seeming, at a little distance, slow,
The waters of the Rhine; but on they go
Fretting and whitening, keener and more keen,
Till madness seizes on the whole wide Flood,
Turned to a fearful Thing whose nostrils breathe   10
Blasts of tempestuous smoke—wherewith he tries
To hide himself but only magnifies;
And doth in more conspicuous torment writhe,
Deafening the region in his ireful mood.

---

1   "The Jung-frau." WW

XXXIV. Troubles of Charles the First.

Such contrast, in whatever track we move,
To the mind's eye Religion doth present;
Now with her own deep quietness content;
Then, like the mountain, thundering from above
Against the ancient Pine-trees of the grove   5
And the Land's humblest comforts. Now her mood
Recals the transformation of the flood,
Whose rage the gentle skies in vain reprove,
Earth cannot check. O terrible excess
Of headstrong will! Can this be Piety?   10
No—some fierce Maniac hath usurp'd her name;
And scourges England struggling to be free:
Her peace destroyed! her hopes a wilderness!
Her blessings curs'd—her glory turn'd to shame!

XXXV. Laud[1]

Pursued by Hate, debarred from friendly care;
An old weak Man for vengeance thrown aside,
Long "in the painful art of dying" tried,
(Like a poor Bird entangled in a Snare
Whose heart still flutters, though his wings forbear   5
To stir in useless struggle) Laud relied
Upon the strength which Innocence supplied,
And in his prison breathed celestial air.
Why tarries then thy Chariot? Wherefore stay,
O Death! the ensanguined yet triumphant wheels,   10
Which thou prepar'st, full often, to convey
(What time a State with madding faction reels)
The Saint or Patriot to the world that heals
All wounds, all perturbations doth allay?

XXXVI. Afflictions of England

Harp! couldst thou venture, on thy boldest string,
The faintest note to echo which the blast
Caught from the hand of Moses as it pass'd
O'er Sinai's top, or from the Shepherd King,

---

1   See WW's note at the end of this volume.

Early awake, by Siloa's brook, to sing   5
Of dread Jehovah; then, should wood and waste
Hear also of that name, and mercy cast
Off to the mountains, like a covering
Of which the Lord was weary. Weep, oh weep,
As good men wept beholding King and Priest   10
Despised by that stern God to whom they raise
Their suppliant hands; but holy is the feast
He keepeth; like the firmament his ways;
His statutes like the chambers of the deep.

Ecclesiastical Sketches
Part III

FROM THE RESTORATION, TO THE PRESENT TIMES

I

I saw the figure of a lovely Maid
Seated alone beneath a darksome Tree,
Whose fondly overhanging canopy
Set off her brightness with a pleasing shade.
Substance she seem'd (and *that* my heart betrayed,   5
For she was one I loved exceedingly;)
But while I gazed in tender reverie
(Or was it sleep that with my Fancy play'd?)
The bright corporeal presence, form, and face,
Remaining still distinct, grew thin and rare,   10
Like sunny mist; at length the golden hair,
Shape, limbs, and heavenly features, keeping pace
Each with the other, in a lingering race
Of dissolution, melted into air.

II. Patriotic Sympathies

Last night, without a voice, this Vision spake
Fear to my Spirit—passion that might seem
To lie dissevered from our present theme;
Yet do I love my Country—and partake
Of kindred agitations for her sake;   5
She visits oftentimes my midnight dream;

Her glory meets me with the earliest beam
Of light, which tells that morning is awake:
If aught impair her beauty or destroy,
Or but forebode destruction, I deplore   10
With filial love the sad vicissitude;
If she hath fallen and righteous Heaven restore
The prostrate, then my spring-time is renewed,
And sorrow bartered for exceeding joy.

III. Charles the Second

Who comes with rapture greeted, and caress'd
With frantic love—his kingdom to regain?
Him Virtue's Nurse, Adversity, in vain
Received, and fostered in her iron breast:
For all she taught of hardiest and of best,   5
Or would have taught, by discipline of pain
And long privation, now dissolves amain,
Or is remembered only to give zest
To wantonness.—Away, Circean revels!
Already stands our Country on the brink   10
Of bigot rage, that all distinction levels
Of truth and falsehood, swallowing the good name,
And, with that draught, the life-blood: misery, shame,
By Poets loathed; from which Historians shrink!

IV. Latitudinarianism

Yet Truth is keenly sought for, and the wind
Charged with rich words poured out in Thought's defence;
Whether the Church inspire that eloquence,
Or a Platonic Piety—confined
To the sole temple of the inward mind;   5
And One there is who builds immortal lays,
Though doomed to tread in solitary ways,
Darkness before, and danger's voice behind!
Yet not alone, nor helpless to repel
Sad thoughts; for from above the starry sphere   10
Come secrets—whispered nightly to his ear;
And the pure spirit of celestial light
Shines through his soul—"that he may see and tell

Of things invisible to mortal sight."

V. Walton's Book of "Lives"

There are no colours in the fairest sky
So fair as these. The feather whence the pen
Was shaped that traced the lives of these good Men,
Dropped from an Angel's wing. With moistened eye
We read of faith and purest charity   5
In Statesman, Priest, and humble Citizen.
O, could we copy their mild virtues, then
What joy to live, what blessedness to die!
Methinks their very Names shine still and bright,
Apart—like glow-worms in the woods of spring,   10
Or lonely tapers shooting far a light
That guides and cheers,—or seen, like stars on high,
Satellites burning in a lucid ring
Around meek Walton's heavenly memory.

VI. Clerical Integrity

Nor shall the eternal roll of praise reject
Those Unconforming; whom one rigorous day
Drives from their Cures, a voluntary prey
To poverty and grief, and disrespect,
And some to want—as if by tempest wreck'd   5
On a wild coast; how destitute! did They
Feel not that Conscience never can betray,
That peace of mind is Virtue's sure effect.
Their Altars they forego, their homes they quit,
Fields which they love, and paths they daily trod,   10
And cast the future upon Providence;
As men the dictate of whose inward sense
Outweighs the world; whom self-deceiving wit
Lures not from what they deem the cause of God.

VII. Acquittal of the Bishops

A voice, from long-expectant thousands sent,
Shatters the air and troubles tower and spire—
For Justice hath absolved the Innocent,
And Tyranny is balked of her desire:

Up—down the busy Thames—rapid as fire   5
Coursing a train of gunpowder—it went,
And transport finds in every street a vent,
Till the whole City rings like one vast quire.
The Fathers urge the People to be still
With outstretched hands and earnest voice—in vain!   10
Yea, many, haply wont to entertain
Small reverence for the Mitre's offices,
And to Religion's self no friendly will,
A Prelate's blessing ask on bended knees.

VIII. William the Third

Calm as an under current—strong to draw
Millions of waves into itself, and run,
From sea to sea, impervious to the sun
And ploughing storm—the spirit of Nassau
(By constant impulse of religious awe   5
Swayed, and thereby enabled to contend
With the wide world's commotions) from its end
Swerves not—diverted by a casual law.
Had mortal action e'er a nobler scope?
The Hero comes to liberate, not defy;   10
And while he marches on with righteous hope,
Conqueror beloved! expected anxiously!
The vacillating Bondman of the Pope
Shrinks from the verdict of his steadfast eye.

IX. Obligations of Civil to Religious Liberty

Ungrateful Country, if thou e'er forget
The sons who for thy civil rights have bled!
How, like a Roman, Sidney bowed his head,
And Russel's milder blood the scaffold wet;
But These had fallen for profitless regret   5
Had not thy holy Church her Champions bred,
And claims from other worlds inspirited
The Star of Liberty to rise. Nor yet
(Grave this within thy heart!) if spiritual things
Be lost, through apathy, or scorn, or fear,   10
Shalt thou thy humbler franchises support,

However hardly won or justly dear;
What came from Heaven to Heaven by nature clings,
And, if dissevered thence, its course is short.

X. Places of Worship

As star that shines dependent upon star
Is to the sky while we look up in love;
As to the deep fair ships which though they move
Seem fixed, to eyes that watch them from afar;
As to the sandy desert fountains are,   5
With palm groves shaded at wide intervals,
Whose fruit around the sun-burnt Native falls
Of roving tired or desultory war;
Such to this British Isle her Christian Fanes,
Each linked to each for kindred services;   10
Her Spires, her Steeple-towers with glittering vanes
Far-kenned, her Chapels lurking among trees,
Where a few villagers on bended knees
Find solace which a busy world disdains.

XI. Pastoral Character[1]

A genial hearth, a hospitable board,
And a refined rusticity, belong
To the neat Mansion, where, his Flock among,
The learned Pastor dwells, their watchful Lord.
Though meek and patient as a sheathèd sword,   5
Though pride's least lurking thought appear a wrong
To human kind; though peace be on his tongue,
Gentleness in his heart; can earth afford
Such genuine state, pre-eminence so free,
As when, arrayed in Christ's authority,   10
He from the Pulpit lifts his awful hand;
Conjures, implores, and labours all he can
For re-subjecting to divine command
The stubborn spirit of rebellious Man?

---

1   See WW's note at the end of this volume.

XII. The Liturgy

Yes, if the intensities of hope and fear
Attract us still, and passionate exercise
Of lofty thoughts, the way before us lies
Distinct with signs—through which, in fixed career,
As through a zodiac, moves the ritual year   5
Of England's Church—stupendous mysteries!
Which whoso travels in her bosom, eyes
As he approaches them, with solemn cheer.
Enough for us to cast a transient glance
The circle through; relinquishing its story   10
For those whom Heaven hath fitted to advance
And, harp in hand, rehearse the King of Glory—
From his mild advent till his countenance
Shall dissipate the seas and mountains hoary. *end of the world*

XIII. Catechizing

From little down to least—in due degree,
Around the Pastor, each in new-wrought vest,
Each with a vernal posy at his breast,
We stood, a trembling, earnest Company!
With low soft murmur, like a distant bee,   5
Some spake, by thought-perplexing fears betrayed;
And some a bold unerring answer made:
How fluttered then thy anxious heart for me,
Beloved Mother! Thou whose happy hand
Had bound the flowers I wore, with faithful tie: 10
Sweet flowers! at whose inaudible command
Her countenance, phantom-like, doth re-appear:
O lost too early for the frequent tear,
And ill requited by this heart-felt sigh!

XIV. Rural Ceremony [1]

With smiles each happy face was overspread,
That trial ended. Give we to a day
Of festal joy one tributary lay;

---

1   "This is still continued in many Churches in Westmoreland. It takes place in the month
    of July, when the floor of the Stalls is strewn with fresh rushes: and hence it is called the
    'Rush-bearing.'" WW

That day when, forth by rustic music led,
The village Children, while the sky is red   5
With evening lights, advance in long array
Through the still Church-yard, each with garland gay,
That, carried sceptre-like, o'ertops the head
Of the proud Bearer. To the wide Church-door,
Charged with these offerings which their Fathers bore   10
For decoration in the Papal time,
The innocent procession softly moves:—
The spirit of Laud is pleased in Heav'n's pure clime,
And Hooker's voice the spectacle approves!

XV. Regrets

Would that our scrupulous Sires had dared to leave
Less scanty measure of those graceful rites
And usages, whose due return invites
A stir of mind too natural to deceive;
Giving the Memory help when she would weave   5
A crown for Hope! I dread the boasted lights
That all too often are but fiery blights,
Killing the bud o'er which in vain we grieve.
Go, seek, when Christmas snows discomfort bring,
The counter Spirit found in some gay Church   10
Green with fresh Holly, every pew a perch
In which the linnet or the thrush might sing,
Merry and loud, and safe from prying search,
Strains offered only to the genial Spring.

XVI. Mutability

From low to high doth dissolution climb,
And sinks from high to low, along a scale
Of awful notes, whose concord shall not fail;
A musical but melancholy chime,
Which they can hear who meddle not with crime,   5
Nor avarice, nor over-anxious care.
Truth fails not; but her outward forms that bear
The longest date do melt like frosty rime,
That in the morning whitened hill and plain
And is no more; drop like the tower sublime   10

Of yesterday, which royally did wear
Its crown of weeds, but could not even sustain
Some casual shout that broke the silent air,
Or the unimaginable touch of Time.

XVII. Old Abbeys

Monastic Domes! following my downward way,
Untouched by due regret I marked your fall!
Now, ruin, beauty, ancient stillness, all
Dispose to judgments temperate as we lay
On our past selves in life's declining day: 5
For as, by discipline of Time made wise,
We learn to tolerate the infirmities
And faults of others, gently as he may
Towards our own the mild Instructor deals,
Teaching us to forget them or forgive.[1]   10
Perversely curious, then, for hidden ill
Why should we break Time's charitable seals?
Once ye were holy, ye are holy still;
Your spirit freely let me drink and live!

XVIII. Congratulation

Thus all things lead to Charity—secured
By THEM who bless'd the soft and happy gale
That landward urged the great Deliverer's sail,
Till in the sunny bay his fleet was moored!
Propitious hour! had we, like them, endured   5
Sore stress of apprehension, with a mind[2]
Sickened by injuries, dreading worse designed,
From month to month trembling and unassured,
How had we then rejoiced! But we have felt,
As a loved substance, their futurity;   10
Good, which they dared not hope for, we have seen;
A State whose generous will through earth is dealt;
A State, which balancing herself between
Licence and slavish order, dares be free.

---

1 "This is borrowed from an affecting passage in Mr. George Dyer's History of Cambridge."
2 "See Burnet, who is unusually animated on this subject; the east wind, so anxiously expected and prayed for, was called the 'Protestant wind.'" WW

XIX. New Churches

But liberty, and triumphs on the Main,
And laurelled Armies—not to be withstood,
What serve they? if, on transitory good
Intent, and sedulous of abject gain,
The State (ah surely not preserved in vain!)   5
Forbear to shape due channels which the Flood
Of sacred Truth may enter—till it brood
O'er the wide realm, as o'er the Egyptian Plain
The all-sustaining Nile. No more—the time
Is conscious of her want; through England's bounds,   10
In rival haste, the wished-for Temples rise!
I hear their Sabbath bells' harmonious chime
Float on the breeze—the heavenliest of all sounds
That hill or vale prolongs or multiplies!

XX. Church to be Erected

Be this the chosen site—the virgin sod,
Moistened from age to age by dewy eve,
Shall disappear—and grateful earth receive
The corner-stone from hands that build to God.
Yon reverend hawthorns, hardened to the rod   5
Of Winter storms yet budding cheerfully;
Those forest oaks of Druid memory,
Shall long survive, to shelter the Abode
Of genuine Faith. Where, haply, 'mid this band
Of daisies, Shepherds sate of yore and wove   10
May-garlands, let the holy Altar stand
For kneeling adoration; while above,
Broods, visibly pourtrayed, the mystic Dove,
That shall protect from Blasphemy the Land.

XXI. Continued

Mine ear has rung, my spirits sunk subdued,
Sharing the strong emotion of the crowd,
When each pale brow to dread hosannas bowed
While clouds of incense mounting veiled the rood,
That glimmered like a pine-tree dimly viewed   5

[handwritten: ! how excessive]

Through Alpine vapours. Such appalling rite
Our Church prepares not, trusting to the might
Of simple truth with grace divine imbued;
Yet will we not conceal the precious Cross,
Like Men ashamed: the Sun with his first smile[1]   10
Shall greet that symbol crowning the low Pile;
And the fresh air of "incense-breathing morn"
Shall wooingly embrace it; and green moss
Creep round its arms through centuries unborn.

XXII. New Church Yard

[handwritten: Presumably Rydal?]

The encircling ground, in native turf array'd,
Is now by solemn consecration given
To social interests, and to favouring Heaven;
And where the rugged Colts their gambols play'd,
And wild Deer bounded through the forest glade,   5
Unchecked as when by merry Outlaw driven,
Shall hymns of praise resound at morn and even;
And soon, full soon, the lonely Sexton's spade
Shall wound the tender sod. Encincture small,
But infinite its grasp of joy and woe!   10
Hopes, fears, in never-ending ebb and flow—
The spousal trembling—and the "dust to dust"—
The prayers—the contrite struggle—and the trust
That to the Almighty Father looks through all!

XXIII. Cathedrals, &c.

Open your Gates ye everlasting Piles!
Types of the spiritual Church which God hath reared;
Not loth we quit the newly-hallowed sward
And humble altar, 'mid your sumptuous aisles
To kneel—or thrid your intricate defiles—   5
Or down the nave to pace in motion slow,
Watching, with upward eyes, the tall tower grow
And mount, at every step, with living wiles
Instinct—to rouse the heart and lead the will
By a bright ladder to the world above.   10

---

1   "The Lutherans have retained the Cross within their Churches; it is to be regretted that we
have not done the same." WW

Open your Gates, ye Monuments of love
Divine! thou Lincoln, on thy sovereign hill!
Thou, stately York! and Ye, whose splendors cheer
Isis and Cam, to patient Science dear!

XXIV. Inside of King's College Chapel, Cambridge

Tax not the royal Saint with vain expense,
With ill-matched aims the Architect who planned,
Albeit labouring for a scanty band
Of white-robed Scholars only, this immense
And glorious Work of fine Intelligence!   5
Give all thou canst; high Heaven rejects the lore
Of nicely-calculated less or more;
So deemed the Man who fashioned for the sense
These lofty pillars—spread that branching roof
Self-poised, and scooped into ten thousand cells,   10
Where light and shade repose, where music dwells
Lingering—and wandering on as loth to die,
Like thoughts whose very sweetness yieldeth proof
That they were born for immortality.

XXV. The Same

What awful pèrspective! while from our sight
Their portraiture the lateral windows hide,
Glimmers their corresponding stone-work, dyed
With the soft chequerings of a sleepy light.
Martyr, or King, or sainted Eremite,   5
Whoe'er ye be, that thus—yourselves unseen—
Imbue your prison-bars with solemn sheen,
Shine on, until ye fade with coming Night!
But, from the arms of silence—list! O list!
The music bursteth into second life—   10
The notes luxuriate—every stone is kiss'd
By sound, or ghost of sound, in mazy strife;
Heart-thrilling strains, that cast before the eye
Of the Devout a veil of ecstasy!

XXVI. Continued

They dreamt not of a perishable home

Who thus could build. Be mine, in hours of fear
Or grovelling thought, to seek a refuge here;
Or through the aisles of Westminster to roam;
Where bubbles burst, and folly's dancing foam   5
Melts, if it cross the threshold; where the wreath
Of awe-struck wisdom droops: or let my path
Lead to that younger Pile, whose sky-like dome
Hath typified by reach of daring art
Infinity's embrace; whose guardian crest,   10
The silent Cross, among the stars shall spread
As now, when she hath *also* seen her breast
Filled with mementos, satiate with its part
Of grateful England's overflowing Dead.

XXVII. Ejaculation

Glory to God! and to the Power who came
In filial duty, clothed with love divine;
That made his human tabernacle shine
Like Ocean burning with purpureal flame;
Or like the Alpine Mount, that takes its name   5
From roseate hues, far kenn'd at morn and even,[1]
In hours of peace, or when the storm is driven
Along the nether region's rugged frame!
Earth prompts—Heaven urges; let us seek the light,
Studious of that pure intercourse begun   10
When first our infant brows their lustre won;
So, like the Mountain, may we grow more bright
From unimpeded commerce with the Sun,
At the approach of all-involving night.

XXVIII. Conclusion

Why sleeps the future, as a snake enrolled,
Coil within coil, at noon-tide? For the Word
Yields, if with unpresumptuous faith explored,
Power at whose touch the sluggard shall unfold
His drowsy rings. Look forth! that Stream behold,   5
That Stream upon whose bosom we have pass'd

---

1   "Some say that Monte Rosa takes its name from a belt of rock at its summit—a very unpoetical and scarcely a probable supposition." WW

Floating at ease while nations have effaced
Nations, and Death has gathered to his fold
Long lines of mighty Kings—look forth, my Soul!
(Nor in that vision be thou slow to trust)   10
The living Waters, less and less by guilt
Stained and polluted, brighten as they roll,
Till they have reached the Eternal City—built
For the perfected Spirits of the just!

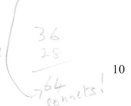

[Poems not included in series as first published]

[*Druid Temple*]

And thus a Structure potent to enchain
The eye of Wonder rose in this fair Isle;
Not built with calculations nice and vain
But in mysterious Nature's boldest style,
Yet orderly as some basaltic Pile   5
That steadfastly repels the fretful main.

The Point at Issue

For what contend the wise? for nothing less
Than that pure Faith dissolve the bonds of Sense;
The Soul restored to God by evidence
Of things not seen—drawn forth from their recess,
Root there, and not in forms, her holiness: 5
That Faith which to the Patriarchs did dispense
Sure guidance, ere a ceremonial fence
Was needful round men thirsting to transgress;
That Faith, more perfect still, with which the Lord
Of all, himself a Spirit, in the youth   10
Of Christian aspiration, deigned to fill
The temples of their hearts—who, with his word
Informed, were resolute to do his will,
And worship him in spirit and in truth.

Revival of Popery

Melts into silent shades the Youth, discrowned
By unrelenting Death. O People keen

For change, to whom the new looks always green!
They cast, they cast with joy upon the ground
Their Gods of wood and stone; and, at the sound   5
Of counter-proclamation, now are seen,
(Proud triumph is it for a sullen Queen!)
Lifting them up, the worship to confound
Of the Most High. Again do they invoke
The Creature, to the Creature glory give;   10
Again with frankincense the altars smoke
Like those the Heathen served; and mass is sung;
And prayer, man's rational prerogative,
Runs through blind channels of an unknown tongue.

Latimer and Ridley

How fast the Marian death-list is unrolled!
See Latimer and Ridley in the might
Of Faith stand coupled for a common flight!
One (like those Prophets whom God sent of old)[1]
Transfigured, from this kindling hath foretold   5
A torch of inextinguishable light;
The other gains a confidence as bold;
And thus they foil their enemy's despite.
The penal instruments, the shows of crime,
Are glorified while this once-mitred pair   10
Of saintly Friends, "the Murtherer's chain partake,
Corded, and burning at the social stake:"
Earth never witnessed object more sublime
In constancy, in fellowship more fair!

Persecution of the Scottish Convenanters

When Alpine Vales threw forth a suppliant cry,
The majesty of England interposed
And the sword stopped; the bleeding wounds were closed;
And Faith preserved her ancient purity.
How little boots that precedent of good,   5
Scorned or forgotten, Thou canst testify,
For England's shame, O Sister Realm! from wood,
Mountain, and moor, and crowded street, where lie

---

1   See WW's note at the end of this volume.

genuine feeling here

The headless martyrs of the Covenant,
Slain by compatriot-protestants that draw   10
From councils senseless as intolerant
Their warrant. Bodies fall by wild sword-law;
But who would force the Soul, tilts with a straw
Against a Champion cased in adamant.

"Down a swift Stream, thus far, a bold design"

Down a swift Stream, thus far, a bold design
Have we pursued, with livelier stir of heart
Than his who sees, borne forward by the Rhine,
The living landscapes greet him, and depart;
Sees spires fast sinking—up again to start!   5
And strives the towers to number, that recline
O'er the dark steeps, or on the horizon line
Striding with shattered crests the eye athwart;—
So have we hurried on with troubled pleasure:
Henceforth, as on the bosom of a stream   10
That slackens, and spreads wide a watery gleam,
We, nothing loth a lingering course to measure,
May gather up our thoughts, and mark at leisure
Features that else had vanished like a dream.

Sacheverell

A sudden conflict rises from the swell
Of a proud slavery met by tenets strained
In Liberty's behalf. Fears, true or feigned,
Spread through all ranks; and lo! the Sentinel
Who loudest rang his pulpit larum bell,   5
Stands at the Bar—absolved by female eyes,
Mingling their Light with graver flatteries,
Lavished on *Him* that England may rebel
Against her ancient virtue. High and Low,
Watch-words of Party, on all tongues are rife;   10
As if a Church, though sprung from heaven, must owe
To opposites and fierce extremes her life,—
Not to the golden mean, and quiet flow
Of truths that soften hatred, temper strife.

Baptism

Blest be the Church, that, watching o'er the needs
Of Infancy, provides a timely shower,
Whose virtue changes to a Christian Flower
The sinful product of a bed of Weeds!
Fitliest beneath the sacred roof proceeds   5
The Ministration; while parental Love
Looks on, and Grace descendeth from above
As the high service pledges now, now pleads.
There, should vain thoughts outspread their wings and fly
To meet the coming hours of festal mirth,   10
The tombs which hear and answer that brief cry,
The Infant's notice of his second birth,
Recal the wandering soul to sympathy
With what Man hopes from Heaven, yet fears from Earth.

Confirmation

The Young-ones gathered in from hill and dale,
With holiday delight on every brow:
'Tis passed away; far other thoughts prevail;
For they are taking the baptismal Vow
Upon their conscious selves; their own lips speak   5
The solemn promise. Strongest sinews fail,
And many a blooming, many a lovely cheek
Under the holy fear of God turns pale,
While on each head his lawn-robed Servant lays
An apostolic hand, and with prayer seals   10
The Covenant. The Omnipotent will raise
Their feeble Souls; and bear with *his* regrets,
Who, looking round the fair assemblage, feels
That ere the Sun goes down their childhood sets.

Confirmation Continued

I saw a Mother's eye intensely bent
Upon a Maiden trembling as she knelt;
In and for whom the pious Mother felt
Things that we judge of by a light too faint:
Tell, if ye may, some star-crowned Muse, or Saint!   5

Tell what rushed in, from what she was relieved—
Then, when her Child the hallowing touch received,
And such vibration to the Mother went
That tears burst forth amain. Did gleams appear?
Opened a vision of that blissful place   10
Where dwells a Sister-child? And was power given
Part of her lost One's glory back to trace
Even to this Rite? For thus *She* knelt, and, ere
The Summer-leaf had faded, passed to Heaven.

Sacrament

By chain yet stronger must the Soul be tied:
One duty more, last stage of this ascent,
Brings to thy food, memorial Sacrament!
The Offspring, haply at the Parent's side;
But not till They, with all that do abide   5
In Heaven, have lifted up their hearts to laud
And magnify the glorious name of God,
Fountain of Grace, whose Son for Sinners died.
Here must my Song in timid reverence pause:
But shrink not, ye, whom to the saving rite   10
The Altar calls; come early under laws
That can secure for you a path of light
Through gloomiest shade; put on (nor dread its weight)
Armour divine, and conquer in your cause!

Emigrant French Clergy

Even while I speak, the sacred roofs of France
Are shattered into dust; and self-exiled
From Altars threatened, levelled, or defiled,
Wander the Ministers of God, as chance
Opens a way for life, or consonance   5
Of Faith invites. More welcome to no land
The fugitives than to the British strand,
Where Priest and Layman with the vigilance
Of true compassion greet them. Creed and test
Vanish before the unreserved embrace   10
Of Catholic humanity:—distrest
They came,—and, while the moral tempest roars

Throughout the Country they have left, our shores
Give to their Faith a dreadless resting-place.

Sponsors

Father! to God himself we cannot give
A holier name! Then lightly do not bear
Both names conjoined—but of thy spiritual care
Be duly mindful; still more sensitive
Do *Thou*, in truth a second *Mother*, strive   5
Against disheartening custom, that by Thee
Watched, and with love and pious industry
Tended at need, the adopted Plant may thrive
For everlasting bloom. Benign and pure
This Ordinance, whether loss it would supply,   10
Prevent omission, help deficiency,
Or seek to make assurance doubly sure.
Shame if the consecrated Vow be found
An idle form, the *Word* an empty sound!

[The three following Sonnets are an intended addition to the "Ecclesiastical
Sketches," the first to stand second; and the two that succeed, seventh and
eighth, in the second part of the Series.—See the Author's Poems.—They are
placed here as having some connection with the foregoing Poem.]

"Deplorable his lot who tills the ground"

Deplorable his lot who tills the ground,
His whole life long tills it, with heartless toil
Of villain-service, passing with the soil
To each new Master, like a steer or hound,
Or like a rooted tree, or stone earth-bound;   5
But mark how gladly, through their own domains,
The Monks relax or break these iron chains;
While Mercy, uttering, through their voice, a sound
Echoed in Heaven, cries out, "Ye Chiefs, abate
These legalized oppressions! Man, whose name   10
And nature God disdained not; Man, whose soul
Christ died for, cannot forfeit his high claim
To live and move exempt from all controul
Which fellow-feeling doth not mitigate!"

The Vaudois

But whence came they who for the Saviour Lord
Have long borne witness as the Scriptures teach?
Ages ere Valdo raised his voice to preach
In Gallic ears the unadulterate Word,
Their fugitive Progenitors explored   5
Subalpine vales, in quest of safe retreats
Where that pure Church survives, though summer heats
Open a passage to the Romish sword,
Far as it dares to follow. Herbs self-sown,
And fruitage gathered from the chestnut wood,   10
Nourish the Sufferers then; and mists, that brood
O'er chasms with new-fallen obstacles bestrown,
Protect them; and the eternal snow that daunts
Aliens, is God's good winter for their haunts.

"Praised be the Rivers, from their mountain-springs"

Praised be the Rivers, from their mountain-springs
Shouting to Freedom, "Plant thy Banners here!"
To harassed Piety, "Dismiss thy fear,
And in our Caverns smooth thy ruffled wings!"
Nor be unthanked their tardiest lingerings   5
'Mid reedy fens wide-spread and marshes drear,
Their own creation, till their long career
End in the sea engulphed. Such welcomings
As came from mighty Po when Venice rose,
Greeted those simple Heirs of truth divine   10
Who near his fountains sought obscure repose,
Yet were prepared as glorious lights to shine,
Should that be needed for their sacred Charge;
Blest Prisoners They, whose spirits are at large!

"Coldly we spake. The Saxons, overpowered"

Coldly we spake. The Saxons, overpowered
By wrong triumphant through its own excess,
From fields laid waste, from house and home devoured
By flames, look up to heaven and crave redress
From God's eternal justice. Pitiless   5

Though men be, there are angels that can feel
For wounds that death alone has power to heal,
For penitent guilt, and innocent distress.
And has a Champion risen in arms to try
His Country's virtue, fought, and breathes no more;   10
Him in their hearts the people canonize;
And far above the mine's most precious ore
The least small pittance of bare mould they prize
Scooped from the sacred earth where his dear relics lie.

Aspects of Christianity in America

I.—The Pilgrim Fathers[1]

Well worthy to be magnified are they
Who, with sad hearts, of friends and country took
A last farewell, their loved abodes forsook,
And hallowed ground in which their fathers lay;
Then to the new-found World explored their way,   5
That so a Church, unforced, uncalled to brook
Ritual restraints, within some sheltering nook
Her Lord might worship and his word obey
In freedom. Men they were who could not bend;
Blest Pilgrims, surely, as they took for guide   10
A will by sovereign Conscience sanctified;
Blest while their Spirits from the woods ascend
Along a Galaxy that knows no end,
But in His glory who for Sinners died.

II. Continued

From Rite and Ordinance abused they fled

---

1   "This and the two following Sonnets are intended to take their place in the Ecclesiastical
Series which the reader may find in the fourth volume of my Poems. American episcopacy,
in union with the church in England, strictly belongs to the general subject; and I here
make my acknowledgments to my American friends, Bishop Doane, and Mr. Henry Reed
of Philadelphia, for having suggested to me the propriety of adverting to it, and pointed
out the virtues and intellectual qualities of Bishop White, which so eminently fitted him for
the great work he undertook. Bishop White was consecrated at Lambeth, Feb. 4, 1787,
by Archbishop Moore; and before his long life was closed, twenty-six bishops had been
consecrated in America by himself. For his character and opinions, see his own numerous
Works, and a "Sermon in commemoration of him, by George Washington Doane, Bishop
of New Jersey."

To Wilds where both were utterly unknown;
But not to them had Providence foreshown
What benefits are missed, what evils bred,
In worship neither raised nor limited   5
Save by Self-will. Lo! from that distant shore,
For Rite and Ordinance, Piety is led
Back to the Land those Pilgrims left of yore,
Led by her own free choice. So Truth and Love
By Conscience governed do their steps retrace.—   10
Fathers! your Virtues, such the power of grace,
Their spirit, in your Children, thus approve.
Transcendent over time, unbound by place,
Concord and Charity in circles move.

III. Concluded.—American Episcopacy

Patriots informed with Apostolic light
Were they, who, when their Country had been freed,
Bowing with reverence to the ancient creed,
Fixed on the frame of England's Church their sight,
And strove in filial love to reunite   5
What force had severed. Thence they fetched the seed
Of Christian unity, and won a meed
Of praise from Heaven. To Thee, O saintly White,
Patriarch of a wide-spreading family,
Remotest lands and unborn times shall turn,   10
Whether they would restore or build—to Thee,
As one who rightly taught how zeal should burn,
As one who drew from out Faith's holiest urn
The purest stream of patient Energy.

"How soon—alas! did Man, created pure—"

How soon—alas! did Man, created pure—
By Angels guarded, deviate from the line
Prescribed to duty:—woeful forfeiture
He made by wilful breach of law divine.
With like perverseness did the Church abjure   5
Obedience to her Lord, and haste to twine,
'Mid Heaven-born flowers that shall for aye endure,
Weeds on whose front the world had fixed her sign.

O Man,—if with thy trials thus it fares,
If good can smooth the way to evil choice,   10
From all rash censure be the mind kept free;
He only judges right who weighs, compares,
And, in the sternest sentence which his voice
Pronounces, ne'er abandons Charity.

"From false assumption rose, and fondly hail'd"

From false assumption rose, and fondly hail'd
By superstition, spread the Papal power;
Yet do not deem the Autocracy prevail'd
Thus only, even in error's darkest hour.
She daunts, forth-thundering from her spiritual tower   5
Brute rapine, or with gentle lure she tames.
Justice and Peace through Her uphold their claims;
And Chastity finds many a sheltering bower.
Realm there is none that if controul'd or sway'd
By her commands partakes not, in degree,   10
Of good, o'er manners arts and arms, diffused:
Yes, to thy domination, Roman See,
Tho' miserably, oft monstrously, abused
By blind ambition, be this tribute paid.

"As faith thus sanctified the warrior's crest"

As faith thus sanctified the warrior's crest
While from the Papal Unity there came,
What feebler means had fail'd to give, one aim
Diffused thro' all the regions of the West;
So does her Unity its power attest   5
By works of Art, that shed, on the outward frame
Of worship, glory and grace, which who shall blame
That ever looked to heaven for final rest?
Hail countless Temples! that so well befit
Your ministry; that, as ye rise and take   10
Form, spirit and character from holy writ,
Give to devotion, wheresoe'er awake,
Pinions of high and higher sweep, and make
The unconverted soul with awe submit.

"Where long and deeply hath been fixed the root"

Where long and deeply hath been fixed the root
In the blest soil of gospel truth, the Tree,
(Blighted or scathed tho' many branches be,
Put forth to wither, many a hopeful shoot)
Can never cease to bear celestial fruit.   5
Witness the Church that oft times, with effect
Dear to the saints, strives earnestly to eject
Her bane, her vital energies recruit.
Lamenting, do not hopelessly repine
When such good work is doomed to be undone,   10
The conquests lost that were so hardly won:—
All promises vouchsafed by Heaven will shine
In light confirmed while years their course shall run,
Confirmed alike in progress and decline.

"Bishops and Priests, blessèd are ye, if deep"

Bishops and Priests, blessèd are ye, if deep
(As yours above all offices is high)
Deep in your hearts the sense of duty lie;
Charged as ye are by Christ to feed and keep
From wolves your portion of his chosen sheep: 5
Labouring as ever in your Master's sight,
Making your hardest task your best delight,
What perfect glory ye in Heaven shall reap!—
But, in the solemn Office which ye sought
And undertook premonished, if unsound   10
Your practice prove, faithless though but in thought,
Bishops and Priests, think what a gulf profound
Awaits you then, if they were rightly taught
Who framed the Ordinance by your lives disowned!

The Marriage Ceremony.

The Vested Priest before the Altar stands;
Approach, come gladly, ye prepared, in sight
Of God and chosen friends, your troth to plight
With the symbolic ring, and willing hands
Solemnly joined. Now sanctify the bands   5

O Father!—to the Espoused thy blessing give,
That mutually assisted they may live
Obedient, as here taught, to thy commands.
So prays the Church, to consecrate a Vow
"The which would endless matrimony make;"   10
Union that shadows forth and doth partake
A mystery potent human love to endow
With heavenly, each more prized for the other's sake;
Weep not, meek Bride! uplift thy timid brow.

Thanksgiving after Childbirth

Woman! the Power who left his throne on high,
And deigned to wear the robe of flesh we wear,
The Power that thro' the straits of Infancy
Did pass dependent on maternal care,
His own humanity with Thee will share,   5
Pleased with the thanks that in his People's eye
Thou offerest up for safe Delivery
From Childbirth's perilous throes. And should the Heir
Of thy fond hopes hereafter walk inclined
To courses fit to make a mother rue   10
That ever he was born, a glance of mind
Cast upon this observance may renew
A better will; and, in the imagined view
Of thee thus kneeling, safety he may find.

Visitation of the Sick

The Sabbath bells renew the inviting peal;
Glad music! yet there be that, worn with pain
And sickness, listen where they long have lain,
In sadness listen. With maternal zeal
Inspired, the Church sends ministers to kneel   5
Beside the afflicted; to sustain with prayer,
And soothe the heart confession hath laid bare—
That pardon, from God's throne, may set its seal
On a true Penitent. When breath departs
From one disburthened so, so comforted,   10
His Spirit Angels greet; and ours be hope
That, if the Sufferer rise from his sick-bed,

Hence he will gain a firmer mind, to cope
With a bad world, and foil the Tempter's arts.

The Commination Service

Shun not this Rite, neglected, yea abhorred,
By some of unreflecting mind, as calling
Man to curse man, (thought monstrous and appalling.)
Go thou and hear the threatenings of the *Lord*;
Listening within his Temple see his sword   5
Unsheathed in wrath to strike the offender's head,
Thy own, if sorrow for thy sin be dead,
Guilt unrepented, pardon unimplored.
Two aspects bears Truth needful for salvation;
Who knows not *that*?—yet would this delicate age   10
Look only on the Gospel's brighter page:
Let light and dark duly our thoughts employ;
So shall the fearful words of Commination
Yield timely fruit of peace and love and joy.

Forms of Prayer at Sea

To kneeling Worshippers no earthly floor
Gives holier invitation than the deck
Of a storm-shattered Vessel saved from Wreck
(When all that Man could do avail'd no more)
By him who raised the Tempest and restrains: 5
Happy the crew who this have felt, and pour
Forth for his mercy, as the Church ordains,
Solemn thanksgiving. Nor will *they* implore
In vain who, for a rightful cause, give breath
To words the Church prescribes aiding the lip   10
For the heart's sake, ere ship with hostile ship
Encounters, armed for work of pain and death.
Suppliants! the God to whom your cause ye trust
Will listen, and ye know that He is just.

Funeral Service

From the Baptismal hour, thro' weal and woe,
The church extends her care to thought and deed;
Nor quits the Body when the Soul is freed,

The mortal weight cast off to be laid low.
Blest Rite for him who hears in faith, "I know   5
That my Redeemer liveth,"—hears each word
That follows—striking on some kindred chord
Deep in the thankful heart;—yet tears will flow.
Man is as grass that springeth up at morn,
Grows green, and is cut down and withereth   10
Ere nightfall—truth that well may claim a sigh,
Its natural echo; but hope comes reborn
At Jesu's bidding. We rejoice, "O Death
Where is thy Sting?—O Grave where is thy Victory?"

Memorials of a Tour on the Continent, 1820.[1]

Dedication

Dear Fellow-Travellers! think not that the Muse
Presents to notice these memorial Lays,
Hoping the general eye thereon will gaze,
As on a mirror that gives back the hues
Of living Nature; no—though free to chuse   5
The greenest bowers, the most inviting ways,
The fairest landscapes and the brightest days,
She felt too deeply what her skill must lose.
For You she wrought;—ye only can supply
The life, the truth, the beauty: she confides   10
In that enjoyment which with you abides,
Trusts to your love and vivid memory;
Thus far contented that for You her verse
Shall lack not power the "meeting soul to pierce!"

                W. WORDSWORTH.

Rydal Mount,
January 1822.

Sonnet. Fish-women

—ON LANDING AT CALAIS[2]

'Tis said, fantastic Ocean doth enfold
The likeness of whate'er on Land is seen;
But, if the Nereid Sisters and their Queen,
Above whose heads the Tide so long hath roll'd,
The Dames resemble whom we here behold,   5
How terrible beneath the opening waves
To sink, and meet them in their fretted caves,
Withered, grotesque, immeasurably old,
And shrill and fierce in accent!—Fear it not;

---

1   For the sources of the reading text and the editor's commentary, see *Sonnet Series and Itinerary Poems, 1820–1845*, ed. Geoffrey Jackson (2004), pp. 351–356, and 419–441.

2   "If in this Sonnet I should seem to have borne a little too hard upon the personal appearance of the worthy Poissardes of Calais, let me take shelter under the authority of my lamented Friend the late Sir George Beaumont. He, a most accurate observer, used to say of them, that their features and countenances seemed to have conformed to those of the creatures they dealt in; at all events the resemblance was striking." WW

For they Earth's fairest Daughters do excel;   10
Pure unmolested beauty is their lot;
Their voices into liquid music swell,
Thrilling each pearly cleft and sparry grot—
The undisturbed Abodes where Sea-nymphs dwell!

Sonnet

BRUGES[1]

Bruges I saw attired with golden light
(Streamed from the west) as with a robe of power:
'Tis passed away;—and now the sunless hour,
That slowly introducing peaceful night
Best suits with fallen grandeur, to my sight   5
Offers her beauty, her magnificence,
And all the graces left her for defence
Against the injuries of time, the spite
Of Fortune, and the desolating storms
Of future War. Advance not—spare to hide,   10
O gentle Power of Darkness! these mild hues;
Obscure not yet these silent avenues
Of stateliest Architecture, where the forms
Of Nun-like Females, with soft motion, glide!

Sonnet

BRUGES

The Spirit of Antiquity, enshrined
In sumptuous Buildings, vocal in sweet Song
And Tales transmitted through the popular tongue,
And with devout solemnities entwined,
Strikes at the seat of grace within the mind: 5
Hence Forms that slide with swan-like ease along;
Hence motions, even amid the vulgar throng,
To an harmonious decency confined:
As if the Streets were consecrated ground,
The City one vast Temple—dedicate   10
To mutual respect in thought and deed;
To leisure, to forbearances sedate;

---

1   See WW's note at the end of this volume.

To social cares from jarring passions freed;
A nobler peace than that in desarts found!

Sonnet

AFTER VISITING THE FIELD OF WATERLOO

A winged Goddess, clothed in vesture wrought
Of rainbow colours; One whose port was bold,
Whose overburthened hand could scarcely hold
The glittering crowns and garlands which it brought,
Hover'd in air above the far-famed Spot.   5
She vanished—All was joyless, blank, and cold;
But if from wind-swept fields of corn that roll'd
In dreary billows, from the meagre cot,
And monuments that soon may disappear,
Meanings we craved which could not there be found;   10
If the wide prospect seemed an envious seal
Of great exploits; we felt as Men *should* feel,
With such vast hoards of hidden carnage near,
And horror breathing from the silent ground!

Sonnet

SCENERY BETWEEN NAMUR AND LIEGE

What lovelier home could gentle Fancy chuse?
Is this the Stream, whose cities, heights, and plains,
War's favorite play-ground, are with crimson stains
Familiar, as the Morn with pearly dews?
The Morn, that now along the silver MEUSE   5
Spreading her peaceful ensigns, calls the Swains
To tend their silent boats and ringing wains,
Or strip the bough whose mellow fruit bestrews
The ripening corn beneath it. As mine eyes
Turn from the fortified and threatening hill,   10
How sweet the prospect of yon watery glade,
With its grey rocks, clustering in pensive shade,
That, shaped like old monastic turrets, rise
From the smooth meadow-ground, serene and still!

Sonnet

Was it to disenchant, and to undo,
That we approached the Seat of Charlemaine?
To sweep from many an old romantic strain
That faith which no devotion may renew!
Why does this puny Church present to view   5
Its feeble columns? and that scanty Chair!
This Sword that One of our weak times might wear;
Objects of false pretence, or meanly true!
If from a Traveller's fortune I might claim
A palpable memorial of that day,   10
Then would I seek the Pyrenean Breach[1]
Which Roland clove with huge two-handed sway,
And to the enormous labor left his name,
Where unremitting frosts the rocky Crescent bleach.

Sonnet

IN THE CATHEDRAL AT COLOGNE

O for the help of Angels to complete
This Temple—Angels governed by a Plan
How gloriously pursued by daring Man,
Studious that He might not disdain the Seat
Who dwells in Heaven! But that inspiring heat   5
Hath failed; and now, ye Powers! whose gorgeous wings
And splendid aspect yon emblazonings
But faintly picture, 'twere an office meet
For you, on these unfinished Shafts to try
The midnight virtues of your harmony:—   10
This vast Design might tempt you to repeat

---

1   In his note WW refers to a work on the Pyrenees by Louis François Elisabeth Ramond de
    Carbonnières, *Observations faites dans les Pyrénéesm oiyr servur de suite à des obser-*
    vations sur les Alpes, insérées dans une traduction des lettres de W. Coxe, sur la Suisse
    (Paris, 1789):
        "Let a wall of rocks be imagined from three to six hundred feet in height, and rising
    between France and Spain, so as physically to separate the two kingdoms—let us fancy
    this wall curved like a crescent with its convexity towards France. Lastly, let us suppose,
    that in the very middle of the wall a breach of 300 feet wide has been beaten down by the
    famous Roland, and we may have a good idea of what the mountaineers call the 'Breche
    de Roland.'"

Charms that call forth upon empyreal ground
Immortal Fabrics—rising to the sound
Of penetrating harps and voices sweet!

Sonnet

AUTHOR'S VOYAGE DOWN THE RHINE (THIRTY YEARS AGO)

The confidence of Youth our only Art,
And Hope gay Pilot of the bold design,
We saw the living Landscapes of the Rhine,
Reach after reach, salute us and depart;
Slow sink the Spires,—and up again they start!   5
But who shall count the Towers as they recline
O'er the dark steeps, or on the horizon line
Striding, with shattered crests, the eye athwart?
More touching still, more perfect was the pleasure,
When hurrying forward till the slack'ning stream   10
Spread like a spacious Mere, we there could measure
A smooth free course along the watery gleam,
Think calmly on the past, and mark at leisure
Features which else had vanished like a dream.

Sonnet

IN A CARRIAGE, UPON THE BANKS OF THE RHINE[1]

Amid this dance of objects sadness steals
O'er the defrauded heart—while sweeping by,
As in a fit of Thespian jollity,
Beneath her vine-leaf crown the green Earth reels:
Backward, in rapid evanescence, wheels   5
The venerable pageantry of Time,
Each beetling rampart—and each tower sublime,
And what the Dell unwillingly reveals
Of lurking cloistral arch, through trees espied
Near the bright River's edge. Yet why repine?   10
Pedestrian liberty shall yet be mine
To muse, to creep, to halt at will, to gaze:

---

1   "'From St. Goar to Bingen—Castles commanding innumerable small fortified villages—
nothing could exceed the delightful variety; but the postilions, who were intoxicated,
whisked us far too fast through those beautiful scenes.'—Extract from Journal." WW
quotes from Mary Wordsworth's entry for July 24, 1820, in her journal.

Freedom which youth with copious hand supplied,
May in fit measure bless my later days.

Hymn

FOR THE BOATMEN, AS THEY APPROACH THE RAPIDS,
UNDER THE CASTLE OF HEIDELBERG

Jesu! bless our slender Boat,
    By the current swept along;
Loud its threatenings—let them not
    Drown the music of a Song
Breathed thy mercy to implore,   5
Where these troubled waters roar!

Lord and Saviour! who art seen
    Bleeding on that precious Rood;
If, while through the meadows green
    Gently wound the peaceful flood,   10
We forgot Thee, do not Thou
Disregard thy Suppliants now!

Hither, like yon ancient Tower
    Watching o'er the River's bed,
Fling the shadow of thy power,   15
    Else we sleep among the Dead;
Traveller on the billowy Sea,
Shield us in our jeopardy!

Guide our Bark among the waves;
    Through the rocks our passage smooth;   20
Where the whirlpool frets and raves
    Let thy love its anger soothe;
All our hope is placed in Thee;
Miserere Domine![1]

---

1 "See the beautiful Song in Mr. Coleridge's Tragedy "The Remorse." Why is the Harp of
    Quantock silent?" WW.
      Coleridge, the "Harp of Quantock," used this refrain ("Lord have mercy!") in the song in
    III.i.68–61 of his play *Remorse* (1813).

Sonnet

LOCAL RECOLLECTION ON THE HEIGHTS NEAR HOCKHEIM[1]

Abruptly paused the Strife;—the field throughout
Resting upon his arms each Warrior stood,
Checked in the very act and deed of blood,
With breath suspended—like a listening Scout.
O Silence! thou wert Mother of a shout   5
That thro' the texture of yon azure dome
Clove its glad way—a cry of harvest home
Uttered to Heaven in ecstasy devout!
The barrier Rhine hath flashed, thro' battle-smoke,
On men who gazed heart-smitten by the view,   10
As if all Germany had felt the shock.
Fly, wretched Gauls! ere they the charge renew
Who have seen (themselves delivered from the yoke)
The unconquerable Stream his course pursue.

Sonnet

THE SOURCE OF THE DANUBE

Not (like his great compeers) indignantly
Doth DANUBE spring to life! The wandering stream
(Who loves the Cross, yet to the Crescent's gleam
Unfolds a willing breast) with infant glee
Slips from his prison walls: and Fancy, free   5
To follow in his track of silver light,
Reaches, with one brief moment's rapid flight,
The vast Encincture of that gloomy sea
Whose rough winds Orpheus soothed; whose waves did greet
So skilfully that they forgot their jars—   10
To waft the heroic progeny of Greece,
When the first Ship sailed for the golden Fleece;
Argo exalted by that daring feat
To a conspicuous height among the stars![2]

1   "The event is thus recorded in the journals of the day: 'When the Austrians took Hockheim,
    in one part of the engagement they got to the brow of the hill, whence they had their first
    view of the Rhine. They instantly halted—not a gun was fired—not a voice heard: but they
    stood gazing on the river with those feelings which the events of the last 15 years at once
    called up. Prince Schwartzenberg rode up to know the cause of this sudden stop, they
    then gave three cheers, rushed after the enemy, and drove them into the water.'" WW
2   "Before this quarter of the Black Forest was inhabited, the source of the Danube might

Sonnet

THE JUNG-FRAU—AND THE RHINE AT SHAUFFHAUSEN

The Virgin Mountain, wearing like a Queen
A brilliant crown of everlasting snow,
Sheds ruin from her sides; and men below
Wonder that aught of aspect so serene[1]
Can link with desolation.—Smooth and green   5
And seeming, at a little distance, slow
The Waters of the Rhine; but on they go
Fretting and whitening, keener and more keen
Till madness seizes on the whole wide Flood
Turned to a fearful Thing, whose nostrils breathe   10
Blasts of tempestuous smoke, with which he tries
To hide himself, but only magnifies:
And doth in more conspicuous torment writhe,
Deafening the region in his "ireful mood."

Memorial,

NEAR THE OUTLET OF THE LAKE OF THUN

"DEM ANDENKEN
MEINES FREUNDES
ALOYS REDING
MDCCCXVIII."

Around a wild and woody hill
A gravelled path-way treading,
We reached a votive Stone that bears
The name of Aloys Reding.[2]

---

have suggested some of those sublime images which Armstrong has so finely described; at present the contrast is most striking. The Spring appears in a capacious stone Basin upon the front of a Ducal palace, with a pleasure-ground opposite; then, passing under the pavement, takes the form of a little, clear, bright, black, vigorous rill, barely wide enough to tempt the agility of a child five years old to leap over it,—and, entering the Garden, it joins, after a course of a few hundred yards, a Stream much more considerable than itself. The copiousness of the Spring at Doneschingen must have procured for it the honour of being named the Source of the Danube." WW

1 "This Sonnet belongs to another publication, but from its fitness for this place is inserted here also. 'Voilà un enfer d'eau,' cried out a German Friend of Ramond, falling on his knees on the scaffold in front of this Waterfall. See Ramond's Translation of Coxe." WW refers to Ramond's *Lettres de M. William Coxe á M. W. Melmoth* . . . (2 vols.; 3d ed., Paris, 1787), I, 16.

2 "Aloys Reding, it will be remembered, was Captain-General of the Swiss forces, which with

Well judged the Friend who placed it there   5
For silence and protection,
And haply with a finer care
Of dutiful affection.

The Sun regards it from the West,
Sinking in summer glory;   10
And, while he sinks, affords a type
Of that pathetic story.

And oft he tempts the patriot Swiss
Amid the grove to linger;
Till all is dim, save this bright Stone   15
Touched by his golden finger.

Sonnet

ON APPROACHING THE STAUB-BACH, LAUTERBRUNNEN[1]

Tracks let me follow far from human-kind
Which these illusive greetings may not reach;
Where only Nature tunes her voice to teach
Careless pursuits, and raptures unconfined.
No Mermaid warbles (to allay the wind   5
That drives some vessel tow'rds a dangerous beach)
More thrilling melodies! no caverned Witch
Chaunting a love-spell, ever intertwined
Notes shrill and wild with art more musical!
Alas! that from the lips of abject Want   10
And Idleness in tatters mendicant
They should proceed—enjoyment to enthral,
And with regret and useless pity haunt
This bold, this pure, this sky-born WATERFALL!

---

a courage and perseverance worthy of the cause, opposed the flagitious, and too suc-
cessful, attempt of Buonaparte to subjugate their country." WW

1   " 'The Staub-bach' is a narrow Stream, which, after a long course on the heights, comes to
a sharp edge of a somewhat overhanging precipice, overleaps it with a bound, and, after
a fall of 930 feet, forms again a rivulet. The vocal powers of these musical Beggars may
seem to be exaggerated; but this wild and savage air was utterly unlike any sounds I had
ever heard: the notes reached me from a distance, and on what occasion they were sung I
could not guess, only they seemed to belong, in some way or other, to the Waterfall—and
reminded me of religious services chaunted to Streams and Fountains in Pagan times."
WW

Sonnet

THE FALL OF THE AAR—HANDEC

From the fierce aspect of this River throwing
His giant body o'er the steep rock's brink,
Back in astonishment and fear we shrink:
But, gradually a calmer look bestowing,
Flowers we espy beside the torrent growing;   5
Flowers that peep forth from many a cleft and chink,
And, from the whirlwind of his anger, drink
Hues ever fresh, in rocky fortress blowing:
They suck, from breath that threatening to destroy
Is more benignant than the dewy eve,   10
Beauty, and life, and motions as of joy:
Nor doubt but HE to whom yon Pine-trees nod
Their heads in sign of worship, Nature's God,
These humbler adorations will receive.

Scene

ON THE LAKE OF BRIENTZ

"What know we of the Blest above
But that they sing and that they love?"
Yet, if they ever did inspire
A mortal hymn, or shaped the choir,
Now, where those harvest Damsels float   5
Homeward in their rugged Boat,
(While all the ruffling winds are fled,
Each slumbering on some mountain's head,)
Now, surely, hath that gracious aid
Been felt, that influence is displayed.   10
Pupils of Heaven, in order stand
The rustic Maidens, every hand
Upon a Sister's shoulder laid,—
To chaunt, as glides the boat along,
A simple, but a touching Song;   15
To chaunt, as Angels do above,
The melodies of Peace in Love!

Engelberg[1]

For gentlest uses, oft-times Nature takes
The work of Fancy from her willing hands;
And even such beautiful creation makes
As renders needless spells and magic wands,
And for the boldest tale belief commands.   5
When first my eyes beheld that famous Hill
The sacred ENGELBERG, celestial Bands,
With intermingling motions soft and still,
Hung round its top, on wings that changed their hues at will.

Clouds do not name those Visitants; they were   10
The very Angels whose authentic lays,
Sung from that heavenly ground in middle air,
Made known the spot where Piety should raise
A holy Structure to the Almighty's praise.
Resplendent Apparition! if in vain   15
My ears did listen, 'twas enough to gaze;
And watch the slow departure of the train,
Whose skirts the glowing Mountain thirsted to detain!

Our Lady of the Snow

Meek Virgin Mother, more benign
Than fairest Star upon the height
Of thy own mountain[2] set to keep
Lone vigils thro' the hours of sleep,
What eye can look upon thy shrine   5
Untroubled at the sight?

These crowded Offerings as they hang
In sign of misery relieved,
Even these, without intent of theirs,
Report of comfortless despairs,   10
Of many a deep and cureless pang
And confidence deceived.

---

1   "'Engelberg,' the Hill of Angels, as the name implies. The Convent whose site was pointed
    out, according to tradition, in this manner, is seated at its base. The Architecture of the
    Building is unimpressive, but the situation is worthy of the honour which the imagination of
    the Mountaineers has conferred upon it." WW
2   "Mount Righi." WW

To Thee, in this aërial cleft,
As to a common centre, tend
All sufferings that no longer rest   15
On mortal succour, all distrest
That pine of human hope bereft,
Nor wish for earthly friend.

And hence, O Virgin Mother mild!
Tho' plenteous flowers around thee blow,   20
Not only from the dreary strife
Of Winter, but the storms of life,
Thee have thy Votaries aptly styled
"Our Lady of the Snow."

Even for the Man who stops not here,   25
But down the irriguous valley hies,
Thy very name, O Lady! flings,
O'er blooming fields and gushing springs,
A holy Shadow soft and dear
Of chastening sympathies!   30

Nor falls that intermingling shade
To Summer gladsomeness unkind,
It chastens only to requite
With gleams of fresher, purer, light;
While, o'er the flower-enamelled glade,   35
More sweetly breathes the wind.

But on!—a tempting downward way,
A verdant path before us lies;
Clear shines the glorious sun above;
Then give free course to joy and love,   40
Deeming the evil of the day
Sufficient for the wise.

Sonnet

THE TOWN OF SCHWYTZ

By antique Fancy trimmed—tho' lowly, bred
To dignity—in thee O SCHWYTZ! are seen
The genuine features of the golden mean;

Equality by Prudence governed,
Or jealous Nature ruling in her stead;   5
And, therefore, art thou blest with peace, serene
As that of the sweet fields and meadows green
In unambitious compass round thee spread!
Majestic BERNE, high on her guardian steep,
Holding a central station of command,   10
Might well by styled this noble Body's HEAD;
Thou, lodg'd 'mid mountainous entrenchments deep,
Its HEART; and ever may the heroic Land
Thy name, O SCHWYTZ, in happy freedom keep![1]

Sonnet

ON HEARING THE "RANZ DES VACHES" ON THE TOP
OF THE PASS OF ST. GOTHARD

I listen—but no faculty of mine
Avails those modulations to detect,
Which, heard in foreign lands, the Swiss affect
With tenderest passion; leaving him to pine
(So fame reports) and die; his sweet-breath'd kine   5
Remembering, and green Alpine pastures deck'd
With vernal flowers. Yet may we not reject
The tale as fabulous.—Here while I recline
Mindful how others love this simple Strain,
Even here, upon this glorious Mountain (named   10
Of God himself from dread pre-eminence)
Aspiring thoughts by memory are reclaimed;
And, thro' the Music's touching influence,
The joys of distant home my heart enchain.

The Church of San Salvador, seen from the Lake of Lugano[2]

Thou sacred Pile! whose turrets rise,
From yon steep Mountain's loftiest stage,
Guarded by lone San Salvador;

---

1 "'Nearly 500 years (says Ebel, speaking of the French Invasion,) had elapsed, when, for
   the first time, foreign Soldiers were seen upon the frontiers of this small Canton, to impose
   upon it the laws of their Governors.'" WW cites Johann Gottfried Ebel, *The Traveller's
   Guide through Switzerland* (London, 1820)
2 For WW's note see the notes at the end of this volume.

Sink (if thou must) as heretofore,
To sulphurous bolts a sacrifice,   5
But ne'er to human rage!

On Horeb's top, on Sinai, deigned
To rest the universal Lord:
Why leap the fountains from their cells
Where everlasting Bounty dwells?   10
That, while the Creature is sustained,
His God may be adored.

Cliffs, fountains, rivers, seasons, times,
Let all remind the soul of heaven;
Our slack devotion needs them all;   15
And Faith, so oft of sense the thrall,
While she, by aid of Nature, climbs,
May hope to be forgiven.

I love, where spreads the village lawn,
Upon some knee-worn Cell to gaze;   20
Hail to the firm unmoving Cross,
Aloft, where pines their branches toss!
And to the Chapel far withdrawn,
That lurks by lonely ways!

Short-sighted Children of the dust   25
We live and move in sorrow's power;
Extinguish that unblest disdain
That scorns the altar, mocks the fane,
Where patient Sufferers bend—in trust
To win a happier hour.   30

Glory, and patriotic Love,
And all the Pomps of this frail "spot
Which men call Earth," have yearned to seek,
Associate with the simply meek,
Religion in the sainted grove,   35
And in the hallowed grot.

Thither, in time of adverse shocks,
Of fainting hopes and backward wills,
Did mighty Tell repair of old—

A Hero cast in Nature's mould,   40
Deliverer of the steadfast rocks
And of the ancient hills!

He,[1] too, of battle-martyrs chief!
Who, to recal his daunted peers,
For victory shaped an open space,   45
By gathering with a wide embrace,
Into his single heart, a sheaf
Of fatal Austrian spears.

Ye Alps, in many a rugged link
Far-stretched, and Thou, majestic Po,   50
Dimly from yon tall Mount descried,
Where'er I wander be my Guide,
Sweet Charity!—that bids us think,
And feel, if we would know!

Fort Fuentes—at the Head of the Lake of Como

Dread hour! when upheaved by war's sulphurous blast,
    This sweet-visaged Cherub of Parian stone
So far from the holy enclosure was cast,
    To couch in this thicket of brambles alone;

To rest where the lizard may bask in the palm   5
    Of his half-open hand pure from blemish or speck;
And the green, gilded snake, without troubling the calm
    Of the beautiful countenance, twine round his neck.

Where haply (kind service to Piety due!)
    When winter the grove of its mantle bereaves,   10
Some Bird (like our own honoured Redbreast) may strew
    The desolate Slumberer with moss and with leaves.

Fuentes once harboured the Good and the Brave,
    Nor to her was the dance of soft pleasure unknown;
Her banners for festal enjoyment did wave   15
    While the thrill of her fifes thro' the mountains was blown:

Now gads the wild vine o'er the pathless Ascent—

---

1 " Arnold WInkelried, at the battle of Sempach, broke an Austrian phalanx in this manner.
    The event is one of the most famous in the annals of Swiss heroism; and pictures and
    prints of it are frequent throughout the country." WW

O silence of Nature, how deep is thy sway
When the whirlwind of human destruction is spent,
  Our tumults appeased, and our strifes passed away!—   20

The Italian Itinerant, and the Swiss Goatherd

PART I

1

Now that the farewell tear is dried,
Heaven prosper thee, be hope thy guide!
Hope be thy guide, adventurous Boy;
The wages of thy travel, joy!
Whether for London bound—to trill   5
Thy mountain notes with simple skill;
Or on thy head to poise a show
Of plaster-craft in seemly row;
The graceful form of milk-white steed,
Or Bird that soared with Ganymede;   10
Or thro' our hamlets thou wilt bear
The sightless Milton, with his hair
Around his placid temples curled;
And Shakespear at his side—a freight,
If clay could think and mind were weight,   15
For him who bore the world!
Hope be thy guide, adventurous Boy;
The wages of thy travel, joy!

2

But thou, perhaps, (alert and free
Tho' serving sage philosophy)   20
Wilt ramble over hill and dale,
A Vender of the well-wrought Scale
Whose sentient tube instructs to time
A purpose to a fickle clime:
Whether thou chuse this useful part,   25
Or minister to finer art,
Tho' robbed of many a cherish'd dream,
And crossed by many a shatter'd scheme,
What stirring wonders wilt thou see

In the proud Isle of liberty!   30
Yet will the Wanderer sometimes pine
With thoughts which no delights can chase,
Recal a Sister's last embrace,
His Mother's neck entwine;
Nor shall forget the Maiden coy   35
That *would* have lov'd the bright-hair'd Boy!

3

My Song, encouraged by the grace
That beams from his ingenuous face,
For this Adventurer scruples not
To prophesy a golden lot;   40
Due recompence, and safe return
To Como's steeps—his happy bourne!
Where he, aloft in Garden glade,
Shall tend, with his own dark-eyed Maid,
The towering maize, and prop the twig   45
That ill supports the luscious fig;
Or feed his eye in paths sun-proof
With purple of the trellis-roof,
That thro' the jealous leaves escapes
From Cadenabbia's pendant grapes.   50
—Oh might he tempt that Goatherd-child
To share his wanderings! *he* whose look
Even yet my heart can scarcely brook,
So touchingly he smiled,
As with a rapture caught from heaven,   55
When Pity's unasked alms were given.

PART II

1

With nodding plumes, and lightly drest
Like Foresters in leaf-green vest,
The Helvetian Mountaineers, on ground
For Tell's dread archery renowned,   60
Before the Target stood—to claim
The guerdon of the steadiest aim.
Loud was the rifle-gun's report,

A startling thunder quick and short!
But, flying thro' the heights around,   65
Echo prolonged a tell-tale sound
Of hearts and hands alike "prepared
The treasures they enjoy to guard!"
And, if there be a favoured hour
When Heroes are allowed to quit   70
The Tomb, and on the clouds to sit
With tutelary power,
On their Descendants shedding grace,
This was the hour, and that the place.

2

But Truth inspired the Bards of old   75
When of an iron age they told,
Which to unequal laws gave birth,
That drove Astræa from the earth.
—A gentle Boy—(perchance with blood
As noble as the best endued,   80
But seemingly a Thing despised;
Even by the sun and air unprized;
For not a tinge or flowery streak
Appeared upon his tender cheek,)
Heart-deaf to those rebounding notes   85
Of pleasure, by his silent Goats—
Sate far apart in forest shed,
Pale, ragged, bare his feet and head,
Mute as the snow upon the hill,
And, as the Saint he prays to, still.   90
Ah, what avails heroic deed?
What liberty? if no defence
Be won for feeble Innocence—
Father of All! if willful Man must read
His punishment in soul-distress,   95
Grant to the morn of life its natural blessedness!

Sonnet

THE LAST SUPPER, BY LEONARDO DA VINCI, IN THE REFECTORY
OF THE CONVENT OF MARIA DELLA GRAZIA—MILAN[1]

Tho' searching damps and many an envious flaw
Have marr'd this Work, the calm etherial grace,
The love deep-seated in the Saviour's face,
The mercy, goodness, have not failed to awe
The Elements; as they do melt and thaw   5
The heart of the Beholder—and erase
(At least for one rapt moment) every trace
Of disobedience to the primal law.
The annunciation of the dreadful truth
Made to the Twelve, survives; the brow, the cheek,   10
And hand reposing on the board in ruth
Of what it utters[2], while the unguilty seek
Unquestionable meanings, still bespeak
A labour worthy of eternal youth!

The Eclipse of the Sun, 1820

High on her speculative Tower
Stood Science waiting for the Hour
When Sol was destined to endure
That darkening of his radiant face
Which Superstition strove to chase,   5
Erewhile, with rites impure.

Afloat beneath Italian skies,
Thro' regions fair as Paradise
We gaily passed,—till Nature wrought
A silent and unlooked-for change,   10
That checked the desultory range
Of joy and sprightly thought.

---

1 "This picture of the Last Supper has not only been grievously injured by time, but parts are said to have been painted over again. These niceties may be left to connoisseurs,—I speak of it as I felt. The copy exhibited in London some years ago, and the engraving by Morghen, are both admirable; but in the original is a power which neither of those works has attained, or even approached." WW

2 "'The hand / *Sang* with the voice, and this the argument.' MILTON." WW quotes from *Paradise Regain'd*, I, ll. 171, 172.

Where'er was dipped the toiling oar
The waves danced round us as before,
As lightly, tho' of altered hue;   15
'Mid recent coolness, such as falls
At noon-tide from umbrageous walls
That screen the morning dew.

No vapour stretched its wings; no cloud
Cast far or near a murky shroud;   20
The sky an azure field displayed;
'Twas sun-light sheathed and gently charmed,
Of all its sparkling rays disarmed,
And as in slumber laid:—

Or something night and day between,   25
Like moon-shine—but the hue was green;
Still moon-shine, without shadow, spread
On jutting rock, and curved shore,
Where gazed the Peasant from his door,
And on the mountain's head.   30

It tinged the Julian steeps—it lay
Upon Lugano's ample bay;
The solemnizing veil was drawn
O'er Villas, Terraces, and Towers,
To Albogasio's olive bowers,   35
Porlezza's verdant lawn.

But Fancy, with the speed of fire,
Hath fled to Milan's loftiest spire,
And there alights 'mid that aërial host
Of figures human and divine,[1]   40
White as the snows of Apennine
Indùrated by frost.

Awe-stricken she beholds the array
That guards the Temple night and day;
Angels she sees that might from heaven have flown;   45
And Virgin Saints—who not in vain
Have striven by purity to gain

---

1   For WW's note see the notes at the end of this volume.

The beatific crown;

Far-stretching files, concentric rings
Each narrowing above each;—the wings—   50
The uplifted palms, the silent marble lips,
The starry zone of sovereign height,
All steeped in this portentous light!
All suffering dim eclipse!

Thus after Man had fallen, (if aught   55
These perishable spheres have wrought
May with that issue be compared)
Throngs of celestial visages,
Darkening like water in the breeze,
A holy sadness shared.   60

See! while I speak, the labouring Sun
His glad deliverance has begun:
The cypress waves its sombre plume
More cheerily; and Town and Tower,
The Vineyard and the Olive bower,   65
Their lustre re-assume!

Oh ye, who guard and grace my Home
While in far-distant Lands we roam,
Enquiring thoughts are turned to you;
Does a clear ether meet your eyes?   70
Or have black vapours hid the skies
And mountains from your view?

I ask in vain—and know far less
If sickness, sorrow, or distress
Have spared my Dwelling to this hour: 75
Sad blindness! but ordained to prove
Our Faith in Heaven's unfailing love
And all-controlling Power.

The Three Cottage Girls

1

How blest the Maid whose heart—yet free

From Love's uneasy sovereignty,
Beats with a fancy running high
Her simple cares to magnify;
Whom Labour, never urged to toil,   5
Hath cherished on a healthful soil;
Who knows not pomp, who heeds not pelf;
Whose heaviest sin it is to look
Askance upon her pretty Self
Reflected in some crystal brook;   10
Whom grief hath spared—who sheds no tear
But in sweet pity; and can hear
Another's praise from envy clear.

2

Such, (but O lavish Nature! why
That dark unfathomable eye,   15
Where lurks a Spirit that replies
To stillest mood of softest skies,
Yet hints at peace to be o'erthrown,
Another's—first, and then her own?)
Such, haply, yon ITALIAN Maid,   20
Our Lady's laggard Votaress,
Halting beneath the chesnut shade
To accomplish there her loveliness:
Nice aid maternal fingers lend;
A Sister serves with slacker hand;   25
Then, glittering like a star, she joins the festal band.

3

How blest (if truth may entertain
Coy fancy with a bolder strain)
The HELVETIAN Girl—who daily braves,
In her light skiff, the tossing waves,   30
And quits the bosom of the deep
Only to climb the rugged steep!
—Say whence that modulated shout?
From Wood-nymph of Diana's throng?
Or does the greeting to a rout   35
Of giddy Bacchanals belong?
Jubilant outcry!—rock and glade

Resounded—but the voice obeyed
The breath of an Helvetian Maid.

4

Her beauty dazzles the thick wood;   40
Her courage animates the flood;
Her step the elastic green-sward meets
Returning unreluctant sweets;
The mountains (as ye heard) rejoice
Aloud, saluted by her voice!   45
Blithe Paragon of Alpine grace,
Be as thou art—for through thy veins
The Blood of Heroes runs its race!
And nobly wilt thou brook the chains
That, for the virtuous, Life prepares;   50
The fetters which the Matron wears;
The Patriot Mother's weight of anxious cares!

5

"Sweet *Highland* Girl! a very shower
Of beauty was thy earthly dower,"[1]
When Thou didst pass before my eyes,   55
Gay Vision under sullen skies,
While Hope and Love around thee played
Near the rough Falls of Inversneyd!
Time cannot thin thy flowing hair,
Nor take one ray of light from Thee;   60
For in my Fancy thou dost share
The gift of Immortality;
And there shall bloom, with Thee allied,
The Votaress by Lugano's side;
And that intrepid Nymph, on Uri's steep, descried!   65

Sonnet

THE COLUMN INTENDED BY BUONAPARTE FOR A TRIUMPHAL EDIFICE IN MILAN, NOW
LYING BY THE WAY-SIDE ON THE SEMPLON PASS

Ambition, following down this far-famed slope

---

1   WW's note cites his earlier poem *To a Highland Girl,* from which these two lines are quoted
    (see vol. 1 of this edition).

Her Pioneer, the snow-dissolving Sun,
While clarions prate of Kingdoms to be won,
Perchance, in future ages, here may stop;
Taught to mistrust her flattering horoscope   5
By admonition from this prostrate Stone;
Memento uninscribed of Pride o'erthrown,
Vanity's hieroglyphic;—a choice trope
In fortune's rhetoric. Daughter of the Rock,
Rest where thy course was stayed by Power Divine!   10
The Soul transported sees, from hint of thine,
Crimes which the great Avenger's hand provoke,
Hears combats whistling o'er the ensanguin'd heath:
What groans! what shrieks! what quietness in death!

Stanzas

COMPOSED IN THE SEMPLON PASS

Vallombrosa! I longed in thy shadiest wood
To slumber, reclined on the moss-covered floor,
To listen to ANIO's precipitous flood,
When the stillness of evening hath softened its roar;
To range thro' the Temples of PÆSTUM, to muse   5
In POMPEII, preserved by her burial in earth,
On pictures to gaze, where they drank in their hues;
And murmur sweet Songs on the ground of their birth!

The beauty of Florence, the grandeur of Rome,
Could I leave them unseen and not yield to regret?   10
With a hope (and no more) for a season to come,
Which ne'er may discharge the magnificent debt?
Thou fortunate Region! whose Greatness inurned,
Awoke to new life from its ashes and dust;
Twice-glorified field! if in sadness I turned   15
From your infinite marvels, the sadness was just.

Now, risen ere the light-footed Chamois retires
From dew-sprinkled grass to heights guarded with snow,
Tow'rd the mists that hang over the land of my Sires,
From the climate of myrtles contented I go.   20
My thoughts become bright, like yon edging of Pine,

Black fringe to a precipice lofty and bare,
Which, as from behind the Sun strikes it, doth shine,
With threads that seem part of his own silver hair.

Tho' the burthen of toil with dear friends we divide,   25
Tho' by the same zephyr our temples are fann'd,
As we rest in the cool orange-bower side by side,
A yearning survives which few hearts shall withstand:
Each step hath its value while homeward we move;—
O joy when the girdle of England appears!   30
What moment in life is so conscious of love,
So rich in the tenderest sweetness of tears?

Sonnet

ECHO, UPON THE GEMMI

What Beast of Chase hath broken from the cover?
Stern GEMMI listens to as full a cry,
As multitudinous a harmony,
As e'er did ring the heights of Latmos over,
When, from the soft couch of her sleeping Lover,   5
Up-starting, Cynthia skimmed the mountain-dew
In keen pursuit—and gave, where'er she flew,
Impetuous motion to the Stars above her.
A solitary Wolf-dog, ranging on
Thro' the bleak concave, wakes this wondrous chime   10
Of aëry voices locked in unison,—
Faints—far off—near—deep—solemn and sublime!
So, from the body of a single deed,
A thousand ghostly fears, and haunting thoughts, proceed!

Processions

SUGGESTED ON A SABBATH MORNING IN THE VALE OF CHAMOUNY

To appease the Gods; or public thanks to yield;
Or to solicit knowledge of events,
Which in her breast futurity concealed;
And that the past might have its true intents
Feelingly told by living monuments;   5
Mankind of yore were prompted to devise

Rites such as yet Persepolis presents
Graven on her cankered walls,—solemnities
That moved in long array before admiring eyes.

The Hebrews, thus, carrying in joyful state   10
Thick boughs of palm, and willows from the brook,
Marched around the Altar—to commemorate
How, when their course they thro' the desart took,
Guided by signs which ne'er the sky forsook,
They lodged in leafy tents and cabins low;   15
Green boughs were borne, while for the blast that shook
Down to the earth the walls of Jericho,
They uttered loud hosannas,—let the trumpets blow!

And thus, in order, 'mid the sacred Grove
Fed in the Libyan Waste by gushing wells,   20
The Priests and Damsels of Ammonian Jove
Provoked responses with shrill canticles;
While, in a Ship begirt with silver bells,
They round his altar bore the horned God,
Old Cham, the solar Deity, who dwells   25
Aloft, yet in a tilting Vessel rode,
When universal sea the mountains overflowed.

Why speak of Roman Pomps? the haughty claims
Of Chiefs triumphant after ruthless wars;
The feast of Neptune—and the Cereal Games,   30
With Images, and Crowns, and empty Cars;
The dancing Salii—on the shields of Mars
Striking with fury; and the deeper dread
Scattered on all sides by the hideous jars
Of Corybantian cymbals, while the head   35
Of Cybele was seen, sublimely turreted!

At length a Spirit more subdued and soft
Appeared, to govern Christian pageantries:
The Cross, in calm procession, borne aloft
Moved to the chaunt of sober litanies.   40
Even such, this day, came wafted on the breeze
From a long train—in hooded vestments fair
Enwrapt—and winding, between Alpine trees

Spiry and dark, around their House of Prayer
Below the icy bed of bright ARGENTIÈRE.   45

But O the fairest pageant of a dream
Did never equal that which met our eyes!
The glacier Pillars with the living Stream
Of white-robed Shapes, seemed linked in solemn guise,[1]
For the same service, by mysterious ties;   50
Numbers exceeding credible account
Of number, stood like spotless Votaries
Prepared to issue from a wintry fount;
The impenetrable heart of that exalted Mount!

They, too, who sent so far a holy gleam   55
While they the Church engirt with motion slow,
A product of that awful Mount did seem,
Poured from his vaults of everlasting snow;
Not virgin-lilies marshalled in bright row,
Not swans descending with the stealthy tide,   60
A livelier sisterly resemblance show
Than the fair Forms, that on the turf did glide,
To that unmoving band—the Shapes aloft descried!

Trembling, I look upon the secret springs
Of that licentious craving in the mind   65
To act the God among external things,
To bind, on apt suggestion, and unbind;
And marvel not that antique Faith inclined
To crowd the world with metamorphosis,
Vouchsafed in pity or in wrath assigned: 70
Such insolent temptations wouldst thou miss,
Avoid these sights; nor brood o'er Fable's dark abyss!

---

1   "This Procession is a part of the sacramental service performed once a month. In the
    Valley of Engelberg we had the good fortune to be present at the Grand Festival of the
    Virgin—but the Procession on that day, though consisting of upwards of 1000 Persons,
    assembled from all the branches of the sequestered Valley, was much less striking (nor-
    withstanding the sublimity of the surrounding scenery): it wanted both the simplicity of the
    other and the accompaniment of the Glacier-columns, whose sisterly resemblance to the
    moving Figures gave it a most beautiful and solemn peculiarity." WW

Elegiac Stanzas

On arriving at Lausanne, we heard of the fate of the young American, whose death is here lamented. He had been our companion for three days; and we separated upon Mount Righi with mutual hope of meeting again in the course of our Tour. GOLDAU, mentioned towards the conclusion of this Piece, is a Village at the foot of Mount Righi, one of those overwhelmed by a mass which fell from the side of the mountain ROSSBERG, a few years ago.

Lulled by the sound of pastoral bells,
Rude Nature's Pilgrims did we go,
From the dread summit of the Queen
Of Mountains, through a deep ravine,
Where, in her holy Chapel, dwells   5
"Our Lady of the Snow."

The sky was blue, the aid was mild;
Free were the streams and green the bowers;
As if, to rough assaults unknown,
The genial spot had *ever* shown   10
A countenance that sweetly smiled,
The face of summer-hours.

And we were gay, our hearts at ease,
With pleasure dancing through the frame;
All that we knew of lively care,   15
Our path that straggled here and there,
Of trouble—but the fluttering breeze,
Of Winter—but a name.

—If foresight could have rent the veil
Of three short days—but hush—no more!   20
Calm is the grave, and calmer none
Than that to which thy cares are gone,
Thou Victim of the stormy gale,
Asleep on ZURICH's shore!

Oh GODDARD! what art thou?—a name—   25
A sunbeam followed by a shade!
Nor more, for aught that time supplies,
The great, the experienced, and the wise;
Too much from this frail earth we claim,
And therefore are betrayed.   30

We met, while festive mirth ran wild,
Where, from a deep Lake's mighty urn,
Forth slips, like an enfranchised Slave,
A sea-green River, proud to lave,
With current swift and undefiled,   35
The Towers of old LUCERNE.

We parted upon solemn ground
Far-lifted tow'rds the unfading sky;
But all our thoughts were *then* of Earth
That gives to common pleasures birth;   40
And nothing in our hearts we found
That prompted even a sigh.

Fetch, sympathizing Powers of air,
Fetch, ye that post o'er seas and lands,
Herbs moistened by Virginian dew,   45
A most untimely sod to strew,
That lacks the ornamental care
Of kindred human hands!

Beloved by every gentle Muse
He left his Trans-atlantic home: 50
Europe, a realized romance,
Had opened on his eager glance;
What present bliss!—what golden views!
What stores for years to come!

Though lodged within no vigorous frame,   55
His soul her daily tasks renewed,
Blithe as the lark on sun-gilt wings
High poised—or as the wren that sings
In shady places, to proclaim
Her modest gratitude.   60

Not vain is sadly-uttered praise;
The words of truth's memorial vow
Are sweet as morning fragrance shed
From flowers 'mid GOLDAU's ruins bred;
Sweet as Eve's fondly-lingering rays,   65
On RIGHI's silent brow.

And, when thy Mother weeps for Thee,
Lost Youth! a solitary Mother;
This tribute from a casual Friend
A not unwelcome aid may lend,   70
To feed the tender luxury,
The rising pang to smother.

Sonnet

SKY-PROSPECT—FROM THE PLAIN OF FRANCE

Lo! in the burning West, the craggy nape
Of a proud Ararat! and, thereupon,
The Ark, her melancholy voyage done!
Yon rampant Cloud mimics a Lion's shape;
There, combats a huge Crocodile—agape   5
A golden spear to swallow! and that brown
And massy Grove, so near yon blazing Town,
Stirs—and recedes—destruction to escape!
Yet all is harmless as the Elysian shades
Where Spirits dwell in undisturb'd repose,   10
Silently disappears, or quickly fades;—
Meek Nature's evening comment on the shows
That for oblivion take their daily birth,
From all the fuming vanities of Earth!

Sonnet

ON BEING STRANDED NEAR THE HARBOUR OF BOULOGNE

Why cast ye back upon the Gallic shore,
Ye furious waves! a patriotic Son
Of England—who in hope her coast had won,
His project crowned, his pleasant travel o'er?
Well—let him pace this noted beach once more,   5
That gave the Roman his triumphal shells;
That saw the Corsican his cap and bells
Haughtily shake—a dreaming Conqueror!
Enough; my Country's Cliffs I can behold,
And proudly think, beside the murmuring sea,   10
Of checked Ambition—Tyranny controuled,
And Folly cursed with endless memory:

These local recollections ne'er can cloy;
Such ground I from my very heart enjoy!

Sonnet

AFTER LANDING—THE VALLEY OF DOVER

Nov. 1820

Where be the noisy followers of the game
Which Faction breeds? the turmoil where? that past
Thro' Europe, echoing from the Newsman's blast,
And filled our hearts with grief for England's shame.
Peace greets us;—rambling on without an aim   5
We mark majestic herds of Cattle free
To ruminate—couched on the grassy lea,
And hear far-off the mellow horn proclaim[1]
The Season's harmless pastime. Ruder sound
Stirs not; enwrapt I gaze—with strange delight,   10
While consciousnesses, not to be disowned,
Here only serve a feeling to invite
That lifts the Spirit to a calmer height,
And makes the rural stillness more profound.

To Enterprize[2]

Keep for the Young the empassioned smile
Shed from thy countenance, as I see thee stand
High on a chalky cliff of Britain's Isle,
A slender Volume grasping in thy hand—
(Perchance the pages that relate   5
The various turns of Crusoe's fate)
Ah, spare the exulting smile,
And drop thy pointing finger bright
As the first flash of beacon-light;
But neither veil thy head in shadows dim,   10
Nor turn thy face away
From One who, in the evening of his day,
To thee would offer no presumptuous hymn!

---

1   "This is a most grateful sight for an Englishman returning to his native land. Every where
    one misses, in the cultivated scenery abroad, the animating and soothing accompaniment
    of animals ranging and selecting their own food at will." WW

2   "'The Italian Itinerant,' &c. . . . led to the train of thought which produced the annexed
    piece." WW refers to *The Italian Itinerant, and the Swiss Goatherd*, above.

I

Bold Spirit! who art free to rove
Among the starry courts of Jove,   15
And oft in splendour dost appear
Embodied to poetic eyes,
While traversing this nether sphere,
Where Mortals call thee ENTERPRIZE.
Daughter of Hope! her favourite Child,   20
Whom she to young Ambition bore,
When Hunter's arrow first defiled
The Grove, and stained the turf with gore;
Thee winged Fancy took, and nursed
On broad Euphrates' palmy shore,   25
Or where the mightier Waters burst
From Caves of Indian mountains hoar!
She wrapp'd thee in a Panther's skin;
And thou (if rightly I rehearse
What wondering Shepherds told in verse)   30
From rocky fortress in mid air
(The food which pleased thee best to win)
Didst oft the flame-eyed Eagle scare
With infant shout,—as often sweep,
Paired with the Ostrich, o'er the plain;   35
And, tired with sport, wouldst sink asleep
Upon the couchant Lion's mane!
With rolling years thy strength increased;
And, far beyond thy native East,
To thee, by varying titles known,   40
As variously thy power was shown,
Did incense-bearing Altars rise,
Which caught the blaze of sacrifice,
From Suppliants panting for the skies!

II

What though this ancient Earth be trod   45
No more by step of Demi-god,
Mounting from glorious deed to deed
As thou from clime to clime didst lead,
Yet still, the bosom beating high,

And the hushed farewell of an eye   50
Where no procrastinating gaze
A last infirmity betrays,
Prove that thy heaven-descended sway
Shall ne'er submit to cold decay.
By thy divinity impelled,   55
The Stripling seeks the tented field;
The aspiring Virgin kneels; and, pale
With awe, receives the hallowed veil,
A soft and tender Heroine
Vowed to severer discipline;   60
Enflamed by thee, the blooming Boy
Makes of the whistling shrouds a toy,
And of the Ocean's dismal breast
A play-ground and a couch of rest;
Thou to his dangers dost enchain,   65
'Mid the blank world of snow and ice,
The Chamois-chaser—awed in vain
By chasm or dizzy precipice;
And hast Thou not with triumph seen
How soaring Mortals glide serene   70
From cloud to cloud, and brave the light
With bolder than Icarian flight?
Or, in their bells of crystal, dive
Where winds and waters cease to strive,
For no unholy visitings,   75
Among the monsters of the Deep,
And all the sad and precious things
Which there in ghastly silence sleep?
—Within our fearless reach are placed
The secrets of the burning Waste,—   80
Egyptian Tombs unlock their Dead,
Nile trembles at his fountain head;
Thou speak'st—and lo! the polar Seas
Unbosom their last mysteries.
—But oh! what transports, what sublime reward,   85
Won from the world of mind, dost thou prepare
For philosophic Sage—or high-souled Bard
Who, for thy service trained in lonely woods,

Hath fed on pageants floating thro' the air,
Or calentured in depth of limpid floods;   90
Nor grieves—tho' doomed, thro' silent night, to bear
The domination of his glorious themes,
Or struggle in the net-work of thy dreams!

III

Dread Minister of wrath!
Who to their destined punishment dost urge   95
The Pharaohs of the earth, the men of hardened heart!
Not unassisted by the flattering stars,
Thou strew'st temptation o'er the path
When they in pomp depart,
With trampling horses and refulgent cars—   100
Soon to be swallowed by the briny surge;
Or cast, for lingering death, on unknown strands;
Or stifled under weight of desart sands—
An Army now, and now a living hill[1]
Heaving with convulsive throes,—   105
It quivers—and is still;
Or to forget their madness and their woes,
Wrapt in a winding-sheet of spotless snows!

IV

Back flows the willing current of my Song:
If to provoke such doom the Impious dare,   110
Why should it daunt a blameless prayer?
—Bold Goddess! range our Youth among;
Nor let thy genuine impulse fail to beat
In hearts no longer young;
Still may a veteran Few have pride   115
In thoughts whose sternness makes them sweet;
In fixed resolves by reason justified;
That to their object cleave like sleet
Whitening a pine-tree's northern side,
While fields are naked far and wide.   120

---

1   "'While the living hill
           Heaved with convulsive throes and all was still.'—
      Dr. Darwin, describing the destruction of the army of Cambyses." WW

V

But, if such homage thou disdain
As doth with mellowing years agree,
One rarely absent from thy Train
More humble favours may obtain
For thy contented Votary.   125
She, who incites the frolic lambs
In presence of their heedless dams,
And to the solitary fawn
Vouchsafes her lessons—bounteous Nymph
That wakes the breeze—the sparkling lymph   130
Doth hurry to the lawn;
She, who inspires that strain of joyance holy
Which the sweet Bird, misnamed the melancholy,
Pours forth in shady groves, shall plead for me;
And vernal mornings opening bright   135
With views of undefined delight,
And cheerful songs, and suns that shine
On busy days, with thankful nights, be mine.

VI

But thou, O Goddess! in thy favourite Isle
(Freedom's impregnable redoubt,   140
The wide Earth's store-house fenced about
With breakers roaring to the gales
That stretch a thousand thousand sails)
Quicken the Slothful, and exalt the Vile!
Thy impulse is the life of Fame;   145
Glad Hope would almost cease to be
If torn from thy society;
And Love, when worthiest of the name,
Is proud to walk the Earth with thee!

[Poems not included in series as first published]

Desultory Stanzas

UPON RECEIVING THE PRECEDING SHEETS FROM THE PRESS

I

Is then the final page before me spread,
Nor further outlet left to mind or heart?
Presumptuous Book! too forward to be read—
How can I give thee licence to depart?
One tribute more;—unbidden feelings start   5
Forth from their coverts—slighted objects rise—
My Spirit is the scene of such wild art
As on Parnassus rules, when lightning flies,
Visibly leading on the thunder's harmonies.

II

All that I saw returns upon my view,   10
All that I heard comes back upon my ear,
All that I felt this moment doth renew;
And where the foot with no unmanly fear
Recoil'd—and wings alone could travel—there
I move at ease, and meet contending themes   15
That press upon me, crossing the career
Of recollections vivid as the dreams
Of midnight,—cities—plains—forests—and mighty streams!

III

Where mortal never breathed I dare to sit
Among the interior Alps, gigantic crew,   20
Who triumphed o'er diluvian power!—and yet
What are they but a wreck and residue,
Whose only business is to perish?—true
To which sad course, these wrinkled Sons of Time
Labour their proper greatness to subdue;   25
Speaking of death alone, beneath a clime
Where life and rapture flow in plenitude sublime.

IV

Fancy hath flung for me an airy bridge

Across thy long deep Valley, furious Rhone!
Arch that *here* rests upon the granite ridge   30
Of Monte Rosa—*there*, on frailer stone
Of secondary birth—the Jung-frau's cone;
And, from that arch down-looking on the Vale,
The aspect I behold of every zone;
A sea of foliage tossing with the gale,   35
Blithe Autumn's purple crown, and Winter's icy mail!

V

Far as St. Maurice, from yon eastern Forks,[1]
Down the main avenue my sight can range:
And all its branchy vales, and all that lurks
Within them, church, and town, and hut, and grange,   40
For my enjoyment meet in vision strange;
Snows—torrents;—to the region's utmost bound,
Life, Death, in amicable interchange—
But list! the avalanche—heart-striking sound!
Tumult by prompt repose and awful silence crown'd!   45

VI

Is not the Chamois suited to his place?
The Eagle worthy of her ancestry?
—Let Empires fall; but ne'er shall Ye disgrace
Your noble birthright, Ye that occupy
Your Council-seats beneath the open sky,   50
On Sarnen's Mount,[2] there judge of fit and right,
In simple democratic majesty;
Soft breezes fanning your rough brows—the might
And purity of nature spread before your sight!

---

1   "Les Fourches, the point at which the two chains of mountains part, that enclose the Valais, which terminates at St. Maurice." WW

2   "Sarnen, one of the two Capitals of the Canton of Underwalden; the spot here alluded to is close to the town, and is called the Landenberg, from the Tyrant of that name, whose chateau formerly stood there. On the 1st of Jan. 1308, the great day which the confederated Heroes had chosen for the deliverance of their Country, all the Castles of the Governors were taken by force or stratagem; and the Tyrants themselves conducted, with their Creatures, to the frontiers, after having witnessed the destruction of their Strong-holds. From that time the Landenberg has been the place where the Legislators of this division of the Canton assemble. The scite, which is well described by Ebel, is one of the most beautiful in Switzerland." WW

VII

From this appropriate Court, renown'd LUCERNE   55
Leads me to pace her honoured Bridge[1]—that cheers
The Patriot's heart with Pictures rude and stern,
An uncouth Chronicle of glorious years.
Like portraiture, from loftier source, endears
That work of kindred frame, which spans the Lake   60
Just at the point of issue, where it fears
The form and motion of a Stream to take;
Where it begins to stir, *yet* voiceless as a Snake.

VIII

Volumes of sound, from the Cathedral roll'd,
This long-roofed Vista penetrate—but see,   65
One after one, its Tablets, that unfold
The whole design of Scripture history;
From the first tasting of the fatal Tree,
Till the bright Star appeared in eastern skies,
Announcing ONE was born Mankind to free;   70
His acts, his wrongs, his final sacrifice;
Lessons for every heart, a Bible for all eyes.

IX

Our pride misleads, our timid likings kill.
—Long may these homely Works devised of old,
These simple Efforts of Helvetian skill,   75
Aid, with congenial influence, to uphold
The State,—the Country's destiny to mould;
Turning, for them who pass, the common dust
Of servile opportunity to gold;
Filling the soul with sentiments august—   80
The beautiful, the brave, the holy, and the just!

X

And those surrounding Mountains—but no more;
Time creepeth softly as the liquid flood;
Life slips from underneath us, like the floor
Of that wide rainbow-arch whereon we stood,   85

---

1 For WW's note see the notes at the end of this volume.

Earth stretched below, Heaven in our neighbourhood.
Go forth, my little Book! pursue thy way;
Go forth, and please the gentle and the good;
Nor be a whisper stifled, if it say
That treasures, yet untouched, may grace some future Lay.   90

Effusion

IN PRESENCE OF THE PAINTED TOWER OF TELL, AT ALTORF

THIS TOWER IS SAID TO STAND UPON THE SPOT WHERE GREW THE LINDEN TREE
AGAINST WHICH HIS SON WAS PLACED, WHEN THE FATHER'S ARCHERY WAS PUT TO
PROOF UNDER CIRCUMSTANCES SO FAMOUS IN SWISS HISTORY.

What though the Italian pencil wrought not here,
Nor such fine skill as did the meed bestow
On Marathonian valour, yet the tear
Springs forth in presence of this gaudy show,
While narrow cares their limits overflow.   5
Thrice happy, Burghers, Peasants, Warriors old,
Infants in arms, and Ye, that as ye go
Home-ward or School-ward, ape what ye behold;
Heroes before your time, in frolic fancy bold!

But when that calm Spectatress from on high   10
Looks down—the bright and solitary Moon,
Who never gazes but to beautify;
And snow-fed torrents, which the blaze of noon
Roused into fury, murmur a soft tune
That fosters peace, and gentleness recals;   15
Then might the passing Monk receive a boon
Of saintly pleasure from these pictured walls,
While, on the warlike groups, the mellowing lustre falls.

How blest the souls who when their trials come
Yield not to terror or despondency,   20
But face like that sweet Boy their mortal doom,
Whose head the ruddy Apple tops, while he
Expectant stands beneath the linden tree,
Not quaking like the timid forest game;
He smiles—the hesitating shaft to free,   25

Assured that Heaven its justice will proclaim,
And to his Father give its own unerring aim.

Composed in one of the Catholic Cantons of Switzerland

Doomed as we are our native dust
To wet with many a bitter shower,
It ill befits us to disdain
The Altar, to deride the Fane,
Where patient Sufferers bend, in trust   5
To win a happier hour.

I love, where spreads the village lawn,
Upon some knee-worn Cell to gaze;
Hail to the firm unmoving Cross,
Aloft, where pines their branches toss!   10
And to the Chapel far withdrawn,
That lurks by lonely ways!

Where'er we roam—along the brink
Of Rhine—or by the sweeping Po,
Through Alpine vale, or champain wide,   15
Whate'er we look on, at our side
Be Charity!—to bid us think,
And feel, if we would know.

After-thought

Oh Life! without thy chequered scene
Of right and wrong, of weal and woe,
Success and failure, could a ground
For magnanimity be found;
For faith, 'mid ruined hopes, serene?   5
Or whence could virtue flow?

Pain entered through a ghastly breach—
Nor while sin lasts must effort cease;
Heaven upon earth's an empty boast;
But, for the bowers of Eden lost,   10
Mercy has placed within our reach
A portion of God's peace.

Incident at Brugès

In Brugès town is many a street
   Whence busy life hath fled;
Where, without hurry, noiseless feet
   The grass-grown pavement tread.
There heard we, halting in the shade   5
   Flung from a Convent-tower,
A harp that tuneful prelude made
   To a voice of thrilling power.

The measure, simple truth to tell,
   Was fit for some gay throng;   10
Though from the same grim turret fell
   The shadow and the song.
When silent were both voice and chords
   The strain seemed doubly dear,
Yet sad as sweet, for *English* words   15
   Had fallen upon the ear.

It was a breezy hour of eve;
   And pinnacle and spire
Quivered and seemed almost to heave,
   Clothed with innocuous fire;   20
But where we stood, the setting sun
   Showed little of his state;
And, if the glory reached the Nun,
   'Twas through an iron grate.

Not always is the heart unwise,   25
   Nor pity idly born,
If even a passing Stranger sighs
   For them who do not mourn.
Sad is thy doom, self-solaced dove,
   Captive, whoe'er thou be!   30
Oh! what is beauty, what is love,
   And opening life to thee?

Such feeling pressed upon my soul,
   A feeling sanctified
By one soft trickling tear that stole   35
   From the Maiden at my side;

Less tribute could she pay than this,
    Borne gaily o'er the sea,
Fresh from the beauty and the bliss
    Of English liberty?   40

At Dover

From the Pier's head, musing—and with increase
Of wonder, long I watched this sea-side Town,
Under the white cliff's battlemented crown,
Hushed to a depth of more than Sabbath peace.
How strange, methought, this orderly release   5
From social noise—quiet elsewhere unknown!
A Spirit whispered, "Doth not Ocean drown
Trivial in solemn sounds? Let wonder cease.
His overpowering murmurs have set free
Thy sense from pressure of life's common din;   10
As the dread voice that speaks from out the sea
Of God's eternal Word, the voice of Time
Deadens—the shocks of tumult, shrieks of crime,
The shouts of folly, and the groans of sin."

Yarrow Revisited, and Other Poems, Composed (two excepted) during a Tour in Scotland, and on the English Border, in the Autumn of 1831[1]

Yarrow Revisited

[The following Stanzas are a memorial of a day passed with Sir Walter Scott, and other Friends visiting the Banks of the Yarrow under his guidance, immediately before his departure from Abbotsford, for Naples.

The title *Yarrow Revisited* will stand in no need of explanation, for Readers acquainted with the Author's previous poems suggested by that celebrated Stream.][2]

The gallant Youth, who may have gained,
    Or seeks, a "Winsome Marrow,"
Was but an Infant in the lap
    When first I looked on Yarrow;
Once more, by Newark's Castle-gate   5
    Long left without a Warder,
I stood, looked, listened, and with Thee,
    Great Minstrel of the Border!

Grave thoughts ruled wide on that sweet day,
    Their dignity installing   10
In gentle bosoms, while sere leaves
    Were on the bough, or falling;
But breezes played, and sunshine gleamed—
    The forest to embolden;
Reddened the fiery hues, and shot   15
    Transparence through the golden.

For busy thoughts the Stream flowed on
    In foamy agitation;
And slept in many a crystal pool
    For quiet contemplation: 20
No public and no private care
    The freeborn mind enthralling,

---

1 WW's notes all appeared in the first edition of the series in 1835. For the sources of the reading text and the editor's commentary, see *Sonnet Series and Itinerary Poems, 1820–1845*, ed. Geoffrey Jackson (2004), pp. 481–488, and 525–536.

2 See *Yarrow Unvisited* and *Yarrow Visited*, in vols. 1 and 2, respectively, of this edition.

We made a day of happy hours,
   Our happy days recalling.

Brisk Youth appeared, the Morn of youth,   25
   With freaks of graceful folly,—
Life's temperate Noon, her sober Eve,
   Her Night not melancholy,
Past, present, future, all appeared
   In harmony united,   30
Like guests that meet, and some from far,
   By cordial love invited.

And if, as Yarrow, through the woods
   And down the meadow ranging,
Did meet us with unaltered face,   35
   Though we were changed and changing;
If, *then*, some natural shadows spread
   Our inward prospect over,
The soul's deep valley was not slow
   Its brightness to recover.   40

Eternal blessings on the Muse,
   And her divine employment!
The blameless Muse, who trains her Sons
   For hope and calm enjoyment;
Albeit sickness lingering yet   45
   Has o'er their pillow brooded;
And Care waylay their steps—a Sprite
   Not easily eluded.

For thee, O SCOTT! compelled to change
   Green Eildon-hill and Cheviot   50
For warm Vesuvio's vine-clad slopes;
   And leave thy Tweed and Teviot
For mild Sorento's breezy waves;
   May classic Fancy, linking
With native Fancy her fresh aid,   55
   Preserve thy heart from sinking!

O ! while they minister to thee,
   Each vying with the other,

May Health return to mellow Age,
 With Strength, her venturous brother;   60
And Tiber, and each brook and rill
 Renowned in song and story,
With unimagined beauty shine,
 Nor lose one ray of glory!

For Thou, upon a hundred streams,   65
 By tales of love and sorrow,
Of faithful love, undaunted truth,
 Hast shed the power of Yarrow;
And streams unknown, hills yet unseen,
 Where'er thy path invite thee,   70
At parent Nature's grateful call,
 With gladness must requite Thee.

A gracious welcome shall be thine,
 Such looks of love and honour
As thy own Yarrow gave to me   75
 When first I gazed upon her;
Beheld what I had feared to see,
 Unwilling to surrender
Dreams treasured up from early days,
 The holy and the tender.   80

And what, for this frail world, were all
 That mortals do or suffer,
Did no responsive harp, no pen,
 Memorial tribute offer?
Yea, what were mighty Nature's self?   85
 Her features, could they win us,
Unhelped by the poetic voice
 That hourly speaks within us?

Nor deem that localised Romance
 Plays false with our affections;   90
Unsanctifies our tears—made sport
 For fanciful dejections:
Ah, no! the visions of the past
 Sustain the heart in feeling
Life as she is—our changeful Life,   95

With friends and kindred dealing.

Bear witness, Ye, whose thoughts that day
    In Yarrow's groves were center'd;
Who through the silent portal arch
    Of mouldering Newark enter'd.   100
And clomb the winding stair that once
    Too timidly was mounted
By the "last Minstrel," (not the last)
    Ere he his Tale recounted!

Flow on for ever, Yarrow Stream!   105
    Fulfil thy pensive duty,
Well pleased that future Bards should chant
    For simple hearts thy beauty,
To dream-light dear while yet unseen,
    Dear to the common sunshine,   110
And dearer still, as now I feel,
    To memory's shadowy moonshine!

I

ON THE DEPARTURE OF SIR WALTER SCOTT FROM ABBOTSFORD, FOR NAPLES

A trouble, not of clouds, or weeping rain,
Nor of the setting sun's pathetic light
Engendered, hangs o'er Eildon's triple height:
Spirits of Power, assembled there, complain
For kindred Power departing from their sight;   5
While Tweed, best pleased in chanting a blithe strain,
Saddens his voice again, and yet again.
Lift up your hearts, ye Mourners! for the might
Of the whole world's good wishes with him goes;
Blessings and prayers in nobler retinue   10
Than sceptred King or laurelled Conqueror knows,
Follow this wondrous Potentate. Be true,
Ye winds of ocean, and the midland sea,
Wafting your Charge to soft Parthenope!

II

A PLACE OF BURIAL IN THE SOUTH OF SCOTLAND

Part fenced by man, part by a rugged steep
That curbs a foaming brook, a Grave-yard lies;
The Hare's best couching-place for fearless sleep;
Which moonlit Elves, far seen by credulous eyes,
Enter in dance. Of Church, or Sabbath ties,   5
No vestige now remains; yet thither creep
Bereft Ones, and in lowly anguish weep
Their prayers out to the wind and naked skies.
Proud tomb is none; but rudely-sculptured knights,
By humble choice of plain old times, are seen   10
Level with earth, among the hillocks green:
Union not sad, when sunny daybreak smites
The spangled turf, and neighbouring thickets ring
With *jubilate* from the choirs of spring!

III

ON THE SIGHT OF A MANSE IN THE SOUTH OF SCOTLAND

Say, ye far-travelled clouds, far-seeing hills,
Among the happiest-looking Homes of men
Scatter'd all Britain over, through deep glen,
On airy upland, and by forest rills,
And o'er wide plains whereon the sky distils   5
Her lark's loved warblings; does aught meet your ken
More fit to animate the Poet's pen,
Aught that more surely by its aspect fills
Pure minds with sinless envy, than the Abode
Of the good Priest: who, faithful through all hours   10
To his high charge, and truly serving God,
Has yet a heart and hand for trees and flowers,
Enjoys the walks his Predecessors trod,
Nor covets lineal rights in lands and towers.

IV

COMPOSED IN ROSLIN CHAPEL, DURING A STORM

The wind is now thy organist;—a clank

(We know not whence) ministers for a bell
To mark some change of service. as the swell
Of music reached its height, and even when sank
The notes, in prelude, ROSLIN! to a blank   5
Of silence, how it thrilled thy sumptuous roof,
Pillars, and arches,—not in vain time-proof,
Though Christian rites be wanting! From what bank
Came those live herbs? by what hand were they sown
Where dew falls not, where rain-drops seem unknown?   10
Yet in the Temple they a friendly niche
Share with their sculptured fellows, that, green-grown,
Copy their beauty more and more, and preach,
Though mute, of all things blending into one.

V

THE TROSACHS

There's not a nook within this solemn Pass,
But were an apt confessional for One
Taught by his summer spent, his autumn gone,
That Life is but a tale of morning grass,
Withered at eve. From scenes of art that chase   5
That thought away, turn, and with watchful eyes
Feed it 'mid Nature's old felicities,
Rocks, rivers, and smooth lakes more clear than glass
Untouched, unbreathed upon. Thrice happy quest,
If from a golden perch of aspen spray   10
(October's workmanship to rival May)
The pensive warbler of the ruddy breast
This moral sweeten by a heaven-taught lay,
Lulling the year, with all its cares, to rest.

VI

The Pibroch's note, discountenanced or mute;
The Roman kilt, degraded to a toy
Of quaint apparel for a half-spoilt boy;
The target mouldering like ungathered fruit;
The smoking steam-boat eager in pursuit,   5
As eagerly pursued; the umbrella spread

To weather-fend the Celtic herdsman's head—
All speak of manners withering to the root,
And some old honours, too, and passions high:
Then may we ask, though pleased that thought should range   10
Among the conquests of civility,
Survives imagination—to the change
Superior? Help to virtue does it give?
If not, O Mortals, better cease to live!

VII

COMPOSED IN THE GLEN OF LOCH ETIVE

This Land of Rainbows, spanning glens whose walls,
Rock-built, are hung with rainbow-coloured mists,
Of far-stretched Meres, whose salt flood never rests,
Of tuneful caves and playful waterfalls,
Of mountains varying momently their crests—   5
Proud be this Land! whose poorest Huts are Halls
Where Fancy entertains becoming guests;
While native song the heroic Past recalls.
Thus, in the net of her own wishes caught,
The Muse exclaimed: but Story now must hide   10
Her trophies, Fancy crouch;—the course of pride
Has been diverted, other lessons taught,
That make the Patriot-spirit bow her head
Where the all-conquering Roman feared to tread.

VIII

COMPOSED AFTER READING A NEWSPAPER OF THE DAY

"People! your chains are severing link by link;
Soon shall the Rich be levelled down—the Poor
Meet them halfway." Vain boast! for These, the more
They thus would rise, must low and lower sink
Till, by repentance stung, they fear to think;   5
While all lie prostrate, save the tyrant few
Bent in quick turns each other to undo,
And mix the poison, they themselves must drink.
Mistrust thyself, vain Country! cease to cry,
"Knowledge will save me from the threatened woe."   10

For, if than other rash ones more thou know,
Yet on presumptuous wing as far would fly
Above thy knowledge as they dared to go,
Thou wilt provoke a heavier penalty.

IX
Eagles

COMPOSED AT DUNOLLIE CASTLE IN THE BAY OF OBAN

Dishonoured Rock and Ruin! that, by law
Tyrannic, keep the Bird of Jove embarred
Like a lone criminal whose life is spared.
Vexed is he, and screams loud. The last I saw
Was on the wing; stooping, he struck with awe   5
Man, bird, and beast; then, with a Consort paired,
From a bold headland, their loved aery's guard,
Flew high above Atlantic waves, to draw
Light from the fountain of the setting sun.
Such was this Prisoner once; and, when his plumes   10
The sea-blast ruffles as the storm comes on,
In spirit, for a moment, he resumes
His rank 'mong freeborn creatures that live free,
His power, his beauty, and his majesty.

X

IN THE SOUND OF MULL

Tradition, be thou mute! Oblivion, throw
Thy veil, in mercy, o'er the records hung
Round strath and mountain, stamped by the ancient tongue
On rock and ruin darkening as we go,—
Spots where a word, ghost-like, survives to show   5
What crimes from hate, or desperate love, have sprung;
From honour misconceived, or fancied wrong,
What feuds, not quenched but fed by mutual woe:
Yet, though a wild vindictive Race, untamed
By civil arts and labour of the pen,   10
Could gentleness be scorned by these fierce Men,
Who, to spread wide the reverence that they claimed

For patriarchal occupations, named
Yon towering Peaks, Shepherds of Etive Glen?"[1]

XI

AT TYNDRUM

Enough of garlands, of the Arcadian crook,
And all that Greece and Italy have sung
Of Swains reposing myrtle groves among!
Ours couch on naked rocks, will cross a brook
Swoln with chill rains, nor ever cast a look   5
This way or that, or give it even a thought
More than by smoothest pathway may be brought
Into a vacant mind. Can written book
Teach what *they* learn? Up, hardy Mountaineer!
And guide the Bard, ambitious to be One   10
Of Nature's privy council, as thou art,
On cloud-sequestered heights, that see and hear
To what dread Powers He delegates his part
On earth, who works in the heaven of heavens, alone.

XII

THE EARL OF BREADALBANE'S RUINED MANSION,
AND FAMILY BURIAL-PLACE, NEAR KILLIN

Well sang the bard who called the Grave, in strains
Thoughtful and sad, the "Narrow House." No style
Of fond sepulchral flattery can beguile
Grief of her sting; nor cheat, where he detains
The sleeping dust, stern Death: how reconcile   5
With truth, or with each other, decked Remains
Of a once warm Abode, and that *new* Pile,
For the departed, built with curious pains
And mausolean pomp? Yet here they stand
Together,—'mid trim walks and artful bowers,   10
To be looked down upon by ancient hills,
That, for the living and the dead, demand
And prompt a harmony of genuine powers;
Concord that elevates the mind, and stills.

---

1   "In Gaelic, Buachaill Eite." WW

XIII

REST AND BE THANKFUL, AT THE HEAD OF GLENCOE

Doubling and doubling with laborious walk,
Who, that has gained at length the wished-for Height,
This brief this simple way-side call can slight,
And rests not thankful? Whether cheered by talk
With some loved Friend, or by the unseen Hawk   5
Whistling to clouds and sky-born streams, that shine
At the sun's outbreak, as with light divine,
Ere they descend to nourish root and stalk
Of valley flowers. Nor, while the limbs repose,
Will we forget that, as the Fowl can keep   10
Absolute stillness, posed aloft in air,
And Fishes front, unmoved, the torrent's sweep,—
So may the Soul, through powers that Faith bestows,
Win rest, and ease, and peace, with bliss that Angels share.

XIV

HIGHLAND HUT

See what gay wild flowers deck this earth-built Cot,
Whose smoke, forth-issuing whence and how it may,
Shines in the greeting of the Sun's first ray
Like wreaths of vapour without stain or blot.
The limpid mountain rill avoids it not;   5
And why shouldst thou? If rightly trained and bred,
Humanity is humble,—finds no spot
Which her Heaven-guided feet refuse to tread.
The walls are cracked, sunk is the flowery roof,
Undressed the pathway leading to the door;   10
But love, as Nature loves, the lonely Poor;
Search, for their worth, some gentle heart wrong-proof,
Meek, patient, kind, and, were its trials fewer,
Belike less happy.—Stand no more aloof!

XV

THE BROWNIE[1]

[Upon a small island not far from the head of Loch Lomond, are some remains of an ancient building, which was for several years the abode of a solitary Individual, one of the last survivors of the Clan of Macfarlane, once powerful in that neighbourhood. Passing along the shore opposite this island in the year 1814, the Author learned these particulars, and that this person then living there had acquired the appellation of *"The Brownie."*[2]]

"How disappeared he?" Ask the newt and toad;
Ask of his fellow men, and they will tell
How he was found, cold as an icicle,
Under an arch of that forlorn abode;
Where he, unpropp'd, and by the gathering flood   5
Of years hemm'd round, had dwelt, prepared to try
Privation's worst extremities, and die
With no one near save the omnipresent God.
Verily so to live was an awful choice—
A choice that wears the aspect of a doom;   10
But in the mould of mercy all is cast
For Souls familiar with the eternal Voice;
And this forgotten Taper to the last
Drove from itself, we trust, all frightful gloom.

XVI

TO THE PLANET VENUS, AN EVENING STAR.
COMPOSED AT LOCH LOMOND

Though joy attend thee orient at the birth
Of dawn, it cheers the lofty spirit most
To watch thy course when Day-light, fled from earth,
In the grey sky hath left his lingering Ghost,
Perplexed as if between a splendour lost   5
And splendour slowly mustering. Since the Sun,
The absolute, the world-absorbing One,
Relinquished half his empire to the Host
Emboldened by thy guidance, holy Star,

---

1   For WW's note see the notes at the end of this volume.
2   "See 'The Brownie's Cell,' in the Author's Poems, . . . to which the following Sonnet is a
     sequel." WW refers to the earlier sonnet by this title in vol. 2.

Holy as princely, who that looks on thee   10
Touching, as now, in thy humility
The mountain borders of this seat of care,
Can question that thy countenance is bright,
Celestial Power, as much with love as light?

XVII

BOTHWELL CASTLE

Immured in Bothwell's Towers, at times the Brave
(So beautiful is Clyde) forgot to mourn
The liberty they lost at Bannockbourn.
Once on those steeps *I* roamed at large,[1] and have
In mind the landscape, as if still in sight;   5
The river glides, the woods before me wave;
But, by occasion tempted, now I crave
Needless renewal of an old delight.
Better to thank a dear and long-past day
For joy its sunny hours were free to give   10
Than blame the present, that our wish hath crost.
Memory, like Sleep, hath powers which dreams obey,
Dreams, vivid dreams, that are not fugitive:
How little that she cherishes is lost!

XVIII

PICTURE OF DANIEL IN THE LION'S DEN, AT HAMILTON PALACE

Amid a fertile region green with wood
And fresh with rivers, well doth it become
The Ducal Owner, in his Palace-home
To naturalise this tawny Lion brood;
Children of Art, that claim strange brotherhood,   5
Couched in their Den, with those that roam at large
Over the burning wilderness, and charge
The wind with terror while they roar for food.
But *these* are satiate, and a stillness drear
Calls into life a more enduring fear;   10
Yet is the Prophet calm, nor would the cave
Daunt him—if his Companions, now be-drowsed

---

1   For WW's note see the notes at the end of this volume.

Yawning and listless, were by hunger roused:
Man placed him here, and God, he knows, can save.

XIX

THE AVON (*A Feeder of the Annan*)

Avon—a precious, an immortal name!
Yet is it one that other Rivulets bear
Like this unheard-of, and their channels wear
Like this contented, though unknown to Fame:
For great and sacred is the modest claim   5
Of streams to Nature's love, where'er they flow;
And ne'er did genius slight them, as they go,
Tree, flower, and green herb, feeding without blame.
But Praise can waste her voice on work of tears,
Anguish, and death: full oft where innocent blood   10
Has mixed its current with the limpid flood,
Her heaven-offending trophies Glory rears;
Never for like distinction may the good
Shrink from *thy* name, pure Rill, with unpleased ears!

XX

SUGGESTED BY A VIEW FROM AN EMINENCE IN INGLEWOOD FOREST

The forest huge of ancient Caledon
Is but a name, nor more is Inglewood,
That swept from hill to hill, from flood to flood:
On her last thorn the nightly Moon has shone;
Yet still, though unappropriate Wild be none,   5
Fair parks spread wide where Adam Bell might deign
With Clym o' the Clough, were they alive again,
To kill for merry feast their venison.
Nor wants the holy Abbot's gliding Shade
His Church with monumental wreck bestrown;   10
The feudal Warrior-chief, a Ghost unlaid,
Hath still his Castle, though a Skeleton,
That he may watch by night, and lessons con
Of Power that perishes, and Rights that fade.

XXI

HART'S-HORN TREE, NEAR PENRITH[1]

Here stood an Oak, that long had borne affixed
To his huge trunk, or, with more subtle art,
Among its withering topmost branches mixed,
The palmy antlers of a hunted Hart,
Whom the dog Hercules pursued—his part　　　　5
Each desperately sustaining, till at last
Both sank and died, the life-veins of the chased
And chaser bursting here with one dire smart.
Mutual the Victory, mutual the Defeat!
High was the trophy hung with pitiless pride;　　　10
Say, rather, with that generous sympathy
That wants not, even in rudest breasts, a seat;
And, for this feeling's sake, let no one chide
Verse that would guard thy memory, *Hart's-horn Tree!*

XXII

COUNTESS'S PILLAR

[On the roadside between Penrith and Appleby, there stands a pillar with the
following inscription:—

"This pillar was erected, in the year 1656, by Anne Countess Dowager
of Pembroke, &c. for a memorial of her last parting with her pious mother,
Margaret Countess Dowager of Cumberland, on the 2d of April, 1616; in
memory whereof she hath left an annuity of 4l. to be distributed to the poor of
the parish of Brougham, every 2d day of April for ever, upon the stone table
placed hard by. Laus Deo!"]

While the Poor gather round, till the end of time
May this bright flower of Charity display
Its bloom, unfolding at the appointed day;
Flower than the loveliest of the vernal prime
Lovelier—transplanted from heaven's purest clime!　　　5
"Charity never faileth:" on that creed,
More than on written testament or deed,
The pious Lady built with hope sublime.
Alms on this stone to be dealt out, *for ever!*
" Laus Deo." Many a Stranger passing by　　　10

1　For WW's note see the end of this volume.

Has with that parting mixed a filial sigh,
Blest its humane Memorial's fond endeavour;
And, fastening on those lines an eye tear-glazed,
Has ended, though no Clerk, with "God be praised!"

XXIII

ROMAN ANTIQUITIES
(FROM THE ROMAN STATION AT OLD PENRITH)

How profitless the relics that we cull,
Troubling the last holds of ambitious Rome,
Unless they chasten fancies that presume
Too high, or idle agitations lull!
Of the world's flatteries if the brain be full,   5
To have no seat for thought were better doom,
Like this old helmet, or the eyeless skull
Of him who gloried in its nodding plume.
Heaven out of view, our wishes what are they?
Our fond regrets, insatiate in their grasp?   10
The Sage's theory? the Poet's lay?
Mere Fibulæ without a robe to clasp;
Obsolete lamps, whose light no time recalls;
Urns without ashes, tearless lacrymals!

Apology

No more: the end is sudden and abrupt,
Abrupt—as without preconceived design
Was the beginning, yet the several Lays
Have moved in order, to each other bound
By a continuous and acknowledged tie   5
Though unapparent, like those Shapes distinct
That yet survive ensculptured on the walls
Of Palace, or of Temple, 'mid the wreck
Of famed Persepolis; each following each,
As might beseem a stately embassy,   10
In set array; these bearing in their hands
Ensign of civil power, weapon of war,
Or gift, to be presented at the Throne
Of the Great King; and others, as they go

In priestly vest, with holy offerings charged,   15
Or leading victims drest for sacrifice.
Nor will the Muse condemn, or treat with scorn
Our ministration, humble but sincere,
That from a threshold loved by every Muse
Its impulse took—that sorrow-stricken door,   20
Whence, as a current from its fountain-head,
Our thoughts have issued, and our feelings flowed,
Receiving, willingly or not, fresh strength
From kindred sources; while around us sighed
(Life's three first seasons having passed away)   25
Leaf-scattering winds, and hoar-frost sprinklings fell,
Foretaste of winter, on the moorland heights;
And every day brought with it tidings new
Of rash change, ominous for the public weal.
Hence, if dejection have too oft encroached   30
Upon that sweet and tender melancholy
Which may itself be cherished and caressed
More than enough, a fault so natural,
Even with the young, the hopeful, or the gay,
For prompt forgiveness will not sue in vain.   35

The Highland Broach

If to Tradition faith be due,
And echoes from old verse speak true,
Ere the meek Saint, Columba, bore
Glad tidings to Iona's shore,
No common light of nature blessed   5
The mountain region of the west,
A land where gentle manners ruled
O'er men in dauntless virtues schooled,
That raised, for centuries, a bar
Impervious to the tide of war;   10
Yet peaceful Arts did entrance gain
Where haughty Force had striven in vain;
And, 'mid the works of skilful hands,
By wanderers brought from foreign lands
And various climes, was not unknown   15
The clasp that fixed the Roman Gown;

The Fibula, whose shape, I ween,
Still in the Highland Broach is seen,
The silver Broach of massy frame,
Worn at the breast of some grave Dame   20
On road or path, or at the door
Of fern-thatched Hut on heathy moor:
But delicate of yore its mould,
And the material finest gold;
As might beseem the fairest Fair,   25
Whether she graced a royal chair,
Or shed, within a vaulted Hall,
No fancied lustre on the wall
Where shields of mighty Heroes hung,
While Fingal heard what Ossian sung.   30

The heroic Age expired—it slept
Deep in its tomb:—the bramble crept
O'er Fingal's hearth; the grassy sod
Grew on the floors his Sons had trod:
Malvina! where art thou? Their state   35
The noblest-born must abdicate,
The fairest, while with fire and sword
Come Spoilers—horde impelling horde,
Must walk the sorrowing mountains, drest
By ruder hands in homelier vest.   40
Yet still the female bosom lent,
And loved to borrow, ornament;
Still was its inner world a place
Reached by the dews of heavenly grace;
Still pity to this last retreat   45
Clove fondly; to his favourite seat
Love wound his way by soft approach,
Beneath a massier Highland Broach.

When alternations came of rage
Yet fiercer, in a darker age;   50
And feuds, where, clan encountering clan,
The weaker perished to a man;
For maid and mother, when despair
Might else have triumphed, baffling prayer,

One small *possession* lacked not power,   55
Provided in a calmer hour,
To meet such need as might befall—
Roof, raiment, bread, or burial:
For woman, even of tears bereft,
The hidden silver Broach was left.   60
As generations come and go,
Their arts, their customs, ebb and flow;
Fate, fortune, sweep strong powers away,
And feeble, of themselves, decay;
What poor abodes the heir-loom hide,   65
In which the castle once took pride!
Tokens, once kept as boasted wealth,
If saved at all, are saved by stealth.
Lo! ships, from seas by nature barred,
Mount along ways by man prepared;   70
And in far-stretching vales, whose streams
Seek other seas, their canvass gleams.
Lo! busy towns spring up, on coasts
Thronged yesterday by airy ghosts;
Soon, like a lingering star forlorn   75
Among the novelties of morn,
While young delights on old encroach,
Will vanish the last Highland Broach.

But when, from out their viewless bed,
Like vapours, years have rolled and spread;   80
And this poor verse, and worthier lays,
Shall yield no light of love or praise,
Then, by the spade, or cleaving plough,
Or torrent from the mountain's brow,
Or whirlwind, reckless what his might   85
Entombs, or forces into light,
Blind Chance, a volunteer ally,
That oft befriends Antiquity,
And clears Oblivion from reproach,
May render back the Highland Broach.[1]   90

---

1   "The exact resemblance which the old Broach (still in use, though rarely met with, among
    the Highlanders) bears to the Roman Fibula must strike every one, and concurs with the
    plaid and kilt to recall to mind the communication which the ancient Romans had with this

[Poem not included in series as published]

The Modern Athens

"Now that a Parthenon ascends, to crown
Our Calton hill, sage Pallas! 'tis most fit
This thy dear City by the name be known
Of modern Athens." But opinions split
Upon this point of taste; and Mother Wit   5
Cries out, "AULD REEKIE, GUID AND HONEST TOWN
Of Ed'nbro', put the sad misnomer down,—
This alias of Conceit—away with it!"
Let none provoke, for questionable smiles
From an outlandish Goddess, the just scorn   10
Of thy staunch gothic Patron, grave St Giles;
—Far better than such heathen foppery
The homeliest Title thou hast ever borne
Before or since the times of, *Wha wants me?*

---

remote country. How much the Broach is sometimes prized by persons in humble stations may be gathered from an occurrence mentioned to me by a female friend. She had had an opportunity of benefiting a poor old woman in her own hut, who, wishing to make a return, said to her daughter, in Erse, in a tone of plaintive earnestness, 'I would give any thing I have, but I *hope* she does not wish for my Broach!' and, uttering these words, she put her hand upon the Broach which fastened her kerchief, and which, she imagined, had attracted the eye of her benefactress." WW

Sonnets Composed or Suggested during a tour in Scotland, in the Summer of 1833[1]

Sonnets

COMPOSED OR SUGGESTED DURING A TOUR IN SCOTLAND,
IN THE SUMMER OF 1833

[Having been prevented by the lateness of the season, in 1831, from visiting Staffa and Iona, the author made these the principal objects of a short tour in the summer of 1833, of which the following series of sonnets is a Memorial. The course pursued was down the Cumberland river Derwent, and to Whitehaven; thence (by the Isle of Man, where a few days were passed) up the Frith of Clyde to Greenock, then to Oban, Staffa, Iona; and back towards England, by Loch Awe, Inverary, Loch Goil-head, Greenock, and through parts of Renfrewshire, Ayrshire, and Dumfries-shire to Carlisle, and thence up the river Eden, and homewards by Ullswater.]

Sonnets, 1833

I

Adieu, Rydalian Laurels! that have grown
And spread as if ye knew that days might come
When ye would shelter in a happy home,
On this fair Mount, a Poet of your own,
One who ne'er ventured for a Delphic crown   5
To sue the God; but, haunting your green shade
All seasons through, is humbly pleased to braid
Ground-flowers, beneath your guardianship, self sown.
Farewell! no Minstrels now with Harp new-strung
For summer wandering quit their household bowers;   10
Yet not for this wants Poesy a tongue
To cheer the Itinerant on whom she pours
Her spirit, while he crosses lonely moors,
Or musing sits forsaken halls among.

---

1 WW's notes are those published with the series in *Yarrow Revisited and Other Poems* (1835). For the sources of the reading text and the editor's commentary, see *Sonnet Series and Itinerary Poems, 1820–1845*, ed. Geoffrey Jackson (2004), pp. 561–572, and 640–655.

II

Why should the Enthusiast, journeying through this Isle,
Repine as if his hour were come too late?
Not unprotected in her mouldering state,
Antiquity salutes him with a smile,
'Mid fruitful fields that ring with jocund toil,   5
And pleasure-grounds where Taste, refined Co-mate
Of Truth and Beauty, strives to imitate,
Far as she may, primeval Nature's style.
Fair land! by Time's parental love made free,
By social Order's watchful arms embraced,   10
With unexampled union meet in thee,
For eye and mind, the present and the past;
With golden prospect for futurity,
If what is rightly reverenced may last.

III

They called Thee merry England, in old time;
A happy people won for thee that name
With envy heard in many a distant clime;
And, spite of change, for me thou keep'st the same
Endearing title, a responsive chime   5
To the heart's fond belief, though some there are
Whose sterner judgments deem that word a snare
For inattentive Fancy, like the lime
Which foolish birds are caught with. Can, I ask,
This face of rural beauty be a mask   10
For discontent, and poverty, and crime;
These spreading towns a cloak for lawless will;
Forbid it, Heaven!—that "merry England" still
May be thy rightful name, in prose and rhyme!

IV

TO THE RIVER GRETA, NEAR KESWICK

Greta, what fearful listening! when huge stones
Rumble along thy bed, block after block:
Or, whirling with reiterated shock,
Combat, while darkness aggravates the groans:

But if thou (like Cocytus from the moans[1]   5
Heard on his rueful margin) thence wert named
The Mourner, thy true nature was defamed,
And the habitual murmur that atones
For thy worst rage, forgotten. Oft as Spring
Decks, on thy sinuous banks, her thousand thrones,   10
Seats of glad instinct and love's carolling,
The concert, for the happy, then may vie
With liveliest peals of birth-day harmony:
To a grieved heart, the notes are benisons.

V

TO THE RIVER DERWENT[2]

Among the mountains were we nursed, loved stream!
Thou near the Eagle's nest—within brief sail,
I, of his bold wing floating on the gale,
Where thy deep voice could lull me! Faint the beam
Of human life when first allowed to gleam   5
On mortal notice.—Glory of the Vale,
Such thy meek outset, with a crown, though frail,
Kept in perpetual verdure by the steam
Of thy soft breath!—Less vivid wreath entwined
Nemæan victor's brow; less bright was worn,   10
Meed of some Roman chief—in triumph borne
With captives chained; and shedding from his car
The sunset splendours of a finished war
Upon the proud enslavers of mankind!

VI

IN SIGHT OF THE TOWN OF COCKERMOUTH (WHERE THE AUTHOR WAS BORN, AND HIS FATHER'S REMAINS ARE LAID)

A point of life between my Parents' dust,
And your's, my buried Little-ones! am I;
And to those graves looking habitually
In kindred quiet I repose my trust.

---

1   For WW's note see the notes at the end of this volume.
2   "This sonnet has already appeared in several editions of the author's poems; but he is tempted to reprint it in this place, as a natural introduction to the two that follow it." WW

Death to the innocent is more than just,   5
And, to the sinner, mercifully bent;
So may I hope, if truly I repent
And meekly bear the ills which bear I must:
And You, my Offspring! that do still remain,
Yet may outstrip me in the appointed race,   10
If e'er, through fault of mine, in mutual pain
We breathed together for a moment's space,
The wrong, by love provoked, let love arraign,
And only love keep in your hearts a place.

VII

ADDRESS FROM THE SPIRIT OF COCKERMOUTH CASTLE

Thou look'st upon me, and dost fondly think,
Poet! that, stricken as both are by years,
We, differing once so much, are now Compeers,
Prepared, when each has stood his time, to sink
Into the dust. Erewhile a sterner link   5
United us; when thou, in boyish play,
Entering my dungeon, didst become a prey
To soul-appalling darkness. Not a blink
Of light was there;—and thus did I, thy Tutor,
Make thy young thoughts acquainted with the grave;   10
While thou wert chasing the wing'd butterfly
Through my green courts; or climbing, a bold suitor,
Up to the flowers whose golden progeny
Still round my shattered brow in beauty wave.

VIII

NUN'S WELL, BRIGHAM

The cattle crowding round this beverage clear
To slake their thirst, with reckless hoofs have trod
The encircling turf into a barren clod;
Through which the waters creep, then disappear,
Born to be lost in Derwent flowing near;   5
Yet, o'er the brink, and round the limestone-cell
Of the pure spring (they call it the "Nun's Well,"
Name that first struck by chance my startled ear)

A tender Spirit broods—the pensive Shade
Of ritual honours to this Fountain paid   10
By hooded Votaries with saintly cheer;[1]
Albeit oft the Virgin-mother mild
Looked down with pity upon eyes beguiled
Into the shedding of "too soft a tear."

IX

TO A FRIEND (ON THE BANKS OF THE DERWENT)

Pastor and Patriot! at whose bidding rise
These modest Walls, amid a flock that need
For one who comes to watch them and to feed
A fixed Abode, keep down presageful sighs.
Threats which the unthinking only can despise,   5
Perplex the Church; but be thou firm,—be true
To thy first hope, and this good work pursue,
Poor as thou art. A welcome sacrifice
Dost Thou prepare, whose sign will be the smoke
Of thy new hearth; and sooner shall its wreaths,   10
Mounting while earth her morning incense breathes,
From wandering fiends of air receive a yoke,
And straightway cease to aspire, than God disdain
This humble tribute as ill-timed or vain.

X

MARY QUEEN OF SCOTS (LANDING AT THE MOUTH OF THE DERWENT, WORKINGTON)[2]

Dear to the Loves, and to the Graces vowed,
The Queen drew back the wimple that she wore;
And to the throng how touchingly she bowed

---

1 "Attached to the church of Brigham was formerly a chantry, which held a moiety of the manor; and in the decayed parsonage some vestiges of monastic architecture are still to be seen." WW

2 "'The fears and impatience of Mary were so great,' says Robertson, 'that she got into a fisher-boat, and with about twenty attendants landed at Workington, in Cumberland; and thence she was conducted with many marks of respect to Carlisle.' The apartment in which the Queen had slept at Workington Hall (where she was received by Sir Henry Curwen as became her rank and misfortunes) was long preserved, out of respect to her memory, as she had left it; and one cannot but regret that some necessary alterations in the mansion could not be effected without its destruction." WW quotes from *The History of Scotland* (1759) by William Robertson.

That hailed her landing on the Cumbrian shore;
Bright as a Star (that, from a sombre cloud   5
Of pine-tree foliage poised in air, forth darts,
When a soft summer gale at evening parts
The gloom that did its loveliness enshroud)
She smiled; but Time, the old Saturnian Seer,
Sighed on the wing as her foot pressed the strand,   10
With step prelusive to a long array
Of woes and degradations hand in hand,
Weeping captivity, and shuddering fear
Stilled by the ensanguined block of Fotheringay!

XI

IN THE CHANNEL, BETWEEN THE COAST OF CUMBERLAND
AND THE ISLE OF MAN

Ranging the Heights of Scawfell or Black-coom,
In his lone course the Shepherd oft will pause,
And strive to fathom the mysterious laws
By which the clouds, arrayed in light or gloom,
On Mona settle, and the shapes assume   5
Of all her peaks and ridges. What He draws
From sense, faith, reason, fancy, of the cause
He will take with him to the silent tomb:
Or, by his fire, a Child upon his knee,
Haply the untaught Philosopher may speak   10
Of the strange sight, nor hide his theory
That satisfies the simple and the meek,
Blest in their pious ignorance, though weak
To cope with Sages undevoutly free.

XII

AT SEA OFF THE ISLE OF MAN.

Bold words affirmed, in days when faith was strong,
And doubts and scruples seldom teazed the brain,
That no adventurer's bark had power to gain
These shores if he approached them bent on wrong;
For, suddenly up-conjured from the Main,   5
Mists rose to hide the Land—that search, though long

And eager, might be still pursued in vain.
O Fancy, what an age was *that* for song!
That age, when not by laws inanimate,
As men believed, the waters were impelled,   10
The air controlled, the stars their courses held,
But element and orb on *acts* did wait
Of *Powers* endued with visible form, instinct
With will, and to their work by passion linked.

XIII

Desire we past illusions to recall?
To reinstate wild Fancy, would we hide
Truths whose thick veil Science has drawn aside?
No,—let this Age, high as she may, install
In her esteem the thirst that wrought man's fall,   5
The universe is infinitely wide;
And conquering Reason, if self-glorified,
Can nowhere move uncrossed by some new wall
Or gulf of mystery, which thou alone,
Imaginative Faith! canst overleap,   10
In progress toward the fount of Love,—the throne
Of Power, whose ministering Spirits records keep
Of periods fixed, and laws established, less
Flesh to exalt than prove its nothingness.

XIV

ON ENTERING DOUGLAS BAY, ISLE OF MAN

"DIGNUM LAUDE VIRU MUSA VETAT MORI."

The feudal Keep, the bastions of Cohorn,
Even when they rose to check or to repel
Tides of aggressive war, oft served as well
Greedy ambition, armed to treat with scorn
Just limits; but yon Tower, whose smiles adorn   5
This perilous bay, stands clear of all offence;
Blest work it is of love and innocence,
A Tower of refuge to the else forlorn.
Spare it, ye waves, and lift the mariner,
Struggling for life, into its saving arms!   10

Spare, too, the human helpers! Do they stir
'Mid your fierce shock like men afraid to die?
No, their dread service nerves the heart it warms,
And they are led by noble HILLARY.[1]

XV

BY THE SEA-SHORE, ISLE OF MAN.

Why stand we gazing on the sparkling Brine
With wonder, smit by its transparency,
And all-enraptured with its purity?
Because the unstained, the clear, the crystalline,
Have ever in them something of benign;   5
Whether in gem, in water, or in sky,
A sleeping infant's brow, or wakeful eye
Of a young maiden, only not divine.
Scarcely the hand forbears to dip its palm
For beverage drawn as from a mountain well: 10
Temptation centres in the liquid Calm;
Our daily raiment seems no obstacle
To instantaneous plunging in, deep Sea!
And revelling in long embrace with Thee.

XVI

ISLE OF MAN

A youth too certain of his power to wade
On the smooth bottom of this clear bright sea,
To sight so shallow, with a bather's glee
Leapt from this rock, and surely, had not aid
Been near, must soon have breathed out life, betrayed   5
By fondly trusting to an element
Fair, and to others more than innocent;
Then had sea-nymphs sung dirges for him laid
In peaceful earth: for, doubtless, he was frank,
Utterly in himself devoid of guile;   10

---

1 "The Tower of Refuge, an ornament to Douglas Bay, was erected chiefly through the
   humanity and zeal of Sir William Hillary; and he also was the founder of the life-boat
   establishment, at that place; by which, under his superintendence, and often by his exer-
   tions at the imminent hazard of his own life, many seamen and passengers have been
   saved." WW

Knew not the double-dealing of a smile;
Nor aught that makes men's promises a blank,
Or deadly snare: and He survives to bless
The Power that saved him in his strange distress.

XVII

THE RETIRED MARINE OFFICER, ISLE OF MAN

Not pangs of grief for lenient time too keen,
Grief that devouring waves had caused, nor guilt
Which they had witnessed, swayed the man who built
This homestead, placed where nothing could be seen,
Nought heard of ocean, troubled or serene.   5
A tired Ship-soldier on paternal land,
That o'er the channel holds august command,
The dwelling raised,—a veteran Marine;
Who, in disgust, turned from the neighbouring sea
To shun the memory of a listless life   10
That hung between two callings. May no strife
More hurtful here beset him, doom'd, though free,
Self-doom'd to worse inaction, till his eye
Shrink from the daily sight of earth and sky!

XVIII

BY A RETIRED MARINER (A FRIEND OF THE AUTHOR)[1]

From early youth I ploughed the restless Main,
My mind as restless and as apt to change;
Through every clime and ocean did I range,
In hope at length a competence to gain;
For poor to Sea I went, and poor I still remain.   5
Year after year I strove, but strove in vain,
And hardships manifold did I endure,
For Fortune on me never deign'd to smile;
Yet I at last a resting-place have found,
With just enough life's comforts to procure,   10
In a snug Cove on this our favoured Isle,

---

1   "This unpretending sonnet is by a gentleman nearly connected with the author, who hopes, as it falls so easily into its place, that both the writer and the reader will excuse its appearance here." WW

A peaceful spot where Nature's gifts abound;
Then sure I have no reason to complain,
Though poor to Sea I went, and poor I still remain.

XIX

AT BALA-SALA, ISLE OF MAN (SUPPOSED TO BE WRITTEN BY
A FRIEND OF THE AUTHOR)

Broken in fortune, but in mind entire
And sound in principle, I seek repose
Where ancient trees this convent-pile[1] enclose,
In ruin beautiful. When vain desire
Intrudes on peace, I pray the eternal Sire   5
To cast a soul-subduing shade on me,
A grey-haired, pensive, thankful Refugee,
A shade but with some sparks of heavenly fire
Once to these cells vouchsafed. And when I note
The old Tower's brow yellowed as with the beams   10
Of sunset ever there, albeit streams
Of stormy weather-stains that semblance wrought,
I thank the silent Monitor, and say
"Shine so, my aged brow, at all hours of the day!"

XX

TYNWALD HILL

Once on the top of Tynwald's formal mound
(Still marked with green turf circles narrowing
Stage above stage) would sit this Island's King,
The laws to promulgate, enrobed and crowned;
While, compassing the little mount around,   5
Degrees and Orders stood, each under each:
Now, like to things within fate's easiest reach,
The power is merged, the pomp a grave has found.
Off with yon cloud, old Snafell! that thine eye[2]

---

1   "Rushen Abbey." WW
2   "The summit of this mountain is well chosen by Cowley, as the scene of the 'Vision,' in which
    the spectral angel discourses with him concerning the government of Oliver Cromwell. 'I
    found myself,' says he, 'on the top of that famous hill in the Island Mona, which has the
    prospect of three great, and not long since most happy, kingdoms. As soon as ever I
    looked upon them, they called forth the sad representation of all the sins and all the miser-

Over three Realms may take its widest range;   10
And let, for them, thy fountains utter strange
Voices, thy winds break forth in prophecy,
If the whole State must suffer mortal change,
Like Mona's miniature of sovereignty.

XXI

Despond who will—*I* heard a voice exclaim,
"Though fierce the assault, and shatter'd the defence,
It cannot be that Britain's social frame,
The glorious work of time and providence,
Before a flying season's rash pretence,   5
Should fall; that She, whose virtue put to shame,
When Europe prostrate lay, the Conqueror's aim,
Should perish, self-subverted. Black and dense
The cloud is; but brings *that* a day of doom
To Liberty? Her sun is up the while,   10
That orb whose beams round Saxon Alfred shone,
Then laugh, ye innocent Vales! ye Streams, sweep on,
Nor let one billow of our heaven-blest Isle
Toss in the fanning wind a humbler plume."

XXII

IN THE FRITH OF CLYDE, AILSA CRAG (JULY 17, 1833)

Since risen from ocean, ocean to defy,
Appeared the Crag of Ailsa, ne'er did morn
With gleaming lights more gracefully adorn
His sides, or wreathe with mist his forehead high:
Now, faintly darkening with the sun's eclipse,   5
Still is he seen, in lone sublimity,
Towering above the sea and little ships;
For dwarfs the tallest seem while sailing by,
Each for her haven; with her freight of Care,
Pleasure, or Grief, and Toil that seldom looks   10
Into the secret of to-morrow's fare;

---

ies that had overwhelmed them these twenty years.' It is not to be denied that the changes now in progress, and the passions, and the way in which they work, strikingly resemble those which led to the disasters the philosophic writer so feelingly bewails. God grant that the resemblance may not become still more striking as months and years advance!" WW

Though poor, yet rich, without the wealth of books,
Or aught that watchful Love to Nature owes
For her mute Powers, fix'd Forms, and transient Shows.

XXIII

ON THE FRITH OF CLYDE (IN A STEAM-BOAT)

Arran! a single-crested Teneriffe,
A St. Helena next—in shape and hue,
Varying her crowded peaks and ridges blue;
Who but must covet a cloud-seat or skiff
Built for the air, or winged Hippogriff,   5
That he might fly, where no one could pursue,
From this dull Monster and her sooty crew;
And, like a God, light on thy topmost cliff.
Impotent wish! which reason would despise
If the mind knew no union of extremes,   10
No natural bond between the boldest schemes
Ambition frames, and heart-humilities.
Beneath stern mountains many a soft vale lies,
And lofty springs give birth to lowly streams.

XXIV

ON REVISITING DUNOLLY CASTLE [1]

The captive Bird was gone;—to cliff or moor
Perchance had flown, delivered by the storm;
Or he had pined, and sunk to feed the worm:
Him found we not; but, climbing a tall tower,
There saw, impaved with rude fidelity   5
Of art mosaic, in a roofless floor,
An Eagle with stretched wings, but beamless eye—
An Eagle that could neither wail nor soar.
Effigies of the Vanished, (shall I dare
To call thee so?) or symbol of past times,   10
That towering courage, and the savage deeds
Those times were proud of, take Thou too a share,

---

1 WW refers the reader to a sonnet in the "former series," *Yarrow Revisited, IX. Eagles*, and
  provides the following note:
      "This ingenious piece of workmanship, as the author afterwards learned, had been
  executed for their own amusement by some labourers employed about the place."

Not undeserved, of the memorial rhymes
That animate my way where'er it leads!

XXV

THE DUNOLLY EAGLE

Not to the clouds, not to the cliff, he flew;
But when a storm, on sea or mountain bred,
Came and delivered him, alone he sped
Into the Castle-dungeon's darkest mew.
Now, near his Master's house in open view   5
He dwells, and hears indignant tempests howl,
Kennelled and chained. Ye tame domestic Fowl,
Beware of him! Thou, saucy Cockatoo,
Look to thy plumage and thy life!—The Roe,
Fleet as the west wind, is for *him* no quarry;   10
Balanced in ether he will never tarry,
Eyeing the sea's blue depths. Poor Bird! even so
Doth Man of Brother-man a creature make,
That clings to slavery for its own sad sake.

XXVI

CAVE OF STAFFA

We saw, but surely, in the motley crowd,
Not One of us has *felt*, the far-famed sight;
How *could* we feel it? each the other's blight,
Hurried and hurrying, volatile and loud.
O for those motions only that invite   5
The Ghost of Fingal to his tuneful Cave!
By the breeze entered, and wave after wave
Softly embosoming the timid light!
And by *one* Votary who at will might stand
Gazing, and take into his mind and heart,   10
With undistracted reverence, the effect
Of those proportions where the almighty hand
That made the worlds, the sovereign Architect,
Has deigned to work as if with human Art!

XXVII

CAVE OF STAFFA[1]

Thanks for the lessons of this Spot—fit school
For the presumptuous thoughts that would assign
Mechanic laws to agency divine;
And, measuring heaven by earth, would overrule
Infinite Power. The pillared vestibule,   5
Expanding yet precise, the roof embowed,
Might seem designed to humble Man, when proud
Of his best workmanship by plan and tool.
Down-bearing with his whole Atlantic weight
Of tide and tempest on the Structure's base,   10
And flashing upwards to its topmost height,
Ocean has proved its strength, and of its grace
In calms is conscious, finding for his freight
Of softest music some responsive place.

XXVIII

CAVE OF STAFFA

Ye shadowy Beings, that have rights and claims
In every cell of Fingal's mystic Grot,
Where are ye? Driven or venturing to the spot,
Our Fathers glimpses caught of your thin Frames,
And, by your mien and bearing, knew your names;   5
And they could hear *his* ghostly song who trod
Earth, till the flesh lay on him like a load,
While he struck his desolate harp without hopes or aims.
Vanished ye are, but subject to recall;
Why keep *we* else the instincts whose dread law   10
Ruled here of yore, till what men felt they *saw*,
Not by black arts but magic natural!
If eyes be still sworn vassals of belief,
Yon light shapes forth a Bard, that shade a Chief.

---

1   "The reader may be tempted to exclaim, "How came this and the two following sonnets to
be written, after the dissatisfaction expressed in the preceding one?" In fact, at the risk of
incurring the reasonable displeasure of the master of the steamboat, the author returned
to the cave, and explored it under circumstances more favourable to those imaginative
impressions, which it is so wonderfully fitted to make upon the mind." WW

XXIX

FLOWERS ON THE TOP OF THE PILLARS AT THE ENTRANCE OF THE CAVE

Hope smiled when your nativity was cast,
Children of Summer! Ye fresh flowers that brave[1]
What Summer here escapes not, the fierce wave,
And whole artillery of the western blast,
Battering the Temple's front, its long-drawn nave   5
Smiting, as if each moment were their last.
But ye, bright flowers, on frieze and architrave
Survive, and once again the Pile stands fast,
Calm as the Universe, from specular Towers
Of heaven contemplated by Spirits pure—   10
Suns and their systems, diverse yet sustained
In symmetry, and fashioned to endure,
Unhurt, the assault of Time with all his hours,
As the supreme Artificer ordained.

XXX

On to Iona!—What can she afford
To *us* save matter for a thoughtful sigh,
Heaved over ruin with stability
In urgent contrast? To diffuse the Word
(Thy Paramount, mighty Nature! and Time's Lord)   5
Her Temples rose, 'mid pagan gloom; but why,
Even for a moment, has our verse deplored
Their wrongs, since they fulfilled their destiny?
And when, subjected to a common doom
Of mutability, those far-famed Piles   10
Shall disappear from both the sister Isles,
Iona's Saints, forgetting not past days,
Garlands shall wear of amaranthine bloom,
While heaven's vast sea of voices chants their praise.

---

1   "Upon the head of the columns which form the front of the cave, rests a body of decom-
posed basaltic matter, which was richly decorated with that large bright flower, the ox-eyed
daisy. The author had noticed the same flower growing with profusion among the bold
rocks on the western coast of the Isle of Man; making a brilliant contrast with their black
and gloomy surfaces." WW

XXXI

IONA (UPON LANDING)

With earnest look, to every voyager,
Some ragged child holds up for sale his store
Of wave-worn pebbles, pleading on the shore
Where once came monk and nun with gentle stir,
Blessings to give, news ask, or suit prefer.   5
But see yon neat trim church, a grateful speck
Of novelty amid this sacred wreck—
Nay spare thy scorn, haughty Philosopher!
Fallen though she be, this Glory of the west,
Still on her sons the beams of mercy shine;   10
And "hopes, perhaps more heavenly bright than thine,
A grace by thee unsought and unpossest,
A faith more fixed, a rapture more divine
Shall gild their passage to eternal rest."[1]

XXXII

THE BLACK STONES OF IONA

[SEE MARTIN'S VOYAGE AMONG THE WESTERN ISLES]

Here on their knees men swore: the stones were black,
Black in the People's minds and words, yet they
Were at that time, as now, in colour grey.
But what is colour, if upon the rack
Of conscience souls are placed by deeds that lack   5
Concord with oaths? What differ night and day
Then, when before the Perjured on his way
Hell opens, and the heavens in vengeance crack
Above his head uplifted in vain prayer
To Saint, or Fiend, or to the Godhead whom   10
He had insulted—Peasant, King, or Thane.
Fly where the culprit may, guilt meets a doom;
And, from invisible worlds at need laid bare,
Come links for social order's awful chain.

---

1   "The four last lines of this sonnet are adopted from a well-known sonnet of Russell, as con-
veying the author's feeling better than any words of his own could do." WW cites sonnet
10 in Thomas Russell's *Sonnets and Miscellaneous Poems* (Oxford, 1789).

XXXIII

Homeward we turn. Isle of Columba's Cell,
Where Christian piety's soul-cheering spark
(Kindled from Heaven between the light and dark
Of time) shone like the morning-star, farewell!—
Remote St. Kilda, art thou visible?   5
No—but farewell to thee, beloved sea-mark
For many a voyage made in Fancy's bark,
When with more hues than in the rainbow dwell
Thou a mysterious intercourse dost hold;
Extracting from clear skies and air serene,   10
And out of sun-bright waves, a lucid veil,
That thickens, spreads, and, mingling fold with fold
Makes known, when thou no longer canst be seen,
Thy whereabout, to warn the approaching sail.

XXXIV

GREENOCK

PER ME SI VA NELLA CITTÀ DOLENTE.

We have not passed into a doleful City,
We who were led to-day down a grim Dell,
By some too boldly named "the Jaws of Hell:"
Where be the wretched Ones, the sights for pity?
These crowded streets resound no plaintive ditty: 5
As from the hive where bees in summer dwell,
Sorrow seems here excluded; and that knell,
It neither damps the gay, nor checks the witty.
Too busy Mart! thus fared it with old Tyre,
Whose Merchants Princes were, whose decks were thrones: 10
Soon may the punctual sea in vain respire
To serve thy need, in union with that Clyde
Whose nursling current brawls o'er mossy stones,
The poor, the lonely Herdsman's joy and pride.

XXXV

"There!" said a Stripling, pointing with meet pride
Towards a low roof with green trees half concealed,
"Is Mossgiel farm; and that's the very field

Where Burns ploughed up the Daisy." Far and wide
A plain below stretched sea-ward, while, descried   5
Above sea-clouds, the Peaks of Arran rose;
And, by that simple notice, the repose
Of earth, sky, sea, and air, was vivified.
Beneath "the random *bield* of clod or stone"
Myriads of Daisies have shone forth in flower   10
Near the lark's nest, and in their natural hour
Have passed away, less happy than the One
That by the unwilling ploughshare died to prove
The tender charm of Poetry and Love

XXXVI

FANCY AND TRADITION

The Lovers took within this ancient grove
Their last embrace; beside those crystal springs
The Hermit saw the Angel spread his wings
For instant flight; the Sage in yon alcove
Sate musing; on that hill the Bard would rove,   5
Not mute, where now the Linnet only sings:
Thus every where to truth Tradition clings,
Or Fancy localises Powers we love.
Were only History licensed to take note
Of things gone by, her meagre monuments   10
Would ill suffice for persons and events:
There is an ampler page for man to quote,
A readier book of manifold contents,
Studied alike in palace and in cot.

XXXVII

THE RIVER EDEN, CUMBERLAND

Eden! till now thy beauty had I viewed
By glimpses only, and confess with shame
That verse of mine, whate'er its varying mood,
Repeats but once the sound of thy sweet name;
Yet fetched from Paradise that honour came,[1]   5

---

1   "It is to be feared that there is more of the poet than the sound etymologist in this deriva-
    tion of the name Eden. On the western coast of Cumberland is a rivulet which enters the
    sea at Moresby, known also in the neighbourhood by the name of Eden. May not the latter

Rightfully borne; for Nature gives thee flowers
That have no rivals among British bowers;
And thy bold rocks are worthy of their fame.
Measuring thy course, fair Stream! at length I pay
To my life's neighbour dues of neighbourhood;   10
But I have traced thee on thy winding way
With pleasure sometimes by the thought restrained
That things far off are toiled for, while a good
Not sought, because too near, is seldom gained.

XXXVIII

MONUMENT OF MRS. HOWARD
(BY NOLLEKINS)
IN WETHERAL CHURCH, NEAR CORBY, ON THE BANKS OF THE EDEN

Stretched on the dying Mother's lap, lies dead
Her new-born Babe, dire issue of bright hope!
But Sculpture here, with the divinest scope
Of luminous faith, heavenward hath raised that head
So patiently; and through one hand has spread   5
A touch so tender for the insensate Child,
Earth's lingering love to parting reconciled,
Brief parting—for the spirit is all but fled;
That we, who contemplate the turns of life
Through this still medium, are consoled and cheered;   10
Feel with the Mother, think the severed Wife
Is less to be lamented than revered;
And own that Art, triumphant over strife
And pain, hath powers to Eternity endeared.

XXXIX

Tranquillity! the sovereign aim wert thou
In heathen schools of philosophic lore;
Heart-stricken by stern destiny of yore
The Tragic Muse thee served with thoughtful vow;
And what of hope Elysium could allow   5

syllable come from the word Dean, a valley? Langdale, near Ambleside, is by the inhabit-
ants called Langden. The former syllable occurs in the name Eamont, a principal feeder of
the Eden; and the stream which flows, when the tide is out, over Cartmel Sands, is called
the Ea." WW

Was fondly seized by Sculpture, to restore
Peace to the Mourner's soul; but He who wore
The crown of thorns around his bleeding brow
Warmed our sad being with his glorious light:
Then Arts, which still had drawn a softening grace   10
From shadowy fountains of the Infinite,
Communed with that Idea face to face;
And move around it now as planets run,
Each in its orbit, round the central Sun.

XL

NUNNERY

The floods are roused, and will not soon be weary;
Down from the Pennine Alps[1] how fiercely sweeps
CROGLIN, the stately Eden's tributary!
He raves, or through some moody passage creeps
Plotting new mischief—out again he leaps   5
Into broad light, and sends, through regions airy,
That voice which soothed the Nuns while on the steeps
They knelt in prayer, or sang to blissful Mary.
That union ceased: then, cleaving easy walks
Through crags, and smoothing paths beset with danger,   10
Came studious Taste; and many a pensive Stranger
Dreams on the banks, and to the river talks.
What change shall happen next to Nunnery Dell?
Canal, and Viaduct, and Railway, tell![2]

XLI

STEAMBOATS, VIADUCTS, AND RAILWAYS

Motions and Means, on land and sea at war
With old poetic feeling, not for this,
Shall ye, by Poets even, be judged amiss!
Nor shall your presence, howsoe'er it mar
The loveliness of Nature, prove a bar   5

---

1   "The chain of Crossfell, which parts Cumberland and Westmore-land from Northumberland
    and Durham." WW
2   "At Corby, a few miles below Nunnery, the Eden is crossed by a magnificent viaduct; and
    another of these works is thrown over a deep glen or ravine at a very short distance from
    the main stream." WW

To the Mind's gaining that prophetic sense
Of future change, that point of vision whence
May be discovered what in soul ye are.
In spite of all that beauty may disown
In your harsh features, Nature doth embrace   10
Her lawful offspring in Man's art; and Time,
Pleased with your triumphs o'er his brother Space,
Accepts from your bold hands the proffered crown
Of hope, and smiles on you with cheer sublime.

XLII

Lowther! in thy majestic Pile are seen
Cathedral pomp and grace, in apt accord
With the baronial castle's sterner mien;
Union significant of God adored,
And charters won and guarded by the sword   5
Of ancient honour; whence that goodly state
Of Polity which wise men venerate,
And will *maintain*, if God his help afford.
Hourly the democratic torrent swells;
For airy promises and hopes suborned   10
The strength of backward-looking thoughts is scorned.
Fall if ye must, ye Towers and Pinnacles,
With what ye symbolise; authentic Story
Will say, Ye disappeared with England's Glory!

XLIII

TO THE EARL OF LONSDALE[1]

"MAGISTRATUS INDICAT VIRUM."

Lonsdale! it were unworthy of a Guest,
Whose heart with gratitude to thee inclines,
If he should speak, by fancy touched, of signs
On thy Abode harmoniously imprest,

---

1   "This sonnet was written immediately after certain trials, which took place at the Cumberland
Assizes, when the Earl of Lonsdale, in consequence of repeated and long continued
attacks upon his character, through the local press, had thought it right to prosecute the
conductors and proprietors of three several journals. A verdict of libel was given in one
case; and in the others, the prosecutions were withdrawn, upon the individuals retracting
and disavowing the charges, expressing regret that they had been made, and promising
to abstain from the like in future." WW

Yet be unmoved with wishes to attest   5
How in thy mind and moral frame agree
Fortitude and that christian Charity
Which, filling, consecrates the human breast.
And if the Motto on thy 'scutcheon teach
With truth, "THE MAGISTRACY SHOWS THE MAN:"   10
That searching test thy public course has stood;
As will be owned alike by bad and good,
Soon as the measuring of life's little span
Shall place thy virtues out of Envy's reach.

XLIV

TO CORDELIA M——, HALLSTEADS, ULLSWATER

Not in the mines beyond the western main,
You tell me, Delia! was the metal sought,
Which a fine skill, of Indian growth, has wrought
Into this flexible yet faithful Chain;
Nor is it silver of romantic Spain   5
You say, but from Helvellyn's depths was brought,
Our own domestic mountain. Thing and thought
Mix strangely; trifles light, and partly vain,
Can prop, as you have learnt, our nobler being:
Yes, Lady, while about your neck is wound   10
(Your casual glance oft meeting) this bright cord,
What witchery, for pure gifts of inward seeing,
Lurks in it, Memory's Helper, Fancy's Lord,
For precious tremblings in your bosom found!

XLV

CONCLUSION

Most sweet it is with unuplifted eyes
To pace the ground, if path be there or none,
While a fair region round the Traveller lies
Which he forbears again to look upon;
Pleased rather with some soft ideal scene,   5
The work of Fancy, or some happy tone
Of meditation, slipping in between
The beauty coming and the beauty gone.

If Thought and Love desert us, from that day
Let us break off all commerce with the Muse;   10
With Thought and Love companions of our way,
Whate'er the senses take or may refuse,
The Mind's internal Heaven shall shed her dews
Of inspiration on the humblest lay.

[Poems not included in series as first published]

The Monument Commonly Called Long Meg and Her Daughters, near the River Eden[1]

A weight of awe not easy to be borne
Fell suddenly upon my Spirit-cast
From the dread bosom of the unknown past,
When first I saw that Sisterhood forlorn;
And Her, whose massy strength and stature scorn   5
The power of years—pre-eminent, and placed
Apart-to overlook the circle vast.
Speak, Giant-mother! tell it to the Morn
While she dispels the cumbrous shades of night;
Let the Moon hear, emerging from a cloud,   10
At whose behest uprose on British ground
Thy Progeny; in hieroglyphic round
Forth-shadowing, some have deemed, the infinite,
The inviolable God, that tames the proud!

Written in a Blank Leaf of Macpherson's Ossian

Oft have I caught from fitful breeze
Fragments of far-off melodies,
With ear not coveting the whole,
A part so charmed the pensive soul:
While a dark storm before my sight   5
Was yielding, on a mountain height

---

1   "The Daughters of Long Meg, placed in a perfect circle eighty yards in diameter, are seventy-two in number, and their height is from three feet to so many yards above ground; a little way out of the circle stands Long Meg herself, a single Stone, eighteen feet high. When the Author first saw this Monument, as he came upon it by surprise, he might overrate its importance as an object; but, though it will not bear a comparison with Stonehenge, he must say, he has not seen any other Relique of those dark ages, which can pretend to rival it in singularity and dignity of appearance." WW

Loose vapours have I watched, that won
Prismatic colours from the sun;
Nor felt a wish that Heaven would show
The image of its perfect bow.   10
What need, then, of these finished Strains?
Away with counterfeit Remains!
An abbey in its lone recess,
A temple of the wilderness,
Wrecks though they be, announce with feeling   15
The majesty of honest dealing.
Spirit of Ossian! if imbound
In language thou may'st yet be found,
If aught (intrusted to the pen
Or floating on the tongues of Men,   20
Albeit shattered and impaired)
Subsist thy dignity to guard,
In concert with memorial claim
Of old grey stone, and high-born name,
That cleaves to rock or pillared cave,   25
Where moans the blast, or beats the wave,
Let Truth, stern Arbitress of all,
Interpret that Original,
And for presumptuous wrongs atone;
Authentic words be given, or none!   30

Time is not blind;—yet He, who spares
Pyramid pointing to the Stars,
Hath preyed with ruthless appetite
On all that marked the primal flight
Of the poetic ecstasy   35
Into the land of mystery.
No tongue is able to rehearse
One measure, Orpheus! of thy verse;
Musæus, stationed with his lyre
Supreme among the Elysian quire,   40
Is, for the dwellers upon earth,
Mute as a Lark ere morning's birth.
Why grieve for these, though passed away
The Music, and extinct the Lay?
When thousands, by severer doom,   45

Full early to the silent tomb
Have sunk, at Nature's call; or strayed
From hope or promise, self-betrayed;
The garland withering on their brows;
Stung with remorse for broken vows;   50
Frantic—else how might they rejoice?
And friendless, by their own sad choice.

Hail, Bards of mightier grasp! on you
I chiefly call, the chosen Few,
Who cast not off the acknowledged guide,   55
Who faltered not, nor turned aside;
Whose lofty Genius could survive
Privation, under sorrow thrive;
In whom the fiery Muse revered
The symbol of a snow-white beard,   60
Bedewed with meditative tears
Dropped from the lenient cloud of years.

Brothers in Soul! though distant times
Produced you, nursed in various climes,
Ye, when the orb of life had waned,   65
A plenitude of love retained;
Hence, while in you each sad regret
By corresponding love was met,
Ye lingered among human kind,
Sweet voices for the passing wind;   70
Departing sunbeams, loth to stop,
Though smiling on the last hill top!

Such to the tender-hearted Maid
Even ere her joys begin to fade;
Such, haply, to the rugged Chief   75
By Fortune crushed, or tamed by grief;
Appears, on Morven's lonely shore,
Dim-gleaming through imperfect lore,
The Son of Fingal; such was blind
Mæonides of ampler mind;   80
Such Milton, to the fountain head
Of Glory by Urania led!

The Somnambulist

1

List, ye who pass by Lyulph's Tower[1]
    At eve; how softly then
Doth Aira-force, that torrent hoarse,
    Speak from the woody glen!
Fit music for a solemn vale!   5
    And holier seems the ground
To him who catches on the gale
The spirit of a mournful tale,
    Embodied in the sound.

2

Not far from that fair site whereon   10
    The Pleasure-house is reared,
As Story says, in antique days,
    A stern-brow'd house appeared;
Foil to a jewel rich in light
    There set, and guarded well;   15
Cage for a bird of plumage bright,
Sweet-voiced, nor wishing for a flight
    Beyond her native dell.

3

To win this bright bird from her cage,
    To make this gem their own,   20
Came Barons bold, with store of gold,
    And Knights of high renown;
But one she prized, and only One;
    Sir Eglamore was he;
Full happy season, when was known,   25
Ye Dales and Hills! to you alone
    Their mutual loyalty—

4

Known chiefly, Aira! to thy glen,
    Thy brook, and bowers of holly;

---

1 "A pleasure-house built by the late Duke of Norfolk upon the banks of Ullswater. FORCE is
    the word used in the Lake District for Water-fall." WW

Where Passion caught what Nature taught,   30
   That all but Love is folly;
Where Fact with Fancy stooped to play,
   Doubt came not, nor regret;
To trouble hours that winged their way,
As if through an immortal day   35
   Whose sun could never set.

5

But in old times Love dwelt not long
   Sequester'd with repose;
Best throve the fire of chaste desire,
   Fanned by the breath of foes.   40
"A conquering lance is beauty's test,
   "And proves the Lover true;"
So spake Sir Eglamore, and pressed
The drooping Emma to his breast,
   And looked a blind adieu.   45

6

They parted.—Well with him it fared
   Through wide-spread regions errant;
A knight of proof in love's behoof,
   The thirst of fame his warrant:
And she her happiness can build   50
   On woman's quiet hours;
Though faint, compared with spear and shield,
The solace beads and masses yield,
   And needlework and flowers.

7

Yet blest was Emma when she heard   55
   Her Champion's praise recounted;
Though brain would swim, and eyes grow dim,
   And high her blushes mounted;
Or when a bold heroic lay
   She warbled from full heart: 60
Delightful blossoms for the May
Of absence! but they will not stay,
   Born only to depart.

8

Hope wanes with her, while lustre fills
   Whatever path he chooses;   65
As if his orb, that owns no curb,
   Received the light hers loses.
He comes not back; an ampler space
   Requires for nobler deeds;
He ranges on from place to place,   70
Till of his doings is no trace
   But what her fancy breeds.

9

His fame may spread, but in the past
   Her spirit finds its centre;
Clear sight she has of what he was,   75
   And that would now content her.
"Still is he my devoted knight?"
   The tear in answer flows;
Month falls on month with heavier weight;
Day sickens round her, and the night   80
   Is empty of repose.

10

In sleep she sometimes walked abroad,
   Deep sighs with quick words blending,
Like that pale Queen whose hands are seen
   With fancied spots contending;   85
But she is innocent of blood,—
   The moon is not more pure
That shines aloft, while through the wood
She thrids her way, the sounding Flood
   Her melancholy lure!   90

11

While 'mid the fern-brake sleeps the doe,
   And owls alone are waking,
In white arrayed, glides on the Maid
   The downward pathway taking,
That leads her to the torrent's side   95
   And to a holly bower;

By whom on this still night descried?
By whom in that lone place espied?
   By thee, Sir Eglamore!

12

A wandering Ghost, so thinks the Knight,   100
   His coming step has thwarted,
Beneath the boughs that heard their vows,
   Within whose shade they parted.
Hush, hush, the busy Sleeper see!
   Perplexed her fingers seem,   105
As if they from the holly tree
Green twigs would pluck, as rapidly
   Flung from her to the stream.

13

What means the Spectre? Why intent
   To violate the Tree,   110
Thought Eglamore, by which I swore
   Unfading constancy?
Here am I, and to-morrow's sun,
   To her I left, shall prove
That bliss is ne'er so surely won   115
As when a circuit has been run
   Of valour, truth, and love.

14

So from the spot whereon he stood,
   He moved with stealthy pace;
And, drawing nigh, with his living eye,   120
   He recognised the face;
And whispers caught, and speeches small,
   Some to the green-leaved tree,
Some muttered to the torrent-fall,—
"Roar on, and bring him with thy call;   125
   "I heard, and so may he!"

15

Soul-shattered was the Knight, nor knew
   If Emma's Ghost it were,

Or boding Shade, or if the Maid
    Her very self stood there.   130
He touched, what followed who shall tell?
    The soft touch snapped the thread
Of slumber—shrieking back she fell,
And the Stream whirled her down the dell
    Along its foaming bed.   135

16

In plunged the Knight! when on firm ground
    The rescued Maiden lay,
Her eyes grew bright with blissful light,
    Confusion passed away;
She heard, ere to the throne of grace   140
    Her faithful Spirit flew,
His voice; beheld his speaking face,
And, dying, from his own embrace,
    She felt that he was true.

17

So was he reconciled to life: 145
    Brief words may speak the rest;
Within the dell he built a cell,
    And there was Sorrow's guest;
In hermits' weeds repose he found,
    From vain temptations free;   150
Beside the torrent dwelling—bound
By one deep heart-controlling sound,
    And awed to piety.

18

Wild stream of Aira, hold thy course,
    Nor fear memorial lays,   155
Where clouds that spread in solemn shade,
    Are edged with golden rays!
Dear art thou to the light of Heaven,
    Though minister of sorrow;
Sweet is thy voice at pensive Even;   160
And thou, in Lovers' hearts forgiven,
    Shalt take thy place with Yarrow!

Stanzas

[St. Bees' Heads, anciently called the Cliff of Baruth, are a conspicuous sea-mark for all vessels sailing in the N.E. Parts of the Irish Sea. In a bay, one side of which is formed by the southern headland, stands the village of St. Bees; a place distinguished, from very early times, for its religious and scholastic foundations.

"St. Bees," say Nicholson and Burns, "had its name from Bega, an holy woman from Ireland, who is said to have founded here, about the year of our Lord 650, a small monastery, where afterwards a church was built in memory of her.

"The aforesaid religious house, being destroyed by the Danes, was restored by William de Meschiens, son of Ranulph, and brother of Ranulph de Meschiens, first Earl of Cumberland after the Conquest; and made a cell of a prior and six Benedictine monks to the Abbey of St. Mary at York."

Several traditions of miracles, connected with the foundation of the first of these religious houses, survive among the people of the neighbourhood; one of which is alluded to in the following Stanzas; and another, of a somewhat bolder and more peculiar character, has furnished the subject of a spirited poem by the Rev. R. Parkinson, M.A., late Divinity Lecturer of St. Bees' College, and now Fellow of the Collegiate Church of Manchester.

After the dissolution of the monasteries, Archbishop Grindal founded a free school at St. Bees, from which the counties of Cumberland and Westmoreland have derived great benefit; and recently, under the patronage of the Earl of Lonsdale, a college has been established there for the education of ministers for the English Church. The old Conventual Church has been repaired under the superintendence of the Rev. Dr. Ainger, the Head of the College; and is well worthy of being visited by any strangers who might be led to the neighbourhood of this celebrated spot.

The form of stanza in the following Piece, and something in the style of versification, are adopted from the "St. Monica," a poem of much beauty upon a monastic subject, by Charlotte Smith: a lady to whom English verse is under greater obligations, than are likely to be either acknowledged or remembered. She wrote little, and that little unambitiously, but with true feeling for nature.]

Stanzas

SUGGESTED IN A STEAM-BOAT OFF ST. BEES' HEADS

1

If Life were slumber on a bed of down,
Toil unimposed, vicissitude unknown,
Sad were our lot: no Hunter of the Hare
Exults like him whose javelin from the lair
Has roused the Lion; no one plucks the Rose,   5
Whose proffered beauty in safe shelter blows
'Mid a trim garden's summer luxuries,
With joy like his who climbs on hands and knees,
For some rare Plant, yon Headland of St. Bees.

2

This independence upon oar and sail,   10
This new indifference to breeze or gale,
This straight-lined progress, furrowing a flat lea,
And regular as if locked in certainty,
Depress the hours. Up, Spirit of the Storm!
That Courage may find something to perform;   15
That Fortitude, whose blood disdains to freeze
At Danger's bidding, may confront the seas,
Firm as the towering Headlands of St. Bees.

3

Dread Cliff of Baruth! *that* wild wish may sleep,
Bold as if Men and Creatures of the Deep   20
Breathed the same Element: too many wrecks
Have struck thy sides, too many ghastly decks
Hast thou looked down upon, that such a thought
Should here be welcome, and in verse enwrought:
With thy stern aspect better far agrees   25
Utterance of thanks that we have past with ease,
As Millions thus shall do, the Headlands of St. Bees.

4

Yet, while each useful Art augments her store,
What boots the gain if Nature should lose more?

And Wisdom, that once held a Christian place   30
In Man's intelligence sublimed by grace?
When Bega sought of yore the Cumbrian coast,
Tempestuous winds her holy errand cross'd;
As high and higher heaved the billows, faith
Grew with them, mightier than the powers of death.   35
She knelt in prayer—the waves their wrath appease;
And, from her vow well weighed in Heaven's decrees,
Rose, where she touched the strand, the Chauntry of St. Bees.

5

"Cruel of heart were they, bloody of hand,"
Who in these Wilds then struggled for command;   40
The strong were merciless, without hope the weak;
Till this bright Stranger came, fair as Day-break,
And as a Cresset true that darts its length
Of beamy lustre from a tower of strength;
Guiding the Mariner through troubled seas,   45
And cheering oft his peaceful reveries,
Like the fixed Light that crowns yon headland of St. Bees.

6

To aid the Votaress, miracles believed
Wrought in men's minds, like miracles achieved;
So piety took root; and Song might tell   50
What humanizing Virtues round her Cell
Sprang up, and spread their fragrance wide around;
How savage bosoms melted at the sound
Of gospel-truth enchained in harmonies
Wafted o'er waves, or creeping through close trees,   55
From her religious Mansion of St. Bees.

7

When her sweet Voice, that instrument of love,
Was glorified, and took its place, above
The silent stars, among the angelic Quire,
Her Chauntry blazed with sacrilegious fire,   60
And perished utterly; but her good deeds
Had sown the spot that witnessed them with seeds

Which lay in earth expectant, till a breeze
With quickening impulse answered their mute pleas,
And lo! a *statelier* Pile, the Abbey of St. Bees.   65

8

There were the naked clothed, the hungry fed;
And Charity extended to the Dead
Her intercessions made for the soul's rest
Of tardy Penitents; or for the best
Among the good (when love might else have slept,   70
Sickened, or died) in pious memory kept.
Thanks to the austere and simple Devotees,
Who, to that service bound by venial fees,
Kept watch before the Altars of St. Bees.

9

Were not, in sooth, their Requiems sacred ties[1]   75
Woven out of passion's sharpest agonies,
Subdued, composed, and formalized by art,
To fix a wiser sorrow in the heart?
The prayer for them whose hour was past away
Said to the Living, profit while ye may!   80
A little part, and that the worst, he sees
Who thinks that priestly cunning holds the keys
That best unlock the secrets of St. Bees.

10

Conscience, the timid being's inmost light,
Hope of the dawn and solace of the night,   85
Cheers these Recluses with a steady ray
In many an hour when judgement goes astray.
Ah! scorn not hastily their rule who try
Earth to despise, and flesh to mortify;
Consume with zeal, in wingèd extacies   90
Of prayer and praise forget their rosaries,
Nor hear the loudest surges of St. Bees.

---

1 For WW's note on "sacred ties" see the notes at the end of this volume.

11

Yet none so prompt to succour and protect
The forlorn Traveller, or Sailor wrecked
On the bare coast; nor do they grudge the boon   95
Which staff and cockle hat and sandal shoon
Claim for the Pilgrim: and, though chidings sharp
May sometimes greet the strolling Minstrel's harp,
It is not then when, swept with sportive ease,
It charms a feast-day throng of all degrees,   100
Brightening the archway of revered St. Bees.

12

How did the Cliffs and echoing Hills rejoice
What time the Benedictine Brethren's voice,
Imploring, or commanding with meet pride,
Summoned the Chiefs to lay their feuds aside,   105
And under one blest ensign serve the Lord
In Palestine. Advance, indignant Sword!
Flaming till thou from Panym hands release
That Tomb, dread centre of all sanctities
Nursed in the quiet Abbey of St. Bees.   110

13

On, Champions, on!—But mark! the passing Day
Submits her intercourse to milder sway,
With high and low whose busy thoughts from far
Follow the fortunes which they may not share.
While in Judea Fancy loves to roam,   115
She helps to make a Holy-land at home:
The Star of Bethlehem from its sphere invites
To sound the crystal depth of maiden rights;
And wedded life, through scriptural mysteries,
Heavenward ascends with all her charities,   120
Taught by the hooded Celibates of St. Bees.

14

Who with the ploughshare clove the barren moors,
And to green meadows changed the swampy shores?
Thinned the rank woods; and for the cheerful Grange

Made room where Wolf and Boar were used to range?   125
Who taught, and showed by deeds, that gentler chains
Should bind the Vassal to his Lord's domains?
The thoughtful Monks, intent their God to please,
For Christ's dear sake, by human sympathies
Poured from the bosom of thy Church, St. Bees!   130

15

But all availed not; by a mandate given
Through lawless will the Brotherhood was driven
Forth from their cells;—their ancient House laid low
In Reformation's sweeping overthrow.
But now once more the local Heart revives,   135
The inextinguishable Spirit strives.
Oh may that Power who hushed the stormy seas,
And cleared a way for the first Votaries,
Prosper the new-born College of St. Bees!

16

Alas! the Genius of our age from Schools   140
Less humble draws her lessons, aims, and rules.
To Prowess guided by her insight keen
Matter and Spirit are as one Machine;
Boastful Idolatress of formal skill
She in her own would merge the eternal will: 145
Expert to move in paths that Newton trod,
From Newton's Universe would banish God.
Better, if Reason's triumphs match with these,
Her flight before the bold credulities
That furthered the first teaching of St. Bees.   150

Memorials of a Tour in Italy. 1837[1]

Memorials of a Tour in Italy

1837

To Henry Crabb Robinson.

Companion! by whose buoyant Spirit cheered,
To whose experience trusting, day by day
Treasures I gained with zeal that neither feared
The toils nor felt the crosses of the way,
These records take, and happy should I be   5
Were but the Gift a meet Return to thee
For kindnesses that never ceased to flow,
And prompt self-sacrifice to which I owe
Far more than any heart but mine can know.

                   W. WORDSWORTH.

RYDAL MOUNT,
  Feb. 14*th,* 1842.

The Tour of which the following Poems are very inadequate remembrances was shortened by report, too well founded, of the prevalence of Cholera at Naples. To make some amends for what was reluctantly left unseen in the South of Italy, we visited the Tuscan Sanctuaries among the Apennines, and the principal Italian Lakes among the Alps. Neither of those lakes, nor of Venice, is there any notice in these Poems, chiefly because I have touched upon them elsewhere. See, in particular, "Descriptive Sketches," "Memorials of a Tour on the Continent in 1820," and a Sonnet upon the extinction of the Venetian Republic.

Musings Near Aquapendente

APRIL 1837[2]

Ye Apennines! with all your fertile vales

---

1 WW's notes are those published with the series in *Poems, Chiefly of Early and Late Years, 1842.* For the sources of the reading text and the editor's commentary, see *Sonnet Series and Itinerary Poems,* 1820–1845, ed. Geoffrey Jackson (2004), pp. 731–739, and 795–809.

2 WW's notes are those published with the series in *Poems, Chiefly of Early and Late*

Deeply embosomed, and your winding shores
Of either sea, an Islander by birth,
A Mountaineer by habit, would resound
Your praise, in meet accordance with your claims   5
Bestowed by Nature, or from man's great deeds
Inherited:—presumptuous thought!—it fled
Like vapour, like a towering cloud dissolved.
Not, therefore, shall my mind give way to sadness;—
Yon snow-white torrent-fall, plumb down it drops   10
Yet ever hangs or seems to hang in air,
Lulling the leisure of that high perched town,
Aquapendente, in her lofty site
Its neighbour and its namesake—town, and flood
Forth flashing out of its own gloomy chasm   15
Bright sunbeams—the fresh verdure of this lawn
Strewn with grey rocks, and on the horizon's verge,
O'er intervenient waste, through glimmering haze,
Unquestionably kenned, that cone-shaped hill
With fractured summit, no indifferent sight   20
To travellers, from such comforts as are thine,
Bleak Radicofani! escaped with joy—
These are before me; and the varied scene
May well suffice, till noon-tide's sultry heat
Relax, to fix and satisfy the mind   25
Passive yet pleased. What! with this Broom in flower
Close at my side. She bids me fly to greet
Her sisters, soon like her to be attired
With golden blossoms opening at the feet
Of my own Fairfield. The glad greeting given,   30
Given with a voice and by a look returned
Of old companionship, Time counts not minutes
Ere, from accustomed paths, familiar fields,
The local Genius hurries me aloft,
Transported over that cloud-wooing hill,   35
Seat Sandal, a fond suitor of the clouds,
With dream-like smoothness, to Helvellyn's top,
There to alight upon crisp moss and range,

Years, 1842. For the sources of the reading text and the editor's commentary, see *Sonnet Series and Itinerary Poems, 1820–1845*, ed. Geoffrey Jackson (2004), pp. 731–739, and 795–809.

Obtaining ampler boon, at every step,
Of visual sovereignty—hills multitudinous,   40
(Not Apennine can boast of fairer) hills
Pride of two nations, wood and lake and plains,
And prospect right below of deep coves shaped
By skeleton arms, that, from the mountain's trunk
Extended, clasp the winds, with mutual moan   45
Struggling for liberty, while undismayed
The shepherd struggles with them. Onward thence
And downward by the skirt of Greenside fell,
And by Glenridding-screes, and low Glencoign,
Places forsaken now, but loving still   50
The muses, as they loved them in the days
Of the old minstrels and the border bards.—
But here am I fast bound;—and let it pass,
The simple rapture;—who that travels far
To feed his mind with watchful eyes could share   55
Or wish to share it?—One there surely was,
"The Wizard of the North," with anxious hope
Brought to this genial climate, when disease
Preyed upon body and mind—yet not the less
Had his sunk eye kindled at those dear words   60
That spake of bards and minstrels; and his spirit
Had flown with mine to old Helvellyn's brow,
Where once together, in his day of strength,
We stood rejoicing, as if earth were free
From sorrow, like the sky above our heads.   65

  Years followed years, and when, upon the eve
Of his last going from Tweed-side, thought turned,
Or by another's sympathy was led,
To this bright land, Hope was for him no friend,
Knowledge no help; Imagination shaped   70
No promise. Still, in more than ear-deep seats,
Survives for me, and cannot but survive
The tone of voice which wedded borrowed words
To sadness not their own, when, with faint smile
Forced by intent to take from speech its edge,   75
He said, "When I am there, although 'tis fair,

"Twill be another Yarrow." Prophecy[1]
More than fulfilled, as gay Campania's shores
Soon witnessed, and the city of seven hills,
Her sparkling fountains, and her mouldering tombs;   80
And more than all, that Eminence which showed
Her splendors, seen, not felt, the while he stood
A few short steps (painful they were) apart
From Tasso's Convent-haven, and retired grave.

   Peace to their Spirits! why should Poesy   85
Yield to the lure of vain regret, and hover
In gloom on wings with confidence outspread
To move in sunshine?—Utter thanks, my Soul!
Tempered with awe, and sweetened by compassion
For them who in the shades of sorrow dwell,   90
That I—so near the term to human life
Appointed by man's common heritage,
Frail as the frailest, one withal (if that
Deserve a thought) but little known to fame—
Am free to rove where Nature's loveliest looks,   95
Art's noblest relics, history's rich bequests,
Failed to reanimate and but feebly cheered
The whole world's Darling—free to rove at will
O'er high and low, and if requiring rest,
Rest from enjoyment only.
                Thanks poured forth   100
For what thus far hath blessed my wanderings, thanks
Fervent but humble as the lips can breathe
Where gladness seems a duty—let me guard
Those seeds of expectation which the fruit
Already gathered in this favoured Land   105
Enfolds within its core. The faith be mine,
That He who guides and governs all, approves
When gratitude, though disciplined to look
Beyond these transient spheres, doth wear a crown
Of earthly hope put on with trembling hand;   110

---

1 "These words were quoted to me from "Yarrow Unvisited," by Sir Walter Scott when I vis-
   ited him at Abbotsford, a day or two before his departure for Italy: and the affecting condi-
   tion in which he was when he looked upon Rome from the Janicular Mount, was reported
   to me by a lady who had the honour of conducting him thither." WW
   For *Yarrow Unvisited*, see vol. 2 of this edition.

Nor is least pleased, we trust, when golden beams,
Reflected through the mists of age, from hours
Of innocent delight, remote or recent,
Shoot but a little way—'tis all they can—
Into the doubtful future. Who would keep   115
Power must resolve to cleave to it through life,
Else it deserts him, surely as he lives.
Saints would not grieve nor guardian angels frown
If one—while tossed, as was my lot to be,
In a frail bark urged by two slender oars   120
Over waves rough and deep, that, when they broke
Dashed their white foam against the palace walls
Of Genoa the superb—should there be led
To meditate upon his own appointed tasks,
However humble in themselves, with thoughts   125
Raised and sustained by memory of Him
Who oftentimes within those narrow bounds
Rocked on the surge, there tried his spirit's strength
And grasp of purpose, long ere sailed his ship
To lay a new world open.
                  Nor less prized   130
Be those impressions which incline the heart
To mild, to lowly, and to seeming weak,
Bend that way her desires. The dew, the storm—
The dew whose moisture fell in gentle drops
On the small hyssop destined to become,   135
By Hebrew ordinance devoutly kept,
A purifying instrument—the storm
That shook on Lebanon the cedar's top,
And as it shook, enabling the blind roots
Further to force their way, endowed its trunk   140
With magnitude and strength fit to uphold
The glorious temple—did alike proceed
From the same gracious will, were both an offspring
Of bounty infinite.
                Between Powers that aim
Higher to lift their lofty heads, impelled   145
By no profane ambition, Powers that thrive
By conflict, and their opposites, that trust

In lowliness—a mid-way tract there lies
Of thoughtful sentiment for every mind
Pregnant with good. Young, Middle-aged, and Old,   150
From century on to century, must have known
The emotion—nay, more fitly were it said—
The blest tranquillity that sunk so deep
Into my spirit, when I paced, enclosed
In Pisa's Campo Santo, the smooth floor   155
Of its Arcades paved with sepulchral slabs,
And through each window's open fret-work looked
O'er the blank Area of sacred earth
Fetched from Mount Calvary, or haply delved
In precincts nearer to the Saviour's tomb,   160
By hands of men, humble as brave, who fought
For its deliverance—a capacious field
That to descendants of the dead it holds
And to all living mute memento breathes,
More touching far than aught which on the walls   165
Is pictured, or their epitaphs can speak,
Of the changed City's long-departed power,
Glory, and wealth, which, perilous as they are,
Here did not kill, but nourished, Piety.
And, high above that length of cloistral roof,   170
Peering in air and backed by azure sky,
To kindred contemplations ministers
The Baptistery's dome, and that which swells
From the Cathedral pile; and with the twain
Conjoined in prospect mutable or fixed   175
(As hurry on in eagerness the feet,
Or pause) the summit of the Leaning-tower.
Not less remuneration waits on him
Who having left the Cemetery stands
In the Tower's shadow, of decline and fall   180
Admonished not without some sense of fear,
Fear that soon vanishes before the sight
Of splendor unextinguished, pomp unscathed,
And beauty unimpaired. Grand in itself,
And for itself, the assemblage, grand and fair   185
To view, and for the mind's consenting eye

A type of age in man, upon its front
Bearing the world-acknowledged evidence
Of past exploits, nor fondly after more
Struggling against the stream of destiny,   190
But with its peaceful majesty content.
—Oh what a spectacle at every turn
The Place unfolds, from pavement skinned with moss,
Or grass-grown spaces, where the heaviest foot
Provokes no echoes, but must softly tread;   195
Where Solitude with Silence paired stops short
Of Desolation, and to Ruin's scythe
Decay submits not.
                              But where'er my steps
Shall wander, chiefly let me cull with care
Those images of genial beauty, oft   200
Too lovely to be pensive in themselves
But by reflexion made so, which do best,
And fitliest serve to crown with fragrant wreaths
Life's cup when almost filled with years, like mine.
—How lovely robed in forenoon light and shade,   205
Each ministering to each, didst thou appear
Savona, Queen of territory fair
As aught that marvellous coast thro' all its length
Yields to the Stranger's eye. Remembrance holds
As a selected treasure thy one cliff,   210
That, while it wore for melancholy crest
A shattered Convent, yet rose proud to have
Clinging to its steep sides a thousand herbs
And shrubs, whose pleasant looks gave proof how kind
The breath of air can be where earth had else   215
Seemed churlish. And behold, both far and near,
Garden and field all decked with orange bloom,
And peach and citron, in Spring's mildest breeze
Expanding; and, along the smooth shore curved
Into a natural port, a tideless sea,   220
To that mild breeze with motion and with voice
Softly responsive; and, attuned to all
Those vernal charms of sight and sound, appeared
Smooth space of turf which from the guardian fort

Sloped seaward, turf whose tender April green,   225
In coolest climes too fugitive, might even here
Plead with the sovereign Sun for longer stay
Than his unmitigated beams allow,
Nor plead in vain, if beauty could preserve,
From mortal change, aught that is born on earth   230
Or doth on time depend.
      While on the brink
Of that high Convent-crested cliff I stood,
Modest Savona! over all did brood
A pure poetic Spirit—as the breeze,
Mild—as the verdure, fresh—the sunshine, bright,   235
Thy gentle Chiabrera!—not a stone,
Mural or level with the trodden floor,
In Church or Chapel, if my curious quest
Missed not the truth, retains a single name
Of young or old, warrior, or saint, or sage,   240
To whose dear memories his sepulchral verse[1]
Paid simple tribute, such as might have flowed
From the clear spring of a plain English heart,
Say rather, one in native fellowship
With all who want not skill to couple grief   245
With praise, as genuine admiration prompts.
The grief, the praise, are severed from their dust,
Yet in his page the records of that worth
Survive, uninjured;—glory then to words,
Honour to word-preserving Arts, and hail   250
Ye kindred local influences that still,
If Hope's familiar whispers merit faith,
Await my steps when they the breezy height
Shall range of philosophic Tusculum;
Or Sabine vales explored inspire a wish   255
To meet the shade of Horace by the side
Of his Bandusian fount; or I invoke
His presence to point out the spot where once
He sate, and eulogized with earnest pen
Peace, leisure, freedom, moderate desires;   260

---

1 "If any English reader should be desirous of knowing how far I am justified in thus describ-
ing the epitaphs of Chiabrera, he will find translated specimens of them in the 5th volume
of my poems." WW

And all the immunities of rural life
Extolled, behind Vacuna's crumbling fane.
Or let me loiter, soothed with what is given,
Nor asking more on that delicious Bay,
Parthenope's Domain—Virgilian haunt,   265
Illustrated with never-dying verse,
And, by the Poet's laurel-shaded tomb,
Age after age to Pilgrims from all lands
Endeared.
       And who—if not a man as cold
In heart as dull in brain—while pacing ground   270
Chosen by Rome's legendary Bards, high minds
Out of her early struggles well inspired
To localize heroic acts—could look
Upon the spots with undelighted eye,
Though even to their last syllable the Lays   275
And very names of those who gave them birth
Have perished?—Verily, to her utmost depth,
Imagination feels what Reason fears not
To recognize, the lasting virtue lodged
In those bold fictions that, by deeds assigned   280
To the Valerian, Fabian, Curian Race,
And others like in fame, created Powers
With attributes from History derived,
By Poesy irradiate, and yet graced,
Through marvellous felicity of skill,   285
With something more propitious to high aims
Than either, pent within her separate sphere,
Can oft with justice claim.
         And not disdaining
Union with those primeval energies
To virtue consecrate, stoop ye from your height   290
Christian Traditions! at my Spirit's call
Descend, and, on the brow of ancient Rome
As she survives in ruin, manifest
Your glories mingled with the brightest hues
Of her memorial halo, fading, fading,   295
But never to be extinct while Earth endures.
O come, if undishonoured by the prayer,

From all her Sanctuaries!—Open for my feet
Ye Catacombs, give to mine eyes a glimpse
Of the Devout, as, mid your glooms convened   300
For safety, they of yore enclasped the Cross
On knees that ceased from trembling, or intoned
Their orisons with voices half-suppressed,
But sometimes heard, or fancies to be heard,
Even at this hour.
          And thou Mamertine prison,   305
Into that vault receive me from whose depth
Issues, revealed in no presumptuous vision,
Albeit lifting human to divine,
A Saint, the Church's Rock, the mystic Keys
Grasped in his hand; and lo! with upright sword   310
Prefiguring his own impendent doom,
The Apostle of the Gentiles; both prepared
To suffer pains with heathen scorn and hate
Inflicted;—blessed Men, for so to Heaven
They follow their dear Lord!
          Time flows—nor winds,   315
Nor stagnates, nor precipitates his course,
But many a benefit borne upon his breast
For human-kind sinks out of sight, is gone,
No one knows how; nor seldom is put forth
An angry arm that snatches good away,   320
Never perhaps to reappear. The Stream
Has to our generation brought and brings
Innumerable gains; yet we, who now
Walk in the light of day, pertain full surely
To a chilled age, most pitiably shut out   325
From that which *is* and actuates, by forms,
Abstractions, and by lifeless fact to fact
Minutely linked with diligence uninspired,
Unrectified, unguided, unsustained,
By godlike insight. To this fate is doomed   330
Science, wide-spread and spreading still as be
Her conquests, in the world of sense made known.
So with the internal mind it fares; and so
With morals, trusting, in contempt or fear

Of vital principle's controlling law,   335
To her pur-blind guide Expediency; and so
Suffers religious faith. Elate with view
Of what is won, we overlook or scorn
The best that should keep pace with it, and must,
Else more and more the general mind will droop,   340
Even as if bent on perishing. There lives
No faculty within us which the Soul
Can spare, and humblest earthly Weal demands,
For dignity not placed beyond her reach,
Zealous co-operation of all means   345
Given or acquired, to raise us from the mire,
And liberate our hearts from low pursuits.
By gross Utilities enslaved we need
More of ennobling impulse from the past,
If to the future aught of good must come   350
Sounder and therefore holier than the ends
Which, in the giddiness of self applause,
We covet as supreme. O grant the crown
That Wisdom wears, or take his treacherous staff
From Knowledge!—If the Muse, whom I have served   355
This day, be mistress of a single pearl
Fit to be placed in that pure diadem;
Then, not in vain, under these chestnut boughs
Reclined, shall I have yielded up my soul
To transports from the secondary founts   360
Flowing of time and place, and paid to both
Due homage; nor shall fruitlessly have striven,
By love of beauty moved, to enshrine in verse
Accordant meditations, which in times
Vexed and disordered, as our own, may shed   365
Influence, at least among a scattered few,
To soberness of mind and peace of heart
Friendly; as here to my repose hath been
This flowering broom's dear neighbourhood, the light
And murmur issuing from yon pendent flood,   370
And all the varied landscape. Let us now
Rise, and to-morrow greet magnificent Rome.[1]

---

1   For WW's note see the notes at the end of this volume.

I

THE PINE OF MONTE MARIO AT ROME[1]

I saw far off the dark top of a Pine
Look like a cloud—a slender stem the tie
That bound it to its native earth—poised high
'Mid evening hues, along the horizon line,
Striving in peace each other to outshine.   5
But when I learned the Tree was living there,
Saved from the sordid axe by Beaumont's care,
Oh, what a gush of tenderness was mine!
The rescued Pine-tree, with its sky so bright
And cloud-like beauty, rich in thoughts of home,   10
Death-parted friends, and days too swift in flight,
Supplanted the whole majesty of Rome
(Then first apparent from the Pincian Height)
Crowned with St. Peter's everlasting Dome.

II

AT ROME

Is this, ye Gods, the Capitolian Hill?
Yon petty Steep in truth the fearful Rock,
Tarpeian named of yore, and keeping still
That name, a local Phantom proud to mock
The Traveller's expectation?—Could our Will   5
Destroy the ideal Power within, 'twere done
Thro' what men see and touch,—slaves wandering on,
Impelled by thirst of all but Heaven-taught skill.
Full oft, our wish obtained, deeply we sigh;
Yet not unrecompensed are they who learn,   10
From that depression raised, to mount on high
With stronger wing, more clearly to discern
Eternal things; and, if need be, defy
Change, with a brow not insolent, though stern.

---

1   "Within a couple of hours of my arrival at Rome, I saw from Monte Pincio, the Pine tree
    as described in the sonnet; and, while expressing admiration at the beauty of its appear-
    ance, I was told by an acquaintance of my fellow-traveller, who happened to join us at the
    moment, that a price had been paid for it by the late Sir G. Beaumont, upon condition that
    the proprietor should not act upon his known intention of cutting it down." WW

III

AT ROME.—REGRETS.—IN ALLUSION TO NIEBUHR
AND OTHER MODERN HISTORIANS

Those old credulities, to nature dear,
Shall they no longer bloom upon the stock
Of History, stript naked as a rock
'Mid a dry desert? What is it we hear?
The glory of Infant Rome must disappear,   5
Her morning splendors vanish, and their place
Know them no more. If Truth, who veiled her face
With those bright beams yet hid it not, must steer
Henceforth a humbler course perplexed and slow;
One solace yet remains for us who came   10
Into this world in days when story lacked
Severe research, that in our hearts we know
How, for exciting youth's heroic flame,
Assent is power, belief the soul of fact.

IV

CONTINUED

Complacent Fictions were they, yet the same
Involved a history of no doubtful sense,
History that proves by inward evidence
From what a precious source of truth it came.
Ne'er could the boldest Eulogist have dared   5
Such deeds to paint, such characters to frame,
But for coeval sympathy prepared
To greet with instant faith their loftiest claim.
None but a noble people could have loved
Flattery in Ancient Rome's pure-minded style: 10
Not in like sort the Runic Scald was moved;
He, nursed 'mid savage passions that defile
Humanity, sang feats that well might call
For the blood-thirsty mead of Odin's riotous Hall.

V

PLEA FOR THE HISTORIAN

Forbear to deem the Chronicler unwise,
Ungentle, or untouched by seemly ruth,
Who, gathering up all that Time's envious tooth
Has spared of sound and grave realities,
Firmly rejects those dazzling flatteries,   5
Dear as they are to unsuspecting Youth,
That might have drawn down Clio from the skies
Her rights to claim, and vindicate the truth.
Her faithful Servants while she walked with men
Were they who, not unmindful of her Sire   10
All-ruling Jove, whate'er their theme might be
Revered her Mother, sage Mnemosyne,
And, at the Muse's will, invoked the lyre
To animate, but not mislead, the pen.[1]

VI

AT ROME

They—who have seen the noble Roman's scorn
Break forth at thought of laying down his head,
When the blank day is over, garreted
In his ancestral palace, where, from morn
To night, the desecrated floors are worn   5
By feet of purse-proud strangers; they—who have read
In one meek smile, beneath a peasant's shed,
How patiently the weight of wrong is borne;
They—who have heard thy lettered sages treat
Of freedom, with mind grasping the whole theme   10
From ancient Rome, downwards through that bright dream
Of Commonwealths, each city a starlike seat
Of rival glory; they—fallen Italy—
Nor must, nor will, nor can, despair of Thee!

---

1   "Quem virum—lyra—
        —sumes celebrare Clio?" WW quotes part of Horace's *Odes*, I, xii, ll. 1–3 ("What
man, Clio, will you choose to praise with your lyre").

VII

NEAR ROME, IN SIGHT OF ST. PETER'S

Long has the dew been dried on tree and lawn;
O'er man and beast a not unwelcome boon
Is shed, the languor of approaching noon;
To shady rest withdrawing or withdrawn
Mute are all creatures, as this couchant fawn,   5
Save insect-swarms that hum in air afloat,
Save that the Cock is crowing, a shrill note,
Startling and shrill as that which roused the dawn.
Heard in that hour, or when, as now, the nerve
Shrinks from the voice as from a mis-timed thing,   10
Oft for a holy warning may it serve,
Charged with remembrance of his sudden sting,
His bitter tears, whose name the Papal Chair
And yon resplendent church are proud to bear.

VIII

AT ALBANO

Days passed—and Monte Calvo would not clear
His head from mist; and, as the wind sobbed through
Albano's dripping Ilex avenue,
My dull forebodings in a Peasant's ear
Found casual vent. She said, "Be of good cheer;   5
Our yesterday's procession did not sue
In vain; the sky will change to sunny blue,
Thanks to our Lady's grace." I smiled to hear,
But not in scorn:—the Matron's Faith may lack
The heavenly sanction needed to ensure   10
Its own fulfilment; but her upward track
Stops not at this low point, nor wants the lure
Of flowers the Virgin without fear may own,
For by her Son's blest hand the seed was sown.

IX

Near Anio's stream, I spied a gentle Dove
Perched on an olive branch, and heard her cooing
'Mid new-born blossoms that soft airs were wooing,

While all things present told of joy and love.
But restless Fancy left that olive grove   5
To hail the exploratory Bird renewing
Hope for the few, who, at the world's undoing,
On the great flood were spared to live and move.
O bounteous Heaven! signs true as dove and bough
Brought to the ark are coming evermore,   10
Even though men seek them not, but, while they plough
This sea of life without a visible shore,
Do neither promise ask nor grace implore
In what alone is ours, the vouchsafed Now.

X

FROM THE ALBAN HILLS, LOOKING TOWARDS ROME

Forgive, illustrious Country! these deep sighs,
Heaved less for thy bright plains and hills bestrown
With monuments decayed or overthrown,
For all that tottering stands or prostrate lies,
Than for like scenes in moral vision shown,   5
Ruin perceived for keener sympathies;
Faith crushed, yet proud of weeds, her gaudy crown;
Virtues laid low, and mouldering energies.
Yet why prolong this mournful strain?—Fallen Power,
Thy fortunes, twice exalted, might provoke   10
Verse to glad notes prophetic of the hour
When thou, uprisen, shalt break thy double yoke,
And enter, with prompt aid from the Most High,
On the third stage of thy great destiny.

XI

NEAR THE LAKE OF THRASYMENE

When here with Carthage Rome to conflict came,
An earthquake, mingling with the battle's shock,
Checked not its rage; unfelt the ground did rock,
Sword dropped not, javelin kept its deadly aim.—
Now all is sun-bright peace. Of that day's shame,   5
Or glory, not a vestige seems to endure,
Save in this Rill that took from blood the name

Which yet it bears, sweet stream! as crystal pure.
So may all trace and sign of deeds aloof   10
From the true guidance of humanity,
Thro' Time and Nature's influence, purify
Their spirit; or, unless they for reproof
Or warning serve, thus let them all, on ground
That gave them being, vanish to a sound.

XII

NEAR THE SAME LAKE

For action born, existing to be tried,
Powers manifold we have that intervene
To stir the heart that would too closely screen
Her peace from images to pain allied.
What wonder if at midnight, by the side   5
Of Sanguinetto or broad Thrasymene,
The clang of arms is heard, and phantoms glide,
Unhappy ghosts in troops by moonlight seen;
And singly thine, O vanquished Chief! whose corse,
Unburied, lay hid under heaps of slain: 10
But who is He?—the Conqueror. Would he force
His way to Rome? Ah, no,—round hill and plain
Wandering, he haunts, at fancy's strong command,
This spot—his shadowy death-cup in his hand.

The Cuckoo at Laverna

MAY 25TH, 1837[1]

List—'twas the Cuckoo.—O with what delight
Heard I that voice! and catch it now, though faint,
Far off and faint, and melting into air,
Yet not to be mistaken. Hark again!

---

1   "Laverna is one of the three famous Convents called the three Tuscan Sanctuaries—
    Camaldoli and Vallombrosa are the other two. Laverna was founded by S Francis of
    Assissi, and the Monks are Franciscans.—In the following verses I am much indebted
    to a passage in a Letter of one of Mrs Corbelins relations—which passage was suggested
    by my own Poem, to the Cuckoo. You will see some account of these sanctuaries in the
    Quarto Volume which you will recollect Lady Charlotte Bury sent me—It contains, as well
    as her poem, drawings by her Husband.—
                              transcribed at Munich April 18th [18]37"
    Manuscript note in WW's hand prefixed to poem in DC MS. 141.

Those louder cries give notice that the Bird,   5
Although invisible as Echo's self,
Is wheeling hitherward. Thanks, happy Creature,
For this unthought-of greeting!
                 While allured
From vale to hill, from hill to vale led on,
We have pursued, through various lands, a long   10
And pleasant course; flower after flower has blown,
Embellishing the ground that gave them birth
With aspects novel to my sight; but still
Most fair, most welcome, when they drank the dew
In a sweet fellowship with kinds beloved,   15
For old remembrance sake. And oft—where Spring
Display'd her richest blossoms among files
Of orange-trees bedecked with glowing fruit
Ripe for the hand, or under a thick shade
Of Ilex, or, if better suited to the hour,   20
The lightsome Olive's twinkling canopy—
Oft have I heard the Nightingale and Thrush
Blending as in a common English grove
Their love-songs; but, where'er my feet might roam,
Whate'er assemblages of new and old,   25
Strange and familiar, might beguile the way,
A gratulation from that vagrant Voice
Was wanting;—and most happily till now.

   For see, Laverna! mark the far-famed Pile,
High on the brink of that precipitous rock,   30
Implanted like a Fortress, as in truth
It is, a Christian Fortress, garrisoned
In faith and hope, and dutiful obedience,
By a few Monks, a stern society,
Dead to the world and scorning earth-born joys.   35
Nay—though the hopes that drew, the fears that drove,
St. Francis, far from Man's resort, to abide
Among these sterile heights of Apennine,
Bound him, nor, since he raised yon House, have ceased
To bind his spiritual Progeny, with rules   40
Stringent as flesh can tolerate and live;
His milder Genius (thanks to the good God

That made us) over those severe restraints
Of mind, that dread heart-freezing discipline,
Doth sometimes here predominate, and works   45
By unsought means for gracious purposes;
For earth through heaven, for heaven, by changeful earth,
Illustrated, and mutually endeared.

   Rapt though He were above the power of sense,
Familiarly, yet out of the cleansed heart   50
Of that once sinful Being overflowed
On sun, moon, stars, the nether elements,
And every shape of creature they sustain,
Divine affections; and with beast and bird
(Stilled from afar—such marvel story tells—   55
By casual outbreak of his passionate words,
And from their own pursuits in field or grove
Drawn to his side by look or act of love
Humane, and virtue of his innocent life)
He wont to hold companionship so free,   60
So pure, so fraught with knowledge and delight,
As to be likened in his Followers' minds
To that which our first Parents, ere the fall
From their high state darkened the Earth with fear,
Held with all Kinds in Eden's blissful bowers.   65

   Then question not that, 'mid the austere Band,
Who breathe the air he breathed, tread where he trod,
Some true Partakers of his loving spirit
Do still survive, and, with those gentle hearts
Consorted, Others, in the power, the faith,   70
Of a baptized imagination, prompt
To catch from Nature's humblest monitors
Whate'er they bring of impulses sublime.

   Thus sensitive must be the Monk, though pale
With fasts, with vigils worn, depressed by years,   75
Whom in a sunny glade I chanced to see,
Upon a pine-tree's storm-uprooted trunk,
Seated alone, with forehead sky-ward raised,
Hands clasped above the crucifix he wore
Appended to his bosom, and lips closed   80

By the joint pressure of his musing mood
And habit of his vow. That ancient Man—
Nor haply less the Brother whom I marked,
As we approached the Convent gate, aloft
Looking far forth from his aerial cell,   85
A young Ascetic—Poet, Hero, Sage,
He might have been, Lover belike he was—
If they received into a conscious ear
The notes whose first faint greeting startled me,
Whose sedulous iteration thrilled with joy   90
My heart—may have been moved like me to think,
Ah! not like me who walk in the world's ways,
On the great Prophet, styled the Voice of One
Crying amid the wilderness, and given,
Now that their snows must melt, their herbs and flowers   95
Revive, their obstinate winter pass away,
That awful name to Thee, thee, simple Cuckoo,
Wandering in solitude, and evermore
Foretelling and proclaiming, ere thou leave
This thy last haunt beneath Italian skies   100
To carry thy glad tidings over heights
Still loftier, and to climes more near the Pole.

   Voice of the Desert, fare-thee-well; sweet Bird!
If that substantial title please thee more,
Farewell!—but go thy way, no need hast thou   105
Of a good wish sent after thee; from bower
To bower as green, from sky to sky as clear,
Thee gentle breezes waft—or airs that meet
Thy course and sport around thee softly fan—
Till Night, descending upon hill and vale,   110
Grants to thy mission a brief term of silence,
And folds thy pinions up in blest repose.

XIII

AT THE CONVENT OF CAMALDOLI[1]

Grieve for the Man who hither came bereft,
And seeking consolation from above;

---

1   For WW's note see the notes at the end of this volume.

Nor grieve the less that skill to him was left
To paint this picture of his lady-love:
Can she, a blessed saint, the work approve?   5
And O, good brethren of the cowl, a thing
So fair, to which with peril he must cling,
Destroy in pity, or with care remove.
That bloom—those eyes—can they assist to bind
Thoughts that would stray from Heaven? The dream must cease   10
To be; by Faith, not sight, his soul must live;
Else will the enamoured Monk too surely find
How wide a space can part from inward peace
The most profound repose his cell can give.

XIV

CONTINUED

The world forsaken, all its busy cares
And stirring interests shunned with desperate flight,
All trust abandoned in the healing might
Of virtuous action; all that courage dares,
Labour accomplishes, or patience bears—   5
Those helps rejected, they, whose minds perceive
How subtly works man's weakness, sighs may heave
For such a One beset with cloistral snares.
Father of Mercy! rectify his view,
If with his vows this object ill agree;   10
Shed over it thy grace, and so subdue
Imperious passion in a heart set free;
That earthly love may to herself be true,
Give him a soul that cleaveth unto thee.

XV

AT THE EREMITE OR UPPER CONVENT OF CAMALDOLI [1]

What aim had they, the Pair of Monks, in size

---

1   "In justice to the Benedictines of Camaldoli, by whom strangers are so hospitably enter-
tained, I feel obliged to notice, that I saw among them no other figures at all resembling,
in size and complexion, the two Monks described in this Sonnet. What was their office,
or the motive which brought them to this place of mortification, which they could not have
approached without being carried in this or some other way, a feeling of delicacy pre-
vented me from inquiring. An account has before been given of the hermitage they were

Enormous, dragged, while side by side they sate,
By panting steers up to this convent gate?
How, with empurpled cheeks and pampered eyes,
Dare they confront the lean austerities   5
Of Brethren who, here fixed, on Jesu wait
In sackcloth, and God's anger deprecate
Through all that humbles flesh and mortifies?
Strange contrast!—verily the world of dreams,
Where mingle, as for mockery combined,   10
Things in their very essences at strife,
Shows not a sight incongruous as the extremes
That everywhere, before the thoughtful mind,
Meet on the solid ground of waking life.

At Vallombrosa

> Thick as autumnal leaves that strew the brooks
> In Vallombrosa, where Etrurian shades
> High over-arch'd embower.[1]
>   PARADISE LOST

"Vallombrosa—I longed in thy shadiest wood
To slumber, reclined on the moss-covered floor!"[2]
Fond wish that was granted at last, and the Flood,
That lulled me asleep, bids me listen once more.
Its murmur how soft! as it falls down the steep,   5
Near that Cell—yon sequestered Retreat high in air—
Where our Milton was wont lonely vigils to keep
For converse with God, sought through study and prayer.

The Monks still repeat the tradition with pride,
And its truth who shall doubt? for his Spirit is here;   10
In the cloud-piercing rocks doth her grandeur abide,
In the pines pointing heavenward her beauty austere;
In the flower-besprent meadows his genius we trace
Turned to humbler delights, in which youth might confide,
That would yield him fit help while prefiguring that Place   15

---

about to enter. It was visited by us towards the end of the month of May; yet snow was
lying thick under the pine-trees, within a few yards of the gate." WW
1   For WW's note see the notes at the end of this volume.
2   "See for the two *first lines*, "Stanzas composed in the Simplon Pass." WW (see the poem
by this title, above).

Where, if Sin had not entered, Love never had died.

When with life lengthened out came a desolate time,
And darkness and danger had compassed him round,
With a thought he might flee to these haunts of his prime,
And here once again a kind of shelter be found. 20
And let me believe that when nightly the Muse
Would waft him to Sion, the glorified hill,
Here also, on some favoured height, they would choose
To wander, and drink inspiration at will.

Vallombrosa! of thee I first heard in the page 25
Of that holiest of Bards; and the name for my mind
Had a musical charm, which the winter of age
And the changes it brings had no power to unbind.
And now, ye Miltonian shades! under you
I repose, nor am forced from sweet fancy to part, 30
While your leaves I behold and the brooks they will strew,
And the realised vision is clasped to my heart.

Even so, and unblamed, we rejoice as we may
In Forms that must perish, frail objects of sense;
Unblamed—if the Soul be intent on the day 35
When the Being of Beings shall summon her hence.
For he and he only with wisdom is blest
Who, gathering true pleasures wherever they grow,
Looks up in all places, for joy or for rest,
To the Fountain whence Time and Eternity flow. 40

XVI

AT FLORENCE

Under the shadow of a stately Pile,
The dome of Florence, pensive and alone,
Nor giving heed to aught that passed the while,
I stood, and gazed upon a marble stone,
The laurelled Dante's favourite seat. A throne, 5
In just esteem, it rivals; though no style
Be there of decoration to beguile
The mind, depressed by thought of greatness flown.
As a true man, who long had served the lyre,

I gazed with earnestness, and dared no more.   10
But in his breast the mighty Poet bore
A Patriot's heart, warm with undying fire.
Bold with the thought, in reverence I sate down,
And, for a moment, filled that empty Throne.

XVII

BEFORE THE PICTURE OF THE BAPTIST, BY RAPHAEL, IN THE GALLERY AT FLORENCE

The Baptist might have been ordain'd to cry
Forth from the towers of that huge Pile, wherein
His Father served Jehovah; but how win
Due audience, how for aught but scorn defy
The obstinate pride and wanton revelry   5
Of the Jerusalem below, her sin
And folly, if they with united din
Drown not at once mandate and prophecy?
Therefore the Voice spake from the Desert, thence
To her, as to her opposite in peace,   10
Silence, and holiness, and innocence,
To her and to all Lands its warning sent,
Crying with earnestness that might not cease,
Make straight a highway for the Lord—repent!

XVIII

AT FLORENCE.—FROM MICHAEL ANGELO

Rapt above earth by power of one fair face,
Hers in whose sway alone my heart delights,
I mingle with the blest on those pure heights
Where Man, yet mortal, rarely finds a place.
With Him who made the work that work accords   5
So well, that by its help and through his grace
I raise my thoughts, inform my deeds and words,
Clasping her beauty in my soul's embrace.
Thus, if from two fair eyes mine cannot turn,
I feel how in their presence doth abide   10
Light which to God is both the way and guide;
And, kindling at their lustre, if I burn,

My noble fire emits the joyful ray
That through the realms of glory shines for aye.

XIX

AT FLORENCE.——FROM M. ANGELO

Eternal Lord! eased of a cumbrous load,
And loosened from the world, I turn to Thee;
Shun, like a shattered bark, the storm, and flee
To thy protection for a safe abode.
The crown of thorns, hands pierced upon the tree,   5
The meek, benign, and lacerated face,
To a sincere repentance promise grace,
To the sad soul give hope of pardon free.
With justice mark not Thou, O Light divine,
My fault, nor hear it with thy sacred ear;   10
Neither put forth that way thy arm severe;
Wash with thy blood my sins; thereto incline
More readily the more my years require
Help, and forgiveness speedy and entire.

Among the Ruins of a Convent in the Apennines

Ye trees! whose slender roots entwine
    Altars that piety neglects;
Whose infant arms enclasp the shrine
    Which no devotion now respects;
If not a straggler from the herd   5
Here ruminate, nor shrouded bird,
Chaunting her low-voiced hymn, take pride
In aught that ye would grace or hide—
How sadly is your love misplaced,
Fair trees, your bounty run to waste!   10

And ye, wild Flowers! that no one heeds,
And ye—full often spurned as weeds—
In beauty clothed, or breathing sweetness
From fractured arch and mouldering wall—
Do but more touchingly recal   15
Man's headstrong violence and Time's fleetness,
And make the precincts ye adorn

Appear to sight still more forlorn.

XX

AT BOLOGNA, IN REMEMBRANCE OF THE LATE INSURRECTIONS

Ah why deceive ourselves! by no mere fit
Of sudden passion roused shall men attain
True freedom where for ages they have lain
Bound in a dark abominable pit,
With life's best sinews more and more unknit.   5
Here, there, a banded few who loathe the chain
May rise to break it: effort worse than vain
For thee, O great Italian nation, split
Into those jarring fractions.—Let thy scope
Be one fixed mind for all; thy rights approve   10
To thy own conscience gradually renewed;
Learn to make Time the father of wise Hope;
Then trust thy cause to the arm of Fortitude,
The light of Knowledge, and the warmth of Love.

XXI

CONTINUED

Hard task! exclaim the undisciplined, to lean
On Patience coupled with such slow endeavour,
That long-lived servitude must last for ever.
Perish the grovelling few, who, prest between
Wrongs and the terror of redress, would wean   5
Millions from glorious aims. Our chains to sever
Let us break forth in tempest now or never!—
What, is there then no space for golden mean
And gradual progress?—Twilight leads to day,
And, even within the burning zones of earth,   10
The hastiest sunrise yields a temperate ray;
The softest breeze to fairest flowers gives birth:
Think not that Prudence dwells in dark abodes,
She scans the future with the eye of gods.

XXII

CONCLUDED

As leaves are to the tree whereon they grow
And wither, every human generation
Is to the Being of a mighty nation,
Locked in our world's embrace through weal and woe;
Thought that should teach the zealot to forego   5
Rash schemes, to abjure all selfish agitation,
And seek through noiseless pains and moderation
The unblemished good they only can bestow.
Alas! with most, who weigh futurity
Against time present, passion holds the scales: 10
Hence equal ignorance of both prevails,
And nations sink; or, struggling to be free,
Are doomed to flounder on, like wounded whales
Tossed on the bosom of a stormy sea.

XXIII

IN LOMBARDY

See, where his difficult way that Old Man wins
Bent by a load of Mulberry-leaves!—most hard
Appears *his* lot, to the small Worm's compared,
For whom his toil with early day begins.
Acknowledging no task-master, at will   5
(As if her labour and her ease were twins)
She seems to work, at pleasure to lie still,
And softly sleeps within the thread she spins.
So fare they—the Man serving as her Slave.
Ere long their fates do each to each conform: 10
Both pass into new being,—but the Worm,
Transfigured, sinks into a hopeless grave;
His volant Spirit will, he trusts, ascend
To bliss unbounded, glory without end.

XXIV

AFTER LEAVING ITALY

Fair Land! Thee all men greet with joy; how few,

Whose souls take pride in freedom, virtue, fame,
Part from thee without pity dyed in shame:
I could not—while from Venice we withdrew,
Led on till an Alpine strait confined our view   5
Within its depths, and to the shore we came
Of Lago Morto, dreary sight and name,
Which o'er sad thoughts a sadder colouring threw.
Italia! on the surface of thy spirit,
(Too aptly emblemed by that torpid lake)   10
Shall a few partial breezes only creep?—
Be its depths quickened; what thou dost inherit
Of the world's hopes, dare to fulfil; awake,
Mother of Heroes, from thy death-like sleep!

XXV

CONTINUED

As indignation mastered grief, my tongue
Spake bitter words; words that did ill agree
With those rich stores of Nature's imagery,
And divine Art, that fast to memory clung—
Thy gifts, magnificent Region, ever young   5
In the sun's eye, and in his sister's sight
How beautiful! how worthy to be sung
In strains of rapture, or subdued delight!
I feign not; witness that unwelcome shock
That followed the first sound of German speech,   10
Caught the far-winding barrier Alps among.
In that announcement, greeting seemed to mock
Parting; the casual word had power to reach
My heart, and filled that heart with conflict strong.

[Poems not included in series as first published]

The Pillar of Trajan

Where Towers are crushed, and unforbidden weeds
O'er mutilated arches shed their seeds;
And Temples, doomed to milder change, unfold
A new magnificence that vies with old;
Firm in its pristine majesty hath stood   5
A votive column, spared by fire and flood;—
And, though the passions of Man's fretful race
Have never ceased to eddy round its base,
Not injured more by touch of meddling hands
Than a lone Obelisk, 'mid Nubian sands,   10
Or aught in Syrian deserts left to save,
From death the memory of the Good and Brave.
Historic figures round the shaft embost
Ascend, with lineaments in air not lost:
Still as he turns, the charmed Spectator sees   15
Group winding after group with dream-like ease;
Triumphs in sunbright gratitude displayed,
Or softly stealing into modest shade.
—So, pleased with purple clusters to entwine
Some lofty elm-tree, mounts the daring vine;   20
The woodbine so, with spiral grace, and breathes
Wide-spreading odours from her flowery wreaths.

Borne by the Muse from rills in shepherds' ears
Murmuring but one smooth story for all years,
I gladly commune with the mind and heart   25
Of him who thus survives by classic art,
His actions witness, venerate his mien,
And study Trajan as by Pliny seen;
Behold how fought the Chief whose conquering sword
Stretched far as Earth might own a single lord;   30
In the delight of moral prudence schooled,
How feelingly at home the Sovereign ruled;
Best of the good—in Pagan faith allied
To more than Man, by virtue deified.

Memorial Pillar! 'mid the wrecks of Time   35

Preserve thy charge with confidence sublime—
The exultations, pomps, and cares of Rome,
Whence half the breathing world received its doom;
Things that recoil from language; that, if shewn
By apter pencil, from the light had flown.   40
A Pontiff, Trajan *here* the Gods implores,
There greets an Embassy from Indian shores;
Lo! he harangues his cohorts—*there* the storm
Of battle meets him in authentic form!
Unharnessed, naked, troops of Moorish horse   45
Sweep to the charge; more high, the Dacian force,
To hoof and finger mailed;—yet, high or low,
None bleed, and none lie prostrate but the foe;
In every Roman, through all turns of fate,
Is Roman dignity inviolate;   50
Spirit in Him pre-eminent, who guides,
Supports, adorns, and over all presides;
Distinguished only by inherent State
From honoured Instruments that round him wait;
Rise as he may, his grandeur scorns the test   55
Of outward symbol, nor will deign to rest
On aught by which another is deprest.[1]
—Alas! that One thus disciplined could toil
To enslave whole Nations on their native soil;
So emulous of Macedonian fame,   60
That, when his age was measured with his aim,
He drooped, 'mid else unclouded victories,
And turned his eagles back with deep-drawn sighs:
O weakness of the Great! O folly of the Wise!

Where now the haughty Empire that was spread   65
With such fond hope? her very speech is dead;
Yet glorious Art the sweep of Time defies,
And Trajan still, through various enterprise,
Mounts, in this fine illusion, tow'rd the skies:
Still are we present with the imperial Chief,   70
Nor cease to gaze upon the bold Relief

---

1   "Here and infra; see Forsythe." WW drew details for the poem from Joseph Forsyth's
Remarks on Antiquities, Arts, and Letters during an Excursion [*in*] *Italy in 1802* [*and 1803*]
(London, 1816).

Till Rome, to silent marble unconfined,
Becomes with all her years a vision of the Mind.

Composed on May-morning, 1838[1]

If with old love of you, dear Hills! I share
New love of many a rival image brought
From far, forgive the wanderings of my thought:
Nor art thou wrong'd, sweet May! when I compare
Thy present birth-morn with thy last, so fair,   5
So rich to me in favours. For my lot
Then was, within the famed Egerian Grot
To sit and muse, fanned by its dewy air
Mingling with thy soft breath! That morning, too,
Warblers I heard their joy unbosoming   10
Amid the sunny, shadowy, Colyseum;
Heard them, unchecked by aught of sombre hue,
For victories there won by flower-crowned Spring,
Chant in full choir their innocent TE DEUM.

---

1   In his *Poems* (1845) WW paired this sonnet with "Life with yon Lambs, like day, is just
     begun," published in *Poems of Early and Late Years* (1842). See *Composed on the Same
     Morning*, below.

Sonnets upon the Punishment of Death. In Series.[1]

I

SUGGESTED BY THE VIEW OF LANCASTER CASTLE (ON THE ROAD
FROM THE SOUTH)

This Spot—at once unfolding sight so fair
Of sea and land, with yon grey towers that still
Rise up as if to lord it over air—
Might soothe in human breasts the sense of ill,
Or charm it out of memory; yea, might fill   5
The heart with joy and gratitude to God
For all his bounties upon man bestowed:
Why bears it then the name of "Weeping Hill"?
Thousands, as toward yon old Lancastrian Towers,
A prison's crown, along this way they past   10
For lingering durance or quick death with shame,
From this bare eminence thereon have cast
Their first look—blinded as tears fell in showers
Shed on their chains; and hence that doleful name.

II

Tenderly do we feel by Nature's law
For worst offenders: though the heart will heave
With indignation, deeply moved we grieve,
In after thought, for Him who stood in awe
Neither of God nor man, and only saw,   5
Lost wretch, a horrible device enthroned
On proud temptations, till the victim groaned
Under the steel his hand had dared to draw.
But O, restrain compassion, if its course,
As oft befals, prevent or turn aside   10
Judgments and aims and acts whose higher source
Is sympathy with the unforewarned, who died
Blameless—with them that shuddered o'er his grave,
And all who from the law firm safety crave.

---

1 For the sources of the reading text and the editor's commentary, see *Sonnet Series and
Itinerary Poems, 1820–1845*, ed. Geoffrey Jackson (2004), pp. 865–868, and 878–879.

III

The Roman Consul doomed his sons to die
Who had betrayed their country. The stern word
Afforded (may it through all time afford)
A theme for praise and admiration high.
Upon the surface of humanity   5
He rested not; its depths his mind explored;
He felt; but his parental bosom's lord
Was Duty,—Duty calmed his agony.
And some, we know, when they by wilful act
A single human life have wrongly taken,   10
Pass sentence on themselves, confess the fact,
And, to atone for it, with soul unshaken
Kneel at the feet of Justice, and, for faith
Broken with all mankind, solicit death.

IV

Is *Death*, when evil against good has fought
With such fell mastery that a man may dare
By deeds the blackest purpose to lay bare,—
Is Death, for one to that condition brought,
For him, or any one, the thing that ought   5
To be *most* dreaded? Lawgivers, beware,
Lest, capital pains remitting till ye spare
The murderer, ye, by sanction to that thought
Seemingly given, debase the general mind;
Tempt the vague will tried standards to disown,   10
Nor only palpable restraints unbind,
But upon Honour's head disturb the crown,
Whose absolute rule permits not to withstand
In the weak love of life his least command.

V

Not to the object specially designed,
Howe'er momentous in itself it be,
Good to promote or curb depravity,
Is the wise Legislator's view confined.
His Spirit, when most severe, is oft most kind;   5

As all Authority in earth depends
On Love and Fear, their several powers he blends,
Copying with awe the one Paternal mind.
Uncaught by processes in show humane,
He feels how far the act would derogate   10
From even the humblest functions of the State;
If she, self-shorn of Majesty, ordain
That never more shall hang upon her breath
The last alternative of Life or Death.

VI

Ye brood of conscience—Spectres! that frequent
The bad Man's restless walk, and haunt his bed—
Fiends in your aspect, yet beneficent
In act, as hovering Angels when they spread
Their wings to guard the unconsciousInnocent—   5
Slow be the Statutes of the land to share
A laxity that could not but impair
Your power to punish crime, and so prevent.
And ye, Beliefs! coiled serpent-like about
The adage on all tongues, "Murder will out,"   10
How shall your ancient warnings work for good
In the full might they hitherto have shown,
If for deliberate shedder of man's blood
Survive not Judgment that requires his own?

VII

Before the world had past her time of youth,
While polity and discipline were weak,
The precept eye for eye, and tooth for tooth,
Came forth—a light, though but as of day-break,
Strong as could then be borne. A Master meek   5
Proscribed the spirit fostered by that rule,
Patience *his* law, long-suffering *his* school,
And love the end, which all through peace must seek.
But lamentably do they err who strain
His mandates, given rash impulse to controul   10
And keep vindictive thirstings from the soul,
So far that, if consistent in their scheme,

They must forbid the State to inflict a pain,
Making of social order a mere dream.

VIII

Fit retribution, by the moral code
Determined, lies beyond the State's embrace,
Yet, as she may, for each peculiar case
She plants well-measured terrors in the road
Of wrongful acts. Downward it is and broad,   5
And, the main fear once doomed to banishment,
Far oftener then, bad ushering worse event,
Blood would be spilt that in his dark abode
Crime might lie better hid. And, should the change
Take from the horror due to a foul deed,   10
Pursuit and evidence so far must fail,
And, guilt escaping, passion then might plead
In angry spirits for her old free range,
And the "wild justice of revenge" prevail.

IX

Though to give timely warning and deter
Is one great aim of penalty, extend
Thy mental vision further and ascend
Far higher, else full surely thou shalt err.
What is a State? The wise behold in her   5
A creature born of time, that keeps one eye
Fixed on the Statutes of Eternity,
To which her judgments reverently defer.
Speaking through Law's dispassionate voice the State
Endues her conscience with external life   10
And being, to preclude or quell the strife
Of individual will, to elevate
The grovelling mind, the erring to recal,
And fortify the moral sense of all.

X

Our bodily life, some plead, that life the shrine
Of an immortal spirit, is a gift
So sacred, so informed with light divine,

That no tribunal, though most wise to sift
Deed and intent, should turn the Being adrift   5
Into that world where penitential tear
May not avail, nor prayer have for God's ear
A voice—that world whose veil no hand can lift
For earthly sight. "Eternity and Time,"
They urge, "have interwoven claims and rights   10
Not to be jeopardised through foulest crime:
The sentence rule by mercy's heaven-born lights."
Even so; but measuring not by finite sense
Infinite Power, perfect Intelligence.

XI

Ah, think how one compelled for life to abide
Locked in a dungeon needs must eat the heart
Out of his own humanity, and part
With every hope that mutual cares provide;
And, should a less unnatural doom confide   5
In life-long exile on a savage coast,
Soon the relapsing penitent may boast
Of yet more heinous guilt, with fiercer pride.
Hence thoughtful Mercy, Mercy sage and pure,
Sanctions the forfeiture that Law demands,   10
Leaving the final issue in *His* hands
Whose goodness knows no change, whose love is sure,
Who sees, foresees; who cannot judge amiss,
And wafts at will the contrite soul to bliss.

XII

See the Condemned alone within his cell
And prostrate at some moment when remorse
Stings to the quick, and, with resistless force,
Assaults the pride she strove in vain to quell.
Then mark him, him who could so long rebel,   5
The crime confessed, a kneeling Penitent
Before the Altar, where the Sacrament
Softens his heart, till from his eyes outwell
Tears of salvation. Welcome death! while Heaven
Does in this change exceedingly rejoice;   10

While yet the solemn heed the State hath given
Helps him to meet the last Tribunal's voice
In faith, which fresh offences, were he cast
On old temptations, might for ever blast.

XIII

CONCLUSION

Yes, though He well may tremble at the sound
Of his own voice, who from the judgment-seat
Sends the pale Convict to his last retreat
In death; though Listeners shudder all around,
They know the dread requital's source profound;   5
Nor is, they feel, its wisdom obsolete—
(Would that it were!) the sacrifice unmeet
For Christian Faith. But hopeful signs abound;
The social rights of man breathe purer air;
Religion deepens her preventive care;   10
Then, moved by needless fear of past abuse,
Strike not from Law's firm hand that awful rod,
But leave it thence to drop for lack of use:
Oh, speed the blessed hour, Almighty God!

XIV

APOLOGY

The formal World relaxes her cold chain
For One who speaks in numbers; ampler scope
His utterance finds; and, conscious of the gain,
Imagination works with bolder hope
The cause of grateful reason to sustain;   5
And, serving Truth, the heart more strongly beats
Against all barriers which his labour meets
In lofty place, or humble Life's domain.
Enough;—before us lay a painful road,
And guidance have I sought in duteous love   10
From Wisdom's heavenly Father. Hence hath flowed
Patience, with trust that, whatsoe'er the way
Each takes in this high matter, all may move
Cheered with the prospect of a brighter day.

Sonnets Dedicated to Liberty and Order[1]

I

COMPOSED AFTER READING A NEWSPAPER OF THE DAY

"People! your chains are severing link by link;
Soon shall the Rich be levelled down—the Poor
Meet them half way." Vain boast! for These, the more
They thus would rise, must low and lower sink
Till, by repentance stung, they fear to think;   5
While all lie prostrate, save the tyrant few
Bent in quick turns each other to undo,
And mix the poison, they themselves must drink.
Mistrust thyself, vain Country! cease to cry,
"Knowledge will save me from the threatened woe."   10
For, if than other rash ones more thou know,
Yet on presumptuous wing as far would fly
Above thy knowledge as they dared to go,
Thou wilt provoke a heavier penalty.

II

UPON THE LATE GENERAL FAST. MARCH, 1832

Reluctant call it was; the rite delayed;
And in the Senate some there were who doffed
The last of their humanity, and scoffed
At providential judgments, undismayed
By their own daring. But the People prayed   5
As with one voice; their flinty heart grew soft
With penitential sorrow, and aloft
Their spirit mounted, crying, "God us aid!"
Oh that with aspirations more intense,
Chastised by self-abasement more profound,   10
This People, once so happy, so renowned
For liberty, would seek from God defence
Against far heavier ill, the pestilence

[handwritten annotation: not what you thought as a young man, what brought change; thought as a young revolution necessary]

---

1 WW's notes are those published with the series in *Poems*, 1845. For the sources of the
reading text and the editor's commentary, see *Sonnet Series and Itinerary Poems, 1820–
1845*, ed. Geoffrey Jackson (2004), pp. 899–903, and 914–917.

Of revolution, impiously unbound!

III

Said Secrecy to Cowardice and Fraud,
Falsehood and Treachery, in close council met,
Deep under ground, in Pluto's cabinet,
"The frost of England's pride will soon be thawed;
"Hooded the open brow that overawed   5
"Our schemes; the faith and honour, never yet
"By us with hope encountered, be upset;—
"For once I burst my bands, and cry, applaud!"
Then whispered she, "The Bill is carrying out!"
They heard, and, starting up, the Brood of Night   10
Clapped hands, and shook with glee their matted locks;
All Powers and Places that abhor the light
Joined in the transport, echoed back their shout,
Hurrah for ———, hugging his Ballot-box!

IV

Blest Statesman He, whose Mind's unselfish will
Leaves him at ease among grand thoughts; whose eye
Sees that, apart from Magnanimity,
Wisdom exists not; nor the humbler skill
Of Prudence, disentangling good and ill   5
With patient care. What tho' assaults run high,
They daunt not him who holds his ministry,
Resolute, at all hazards, to fulfil
Its duties;—prompt to move, but firm to wait,—
Knowing, things rashly sought are rarely found;   10
That, for the functions of an ancient State—
Strong by her charters, free because imbound,
Servant of Providence, not slave of Fate—
Perilous is sweeping change, all chance unsound.[1]

---

1   "'All change is perilous, and all chance unsound.' SPENSER." WW

V

IN ALLUSION TO VARIOUS RECENT HISTORIES AND NOTICES
OF THE FRENCH REVOLUTION

Portentous change when History can appear
As the cool Advocate of foul device;
Reckless audacity extol, and jeer
At consciences perplexed with scruples nice!
They who bewail not, must abhor, the sneer   5
Born of Conceit, Power's blind Idolater;
Or haply sprung from vaunting Cowardice
Betrayed by mockery of holy fear.
Hath it not long been said the wrath of Man
Works not the righteousness of God? Oh bend,   10
Bend, ye Perverse! to judgments from on High,
Laws that lay under Heaven's perpetual ban
All principles of action that transcend
The sacred limits of humanity.

VI

CONTINUED

Who ponders National events shall find
An awful balancing of loss and gain,
Joy based on sorrow, good with ill combined,
And proud deliverance issuing out of pain
And direful throes; as if the All-ruling Mind,   5
With whose perfection it consists to ordain
Volcanic burst, earthquake, and hurricane,
Dealt in like sort with feeble human kind
By laws immutable. But woe for him
Who thus deceived shall lend an eager hand   10
To social havoc. Is not Conscience ours,
And Truth, whose eye guilt only can make dim;
And Will, whose office, by divine command,
Is to control and check disordered Powers?

VII

CONCLUDED

Long-favoured England! be not thou misled
By monstrous theories of alien growth,
Lest alien frenzy seize thee, waxing wroth,
Self-smitten till thy garments reek dyed red
With thy own blood, which tears in torrents shed   5
Fail to wash out, tears flowing ere thy troth
Be plighted, not to ease but sullen sloth,
Or wan despair—the ghost of false hope fled
Into a shameful grave. Among thy youth,
My Country! if such warning be held dear,   10
Then shall a Veteran's heart be thrilled with joy,
One who would gather from eternal truth,
For time and season, rules that work to cheer—
Not scourge, to save the People—not destroy

VIII

Men of the Western World! in Fate's dark book[1]
Whence these opprobrious leaves of dire portent?
Think ye your British Ancestors forsook
Their native Land, for outrage provident;
From unsubmissive necks the bridle shook   5
To give, in their Descendants, freer vent
And wider range to passions turbulent,
To mutual tyranny a deadlier look?
Nay, said a voice, soft as the south wind's breath,
Dive through the stormy surface of the flood   10
To the great current flowing underneath;
Explore the countless springs of silent good;
So shall the truth be better understood,
And thy grieved Spirit brighten strong in faith.

---

1   "These lines were written several years ago, when reports prevailed of cruelties committed in many parts of America, by men making a law of their own passions. A far more formidable, as being a more deliberate mischief, has appeared among those States which have lately broken faith with the public creditor in a manner so infamous. I cannot, however, but look at both evils under a similar relation to inherent good, and hope that the time is not distant when our brethren of the West will wipe off this stain from their name and nation." WW

IX

TO THE PENNSYLVANIANS

Days undefiled by luxury or sloth,
Firm self-denial, manners grave and staid,
Rights equal, laws with cheerfulness obeyed,
Words that require no sanction from an oath,
And simple honesty a common growth—   5
This high repute, with bounteous Nature's aid,
Won confidence, now ruthlessly betrayed
At will, your power the measure of your troth!—
All who revere the memory of Penn
Grieve for the land on whose wild woods his name   10
Was fondly grafted with a virtuous aim,
Renounced, abandoned by degenerate Men
For state-dishonour black as ever came
To upper air from Mammon's loathsome den.

X

AT BOLOGNA, IN REMEMBRANCE OF THE LATE INSURRECTIONS, 1831

I

Ah why deceive ourselves! by no mere fit
Of sudden passion roused shall men attain
True freedom where for ages they have lain
Bound in a dark abominable pit,
With life's best sinews more and more unknit.   5
Here, there, a banded few who loathe the chain
May rise to break it: effort worse than vain
For thee, O great Italian nation, split
Into those jarring fractions.—Let thy scope
Be one fixed mind for all; thy rights approve   10
To thy own conscience gradually renewed;
Learn to make Time the father of wise Hope;
Then trust thy cause to the arm of Fortitude,
The light of Knowledge, and the warmth of Love.

XI

CONTINUED

II

Hard task! exclaim the undisciplined, to lean
On Patience coupled with such slow endeavour,
That long-lived servitude must last for ever.
Perish the grovelling few, who, prest between
Wrongs and the terror of redress, would wean   5
Millions from glorious aims. Our chains to sever
Let us break forth in tempest now or never!—
What, is there then no space for golden mean
And gradual progress?—Twilight leads to day,
And, even within the burning zones of earth,   10
The hastiest sunrise yields a temperate ray;
The softest breeze to fairest flowers gives birth:
Think not that Prudence dwells in dark abodes,
She scans the future with the eye of gods.

XII

CONCLUDED

III

As leaves are to the tree whereon they grow
And wither, every human generation
Is to the Being of a mighty nation,
Locked in our world's embrace through weal and woe;
Thought that should teach the zealot to forego   5
Rash schemes, to abjure all selfish agitation,
And seek through noiseless pains and moderation
The unblemished good they only can bestow.
Alas! with most, who weigh futurity
Against time present, passion holds the scales: 10
Hence equal ignorance of both prevails,
And nations sink; or, struggling to be free,
Are doomed to flounder on, like wounded whales
Tossed on the bosom of a stormy sea.

XIII

Young England—what is then become of Old,
Of dear Old England? Think they she is dead,
Dead to the very name? Presumption fed
On empty air! That name will keep its hold
In the true filial bosom's inmost fold   5
For ever.—The Spirit of Alfred, at the head
Of all who for her rights watch'd, toil'd and bled,
Knows that this prophecy is not too bold.
What—how! shall she submit in will and deed
To Beardless Boys—an imitative race,   10
The *servum pecus* of a Gallic breed?
Dear Mother! if thou *must* thy steps retrace,
Go where at least meek Innocency dwells;
Let Babes and Sucklings be thy oracles.

XIV

Feel for the wrongs to universal ken
Daily exposed, woe that unshrouded lies;
And seek the Sufferer in his darkest den,
Whether conducted to the spot by sighs
And moanings, or he dwells (as if the wren   5
Taught him concealment) hidden from all eyes
In silence and the awful modesties
Of sorrow;—feel for all, as brother Men!
Rest not in hope want's icy chain to to thaw
By casual boons and formal charities;   10
Learn to be just, just through impartial law;
Far as ye may, erect and equalise;
And what ye cannot reach by statute, draw
Each from his fountain of self-sacrifice!

Last Poems (1821–1850)[1]

Decay of Piety

Oft have I seen, ere Time had ploughed my cheek,
Matrons and Sires—who, punctual to the call
Of their loved Church, on Fast or Festival
Through the long year the House of Prayer would seek:
By Christmas snows, by visitation bleak   5
Of Easter winds, unscared, from Hut or Hall
They came to lowly bench or sculptured Stall,
But with one fervour of devotion meek.
I see the places where they once were known,
And ask, surrounded even by kneeling crowds,   10
Is ancient Piety for ever flown?
Alas! even then they seemed like fleecy clouds
That, struggling through the western sky, have won
Their pensive light from a departed sun!

"Not Love, nor War, nor the tumultuous swell"

Not Love, nor War, nor the tumultuous swell
Of civil conflict, nor the wrecks of change,
Nor Duty struggling with afflictions strange,
Not these alone inspire the tuneful shell;
But where untroubled peace and concord dwell,   5
There also is the Muse not loth to range,
Watching the blue smoke of the elmy grange,
Skyward ascending from the twilight dell.
Meek aspirations please her, lone endeavour,
And sage content, and placid melancholy;   10
She loves to gaze upon a crystal river,
Diaphanous, because it travels slowly;
Soft is the music that would charm for ever;
The flower of sweetest smell is shy and lowly.

---

1   For the sources of the reading text and the editor's commentary, see *Last Poems, 1821–1850*, ed. Jared Curtis, with Apryl Lee Denny and Jill Heydt-Stevenson, associate editors (1999).

A Parsonage in Oxfordshire[1]

Where holy ground begins—unhallowed ends,
Is marked by no distinguishable line;
The turf unites—the pathways intertwine;
And, wheresoe'er the stealing footstep tends,
Garden, and that Domain where Kindred, Friends,   5
And Neighbours rest together, here confound
Their several features—mingled like the sound
Of many waters, or as evening blends
With shady night. Soft airs, from shrub and flower,
Waft fragrant greetings to each silent grave;   10
Meanwhile between those Poplars, as they wave
Their lofty summits, comes and goes a sky
Bright as the glimpses of Eternity,
To Saints accorded in their mortal hour.

Recollection of the Portrait of King Henry Eighth, Trinity Lodge, Cambridge

The imperial Stature, the colossal stride,
Are yet before me; yet do I behold
The broad full visage, chest of amplest mould,
The vestments 'broidered with barbaric pride:
And lo! a poniard, at the Monarch's side,   5
Hangs ready to be grasped in sympathy
With the keen threatenings of that fulgent eye,
Below the white-rimmed bonnet, far descried.
Who trembles now at thy capricious mood?
Mid those surrounding worthies, haughty King!   10
We rather think, with grateful mind sedate,
How Providence educeth, from the spring
Of lawless will, unlooked-for streams of good,
Which neither force shall check, nor time abate.

[Translation of the Sestet of a Sonnet by Tasso]

Camoëns, he the accomplished and the good,
Gave to thy Fame a more illustrious flight
Than that brave vessel though she sailed so far,

---

1 WW included this sonnet in his note to *Pastoral Character*, sonnet III.xi. of *Ecclesiastical Sketches* in 1822.

Through him her course along the austral flood
Is known to all beneath the polar star   5
Through him the antipodes in thy name delight.

"A volant Tribe of Bards on earth are found"

A volant Tribe of Bards on earth are found,
Who, while the flattering Zephyrs round them play,
On "coignes of vantage" hang their nests of clay;
How quickly from that aery hold unbound,
Dust for oblivion! To the solid ground   5
Of nature trusts the Mind that builds for aye;
Convinced that there, there only, she can lay
Secure foundations. As the year runs round,
Apart she toils within the chosen ring;
While the stars shine, or while day's purple eye   10
Is gently closing with the flowers of spring;
Where even the motion of an Angel's wing
Would interrupt the intense tranquillity
Of silent hills, and more than silent sky.

"Queen and Negress chaste and fair!"

Queen and Negress chaste and fair!
   Christophe now is laid asleep
Seated in a British Chair
State in humbler manner keep
   Shine for Clarkson's pure delight   5
   Negro Princess, ebon bright!
Lay thy Diadem apart
   Pomp has been a sad Deceiver
Through thy Champion's faithful heart
Joy be poured, and thou the Giver   10
   Thou that mak'st a day of night
   Sable Princess, ebon bright!
Let not "Wilby's" holy shade
   Interpose at Envy's call,
Hayti's shining Queen was made   15
To illumine Playford Hall
   Bless it then with constant light
   Negress excellently bright!

[Epigrams on Byron's *Cain*]

i. *"Critics, right honourable Bard! decree"*

Critics, right honourable Bard! decree
Laurels to some, a nightshade wreath to thee,
Whose Muse a sure though late revenge hath ta'en
Of harmless Abel's death by murdering Cain.

ii.
On Cain a Mystery dedicated to Sir Walter Scott

A German Haggis—from Receipt
Of him who cook'd "The death of Abel"
And sent "warm–reeking rich" and sweet
From Venice to Sir Walter's table.

iii.
After reading a luscious scene of the above—
The Wonder explained

What! Adam's eldest Son in this sweet strain!
Yes—did you never hear of Sugar-Cain?

iv.
On a Nursery piece of the same, by a Scottish Bard—

Dont wake little Enoch,
Or he'll give you a wee knock!
For the pretty sweet Lad
As he lies in his Cradle
Is more like to his Dad   5
Than a Spoon to a Ladle.

"Thus far I write to please my Friend"

Thus far I write to please my Friend;
And now to please myself I end.

"By Moscow self–devoted to a blaze"

By Moscow self–devoted to a blaze
Of dreadful sacrifice; by Russian blood

Lavished in fight with desperate hardihood;
The unfeeling Elements no claim shall raise
To rob our Human–nature of just praise   5
For what she did and suffered. Pledges sure
Of a deliverance absolute and pure
She gave, if Faith might tread the beaten ways
Of Providence. But now did the Most High
Exalt his still small Voice;—to quell that Host   10
Gathered his Power, a manifest Ally;
He whose heaped waves confounded the proud boast
Of Pharaoh, said to Famine, Snow, and Frost,
Finish the strife by deadliest Victory!

"These Vales were saddened with no common gloom"

In the Burial-ground of this Church are deposited the Remains of Jemima A.
D. second daughter of Sir Egerton Brydges Bart—of Lee Priory, Kent—who
departed this life at Rydal May 25th 1822 Ag: 28 years. This memorial is
erected by her afflicted husband Edw[d] Quillinan

These Vales were saddened with no common gloom
When good Jemima perished in her bloom;
When (such the awful will of heaven) she died   *genuinely affecting*
By flames breathed on her from her own fire-side.
On Earth we dimly see, and but in part   5
We know, yet Faith sustains the sorrowing heart;
And she, the pure, the patient and the meek,
Might have fit Epitaph could feelings speak;
If words could tell and monuments record,
How treasures lost are inwardly deplored,   10
No name by grief's fond eloquence adorn'd,
More than Jemima's would be praised and mourn'd;
The tender virtues of her blameless life,
Bright in the Daughter, brighter in the Wife,
And in the cheerful Mother brightest shone: 15
That light hath past away—the will of God be done!

To the Lady —————,

ON SEEING THE FOUNDATION PREPARING FOR THE ERECTION
OF ————— CHAPEL, WESTMORELAND [1]

Blest is this Isle—our native Land;
Where battlement and moated gate
Are objects only for the hand
Of hoary Time to decorate;
Where shady hamlet, town that breathes   5
Its busy smoke in social wreaths,
No rampart's stern defence require,
Nought but the heaven-directed Spire,
And steeple Tower (with pealing bells
Far heard)—our only Citadels.   10

O Lady! from a noble line
Of Chieftains sprung, who stoutly bore
The spear, yet gave to works divine
A bounteous help in days of yore,
(As records mouldering in the Dell   15
Of Nightshade[2] haply yet may tell)
Thee kindred aspirations moved
To build, within a Vale beloved,
For Him upon whose high behests
All peace depends, all safety rests.   20

Well may the Villagers rejoice!
Nor heat, nor cold, nor weary ways,
Will be a hindrance to the voice
That would unite in prayer and praise;
More duly shall wild-wandering Youth   25
Receive the curb of sacred truth,
Shall tottering Age, bent earthward, hear
The Promise, with uplifted ear;
And all shall welcome the new ray
Imparted to their Sabbath-day.   30

---

1   In 1840 the title became *To the Lady Fleming, On Seeing the Foundation Preparing for the Erection of Rydal Chapel, Westmoreland.*
2   "Beckangs Ghyll—or the Vale of Nightshade—in which stands St. Mary's Abbey, in Low Furness." WW

Even Strangers, slackening here their pace,
Shall hail this work of pious care,
Lifting its front with modest grace
To make a fair recess more fair;
And to exalt the passing hour;   35
Or soothe it, with a healing power
Drawn from the Sacrifice fulfilled,
Before this rugged soil was tilled,
Or human habitation rose
To interrupt the deep repose!   40

Nor yet the corner stone is laid
With solemn rite; but Fancy sees
The tower time-stricken, and in shade
Embosomed of coeval trees;
Hears, o'er the lake, the warning clock   45
As it shall sound with gentle shock
At evening, when the ground beneath
Is ruffled o'er with cells of Death;
Where happy Generations lie,
Here tutored for Eternity.   50

Lives there a Man whose sole delights
Are trivial pomp and city noise,
Hardening a heart that loathes or slights
What every natural heart enjoys?
Who never caught a noon-tide dream   55
From murmur of a running stream;
Could strip, for aught the prospect yields
To him, their verdure from the fields;
And take the radiance from the clouds
In which the Sun his setting shrouds.   60

A Soul so pitiably forlorn,
If such do on this earth abide,
May season apathy with scorn,
May turn indifference to pride,
And still be not unblest—compared   65
With him who grovels, self-debarred
From all that lies within the scope
Of holy faith and Christian hope;

Or, shipwrecked, kindles on the coast
False fires, that others may be lost.   70

Alas! that such perverted zeal
Should spread on Britain's favoured ground!
That public order, private weal,
Should e'er have felt or feared a wound
From champions of the desperate law   75
Which from their own blind hearts they draw;
Who tempt their reason to deny
God, whom their passions dare defy,
And boast that *they alone* are free
Who reach this dire extremity!   80

But turn we from these "bold bad" men;
The way, mild Lady! that hath led
Down to their "dark opprobrious den,"
Is all too rough for Thee to tread.
Softly as morning vapours glide   85
Through Mosedale-cove from Carrock's side,
Should move the tenour of *his* song
Who means to Charity no wrong;
Whose offering gladly would accord
With this day's work, in thought and word.   90

Heaven prosper it! may peace, and love,
And hope, and consolation, fall,
Through its meek influence, from above,
And penetrate the hearts of all;
All who, around the hallowed Fane,   95
Shall sojourn in this fair domain;
Grateful to Thee, while service pure,
And ancient ordinance, shall endure,
For opportunity bestowed
To kneel together, and adore their God.   100

On the Same Occasion

Oh! gather whencesoe'er ye safely may
The help which slackening Piety requires;
Nor deem that he perforce must go astray
Who treads upon the footmarks of his Sires.

Our churches, invariably perhaps, stand east and west, but *why* is by few persons *exactly* known; nor, that the degree of deviation from due east often noticeable in the ancient ones was determined, in each particular case, by the point in the horizon, at which the sun rose upon the day of the Saint to whom the church was dedicated. These observances of our Ancestors, and the causes of them, are the subject of the following stanzas.

When in the antique age of bow and spear
And feudal rapine clothed with iron mail,
Came Ministers of peace, intent to rear
The mother Church in yon sequestered vale;

Then, to her Patron Saint a previous rite   5
Resounded with deep swell and solemn close,
Through unremitting vigils of the night,
Till from his couch the wished-for Sun uprose.

He rose, and straight—as by divine command,
They who had waited for that sign to trace   10
Their work's foundation, gave with careful hand
To the high Altar its determined place;

Mindful of Him who in the Orient born
There lived, and on the cross his life resigned,
And who, from out the regions of the Morn,   15
Issuing in pomp, shall come to judge Mankind.

So taught *their* creed;—nor failed the eastern sky,
Mid these more awful feelings, to infuse
The sweet and natural hopes that shall not die
Long as the Sun his gladsome course renews.   20

For us hath such prelusive vigil ceased;
Yet still we plant, like men of elder days,
Our Christian Altar faithful to the East,
Whence the tall window drinks the morning rays;

That obvious emblem giving to the eye   25
Of meek devotion, which erewhile it gave,
That symbol of the dayspring from on high,
Triumphant o'er the darkness of the grave.

Memory

A pen—to register; a key—
That winds through secret wards;
Are well assigned to Memory
By allegoric Bards.

As aptly, also, might be given   5
A Pencil to her hand;
That, softening objects, sometimes even
Outstrips the heart's demand;

That smooths foregone distress, the lines
Of lingering care subdues,   10
Long-vanished happiness refines,
And clothes in brighter hues:

Yet, like a tool of Fancy, works
Those Spectres to dilate
That startle Conscience, as she lurks   15
Within her lonely seat.

O! that our lives, which flee so fast,
In purity were such,
That not an image of the past
Should fear that pencil's touch!   20

Retirement then might hourly look
Upon a soothing scene,
Age steal to his allotted nook,
Contented and serene;

With heart as calm as Lakes that sleep,   25
In frosty moonlight glistening;
Or mountain Rivers, where they creep
Along a channel smooth and deep,
To their own far-off murmurs listening.

"First Floweret of the year is that which shows"

First Floweret of the year is that which shows
Its rival whiteness mid surrounding snows;
To guide the shining company of heaven,

Brightest as first appears the star of Even;
Upon imperial brows the richest gem   5
Stands ever foremost in the diadem;
How, then, could mortal so unfit engage
To take his station in this leading page,
For others marshal with his *pen* the way
Which shall be trod in many a future day!   10
Why was not some fair Lady call'd to write
Dear words—for Memory characters of light—
Lines which enraptur'd Fancy might explore
And half create her image?—but no more;
Strangers! forgive the deed, an unsought task,   15
For what you look on, Friendship deigned to ask.

"How rich that forehead's calm expanse!"

How rich that forehead's calm expanse!
How bright that Heaven-directed glance!
—Waft her to Glory, wingèd Powers,
Ere Sorrow be renewed,
And intercourse with mortal hours   5
Bring back a humbler mood!
So looked Cecilia when she drew
An Angel from his station;
So looked—not ceasing to pursue
Her tuneful adoration!   10

But hand and voice alike are still;
No sound *here* sweeps away the will
That gave it birth;—in service meek
One upright arm sustains the cheek,
And one across the bosom lies—   15
That rose, and now forgets to rise,
Subdued by breathless harmonies
Of meditative feeling;
Mute strains from worlds beyond the skies,
Through the pure light of female eyes   20
Their sanctity revealing!

A Flower Garden

Tell me, ye Zephyrs! that unfold,
While fluttering o'er this gay Recess,
Pinions that fanned the teeming mould
Of Eden's blissful wilderness,
Did only softly-stealing Hours   5
There close the peaceful lives of flowers?

Say, when the *moving* Creatures saw
All kinds commingled without fear,
Prevailed a like indulgent law
For the still Growths that prosper here?   10
Did wanton Fawn and Kid forbear
The half-blown Rose, the Lily spare?

Or peeped they often from their beds
And prematurely disappeared,
Devoured like pleasure ere it spreads   15
A bosom to the Sun endeared?
If such their harsh untimely doom,
It falls not *here* on bud or bloom.

All Summer long the happy Eve
Of this fair Spot her flowers may bind,   20
Nor e'er, with ruffled fancy, grieve,
From the next glance she casts, to find
That love for little Things by Fate
Is rendered vain as love for great.

Yet, where the guardian Fence is wound,   25
So subtly is the eye beguiled
It sees not nor suspects a Bound,
No more than in some forest wild;
Free as the light in semblance—crost
Only by art in nature lost.   30

And, though the jealous turf refuse
By random footsteps to be prest,
And feeds on never-sullied dews,
Ye, gentle breezes from the West,
With all the ministers of Hope,   35

Are tempted to this sunny slope!

And hither throngs of Birds resort;
Some, inmates lodged in shady nests,
Some, perched on stems of stately port
That nod to welcome transient guests;   40
While Hare and Leveret, seen at play,
Appear not more shut out than they.

Apt emblem (for reproof of pride)
This delicate Enclosure shows
Of modest kindness, that would hide   45
The firm protection she bestows;
Of manners, like its viewless fence,
Ensuring peace to innocence.

Thus spake the moral Muse—her wing
Abruptly spreading to depart,   50
She left that farewell offering,
Memento for some docile heart;
That may respect the good old Age
When Fancy was Truth's willing Page;
And Truth would skim the flowery glade,   55
Though entering but as Fancy's Shade.

To ———

Let other Bards of Angels sing,[1]
    Bright Suns without a spot;
But thou art no such perfect Thing;
    Rejoice that thou art not!

Such if thou wert in all men's view,   5
    A universal show,
What would my Fancy have to do,
    My Feelings to bestow?

The world denies that Thou art fair;
    So, Mary, let it be   10
If nought in loveliness compare
    With what thou art to me.

---

1   WW's manuscript note identifies Mary Wordsworth as the addressee.

True beauty dwells in deep retreats,
   Whose veil is unremoved
Till heart with heart in concord beats,   15
   And the Lover is beloved.

To ——

Look at the fate of summer Flowers,[1]
Which blow at daybreak, droop ere even-song;
And, grieved for their brief date, confess that ours,
Measured by what we are and ought to be,
Measured by all that trembling we foresee,   5
   Is not so long!

If human Life do pass away,
Perishing yet more swiftly than the Flower,
Whose frail existence is but of a day;
What space hath Virgin's Beauty to disclose   10
Her sweets, and triumph o'er the breathing Rose?
   Not even an hour!

The deepest grove whose foliage hid
The happiest Lovers Arcady might boast,
Could not the entrance of this thought forbid: 15
O be thou wise as they, soul-gifted Maid!
Nor rate too high what must so quickly fade,
   So soon be lost.

Then shall Love teach some virtuous Youth
"To draw out of the Object of his eyes,"   20
The whilst on Thee they gaze in simple truth,
Hues more exalted, "a refinèd Form,"
That dreads not age, nor suffers from the worm,
   And never dies.

To Rotha Q ——[2]

Rotha, my Spiritual Child! this head was grey
When at the sacred Font for Thee I stood;

---

1 WW's manuscript note states that he addressed the poem to "dear friends" who were given
    to attaching undue importance to "personal beauty."
2 Addressed to Rotha Quillinan, the daughter of WW's son-in-law Edward and his first wife.
    She was named after the mountain stream of l. 9.

Pledged till thou reach the verge of womanhood,
And shalt become thy own sufficient stay:
Too late, I feel, sweet Orphan! was the day   5
For stedfast hope the contract to fulfil;
Yet shall my blessing hover o'er thee still,
Embodied in the music of this Lay,
Breathed forth beside the peaceful mountain Stream
Whose murmur soothed thy languid Mother's ear   10
After her throes, this Stream of name more dear
Since thou dost bear it,—a memorial theme
For others; for thy future self a spell
To summon fancies out of Time's dark cell.

Composed among the Ruins of a Castle in North Wales

Through shattered galleries, 'mid roofless halls,
Wandering with timid footstep oft betrayed,
The Stranger sighs, nor scruples to upbraid
Old Time, though He, gentlest among the Thralls
Of Destiny, upon these wounds hath laid   5
His lenient touches, soft as light that falls,
From the wan Moon, upon the Towers and Walls,
Light deepening the profoundest sleep of shade.
Relic of Kings! Wreck of forgotten Wars,
To winds abandoned and the prying Stars,   10
Time *loves* Thee! at his call the Seasons twine
Luxuriant wreaths around thy forehead hoar;
And, though past pomp no changes can restore,
A soothing recompense, his gift, is Thine!

To the Lady E. B. and the Hon. Miss P

COMPOSED IN THE GROUNDS OF PLASS NEWIDD, NEAR LLANGOLLIN, 1824

A Stream, to mingle with your favourite Dee,
Along the Vale of Meditation flows;
So styled by those fierce Britons, pleased to see
In Nature's face the expression of repose;
Or haply there some pious Hermit chose   5
To live and die, the peace of Heaven his aim;
To whom the wild sequestered region owes,
At this late day, its sanctifying name.

GLYN CAFAILLGAROCH, in the Cambrian tongue,
In ours the *Vale of Friendship*, let *this* spot   10
Be named; where, faithful to a low-roofed Cot,
On Deva's banks, ye have abode so long;
Sisters in love—a love allowed to climb,
Even on this Earth, above the reach of Time!

To the Torrent at the Devil's Bridge, North Wales

How art thou named? In search of what strange land
From what huge height, descending? Can such force
Of waters issue from a British source,
Or hath not Pindus fed Thee, where the band
Of Patriots scoop their freedom out, with hand   5
Desperate as thine? Or come the incessant shocks
From that young Stream, that smites the throbbing rocks
Of Viamala? There I seem to stand,
As in Life's Morn; permitted to behold,
From the dread chasm, woods climbing above woods   10
In pomp that fades not, everlasting snows,
And skies that ne'er relinquish their repose;
Such power possess the Family of floods
Over the minds of Poets, young or old!

To ———

O dearer far than light and life are dear,[1]
Full oft our human foresight I deplore;
Trembling, through my unworthiness, with fear
That friends, by death disjoined, may meet no more!

Misgivings, hard to vanquish or control,   5
Mix with the day, and cross the hour of rest;
While all the future, for thy purer soul,
With "sober certainties" of love is blest.

If a faint sigh, not meant for human ear,
Tell that these words thy humbleness offend,   10
Cherish me still—else faltering in the rear
Of a steep march; uphold me to the end.

---

1 Addressed to Thomas Hutchinson, brother of Mary Wordsworth.

Peace settles where the Intellect is meek,
And Love is dutiful in thought and deed;
Through Thee communion with that Love I seek;   15
The faith Heaven strengthens where *he* moulds the creed.

The Contrast

Within her gilded cage confined,
I saw a dazzling Belle,
A Parrot of that famous kind
Whose name is Non-pareil.

Like beads of glossy jet her eyes;   5
And, smoothed by Nature's skill,
With pearl or gleaming agate vies
Her finely-curvèd bill.

Her plumy Mantle's living hues
In mass opposed to mass,   10
Outshine the splendour that imbues
The robes of pictured glass.

And, sooth to say, an apter Mate
Did never tempt the choice
Of feathered Thing most delicate   15
In figure and in voice.

But, exiled from Australian Bowers,
And singleness her lot,
She trills her song with tutored powers,
Or mocks each casual note.   20

No more of pity for regrets
With which she may have striven!
Now but in wantonness she frets,
Or spite, if cause be given;

Arch, volatile, a sportive Bird   25
By social glee inspired;
Ambitious to be seen or heard,
And pleased to be admired!

———————

This moss-lined shed, green, soft, and dry,
Harbours a self-contented Wren,   30
Not shunning man's abode, though shy,
Almost as thought itself, of human ken.

Strange places, coverts unendeared
She never tried; the very nest
In which this Child of Spring was reared,   35
Is warmed, thro' winter, by her feathery breast.

To the bleak winds she sometimes gives
A slender unexpected strain;
That tells the Hermitess still lives,
Though she appear not, and be sought in vain.   40

Say, Dora! tell me by yon placid Moon,
If called to choose between the favoured pair,
Which would you be,—the Bird of the Saloon,
By Lady fingers tended with nice care,
Caressed, applauded, upon dainties fed,   45
Or Nature's DARKLING of this mossy Shed?

The Infant M——— M———[1]

Unquiet Childhood here by special grace
Forgets her nature, opening like a flower
That neither feeds nor wastes its vital power
In painful struggles. Months each other chase,
And nought untunes that Infant's voice; a trace   5
Of fretful temper sullies not her cheek;
Prompt, lively, self-sufficing, yet so meek
That one enrapt with gazing on her face,
(Which even the placid innocence of Death
Could scarcely make more placid, Heaven more bright,)   10
Might learn to picture, for the eye of faith,
The Virgin, as she shone with kindred light;
A Nursling couched upon her Mother's knee,
Beneath some shady Palm of Galilee.

---

1 Addressed to Mary Monkhouse, daughter of WW's friend Thomas Monkhouse. She was
   born December 21, 1821.

Cenotaph

In affectionate remembrance of Frances Fermor, whose remains are deposited in the church of Claines, near Worcester, this stone is erected by her sister, Dame Margaret, wife of Sir George Beaumont, Bart., who, feeling not less than the love of a brother for the deceased, commends this memorial to the care of his heirs and successors in the possession of this place.

By vain affections unenthralled,
Though resolute when duty called
To meet the world's broad eye,
Pure as the holiest cloistered nun
That ever feared the tempting sun,   5
Did Fermor live and die.

This Tablet, hallowed by her name,
One heart-relieving tear may claim;
But if the pensive gloom
Of fond regret be still thy choice,   10
Exalt thy spirit, hear the voice
Of Jesus from her tomb!
"I AM THE WAY, THE TRUTH, AND THE LIFE."

Elegiac Stanzas. 1824[1]

O for a dirge! But why complain?
Ask rather a triumphal strain
When FERMOR's race is run;
A garland of immortal boughs
To bind around the Christian's brows,   5
Whose glorious work is done.

We pay a high and holy debt;
No tears of passionate regret
Shall stain this votive lay;
Ill-worthy, Beaumont! were the grief   10
That flings itself on wild relief
When Saints have passed away.

Sad doom, at Sorrow's shrine to kneel,
For ever covetous to feel,
And impotent to bear: 15

---

1   The subject here, as in the preceding poem, is Frances Fermor.

Such once was hers—to think and think
On severed love, and only sink
From anguish to despair!

But nature to its inmost part
Had Faith refined, and to her heart   20
A peaceful cradle given;
Calm as the dew-drop's, free to rest
Within a breeze-fanned rose's breast
Till it exhales to heaven.

Was ever Spirit that could bend   25
So graciously?—that could descend,
Another's need to suit,
So promptly from her lofty throne?—
In works of love, in these alone,
How restless, how minute!   30

Pale was her hue; yet mortal cheek
Ne'er kindled with a livelier streak
When aught had suffered wrong,—
When aught that breathes had felt a wound;
Such look the Oppressor might confound,   35
However proud and strong.

But hushed be every thought that springs
From out the bitterness of things;
Her quiet is secure;
No thorns can pierce her tender feet,   40
Whose life was, like the violet sweet,
As climbing jasmine, pure;—

As snowdrop on an infant's grave,
Or lily heaving with the wave
That feeds it and defends;   45
As Vesper, ere the star hath kissed
The mountain top, or breathed the mist
That from the vale ascends.
Thou takest not away, O Death!

Thou strik'st—and absence perisheth,   50
Indifference is no more;

The future brightens on our sight;
For on the past hath fallen a light
That tempts us to adore.

"Why, Minstrel, these untuneful murmurings—"

"Why, Minstrel, these untuneful murmurings—
Dull, flagging notes that with each other jar?"
"Think, gentle Lady, of a Harp so far
From its own Country, and forgive the strings."
A simple answer! but even so forth springs,   5
From the Castalian fountain of the heart,
The Poetry of Life, and all that Art
Divine of words quickening insensate Things.
From the submissive necks of guiltless Men
Stretched on the block, the glittering axe recoils;   10
Sun, Moon, and Stars, all struggle in the toils
Of mortal sympathy; what wonder then
If the poor Harp distempered music yields
To its sad Lord, far from his native Fields?

A Morning Exercise

Fancy, who leads the pastimes of the glad,
Full oft is pleased a wayward dart to throw;
Sending sad shadows after things not sad,
Peopling the harmless fields with signs of woe:
Beneath her sway, a simple forest cry   5
Becomes an echo of Man's misery.

  Blithe Ravens croak of death; and when the Owl
Tries his two voices for a favourite strain—
Tu-whit—Tu-whoo! the unsuspecting fowl
Forebodes mishap, or seems but to complain;   10
Fancy, intent to harass and annoy,
Can thus pervert the evidence of joy.

  Through border wilds where naked Indians stray,
Myriads of notes attest her subtle skill;
A feathered Task-master cried, "WORK AWAY!"   15

And, in thy iteration, "WHIP POOR WILL,"[1]
Is heard the Spirit of a toil-worn Slave,
Lashed out of life, not quiet in the grave!

What wonder? at her bidding, ancient lays
Steeped in dire griefs the voice of Philomel;   20
And that fleet Messenger of summer days,
The Swallow, twittered subject to like spell;
But ne'er could Fancy bend the buoyant Lark
To melancholy service—hark! O hark!

The daisy sleeps upon the dewy lawn,   25
Not lifting yet the head that evening bowed;
But *He* is risen, a later star of dawn,
Glittering and twinkling near yon rosy cloud;
Bright gem instinct with music, vocal spark;
The happiest Bird that sprang out of the Ark!   30

Hail, blest above all kinds!—Supremely skilled
Restless with fixed to balance, high with low,
Thou leav'st the Halcyon free her hopes to build
On such forbearance as the deep may show;
Perpetual flight, unchecked by earthly ties,   35
Leavest to the wandering Bird of Paradise.

Faithful, though swift as lightning, the meek Dove;
Yet more hath Nature reconciled in thee;
So constant with thy downward eye of love,
Yet, in aerial singleness, so free;   40
So humble, yet so ready to rejoice
In power of wing and never-wearied voice!

How would it please old Ocean to partake,
With Sailors longing for a breeze in vain,
The harmony that thou best lovest to make   45
Where earth resembles most his blank domain!
Urania's self might welcome with pleased ear
These matins mounting towards her native sphere.

---

1 "See Waterton's Wanderings in South America." WW refers to Charles Waterton's
*Wanderings in South America, the North-West of the United States, and the Antilles, in the
Years 1812, 1816, 1820 and 1824* (London, 1825).

Chanter by Heaven attracted, whom no bars
To day-light known deter from that pursuit,   50
'Tis well that some sage instinct, when the stars
Come forth at evening, keeps Thee still and mute;
For not an eyelid could to sleep incline
Were thou among them singing as they shine!

To a Sky-lark

Ethereal Minstrel! Pilgrim of the sky!
Dost thou despise the earth where cares abound?
Or, while the wings aspire, are heart and eye
Both with thy nest upon the dewy ground?
Thy nest which thou canst drop into at will,   5
Those quivering wings composed, that music still!

To the last point of vision, and beyond,
Mount, daring Warbler! that love-prompted strain,
('Twixt thee and thine a never-failing bond)
Thrills not the less the bosom of the plain: 10
Yet might'st thou seem, proud privilege! to sing
All independent of the leafy spring.

Leave to the Nightingale her shady wood;
A privacy of glorious light is thine;
Whence thou dost pour upon the world a flood   15
Of harmony, with rapture more divine;
Type of the wise who soar, but never roam;
True to the kindred points of Heaven and Home!

"While they, her Playmates once, light-hearted tread"

While they, her Playmates once, light-hearted tread
The mountain turf and river's flowery marge;
Or float with music in the festal barge;
Rein the proud steed, or through the dance are led;
Is Anna doomed to press a weary bed—   5
Till oft her guardian Angel, to some Charge
More urgent called, will stretch his wings at large,
And Friends too rarely prop the languid head.
Yet Genius is no feeble comforter:
The presence even of a stuffed Owl for her   10

Can cheat the time; sending her fancy out
To ivied castles and to moonlight skies,
Though he can neither stir a plume, nor shout,
Nor veil, with restless film, his staring eyes.

To ———[1]

Such age how beautiful! O Lady bright,
Whose mortal lineaments seem all refined
By favouring Nature and a saintly Mind
To something purer and more exquisite
Than flesh and blood; whene'er thou meet'st my sight,   5
When I behold thy blanched unwithered cheek,
Thy temples fringed with locks of gleaming white,
And head that droops because the soul is meek,
Thee with the welcome Snowdrop I compare;
That Child of Winter, prompting thoughts that climb   10
From desolation tow'rds the genial prime;
Or with the Moon conquering earth's misty air,
And filling more and more with crystal light
As pensive Evening deepens into night.

"Ere with cold beads of midnight dew"

Ere with cold beads of midnight dew
    Had mingled tears of thine,
I grieved, fond Youth! that thou shouldst sue
    To haughty Geraldine.

Immoveable by generous sighs,   5
    She glories in a train
Who drag, beneath our native skies,
    An Oriental Chain.

Pine not like them with arms across,
    Forgetting in thy care   10
How the fast-rooted trees can toss
    Their branches in mid air.

The humblest Rivulet will take
    Its own wild liberties;

---

1   Addressed to Lady Fitzgerald, as described to WW by his friend Lady Beaumont.

And, every day, the imprisoned Lake   15
  Is flowing in the breeze.

Then, crouch no more on suppliant knee,
  But scorn with scorn outbrave;
A Briton, even in love, should be
  A subject, not a slave!   20

Inscription

The massy Ways, carried across these Heights
By Roman Perseverance, are destroyed,
Or hidden under ground, like sleeping worms.
How venture then to hope that Time will spare
This humble Walk? Yet on the mountain's side   5
A Poet's hand first shaped it; and the steps
Of that same Bard, repeated to and fro
At morn, at noon, and under moonlight skies,
Through the vicissitudes of many a year,
Forbade the weeds to creep o'er its grey line.   10
No longer, scattering to the heedless winds
The vocal raptures of fresh poesy,
Shall he frequent these precincts; locked no more
In earnest converse with beloved Friends,
Here will he gather stores of ready bliss,   15
As from the beds and borders of a garden
Choice flowers are gathered! But, if Power may spring
Out of a farewell yearning favoured more
Than kindred wishes mated suitably
With vain regrets, the Exile would consign   20
This Walk, his loved possession, to the care
Of those pure Minds that reverence the Muse.

"Strange visitation! at Jemima's lip"[1]

Strange visitation! at *Jemima's* lip

---

1   "This Sonnet, as Poetry, explains itself, yet the scene of the incident having been a wild
wood, it may be doubted, as a point of natural history, whether the bird was aware that his
attentions were bestowed upon a human, or even a living, creature. But a Redbreast will
perch upon the foot of a gardener at work, and alight on the handle of the spade when his
hand is half upon it—this I have seen. And under my own roof I have witnessed affecting
instances of the creature's friendly visits to the chambers of sick persons, as described in
the Author's poems, [*The Redbreast. (Suggested in a Westmoreland Cottage.*), included

Thus hadst thou pecked, wild Redbreast! Love might say,
A half-blown rose had tempted thee to sip
Its glistening dews; but hallowed is the clay
Which the Muse warms; and I, whose head is grey,   5
Am not unworthy of thy fellowship;
Nor could I let one thought—one motion—slip
That might thy sylvan confidence betray.
For are we not all His, without whose care
Vouchsafed no sparrow falleth to the ground?   10
Who gives his Angels wings to speed through air,
And rolls the planets through the blue profound;
Then peck or perch, fond Flutterer! nor forbear
To trust a Poet in still vision bound.

"When Philoctetes in the Lemnian Isle"

When Philoctetes in the Lemnian Isle
Lay couched;—upon that breathless Monument,
On him, or on his fearful bow unbent,
Some wild Bird oft might settle, and beguile
The rigid features of a transient smile,   5
Disperse the tear, or to the sigh give vent,
Slackening the pains of ruthless banishment
From home affections, and heroic toil.
Nor doubt that spiritual Creatures round us move,
Griefs to allay that Reason cannot heal;   10
And very Reptiles have sufficed to prove
To fettered Wretchedness, that no Bastile
Is deep enough to exclude the light of love,
Though Man for Brother Man has ceased to feel.

Retirement

If the whole weight of what we think and feel,
Save only far as thought and feeling blend
With action, were as nothing, patriot Friend!
From thy remonstrance would be no appeal;

---

below]. One of these welcome intruders used frequently to roost upon a nail in the wall, from which a picture had hung, and was ready, as morning came, to pipe his song in the hearing of the Invalid, who had been long confined to her room. These attachments to a particular person, when marked and continued, used to be reckoned ominous; but the superstition is passing away." WW added this note in 1838.

But to promote and fortify the weal   5
Of our own Being, is her paramount end;
A truth which they alone shall comprehend
Who shun the mischief which they cannot heal.
Peace in these feverish times is sovereign bliss;
Here, with no thirst but what the stream can slake,   10
And startled only by the rustling brake,
Cool air I breathe; while the unincumbered Mind,
By some weak aims at services assigned
To gentle Natures, thanks not Heaven amiss.

"Fair Prime of life! were it enough to gild"

Fair Prime of life! were it enough to gild
With ready sunbeams every straggling shower;
And, if an unexpected cloud should lower,
Swiftly thereon a rainbow arch to build
For Fancy's errands,—then, from fields half-tilled   5
Gathering green weeds to mix with poppy flower,
Thee might thy Minions crown, and chant thy power,
Unpitied by the wise, all censure stilled.
Ah! show that worthier honours are thy due;
Fair Prime of Life! arouse the deeper heart;   10
Confirm the Spirit glorying to pursue
Some path of steep ascent and lofty aim;
And, if there be a joy that slights the claim
Of grateful memory, bid that joy depart.

"Go back to antique Ages, if thine eyes"

Go back to antique Ages, if thine eyes
The genuine mien and character would trace
Of the rash Spirit that still holds her place,
Prompting the World's audacious vanities!
See, at her call, the Tower of Babel rise;   5
The Pyramid extend its monstrous base,
For some Aspirant of our short-lived race,
Anxious an aery name to immortalize.
There, too, ere wiles and politic dispute
Gave specious colouring to aim and act,   10
See the first mighty Hunter leave the brute

To chase mankind, with men in armies packed
For his field-pastime, high and absolute,
While, to dislodge his game, cities are sacked!

"Are States oppress'd afflicted and degraded"

Are States oppress'd afflicted and degraded
Lo! while before Minerva's altar quake
The conscious Tyrants, like a vengeful snake
Leaps forth the Sword that lurk'd with myrtles braided!
Thence to the Capitol by Fancy aided   5
The hush'd design of Brutus to partake
Or watch the Hero of the Helvetian Lake
'Till from that rocky couch with pine oershaded
He starts and grasps his deadly Carabine
Nor let thy thirst forego the draught divine   10
Of Liberty which like a liquid Fountain
Refresh'd Pelayo on the illustrious mountain;
The Swede within the Dalecarlian mine
When every hope but his was shrunk and faded.

Ode,

COMPOSED ON MAY MORNING

While from the purpling east departs
   The Star that led the dawn,
Blithe Flora from her couch upstarts,
   For May is on the lawn.
A quickening hope, a freshening glee,   5
   Foreran the expected Power,
Whose first-drawn breath, from bush and tree,
   Shakes off that pearly shower.

All Nature welcomes Her whose sway,
   Tempers the year's extremes;   10
Who scattereth lusters o'er noon-day,
   Like morning's dewy gleams;
While mellow warble, sprightly trill,
   The tremulous heart excite;
And hums the balmy air to still   15
   The balance of delight.

Time was, blest Power! when Youths and Maids
   At peep of dawn would rise,
And wander forth, in forest glades
   Thy birth to solemnize.   20
Though mute the song—to grace the rite
   Untouched the hawthorn bough,
Thy Spirit triumphs o'er the slight;
   Man changes, but not Thou!

Thy feathered Lieges bill and wings   25
   In love's disport employ;
Warmed by thy influence, creeping Things
   Awake to silent joy:
Queen art thou still for each gay Plant
   Where the slim wild Deer roves;   30
And served in depths where Fishes haunt
   Their own mysterious groves.

Cloud-piercing Peak, and trackless Heath,
   Instinctive homage pay;
Nor wants the dim-lit Cave a wreath   35
   To honour Thee, sweet May!
Where Cities fanned by thy brisk airs
   Behold a smokeless sky,
Their puniest Flower-pot-nursling dares
   To open a bright eye.   40

And if, on this thy natal morn,
   The Pole, from which thy name
Hath not departed, stands forlorn
   Of song and dance and game,
Still from the village-green a vow   45
   Aspires to thee addrest,
Wherever peace is on the brow,
   Or love within the breast.

Yes! where Love nestles thou canst teach
   The soul to love the more;   50
Hearts also shall thy lessons reach
   That never loved before.
Stript is the haughty One of pride,

The bashful freed from fear,
While rising, like the ocean-tide,   55
  In flows the joyous year.

Hush, feeble lyre! weak words, refuse
  The service to prolong!
To yon exulting Thrush the Muse
  Intrusts the imperfect song;   60
His voice shall chant, in accents clear,
  Throughout the live-long day,
Till the first silver Star appear,
  The sovereignty of May.

To May

Though many suns have risen and set
  Since thou, blithe May, wert born,
And Bards, who hailed thee, may forget
  Thy gifts, thy beauty scorn;
There are who to a birthday strain   5
  Confine not harp and voice,
But evermore throughout thy reign
  Are grateful and rejoice!

Delicious odours! music sweet,
  Too sweet to pass away!   10
Oh for a deathless song to meet
  The soul's desire—a lay
That, when a thousand years are told,
  Should praise thee, genial Power!
Through summer heat, autumnal cold,   15
  And winter's dreariest hour.

Earth, Sea, thy presence feel—nor less,
  If yon ethereal blue
With its soft smile the truth express,
  The Heavens have felt it too.   20
The inmost heart of man if glad
  Partakes a livelier cheer;
And eyes that cannot but be sad
  Let fall a brightened tear.

Since thy return, through days and weeks   25
  Of hope that grew by stealth,
How many wan and faded cheeks
  Have kindled into health!
The Old, by thee revived, have said,
  "Another year is ours;"   30
And wayworn Wanderers, poorly fed,
  Have smiled upon thy flowers.

Who tripping lisps a merry song
  Amid his playful peers?
The tender Infant who was long   35
  A prisoner of fond fears;
But now, when every sharp-edged blast
  Is quiet in its sheath,
His Mother leaves him free to taste
  Earth's sweetness in thy breath.   40

Thy help is with the Weed that creeps
  Along the humblest ground;
No Cliff so bare but on its steeps
  Thy favours may be found;
But most on some peculiar nook   45
  That our own hands have drest,
Thou and thy train are proud to look,
  And seem to love it best.

And yet how pleased we wander forth
  When May is whispering, "Come!   50
Choose from the bowers of virgin earth
  The happiest for your home;
Heaven's bounteous love through me is spread
  From sunshine, clouds, winds, waves,
Drops on the mouldering turret's head,   55
  And on your turf-clad graves!"

Such greeting heard, away with sighs
  For lilies that must fade,
Or "the rathe primrose as it dies
  Forsaken" in the shade!   60
Vernal fruitions and desires

Are linked in endless chase;
   While, as one kindly growth retires,
     Another takes its place.

And what if thou, sweet May, hast known   65
   Mishap by worm and blight;
If expectations newly blown
   Have perished in thy sight;
If loves and joys, while up they sprung,
   Were caught as in a snare;   70
Such is the lot of all the young,
   However bright and fair.

Lo! Streams that April could not check
   Are patient of thy rule;
Gurgling in foamy water-break,   75
   Loitering in glassy pool:
By thee, thee only, could be sent
   Such gentle Mists as glide,
Curling with unconfirmed intent,
   On that green mountain's side.   80

How delicate the leafy veil
   Through which yon House of God
Gleams 'mid the peace of this deep dale
   By few but shepherds trod!
And lowly Huts, near beaten ways,   85
   No sooner stand attired
In thy fresh wreaths, than they for praise
   Peep forth, and are admired.

Season of fancy and of hope,
   Permit not for one hour   90
A blossom from thy crown to drop,
   Nor add to it a flower!
Keep, lovely May, as if by touch
   Of self-restraining art,
This modest charm of not too much,   95
   Part seen, imagined part!

"Once I could hail (howe'er serene the sky)"

"Late, late yestreen I saw the new moone
Wi' the auld moone in hir arme."
        Ballad of Sir Patrick Spence, Percy's Reliques.[1]

Once I could hail (howe'er serene the sky)
The Moon re-entering her monthly round,
No faculty yet given me to espy
The dusky Shape within her arms imbound,
That thin memento of effulgence lost   5
Which some have named her Predecessor's Ghost.

Young, like the Crescent that above me shone,
Nought I perceived within it dull or dim;
All that appeared was suitable to One
Whose fancy had a thousand fields to skim;   10
To expectations spreading with wild growth,
And hope that kept with me her plighted troth.

I saw (ambition quickening at the view)
A silver boat launched on a boundless flood;
A pearly crest, like Dian's when it threw   15
Its brightest splendour round a leafy wood;
But not a hint from under-ground, no sign
Fit for the glimmering brow of Proserpine.

Or was it Dian's self that seemed to move
Before me? nothing blemished the fair sight;   20
On her I looked whom jocund Fairies love,
Cynthia, who puts the *little* stars to flight,
And by that thinning magnifies the great,
For exaltation of her sovereign state.

And when I learned to mark the spectral Shape   25
As each new Moon obeyed the call of Time,
If gloom fell on me, swift was my escape;
Such happy privilege hath Life's gay Prime,
To see or not to see, as best may please
A buoyant Spirit, and a heart at ease.   30

---

1   WW cites Thomas Percy's *Reliques of Ancient English Poetry* (3 vols.; London, 1765).

Now, dazzling Stranger! when thou meet'st my glance,
Thy dark Associate ever I discern;
Emblem of thoughts too eager to advance
While I salute my joys, thoughts sad or stern;
Shades of past bliss, or phantoms that to gain   35
Their fill of promised lustre wait in vain.

So changes mortal Life with fleeting years;
A mournful change, should Reason fail to bring
The timely insight that can temper fears,
And from vicissitude remove its sting;   40
While Faith aspires to seats in that Domain
Where joys are perfect, neither wax nor wane.

"The Lady whom you here behold"

The Lady whom you here behold
Was once Pigmalion's Wife
He made her first from marble cold
And Venus gave her life.

When fate remov'd her from his arms   5
Thro' sundry Forms she pass'd
And conquering hearts by various charms
This shape she took at last.

We caught her, true tho' strange th' account
Among a troop of Fairies   10
Who nightly frisk on our green Mount
And practise strange vagaries.

Her raiment then was scant, so we
Bestowed some pains upon her
Part for the sake of decency   15
And part to do her honor.

But as no doubt 'twas for her sins
We found her in such plight
She shall do penance stuck with pins
And serve you day and night.   20

To ——— [1]

Happy the feeling from the bosom thrown
In perfect shape whose beauty Time shall spare
Though a breath made it, like a bubble blown
For summer pastime into wanton air;
Happy the thought best likened to a stone   5
Of the sea-beach, when, polished with nice care,
Veins it discovers exquisite and rare,
Which for the loss of that moist gleam atone
That tempted first to gather it. O chief
Of Friends! such feelings if I here present,   10
Such thoughts, with others mixed less fortunate;
Then smile into my heart a fond belief
That Thou, if not with partial joy elate,
Receiv'st the gift for more than mild content!

To S. H. [2]

Excuse is needless when with love sincere
Of occupation, not by fashion led,
Thou turn'st the Wheel that slept with dust o'erspread;
My nerves from no such murmur shrink,—tho' near,
Soft as the Dorhawk's to a distant ear,   5
When twilight shades bedim the mountain's head.
She who was feigned to spin our vital thread
Might smile, O Lady! on a task once dear
To household virtues. Venerable Art,
Torn from the Poor! yet will kind Heaven protect   10
Its own, not left without a guiding chart,
If Rulers, trusting with undue respect
To proud discoveries of the Intellect,
Sanction the pillage of man's ancient heart.

"Prithee gentle Lady list"

Prithee gentle Lady list
To a small Ventriloquist
I whose pretty voice you hear
From this paper speaking clear

---

1   Probably addressed to Mary Wordsworth.
2   Sara Hutchinson, WW's sister-in-law.

Have a mother, once a Statue!   5
I thus boldly looking at you
Do the name of Paphus bear
Fam'd Pygmalion's son and heir
By that wondrous marble wife
That from Venus took her life   10
Cupid's nephew then am I
Nor unskilled his darts to ply
But from him I crav'd no warrant
Coming thus to seek my parent
Not equipp'd with bow and quiver   15
Her by menace to deliver
But resolv'd with filial care
Her captivity to share
Hence while on your Toilet she
Is doom'd a Pincushion to be   20
By her side I'll take my place
As a humble Needlecase
Furnish'd too with dainty thread
For a Sempstress thorough bred
Then let both be kindly treated   25
Till the Term for which she's fated
Durance to sustain be over
So will I ensure a Lover
Lady! to your heart's content
But on harshness are you bent?   30
Bitterly shall you repent
When to Cyprus back I go
And take up my Uncle's bow.

Conclusion

TO ———————[1]

If these brief Records, by the Muses' art
Produced as lonely Nature or the strife
That animates the scenes of public life
Inspired, may in thy leisure claim a part;
And if these Transcripts of the private heart   5

---

1   The sonnet concluded the Miscellaneous Sonnets in WW's *Poetical Works* (1827) and
    reflects back on them at the close of that series.

Have gained a sanction from thy falling tears,
Then I repent not: but my soul hath fears
Breathed from eternity; for as a dart
Cleaves the blank air, Life flies: now every day
Is but a glimmering spoke in the swift wheel   10
Of the revolving week. Away, away,
All fitful cares, all transitory zeal;
So timely Grace the immortal wing may heal,
And honour rest upon the senseless clay.

Address

TO KILCHURN CASTLE UPON LOCH AWE

"From the top of the hill a most impressive scene opened upon our view,—a
ruined Castle on an Island at some distance from the shore, backed by a
Cove of the Mountain Cruachan, down which came a foaming stream. The
Castle occupied every foot of the Island that was visible to us, appearing to
rise out of the Water,—mists rested upon the mountain side, with spots of
sunshine; there was a mild desolation in the low-grounds, a solemn gran-
deur in the mountains, and the Castle was wild, yet stately—not disman-
tled of Turrets—nor the walls broken down, though obviously a ruin."
Extract from the Journal of my Companion.

Child of loud-throated War! the mountain Stream
Roars in thy hearing; but thy hour of rest
Is come, and thou art silent in thy age;
Save when the winds sweep by and sounds are caught
Ambiguous, neither wholly thine nor theirs.   5
Oh! there is life that breathes not; Powers there are
That touch each other to the quick in modes
Which the gross world no sense hath to perceive,
No soul to dream of. What art Thou, from care   10
Cast off—abandoned by thy rugged Sire,
Nor by soft Peace adopted; though, in place
And in dimension, such that thou might'st seem
But a mere footstool to yon sovereign Lord,
Huge Cruachan, (a thing that meaner Hills   15
Might crush, nor know that it had suffered harm;)
Yet he, not loth, in favour of thy claims
To reverence suspends his own; submitting
All that the God of Nature hath conferred,

All that he has in common with the Stars,   20
To the memorial majesty of Time
Impersonated in thy calm decay!

Take, then, thy seat, Vicegerent unreproved!
Now, while a farewell gleam of evening light
Is fondly lingering on thy shattered front,   25
Do thou, in turn, be paramount; and rule
Over the pomp and beauty of a scene
Whose mountains, torrents, lake, and woods, unite
To pay thee homage; and with these are joined,
In willing admiration and respect,   30
Two Hearts, which in thy presence might be called
Youthful as Spring. Shade of departed Power,
Skeleton of unfleshed humanity,
The Chronicle were welcome that should call
Into the compass of distinct regard   35
The toils and struggles of thy infancy!
Yon foaming flood seems motionless as Ice;
Its dizzy turbulence eludes the eye,
Frozen by distance; so, majestic Pile,
To the perception of this Age, appear   40
Thy fierce beginnings, softened and subdued
And quieted in character; the strife,
The pride, the fury uncontrollable,
Lost on the aërial heights of the Crusades![1]

"Scorn not the Sonnet; Critic, you have frowned"

Scorn not the Sonnet; Critic, you have frowned,
Mindless of its just honours;—with this Key
Shakspeare unlocked his heart; the melody
Of this small Lute gave ease to Petrarch's wound;
A thousand times this Pipe did Tasso sound;   5
Camöens soothed with it an Exile's grief;
The Sonnet glittered a gay myrtle Leaf
Amid the cypress with which Dante crowned
His visionary brow: a glow-worm Lamp,
It cheered mild Spenser, called from Faery-land   10

---

1 "The Tradition is, that the Castle was built by a Lady during the absence of her Lord in Palestine." WW

To struggle through dark ways; and when a damp
Fell round the path of Milton, in his hand
The Thing became a Trumpet, whence he blew
Soul-animating strains—alas, too few!

"There is a pleasure in poetic pains"

There is a pleasure in poetic pains
Which only Poets know;—'twas rightly said;
Whom could the Muses else allure to tread
Their smoothest paths, to wear their lightest chains?
When happiest Fancy has inspired the Strains,   5
How oft the malice of one luckless word
Pursues the Enthusiast to the social board,
Haunts him belated on the silent plains!
Yet he repines not, if his thought stand clear
At last of hindrance and obscurity,   10
Fresh as the Star that crowns the brow of Morn;
Bright, speckless as a softly-moulded tear
The moment it has left the Virgin's eye,
Or rain-drop lingering on the pointed Thorn.

To the Cuckoo

Not the whole warbling grove in concert heard
When sunshine follows shower, the breast can thrill
Like the first summons, Cuckoo! of thy bill,
With its twin notes inseparably paired.
The Captive, 'mid damp vaults unsunned, unaired,   5
Measuring the periods of his lonely doom,
That cry can reach; and to the sick man's room
Sends gladness, by no languid smile declared.
The lordly Eagle-race through hostile search
May perish; time may come when never more   10
The wilderness shall hear the Lion roar;
But, long as Cock shall crow from household perch
To rouse the dawn, soft gales shall speed thy wing,
And thy erratic voice be faithful to the Spring! ✝

"In my mind's eye a Temple, like a cloud"

In my mind's eye a Temple, like a cloud

✝ no longer in Friars,
Bank!
11/21

Slowly surmounting some invidious hill,
Rose out of darkness: the bright Work stood still,
And might of its own beauty have been proud,
But it was fashioned and to God was vowed   5
By virtues that diffused, in every part,
Spirit divine through forms of human art:
Faith had her arch—her arch, when winds blow loud,
Into the consciousness of safety thrilled;
And Love her towers of dread foundation laid   10
Under the grave of things; Hope had her spire
Star-high, and pointing still to something higher;
Trembling I gazed, but heard a voice—it said,
Hell-gates are powerless Phantoms when *we* build.

On Seeing a Needlecase in the Form of a Harp,

THE WORK OF E. M. S.[1]

Frowns are on every Muse's face,
    Reproaches from their lips are sent,
That mimickry should thus disgrace
    The noble Instrument.

A very Harp in all but size!   5
    Needles for strings in apt gradation!
Minerva's self would stigmatize
    The unclassic profanation.

Even her *own* Needle that subdued
    Arachne's rival spirit,   10
Though wrought in Vulcan's happiest mood,
    Like station could not merit.

And this, too, from the Laureate's Child,
    A living Lord of melody!
How will her Sire be reconciled   15
    To the refined indignity?

I spake, when whispered a low voice,
    "Bard! moderate your ire;
"Spirits of all degrees rejoice

---

1 Edith May Southey was the daughter of Robert Southey of Greta Hall, Keswick.

"In presence of the Lyre.   20

"The Minstrels of Pygmean bands,
    "Dwarf Genii, moonlight-loving Fays,
"Have shells to fit their tiny hands
    "And suit their slender lays.

"Some, still more delicate of ear,   25
    "Have lutes (believe my words)
"Whose framework is of gossamer,
    "While sunbeams are the chords.

"Gay Sylphs this Miniature will court,
    "Made vocal by their brushing wings,   30
"And sullen Gnomes will learn to sport
    "Around its polished strings;

"Whence strains to love-sick Maiden dear,
    "While in her lonely Bower she tries
"To cheat the thought she cannot cheer,   35
    "By fanciful embroideries.

"Trust, angry Bard! a knowing Sprite,
    "Nor think the Harp her lot deplores;
"Though mid the stars the Lyre shines bright,
    "Love *stoops* as fondly as he soars."   40

"Her only Pilot the soft breeze the Boat"

Her only Pilot the soft breeze the Boat
Lingers, but Fancy is well satisfied;
With keen-eyed Hope, with Memory, at her side,
And the glad Muse at liberty to note
All that to each is precious, as we float   5
Gently along; regardless who shall chide
If the Heavens smile, and leave us free to glide,
Happy Associates breathing air remote
From trivial cares. But, Fancy and the Muse,
Why have I crowded this small Bark with you   10
And others of your kind, Ideal Crew!
While here sits One whose brightness owes its hues
To flesh and blood; no Goddess from above,

No fleeting Spirit, but my own true Love?

Farewell Lines

"High bliss is only for a higher state,"
But, surely, if severe afflictions borne
With patience merit the reward of peace,
Peace ye deserve; and may the solid good,
Sought by a wise though late exchange, and here   5
With bounteous hand beneath a cottage-roof
To you accorded, never be withdrawn,
Nor for the world's best promises renounced.
Most soothing was it for a welcome friend,
Fresh from the crowded city, to behold   10
That lonely union, privacy so deep,
Such calm employments, such entire content.
So, when the rain is over, the storm laid,
A pair of herons oft-times have I seen,
Upon a rocky islet, side by side,   15
Drying their feathers in the sun, at ease;
And so, when night with grateful gloom had fallen,
Two glowworms in such nearness that they shared,
As seemed, their soft self-satisfying light,
Each with the other, on the dewy ground,   20
Where He that made them blesses their repose.
When wandering among lakes and hills I note,
Once more, those creatures thus by nature paired,
And guarded in their tranquil state of life,
Even, as your happy presence to my mind   25
Their union brought, will they repay the debt,
And send a thankful spirit back to you,
With hope that we, dear Friends! shall meet again.

Extract from the Strangers book
Station Winandermere

"Lord & Lady Darlington, Lady Vane, Miss Taylor & Cap^n Stamp pronounce this Lake superior to Lac de Geneve, Lago de Como, Lago Maggiore, L'Eau de Zurick, Loch Lomond, Loch Ketterine or the Lakes of Killarney"—

ON SEEING THE ABOVE

My Lord and Lady Darlington
I would not speak in snarling tone
Nor to you good Lady Vane
Would I give one moment's pain
Nor Miss Taylor Captain Stamp   5
Would I your flights of *memory* cramp
Yet having spent a summer's day
On the green margin of Loch Tay
And doubled (prospects ever bettering)
The mazy reaches of Loch Ketterine   10
And more than once been free at Luss
Loch Lomond's beauties to discuss
And *wish'd* at least to hear the blarney
Of the sly boatmen of Killarney
And dipt my hand in dancing wave   15
Of "Eau de Zurich Lac Genêve"
And bow'd to many a Major Domo
On stately terraces of Como
And seen the Simplon's forehead hoary
Reclinèd on Lago Maggiore   20
At breathless eventide at rest
On the broad water's placid breast
I, not insensible Heaven knows
To the charms this station shows,
Must tell you Cap^n Lord and Ladies,   25
For honest truth one Poet's trade is,
That your praise appears to me
Folly's own Hyperbole—!

"Four fiery steeds impatient of the rein"

Four fiery steeds impatient of the rein
Whirled us o'er sunless ground beneath a sky
As void of sunshine, when, from that wide Plain,
Clear tops of far-off Mountains we descry,
Like a Sierra of cerulean Spain,   5
All light and lustre. Did no heart reply?
Yes, there was One;—for One, asunder fly
The thousand links of that ethereal chain;

And green vales open out, with grove and field,
And the fair front of many a happy Home;   10
Such tempting spots as into vision come
While Soldiers, of the weapons that they wield
Weary, and sick of strifeful Christendom,
Gaze on the moon by parting clouds revealed.

Roman Antiquities Discovered,
AT BISHOPSTONE, HEREFORDSHIRE

While poring Antiquarians search the ground
Upturned with curious pains, the Bard, a Seer,
Takes fire:—The men that have been reappear;
Romans for travel girt, for business gowned,
And some recline on couches, myrtle-crowned,   5
In festal glee: why not? For fresh and clear,
As if its hues were of the passing year,
Dawns this time-buried pavement. From that mound
Hoards may come forth of Trajans, Maximins,
Shrunk into coins with all their warlike toil: 10
Or a fierce impress issues with its foil
Of tenderness—the Wolf, whose suckling Twins
The unlettered Ploughboy pities when he wins
The casual treasure from the furrowed soil.

St. Catherine of Ledbury

When human touch, as monkish books attest,
Nor was applied nor could be, Ledbury bells
Broke forth in concert flung adown the dells,
And upward, high as Malvern's cloudy crest;
Sweet tones, and caught by a noble Lady blest   5
To rapture! Mabel listened at the side
Of her loved Mistress: soon the music died,
And Catherine said, "Here I set up my rest."
Warned in a dream, the Wanderer long had sought
A home that by such miracle of sound   10
Must be revealed:—she heard it now, or felt
The deep, deep joy of a confiding thought;
And there, a saintly Anchoress she dwelt
Till she exchanged for heaven that happy ground.

To ———[1]

[Miss not the occasion; by the forelock take
That subtile Power, the never-halting Time,
Lest a mere moment's putting-off should make
Mischance almost as heavy as a crime.]

"Wait, prithee, wait!" this answer Lesbia threw
Forth to her Dove, and took no further heed;
Her eye was busy, while her fingers flew
Across the harp, with soul-engrossing speed;
But from that bondage when her thoughts were freed   5
She rose, and toward the close-shut casement drew,
Whence the poor unregarded Favorite, true
To old affections, had been heard to plead
With flapping wing for entrance. What a shriek
Forced from that voice so lately tuned to a strain   10
Of harmony!—a shriek of terror, pain,
And self-reproach!—for, from aloft, a Kite
Pounced, and the Dove, which from its ruthless beak
She could not rescue, perished in her sight!

Filial Piety

Untouched through all severity of cold,
Inviolate, whate'er the cottage hearth
Might need for comfort, or for festal mirth,
That Pile of Turf is half a century old:
Yes, Traveller! fifty winters have been told   5
Since suddenly the dart of death went forth
'Gainst him who raised it,—his last work on earth;
Thence by his Son more prized than aught which gold
Could purchase—watched, preserved by his own hands,
That, faithful to the Structure, still repair   10
Its waste.—Though crumbling with each breath of air,
In annual renovation thus it stands—
Rude Mausoleum! but wrens nestle there,
And red-breasts warble when sweet sounds are rare.

---

1   Addressed to Ellen Loveday Walker.

A Grave-stone upon the Floor in the Cloisters
of Worcester Cathedral

"*MISERRIMUS!*" and neither name nor date,
Prayer, text, or symbol, graven upon the stone;
Nought but that word assigned to the unknown,
That solitary word—to separate
From all, and cast a cloud around the fate   5
Of him who lies beneath. Most wretched one,
Who chose his Epitaph? Himself alone
Could thus have dared the grave to agitate,
And claim, among the dead, this awful crown;
Nor doubt that He marked also for his own,   10
Close to these cloistral steps a burial-place,
That every foot might fall with heavier tread,
Trampling upon his vileness. Stranger, pass
Softly!—To save the contrite, Jesus bled.

The Wishing-gate[1]

In the vale of Grasmere, by the side of the high-way, leading to Ambleside,
is a gate, which, time out of mind, has been called the wishing-gate, from a
belief that wishes formed or indulged there have a favourable issue.

Hope rules a land for ever green:
All powers that serve the bright-eyed Queen
Are confident and gay;
Clouds at her bidding disappear;
Points she to aught?—the bliss draws near,   5
And Fancy smooths the way.

Not such the land of wishes—there
Dwell fruitless day-dreams, lawless prayer,
And thoughts with things at strife;
Yet how forlorn should *ye* depart,   10
Ye superstitions of the *heart*,
How poor were human life!

When magic lore abjured its might,
Ye did not forfeit one dear right,
One tender claim abate;   15

---

1 See "The Wishing-gate Destroyed," below, and WW's note to that poem.

Witness this symbol of your sway,
Surviving near the public way,
The rustic Wishing-gate!

Inquire not if the faery race
Shed kindly influence on the place,   20
Ere northward they retired;
If here a warrior left a spell,
Panting for glory as he fell;
Or here a saint expired.

Enough that all around is fair,   25
Composed with Nature's finest care,
And in her fondest love;
Peace to embosom and content,
To overawe the turbulent,
The selfish to reprove.   30

Yea! even the Stranger from afar,
Reclining on this moss-grown bar,
Unknowing, and unknown,
The infection of the ground partakes,
Longing for his Belov'd—who makes   35
All happiness her own.

Then why should conscious Spirits fear
The mystic stirrings that are here,
The ancient faith disclaim?
The local Genius ne'er befriends   40
Desires whose course in folly ends,
Whose just reward is shame.

Smile if thou wilt, but not in scorn,
If some, by ceaseless pains outworn,
Here crave an easier lot;   45
If some have thirsted to renew
A broken vow, or bind a true,
With firmer, holier knot.

And not in vain, when thoughts are cast
Upon the irrevocable past,   50
Some penitent sincere

May for a worthier future sigh,
While trickles from his downcast eye
No unavailing tear.

The Worldling, pining to be freed   55
From turmoil, who would turn or speed
The current of his fate,
Might stop before this favoured scene,
At Nature's call, nor blush to lean
Upon the Wishing-gate.   60

The Sage, who feels how blind, how weak
Is man, though loth such help to seek,
Yet, passing, here might pause,
And yearn for insight to allay
Misgiving, while the crimson day   65
In quietness withdraws;

Or when the church-clock's knell profound
To Time's first step across the bound
Of midnight makes reply;
Time pressing on with starry crest,   70
To filial sleep upon the breast
Of dread eternity!

A Tradition of Darley Dale, Derbyshire

'Tis said that to the brow of yon fair hill
Two Brothers clomb, and, turning face from face,
Nor one look more exchanging, grief to still
Or feed, each planted on that lofty place
A chosen Tree; then, eager to fulfil   5
Their courses, like two new-born rivers, they
In opposite directions urged their way
Down from the far-seen mount. No blast might kill
Or blight that fond memorial;—the trees grew,
And now entwine their arms; but ne'er again   10
Embraced those Brothers upon earth's wide plain;
Nor aught of mutual joy or sorrow knew
Until their spirits mingled in the sea
That to itself takes all—Eternity.

"The unremitting voice of nightly streams"

The unremitting voice of nightly streams
That wastes so oft, we think, its tuneful powers,
If neither soothing to the worm that gleams
Through dewy grass, nor small birds hushed in bowers,
Nor unto silent leaves and drowsy flowers,—   5
That voice of unpretending harmony
(For who what is shall measure by what seems
To be, or not to be,
Or tax high Heaven with prodigality?)
Wants not a healing influence that can creep   10
Into the human breast, and mix with sleep
To regulate the motion of our dreams
For kindly issues—as through every clime
Was felt near murmuring brooks in earliest time;
As at this day, the rudest swains who dwell   15
Where torrents roar, or hear the tinkling knell
Of water-breaks, with grateful heart could tell.

The Gleaner (Suggested by a Picture)

That happy gleam of vernal eyes,
Those locks from summer's golden skies,
    That o'er thy brow are shed;
That cheek—a kindling of the morn,
That lip—a rose-bud from the thorn,   5
    I saw;—and Fancy sped
To scenes Arcadian, whispering, through soft air,
Of bliss that grows without a care,
Of happiness that never flies—
How can it where love never dies?   10
Of promise whispering, where no blight
Can reach the innocent delight;
Where pity, to the mind conveyed
In pleasure, is the darkest shade
That Time, unwrinkled Grandsire, flings   15
From his smoothly-gliding wings.

What mortal form, what earthly face,
Inspired the pencil, lines to trace,

And mingle colours, that should breed
Such rapture, nor want power to feed;   20
For had thy charge been idle flowers,
Fair Damsel, o'er my captive mind,
To truth and sober reason blind,
'Mid that soft air, those long-lost bowers,
The sweet illusion might have hung, for hours.   25

—Thanks to this tell-tale sheaf of corn,
That touchingly bespeaks thee born
Life's daily tasks with them to share
Who, whether from their lowly bed
They rise, or rest the weary head,   30
Ponder the blessing they entreat
From Heaven, and *feel* what they repeat,
While they give utterance to the prayer
That asks for daily bread.

The Triad[1]

Show me the noblest Youth of present time,
Whose trembling fancy would to love give birth;
Some God or Hero, from the Olympian clime
Returned, to seek a Consort upon earth;
Or, in no doubtful prospect, let me see   5
The brightest star of ages yet to be,
And I will mate and match him blissfully.

I will not fetch a Naiad from a flood
Pure as herself—(song lacks not mightier power)
Nor leaf-crowned Dryad from a pathless wood,   10
Nor Sea-nymph glistening from her coral bower;
Mere Mortals bodied forth in vision still,
Shall with Mount Ida's triple lustre fill
The chaster coverts of a British hill.

"Appear!—obey my lyre's command!   15
Come, like the Graces, hand in hand!
For ye, though not by birth allied,

---

1   WW identified the three young women addressed in the poem as Edith May Southey,
    daughter of Robert Southey, his own daughter Dora, and Sara Coleridge, daughter of
    Samuel T. Coleridge.

Are Sisters in the bond of love;
And not the boldest tongue of envious pride
In you those interweavings could reprove   20
Which They, the progeny of Jove,
Learnt from the tuneful spheres that glide
In endless union earth and sea above."—
—I speak in vain,—the pines have hushed their waving:
A peerless Youth expectant at my side,   25
Breathless as they, with unabated craving
Looks to the earth, and to the vacant air;
And, with a wandering eye that seems to chide,
Asks of the clouds what Occupants they hide:—
But why solicit more than sight could bear,   30
By casting on a moment all we dare?
Invoke we those bright Beings one by one,
And what was boldly promised, truly shall be done.

"Fear not this constraining measure!
Drawn by a poetic spell,   35
Lucida! from domes of pleasure,
Or from cottage-sprinkled dell,
Come to regions solitary,
Where the eagle builds her aery,
Above the hermit's long-forsaken cell!"   40
—She comes!—behold
That Figure, like a ship with silver sail!
Nearer she draws—a breeze uplifts her veil—
Upon her coming wait
As pure a sunshine and as soft a gale   45
As e'er, on herbage covering earthly mould,
Tempted the bird of Juno to unfold
His richest splendour, when his veering gait
And every motion of his starry train
Seem governed by a strain   50
Of music, audible to him alone.—
O Lady, worthy of earth's proudest throne!
Nor less, by excellence of nature, fit
Beside an unambitious hearth to sit
Domestic queen, where grandeur is unknown;   55
What living man could fear

The worst of Fortune's malice, wert thou near,
Humbling that lily stem, thy sceptre meek,
That its fair flowers may brush from off his cheek
The too, too happy tear?   60
——Queen and handmaid lowly!
Whose skill can speed the day with lively cares,
And banish melancholy
By all that mind invents or hand prepares;
O thou, against whose lip, without its smile,   65
And in its silence even, no heart is proof;
Whose goodness, sinking deep, would reconcile
The softest Nursling of a gorgeous palace
To the bare life beneath the hawthorn roof
Of Sherwood's archer, or in caves of Wallace—   70
Who that hath seen thy beauty could content
His soul with but a *glimpse* of heavenly day?
Who that hath loved thee, but would lay
His strong hand on the wind, if it were bent
To take thee in thy Majesty away?   75
—Pass onward (even the glancing deer
Till we depart intrude not here;)
That mossy slope, o'er which the woodbine throws
A canopy, is smoothed for thy repose!"

Glad moment is it when the throng   80
Of warblers in full concert strong
Strive, and not vainly strive, to rout
The lagging shower, and force coy Phœbus out,
Met by the rainbow's form divine,
Issuing from her cloudy shrine;—   85
So may the thrillings of the lyre
Prevail to further our desire,
While to these shades a Nymph I call,
The youngest of the lovely Three.—
"Come, if the notes thine ear may pierce;   90
Submissive to the might of verse,
By none more deeply felt than thee!"
—I sang; and lo! from pastimes virginal
She hastens to the tents
Of nature, and the lonely elements.   95

Air sparkles round her with a dazzling sheen,
And mark her glowing cheek, her vesture green!
And, as if wishful to disarm
Or to repay the potent charm,
She bears the stringèd lute of old romance,   100
That cheered the trellised arbour's privacy,
And soothed war-wearied knights in raftered hall.
How light her air! how delicate her glee!
So tripped the Muse, inventress of the dance;
So, truant in waste woods, the blithe Euphrosyne!   105

But the ringlets of that head
Why are they ungarlanded?
Why bedeck her temples less
Than the simplest shepherdess?
Is it not a brow inviting   110
Choicest flowers that ever breathed,
Which the myrtle would delight in
With Idalian rose enwreathed?
But her humility is well content
With *one* wild floweret (call it not forlorn)   115
FLOWER OF THE WINDS, beneath her bosom worn;
Yet is it more for love than ornament.

Open, ye thickets! let her fly,
Swift as a Thracian Nymph o'er field and height!
For She, to all but those who love Her shy,   120
Would gladly vanish from a Stranger's sight;
Though where she is beloved, and loves, as free
As bird that rifles blossoms on a tree,
Turning them inside out with arch audacity.

Alas! how little can a moment show   125
Of an eye where feeling plays
In ten thousand dewy rays;
A face o'er which a thousand shadows go!
—She stops—is fastened to that rivulet's side;
And there (while, with sedater mien,   130
O'er timid waters that have scarcely left
Their birth-place in the rocky cleft
She bends) at leisure may be seen

Features to old ideal grace allied,
Amid their smiles and dimples dignified—   135
Fit countenance for the soul of primal truth,
The bland composure of eternal youth!

What more changeful than the sea?
But over his great tides
Fidelity presides;   140
And this light-hearted Maiden constant is as he.—
High is her aim as heaven above,
And wide as ether her good-will,
And, like the lowly reed, her love
Can drink its nurture from the scantiest rill;   145
Insight as keen as frosty star
Is to *her* charity no bar,
Nor interrupts her frolic graces
When she is, far from these wild places,
Encircled by familiar faces.   150

O the charm that manners draw,
Nature, from thy genuine law!
If from what her hand would do,
Her voice would utter, there ensue
Aught untoward or unfit,   155
She, in benign affections pure,
In self-forgetfulness secure,
Sheds round the transient harm or vague mischance
A light unknown to tutored elegance:
Her's is not a cheek shame-stricken,   160
But her blushes are joy-flushes—
And the fault (if fault it be)
Only ministers to quicken
Laughter-loving gaiety,
And kindle sportive wit—   165
Leaving this Daughter of the mountains free
As if she knew that Oberon king of Faery
Had crossed her purpose with some quaint vagary,
And heard his viewless bands
Over their mirthful triumph clapping hands.   170

"Last of the Three, though eldest born,

Reveal thyself, like pensive morn,
Touched by the skylark's earliest note,
Ere humbler gladness be afloat.
But whether in the semblance drest   175
Of dawn—or eve, fair vision of the west,
Come with each anxious hope subdued
By woman's gentle fortitude,
Each grief, through meekness, settling into rest.
—Or I would hail thee when some high-wrought page   180
Of a closed volume lingering in thy hand
Has raised thy spirit to a peaceful stand
Among the glories of a happier age."
—Her brow hath opened on me—see it there,
Brightening the umbrage of her hair;   185
So gleams the crescent moon, that loves
To be descried through shady groves.
—Tenderest bloom is on her cheek;
Wish not for a richer streak—
Nor dread the depth of meditative eye;   190
But let thy love, upon that azure field
Of thoughtfulness and beauty, yield
Its homage offered up in purity.—
What would'st thou more? In sunny glade
Or under leaves of thickest shade,   195
Was such a stillness e'er diffused
Since earth grew calm while angels mused?
Softly she treads, as if her foot were loth
To crush the mountain dew-drops, soon to melt
On the flower's breast; as if she felt   200
That flowers themselves, whate'er their hue,
With all their fragrance, all their glistening,
Call to the heart for inward listening;
And though for bridal wreaths and tokens true
Welcomed wisely—though a growth   205
Which the careless shepherd sleeps on,
As fitly spring from turf the mourner weeps on,
And without wrong are cropped the marble tomb to strew.
The charm is over; the mute phantoms gone,
Nor will return—but droop not, favoured Youth;   210

The apparition that before thee shone
Obeyed a summons covetous of truth.
From these wild rocks thy footsteps I will guide
To bowers in which thy fortune may be tried,
And one of the bright Three become thy happy Bride!   215

Stanzas

ON

THE POWER OF SOUND

[handwritten margin note: Impossible to work out any logical meaning in these verses!]

Argument.

   The Ear addressed, as occupied by a spiritual functionary, in communion
with sounds, individual, or combined in studied harmony.—Sources and
effects of those sounds (to the close of 6th Stanza).—The power of music,
whence proceeding, exemplified in the idiot.—Origin of music, and its
effect in early ages—how produced (to the middle of 10th Stanza).—The
mind recalled to sounds acting casually and severally.—Wish uttered (11th
Stanza) that these could be united into a scheme or system for moral inter-
ests and intellectual contemplation.—(Stanza 12th.) The Pythagorean theory
of numbers and music, with their supposed power over the motions of the
universe—imaginations consonant with such a theory.—Wish expressed (in
11th Stanza) realised, in some degree, by the representation of all sounds
under the form of thanksgiving to the Creator.—(Last Stanza) the destruction
of earth and the planetary system—the survival of audible harmony, and its
support in the Divine Nature, as revealed in Holy Writ.

On the Power of Sound

1

Thy functions are etherial,
As if within thee dwelt a glancing Mind,
Organ of Vision! And a Spirit aerial
Informs the cell of hearing, dark and blind;
Intricate labyrinth, more dread for thought   5
To enter than oracular cave;
Strict passage, through which sighs are brought,
And whispers, for the heart, their slave;
And shrieks, that revel in abuse
Of shivering flesh; and warbled air,   10

Whose piercing sweetness can unloose
The chains of frenzy, or entice a smile
Into the ambush of despair;
Hosannas pealing down the long-drawn aisle,
And requiems answered by the pulse that beats   15
Devoutly, in life's last retreats!

2

The headlong Streams and Fountains
Serve Thee, Invisible Spirit, with untired powers;
Cheering the wakeful Tent on Syrian mountains,
They lull perchance ten thousand thousand flowers.   20
That roar, the prowling Lion's *Here I am*,
How fearful to the desert wide!
That bleat, how tender! of the Dam
Calling a straggler to her side.
Shout, Cuckoo! let the vernal soul   25
Go with thee to the frozen zone;
Toll from thy loftiest perch, lone Bell-bird, toll!
At the still hour to Mercy dear,
Mercy from her twilight throne
Listening to Nun's faint sob of holy fear,   30
To Sailor's prayer breathed from a darkening sea,
Or Widow's cottage lullaby.

3

Ye Voices, and ye Shadows,
And Images of voice—to hound and horn
From rocky steep and rock-bestudded meadows   35
Flung back, and, in the sky's blue caves, reborn,
On with your pastime! till the church-tower bells
A greeting give of *measured* glee;
And milder echoes from their cells
Repeat the bridal symphony.   40
Then, or far earlier, let us rove
Where mists are breaking up or gone,
And from aloft look down into a cove
Besprinkled with a careless quire,
Happy Milk-maids, one by one   45

Scattering a ditty each to her desire,
A liquid concert matchless by nice Art,
A stream as if from one full heart.

4

Blest be the song that brightens
The blind Man's gloom, exalts the Veteran's mirth;   50
Unscorned the Peasant's whistling breath, that lightens
His duteous toil of furrowing the green earth.
For the tired Slave, Song lifts the languid oar,
And bids it aptly fall, with chime
That beautifies the fairest shore,   55
And mitigates the harshest clime.
Yon Pilgrims see—in lagging file
They move; but soon the appointed way
A choral *Ave Marie* shall beguile,
And to their hope the distant shrine   60
Glisten with a livelier ray:
Nor friendless He, the Prisoner of the Mine,
Who from the well-spring of his own clear breast
Can draw, and sing his griefs to rest.

5

When civic renovation   65
Dawns on a kingdom, and for needful haste
Best eloquence avails not, Inspiration
Mounts with a tune, that travels like a blast
Piping through cave and battlemented tower;
Then starts the Sluggard, pleased to meet   70
That voice of Freedom, in its power
Of promises, shrill, wild, and sweet!
Who, from a martial *pageant*, spreads
Incitements of a battle-day,
Thrilling the unweaponed crowd with plumeless heads;   75
Even She whose Lydian airs inspire
Peaceful striving, gentle play
Of timid hope and innocent desire
Shot from the dancing Graces, as they move
Fanned by the plausive wings of Love.   80

6

How oft along thy mazes,
Regent of Sound, have dangerous Passions trod!
O Thou, through whom the Temple rings with praises,
And blackening clouds in thunder speak of God,
Betray not by the cozenage of sense   85
Thy Votaries, wooingly resigned
To a voluptuous influence
That taints the purer, better mind;
But lead sick Fancy to a harp
That hath in noble tasks been tried;   90
And, if the Virtuous feel a pang too sharp,
Soothe it into patience,—stay
The uplifted arm of Suicide;
And let some mood of thine in firm array
Knit every thought the impending issue needs,   95
Ere Martyr burns, or Patriot bleeds!

7

As Conscience, to the centre
Of Being, smites with irresistible pain,
So shall a solemn cadence, if it enter
The mouldy vaults of the dull Idiot's brain,   100
Transmute him to a wretch from quiet hurled—
Convulsed as by a jarring din;
And then aghast, as at the world
Of reason partially let in
By concords winding with a sway   105
Terrible for sense and soul!
Or, awed he weeps, struggling to quell dismay.
Point not these mysteries to an Art
Lodged above the starry pole;
Pure modulations flowing from the heart   110
Of divine Love, where Wisdom, Beauty, Truth
With Order dwell, in endless youth?

8

Oblivion may not cover
All treasures hoarded by the Miser, Time.

Orphean Insight! Truth's undaunted Lover, 115
To the first leagues of tutored passion climb,
When Music deigned within this grosser sphere
Her subtle essence to enfold,
And Voice and Shell drew forth a tear
Softer than Nature's self could mould. 120
Yet *strenuous* was the infant Age:
Art, daring because souls could feel,
Stirred nowhere but an urgent equipage
Of rapt imagination sped her march
Through the realms of woe and weal: 125
Hell to the lyre bowed low; the upper arch
Rejoiced that clamorous spell and magic verse
Her wan disasters could disperse.

9

The Gift to King Amphion
That walled a city with its melody 130
Was for belief no dream; thy skill, Arion!
Could humanise the creatures of the sea,
Where men were monsters. A last grace he craves,
Leave for one chant;— the dulcet sound
Steals from the deck o'er willing waves, 135
And listening Dolphins gather round.
Self-cast, as with a desperate course,
'Mid that strange audience, he bestrides
A proud One docile as a managed horse;
And singing, while the accordant hand 140
Sweeps his harp, the Master rides;
So shall he touch at length a friendly strand,
And he, with his Preserver, shine star-bright
In memory, through silent night.

10

The pipe of Pan, to Shepherds 145
Couched in the shadow of Menalian Pines,
Was passing sweet; the eyeballs of the Leopards,
That in high triumph drew the Lord of vines,
How did they sparkle to the cymbal's clang!

While Fauns and Satyrs beat the ground   150
In cadence,—and Silenus swang
This way and that, with wild-flowers crowned.
To life, to *life* give back thine Ear:
Ye who are longing to be rid
Of Fable, though to truth subservient, hear   155
The little sprinkling of cold earth that fell
Echoed from the coffin lid;
The Convict's summons in the steeple knell;
"The vain distress-gun," from a leeward shore,
Repeated—heard, and heard no more!   160

11

For terror, joy, or pity,
Vast is the compass, and the swell of notes:
From the Babe's first cry to voice of regal City,
Rolling a solemn sea-like bass, that floats
Far as the woodlands—with the trill to blend   165
Of that shy Songstress, whose love-tale
Might tempt an Angel to descend,
While hovering o'er the moonlight vale.
O for some soul-affecting scheme
Of *moral* music, to unite   170
Wanderers whose portion is the faintest dream
Of memory!—O that they might stoop to bear
Chains, such precious chains of sight
As laboured minstrelsies through ages wear!
O for a balance fit the truth to tell   175
Of the Unsubstantial, pondered well!

12

By one pervading Spirit
Of tones and numbers all things are controlled,
As Sages taught, where faith was found to merit
Initiation in that mystery old.   180
The Heavens, whose aspect makes our minds as still
As they themselves *appear* to be,
Innumerable voices fill
With everlasting harmony;

The towering Headlands, crowned with mist,   185
Their feet among the billows, know
That Ocean is a mighty harmonist;
Thy pinions, universal Air,
Ever waving to and fro,
Are delegates of harmony, and bear   190
Strains that support the Seasons in their round;
Stern Winter loves a dirge-like sound.

13

Break forth into thanksgiving,
Ye banded Instruments of wind and chords;
Unite, to magnify the Ever-living,   195
Your inarticulate notes with the voice of words!
Nor hushed be service from the lowing mead,
Nor mute the forest hum of noon;
Thou too be heard, lone Eagle! freed
From snowy peak and cloud, attune   200
Thy hungry barkings to the hymn
Of joy, that from her utmost walls
The six-days' Work, by flaming Seraphim,
Transmits to Heaven! As Deep to Deep
Shouting through one valley calls,   205
All worlds, all natures, mood and measure keep
For praise and ceaseless gratulation, poured
Into the ear of God, their Lord!

14

A Voice to Light gave Being;
To Time, and Man his earth-born Chronicler;   210
A Voice shall finish doubt and dim foreseeing,
And sweep away life's visionary stir;
The Trumpet (we, intoxicate with pride,
Arm at its blast for deadly wars)
To archangelic lips applied,   215
The grave shall open, quench the stars.
O Silence! are Man's noisy years
No more than moments of thy life?
Is Harmony, blest Queen of smiles and tears,

With her smooth tones and discords just,   220
Tempered into rapturous strife,
Thy destined Bond-slave? No! though Earth be dust
And vanish, though the Heavens dissolve, her stay
Is in the Word, that shall not pass away.

The Egyptian Maid;

OR,

THE ROMANCE OF THE WATER LILY

[FOR THE NAME AND PERSONS IN THE FOLLOWING POEM, SEE THE "HISTORY OF THE
RENOWNED PRINCE ARTHUR AND HIS KNIGHTS OF THE ROUND TABLE;" FOR THE
REST THE AUTHOR IS ANSWERABLE; ONLY IT MAY BE PROPER TO ADD, THAT THE
LOTUS, WITH THE BUST OF THE GODDESS APPEARING TO RISE OUT OF THE FULL-BLOWN
FLOWER, WAS SUGGESTED BY THE BEAUTIFUL WORK OF ANCIENT ART, ONCE INCLUDED
AMONG THE TOWNLEY MARBLES, AND NOW IN THE BRITISH MUSEUM.]

While Merlin paced the Cornish sands,
Forth-looking toward the Rocks of Scilly,
The pleased Enchanter was aware
Of a bright Ship that seemed to hang in air,
Yet was she work of mortal hands,   5
And took from men her name—THE WATER LILY.

Soft was the wind, that landward blew;
And, as the Moon, o'er some dark hill ascendant,
Grows from a little edge of light
To a full orb, this Pinnace bright,   10
Became, as nearer to the Coast she drew,
More glorious, with spread sail and streaming pendant.

Upon this wingèd Shape so fair
Sage Merlin gazed with admiration:
Her lineaments, thought he, surpass   15
Aught that was ever shown in magic glass;
Was ever built with patient care;
Or, at a touch, set forth with wondrous transformation.

Now, though a Mechanist, whose skill
Shames the degenerate grasp of modern science,   20
Grave Merlin (and belike the more

For practising occult and perilous lore)
Was subject to a freakish will
That sapped good thoughts, or scared them with defiance.

Provoked to envious spleen, he cast   25
An altered look upon the advancing Stranger
Whom he had hailed with joy, and cried,
"My Art shall help to tame her pride—"
Anon the breeze became a blast,
And the waves rose, and sky portended danger.   30

With thrilling word, and potent sign
Traced on the beach, his work the Sorcerer urges;
The clouds in blacker clouds are lost,
Like spiteful Fiends that vanish, crossed
By Fiends of aspect more malign;   35
And the winds roused the Deep with fiercer scourges.

But worthy of the name she bore
Was this Sea-flower, this buoyant Galley;
Supreme in loveliness and grace
Of motion, whether in the embrace   40
Of trusty anchorage, or scudding o'er
The main flood roughened into hill and valley.

Behold, how wantonly she laves
Her sides, the Wizard's craft confounding;
Like something out of Ocean sprung   45
To be for ever fresh and young,
Breasts the sea-flashes, and huge waves
Top-gallant high, rebounding and rebounding!

But Ocean under magic heaves,
And cannot spare the Thing he cherished: 50
Ah! what avails that She was fair,
Luminous, blithe, and debonair?
The storm has stripped her of her leaves;
The Lily floats no longer!—She hath perished.

Grieve for her,—She deserves no less;   55
So like, yet so unlike, a living Creature!
No heart had she, no busy brain;

Though loved, she could not love again;
Though pitied, *feel* her own distress;
Nor aught that troubles us, the fools of Nature.   60

Yet is there cause for gushing tears;
So richly was this Galley laden;
A fairer than Herself she bore,
And, in her struggles, cast ashore;
A lovely One, who nothing hears   65
Of wind or wave—a meek and guileless Maiden.

Into a cave had Merlin fled
From mischief, caused by spells himself had muttered;
And, while repentant all too late,
In moody posture there he sate,   70
He heard a voice, and saw, with half-raised head,
A Visitant by whom these words were uttered:

"On Christian service this frail Bark
Sailed" (hear me, Merlin!) "under high protection,
Though on her prow a sign of heathen power   75
Was carved—a Goddess with a Lily flower,
The old Egyptian's emblematic mark
Of joy immortal and of pure affection.

"Her course was for the British strand,
Her freight it was a Damsel peerless;   80
God reigns above, and Spirits strong
May gather to avenge this wrong
Done to the Princess, and her Land
Which she in duty left, though sad not cheerless.

"And to Caerleon's loftiest tower   85
Soon will the Knights of Arthur's Table
A cry of lamentation send;
And all will weep who there attend,
To grace that Stranger's bridal hour,
For whom the sea was made unnavigable.   90

"Shame! should a Child of Royal Line
Die through the blindness of thy malice:"
Thus to the Necromancer spake

Nina, the Lady of the Lake,
A gentle Sorceress, and benign,   95
Who ne'er embittered any good man's chalice.

"What boots," continued she, "to mourn?
To expiate thy sin endeavour!
From the bleak isle where she is laid,
Fetched by our art, the Egyptian Maid   100
May yet to Arthur's court be borne
Cold as she is, ere life be fled for ever.

"My pearly Boat, a shining Light,
That brought me down that sunless river,
Will bear me on from wave to wave,   105
And back with her to this sea-cave;
Then Merlin! for a rapid flight
Through air to thee my charge will I deliver.

"The very swiftest of thy Cars
Must, when my part is done, be ready;   110
Meanwhile, for further guidance, look
Into thy own prophetic book;
And, if that fail, consult the Stars
To learn thy course; farewell! be prompt and steady."

This scarcely spoken, she again   115
Was seated in her gleaming Shallop,
That, o'er the yet-distempered Deep,
Pursued its way with bird-like sweep,
Or like a steed, without a rein,
Urged o'er the wilderness in sportive gallop.   120

Soon did the gentle Nina reach
That Isle without a house or haven;
Landing, she found not what she sought,
Nor saw of wreck or ruin aught
But a carved Lotus cast upon the shore   125
By the fierce waves, a flower in marble graven.

Sad relique, but how fair the while!
For gently each from each retreating
With backward curve, the leaves revealed

The bosom half, and half concealed,   130
Of a Divinity, that seemed to smile
On Nina as she passed, with hopeful greeting.

No quest was hers of vague desire,
Of tortured hope and purpose shaken;
Following the margin of a bay,   135
She spied the lonely Cast-away,
Unmarred, unstripped of her attire,
But with closed eyes,—of breath and bloom forsaken.

Then Nina, stooping down, embraced,
With tenderness and mild emotion,   140
The Damsel, in that trance embound;
And, while she raised her from the ground,
And in the pearly shallop placed,
Sleep fell upon the air, and stilled the ocean.

The turmoil hushed, celestial springs   145
Of music opened, and there came a blending
Of fragrance, underived from earth,
With gleams that owed not to the Sun their birth,
And that soft rustling of invisible wings
Which Angels make, on works of love descending.   150

And Nina heard a sweeter voice
Than if the Goddess of the Flower had spoken:
"Thou hast achieved, fair Dame! what none
Less pure in spirit could have done;
Go, in thy enterprise rejoice!   155
Air, earth, sea, sky, and heaven, success betoken."

So cheered she left that Island bleak,
A bare rock of the Scilly cluster;
And, as they traversed the smooth brine,
The self-illumined Brigantine   160
Shed, on the Slumberer's cold wan cheek
And pallid brow, a melancholy lustre.

Fleet was their course, and when they came
To the dim cavern, whence the river
Issued into the salt-sea flood,   165

Merlin, as fixed in thought he stood,
Was thus accosted by the Dame:
"Behold to thee my Charge I now deliver!

"But where attends thy chariot—where?"
Quoth Merlin, "Even as I was bidden,   170
So have I done; as trusty as thy barge
My vehicle shall prove—O precious Charge!
If this be sleep, how soft! if death, how fair!
Much have my books disclosed, but the end is hidden."

He spake, and gliding into view   175
Forth from the grotto's dimmest chamber
Came two mute Swans, whose plumes of dusky white
Changed, as the pair approached the light,
Drawing an ebon car, their hue
(Like clouds of sunset) into lucid amber.   180

Once more did gentle Nina lift
The Princess, passive to all changes:
The car received her; then up-went
Into the ethereal element
The Birds with progress smooth and swift   185
As thought, when through bright regions memory ranges.

Sage Merlin, at the Slumberer's side,
Instructs the Swans their way to measure;
And soon Caerleon's towers appeared,
And notes of minstrelsy were heard   190
From rich pavilions spreading wide,
For some high day of long-expected pleasure.

Awe-stricken stood both Knights and Dames
Ere on firm ground the car alighted;
Eftsoons astonishment was past,   195
For in that face they saw the last
Last lingering look of clay, that tames
All pride, by which all happiness is blighted.

Said Merlin, "Mighty King, fair Lords,
Away with feast and tilt and tourney!   200
Ye saw, throughout this Royal House,

Ye heard, a rocking marvellous
Of turrets, and a clash of swords
Self-shaken, as I closed my airy journey.

"Lo! by a destiny well known   205
To mortals, joy is turned to sorrow;
This is the wished-for Bride, the Maid
Of Egypt, from a rock conveyed
Where she by shipwreck had been thrown;
Ill sight! but grief may vanish ere the morrow."   210

"Though vast thy power, thy words are weak,"
Exclaimed the King, "a mockery hateful;
Dutiful Child! her lot how hard!
Is this her piety's reward?
Those watery locks, that bloodless cheek!   215
O winds without remorse! O shore ungrateful!

"Rich robes are fretted by the moth;
Towers, temples, fall by stroke of thunder;
Will that, or deeper thoughts, abate
A Father's sorrow for her fate?   220
He will repent him of his troth;
His brain will burn, his stout heart split asunder.

"Alas! and I have caused this woe;
For, when my prowess from invading Neighbours
Had freed his Realm, he plighted word   225
That he would turn to Christ our Lord,
And his dear Daughter on a Knight bestow
Whom I should choose for love and matchless labours.

"Her birth was heathen, but a fence
Of holy Angels round her hovered;   230
A Lady added to my court
So fair, of such divine report
And worship, seemed a recompence
For fifty kingdoms by my sword recovered.

"Ask not for whom, O champions true!   235
She was reserved by me her life's betrayer;
She who was meant to be a bride

Is now a corse; then put aside
Vain thoughts, and speed ye, with observance due
Of Christian rites, in Christian ground to lay her."   240

"The tomb," said Merlin, "may not close
Upon her yet, earth hide her beauty;
Not froward to thy sovereign will
Esteem me, Liege! if I, whose skill
Wafted her hither, interpose   245
To check this pious haste of erring duty.

"My books command me to lay bare
The secret thou art bent on keeping;
Here must a high attest be given,
What Bridegroom was for her ordained by Heaven;   250
And in my glass significants there are
Of things that may to gladness turn this weeping.

"For this, approaching, One by One,
Thy Knights must touch the cold hand of the Virgin;
So, for the favoured One, the Flower may bloom   255
Once more; but, if unchangeable her doom,
If life departed be for ever gone,
Some blest assurance, from this cloud emerging,

May teach him to bewail his loss;
Not with a grief that, like a vapour, rises   260
And melts; but grief devout that shall endure,
And a perpetual growth secure
Of purposes which no false thought shall cross,
A harvest of high hopes and noble enterprises."

"So be it," said the King;—"anon,   265
Here, where the Princess lies, begin the trial;
Knights each in order as ye stand
Step forth."—To touch the pallid hand
Sir Agravaine advanced; no sign he won
From Heaven or Earth;—Sir Kaye had like denial.   270

Abashed, Sir Dinas turned away;
Even for Sir Percival was no disclosure;
Though he, devoutest of all Champions, ere

He reached that ebon car, the bier
Whereon diffused like snow the Damsel lay,   275
Full thrice had crossed himself in meek composure.

Imagine (but ye Saints! who can?)
How in still air the balance trembled;
The wishes, peradventure the despites
That overcame some not ungenerous Knights;   280
And all the thoughts that lengthened out a span
Of time to Lords and Ladies thus assembled.

What patient confidence was here!
And there how many bosoms panted!
While drawing toward the Car Sir Gawaine, mailed   285
For tournament, his Beaver vailed,
And softly touched; but, to his princely cheer
And high expectancy, no sign was granted.

Next, disencumbered of his harp,
Sir Tristram, dear to thousands as a brother,   290
Came to proof, nor grieved that there ensued
No change;—the fair Izonda he had wooed
With love too true, a love with pangs too sharp,
From hope too distant, not to dread another.

Not so Sir Launcelot;—from Heaven's grace   295
A sign he craved, tired slave of vain contrition;
The royal Guinever looked passing glad
When his touch failed.—Next came Sir Galahad;
He paused, and stood entranced by that still face
Whose features he had seen in noontide vision.   300

For late, as near a murmuring stream
He rested 'mid an arbour green and shady,
Nina, the good Enchantress, shed
A light around his mossy bed;
And, at her call, a waking dream   305
Prefigured to his sense the Egyptian Lady.

Now, while his bright-haired front he bowed,
And stood, far-kenned by mantle furred with ermine,
As o'er the insensate Body hung

The enrapt, the beautiful, the young,   310
  Belief sank deep into the crowd
That he the solemn issue would determine.

  Nor deem it strange; the Youth had worn
  That very mantle on a day of glory,
  The day when he achieved that matchless feat,   315
  The marvel of the PERILOUS SEAT,
  Which whosoe'er approached of strength was shorn,
Though King or Knight the most renowned in story.

  He touched with hesitating hand,
  And lo! those Birds, far-famed through Love's dominions,   320
  The Swans, in triumph clap their wings;
  And their necks play, involved in rings,
  Like sinless snakes in Eden's happy land;—
"Mine is she," cried the Knight;—again they clapped their pinions.

  "Mine was she—mine she is, though dead,   325
  And to her name my soul shall cleave in sorrow;"
  Whereat, a tender twilight streak
  Of colour dawned upon the Damsel's cheek;
  And her lips, quickening with uncertain red,
Seemed from each other a faint warmth to borrow.   330

  Deep was the awe, the rapture high,
  Of love emboldened, hope with dread entwining,
  When, to the mouth, relenting Death
  Allowed a soft and flower-like breath,
  Precursor to a timid sigh,   335
To lifted eyelids, and a doubtful shining.

  In silence did King Arthur gaze
  Upon the signs that pass away or tarry;
  In silence watched the gentle strife
  Of Nature leading back to life;   340
  Then eased his Soul at length by praise
Of God, and Heaven's pure Queen—the blissful Mary.

  Then said he, "Take her to thy heart
  Sir Galahad! a treasure that God giveth,
  Bound by indissoluble ties to thee   345

Through mortal change and immortality;
Be happy and unenvied, thou who art
A goodly Knight that hath no Peer that liveth!"

Not long the Nuptials were delayed;
And sage tradition still rehearses   350
The pomp the glory of that hour
When toward the Altar from her bower
King Arthur led the Egyptian Maid,
And Angels carolled these far-echoed verses;—

Who shrinks not from alliance   355
Of evil with good Powers,
To God proclaims defiance,
And mocks whom he adores.

A Ship to Christ devoted
From the Land of Nile did go;   360
Alas! the bright Ship floated,
An Idol at her Prow.

By magic domination,
The Heaven-permitted vent
Of purblind mortal passion,   365
Was wrought her punishment.

The Flower, the Form within it,
What served they in her need?
Her port she could not win it,
Nor from mishap be freed.   370

The tempest overcame her,
And she was seen no more;
But gently gently blame her,
She cast a Pearl ashore.

The Maid to Jesu hearkened,   375
And kept to him her faith,
Till sense in death was darkened,
Or sleep akin to death.

But Angels round her pillow

Kept watch, a viewless band;   380
And, billow favouring billow,
She reached the destined strand.

Blest Pair! whate'er befall you,
Your faith in Him approve
Who from frail earth can call you,   385
To bowers of endless love!

A Jewish Family

(IN A SMALL VALLEY OPPOSITE ST. GOAR, UPON THE RHINE)

Genius of Raphael! if thy wings
    Might bear thee to this glen,
With faithful memory left of things
    To pencil dear and pen,
Thou wouldst forego the neighbouring Rhine,   5
    And all his majesty,
A studious forehead to incline
    O'er this poor family.

The Mother—her thou must have seen,
    In spirit, ere she came   10
To dwell these rifted rocks between,
    Or found on earth a name;
An image, too, of that sweet Boy,
    Thy inspirations give:
Of playfulness, and love, and joy,   15
    Predestined here to live.

Downcast, or shooting glances far,
    How beautiful his eyes,
That blend the nature of the star
    With that of summer skies!   20
I speak as if of sense beguiled;
    Uncounted months are gone,
Yet am I with the Jewish Child,
    That exquisite Saint John.

I see the dark brown curls, the brow,   25
    The smooth transparent skin,

Refined, as with intent to show
  The holiness within;
The grace of parting Infancy
  By blushes yet untamed;   30
Age faithful to the mother's knee,
  Nor of her arms ashamed.

Two lovely Sisters, still and sweet
  As flowers, stand side by side;
Their soul–subduing looks might cheat   35
  The Christian of his pride:
Such beauty hath the Eternal poured
  Upon them not forlorn,
Though of a lineage once abhorred,
  Nor yet redeemed from scorn.   40

Mysterious safeguard, that, in spite
  Of poverty and wrong,
Doth here preserve a living light,
  From Hebrew fountains sprung;
That gives this ragged group to cast   45
  Around the dell a gleam
Of Palestine, of glory past,
  And proud Jerusalem!

The Poet and the Caged Turtledove

As often as I murmur here
  My half-formed melodies,
Straight from her osier mansion near,
  The Turtledove replies:
Though silent as a leaf before,   5
  The captive promptly coos;
Is it to teach her own soft lore,
  Or second my weak Muse?

I rather think, the gentle Dove
  Is murmuring a reproof,   10
Displeased that I from lays of love
  Have dared to keep aloof;
That I, a Bard of hill and dale,

Have caroll'd, fancy free,
As if nor dove, nor nightingale,   15
  Had heart or voice for me.

If such thy meaning, O forbear,
  Sweet Bird! to do me wrong;
Love, blessed Love, is every where
  The spirit of my song: 20
'Mid grove, and by the calm fireside,
  Love animates my lyre;
That coo again!—'tis not to chide,
  I feel, but to inspire.

Written in Mrs. Field's Album
Opposite a Pen-and-ink Sketch in the Manner of
a Rembrandt Etching done by Edmund Field

That gloomy cave, that gothic nich,
Those trees that forward lean
As if enamoured of the brook—
How soothing is the scene!
No witchery of inky words   5
Can such illusions yield;
Yet all (ye Landscape Poets blush!)
Was penned by Edmund Field.

The Russian Fugitive

[Peter Henry Bruce, having given in his entertaining Memoirs the substance
of the following Tale, affirms, that, besides the concurring reports of others,
he had the story from the Lady's own mouth.

  The Lady Catherine, mentioned towards the close, was the famous Catherine,
then bearing that name as the acknowledged Wife of Peter the Great.]

The Russian Fugitive

PART I

1

Enough of rose-bud lips, and eyes
  Like harebells bathed in dew,
Of cheek that with carnation vies,

And veins of violet hue;
Earth wants not beauty that may scorn
   A likening to frail flowers;
Yea, to the stars, if they were born
   For seasons and for hours.

5

2

Through Moscow's gates, with gold unbarred,
   Stepped one at dead of night,
Whom such high beauty could not guard
   From meditated blight;
By stealth she passed, and fled as fast
   As doth the hunted fawn,
Nor stopped, till in the dappling east
   Appeared unwelcome dawn.

10

15

3

Seven days she lurked in brake and field,
   Seven nights her course renewed,
Sustained by what her scrip might yield,
   Or berries of the wood;
At length, in darkness travelling on,
   When lowly doors were shut,
The haven of her hope she won,
   Her Foster-mother's hut.

20

4

"To put your love to dangerous proof
   I come," said she, "from far;
For I have left my Father's roof,
   In terror of the Czar."
No answer did the Matron give,
   No second look she cast;
She hung upon the Fugitive,
   Embracing and embraced.

25

30

5

She led her Lady to a seat
   Beside the glimmering fire,

Bathed duteously her wayworn feet,   35
   Prevented each desire:
The cricket chirped, the house-dog dozed,
   And on that simple bed,
Where she in childhood had reposed,
   Now rests her weary head.   40

6

When she, whose couch had been the sod,
   Whose curtain pine or thorn,
Had breathed a sigh of thanks to God,
   Who comforts the forlorn;
While over her the Matron bent   45
   Sleep sealed her eyes, and stole
Feeling from limbs with travel spent,
   And trouble from the soul.

7

Refreshed, the Wanderer rose at morn,
   And soon again was dight   50
In those unworthy vestments worn
   Through long and perilous flight;
And "O beloved Nurse," she said,
   "My thanks with silent tears
Have unto Heaven and You been paid: 55
   Now listen to my fears!

8

"Have you forgot"—and here she smiled—
   "The babbling flatteries
You lavished on me when a child
   Disporting round your knees?   60
I was your lambkin, and your bird,
   Your star, your gem, your flower;
Light words, that were more lightly heard
   In many a cloudless hour!

9

"The blossom you so fondly praised   65

Is come to bitter fruit;
   A mighty One upon me gazed;
     I spurned his lawless suit,
And must be hidden from his wrath:
     You, Foster-father dear,   70
Will guide me in my forward path;
     I may not tarry here!

10

"I cannot bring to utter woe
     Your proved fidelity."—
"Dear Child, sweet Mistress, say not so!   75
     For you we both would die."
"Nay, nay, I come with semblance feigned
     And cheek embrowned by art;
Yet, being inwardly unstained,
     With courage will depart."   80

11

"But whither would you, could you, flee?
     A poor Man's counsel take;
The Holy Virgin gives to me
     A thought for your dear sake;
Rest shielded by our Lady's grace;   85
     And soon shall you be led
Forth to a safe abiding-place,
     Where never foot doth tread."

The Russian Fugitive

PART II

1

The Dwelling of this faithful pair
     In a straggling village stood,   90
For One who breathed unquiet air
     A dangerous neighbourhood;
But wide around lay forest ground
     With thickets rough and blind;

And pine-trees made a heavy shade   95
  Impervious to the wind.

2

And there, sequestered from the sight,
  Was spread a treacherous swamp,
On which the noonday sun shed light
  As from a lonely lamp;   100
And midway in the unsafe morass,
  A single Island rose
Of firm dry ground, with healthful grass
  Adorned, and shady boughs.

3

The Woodman knew, for such the craft   105
  This Russian Vassal plied,
That never fowler's gun, nor shaft
  Of archer, there was tried;
A sanctuary seemed the spot
  From all intrusion free;   110
And there he planned an artful Cot
  For perfect secrecy.

4

With earnest pains unchecked by dread
  Of Power's far-stretching hand,
The bold good Man his labour sped   115
  At nature's pure command;
Heart-soothed, and busy as a wren,
  While, in a hollow nook,
She moulds her sight-eluding den
  Above a murmuring brook.   120

5

His task accomplished to his mind,
  The twain ere break of day
Creep forth, and through the forest wind
  Their solitary way;
Few words they speak, nor dare to slack   125

Their pace from mile to mile,
Till they have crossed the quaking marsh,
    And reached the lonely Isle.

6

The sun above the pine-trees showed
    A bright and cheerful face;   130
And Ina looked for her abode,
    The promised hiding-place;
She sought in vain, the Woodman smiled;
    No threshold could be seen,
Nor roof, nor window; all seemed wild   135
    As it had ever been.

7

Advancing, you might guess an hour,
    The front with such nice care
Is masked, "if house it be or bower,"
    But in they entered are;   140
As shaggy as were wall and roof
    With branches intertwined,
So smooth was all within, air-proof,
    And delicately lined.

8

And hearth was there, and maple dish,   145
    And cups in seemly rows,
And couch—all ready to a wish
    For nurture or repose;
And Heaven doth to her virtue grant
    That here she may abide   150
In solitude, with every want
    By cautious love supplied.

9

No Queen, before a shouting crowd,
    Led on in bridal state,
E'er struggled with a heart so proud,   155
    Entering her palace gate;

Rejoiced to bid the world farewell,
 No saintly Anchoress
E'er took possession of her cell
 With deeper thankfulness.   160

10

"Father of all, upon thy care
 And mercy am I thrown;
Be thou my safeguard!"—such her prayer
 When she was left alone,
Kneeling amid the wilderness   165
 When joy had passed away,
And smiles, fond efforts of distress
 To hide what they betray!

11

The prayer is heard, the Saints have seen,
 Diffused through form and face,   170
Resolves devotedly serene;
 That monumental grace
Of Faith, which doth all passions tame
 That Reason *should* control;
And shows in the untrembling frame   175
 A statue of the soul.

The Russian Fugitive

PART III

1

'Tis sung in ancient minstrelsy
 That Phœbus wont to wear
"The leaves of any pleasant tree
 Around his golden hair,"[1]   180
Till Daphne, desperate with pursuit
 Of his imperious love,
At her own prayer transformed, took root,
 A laurel in the grove.

---

1 "From Golding's Translation of Ovid's Metamorphoses. See also his Dedicatory Epistle
 prefixed to the same work." WW refers to Arthur Golding's translation, first published in
 1565.

2

Then did the Penitent adorn   185
   His brow with laurel green;
And 'mid his bright locks never shorn
   No meaner leaf was seen;
And Poets sage, through every age,
   About their temples wound   190
The bay; and Conquerors thanked the Gods,
   With laurel chaplets crowned.

3

Into the mists of fabling Time
   So far runs back the praise
Of Beauty, that disdains to climb   195
   Along forbidden ways;
That scorns temptation; power defies
   Where mutual love is not;
And to the tomb for rescue flies
   When life would be a blot.   200

4

To this fair Votaress, a fate
   More mild doth Heaven ordain
Upon her Island desolate;
   And words, not breathed in vain,
Might tell what intercourse she found,   205
   Her silence to endear;
What birds she tamed, what flowers the ground
   Sent forth her peace to cheer.

5

To one mute Presence, above all,
   Her soothed affections clung,   210
A picture on the Cabin wall
   By Russian usage hung—
The Mother-maid, whose countenance bright
   With love abridged the day;
And, communed with by taper light,   215
   Chased spectral fears away.

6

And oft, as either Guardian came,
    The joy in that retreat
Might any common friendship shame,
    So high their hearts would beat;   220
And to the lone Recluse, whate'er
    They brought, each visiting
Was like the crowding of the year
    With a new burst of spring.

7

But, when she of her Parents thought,   225
    The pang was hard to bear;
And, if with all things not enwrought,
    That trouble still is near.
Before her flight she had not dared
    Their constancy to prove,   230
Too much the heroic Daughter feared
    The weakness of their love.

8

Dark is the Past to them, and dark
    The Future still must be,
Till pitying Saints conduct her bark   235
    Into a safer sea—
Or gentle Nature close her eyes,
    And set her Spirit free
From the altar of this sacrifice,
    In vestal purity.   240

9

Yet, when above the forest-glooms
    The white swans southward passed,
High as the pitch of their swift plumes
    Her fancy rode the blast;
And bore her tow'rd the fields of France,   245
    Her Father's native land,
To mingle in the rustic dance,
    The happiest of the band!

10

Of those belovèd fields she oft
   Had heard her Father tell   250
In phrase that now with echoes soft
   Haunted her lonely Cell;
She saw the hereditary bowers,
   She heard the ancestral stream;
The Kremlin and its haughty towers   255
   Forgotten like a dream!

The Russian Fugitive

PART IV

1

The ever-changing Moon had traced
   Twelve times her monthly round,
When through the unfrequented Waste
   Was heard a startling sound;   260
A shout thrice sent from one who chased
   At speed a wounded Deer,
Bounding through branches interlaced,
   And where the wood was clear.

2

The fainting Creature took the marsh,   265
   And toward the Island fled,
While plovers screamed with tumult harsh
   Above his antlered head;
This, Ina saw; and, pale with fear,
   Shrunk to her citadel;   270
The desperate Deer rushed on, and near
   The tangled covert fell.

3

Across the marsh, the game in view,
   The Hunter followed fast,
Nor paused, till o'er the Stag he blew   275
   A death-proclaiming blast;

Then, resting on her upright mind,
   Came forth the Maid—"In me
Behold," she said, "a stricken Hind
   Pursued by destiny!   280

4

"From your deportment, Sir! I deem
   That you have worn a sword,
And will not hold in light esteem
   A suffering woman's word;
There is my covert, there perchance   285
   I might have lain concealed,
My fortunes hid, my countenance
   Not even to you revealed.

5

"Tears might be shed, and I might pray,
   Crouching and terrified,   290
That what has been unveiled to day,
   You would in mystery hide;
But I will not defile with dust
   The knee that bends to adore
The God in heaven;—attend, be just: 295
   This ask I, and no more!

6

"I speak not of the winter's cold,
   For summer's heat exchanged,
While I have lodged in this rough hold,
   From social life estranged;   300
Nor yet of trouble and alarms:
   High Heaven is my defence;
And every season has soft arms
   For injured Innocence.

7

"From Moscow to the Wilderness   305
   It was my choice to come,
Lest virtue should be harbourless,

And honour want a home;
And happy were I, if the Czar
   Retain his lawless will,   310
To end life here like this poor Deer,
   Or a Lamb on a green hill."

8

"Are you the Maid," the Stranger cried,
   "From Gallic Parents sprung,
Whose vanishing was rumoured wide,   315
   Sad theme for every tongue;
Who foiled an Emperor's eager quest?
   You, Lady, forced to wear
These rude habiliments, and rest
   Your head in this dark lair!"   320

9

But wonder, pity, soon were quelled;
   And in her face and mien
The soul's pure brightness he beheld
   Without a veil between:
He loved, he hoped,—a holy flame   325
   Kindled 'mid rapturous tears;
The passion of a moment came
   As on the wings of years.

10

"Such bounty is no gift of chance,"
   Exclaimed he; "righteous Heaven,   330
Preparing your deliverance,
   To me the charge hath given.
The Czar full oft in words and deeds
   Is stormy and self-willed;
But, when the Lady Catherine pleads,   335
   His violence is stilled.

11

"Leave open to my wish the course,
   And I to her will go;

From that humane and heavenly source,
 Good, only good, can flow."   340
Faint sanction given, the Cavalier
 Was eager to depart,
Though question followed question, dear
 To the Maiden's filial heart.

12

Light was his step,—his hopes, more light,   345
 Kept pace with his desires;
And the third morning gave him sight
 Of Moscow's glittering spires.
He sued:—heart-smitten by the wrong,
 To the lorn Fugitive   350
The Emperor sent a pledge as strong
 As sovereign power could give.

13

O more than mighty change! If e'er
 Amazement rose to pain,
And over-joy produced a fear   355
 Of something void and vain,
'Twas when the Parents, who had mourned
 So long the lost as dead,
Beheld their only Child returned,
 The household floor to tread.   360

14

Soon gratitude gave way to love
 Within the Maiden's breast:
Delivered and Deliverer move
 In bridal garments drest;
Meek Catherine had her own reward;   365
 The Czar bestowed a dower;
And universal Moscow shared
 The triumph of that hour.

15

Flowers strewed the ground; the nuptial feast

Was held with costly state;   370
And there, 'mid many a noble Guest,
   The Foster-parents sate;
Encouraged by the imperial eye,
   They shrank not into shade;
Great was their bliss, the honour high   375
   To them and nature paid!

The Primrose of the Rock

A Rock there is whose homely front
   The passing Traveller slights;
Yet there the Glow-worms hang their lamps,
   Like stars, at various heights;
And one coy Primrose to that Rock   5
   The vernal breeze invites.

What hideous warfare hath been waged,
   What kingdoms overthrown,
Since first I spied that Primrose-tuft
   And marked it for my own;   10
A lasting link in Nature's chain
   From highest Heaven let down!

The Flowers, still faithful to the stems,
   Their fellowship renew;
The stems are faithful to the root,   15
   That worketh out of view;
And to the rock the root adheres
   In every fibre true.

Close clings to earth the living rock,
   Though threatening still to fall;   20
The earth is constant to her sphere;
   And God upholds them all:
So blooms this lonely Plant, nor dreads
   Her annual funeral.

*   *   *   *   *

Here closed the meditative Strain;   25
   But air breathed soft that day,
The hoary mountain-heights were cheered,

The sunny vale looked gay;
And to the Primrose of the Rock
   I gave this after-lay.   30

I sang, Let myraids of bright flowers,
   Like Thee, in field and grove
Revive unenvied,—mightier far
   Than tremblings that reprove
Our vernal tendencies to hope   35
   Is God's redeeming love:

That love which changed, for wan disease,
   For sorrow that had bent
O'er hopeless dust, for withered age,
   Their moral element,   40
And turned the thistles of a curse
   To types beneficent.

Sin-blighted though we are, we too,
   The reasoning Sons of Men,
From one oblivious winter called   45
   Shall rise, and breathe again;
And in eternal summer lose
   Our threescore years and ten.

To humbleness of heart descends
   This prescience from on high,   50
The faith that elevates the Just,
   Before and when they die;
And makes each soul a separate heaven,
   A court for Deity.

The Armenian Lady's Love

[The subject of the following poem is from the Orlandus of the author's friend, Kenelm Henry Digby;[1] and the liberty is taken of inscribing it to him as an acknowledgment, however unworthy, of pleasure and instruction derived from his numerous and valuable writings, illustrative of the piety and chivalry of the olden time.]

---

1 Author of *The Broad Stone of Honour: The True Sense and Practice of Chilvary* (London, 1826, 1828, 1829)

1

You have heard "a Spanish Lady
    How she wooed an English Man;"[1]
Hear now of a fair Armenian,
    Daughter of the proud Soldàn;
How she loved a Christian Slave, and told her pain   5
By word, look, deed, with hope that he might love again.

2

"Pluck that rose, it moves my liking,"
    Said she, lifting up her veil;
"Pluck it for me, gentle Gardener,
    Ere it wither and grow pale."   10
"Princess fair, I till the ground, but may not take
From twig or bed an humbler flower, even for your sake."

3

"Grieved am I, submissive Christian!
    To behold thy captive state;
Women, in your land, may pity   15
    (May they not?) the unfortunate."
"Yes, kind Lady! otherwise Man could not bear
Life, which to every one that breathes is full of care."

4

"Worse than idle is compassion
    If it end in tears and sighs;   20
Thee from bondage would I rescue
    And from vile indignities;
Nurtured, as thy mien bespeaks, in high degree,
Look up—and help a hand that longs to set thee free."

5

"Lady, dread the wish, nor venture   25
    In such peril to engage;
Think how it would stir against you

---

1   "See, in Percy's Reliques, that fine old ballad, 'The Spanish Lady's Love;' from which Poem
    the form of stanza, as suitable to dialogue, is adopted." WW refers to Thomas Percy,
    Reliques of Ancient English Poetry (London, 1765).

Your most loving Father's rage:
Sad deliverance would it be, and yoked with shame,
Should troubles overflow on her from whom it came."   30

6

"Generous Frank! the just in effort
    Are of inward peace secure;
Hardships for the brave encountered,
    Even the feeblest may endure:
If Almighty Grace through me thy chains unbind,   35
My Father for slave's work may seek a slave in mind."

7

"Princess, at this burst of goodness,
    My long-frozen heart grows warm!"
"Yet you make all courage fruitless,
    Me to save from chance of harm: 40
Leading such Companion I that gilded Dome,
Yon Minarets, would gladly leave for his worst home."

8

"Feeling tunes your voice, fair Princess!
    And your brow is free from scorn,
Else these words would come like mockery,   45
    Sharper than the pointed thorn."
"Whence the undeserved mistrust? Too wide apart
Our faith hath been,—O would that eyes could see the heart!"

9

"Tempt me not, I pray; my doom is
    These base implements to wield;   50
Rusty Lance, I ne'er shall grasp thee,
    Ne'er assoil my cobwebb'd shield!
Never see my native land, nor castle towers,
Nor Her who thinking of me there counts widowed hours."

10

"Prisoner! pardon youthful fancies;   55
    Wedded? If you can, say no!—

Blessed is and be your Consort;
   Hopes I cherished let them go!
Handmaid's privilege would leave my purpose free,
Without another link to my felicity."   60

11

"Wedded love with loyal Christians,
   Lady, is a mystery rare;
Body, heart, and soul in union,
   Make one being of a pair."
"Humble love in me would look for no return,   65
Soft as a guiding star that cheers, but cannot burn."

12

"Gracious Allah! by such title
   Do I dare to thank the God,
Him who thus exalts thy spirit,
   Flower of an unchristian sod!   70
Or hast thou put off wings which thou in heaven dost wear?
What have I seen, and heard, or dreamt? where am I? where?"

13

Here broke off the dangerous converse:
   Less impassioned words might tell
How the Pair escaped together,   75
   Tears not wanting, nor a knell
Of sorrow in her heart while through her Father's door,
And from her narrow world, she passed for evermore.

14

But affections higher, holier,
   Urged her steps; she shrunk from trust   80
In a sensual creed that trampled
   Woman's birthright into dust.
Little be the wonder then, the blame be none,
If she, a timid Maid, hath put such boldness on.

15

Judge both Fugitives with knowledge: 85

In those old romantic days
   Mighty were the soul's commandments
     To support, restrain, or raise.
Foes might hang upon their path, snakes rustle near,
But nothing from their inward selves had they to fear.   90

16

Thought infirm ne'er came between them,
   Whether printing desert sands
With accordant steps, or gathering
   Forest-fruit with social hands;
Or whispering like two reeds that in the cold moonbeam   95
Bend with the breeze their heads, beside a crystal stream.

17

On a friendly deck reposing
   They at length for Venice steer;
There, when they had closed their voyage,
   One, who daily on the Pier   100
Watched for tidings from the East, beheld his Lord,
Fell down and clasped his knees for joy, not uttering word.

18

Mutual was the sudden transport;
   Breathless questions followed fast,
Years contracting to a moment,   105
   Each word greedier than the last;
"Hie thee to the Countess, Friend! return with speed,
And of this Stranger speak by whom her Lord was freed.

19

"Say that I, who might have languished,
   Drooped and pined till life was spent,   110
Now before the gates of Stolberg
   My Deliverer would present
For a crowning recompence, the precious grace
Of her who in my heart still holds her ancient place.

20

"Make it known that my Companion   115

Is of royal Eastern blood,
　　Thirsting after all perfection,
　　　Innocent, and meek, and good,
Though with misbelievers bred; but that dark night
Will Holy Church disperse by beams of Gospel Light."   120

21

Swiftly went that grey-haired Servant,
　　Soon returned a trusty Page
Charged with greetings, benedictions,
　　Thanks and praises, each a gage
For a sunny thought to cheer the Stranger's way,   125
Her virtuous scruples to remove, her fears allay.

22

Fancy (while, to banners floating
　　High on Stolberg's Castle walls,
Deafening noise of welcome mounted,
　　Trumpets, Drums, and Atabals,)   130
The devout embraces still, while such tears fell
As made a meeting seem most like a dear farewell.

23

Through a haze of human nature,
　　Glorified by heavenly light,
Looked the beautiful Deliverer   135
　　On that overpowering sight,
While across her virgin cheek pure blushes strayed,
For every tender sacrifice her heart had made.

24

On the ground the weeping Countess
　　Knelt, and kissed the Stranger's hand;   140
Act of soul-devoted homage,
　　Pledge of an eternal band:
Nor did aught of future days that kiss belie,
Which, with a generous shout, the crowd did ratify.

25

Constant to the fair Armenian,	145

Constant to the fair Armenian,   145
    Gentle pleasures round her moved,
Like a tutelary Spirit
    Reverenced, like a Sister, loved.
Christian meekness smoothed for all the path of life,
Who, loving most, should wiseliest love, their only strife.   150

26

Mute Memento of that union
    In a Saxon Church survives,
Where a cross-legged Knight lies sculptured
    As between two wedded Wives—
Figures with armorial signs of race and birth,   155
And the vain rank the Pilgrims bore while yet on earth.

Rural Illusions

1

Sylph was it? or a Bird more bright
    Than those of fabulous stock?
A second darted by;—and lo!
    Another of the flock,
Through sunshine flitting from the bough   5
    To nestle in the rock.
Transient deception! a gay freak
    Of April's mimicries!
Those brilliant Strangers, hailed with joy
    Among the budding trees,   10
Proved last year's leaves, pushed from the spray
    To frolic on the breeze.

2

Maternal Flora! show thy face,
    And let thy hand be seen
Which sprinkles here these tiny flowers,   15
    That, as they touch the green,
Take root (so seems it) and look up

In honour of their Queen.
Yet, sooth, those little starry specks,
    That not in vain aspired   20
To be confounded with live growths,
    Most dainty, most admired,
Were only blossoms dropped from twigs
    Of their own offspring tired.

3

Not such the World's illusive shows;   25
    Her wingless flutterings,
Her blossoms which, though shed, outbrave
    The Floweret as it springs,
For the Undeceived, smile as they may,
    Are melancholy things: 30
But gentle Nature plays her part
    With ever-varying wiles,
And transient feignings with plain truth
    So well she reconciles,
That those fond Idlers most are pleased   35
    Whom oftenest she beguiles.

This Lawn, &c.

This Lawn, a carpet all alive
With shadows flung from leaves—to strive
    In dance, amid a press
Of sunshine—an apt emblem yields
Of Worldlings revelling in the fields   5
    Of strenuous idleness;

Less quick the stir when tide and breeze
Encounter, and to narrow seas
    Forbid a moment's rest;
The medley less when boreal Lights   10
Glance to and fro like aery Sprites
    To feats of arms addrest!

Yet, spite of all this eager strife,
This ceaseless play, the genuine life

That serves the steadfast hours,   15
Is in the grass beneath, that grows
Unheeded, and the mute repose
    Of sweetly-breathing flowers.

Presentiments

Presentiments! they judge not right
Who deem that ye from open light
    Retire in fear of shame;
All *heaven-born* Instincts shun the touch
Of vulgar sense, and, being such,   5
    Such privilege ye claim.

The tear whose source I could not guess,
The deep sigh that seemed fatherless,
    Were mine in early days;
And now, unforced by Time to part   10
With Fancy, I obey my heart,
    And venture on your praise.

What though some busy Foes to good,
Too potent over nerve and blood,
    Lurk near you, and combine   15
To taint the health which ye infuse,
This hides not from the moral Muse
    Your origin divine.

How oft from you, derided Powers!
Comes Faith that in auspicious hours   20
    Builds castles, not of air;
Bodings unsanctioned by the will
Flow from your visionary skill,
    And teach us to beware.

The bosom-weight, your stubborn gift,   25
That no philosophy can lift,
    Shall vanish, if ye please,
Like morning mist; and, where it lay,
The spirits at your bidding play
    In gaiety and ease.   30

Star-guided Contemplations move
Through space, though calm, not raised above
 Prognostics that ye rule;
The naked Indian of the Wild,
And haply, too, the cradled Child,   35
 Are pupils of your school.

But who can fathom your intents,
Number their signs or instruments?
 A rainbow, a sunbeam,
A subtle smell that Spring unbinds,   40
Dead pause abrupt of midnight winds,
 An echo, or a dream.

The laughter of the Christmas hearth
With sighs of self-exhausted mirth
 Ye feelingly reprove;   45
And daily, in the conscious breast,
Your visitations are a test
 And exercise of love.

When some great change gives boundless scope
To an exulting Nation's hope,   50
 Oft, startled and made wise
By your low-breathed interpretings,
The simply-meek foretaste the springs
 Of bitter contraries.

Ye daunt the proud array of War,   55
Pervade the lonely Ocean far
 As sail hath been unfurled;
For Dancers in the festive hall
What ghastly Partners hath your call
 Fetched from the shadowy world!   60

'Tis said, that warnings ye dispense,
Emboldened by a keener sense;
 That men have lived for whom,
With dread precision, ye made clear
The hour that in a distant year   65
 Should knell them to the tomb.

Unwelcome Insight! Yet there are
Blest times when mystery is laid bare,
   Truth shows a glorious face,
While on that Isthmus which commands   70
The councils of both worlds she stands,
   Sage Spirits! by your grace.

God, who instructs the Brutes to scent
All changes of the element,
   Whose wisdom fixed the scale   75
Of Natures, for our wants provides
By higher, sometimes humbler, guides,
   When lights of Reason fail.

Gold and Silver Fishes,
IN A VASE

The soaring Lark is blest as proud
   When at Heaven's gate she sings;
The roving Bee proclaims aloud
   Her flight by vocal wings;
While Ye, in lasting durance pent,   5
   Your silent lives employ
For something "more than dull content
   Though haply less than joy."

Yet might your glassy prison seem
   A place where joy is known,   10
Where golden flash and silver gleam
   Have meanings of their own;
While, high and low, and all about,
   Your motions, glittering Elves!
Ye weave—no danger from without,   15
   And peace among yourselves.

Type of a sunny human breast
   Is your transparent Cell;
Where Fear is but a transient Guest,
   No sullen Humours dwell;   20
Where, sensitive of every ray
   That smites this tiny sea,

Your scaly panoplies repay
   The loan with usury.

How beautiful! Yet none knows why   25
   This ever-graceful change,
Renewed—renewed incessantly—
   Within your quiet range.
Is it that ye with conscious skill
   For mutual pleasure glide;   30
And sometimes, not without your will,
   Are dwarfed, or magnified?

Fays—Genii of gigantic size—
   And now, in twilight dim,
Clustering like constellated Eyes   35
   In wings of Cherubim,
When they abate their fiery glare:
   Whate'er your forms express,
Whate'er ye seem, whate'er ye are,
   All leads to gentleness.   40

Cold though your nature be, 'tis pure;
   Your birthright is a fence
From all that haughtier kinds endure
   Through tyranny of sense.
Ah! not alone by colours bright   45
   Are Ye to Heaven allied,
When, like essential Forms of light,
   Ye mingle, or divide.

For day-dreams soft as e'er beguiled
   Day-thoughts while limbs repose;   50
For moonlight fascinations mild
   Your gift, ere shutters close;
Accept, mute Captives! thanks and praise;
   And may this tribute prove
That gentle admirations raise   55
   Delight resembling love.

Liberty
(SEQUEL TO THE ABOVE)

[ADDRESSED TO A FRIEND; THE GOLD AND SILVER FISHES HAVING BEEN REMOVED
TO A POOL IN THE PLEASURE-GROUND OF RYDAL MOUNT.]

"THE LIBERTY OF A PEOPLE CONSISTS IN BEING GOVERNED BY LAWS WHICH THEY
HAVE MADE FOR THEMSELVES, UNDER WHATEVER FORM IT BE OF GOVERNMENT. THE
LIBERTY OF A PRIVATE MAN, IN BEING MASTER OF HIS OWN TIME AND ACTIONS, AS FAR
AS MAY CONSIST WITH THE LAWS OF GOD AND OF HIS COUNTRY. OF THIS LATTER WE
ARE HERE TO DISCOURSE." COWLEY.

Those breathing Tokens of your kind regard,
(Suspect not, Anna, that their fate is hard;
Not soon does aught to which mild fancies cling,
In lonely spots, become a slighted thing;)
Those silent Inmates now no longer share,   5
Nor do they need, our hospitable care,
Removed in kindness from their glassy Cell
To the fresh waters of a living Well;
That spreads into an elfin pool opaque
Of which close boughs a glimmering mirror make,   10
On whose smooth breast with dimples light and small
The fly may settle, leaf or blossom fall.
—*There* swims, of blazing sun and beating shower
Fearless (but how obscured!) the golden Power,
That from his bauble prison used to cast   15
Gleams by the richest jewel unsurpast;
And near him, darkling like a sullen Gnome,
The silver Tenant of the crystal dome;
Dissevered both from all the mysteries
Of hue and altering shape that charmed all eyes.   20
They pined, perhaps, they languished while they shone;
And, if not so, what matters beauty gone
And admiration lost, by change of place
That brings to the inward Creature no disgrace?
But if the change restore his birthright, then,   25
Whate'er the difference, boundless is the gain.
Who can divine what impulses from God
Reach the caged Lark, within a town-abode,
From his poor inch or two of daisied sod?
O yield him back his privilege! No sea   30

Swells like the bosom of a man set free;
A wilderness is rich with liberty.
Roll on, ye spouting Whales, who die or keep
Your independence in the fathomless Deep!
Spread, tiny Nautilus, the living sail;   35
Dive, at thy choice, or brave the freshening gale!
If unreproved the ambitious Eagle mount
Sunward to seek the daylight in its fount,
Bays, gulfs, and Ocean's Indian width, shall be,
Till the world perishes, a field for thee!   40

   While musing here I sit in shadow cool,
And watch these mute Companions, in the pool,
Among reflected boughs of leafy trees,
By glimpses caught—disporting at their ease—
Enlivened, braced, by hardy luxuries,   45
I ask what warrant fixed them (like a spell
Of witchcraft fixed them) in the crystal Cell;
To wheel with languid motion round and round,
Beautiful, yet in a mournful durance bound.
Their peace, perhaps, our lightest footfall marred;   50
On their quick sense our sweetest music jarred;
And whither could they dart, if seized with fear?
No sheltering stone, no tangled root was near.
When fire or taper ceased to cheer the room,
They wore away the night in starless gloom;   55
And, when the sun first dawned upon the streams,
How faint their portion of his vital beams!
Thus, and unable to complain, they fared,
While not one joy of ours by them was shared.

   Is there a cherished Bird (I venture now   60
To snatch a sprig from Chaucer's reverend brow)—
Is there a brilliant Fondling of the cage,
Though sure of plaudits on his costly stage,
Though fed with dainties from the snow-white hand
Of a kind Mistress, fairest of the land,   65
But gladly would escape; and, if need were,
Scatter the colours from the plumes that bear
The emancipated captive through blithe air

Into strange woods, where he at large may live
On best or worst which they and Nature give?   70
The Beetle loves his unpretending track,
The Snail the house he carries on his back:
The far-fetched Worm with pleasure would disown
The bed we give him, though of softest down;
A noble instinct; in all Kinds the same,   75
All Ranks! What Sovereign, worthy of the name,
If doomed to breathe against his lawful will
An element that flatters him—to kill,
But would rejoice to barter outward show
For the least boon that freedom can bestow?   80

   But most the Bard is true to inborn right,
Lark of the dawn, and Philomel of night,
Exults in freedom, can with rapture vouch
For the dear blessings of a lowly couch,
A natural meal—days, months, from Nature's hand;   85
Time, place, and business, all at his command!
Who bends to happier duties, who more wise
Than the industrious Poet, taught to prize,
Above all grandeur, a pure life uncrossed
By cares in which simplicity is lost?   90
That life—the flowery path which winds by stealth,
Which Horace needed for his spirit's health;
Sighed for, in heart and genius, overcome
By noise, and strife, and questions wearisome,
And the vain splendours of Imperial Rome?   95
Let easy mirth his social hours inspire,
And fiction animate his sportive lyre,
Attuned to verse that crowning light Distress
With garlands cheats her into happiness;
Give me the humblest note of those sad strains   100
Drawn forth by pressure of his gilded chains,
As a chance sunbeam from his memory fell
Upon the Sabine Farm he loved so well;
Or when the prattle of Bandusia's spring
Haunted his ear—he only listening—   105
He proud to please, above all rivals, fit
To win the palm of gaiety and wit;

He, doubt not, with involuntary dread,
Shrinking from each new favour to be shed,
By the World's Ruler, on his honoured head!   110

In a deep vision's intellectual scene,
Such earnest longings and regrets as keen
Depressed the melancholy Cowley, laid
Under a fancied yew-tree's luckless shade;
A doleful bower for penitential song,   115
Where Man and Muse complained of mutual wrong;
While Cam's ideal current glided by,
And antique Towers nodded their foreheads high,
Citadels dear to studious privacy.
But Fortune, who had long been used to sport   120
With this tried Servant of a thankless Court,
Relenting met his wishes; and to You
The *remnant* of his days at least was true;
You, whom, though long deserted, he loved best;
You, Muses, Books, Fields, Liberty, and Rest!   125
But happier they who, fixing hope and aim
On the humanities of peaceful fame,
Enter *betimes* with more than martial fire
The generous course, aspire, and still aspire;
Upheld by warnings heeded not too late   130
Stifle the contradictions of their fate,
And to one purpose cleave, their Being's godlike mate!

Thus, gifted Friend, but with the placid brow
That Woman ne'er should forfeit, keep thy vow;
With modest scorn reject whate'er would blind   135
The ethereal eyesight, cramp the wingèd mind!
Then, with a blessing granted from above
To every act, word, thought, and look of love,
Life's book for Thee may lie unclosed, till age
Shall with a thankful tear bedrop its latest page.[1]   140

---

1 "There is now, alas! no possibility of the anticipation, with which the above Epistle con-
   cludes, being realised: nor were the verses ever seen by the Individual for whom they
   were intended. She accompanied her husband, the Rev. Wm. Fletcher, to India, and died
   of cholera, at the age of thirty-two or thirty-three years, on her way from Shalapore to
   Bombay, deeply lamented by all who knew her.
       Her enthusiasm was ardent, her piety steadfast; and her great talents would have ena-
   bled her to be eminently useful in the difficult path of life to which she had been called. The

Humanity (Written in the Year 1829)

Not from his fellows only man may learn
Rights to compare and duties to discern:
All creatures and all objects, in degree,
Are friends and patrons of humanity.—MS.

[The Rocking-stones, alluded to in the beginning of the following verses, are
supposed to have been used, by our British ancestors, both for judicial and
religious purposes. Such stones are not uncommonly found, at this day, both
in Great Britain and in Ireland.]

What though the Accused, upon his own appeal
To righteous Gods when Man has ceased to feel,
Or at a doubting Judge's stern command,
Before the STONE OF POWER no longer stand—
To take his sentence from the balanced Block,   5
As, at his touch, it rocks, or seems to rock;
Though, in the depths of sunless groves, no more
The Druid-priest the hallowed Oak adore;
Yet, for the Initiate, rocks and whispering trees
Do still perform mysterious offices!   10
And still in beast and bird a function dwells,
That, while we look and listen, sometimes tells
Upon the heart, in more authentic guise
Than Oracles, or wingèd Auguries,
Spake to the Science of the ancient wise.   15
Not uninspired appear their simplest ways;
Their voices mount symbolical of praise—
To mix with hymns that Spirits make and hear;
And to fallen Man their innocence is dear.
Enraptured Art draws from those sacred springs   20
Streams that reflect the poetry of things!
Where Christian Martyrs stand in hues portrayed,
That, might a wish avail, would never fade,
Borne in their hands the Lily and the Palm
Shed round the Altar a celestial calm;   25
There, too, behold the Lamb and guileless Dove

opinion she entertained of her own performances, given to the world under her maiden
name, Jewsbury, was modest and humble, and, indeed, far below their merits; as is often
the case with those who are making trial of their powers with a hope to discover what they
are best fitted for. In one quality, viz., quickness in the motions of her mind, she was in the
author's estimation unequalled." WW

Prest in the tenderness of virgin love
To saintly bosoms!—Glorious is the blending
Of right Affections, climbing or descending
Along a scale of light and life, with cares   30
Alternate; carrying holy thoughts and prayers
Up to the sovereign seat of the Most High;
Descending to the worm in charity;[1]
Like those good Angels whom a dream of night
Gave, in the Field of Luz, to Jacob's sight;   35
All, while *he* slept, treading the pendent stairs
Earthward or heavenward, radiant Messengers,
That, with a perfect will in one accord
Of strict obedience, served the Almighty Lord;
And with untired humility forbore   40
The ready service of the wings they wore.

What a fair World were ours for Verse to paint,
If Power could live at ease with self-restraint!
Opinion bow before the naked sense
Of the greatest Vision,—faith in Providence;   45
Merciful over all existence, just
To the least particle of sentient dust;
And, fixing by immutable decrees,
Seedtime and harvest for his purposes!
Then would be closed the restless oblique eye   50
That looks for evil like a treacherous spy;
Disputes would then relax, like stormy winds
That into breezes sink; impetuous Minds
By discipline endeavour to grow meek
As Truth herself, whom they profess to seek.   55
Then Genius, shunning fellowship with Pride,
Would braid his golden locks at Wisdom's side;
Love ebb and flow untroubled by caprice;
And not alone *harsh* tyranny would cease,
But unoffending creatures find release   60
From *qualified* oppression, whose defence
Rests on a hollow plea of recompence;

---

1   "The author is indebted, here, to a passage in one of Mr. Digby's valuable works." WW
    refers to Kenelm Henry Digby, author of *The Broad Stone of Honour: The True Sense and
    Practice of Chilvary* (London, 1826, 1828,1829).

Thought-tempered wrongs, for each humane respect
Oft worse to bear, or deadlier in effect.
Witness those glances of indignant scorn   65
From some high-minded Slave, impelled to spurn
The kindness that would make him less forlorn;
Or, if the soul to bondage be subdued,
His look of pitable gratitude!

   Alas for thee, bright Galaxy of Isles,   70
Where day departs in pomp, returns with smiles—
To greet the flowers and fruitage of a land,
As the sun mounts, by sea-born breezes fanned;
A land whose azure mountain-tops are seats
For Gods in council, whose green vales, Retreats   75
Fit for the Shades of Heroes, mingling there
To breathe Elysian peace in upper air.
   Though cold as winter, gloomy as the grave,
Stone-walls a Prisoner make, but not a Slave.
Shall Man assume a property in Man?   80
Lay on the moral Will a withering ban?
Shame that our laws at distance should protect
Enormities, which they at home reject!
"Slaves cannot breathe in England"—a proud boast!
And yet a mockery! if, from coast to coast,   85
Though *fettered* slave be none, her floors and soil
Groan underneath a weight of slavish toil,
For the poor Many, measured out by rules
Fetched with cupidity from heartless schools,
That to an Idol, falsely called "the Wealth   90
Of Nations," sacrifice a People's health,
Body and mind and soul; a thirst so keen
Is ever urging on the vast machine
Of sleepless Labour, 'mid whose dizzy wheels
The Power least prized is that which thinks and feels.   95

   Then, for the pastimes of this delicate age,
And all the heavy or light vassalage
Which for their sakes we fasten, as may suit
Our varying moods, on human kind or brute,
'Twere well in little, as in great, to pause,   100

Lest Fancy trifle with eternal laws.
There are to whom even garden, grove, and field,
Perpetual lessons of forbearance yield;
Who would not lightly violate the grace
The lowliest flower possesses in its place;   105
Nor shorten the sweet life, too fugitive,
Which nothing less than Infinite Power could give.

"Why art thou silent! Is thy love a plant"

Why art thou silent! Is thy love a plant
Of such weak fibre that the treacherous air
Of absence withers what was once so fair?
Is there no debt to pay, no boon to grant?
Yet have my thoughts for thee been vigilant   5
(As would my deeds have been) with hourly care,
The mind's least generous wish a mendicant
For nought but what thy happiness could spare.
Speak, though this soft warm heart, once free to hold
A thousand tender pleasures, thine and mine,   10
Be left more desolate, more dreary cold
Than a forsaken bird's-nest filled with snow
'Mid its own bush of leafless eglantine;
Speak, that my torturing doubts their end may know!

Inscription

INTENDED FOR A STONE IN THE GROUNDS OF RYDAL MOUNT

In these fair Vales hath many a Tree
   At Wordsworth's suit been spared;
And from the Builder's hand this Stone,
For some rude beauty of its own,
   Was rescued by the Bard: 5
So let it rest,—and time will come
   When here the tender-hearted
May heave a gentle sigh for him,
   As one of the departed.

Elegiac Musings

IN THE GROUNDS OF COLEORTON HALL, THE SEAT OF
THE LATE SIR GEORGE BEAUMONT, BART.

[IN THESE GROUNDS STANDS THE PARISH CHURCH, WHEREIN IS A MURAL MONU-
MENT, THE INSCRIPTION UPON WHICH, IN DEFERENCE TO THE EARNEST REQUEST OF THE
DECEASED, IS CONFINED TO NAME, DATES, AND THESE WORDS:—"ENTER NOT INTO
JUDGMENT WITH THY SERVANT, O LORD!"]

With copious eulogy in prose or rhyme
Graven on the tomb we struggle against Time,
Alas, how feebly! but our feelings rise
And still we struggle when a good man dies:
Such offering Beaumont dreaded and forbade,   5
A spirit meek in self-abasement clad.
Yet here at least, though few have numbered days
That shunned so modestly the light of praise,
His graceful manners, and the temperate ray
Of that arch fancy which would round him play,   10
Brightening a converse never known to swerve
From courtesy and delicate reserve;
That sense—the bland philosophy of life
Which checked discussion ere it warmed to strife;
Those fine accomplishments, and varied powers,   15
Might have their record among sylvan bowers.
—Oh, fled for ever! vanished like a blast
That shook the leaves in myriads as it passed;
Gone from this world of earth, air, sea, and sky,
From all its spirit-moving imagery,   20
Intensely studied with a Painter's eye,
A Poet's heart; and, for congenial view,
Portrayed with happiest pencil, not untrue
To common recognitions while the line
Flowed in a course of sympathy divine—   25
Oh! severed too abruptly from delights
That all the seasons shared with equal rights—
Rapt in the grace of undismantled age,
From soul-felt music, and the treasured page,
Lit by that evening lamp which loved to shed   30
Its mellow lustre round thy honoured head,
While Friends beheld thee give with eye, voice, mien,

More than theatric force to Shakspeare's scene—
Rebuke us not!—The mandate is obeyed
That said, "Let praise be mute where I am laid;"   35
The holier deprecation, given in trust
To the cold Marble, waits upon thy dust;
Yet have we found how slowly genuine grief
From *silent* admiration wins relief.
Too long abashed thy Name is like a Rose   40
That doth "within itself its sweetness close;"
A drooping Daisy changed into a cup
In which her bright-eyed beauty is shut up.
Within these Groves, where still are flitting by
Shades of the Past, oft noticed with a sigh,   45
Shall stand a votive Tablet, haply free,
When towers and temples fall, to speak of Thee!
If sculptured emblems of our mortal doom
Recall not there the wisdom of the Tomb,
Green ivy, risen from out the cheerful earth,   50
Shall fringe the lettered stone; and herbs spring forth,
Whose fragrance, by soft dews and rain unbound,
Shall penetrate the heart without a wound;
While truth and love their purposes fulfil,
Commemorating genius, talent, skill,   55
That could not lie concealed where Thou wert known;
Thy virtues *He* must judge, and *He* alone,
The God upon whose mercy they are thrown.

"Chatsworth! thy stately mansion, and the pride"

Chatsworth! thy stately mansion, and the pride
Of thy domain, strange contrast do present
To house and home in many a craggy rent
Of the wild Peak; where new–born waters glide
Through fields whose thrifty Occupants abide   5
As in a dear and chosen banishment,
With every semblance of entire content;
So kind is simple Nature, fairly tried!
Yet He whose heart in childhood gave her troth
To pastoral dales, thin set with modest farms,   10
May learn, if judgement strengthen with his growth,

That, not for Fancy only, pomp hath charms;
And, strenuous to protect from lawless harms
The extremes of favoured life, may honour both.

To B. R. Haydon, Esq. On Seeing his Picture of Napoleon Buonaparte on the Island of St. Helena

Haydon! let worthier judges praise the skill
Here by thy pencil shown in truth of lines
And charm of colours; I applaud those signs
Of thought, that give the true poetic thrill;
That unencumbered whole of blank and still,   5
Sky without cloud—ocean without a wave;
And the one Man that laboured to enslave
The World, sole-standing high on the bare hill—
Back turned, arms folded, the unapparent face
Tinged, we may fancy, in this dreary place   10
With light reflected from the invisible sun
Set like his fortunes; but not set for aye
Like them. The unguilty Power pursues his way,
And before *him* doth dawn perpetual run.

Epitaph

By a blest Husband guided, Mary came
From nearest kindred, * * * * * * her new name;[1]
She came, though meek of soul, in seemly pride
Of happiness and hope, a youthful Bride.
O dread reverse! if aught *be* so, which proves   5
That God will chasten whom he dearly loves.
Faith bore her up through pains in mercy given,
And troubles that were each a step to Heaven:
Two Babes were laid in earth before she died;
A third now slumbers at the Mother's side;   10
Its Sister-twin survives, whose smiles afford
A trembling solace to her widowed Lord.

Reader! if to thy bosom cling the pain

---

1 WW replaced the asterisks with the last name of Mary Elizabeth (Carleton) Vernon, a woman raised in Grasmere, in the third edition of *Yarrow Revisited, and Other Poems* (London, 1839). The epitaph was inscribed on a tablet in St. Mary's Church in Sprawley, near Hanbury, England.

Of recent sorrow combated in vain;
Or if thy cherished grief have failed to thwart   15
Time still intent on his insidious part,
Lulling the Mourner's best good thoughts asleep,
Pilfering regrets we would, but cannot, keep;
Bear with Him—judge *Him* gently who makes known
His bitter loss by this memorial Stone;   20
And pray that in his faithful breast the grace
Of resignation find a hallowed place.

Devotional Incitements

"Not to the earth confined,
  "Ascend to heaven."

Where will they stop, those breathing Powers,
The Spirits of the new-born flowers?
They wander with the breeze, they wind
Where'er the streams a passage find;
Up from their native ground they rise   5
In mute aërial harmonies;
From humble violet modest thyme
Exhaled, the essential odours climb,
As if no space below the sky
Their subtle flight could satisfy: 10
Heaven will not tax our thoughts with pride
If like ambition be *their* guide.

Roused by this kindliest of May-showers,
The spirit-quickener of the flowers,
That with moist virtue softly cleaves   15
The buds, and freshens the young leaves,
The Birds pour forth their souls in notes
Of rapture from a thousand throats,
Here checked by too impetuous haste,
While there the music runs to waste,   20
With bounty more and more enlarged,
Till the whole air is overcharged;
Give ear, O Man! to their appeal
And thirst for no inferior zeal,
Thou, who canst *think*, as well as feel.   25

Mount from the earth; aspire! aspire!
So pleads the town's cathedral choir,
In strains that from their solemn height
Sink, to attain a loftier flight;
While incense from the altar breathes   30
Rich fragrance in embodied wreaths;
Or, flung from swinging censer, shrouds
The taper lights, and curls in clouds
Around angelic Forms, the still
Creation of the painter's skill,   35
That on the service wait concealed
One moment, and the next revealed.
—Cast off your bonds, awake, arise,
And for no transient ecstasies!
What else can mean the visual plea   40
Of still or moving imagery?
The iterated summons loud,
Not wasted on the attendant crowd,
Nor wholly lost upon the throng
Hurrying the busy streets along?   45

   Alas! the sanctities combined
By art to unsensualise the mind,
Decay and languish; or, as creeds
And humours change, are spurned like weeds:
The solemn rites, the awful forms,   50
Founder amid fanatic storms;
The priests are from their altars thrust,
The temples levelled with the dust:
Yet evermore, through years renewed
In undisturbed vicissitude   55
Of seasons balancing their flight
On the swift wings of day and night,
Kind Nature keeps a heavenly door
Wide open for the scattered Poor.
Where flower-breathed incense to the skies   60
Is wafted in mute harmonies;
And ground fresh cloven by the plough
Is fragrant with a humbler vow;
Where birds and brooks from leafy dells

Chime forth unwearied canticles,   65
And vapours magnify and spread
The glory of the sun's bright head;
Still constant in her worship, still
Conforming to the almighty Will,
Whether men sow or reap the fields,   70
Her admonitions Nature yields;
That not by bread alone we live,
Or what a hand of flesh can give;
That every day should leave some part
Free for a sabbath of the heart;   75
So shall the seventh be truly blest,
From morn to eve, with hallowed rest.

To the Author's Portrait

[Painted at Rydal Mount, by W. Pickersgill, Esq., for St. John's College,
Cambridge.]

Go, faithful Portrait! and where long hath knelt
Margaret, the saintly Foundress, take thy place;
And, if Time spare the colours for the grace
Which to the work surpassing skill hath dealt,
Thou, on thy rock reclined, though Kingdoms melt   5
And States be torn up by the roots, wilt seem
To breathe in rural peace, to hear the stream,
To think and feel as once the Poet felt.
Whate'er thy fate, those features have not grown
Unrecognised through many a household tear,   10
More prompt more glad to fall than drops of dew
By morning shed around a flower half blown;
Tears of delight, that testified how true
To life thou art, and, in thy truth, how dear!

[Four Poems Written in Response to the Reform Movement, December
1832]

i. "For Lubbock vote—no legislative Hack"

For Lubbock vote—no legislative Hack
The dupe of History—that old Almanack!
The Sage has read the Stars with skill so true

That Men may trust him, and be certain, too,
The almanack He'll follow must be *new*.   5

ii. *"If this great world of joy and pain"*

If this great world of joy and pain
    Revolve in one sure track;
If Freedom, set, will rise again,
    And Virtue, flown, come back;
Woe to the purblind crew who fill   5
    The heart with each day's care;
Nor gain, from past or future, skill
    To bear, and to forbear!

iii. *"Now that Astrology is out of date"*

Now that Astrology is out of date,
What have the Stars to do with Church and State?
In Parliament should Lubbock go astray,
Twould be an odd excuse for Friends to say,
"He's wondrous knowing in *The Milky Way!*"   5

iv. *Question and Answer*

"Can Lubbock fail to make a good M.P,
A Whig so clever in Astronomy?"
"*Baillie*, a Brother-sage, went forth as keen
Of change—for what reward?—the Guillotine:
Not Newton's Genius could have saved his head   5
From falling by the "Mouvement" he had led."

Thought on the Seasons

Flattered with promise of escape
    From every hurtful blast,
Spring takes, O sprightly May! thy shape,
    Her loveliest and her last.

Less fair is summer riding high   5
    In fierce solstitial power,
Less fair than when a lenient sky
    Brings on her parting hour.

When earth repays with golden sheaves
   The labours of the plough,   10
And ripening fruits and forest leaves
   All brighten on the bough,

What pensive beauty autumn shows,
   Before she hears the sound
Of winter rushing in, to close   15
   The emblematic round!

Such be our Spring, our Summer such;
   So may our Autumn blend
With hoary Winter, and Life touch,
   Through heaven-born hope, her end!   20

A Wren's Nest

Among the dwellings framed by birds
   In field or forest with nice care,
Is none that with the little Wren's
   In snugness may compare.

No door the tenement requires,   5
   And seldom needs a laboured roof;
Yet is it to the fiercest sun
   Impervious and storm-proof.

So warm, so beautiful withal,
   In perfect fitness for its aim,   10
That to the Kind by special grace
   Their instinct surely came.

And when for their abodes they seek
   An opportune recess,
The Hermit has no finer eye   15
   For shadowy quietness.

These find, 'mid ivied Abbey walls,
   A canopy in some still nook;
Others are pent-housed by a brae
   That overhangs a brook.   20

There to the brooding Bird her Mate

Warbles by fits his low clear song;
   And by the busy Streamlet both
     Are sung to all day long.

Or in sequestered lanes they build,   25
   Where, till the flitting Bird's return,
Her eggs within the nest repose,
     Like relics in an urn.

But still, where general choice is good,
   There is a better and a best;   30
And, among fairest objects, some
     Are fairer than the rest;

This, one of those small Builders proved
   In a green covert, where, from out
The forehead of a pollard oak,   35
     The leafy antlers sprout;

For She who planned the mossy Lodge,
   Mistrusting her evasive skill,
Had to a Primrose looked for aid
     Her wishes to fulfil.   40

High on the trunk's projecting brow,
   And fixed an infant's span above
The budding flowers, peeped forth the nest
     The prettiest of the grove!

The treasure proudly did I show   45
   To some whose minds without disdain
Can turn to little things, but once
     Looked up for it in vain:

'Tis gone—a ruthless Spoiler's prey,
   Who heeds not beauty, love, or song,   50
'Tis gone! (so seemed it) and we grieved
     Indignant at the wrong.

Just three days after, passing by
   In clearer light the moss-built cell
I saw, espied its shaded mouth,   55

And felt that all was well.

The Primrose for a veil had spread
   The largest of her upright leaves;
And thus, for purposes benign,
   A simple Flower deceives.   60

Concealed from friends who might disturb
   Thy quiet with no ill intent,
Secure from evil eyes and hands
   On barbarous plunder bent,

Rest, mother-bird! and when thy young   65
   Take flight, and thou art free to roam,
When withered is the guardian flower,
   And empty thy late home,

Think how ye prospered, thou and thine,
   Amid the unviolated grove   70
Housed near the growing primrose tuft
   In foresight, or in love.

Evening Voluntaries

I

Calm is the fragrant air, and loth to lose
Day's grateful warmth, tho' moist with falling dews.
Look for the stars, you'll say that there are none;
Look up a second time, and, one by one,
You mark them twinkling out with silvery light,   5
And wonder how they could elude the sight.
The birds, of late so noisy in their bowers,
Warbled a while with faint and fainter powers,
But now are silent as the dim-seen flowers:
Nor does the Village Church-clock's iron tone   10
The time's and season's influence disown;
Nine beats distinctly to each other bound
In drowsy sequence; how unlike the sound
That, in rough winter, oft inflicts a fear
On fireside Listeners, doubting what they hear!   15

The Shepherd, bent on rising with the sun,
Had closed his door before the day was done,
And now with thankful heart to bed doth creep,
And join his little Children in their sleep.
The Bat, lured forth where trees the lane o'ershade,   20
Flits and reflits along the close arcade;
Far-heard the Dor-hawk chases the white Moth
With burring note, which Industry and Sloth
Might both be pleased with, for it suits them both.
Wheels and the tread of hoofs are heard no more;   25
One Boat there was, but it will touch the shore
With the next dipping of its slackened oar;
Faint sound, that, for the gayest of the gay,
Might give to serious thought a moment's sway,
As a last token of Man's toilsome day!   30

II

Not in the lucid intervals of life
That come but as a curse to Party-strife;
Not in some hour when Pleasure with a sigh
Of langour puts his rosy garland by;
Not in the breathing-times of that poor Slave   5
Who daily piles up wealth in Mammon's cave,
Is Nature felt, or can be; nor do words,
Which practised Talent readily affords,
Prove that her hand has touched responsive chords;
Nor has her gentle beauty power to move   10
With genuine rapture and with fervent love
The soul of Genius, if he dares to take
Life's rule from passion craved for passion's sake;
Untaught that meekness is the cherished bent
Of all the truly Great and all the Innocent.   15
But who is innocent? By grace divine,
Not otherwise, O Nature! we are thine,
Through good and evil thine, in just degree
Of rational and manly sympathy.
To all that Earth from pensive hearts is stealing,   20
And Heaven is now to gladdened eyes revealing,
Add every charm the Universe can show

Through every change its aspects undergo,
Care may be respited, but not repealed;
No perfect cure grows on the bounded field.   25
Vain is the pleasure, a false calm the peace,
If He, through whom alone our conflicts cease,
Our virtuous hopes without relapse advance,
Come not to speed the Soul's deliverance;
To the distempered Intellect refuse   30
His gracious help, or give what we abuse.

III

(BY THE SIDE OF RYDAL MERE)

The Linnet's warble, sinking towards a close,
Hints to the Thrush 'tis time for their repose;
The shrill-voiced Thrush is heedless, and again
The Monitor revives his own sweet strain;
But both will soon be mastered, and the copse   5
Be left as silent as the mountain-tops,
Ere some commanding Star dismiss to rest
The throng of Rooks, that now, from twig or nest,
(After a steady flight on home-bound wings,
And a last game of mazy hoverings   10
Around their ancient grove) with cawing noise
Disturb the liquid music's equipoise.
O Nightingale! Who ever heard thy song
Might here be moved, till Fancy grows so strong
That listening sense is pardonably cheated   15
Where wood or stream by thee was never greeted.
Surely, from fairest spots of favoured lands,
Were not some gifts withheld by jealous hands,
This hour of deepening darkness here would be,
As a fresh morning for new harmony;   20
And Lays as prompt would hail the dawn of night;
A *dawn* she has both beautiful and bright,
When the East kindles with the full moon's light.

Wanderer by spring with gradual progress led,
For sway profoundly felt as widely spread;   25
To king, to peasant, to rough sailor, dear,

And to the soldier's trumpet-wearied ear;
How welcome wouldst thou be to this green Vale
Fairer than Tempe! Yet, sweet Nightingale!
From the warm breeze that bears thee on alight   30
At will, and stay thy migratory flight;
Build, at thy choice, or sing, by pool or fount,
Who shall complain, or call thee to account?
The wisest, happiest, of our kind are they
That ever walk content with Nature's way,   35
God's goodness measuring bounty as it may;
For whom the gravest thought of what they miss,
Chastening the fulness of a present bliss,
Is with that wholesome office satisfied,
While unrepining sadness is allied   40
In thankful bosoms to a modest pride.

IV

Soft as a cloud is yon blue Ridge—the Mere
Seems firm as solid crystal, breathless, clear,
And motionless; and, to the gazer's eye,
Deeper than Ocean, in the immensity
Of its vague mountains and unreal sky!   5
But, from the process in that still retreat,
Turn to minuter changes at our feet;
Observe how dewy Twilight has withdrawn
The crowd of daisies from the shaven lawn,
And has restored to view its tender green,   10
That, while the sun rode high, was lost beneath their dazzling sheen.
—An emblem this of what the sober Hour
Can do for minds disposed to feel its power!
Thus oft, when we in vain have wish'd away
The petty pleasures of the garish day,   15
Meek Eve shuts up the whole usurping host
(Unbashful dwarfs each glittering at his post)
And leaves the disencumbered spirit free
To reassume a staid simplicity.
'Tis well—but what are helps of time and place,   20
When wisdom stands in need of nature's grace;
Why do good thoughts, invoked or not, descend,

Like Angels from their bowers, our virtues to befriend;
If yet To-morrow, unbelied, may say,
"I come to open out, for fresh display,   25
The elastic vanities of yesterday?"

V

The leaves that rustled on this oak-crowned hill,
And sky that danced among those leaves, are still;
Rest smooths the way for sleep; in field and bower
Soft shades and dews have shed their blended power
On drooping eyelid and the closing flower;   5
Sound is there none at which the faintest heart
Might leap, the weakest nerve of superstition start;
Save when the Owlet's unexpected scream
Pierces the ethereal vault; and 'mid the gleam
Of unsubstantial imagery—the dream,   10
From the hushed vale's realities, transferred
To the still lake, the imaginative Bird
Seems, 'mid inverted mountains, not unheard.

Grave Creature! whether, while the moon shines bright
On thy wings opened wide for smoothest flight,   15
Thou art discovered in a roofless tower,
Rising from what may once have been a Lady's bower:
Or spied where thou sit'st moping in thy mew
At the dim centre of a churchyard yew;
Or, from a rifted crag or ivy tod   20
Deep in a forest, thy secure abode,
Thou giv'st, for pastime's sake, by shriek or shout,
A puzzling notice of thy whereabout;
May the night never come, the day be seen,
When I shall scorn thy voice or mock thy mien!   25
In classic ages men perceived a soul
Of sapience in thy aspect, headless Owl!
Thee Athens reverenced in the studious grove;
And, near the golden sceptre grasped by Jove,
His Eagle's favourite perch, while round him sate   30
The Gods revolving the decrees of Fate,
Thou, too, wert present at Minerva's side—
Hark to that second larum! far and wide

The elements have heard, and rock and cave replied.

VI

The Sun, that seemed so mildly to retire,
Flung back from distant climes a streaming fire,
Whose blaze is now subdued to tender gleams,
Prelude of night's approach with soothing dreams.
Look round;—of all the clouds not one is moving;   5
'Tis the still hour of thinking, feeling, loving.
Silent, and stedfast as the vaulted sky,
The boundless plain of waters seems to lie:—
Comes that low sound from breezes rustling o'er
The grass-crowned headland that conceals the shore!   10
No 'tis the earth-voice of the mighty sea,
Whispering how meek and gentle he *can* be!

   Thou Power supreme! who, arming to rebuke
Offenders, dost put off the gracious look,
And clothe thyself with terrors like the flood   15
Of ocean roused into his fiercest mood,
Whatever discipline thy Will ordain
For the brief course that must for me remain;
Teach me with quick-eared spirit to rejoice
In admonitions of thy softest voice!   20
Whate'er the path these mortal feet may trace,
Breathe through my soul the blessing of thy grace,
Glad, through a perfect love, a faith sincere
Drawn from the wisdom that begins with fear;
Glad to expand, and, for a season, free   25
From finite cares, to rest absorbed in Thee!

VII

(BY THE SEA-SIDE)

The sun is couched, the sea-fowl gone to rest,
And the wild storm hath somewhere found a nest;
Air slumbers—wave with wave no longer strives,
Only a heaving of the deep survives,
A tell-tale motion! soon will it be laid,   5
And by the tide alone the water swayed.

Stealthy withdrawings, interminglings mild
Of light with shade in beauty reconciled—
Such is the prospect far as sight can range,
The soothing recompence, the welcome change.   10
Where now the ships that drove before the blast,
Threatened by angry breakers as they passed;
And by a train of flying clouds bemocked;
Or, in the hollow surge, at anchor rocked
As on a bed of death? Some lodge in peace,   15
Saved by His care who bade the tempest cease;
And some, too heedless of past danger, court
Fresh gales to waft them to the far-off port;
But near, or hanging sea and sky between,
Not one of all those wingèd Powers is seen,   20
Seen in her course, nor 'mid this quiet heard;
Yet oh! how gladly would the air be stirred
By some acknowledgment of thanks and praise,
Soft in its temper as those vesper lays
Sung to the Virgin while accordant oars   25
Urge the slow bark along Calabrian shores;
A sea-born service through the mountains felt
Till into one loved vision all things melt:
Or like those hymns that soothe with graver sound
The gulfy coast of Norway iron-bound;   30
And, from the wide and open Baltic, rise
With punctual care, Lutherian harmonies.
Hush, not a voice is here! but why repine,
Now when the star of eve comes forth to shine
On British waters with that look benign?   35
Ye mariners, that plough your onward way,
Or in the haven rest, or sheltering bay,
May *silent* thanks at least to God be given
With a full heart, "our thoughts are heard in heaven!"

VIII

The sun has long been set,[1]
    The stars are out by twos and threes,

---

1   For WW's explanatory note for VIII and IX, see the notes at the end of this volume. WW
    first published a version of "The sun has long been set" in *Poems, in Two Volumes* in 1807
    (see vol. 1 of this edition).

The little birds are piping
   Among the bushes and trees;
There's a cuckoo, and one or two thrushes,   5
And a far-off wind that rushes,
And a sound of water that gushes,
And the Cuckoo's sovereign cry
Fills all the hollow of the sky.

Who would "go parading"   10
In London, "and masquerading,"
On such a night of June
With that beautiful soft half-moon,
And all these innocent blisses,
On such a night as this is?   15

IX

Throned in the Sun's descending car[1]
What Power unseen diffuses far
This tenderness of mind?
What Genius smiles on yonder flood?
What God in whispers from the wood   5
Bids every thought be kind?

O ever pleasing Solitude,
Companion of the wise and good,
Thy shades, thy silence, now be mine,
   Thy charms my only theme;   10
My haunt the hollow cliff whose Pine
   Waves o'er the gloomy stream;
Whence the scared Owl on pinions grey
   Breaks from the rustling boughs,
And down the lone vale sails away   15
   To more profound repose!

Composed by the Sea-shore

What mischief cleaves to unsubdued regret,
How fancy sickens by vague hopes beset;
How baffled projects on the spirit prey,

---

1 For WW's comment on this poem see the notes at the end of this volume.

And fruitless wishes eat the heart away,
The sailor knows; he best whose lot is cast   5
On the relentless sea that holds him fast
On chance dependent, and the fickle star
Of power, through long and melancholy war.
O sad it is, in sight of foreign shores,
Daily to think on old familiar doors,   10
Hearths loved in childhood and ancestral floors;
Or, tossed about along a waste of foam,
To ruminate on that delightful home
Which with the dear Betrothèd *was* to come;
Or came and was, and is, yet meets the eye   15
Never but in the world of memory;
Or in a dream recalled, whose smoothest range
Is crossed by knowledge, or by dread, of change,
And if not so, whose perfect joy makes sleep
A thing too bright for breathing man to keep.   20
Hail to the virtues which that perilous life
Extracts from Nature's elemental strife;
And welcome glory won in battles fought
As bravely as the foe was keenly sought.
But to each gallant Captain and his crew   25
A less imperious sympathy is due,
Such as my verse now yields, while moonbeams play
On the mute sea in this unruffled bay;
Such as will promptly flow from every breast,
Where good men, disappointed in the quest   30
Of wealth and power and honours, long for rest;
Or having known the splendours of success,
Sigh for the obscurities of happiness.

To ———,

UPON THE BIRTH OF HER FIRST-BORN CHILD, MARCH, 1833 [1]

"Tum porro puer, ut sævis projectus ab undis
Navita; nudus humi jacet," &c.—Lucretius.

Like a shipwreck'd Sailor tost
By rough waves on a perilous coast,

---

1   Addressed to Isabella, wife of WW's son John, on the occasion of the birth of Jane, WW's
   first grandchild.

Lies the Babe, in helplessness
And in tenderest nakedness,
Flung by labouring nature forth   5
Upon the mercies of the earth.
Can its eyes beseech? no more
Than the hands are free to implore:
Voice but serves for one brief cry,
Plaint was it? or prophecy   10
Of sorrow that will surely come?
Omen of man's grievous doom!

   But, O Mother! by the close
Duly granted to thy throes;
By the silent thanks now tending   15
Incense-like to Heaven, descending
Now to mingle and to move
With the gush of earthly love,
As a debt to that frail Creature,
Instrument of struggling Nature   20
For the blissful calm, the peace
Known but to this *one* release;
Can the pitying spirit doubt
That for human-kind springs out
From the penalty a sense   25
Of more than mortal recompence?

   As a floating summer cloud,
Though of gorgeous drapery proud,
To the sun-burnt traveller,
Or the stooping labourer,   30
Ofttimes makes its bounty known
By its shadow round him thrown;
So, by chequerings of sad cheer,
Heavenly guardians, brooding near,
Of their presence tell—too bright   35
Haply for corporeal sight!
Ministers of grace divine
Feelingly their brows incline
O'er this seeming Castaway
Breathing, in light of day,   40

Something like the faintest breath
That has power to baffle death—
Beautiful, while very weakness
Captivates like passive meekness!

And, sweet Mother! under warrant   45
Of the universal Parent,
Who repays in season due
Them who have, like thee, been true
To the filial chain let down
From his everlasting throne,   50
Angels hovering round thy couch,
With their softest whispers vouch,
That, whatever griefs may fret,
Cares entangle, sins beset
This thy first-born, and with tears   55
Stain her cheek in future years,
Heavenly succour, not denied
To the Babe, whate'er betide,
Will to the Woman be supplied!

Mother! blest be thy calm ease;   60
Blest the starry promises,
And the firmament benign
Hallowed be it, where they shine!
Yes, for them whose souls have scope
Ample for a wingèd hope,   65
And can earthward bend an ear
For needful listening, pledge is here,
That, if thy new-born Charge shall tread
In thy footsteps, and be led
By that other Guide, whose light   70
Of manly virtues, mildly bright,
Gave him first the wished-for part
In thy gentle virgin heart,
Then, amid the storms of life
Presignified by that dread strife   75
Whence ye have escaped together,
She may look for serene weather;
In all trials sure to find

Comfort for a faithful mind;
Kindlier issues, holier rest,   80
Than even now await her prest,
Conscious Nursling, to thy breast!

die!

The Warning

A SEQUEL TO THE FOREGOING. MARCH, 1833 [1]

List, the winds of March are blowing;
Her ground-flowers shrink, afraid of showing
Their meek heads to the nipping air,
Which ye feel not, happy pair!
Sunk into a kindly sleep.   5
We, meanwhile, our hope will keep;
And if Time leagued with adverse Change
(Too busy fear!) shall cross its range,
Whatsoever check they bring,
Anxious duty hindering,   10
To like hope our prayers will cling.

   Thus, while the ruminating spirit feeds
Upon each home-event as life proceeds,
Affections pure and holy in their source
Gain a fresh impulse, run a livelier course;   15
Hopes that within the Father's heart prevail,
Are in the experienced Grandsire's slow to fail;
And if the harp pleased his gay youth, it rings
To his grave touch with no unready strings,
While thoughts press on, and feelings overflow,   20
And quick words round him fall like flakes of snow.

   Thanks to the Powers that yet maintain their sway,
And have renewed the tributary Lay.
Truths of the heart flock in with eager pace,
And FANCY greets them with a fond embrace;   25
Swift as the rising sun his beams extends
She shoots the tidings forth to distant friends;
Their gifts she hails (deemed precious, as they prove
For the unconscious Babe an unbelated love!)

---

1 Sequel to *To* ———, *Upon the Birth of her First-born Child, March,* 1833.

But from this peaceful centre of delight   30
Vague sympathies have urged her to take flight.
She rivals the fleet Swallow, making rings
In the smooth lake where'er he dips his wings:
—Rapt into upper regions, like the Bee
That sucks from mountain heath her honey fee;   35
Or, like the warbling Lark intent to shroud
His head in sunbeams or a bowery cloud,
She soars—and here and there her pinions rest
On proud towers, like this humble cottage, blest
With a new visitant, an infant guest—   40
Towers where red streamers flout the breezy sky
In pomp foreseen by her creative eye,
When feasts shall crowd the Hall, and steeple bells
Glad proclamation make, and heights and dells
Catch the blithe music as it sinks or swells;   45
And harboured ships, whose pride is on the sea,
Shall hoist their topmast flags in sign of glee,
Honouring the hope of noble ancestry.

   But who (though neither reckoning ills assigned
By Nature, nor reviewing in the mind   50
The track that was, and is, and must be, worn
With weary feet by all of woman born)—
Shall *now* by such a gift with joy be moved,
Nor feel the fulness of that joy reproved?
Not He, whose last faint memory will command   55
The truth that Britain was his native land;
Whose infant soul was tutored to confide
In the cleansed faith for which her martyrs died;
Whose boyish ear the voice of her renown
With rapture thrilled; whose Youth revered the crown   60
Of Saxon liberty that Alfred wore,
Alfred, dear Babe, thy great Progenitor!
—Not He, who from her mellowed practice drew
His social sense of just, and fair, and true;
And saw, thereafter, on the soil of France   65
Rash Polity begin her maniac dance,
Foundations broken up, the deeps run wild,
Nor grieved to see, (himself not unbeguiled)—

Woke from the dream, the dreamer to upbraid,
And learn how sanguine expectations fade   70
When novel trusts by folly are betrayed,—
To see presumption, turning pale, refrain
From further havoc, but repent in vain,—
Good aims lie down, and perish in the road
Where guilt had urged them on, with ceaseless goad,   75
Till undiscriminating Ruin swept
The Land, and Wrong perpetual vigils kept;
With proof before her that on public ends
Domestic virtue vitally depends.

  Can such a one, dear Babe! though glad and proud   80
To welcome Thee, repel the fears that crowd
Into his English breast, and spare to quake
Not for his own, but for thy innocent sake?
Too late—or, should the providence of God
Lead, through blind ways by sin and sorrow trod,   85
Justice and peace to a secure abode,
Too soon—thou com'st into this breathing world;
Ensigns of mimic outrage are unfurled.
Who shall preserve or prop the tottering Realm?
What hand suffice to govern the state-helm?   90
If, in the aims of men, the surest test
Of good or bad (whate'er be sought for or profest)
Lie in the means required, or ways ordained,
For compassing the end, else never gained;
Yet governors and govern'd both are blind   95
To this plain truth, or fling it to the wind;
If to expedience principle must bow;
Past, future, shrinking up beneath the incumbent Now;
If cowardly concession still must feed
The thirst for power in men who ne'er concede;   100
If generous Loyalty must stand in awe
Of subtle Treason, with his mask of law;
Or with bravado insolent and hard,
Provoking punishment, to win reward;
If office help the factious to conspire,   105
And they who should extinguish, fan the fire—
Then, will the sceptre be a straw, the crown

Sit loosely, like the thistle's crest of down;
To be blown off at will, by Power that spares it
In cunning patience, from the head that wears it.   110

   Lost people, trained to theoretic feud;
Lost above all, ye labouring multitude!
Bewildered whether ye, by slanderous tongues
Deceived, mistake calamities for wrongs;
And over fancied usurpations brood,   115
Oft snapping at revenge in sullen mood;
Or, from long stress of real injuries fly
To desperation for a remedy;
In bursts of outrage spread your judgments wide,
And to your wrath cry out, "Be thou our guide;"   120
Or, bound by oaths, come forth to tread earth's floor
In marshalled thousands, darkening street and moor
With the worst shape mock-patience ever wore;
Or, to the giddy top of self-esteem
By Flatterers carried, mount into a dream   125
Of boundless suffrage, at whose sage behest
Justice shall rule, disorder be supprest,
And every man sit down as Plenty's Guest!
—O for a bridle bitted with remorse
To stop your Leaders in their headstrong course!   130
Oh may the Almighty scatter with his grace
These mists, and lead you to a safer place,
By paths no human wisdom can foretrace!
May He pour round you, from worlds far above
Man's feverish passions, his pure light of love,   135
That quietly restores the natural mien
To hope, and makes truth willing to be seen!
Else shall your blood-stained hands in frenzy reap
Fields gaily sown when promises were cheap.
Why is the Past belied with wicked art,   140
The Future made to play so false a part,
Among a people famed for strength of mind,
Foremost in freedom, noblest of mankind?
We act as if we joyed in the sad tune
Storms make in rising, valued in the moon   145
Nought but her changes. Thus, ungrateful Nation!

If thou persist, and, scorning moderation,
Spread for thyself the snares of tribulation,
Whom, then, shall meekness guard? What saving skill
Lie in forbearance, strength in standing still?   150
—Soon shall the Widow (for the speed of Time
Nought equals when the hours are winged with crime)
Widow, or Wife, implore on tremulous knee,
From him who judged her Lord, a like decree;
The skies will weep o'er old men desolate: 155
Ye Little-ones! Earth shudders at your fate,
Outcasts and homeless orphans——

    But turn, my Soul, and from the sleeping Pair
Learn thou the beauty of omniscient care!
Be strong in faith, bid anxious thoughts lie still;   160
Seek for the good and cherish it—the ill
Oppose, or bear with a submissive will.

"He who defers his work from day to day"

He who defers his work from day to day
Does on a river's bank expecting stay,
Till the whole Stream which stopped him shall be gone
Which runs and as it runs for ever will run on.

To the Utilitarians

Avaunt this œconomic rage!
What would it bring?—an iron age,
Where Fact with heartless search explored
Shall be Imagination's Lord,
And sway with absolute controul,   5
The god-like Functions of the Soul.
Not *thus* can knowledge elevate
Our Nature from her fallen state.
With sober Reason Faith unites
To vindicate the ideal rights   10
Of Human-kind—the true agreeing
Of objects with internal seeing,
Of effort with the end of Being.—

The Labourer's Noon-day Hymn

Up to the throne of God is borne
The voice of praise at early morn,
And he accepts the punctual hymn
Sung as the light of day grows dim.

Nor will he turn his ear aside   5
From holy offerings at noontide:
Then here reposing let us raise
A song of gratitude and praise.

What though our burthen be not light
We need not toil from morn to night;   10
The respite of the mid-day hour
Is in the thankful Creature's power.

Blest are the moments, doubly blest,
That, drawn from this one hour of rest,
Are with a ready heart bestowed   15
Upon the service of our God!

Why should we crave a hallowed spot?
An Altar is in each man's cot,
A Church in every grove that spreads
Its living roof above our heads.   20

Look up to Heaven! the industrious Sun
Already half his race hath run;
He cannot halt nor go astray,
But our immortal Spirits may.

Lord! since his rising in the East,   25
If we have faltered or transgressed,
Guide, from thy love's abundant source,
What yet remains of this day's course:

Help with thy grace, through life's short day
Our upward and our downward way;   30
And glorify for us the west,
When we shall sink to final rest.

Love Lies Bleeding

You call it, "Love lies bleeding,"—so you may,
Though the red Flower, not prostrate, only droops,
As we have seen it here from day to day,
From month to month, life passing not away:
A flower how rich in sadness! Even thus stoops,   5
(Sentient by Grecian sculpture's marvellous power)
Thus leans, with hanging brow and body bent
Earthward in uncomplaining languishment,
The dying Gladiator. So, sad Flower!
('Tis Fancy guides me willing to be led,   10
    Though by a slender thread,)
So drooped Adonis bathed in sanguine dew
Of his death-wound, when he from innocent air
The gentlest breath of resignation drew;
While Venus in a passion of despair   15
Rent, weeping over him, her golden hair
Spangled with drops of that celestial shower.
She suffered, as Immortals sometimes do;
But pangs more lasting far, *that* Lover knew
Who first, weighed down by scorn, in some lone bower   20
Did press this semblance of unpitied smart
Into the service of his constant heart,
His own dejection, downcast Flower! could share
With thine, and gave the mournful name which thou wilt ever bear.

Companion to the Foregoing

Never enlivened with the liveliest ray
That fosters growth or checks or cheers decay,
Nor by the heaviest rain-drops more deprest,
This Flower, that first appeared as summer's guest,
Preserved her beauty among summer leaves,   5
And to her mournful habits fondly cleaves.
When files of stateliest plants have ceased to bloom,
One after one submitting to their doom,
When her coevals each and all are fled,
What keeps her thus reclined upon her lonesome bed?   10
    The old mythologists, more impress'd than we
Of this late day by character in tree

Or herb, that claimed peculiar sympathy,
Or by the silent lapse of fountain clear,
Or with the language of the viewless air   15
By bird or beast made vocal, sought a cause
To solve the mystery, not in Nature's laws
But in Man's fortunes. Hence a thousand tales
Sung to the plaintive lyre in Grecian vales.
Nor doubt that something of their spirit swayed   20
The fancy-stricken youth or heart-sick maid,
Who, while each stood companionless and eyed
This undeparting Flower in crimson dyed,
Thought of a wound which death is slow to cure,
A fate that has endured and will endure,   25
And, patience coveting yet passion feeding,
Called the dejected Lingerer, *Love lies bleeding.*

Written in an Album

Small service is true service while it lasts;
    Of Friends, however humble, scorn not one:
The Daisy, by the shadow that it casts,
    Protects the lingering dew-drop from the Sun.

Lines

SUGGESTED BY A PORTRAIT FROM THE PENCIL OF F. STONE

Beguiled into forgetfulness of care
Due to the day's unfinished task, of pen
Or book regardless, and of that fair scene
In Nature's prodigality displayed
Before my window, oftentimes and long   5
I gaze upon a Portrait whose mild gleam
Of beauty never ceases to enrich
The common light; whose stillness charms the air,
Or seems to charm it, into like repose;
Whose silence, for the pleasure of the ear,   10
Surpasses sweetest music. There she sits
With emblematic purity attired
In a white vest, white as her marble neck
Is, and the pillar of the throat *would be*

But for the shadow by the drooping chin   15
Cast into that recess—the tender shade
The shade and light, both there and every where,
And through the very atmosphere she breathes,
Broad, clear, and toned harmoniously, with skill
That might from nature have been learnt in the hour   20
When the lone Shepherd sees the morning spread
Upon the mountains. Look at her, whoe'er
Thou be, that kindling with a poet's soul
Hast loved the painter's true Promethean craft
Intensely—from Imagination take   25
The treasure, what mine eyes behold see thou,
Even though the Atlantic Ocean roll between.

   A silver line, that runs from brow to crown,
And in the middle parts the braided hair,
Just serves to show how delicate a soil   30
The golden harvest grows in; and those eyes,
Soft and capacious as a cloudless sky
Whose azure depth their colour emulates,
Must needs be conversant with *upward* looks,
Prayer's voiceless service; but now, seeking nought   35
And shunning nought, their own peculiar life
Of motion they renounce, and with the head
Partake its inclination towards earth
In humble grace, and quiet pensiveness
Caught at the point where it stops short of sadness.   40

   Offspring of soul-bewitching Art, make me
Thy confidant! say, whence derived that air
Of calm abstraction? Can the ruling thought
Be with some lover far away, or one
Crossed by misfortune, or of doubted faith?   45
Inapt conjecture! Childhood here, a moon
Crescent in simple loveliness serene,
Has but approached the gates of womanhood,
Not entered them; her heart is yet unpierced
By the blind Archer-god, her fancy free: 50
The fount of feeling, if unsought elsewhere,
Will not be found.

                    Her right hand, as it lies
Across the slender wrist of the left arm
Upon her lap reposing, holds—but mark
How slackly, for the absent mind permits   55
No firmer grasp—a little wild-flower, joined
As in a posy, with a few pale ears
Of yellowing corn, the same that overtopped
And in their common birthplace sheltered it
'Till they were plucked together; a blue flower   60
Called by the thrifty husbandman a weed ;
But Ceres, in her garland, might have worn
That ornament, unblamed. The floweret, held
In scarcely conscious fingers, was, she knows,
(Her Father told her so) in Youth's gay dawn   65
Her Mother's favourite; and the orphan Girl,
In her own dawn—a dawn less gay and bright,
Loves it while there in solitary peace
She sits, for that departed Mother's sake.
—Not from a source less sacred is derived   70
(Surely I do not err) that pensive air
Of calm abstraction through the face diffused
And the whole person.

                  Words have something told
More than the pencil can, and verily
More than is needed, but the precious Art   75
Forgives their interference—Art divine,
That both creates and fixes, in despite
Of Death and Time, the marvels it hath wrought.

   Strange contrasts have we in this world of ours!
That posture, and the look of filial love   80
Thinking of past and gone, with what is left
Dearly united, might be swept away
From this fair Portrait's fleshly Archetype,
Even by an innocent fancy's slightest freak
Banished, nor ever, haply, be restored   85
To their lost place, or meet in harmony
So exquisite; but *here* do they abide,
Enshrined for ages. Is not then the Art

Godlike, a humble branch of the divine,
In visible quest of immortality,   90
Stretched forth with trembling hope? In every realm,
From high Gibraltar to Siberian plains,
Thousands, in each variety of tongue
That Europe knows, would echo this appeal;
One above all, a Monk who waits on God   95
In the magnific Convent built of yore[1]
To sanctify the Escurial palace. He,
Guiding, from cell to cell and room to room,
A British Painter (eminent for truth
In character, and depth of feeling, shown   100
By labours that have touched the hearts of kings,
And are endeared to simple cottagers)
Left not unvisited a glorious work,
Our Lord's Last Supper, beautiful as when first
The appropriate Picture, fresh from Titian's hand,   105
Graced the Refectory: and there, while both
Stood with eyes fixed upon that Masterpiece,
The hoary Father in the Stranger's ear
Breathed out these words:—"Here daily do we sit,
Thanks given to God for daily bread, and here   110
Pondering the mischiefs of these restless Times,
And thinking of my Brethren, dead, dispersed,
Or changed and changing, I not seldom gaze
Upon this solemn Company unmoved
By shock of circumstance, or lapse of years,   115
Until I cannot but believe that they—
They are in truth the Substance, we the Shadows."

    So spake the mild Jeronymite, his griefs
Melting away within him like a dream
Ere he had ceased to gaze, perhaps to speak: 120
And I, grown old, but in a happier land,
Domestic Portrait! have to verse consigned
In thy calm presence those heart-moving words:

---

1   "The pile of buildings, composing the palace and convent of San Lorenzo, has, in common
    usage, lost its proper name in that of the *Escurial*, a village at the foot of the hill upon which
    the splendid edifice, built by Philip the Second, stands. It need scarcely be added, that
    Wilkie is the painter alluded to." WW

Words that can soothe, more than they agitate;
Whose spirit, like the angel that went down   125
Into Bethesda's pool, with healing virtue
Informs the fountain in the human breast
That by the visitation was disturbed.
——But why this stealing tear? Companion mute,
On thee I look, not sorrowing; fare thee well,   130
My Song's Inspirer, once again farewell!

The Foregoing Subject Resumed[1]

Among a grave fraternity of Monks,
For One, but surely not for One alone,
Triumphs, in that great work, the Painter's skill,
Humbling the body, to exalt the soul;
Yet representing, amid wreck and wrong   5
And dissolution and decay, the warm
And breathing life of flesh, as if already
Clothed with impassive majesty, and graced
With no mean earnest of a heritage
Assigned to it in future worlds. Thou, too,   10
With thy memorial flower, meek Portraiture!
From whose serene companionship I passed,
Pursued by thoughts that haunt me still; thou also—
Though but a simple object, into light
Called forth by those affections that endear   15
The private hearth; though keeping thy sole seat
In singleness, and little tried by time,
Creation, as it were, of yesterday—
With a congenial function art endued
For each and all of us, together joined,   20
In course of nature, under a low roof
By charities and duties that proceed
Out of the bosom of a wiser vow.
To a like salutary sense of awe,

---

1 "In the class entitled "Musings," in Mr. Southey's Minor Poems, is one upon his own minia-
ture Picture, taken in childhood, and another upon a landscape painted by Gaspar Poussin.
It is possible that every word of the above verses, though similar in subject, might have
been written had the author been unacquainted with those beautiful effusions of poetic
sentiment. But, for his own satisfaction, he must be allowed thus publicly to acknowledge
the pleasure those two poems of his Friend have given him, and the grateful influence they
have upon his mind as often as he reads them, or thinks of them." WW

Or sacred wonder, growing with the power   25
Of meditation that attempts to weigh,
In faithful scales, things and their opposites,
Can thy enduring quiet gently raise
A household small and sensitive,—whose love,
Dependent as in part its blessings are   30
Upon frail ties dissolving or dissolved
On earth, will be revived, we trust, in heaven.

"Desponding Father! mark this altered bough"

Desponding Father! mark this altered bough,
So beautiful of late, with sunshine warmed,
Or moist with dews; what more unsightly now,
Its blossoms shrivelled, and its fruit, if formed,
Invisible? yet Spring her genial brow   5
Knits not o'er that discolouring and decay
As false to expectation. Nor fret thou
At like unlovely process in the May
Of human life: a Stripling's graces blow,
Fade and are shed, that from their timely fall   10
(Misdeem it not a cankerous change) may grow
Rich mellow bearings, that for thanks shall call;
In *all* men, sinful is it to be slow
To hope—in *Parents*, sinful above all.

ditto to supra

Lines

Lady! a Pen, perhaps, with thy regard,
Among the Favoured, favoured not the least,
Left, 'mid the Records of this Book inscribed,
Deliberate traces, registers of thought
And feeling, suited to the place and time   5
That gave them birth:—months passed, and still this hand,
That had not been too timid to imprint
Words which the virtues of thy Lord inspired,
Was yet not bold enough to write of Thee.

---

1   WW identified the Countess Lonsdale in the third edition of *Yarrow Revisited, and Other Poems* (1839).

And why that scrupulous reserve? In sooth   10
The blameless cause lay in the Theme itself.
Flowers are there many that delight to strive
With the sharp wind, and seem to court the shower,
Yet are by nature careless of the sun
Whether he shine on them or not; and some,   15
Where'er he moves along the unclouded sky,
Turn a broad front full on his flattering beams:
Others do rather from their notice shrink,
Loving the dewy shade,—a humble Band,
Modest and sweet, a Progeny of earth,   20
Congenial with thy mind and character,
High-born Augusta!

             Towers, and stately Groves,
Bear witness for me; thou, too, Mountain-stream!
From thy most secret haunts; and ye Parterres,
Which she is pleased and proud to call her own;   25
Witness how oft upon my noble Friend
Mute offerings, tribute from an inward sense
Of admiration and respectful love,
Have waited, till the affections could no more
Endure that silence, and broke out in song;   30
Snatches of music taken up and dropt
Like those self-solacing those under notes
Trilled by the redbreast, when autumnal leaves
Are thin upon the bough. Mine, only mine,
The pleasure was, and no one heard the praise,   35
Checked, in the moment of its issue checked;
And reprehended by a fancied blush
From the pure qualities that called it forth.

  Thus Virtue lives debarred from Virtue's meed;
Thus, Lady, is retiredness a veil   40
That, while it only spreads a softening charm
O'er features looked at by discerning eyes,
Hides half their beauty from the common gaze;
And thus, even on the exposed and breezy hill
Of lofty station, female goodness walks,   45
When side by side with lunar gentleness,

As in a cloister. Yet the grateful Poor
(Such the immunities of low estate,
Plain Nature's enviable privilege,
Her sacred recompence for many wants)   *how can he think this way?*   50
Open their hearts before Thee, pouring out
All that they think and feel, with tears of joy;
And benedictions not unheard in Heaven:
And friend in the ear of friend, where speech is free
To follow truth, is eloquent as they.   55

Then let the Book receive in these prompt lines
A just memorial; and thine eyes consent
To read that they, who mark thy course, behold
A life declining with the golden light
Of summer, in the season of sere leaves;   60
See cheerfulness undamped by stealing Time;
See studied kindness flow with easy stream,
Illustrated with inborn courtesy;
And an habitual disregard of self
Balanced by vigilance for others' weal.   65

And shall the verse not tell of lighter gifts
With these ennobling attributes conjoined
And blended, in peculiar harmony,
By Youth's surviving spirit? What agile grace!
A nymph-like liberty, in nymph-like form,   70
Beheld with wonder; whether floor or path
Thou tread, or on the managed steed art borne,
Fleet as the shadows, over down or field,
Driven by strong winds at play among the clouds.

Yet one word more—one farewell word—a wish   75
Which came, but it has passed into a prayer,
That, as thy sun in brightness is declining,
So, at an hour yet distant for *their* sakes
Whose tender love, here faltering on the way
Of a diviner love, will be forgiven,—   80
So may it set in peace, to rise again
For everlasting glory won by faith.

"Fairy skill"

Fairy skill,
Fairy's hand,
And a quill
From fairy-land,
Album small!   5
Are needed all
To write in you;
So adieu
    W.W.—

The Redbreast

(SUGGESTED IN A WESTMORELAND COTTAGE)

Driven in by Autumn's sharpening air,
From half-stripped woods and pastures bare,
Brisk Robin seeks a kindlier home:
Not like a beggar is he come,
But enters as a looked-for guest,   5
Confiding in his ruddy breast,
As if it were a natural shield
Charged with a blazon on the field,
Due to that good and pious deed
Of which we in the Ballad read.   10
But pensive fancies putting by,
And wild-wood sorrows, speedily
He plays the expert ventriloquist;
And, caught by glimpses now—now missed,
Puzzles the listener with a doubt   15
If the soft voice he throws about
Comes from within doors of without!
Was ever such a sweet confusion,
Sustained by delicate illusion?
He's at your elbow—to your feeling   20
The notes are from the floor or ceiling;
And there's a riddle to be guessed,
'Till you have marked his heaving breast,
Where tiny sinking, and faint swell,
Betray the Elf that loves to dwell   25

In Robin's bosom, as a chosen cell.

Heart-pleased we smile upon the Bird
If seen, and with like pleasure stirred
Commend him, when he's only heard.
But small and fugitive *our* gain   30
Compared with *his* who long hath lain,
With languid limbs and patient head,
Reposing on a lone sick-bed;
Where now he daily hears a strain
That cheats him of too busy cares,   35
Eases his pain, and helps his prayers.
And who but this dear Bird beguiled
The fever of that pale-faced Child?
Now cooling, with his passing wing,
Her forhead, like a breeze of Spring;   40
Recalling now, with descant soft
Shed round her pillow from aloft,
Sweet thoughts of angels hovering nigh,
And the invisible sympathy
Of "Mathew, Mark, and Luke, and John,   45
Blessing the bed she lies upon:"[1]
And sometimes, just as listening ends
In slumber, with the cadence blends
A dream of that low-warbled hymn
Which Old-folk, fondly pleased to trim   50
Lamps of faith now burning dim,
Say that the Cherubs carved in stone,
When clouds gave way at dead of night,
And the moon filled the church with light,
Used to sing in heavenly tone,   55
Above and round the sacred places
They guard, with wingèd baby-faces.

Thrice-happy Creature! in all lands
Nurtured by hospitable hands:
Free entrance to this cot has he,   60

---

1   "The words—
          'Mathew, Mark, and Luke, and John,
              Bless the bed that I lie on,'
     are part of a child's prayer, still in general use through the northern counties." WW

Entrance and exit both *yet* free;
And, when the keen unruffled weather
That thus brings man and bird together,
Shall with its pleasantness be past,
And casement closed and door made fast,   65
To keep at bay the howling blast,
He needs not fear the season's rage,
For the whole house is Robin's cage.
Whether the bird flit here or there,
O'er table *lilt*, or perch on chair,   70
Though some may frown, and make a stir
To scare him as a trespasser,
And he belike will flinch or start,
Good friends he has to take his part;
One chiefly, who with voice and look   75
Pleads for him from the chimney nook,
Where sits the Dame, and wears away
Her long and vacant holiday;
With images about her heart,
Reflected, from the years gone by,   80
On human nature's second infancy.

Upon Seeing a Coloured Drawing of the Bird of Paradise in an Album

Who rashly strove thy Image to portray?
Thou buoyant minion of the tropic air;
How could he think of the live creature—gay
With a divinity of colours—drest
In all her brightness, from the dancing crest   5
Far as the last gleam of the filmy train
Extended and extending to sustain
The motions that it graces—and forbear
To drop his pencil! Flowers of every clime
Depicted on these pages smile at time;   10
And gorgeous insects copied with nice care
Are here, and likenesses of many a shell
Tossed ashore by restless waves,
Or in the diver's grasp fetched up from caves
Where sea-nymphs might be proud to dwell: 15

But whose rash hand (again I ask) could dare,
'Mid casual tokens and promiscuous shows,
To circumscribe this shape in fixed repose;
Could imitate for indolent survey,
Perhaps for touch profane,   20
Plumes that might catch, but cannot keep a stain;
And, with cloud-streaks lightest and loftiest, share
The sun's first greeting, his last farewell ray!

   Resplendent Wanderer! followed with glad eyes
Where'er her course; mysterious Bird!   25
To whom, by wondering Fancy stirred,
Eastern Islanders have given
A holy name—the Bird of Heaven!
And even a title higher still,
The Bird of God! whose blessed will   30
She seems performing as she flies
Over the earth and through the skies
In never-wearied search of Paradise—
Region that crowns her beauty, with the name
She bears for *us*—for us how blest,   35
How happy at all seasons, could like aim
Uphold our Spirits urged to kindred flight
On wings that fear no glance of God's pure sight,
No tempest from his breath, their promised rest
Seeking with indefatigable quest   40
Above a world that deems itself most wise
When most enslaved by gross realities.

Airey-force Valley

   —Not a breath of air
Ruffles the bosom of this leafy glen.
From the brook's margin, wide around, the trees
Are stedfast as the rocks; the brook itself,
Old as the hills that feed it from afar,   5
Doth rather deepen than disturb the calm
Where all things else are still and motionless.
And yet, even now, a little breeze, perchance
Escaped from boisterous winds that rage without,
Has entered, by the sturdy oaks unfelt;   10

But to its gentle touch how sensitive
Is the light ash! that, pendent from the brow
Of yon dim cave, in seeming silence makes
A soft eye-music of slow-waving boughs,
Powerful almost as vocal harmony   15
To stay the wanderer's steps and soothe his thoughts.

To the Moon

(COMPOSED BY THE SEA-SIDE,—ON THE COAST OF CUMBERLAND)

Wanderer! that stoop'st so low, and com'st so near
To human life's unsettled atmosphere;
Who lov'st with Night and Silence to partake,
So might it seem, the cares of them that wake;
And, through the cottage-lattice softly peeping,   5
Dost shield from harm the humblest of the sleeping;
What pleasure once encompassed those sweet names
Which yet in thy behalf the Poet claims,
An idolizing dreamer as of yore!—
I slight them all; and, on this sea-beat shore   10
Sole-sitting, only can to thoughts attend
That bid me hail thee as the SAILOR'S FRIEND;
So call thee for heaven's grace through thee made known
By confidence supplied and mercy shown,
When not a twinkling star or beacon's light   15
Abates the perils of a stormy night;
And for less obvious benefits, that find
Their way, with thy pure help, to heart and mind;
Both for the adventurer starting in life's prime;
And veteran ranging round from clime to clime,   20
Long-baffled hope's slow fever in his veins,
And wounds and weakness oft his labour's sole remains.

   The aspiring Mountains and the winding Streams
Empress of Night! are gladdened by thy beams;
A look of thine the wilderness pervades,   25
And penetrates the forest's inmost shades;
Thou, chequering peaceably the minster's gloom,
Guid'st the pale Mourner to the lost one's tomb;
Canst reach the Prisoner—to his grated cell

Welcome, though silent and intangible!—   30
And lives there one, of all that come and go
On the great waters toiling to and fro,
One, who has watched thee at some quiet hour
Enthroned aloft in undisputed power,
Or crossed by vapoury streaks and clouds that move   35
Catching the lustre they in part reprove—
Nor sometimes felt a fitness in thy sway
To call up thoughts that shun the glare of day,
And make the serious happier than the gay?

   Yes, lovely Moon! if thou so mildly bright   40
Dost rouse, yet surely in thy own despite,
To fiercer mood the phrenzy-stricken brain,
Let me a compensating faith maintain;
That there's a sensitive, a tender, part
Which thou canst touch in every human heart,   45
For healing and composure.—But, as least
And mightiest billows ever have confessed
Thy domination; as the whole vast Sea
Feels through her lowest depths thy sovereignty;
So shines that countenance with especial grace   50
On them who urge the keel her *plains* to trace
Furrowing its way right onward. The most rude,
Cut off from home and country, may have stood—
Even till long gazing hath bedimmed his eye,
Or the mute rapture ended in a sigh—   55
Touched by accordance of thy placid cheer,
With some internal lights to memory dear,
Or fancies stealing forth to soothe the breast
Tired with its daily share of earth's unrest,—
Gentle awakenings, visitations meek;   60
A kindly influence whereof few will speak,
Though it can wet with tears the hardiest cheek.

   And when thy beauty in the shadowy cave
Is hidden, buried in its monthly grave;
Then, while the Sailor, mid an open sea   65
Swept by a favouring wind that leaves thought free,
Paces the deck—no star perhaps in sight,

And nothing save the moving ship's own light
To cheer the long dark hours of vacant night—
Oft with his musings does thy image blend,   70
In his mind's eye thy crescent horns ascend,
And thou art still, O Moon, that SAILOR'S FRIEND!

To the Moon

(RYDAL)

Queen of the stars!—so gentle, so benign,
That ancient Fable did to thee assign,
When darkness creeping o'er thy silver brow
Warned thee these upper regions to forego,
Alternate empire in the shades below—   5
A Bard, who, lately near the wide-spread sea
Traversed by gleaming ships, looked up to thee
With grateful thoughts, doth now thy rising hail
From the close confines of a shadowy vale.
Glory of night, conspicuous yet serene,   10
Nor less attractive when by glimpses seen
Through cloudy umbrage, well might that fair face,
And all those attributes of modest grace,
In days when Fancy wrought unchecked by fear,
Down to the green earth fetch thee from thy sphere,   15
To sit in leafy woods by fountains clear!

   O still belov'd (for thine, meek Power, are charms
That fascinate the very Babe in arms,
While he, uplifted towards thee, laughs outright,
Spreading his little palms in his glad Mother's sight)   20
O still belov'd, once worshipped! Time, that frowns
In his destructive flight on earthly crowns,
Spares thy mild splendour; still those far-shot beams
Tremble on dancing waves and rippling streams
With stainless touch, as chaste as when thy praise   25
Was sung by Virgin-choirs in festal lays;
And through dark trials still dost thou explore
Thy way for increase punctual as of yore,
When teeming Matrons—yielding to rude faith
In mysteries of birth and life and death   30

And painful struggle and deliverance—prayed
Of thee to visit them with lenient aid.
What though the rites be swept away, the fanes
Extinct that echoed to the votive strains;
Yet thy mild aspect does not, cannot cease,   35
Love to promote and purity and peace;
And Fancy, unreproved, even yet may trace
Faint types of suffering in thy beamless face.

    Then, silent Monitress! let us—not blind
To worlds unthought of till the searching mind   40
Of Science laid them open to mankind—
Told, also, how the voiceless heavens declare
God's glory; and acknowledging thy share
In that blest charge; let us—without offence
To aught of highest, holiest, influence—   45
Receive whatever good 'tis given thee to dispense.
May sage and simple, catching with one eye
The moral intimations of the sky,
Learn from thy course, where'er their own be taken,
'To look on tempests, and be never shaken;'   50
To keep with faithful step the appointed way
Eclipsing or eclipsed, by night or day,
And from example of thy monthly range
Gently to brook decline and fatal change;
Meek, patient, stedfast, and with loftier scope,   55
Than thy revival yields, for gladsome hope!

"To a good Man of most dear memory"[1]

To a good Man of most dear memory
This Stone is sacred. Here he lies apart
From the great city where he first drew breath,
Was reared and taught; and humbly earned his bread,
To the strict labours of the merchant's desk   5
By duty chained. Not seldom did those tasks
Tease, and the thought of time so spent depress,
His spirit, but the recompence was high;
Firm Independence, Bounty's rightful sire;

---

1   Charles Lamb died December 27, 1834.

Affections, warm as sunshine, free as air;   10
And when the precious hours of leisure came,
Knowledge and wisdom, gained from converse sweet
With books, or while he ranged the crowded streets
With a keen eye, and overflowing heart:
So genius triumphed over seeming wrong,   15
And poured out truth in works by thoughtful love
Inspired—works potent over smiles and tears.
And as round mountain-tops the lightning plays,
Thus innocently sported, breaking forth
As from a cloud of some grave sympathy,   20
Humour and wild instinctive wit, and all
The vivid flashes of his spoken words.
From the most gentle creature nursed in fields
Had been derived the name he bore—a name,
Wherever christian altars have been raised,   25
Hallowed to meekness and to innocence;
And if in him meekness at times gave way,
Provoked out of herself by troubles strange,
Many and strange, that hung about his life;
Still, at the centre of his being, lodged   30
A soul by resignation sanctified:
And if too often, self-reproached, he felt
That innocence belongs not to our kind,
A power that never ceased to abide in him,
Charity, 'mid the multitude of sins   35
That she can cover, left not his exposed
To an unforgiving judgment from just Heaven.
O, he was good, if e'er a good Man lived!
                    *   *   *   *   *
From a reflecting mind and sorrowing heart
Those simple lines flowed with an earnest wish,   40
Though but a doubting hope, that they might serve
Fitly to guard the precious dust of him
Whose virtues called them forth. That aim is missed;
For much that truth most urgently required
Had from a faltering pen been asked in vain: 45
Yet, haply, on the printed page received,
The imperfect record, there, may stand unblamed

As long as verse of mine shall breathe the air
Of memory, or see the light of love.

    Thou wert a scorner of the fields, my Friend!   50
But more in show than truth; and from the fields,
And from the mountains, to thy rural grave
Transported, my soothed spirit hovers o'er
Its green untrodden turf, and blowing flowers;
And taking up a voice shall speak (tho' still   55
Awed by the theme's peculiar sanctity
Which words less free presumed not even to touch)
Of that fraternal love, whose heaven-lit lamp
From infancy, through manhood, to the last
Of threescore years, and to thy latest hour,   60
Burnt on with ever-strengthening light, enshrined
Within thy bosom.
                     'Wonderful' hath been
The love established between man and man,
'Passing the love of women;' and between
Man and his help-mate in fast wedlock joined   65
Through God, is raised a spirit and soul of love
Without whose blissful influence Paradise
Had been no Paradise; and earth were now
A waste where creatures bearing human form,
Direst of savage beasts, would roam in fear,   70
Joyless and comfortless. Our days glide on;
And let him grieve who cannot choose but grieve
That he hath been an Elm without his Vine,
And her bright dower of clustering charities,
That, round his trunk and branches, might have clung   75
Enriching and adorning. Unto thee
Not so enriched, not so adorned, to thee
Was given (say rather thou of later birth
Wert given to her) a Sister—'tis a word
Timidly uttered, for she *lives*, the meek,   80
The self-restraining, and the ever-kind;
In whom thy reason and intelligent heart
Found—for all interests, hopes, and tender cares,
All softening, humanising, hallowing powers,
Whether withheld, or for her sake unsought—   85

More than sufficient recompence!
                              Her love
(What weakness prompts the voice to tell it here?)
Was as the love of mothers; and when years,
Lifting the boy to man's estate, had called
The long-protected to assume the part   90
Of a protector, the first filial tie
Was undissolved; and, in or out of sight,
Remained imperishably interwoven
With life itself. Thus, 'mid a shifting world,
Did they together testify of time   95
And season's difference—a double tree
With two collateral stems sprung from one root;
Such were they—such thro' life they *might* have been
In union, in partition only such;
Otherwise wrought the will of the Most High;   100
Yet, thro' all visitations and all trials,
Still they were faithful; like two vessels launched
From the same beach one ocean to explore
With mutual help, and sailing—to their league
True, as inexorable winds, or bars   105
Floating or fixed of polar ice, allow.

    But turn we rather, let my spirit turn
With thine, O silent and invisible Friend!
To those dear intervals, nor rare nor brief,
When reunited, and by choice withdrawn   110
From miscellaneous converse, ye were taught
That the remembrance of foregone distress,
And the worse fear of future ill (which oft
Doth hang around it, as a sickly child
Upon its mother) may be both alike   115
Disarmed of power to unsettle present good
So prized, and things inward and outward held
In such an even balance, that the heart
Acknowledges God's grace, his mercy feels,
And in its depth of gratitude is still.   120

    O gift divine of quiet sequestration!
The hermit, exercised in prayer and praise,

And feeding daily on the hope of heaven,
Is happy in his vow, and fondly cleaves
To life-long singleness; but happier far   125
Was to your souls, and, to the thoughts of others,
A thousand times more beautiful appeared,
Your *dual* loneliness. The sacred tie
Is broken; yet why grieve? for Time but holds
His moiety in trust, till Joy shall lead   130
To the blest world where parting is unknown.

Extempore Effusion upon the Death of James Hogg

When first, descending from the moorlands,
I saw the Stream of Yarrow glide
Along a bare and open valley,
The Ettrick Shepherd was my guide.

When last along its banks I wandered,   5
Through groves that had begun to shed
Their golden leaves upon the pathways,
My steps the border minstrel led.

The mighty Minstrel breathes no longer,
Mid mouldering ruins low he lies;   10
And death upon the braes of Yarrow,
Has closed the Shepherd-poet's eyes:

Nor has the rolling year twice measured,
From sign to sign, its stedfast course,
Since every mortal power of Coleridge   15
Was frozen at its marvellous source;

The 'rapt One, of the godlike forehead,
The heaven-eyed creature sleeps in earth:
And Lamb, the frolic and the gentle,
Has vanished from his lonely hearth.   20

Like clouds that rake the mountain-summits,
Or waves that own no curbing hand,
How fast has brother followed brother,
From sunshine to the sunless land!

Yet I, whose lids from infant slumbers   25
Were earlier raised, remain to hear
A timid voice, that asks in whispers,
"Who next will drop and disappear?"

Our haughty life is crowned with darkness,
Like London with its own black wreath,   30
On which with thee, O Crabbe! forth-looking,
I gazed from Hampstead's breezy heath.

As if but yesterday departed,
Thou too art gone before; but why,
O'er ripe fruit, seasonably gathered,   35
Should frail survivors heave a sigh?

Mourn rather for that holy Spirit,
Sweet as the spring, as ocean deep;
For Her who, ere her summer faded,
Has sunk into a breathless sleep.   40

No more of old romantic sorrows,
For slaughtered Youth or love-lorn Maid!
With sharper grief is Yarrow smitten,
And Ettrick mourns with her their Poet dead.[1]

At the Grave of Burns

1803

I shiver, Spirit fierce and bold,
At thought of what I now behold:
As vapours breathed from dungeons cold
    Strike pleasure dead,
So sadness comes from out the mould   5
    Where Burns is laid.

And have I then thy bones so near,
And thou forbidden to appear?
As if it were thyself that's here,
    I shrink with pain;   10

---

1   In a note WW identified the five poets elegized in this poem: "Walter Scott died 21st Sept.
     1832. S. T. Coleridge 25th July, 1834. Charles Lamb 27th Dec. 1834. Geo. Crabbe 3rd
     Feb. 1832. Felicia Hemans 16th May, 1835."

And both my wishes and my fear
    Alike are vain.

Off weight—nor press on weight!—away
Dark thoughts!—they came, but not to stay;
With chastened feelings would I pay   15
    The tribute due
To him, and aught that hides his clay
    From mortal view.

Fresh as the flower, whose modest worth
He sang, his genius "glinted" forth,   20
Rose like a star that touching earth,
    For so it seems,
Doth glorify its humble birth
    With matchless beams.

The piercing eye, the thoughtful brow,   25
The struggling heart, where be they now?—
Full soon the Aspirant of the plough,
    The prompt, the brave,
Slept, with the obscurest, in the low
    And silent grave.   30

Well might I mourn that He was gone
Whose light I hailed when first it shone,
When, breaking forth as nature's own,
    It showed my youth
How Verse may build a princely throne   35
    On humble truth.

Alas! where'er the current tends,
Regret pursues and with it blends,—
Huge Criffel's hoary top ascends
    By Skiddaw seen,—   40
Neighbours we were, and loving friends
    We might have been;

True friends though diversely inclined;
But heart with heart and mind with mind,
Where the main fibres are entwined,   45
    Through Nature's skill,

May even by contraries be joined
    More closely still.

The tear will start, and let it flow;
Thou "poor Inhabitant below,"   50
At this dread moment—even so—
    Might we together
Have sate and talked where gowans blow,
    Or on wild heather.

What treasures would have then been placed   55
Within my reach; of knowledge graced
By fancy what a rich repast!
    But why go on?—
Oh! spare to sweep, thou mournful blast,
    His grave grass-grown.   60

There, too, a Son, his joy and pride,
(Not three weeks past the Stripling died,)
Lies gathered to his Father's side,
    Soul-moving sight!
Yet one to which is not denied   65
    Some sad delight.

For he is safe, a quiet bed
Hath early found among the dead,
Harboured where none can be misled,
    Wronged, or distrest;   70
And surely here it may be said
    That such are blest.

And oh for Thee, by pitying grace
Checked oft-times in a devious race,
May He who halloweth the place   75
    Where Man is laid
Receive thy Spirit in the embrace
    For which it prayed!

Sighing I turned away; but ere
Night fell I heard, or seemed to hear,   80
Music that sorrow comes not near,
    A ritual hymn,

Chaunted in love that casts out fear
    By Seraphim.

Thoughts

SUGGESTED THE DAY FOLLOWING ON THE BANKS OF NITH,
NEAR THE POET'S RESIDENCE

Too frail to keep the lofty vow
That must have followed when his brow
Was wreathed—"The Vision" tells us how—
    With holly spray,
He faultered, drifted to and fro,   5
    And passed away.

Well might such thoughts, dear Sister, throng
Our minds when, lingering all too long,
Over the grave of Burns we hung
    In social grief—   10
Indulged as if it were a wrong
    To seek relief.

But, leaving each unquiet theme
Where gentlest judgments may misdeem,
And prompt to welcome every gleam   15
    Of good and fair,
Let us beside this limpid Stream
    Breathe hopeful air.

Enough of sorrow, wreck, and blight;
Think rather of those moments bright   20
When to the consciousness of right
    His course was true,
When Wisdom prospered in his sight
    And virtue grew.

Yes, freely let our hearts expand,   25
Freely as in youth's season bland,
When side by side, his Book in hand,
    We wont to stray,
Our pleasure varying at command
    Of each sweet Lay.   30

How oft inspired must he have trod
These pathways, yon far-stretching road!
There lurks his home; in that Abode,
    With mirth elate,
Or in his nobly-pensive mood,   35
    The Rustic sate.

Proud thoughts that Image overawes,
Before it humbly let us pause,
And ask of Nature, from what cause
    And by what rules   40
She trained her Burns to win applause
    That shames the Schools.

Through busiest street and loneliest glen
Are felt the flashes of his pen;
He rules mid winter snows, and when   45
    Bees fill their hives;
Deep in the general heart of men
    His power survives.

What need of fields in some far clime
Where Heroes, Sages, Bards sublime,   50
And all that fetched the flowing rhyme
    From genuine springs,
Shall dwell together till old Time
    Folds up his wings?

Sweet Mercy! to the gates of Heaven   55
This Minstrel lead, his sins forgiven;
The rueful conflict, the heart riven
    With vain endeavour,
And memory of Earth's bitter leaven,
    Effaced for ever.   60

But why to Him confine the prayer,
When kindred thoughts and yearnings bear
On the frail heart the purest share
    With all that live?—
The best of what we do and are,   65
    Just God, forgive!

A Night Thought.

Lo! where the Moon along the sky
Sails with her happy destiny;
Oft is she hid from mortal eye
   Or dimly seen,
But when the clouds asunder fly   5
   How bright her mien!

Far different we—a froward race,
Thousands though rich in Fortune's grace
With cherished sullenness of pace
   Their way pursue,   10
Ingrates who wear a smileless face
   The whole year through.

If kindred humours e'er would make
My spirit droop for drooping's sake,
From Fancy following in thy wake,   15
   Bright ship of heaven!
A counter impulse let me take
   And be forgiven.

On an Event in Col: Evans's redoubted performances in Spain

The Ball whizzed by—it grazed his ear,
   And whispered as it flew,
I only touch—not take—don't fear
For both, my honest Buccaneer!
   Are to the Pillory due.

November, 1836

Even so for me a Vision sanctified
The sway of Death; long ere mine eyes had seen
Thy countenance—the still rapture of thy mien—
When thou, dear Sister! wert become Death's Bride:
No trace of pain or languor could abide   5
That change:—age on thy brow was smoothed—thy cold
Wan cheek at once was privileged to unfold
A loveliness to living youth denied.
Oh! if within me hope should e'er decline,

The lamp of faith, lost Friend! too faintly burn;   10
Then may that heaven-revealing smile of thine,
The bright assurance, visibly return:
And let my spirit in that power divine
Rejoice, as, through that power, it ceased to mourn.

The Widow on Windermere Side

I

How beautiful, when up a lofty height
Honour ascends among the humblest poor,
And feeling sinks as deep! See there the door
Of One, a Widow, left beneath a weight
Of blameless debt. On evil Fortune's spite   5
She wasted no complaint, but strove to make
A just repayment, both for conscience-sake
And that herself and hers should stand upright
In the world's eye. Her work when daylight failed
Paused not, and through the depth of night she kept   10
Such earnest vigils, that belief prevailed
With some, the noble creature never slept;
But, one by one, the hand of death assailed
Her children from her inmost heart bewept.

II

The Mother mourned, nor ceased her tears to flow,   15
Till a winter's noon-day placed her buried Son
Before her eyes, last child of many gone—
His raiment of angelic white, and lo!
His very feet bright as the dazzling snow
Which they are touching; yea far brighter, even   20
As that which comes, or seems to come, from heaven,
Surpasses aught these elements can show.
Much she rejoiced, trusting that from that hour
Whate'er befel she could not grieve or pine;
But the Transfigured, in and out of season,   25
Appeared, and spiritual presence gained a power
Over material forms that mastered reason.
Oh, gracious Heaven, in pity make her thine!

III

But why that prayer? as if to her could come *(is)* *Connected!*
No good but by the way that leads to bliss *(a)*   30
Through Death,—so judging we should judge amiss.
Since reason failed want is her threatened doom,
Yet frequent transports mitigate the gloom:
Nor of those maniacs is she one that kiss
The air or laugh upon a precipice;   35
No, passing through strange sufferings toward the tomb,
She smiles as if a martyr's crown were won:
Oft, when light breaks through clouds or waving trees,
With outspread arms and fallen upon her knees
The Mother hails in her descending Son   40
An Angel, and in earthly ecstacies
Her own angelic glory seems begun.

To the Planet Venus,

UPON ITS APPROXIMATION (AS AN EVENING STAR) TO THE EARTH,
JANUARY 1838

What strong allurement draws, what spirit guides
Thee, Vesper! brightening still, as if the nearer
Thou com'st to man's abode the spot grew dearer
Night after night? True is it, Nature hides
Her treasures less and less—Man now presides,   5
In power, where once he trembled in his weakness;
Knowledge advances with gigantic strides;
But are we aught enriched in love and meekness?
Aught dost thou see, bright Star! of pure and wise
More than in humbler times graced human story;   10
That makes our hearts more apt to sympathise
With heaven, our souls more fit for future glory,
When earth shall vanish from our closing eyes,
Ere we lie down in our last dormitory?

"Wouldst Thou be gathered to Christ's chosen flock"

Wouldst Thou be gathered to Christ's chosen flock
Shun the broad way too easily explored
And let thy path be hewn out of the rock

The living Rock of God's eternal WORD.

1838

"Oh what a Wreck! how changed in mien and speech!"

Oh what a Wreck! how changed in mien and speech![1]
Yet—though dread Powers, that work in mystery, spin
Entanglings of the brain; though shadows stretch
O'er the chilled heart—reflect; far, far within
Hers is a holy Being, freed from Sin.   5
She is not what she seems, a forlorn wretch,
But delegated Spirits comfort fetch
To Her from heights that Reason may not win.
Like Children, She is privileged to hold
Divine communion; both do live and move,   10
Whate'er to shallow Faith their ways unfold,
Inly illumined by Heaven's pitying love;
Love pitying innocence not long to last,
In them—in Her our sins and sorrows past.

Valedictory Sonnet[2]

Serving no haughty Muse, my hands have here
Disposed some cultured Flowerets (drawn from spots
Where they bloomed singly, or in scattered knots)
Each kind in several beds of one parterre;
Both to allure the casual Loiterer,   5
And that, so placed, my nurslings may requite
Studious regard with opportune delight,
Nor be unthanked, unless I fondly err.
But, metaphor dismissed, and thanks apart,
Reader, farewell! My last words let them be,—   10
If in this book Fancy and Truth agree;
If simple Nature trained by careful Art
Through It have won a passage to thy heart;
Grant me thy love, I crave no other fee!

---

1   WW pays tribute to Edith Southey, Robert Southey's wife.
2   WW ended a section of sonnets in *Poems of Early and Late Years* (1842) with this sonnet.

"Said red-ribbon'd Evans"

Said red-ribbon'd Evans
'My legions in Spain
Were at sixes and sevens;
Now they're famished or slain:
But no fault of mine,   5
For like brave Philip Sidney
In campaigning I shine,
A true knight of his kidney.
Sound flogging and fighting;
No Chief, on my troth,   10
Eer took such delight in
As I in them both.
Fontarabbia can tell
How my eyes watched the foe,
Hernani knows well   15
That our feet were not slow
Our hospitals, too,
Are matchless in story,
Where her thousands fate slew
All panting for glory."   20
Alas for this Hero
His fame touched the skies,
Then fell below Zero;
Never never to rise!
For him to Westminster   25
Did Prudence convey,
There safe as a Spinster
The Patriot to play.
But why be so glad on
His feats, or his fall?   30
He's got his red ribbon
And laughs at us all.—

"Hark! 'tis the Thrush, undaunted, undeprest"

Hark! 'tis the Thrush, undaunted, undeprest,
By twilight premature of cloud and rain;
Nor does that roaring wind deaden his strain
Who carols thinking of his Love and nest,

And seems, as more incited, still more blest.   5
Thanks, thou hast snapped a fire-side Prisoner's chain,
Exulting Warbler! eased a fretted brain,
And in a moment charmed my cares to rest.
Yes, I will forth, bold Bird! and front the blast,
That we may sing together, if thou wilt,   10
So loud, so clear, my Partner through life's day,
Mute in her nest love-chosen, if not love-built
Like thine, shall gladden, as in seasons past,
Thrilled by loose snatches of the social Lay.
                    RYDAL MOUNT, 1838.

" 'Tis He whose yester-evening's high disdain"

'Tis He whose yester-evening's high disdain
Beat back the roaring storm—but how subdued
His day-break note, a sad vicissitude!
Does the hour's drowsy weight his glee restrain?
Or, like the nightingale, her joyous vein   5
Pleased to renounce, does this dear Thrush attune
His voice to suit the temper of yon Moon
Doubly depressed, setting, and in her wane?
Rise, tardy Sun! and let the Songster prove
(The balance trembling between night and morn   10
No longer) with what ecstasy upborne
He can pour forth his spirit. In heaven above,
And earth below, they best can serve true gladness
Who meet most feelingly the calls of sadness.

A Plea for Authors. May, 1838

Failing impartial measure to dispense
To every suitor, Equity is lame;
And social Justice, stript of reverence
For natural rights, a mockery and a shame;
Law but a servile dupe of false pretence,   5
If, guarding grossest things from common claim
Now and for ever, She, to works that came
From mind and spirit, grudge a short-lived fence.
"What! lengthened privilege, a lineal tie
For *books!*" Yes, heartless Ones, or be it proved   10

That 'tis a fault in Us to have lived and loved
Like others, with like temporal hopes to die;
No public harm that Genius from her course
Be turned; and streams of truth dried up, even at their source!

Protest against the Ballot
1838

Forth rushed, from Envy sprung and Self-conceit,
A Power misnamed the SPIRIT OF REFORM,
And through the astonished Island swept in storm,
Threatening to lay all Orders at her feet
That crossed her way. Now stoops she to entreat   5
License to hide at intervals her head,
Where she may work, safe, undisquieted,
In a close Box, covert for Justice meet.
St. George of England! keep a watchful eye
Fixed on the Suitor; frustrate her request—   10
Stifle her hope; for, if the State comply,
From such Pandorian gift may come a Pest
Worse than the Dragon that bowed low his crest,
Pierced by the spear in glorious victory.

Composed on the same Morning[1]

Life with yon Lambs, like day, is just begun,
Yet Nature seems to them a heavenly guide.
Does joy approach? they meet the coming tide;
And sullenness avoid, as now they shun
Pale twilight's lingering glooms,—and in the sun   5
Couch near their dams, with quiet satisfied;
Or gambol—each with his shadow at his side
Varying its shape wherever he may run.
As they from turf yet hoar with sleepy dew
All turn, and court the shining and the green,   10
Where herbs look up, and opening flowers are seen;
Why to God's goodness cannot We be true,
And so, His gifts and promises between,
Feed to the last on pleasures ever new?

---

1   WW originally paired this sonnet with *Composed on a May-Morning. 1838* ("If with old love
   of you, dear Hills! I share"), in *Memorials of a Tour in Italy*, above.

A Poet to his Grandchild

(SEQUEL TO THE FOREGOING)[1]

"Son of my buried Son, while thus thy hand
"Is clasping mine, it saddens me to think
"How Want may press thee down, and with thee sink
"Thy Children left unfit, through vain demand
"Of culture, even to feel or understand   5
"My simplest Lay that to their memory
"May cling;—hard fate! which haply need not be
"Did Justice mould the Statutes of the Land.
"A Book time-cherished and an honoured name
"Are high rewards; but bound they nature's claim   10
"Or Reasons? No—hopes spun in timid line
"From out the bosom of a modest home
"Extend through unambitious years to come,
"My careless Little-one, for thee and thine!"

                                        May 23rd.

"Come gentle Sleep, Death's image tho' thou art"[2]

Come gentle Sleep, Death's image tho' thou art
Come share my couch nor speedily depart
How sweet thus living without life to lie
Thus without death how sweet it is to die.

[Two Translations from Michael Angelo]

i. "Grateful is Sleep; more grateful still to be"

Grateful is Sleep; more grateful still to be
Of marble; for while Shameless wrong and woe
Prevail 'tis best to neither hear nor see:
Then, wake me not, I pray you. Hush, speak low.

---

1   Sequel to *A Plea for Authors. May,* 1838.
2   From the Latin of Thomas Warton.

ii. Michael Angelo in reply to the passage upon his statue
of Night sleeping

Night speaks.

Grateful is Sleep, my life in stone bound fast
More grateful still: while wrong and shame shall last
On me can time no happier state bestow
Than to be left unconscious of the woe
Ah then lest you awaken me, speak low.   5

With a Small Present

A prized memorial this slight work may prove
As bought in Charity and given in Love.

"A sad and lovely face, with upturn'd eyes"

A sad and lovely face, with upturn'd eyes,
Tearless, yet full of grief.—How heavenly fair
How saintlike is the look those features wear!
Such sorrow is more lovely in its guise
Than joy itself—for underneath it lies   5
A calmness that betokens strength to bear
Earth's petty grievances—its toil and care:—
A spirit that can look through clouded skies,
And see the blue beyond.—Type of that grace
That lit *Her* holy features, from whose womb   10
Issued the blest Redeemer of our race—
How little dost thou speak of earthly gloom!
As little as the unblemish'd Queen of Night,
When envious clouds shut out her silver light.

Sonnet presumably by M–A – but powerful & eloquent

"Lo! where she stands fixed in a saint-like trance"

Lo! where she stands fixed in a saint-like trance,
One upward hand, as if she needed rest
From rapture, lying softly on her breast!
Nor wants her eyeball an ethereal glance;
But not the less—nay more—that countenance,   5
While thus illumined, tells of painful strife
For a sick heart made weary of this life
By love, long crossed with adverse circumstance.

—Would she were now as when she hoped to pass
At God's appointed hour to them who tread   10
Heaven's sapphire pavement, yet breathed well content,
Well pleased, her foot should print earth's common grass,
Lived thankful for day's light, for daily bread,
For health, and time in obvious duty spent.

To a Painter[1]

All praise the Likeness by thy skill portrayed;
But 'tis a fruitless task to paint for me,
Who, yielding not to changes Time has made,
By the habitual light of memory see
Eyes unbedimmed, see bloom that cannot fade,   5
And smiles that from their birth-place ne'er shall flee
Into the land where ghosts and phantoms be;
And, seeing this, own nothing in its stead.
Couldst thou go back into far-distant years,
Or share with me, fond thought! that inward eye,   10
Then, and then only, Painter! could thy Art
The visual powers of Nature satisfy,
Which hold, whate'er to common sight appears,
Their sovereign empire in a faithful heart.

On the same Subject

Though I beheld at first with blank surprise
This Work, I now have gazed on it so long   *heartfelt*
I see its truth with unreluctant eyes;
O, my Belovèd! I have done thee wrong,
Conscious of blessedness, but, whence it sprung,   5
Ever too heedless, as I now perceive:
Morn into noon did pass, noon into eve,
And the old day was welcome as the young,
As welcome, and as beautiful—in sooth
More beautiful, as being a thing more holy: 10
Thanks to thy virtues, to the eternal youth
Of all thy goodness, never melancholy;
To thy large heart and humble mind, that cast

---

1   WW wrote this and the following sonnet on seeing the portrait of Mary Wordsworth painted
    by the miniature portrait painter, Margaret Gillies (1803–1887).

Into one vision, future, present, past.

[Four Poems on a Portrait][1]

"More may not be by human Art exprest"

More may not be by human Art exprest
But Love, far mightier Power, can add the rest,
Add to the picture which those lines present
All that is wanting for my heart's content:
The braided hair a majesty displays   5
Of brow that thinks and muses while I gaze,
And O what meekness in those lips that share
A seeming intercourse with vital air,
Such faint sweet sign of life as Nature shows
A sleeping infant or the breathing rose;   10
And in that eye where others gladly see
Earth's purest light Heaven opens upon me.

"Art, Nature, Love here claim united praise"

Art, Nature, Love here claim united praise.
The forehead thinks—it muses while I gaze,
And the light breaking from the eyes to me
For hearts content is all it seems to be,
O that the lips though motionless might share   5
Some vital intercourse with silent air
Such faint sweet sign of life as Nature shows
The sleeping infant or the breathing rose.—

Upon the sight of the Portrait of a female Friend—

Upon those lips, those placid lips, I look,
Nor grieve that they are still and mute as death,
I gaze—I read as in an Angel's Book,
And ask not speech from them, but long for breath.
                    WM WORDSWORTH—
Ambleside,
    10th July,
      1840

---

1 The following poems on painting arose out of several portraits done by Margaret Gillies
   during her visit to Rydal Mount in the fall and winter of 1839.

Upon a Portrait

We gaze, not sad to think that we must die
And part; but that the love this Friend hath sown
Within our hearts, the love whose Flower hath blown
Bright as if heaven were ever in its eye
Shall pass so soon from human memory   5
And not by strangers to our blood alone
But by our best descendants be unknown
Unthought-of this may surely claim a sigh.
But blessed Art! we yield not to dejection
Thou against time so feelingly dost strive   10
Where'er preserved in this most true reflection
The Image of her Soul is kept alive
Some lingering fragrance of the pure affection,
Whose flower with us will vanish, must survive.

"The Star that comes at close of day to shine"

The Star that comes at close of day to shine
More heavenly bright than when it leads the Morn
Is Friendship's Emblem whether the forlorn
She visiteth; or shedding light benign
Thro' shades that solemnize life's calm decline   5
Doth make the happy happier. This have we
Learnt, Isabel! from thy society
Which now we too unwillingly resign
Tho' for brief absence. But farewell! The page
Glimmers before my sight, thro' thankful tears,   10
Such as start forth, not seldom to approve
Our truth, when we, old yet unchilled by age
Call Thee, tho' known but for a few fleet years
The heart-affianced Sister of our love.

Poor Robin[1]

Now when the primrose makes a splendid show,
And lilies face the March-winds in full blow,
And humbler growths as moved with one desire
Put on, to welcome spring, their best attire,

---

1   "The small wild Geranium, known by that name." WW

Poor Robin is yet flowerless, but how gay   5
With his red stalks upon this sunny day!
And, as his tuft of leaves he spreads, content
With a hard bed and scanty nourishment,
Mixed with the green some shine, not lacking power
To rival summer's brightest scarlet flower;   10
And flowers they well might seem to passers-by
If looked at only with a careless eye;
Flowers—or a richer produce (did it suit
The season) sprinklings of ripe strawberry fruit.

But, while a thousand pleasures come unsought,   15
Why fix upon his want or wealth a thought?
Is the string touched in prelude to a lay
Of pretty fancies that would round him play
When all the world acknowledged elfin sway?
Or does it suit our humour to commend   20
Poor Robin as a sure and crafty friend,
Whose practice teaches, spite of names to show
Bright colours whether they deceive or no?—
Nay, we would simply praise the free good-will
With which, though slighted, he, on naked hill   25
Or in warm valley, seeks his part to fill;
Cheerful alike if bare of flowers as now,
Or when his tiny gems shall deck his brow:
Yet more, we wish that men by men despised,
And such as lift their foreheads overprized,   30
Should sometimes think, where'er they chance to spy
This child of Nature's own humility,
What recompense is kept in store or left
For all that seem neglected or bereft;
With what nice care equivalents are given,   35
How just, how bountiful, the hand of Heaven.
                                        MARCH, 1840.

The Cuckoo-clock

Wouldst thou be taught, when sleep has taken flight,
By a sure voice that can most sweetly tell,
How far-off yet a glimpse of morning light,
And if to lure the truant back be well,

Forbear to covet a Repeater's stroke,   5
That, answering to thy touch, will sound the hour;
Better provide thee with a *Cuckoo-clock*,
For service hung behind thy chamber door;
And in due time the soft spontaneous shock,
The double note, as if with *living* power,   10
Will to composure lead—or make thee blithe as bird in bower.

List, Cuckoo—Cuckoo!—oft though tempests howl,
Or nipping frost remind thee trees are bare,
How cattle pine, and droop the shivering fowl,
Thy spirits will seem to feed on balmy air;   15
I speak with knowledge,—by that Voice beguiled,
Thou wilt salute old memories as they throng
Into thy heart; and fancies, running wild
Through fresh green fields, and budding groves among,
Will make thee happy, happy as a child;   20
Of sunshine wilt thou think, and flowers, and song,
And breathe as in a world where nothing can go wrong.

And know—that, even for him who shuns the day
And nightly tosses on a bed of pain;
Whose joys, from all but memory swept away,   25
Must come unhoped for, if they come again;
Know—that, for him whose waking thoughts, severe
As his distress is sharp, would scorn my theme,
The mimic notes, striking upon his ear
In sleep, and intermingling with his dream,   30
Could from sad regions send him to a dear
Delightful land of verdure, shower and gleam,
To mock the *wandering* Voice beside some haunted stream.

O bounty without measure! while the grace
Of Heaven doth in such wise, from humblest springs,   35
Pour pleasure forth, and solaces that trace
A mazy course along familiar things,
Well may our hearts have faith that blessings come,
Streaming from founts above the starry sky,
With angels when their own untroubled home   40
They leave, and speed on nightly embassy
To visit earthly chambers,—and for whom?

Yea, both for souls who God's forbearance try,
And those that seek his help, and for his mercy sigh.

The Norman Boy

High on a broad unfertile tract of forest-skirted Down,
Nor kept by Nature for herself, nor made by man his own,
From home and company remote and every playful joy,
Served, tending a few sheep and goats, a ragged Norman Boy.

Him never saw I, nor the spot, but from an English Dame,   5
Stranger to me and yet my friend, a simple notice came,
With suit that I would speak in verse of that sequestered child
Whom, one bleak winter's day, she met upon the dreary Wild.

His flock, along the woodland's edge with relics sprinkled o'er
Of last night's snow, beneath a sky threatening the fall of more,   10
Where tufts of herbage tempted each, were busy at their feed,
And the poor Boy was busier still, with work of anxious heed.

There was he, where of branches rent and withered and decayed,
For covert from the keen north wind, his hands a hut had made.
A tiny tenement, forsooth, and frail, as needs must be   15
A thing of such materials framed, by a builder such as he.

The hut stood finished by his pains, nor seemingly lacked aught
That skill or means of his could add, but the architect had wrought
Some limber twigs into a Cross, well-shaped with fingers nice,
To be engrafted on the top of his small edifice.   20

That Cross he now was fastening there, as the surest power and best
For supplying all deficiencies, all wants of the rude nest
In which, from burning heat, or tempest driving far and wide,
The innocent Boy, else shelterless, his lonely head must hide.

That Cross belike he also raised as a standard for the true   25
And faithful service of his heart in the worst that might ensue
Of hardship and distressful fear, amid the houseless waste
Where he, in his poor self so weak, by Providence was placed.

— Here, Lady! might I cease; but nay, let us before we part
With this dear holy Shepherd-boy breathe a prayer of earnest heart,   30
That unto him, where'er shall lie his life's appointed way,
The Cross, fixed in his soul, may prove an all-sufficing stay.

Sequel to the Norman Boy

Just as those final words were penned, the sun broke out in power,
And gladdened all things; but, as chanced, within that very hour,
Air blackened, thunder growled, fire flashed from clouds that hid the sky,
And, for the Subject of my Verse, I heaved a pensive sigh.

Nor could my heart by second thoughts from heaviness be cleared,   5
For bodied forth before my eyes the cross-crowned hut appeared;
And, while around it storm as fierce seemed troubling earth and air,
I saw, within, the Norman Boy kneeling alone in prayer.

The Child, as if the thunder's voice spake with articulate call,
Bowed meekly in submissive fear, before the Lord of All;   10
His lips were moving; and his eyes, upraised to sue for grace,
With soft illumination cheered the dimness of that place.

How beautiful is holiness!—What wonder if the sight,
Almost as vivid as a dream, produced a dream at night!
It came with sleep and showed the Boy, no cherub, not transformed,   15
But the poor ragged Thing whose ways my human heart had warmed.

Me had the dream equipped with wings, so I took him in my arms,
And lifted from the grassy floor, stilling his faint alarms,
And bore him high through yielding air my debt of love to pay,
By giving him, for both our sakes, an hour of holiday.   20

I whispered, "Yet a little while, dear Child! thou art my own,
To show thee some delightful thing, in country or in town.
What shall it be? a mirthful throng, or that holy place and calm
St. Denis, filled with royal tombs, or the Church of Notre Dame?

"St. Ouen's golden Shrine? or choose what else would please thee most   25
Of any wonder Normandy, or all proud France, can boast!"
"My Mother," said the Boy, "was born near to a blessèd Tree,
The Chapel Oak of Allonville; good Angel, show it me!"

On wings, from broad and steadfast poise let loose by this reply,
For Allonville, o'er down and dale, away then did we fly;   30
O'er town and tower we flew, and fields in May's fresh verdure drest;
The wings they did not flag; the Child, though grave, was not deprest.

But who shall show, to waking sense, the gleam of light that broke
Forth from his eyes, when first the Boy looked down on that huge oak,
For length of days so much revered, so famous where it stands   35

For twofold hallowing—Nature's care, and work of human hands?

Strong as an Eagle with my charge I glided round and round
The wide-spread boughs, for view of door, window, and stair that wound
Gracefully up the gnarled trunk; nor left we unsurveyed
The pointed steeple peering forth from the centre of the shade.   40

I lighted—opened with soft touch a grated iron door,
Past softly, leading in the Boy; and, while from roof to floor
From floor to roof all round his eyes the wondering creature cast,
Pleasure on pleasure crowded in, each livelier than the last.

For, deftly framed with the trunk, a sanctuary showed,   45
By light of lamp and precious stones, that glimmered here, there glowed,
Shrine, Altar, Image, Offerings hung in sign of gratitude;
And swift as lightning went the time, ere speech I thus renewed:

"Hither the Afflicted come, as thou hast heard thy Mother say,
And, kneeling, supplication make to our Lady de la Paix;   50
What mournful sighs have here been heard, and, when the voice was stopt
By sudden pangs, what bitter tears have on this pavement dropt!

"Poor Shepherd of the naked Down, a favoured lot is thine,
Far happier lot, dear Boy, than brings full many to this shrine;
From body pains and pains of soul thou needest no release,   55
Thy hours as they flow on are spent, if not in joy, in peace.

"Then offer up thy heart to God in thankfulness and praise,
Give to Him prayers, and many thoughts, in thy most busy days;
And in His sight the fragile Cross, on thy small hut, will be
Holy as that which long hath crowned the Chapel of this Tree;   60

"Holy as that far seen which crowns the sumptuous Church in Rome
Where thousands meet to worship God under a mighty Dome;
He sees the bending multitude, he hears the choral rites,
Yet not the less, in children's hymns and lonely prayer, delights.

"God for his service needeth not proud work of human skill;   65
They please him best who labour most to do in peace his will:
So let us strive to live, and to our Spirits will be given
Such wings as, when our Saviour calls, shall bear us up to heaven."

The Boy no answer made by words, but, so earnest was his look,
Sleep fled, and with it fled the dream—recorded in this book,   70
Lest all that passed should melt away in silence from my mind,

As visions still more bright have done, and left no trace behind.

And though the dream, to thee, poor Boy! to thee from whom it flowed,
Was nothing, nor e'er can be aught, 'twas bounteously bestowed,
If I may dare to cherish hope that gentle eyes will read   75
Not loth, and listening Little-ones, heart-touched, their fancies feed.

At Furness Abbey

in Gill, well deserved!

Here, where, of havoc tired and rash undoing,
Man left this Structure to become Time's prey
A soothing spirit follows in the way
That Nature takes, her counter-work pursuing.
See how her Ivy clasps the sacred Ruin   5
Fall to prevent or beautify decay;
And, on the mouldered walls, how bright, how gay,
The flowers in pearly dews their bloom renewing!
Thanks to the place, blessings upon the hour;
Even as I speak the rising Sun's first smile   10
Gleams on the grass-crowned top of yon tall Tower
Whose cawing occupants with joy proclaim
Prescriptive title to the shattered pile
Where, Cavendish, *thine* seems nothing but a name!

On a Portrait of the Duke of Wellington, upon the Field of Waterloo, by Haydon[1]

By Art's bold privilege Warrior and War-horse stand
On ground yet strewn with their last battle's wreck;
Let the Steed glory while his Master's hand
Lies fixed for ages on his conscious neck;
But by the Chieftain's look, though at his side   5
Hangs that day's treasured sword, how firm a check
Is given to triumph and all human pride!
Yon trophied Mound shrinks to a shadowy speck
In his calm presence! Him the mighty deed
Elates not, brought far nearer the grave's rest,   10
As shows that time-worn face, for he such seed
Has sown as yields, we trust, the fruit of fame
In Heaven; hence no one blushes for thy name,

---

1   Benjamin Robert Haydon (1786–1846) specialized in large historical paintings in oil.

Conqueror, 'mid some sad thoughts, divinely blest!

"Sigh no more Ladies, sigh no more"

Sigh no more Ladies, sigh no more,
Men were deceivers ever!
So says the old Ballad but
Fair Ladies believe it never!

"The Crescent-moon, the Star of Love"

The Crescent-moon, the Star of Love,
Glories of evening, as ye there are seen
With but a span of sky between—
Speak one of you, my doubts remove,
Which is the attendant Page and which the Queen?

"Let more ambitious Poets take the heart"

Let more ambitious Poets take the heart
By storm, my verse would rather win its way
With gentle violence into minds well-pleased
To give it welcome with a prompt return
Of their own sweetness, as March-flowers that shrink   5
From the sharp wind do readily yield up
Their choicest fragrance to a southern breeze
Ruffling their bosoms with its genial breath.

Epitaph in the Chapel-yard of Langdale, Westmoreland

By playful smiles, (alas too oft
A sad heart's sunshine) by a soft
And gentle nature, and a free
Yet modest hand of charity,
Through life was OWEN LLOYD endeared   5
To young and old; and how revered
Had been that pious spirit, a tide
Of humble mourners testified,
When, after pains dispensed to prove
The measure of God's chastening love,   10
Here, brought from far, his corse found rest,—
Fulfilment of his own request;—
Urged less for this Yew's shade, though he

Planted with such fond hope the tree;
Less for the love of stream and rock,   15
Dear as they were, than that his Flock,
When they no more their Pastor's voice
Could hear to guide them in their choice
Through good and evil, help might have,
Admonished, from his silent grave,   20
Of righteousness, of sins forgiven,
For peace on earth and bliss in heaven.

"Though Pulpits and the Desk may fail"

Though Pulpits and the Desk may fail
To reach the hearts of worldly men;
Yet may the grace of God prevail
And touch them through the Poet's pen.
                                    WM. WORDSWORTH
BATH, April 28th, 1841

The Wishing-gate Destroyed[1]

'Tis gone—with old belief and dream
That round it clung, and tempting scheme
      Released from fear and doubt;
And the bright landscape too must lie,
By this blank wall, from every eye,   5
      Relentlessly shut out.

Bear witness ye who seldom passed
That opening—but a look ye cast
      Upon the lake below,
What spirit-stirring power it gained   10
From faith which here was entertained,
      Though reason might say no.

Blest is that ground, where, o'er the springs
Of history, glory claps her wings,
      Fame sheds the exulting tear;   15
Yet earth is wide, and many a nook

---

1   "See 'The Wishing-Gate.' Having been told, upon what I thought good authority, that this
    gate had been destroyed, and the opening where it hung walled up, I gave vent immedi-
    ately to my feelings in these stanzas. But going to the place some time after I found, with
    much delight, my old favourite unmolested." WW's earlier poem is included above.

Unheard of is, like this, a book
   For modest meanings dear.

It was in sooth a happy thought
That grafted, on so fair a spot,   20
   So confident a token
Of coming good;—the charm is fled;
Indulgent centuries spun a thread,
   Which one harsh day has broken.

Alas! for him who gave the word;   25
Could he no sympathy afford,
   Derived from earth or heaven,
To hearts so oft by hope betrayed;
Their very wishes wanted aid
   Which here was freely given?   30

Where, for the love-lorn maiden's wound,
Will now so readily be found
   A balm of expectation?
Anxious for far-off children, where
Shall mothers breathe a like sweet air   35
   Of home-felt consolation?

And not unfelt will prove the loss
'Mid trivial care and petty cross
   And each day's shallow grief;
Though the most easily beguiled   40
Were oft among the first that smiled
   At their own fond belief.

If still the reckless change we mourn,
A reconciling thought may turn
   To harm that might lurk here,   45
Ere judgment prompted from within
Fit aims, with courage to begin,
   And strength to persevere.

Not Fortune's slave is man: our state
Enjoins, while firm resolves await   50
   On wishes just and wise,
That strenuous action follow both,
And life be one perpetual growth

Of heaven-ward enterprise.

So taught, so trained, we boldly face   55
All accidents of time and place;
   Whatever props may fail,
Trust in that sovereign law can spread
New glory o'er the mountain's head,
   Fresh beauty through the vale.   60

That truth informing mind and heart,
The simplest cottager may part,
   Ungrieved, with charm and spell;
And yet, lost Wishing-gate, to thee
The voice of grateful memory   65
   Shall bid a kind farewell!

Sonnet

Though the bold wings of Poesy affect
The clouds and wheel around the mountain tops
Rejoicing, from her loftiest height she drops
Well pleased to skim the plain with wild flowers deckt,
Or muse in solemn grove whose shades protect   5
The lingering dew—there steals along, or stops
Watching the least small bird that round her hops,
Or creeping worm, with sensitive respect.
Her functions are they therefore less divine,
Her thoughts less deep, or void of grave intent   10
Her simplest fancies? Should that fear be thine,
Aspiring Votary, ere thy hand present
One offering, kneel before her modest shrine,
With brow in penitential sorrow bent!

Suggested by a Picture of the Bird of Paradise

The gentlest Poet, with free thoughts endowed,
And a true master of the glowing strain,
Might scan the narrow province with disdain
That to the Painter's skill is here allowed.
This, this the Bird of Paradise! disclaim   5
The daring thought, forget the name;
This the Sun's Bird, whom Glendoveers might own

As no unworthy Partner in their flight
Through seas of ether, where the ruffling sway
Of nether air's rude billows is unknown;   10
Whom Sylphs, if e'er for casual pastime they
Through India's spicy regions wing their way,
Might bow to as their Lord. What character,
O sovereign Nature! I appeal to thee,
Of all thy feathered progeny   15
Is so unearthly, and what shape so fair?
So richly decked in variegated down,
Green, sable, shining yellow, shadowy brown,
Tints softly with each other blended,
Hues doubtfully begun and ended;   20
Or intershooting, and to sight
Lost and recovered, as the rays of light
Glance on the conscious plumes touched here and there?
Full surely, when with such proud gifts of life
Began the pencil's strife,   25
O'erweening Art was caught as in a snare.

A sense of seemingly presumptuous wrong
Gave the first impulse to the Poet's song;
But, of his scorn repenting soon, he drew
A juster judgment from a calmer view;   30
And, with a spirit freed from discontent,
Thankfully took an effort that was meant
Not with God's bounty, Nature's love, to vie,
Or made with hope to please that inward eye
Which ever strives in vain itself to satisfy,   35
But to recal the truth by some faint trace
Of power ethereal and celestial grace,
That in the living Creature find on earth a place.

"Lyre! though such power do in thy magic live"

Lyre! though such power do in thy magic live
    As might from India's farthest plain
    Recal the not unwilling Maid,
        Assist me to detain
        The lovely Fugitive: 5
Check with thy notes the impulse which, betrayed

By her sweet farewell looks, I longed to aid.
Here let me gaze enrapt upon that eye,
The impregnable and awe-inspiring fort
Of contemplation, the calm port   10
By reason fenced from winds that sigh
Among the restless sails of vanity.
But if no wish be hers that we should part,
A humbler bliss would satisfy my heart.
      Where all things are so fair,   15
Enough by her dear side to breathe the air
      Of this Elysian weather;
And, on or in, or near, the brook, espy
    Shade upon the sunshine lying
      Faint and somewhat pensively;   20
    And downward Image gaily vying
      With its upright living tree
Mid silver clouds, and openings of blue sky
As soft almost and deep as her cerulean eye.

Nor less the joy with many a glance   25
Cast up the Stream or down at her beseeching,
To mark its eddying foam-balls prettily distrest
By ever-changing shape and want of rest;
    Or watch, with mutual teaching,
    The current as it plays   30
    In flashing leaps and stealthy creeps
    Adown a rocky maze;
Or note (translucent summer's happiest chance!)
In the slope-channel floored with pebbles bright,
Stones of all hues, gem emulous of gem,   35
So vivid that they take from keenest sight
The liquid veil that seeks not to hide them.

Prelude[1]

In desultory walk through orchard grounds,
Or some deep chestnut grove, oft have I paused
The while a Thrush, urged rather than restrained
By gusts of vernal storm, attuned his song
To his own genial instincts; and was heard   5

1   The poem served as a prelude to WW's *Poems Chiefly of Early and Late Years* (1842).

(Though not without some plaintive tones between)
To utter, above showers of blossom swept
From tossing boughs, the promise of a calm,
Which the unsheltered traveller might receive
With thankful spirit. The descant, and the wind   10
That seemed to play with it in love or scorn,
Encouraged and endeared the strain of words
That haply flowed from me, by fits of silence
Impelled to livelier pace. But now, my Book!
Charged with those lays, and others of like mood,   15
Or loftier pitch if higher rose the theme,
Go, single—yet aspiring to be joined
With thy Forerunners that through many a year
Have faithfully prepared each other's way—
Go forth upon a mission best fulfilled   20
When and wherever, in this changeful world,
Power hath been given to please for higher ends
Than pleasure only; gladdening to prepare
For wholesome sadness, troubling to refine,
Calming to raise; and, by a sapient Art   25
Diffused through all the mysteries of our Being,
Softening the toils and pains that have not ceased
To cast their shadows on our mother Earth
Since the primeval doom. Such is the grace
Which, though unsued for, fails not to descend   30
With heavenly inspiration; such the aim
That Reason dictates; and, as even the wish
Has virtue in it, why should hope to me
Be wanting that sometimes, where fancied ills
Harass the mind and strip from off the bowers   35
Of private life their natural pleasantness,
A Voice devoted to the love whose seeds
Are sown in every human breast, to beauty
Lodged within compass of the humblest sight,
To cheerful intercourse with wood and field,   40
And sympathy with man's substantial griefs—
Will not be heard in vain? And in those days
When unforeseen distress spreads far and wide
Among a People mournfully cast down,

Or into anger roused by venal words   45
In recklessness flung out to overturn
The judgment, and divert the general heart
From mutual good—some strain of thine, my Book!
Caught at propitious intervals, may win
Listeners who not unwillingly admit   50
Kindly emotion tending to console
And reconcile; and both with young and old
Exalt the sense of thoughtful gratitude
For benefits that still survive, by faith
In progress, under laws divine, maintained.   55

RYDAL MOUNT, MARCH 26, 1842

Upon Perusing the Foregoing Epistle Thirty Years after its Composition [1]

Soon did the Almighty Giver of all rest
Take those dear young Ones to a fearless nest;
And in Death's arms has long reposed the Friend
For whom this simple Register was penned.
Thanks to the moth that spared it for our eyes;   5
And Strangers even the slighted Scroll may prize,
Moved by the touch of kindred sympathies.
For—save the calm, repentance sheds o'er strife
Raised by remembrances of misused life,
The light from past endeavours purely willed   10
And by Heaven's favour happily fulfilled;
Save hope that we, yet bound to Earth, may share
The joys of the Departed—what so fair
As blameless pleasure, not without some tears,
Reviewed through Love's transparent veil of years?   15

Sonnet

When Severn's sweeping Flood had overthrown
St Mary's Church the Preacher then would cry,
"Thus, Christian People God his might hath shown
That Ye to Him your love may testify;
Haste, and rebuild the Pile"! But not a stone   5
Resumed its place. Age after Age went by

---

1   Title and poem refer to *Epistle to Sir George Beaumont, Bart. From the South-west Coast of Cumberland.* See the latter poem, above.

And Heaven still lacked its due; though Piety
In secret did, we trust, her loss bemoan.
But now her spirit has put forth its claim
In power, and Poesy would lend her voice   10
Let the new Work be worthy of its aim,
That in its beauty Cardiff may rejoice!
Oh, in the Past if cause there was for shame
Let not our Times halt in their better choice!
                                        WM WORDSWORTH
        Rydal Mount, 23d Janry 1842

"A Poet!—He hath put his heart to school"

A Poet!—He hath put his heart to school,
Nor dares to move unpropped upon the staff
Which Art hath lodged within his hand—must laugh
By precept only, and shed tears by rule.
Thy Art be Nature; the live current quaff,   5
And let the groveller sip his stagnant pool,
In fear that else, when Critics grave and cool
Have killed him, Scorn should write his epitaph.
How does the Meadow-flower its bloom unfold?
Because the lovely little flower is free   10
Down to its root, and, in that freedom, bold;
And so the grandeur of the Forest-tree
Comes not by casting in a formal mould,
But from its *own* divine vitality.

To a Redbreast—(In Sickness)

Stay, little cheerful Robin! stay,
    And at my casement sing,
Though it should prove a farewell lay
    And this our parting spring.

Though I, alas! may ne'er enjoy   5
    The promise in thy song;
A charm, that thought can not destroy,
    Doth to thy strain belong.

Methinks that in my dying hour
    Thy song would still be dear,   10

And with a more than earthly power
  My passing Spirit cheer.

Then, little Bird, this boon confer,
  Come, and my requiem sing,
Nor fail to be the harbinger   15
  Of everlasting Spring.
                  S. H.[1]

"The most alluring clouds that mount the sky"

The most alluring clouds that mount the sky
Owe to a troubled element their forms,
Their hues to sunset. If with raptured eye
We watch their splendor, shall we covet storms,
And wish the Lord of day his slow decline   5
Would hasten, that such pomp may float on high?
Behold, already they forget to shine,
Dissolve—and leave to him who gazed a sigh.
Not loth to thank each moment for its boon
Of pure delight, come whencesoe'er it may,   10
Peace let us seek,—to stedfast things attune
Calm expectations, leaving to the gay
And volatile their love of transient bowers,
The house that cannot pass away be ours.

"Intent on gathering wool from hedge and brake"

Intent on gathering wool from hedge and brake
Yon busy Little-ones rejoice that soon
A poor old Dame will bless them for the boon:
Great is their glee while flake they add to flake
With rival earnestness; far other strife   5
Than will hereafter move them, if they make
Pastime their idol, give their day of life
To pleasure snatched for reckless pleasure's sake.
Can pomp and show allay one heart-born grief?
Pains which the World inflicts can she requite?   10
Not for an interval however brief;

---

1 "S. H." is WW's sister-in-law Sara Hutchinson. He included it in his publications in 1842 and
from 1845, and acknowledged his authorship of the second stanza, ll. 5–12.

The silent thoughts that search for stedfast light,
Love from on high, and Duty in her might,
And Faith—these only yield secure relief.

MARCH 8th, 1842.

The Eagle and the Dove

Shade of Caractacus, if Spirits love
The cause they fought for in their earthly home,
To see the Eagle ruffled by the Dove
May soothe thy memory of the chains of Rome.
These children claim thee for their Sire; the breath   5
Of thy renown, from Cambrian mountains, fans
A flame within them that despises death,
And glorifies the truant Youth of Vannes.
With thy own scorn of tyrants they advance,
But truth divine has sanctified their rage,   10
A silver Cross enchased with Flowers of France,
Their badge, attests the holy fight they wage.
The shrill defiance of the young Crusade
Their veteran foes mock as an idle noise
But unto Faith and Loyalty comes aid   15
From Heaven—gigantic force to beardless Boys.

"What heavenly smiles! O Lady mine"

What heavenly smiles! O Lady mine
Through my very heart they shine;
And, if my brow gives back their light,
Do thou look gladly on the sight;
As the clear Moon with modest pride   5
    Beholds her own bright beams
Reflected from the mountain's side
    And from the headlong streams.

"Wansfell! this Household has a favoured lot"

Wansfell![1]this Household has a favoured lot,
Living with liberty on thee to gaze,
To watch while Morn first crowns thee with her rays,

---

1   "The Hill that rises to the south-east, above Ambleside." WW

Or when along thy breast serenely float
Evening's angelic clouds. Yet ne'er a note   5
Hath sounded (shame upon the Bard!) thy praise
For all that thou, as if from heaven, hast brought
Of glory lavished on our quiet days.
Bountiful Son of Earth! when we are gone
From every object dear to mortal sight,   10
As soon we shall be, may these words attest
How oft, to elevate our spirits, shone
Thy visionary majesties of light,
How in thy pensive glooms our hearts found rest.
                                   Dec. 24, 1842.

"Glad sight wherever new with old"

Glad sight wherever new with old
Is joined through some dear homeborn tie;
The life of all that we behold
Depends upon that mystery.
Vain is the glory of the sky,   5
The beauty vain of field and grove
Unless, while with admiring eye
We gaze, we also learn to love.

To a Lady,

IN ANSWER TO A REQUEST THAT I WOULD WRITE HER A POEM
UPON SOME DRAWINGS THAT SHE HAD MADE OF FLOWERS
IN THE ISLAND OF MADEIRA

Fair Lady! can I sing of flowers
    That in Madeira bloom and fade,
I who ne'er sate within their bowers,
    Nor through their sunny lawns have strayed?
How they in sprightly dance are worn   5
    By Shepherd-groom or May-day queen,
Or holy festal pomps adorn,
    These eyes have never seen.

Yet tho' to me the pencil's art
    No like remembrances can give,   10
Your portraits still may reach the heart

And there for gentle pleasure live;
    While Fancy ranging with free scope
        Shall on some lovely Alien set
A name with us endeared to hope,   15
        To peace, or fond regret.

Still as we look with nicer care,
        Some new resemblance we may trace:
A *Heart's-ease* will perhaps be there,
        A *Speedwell* may not want its place.   20
And so may we, with charmèd mind
        Beholding what your skill has wrought,
Another *Star-of-Bethlehem* find,
        A new *Forget-me-not*.

From earth to heaven with motion fleet   25
        From heaven to earth our thoughts will pass,
A *Holy-thistle* here we meet
        And there a *Shepherd's weather-glass*;
And haply some familiar name
        Shall grace the fairest, sweetest, plant   30
Whose presence cheers the drooping frame
        Of English Emigrant.

Gazing she feels its power beguile
        Sad thoughts, and breathes with easier breath;
Alas! that meek that tender smile   35
        Is but a harbinger of death:
And pointing with a feeble hand
        She says, in faint words by sighs broken,
Bear for me to my native land
        This precious Flower, true love's last token.   40

"While beams of orient light shoot wide and high"

While beams of orient light shoot wide and high,
Deep in the vale a little rural Town[1]
Breathes forth a cloud-like creature of its own,
That mounts not toward the radiant morning sky,
But, with a less ambitious sympathy,   5

---

1   "Ambleside." WW

Hangs o'er its Parent waking to the cares
Troubles and toils that every day prepares.
So Fancy, to the musing Poet's eye,
Endears that Lingerer. And how blest her sway
(Like influence never may my soul reject)   10
If the calm Heaven, now to its zenith decked
With glorious forms in numberless array,
To the lone shepherd on the hills disclose
Gleams from a world in which the saints repose.
                                             Jan 1, 1843.

Grace Darling[1]

Among the dwellers in the silent fields
The natural heart is touched, and public way
And crowded street resound with ballad strains,
Inspired by ONE whose very name bespeaks
Favour divine, exalting human love;   5
Whom, since her birth on bleak Northumbria's coast,
Known unto few but prized as far as known,
A single Act endears to high and low
Through the whole land—to Manhood, moved in spite
Of the world's freezing cares—to generous Youth—   10
To Infancy, that lisps her praise—to Age
Whose eye reflects it, glistening through a tear
Of tremulous admiration. Such true fame
Awaits her *now*; but, verily, good deeds
Do no imperishable record find   15
Save in the rolls of heaven, where hers may live
A theme for angels, when they celebrate
The high-souled virtues which forgetful earth
Has witness'd. Oh! that winds and waves could speak
Of things which their united power called forth   20
From the pure depths of her humanity!
A Maiden gentle, yet, at duty's call,
Firm and unflinching, as the Lighthouse reared
On the Island-rock, her lonely dwelling-place;
Or like the invincible Rock itself that braves,   25

---

1   The poem is closely based on accounts of the event September 7, 1838, that appeared in
    the newspapers of the day.

Age after age, the hostile elements,
As when it guarded holy Cuthbert's cell.

All night the storm had raged, nor ceased, nor paused,
When, as day broke, the Maid, through misty air,
Espies far off a Wreck, amid the surf,   30
Beating on one of those disastrous isles—
Half of a Vessel, half—no more; the rest
Had vanished, swallowed up with all that there
Had for the common safety striven in vain,
Or thither thronged for refuge. With quick glance   35
Daughter and Sire through optic-glass discern,
Clinging about the remnant of this Ship,
Creatures—how precious in the Maiden's sight!
For whom, belike, the old Man grieves still more
Than for their fellow-sufferers engulfed   40
Where every parting agony is hushed,
And hope and fear mix not in further strife.
"But courage, Father! let us out to sea—
A few may yet be saved." The Daughter's words,
Her earnest tone, and look beaming with faith,   45
Dispel the Father's doubts: nor do they lack
The noble-minded Mother's helping hand
To launch the boat; and with her blessing cheered,
And inwardly sustained by silent prayer,
Together they put forth, Father and Child!   50
Each grasps an oar, and struggling on they go—
Rivals in effort; and, alike intent
Here to elude and there surmount, they watch
The billows lengthening, mutually crossed
And shattered, and re-gathering their might;   55
As if the tumult, by the Almighty's will
Were, in the conscious sea, roused and prolonged
That woman's fortitude—so tried, so proved—
May brighten more and more!

                           True to the mark,
They stem the current of that perilous gorge,   60
Their arms still strengthening with the strengthening heart,
Though danger, as the Wreck is near'd, becomes

More imminent. Not unseen do they approach;
And rapture, with varieties of fear
Incessantly conflicting, thrills the frames   65
Of those who, in that dauntless energy,
Foretaste deliverance; but the least perturbed
Can scarcely trust his eyes, when he perceives
That of the pair—tossed on the waves to bring
Hope to the hopeless, to the dying, life—   70
One is a Woman, a poor earthly sister,
Or, be the Visitant other than she seems,
A guardian Spirit sent from pitying Heaven,
In woman's shape. But why prolong the tale,
Casting weak words amid a host of thoughts   75
Armed to repel them? Every hazard faced
And difficulty mastered, with resolve
That no one breathing should be left to perish,
This last remainder of the crew are all
Placed in the little boat, then o'er the deep   80
Are safely borne, landed upon the beach,
And, in fulfilment of God's mercy, lodged
Within the sheltering Lighthouse.—Shout, ye Waves!
Send forth a song of triumph. Waves and Winds,
Exult in this deliverance wrought through faith   85
In Him whose Providence your rage hath served!
Ye screaming Sea-mews, in the concert join!
And would that some immortal Voice—a Voice
Fitly attuned to all that gratitude
Breathes out from floor or couch, through pallid lips   90
Of the survivors—to the clouds might bear—
Blended with praise of that parental love,
Beneath whose watchful eye the Maiden grew
Pious and pure, modest and yet so brave,
Though young so wise, though meek so resolute—   95
Might carry to the clouds and to the stars,
Yea, to celestial Choirs, GRACE DARLING's name!

Inscription

FOR A MONUMENT IN CROSTHWAITE CHURCH, IN
THE VALE OF KESWICK[1]

Ye vales and hills whose beauty hither drew
The poet's steps, and fixed him here, on you,
His eyes have closed! And ye, lov'd books, no more
Shall Southey feed upon your precious lore,
To works that ne'er shall forfeit their renown,   5
Adding immortal labours of his own—
Whether he traced historic truth, with zeal
For the State's guidance, or the Church's weal,
Or Fancy, disciplined by studious art,
Inform'd his pen, or wisdom of the heart,   10
Or judgments sanctioned in the Patriot's mind
By reverence for the rights of all mankind.
Wide were his aims, yet in no human breast
Could private feelings meet for holier rest.
His joys, his griefs, have vanished like a cloud   15
From Skiddaw's top; but he to heaven was vowed
Through his industrious life, and Christian faith
Calmed in his soul the fear of change and death.

To the Rev. Christopher Wordsworth, D.D.

MASTER OF HARROW SCHOOL, AFTER THE PERUSAL OF HIS
THEOPHILUS ANGLICANUS, RECENTLY PUBLISHED

Enlightened Teacher,[2] gladly from thy hand
Have I received this proof of pains bestowed
By Thee to guide thy Pupils on the road
That, in our native isle, and every land,
The Church, when trusting in divine command   5
And in her Catholic attributes, hath trod:
O may these lessons be with profit scanned
To thy heart's wish, thy labour blest by God!
So the bright faces of the young and gay
Shall look more bright—the happy, happier still;   10
Catch, in the pauses of their keenest play,

---

1   Robert Southey died March 21, 1843.
2   WW's nephew.

Motions of thought which elevate the will
And, like the Spire that from your classic Hill
Points heavenward, indicate the end and way.
  Rydal Mount, Dec. 11, 1843.

"So fair, so sweet, withal so sensitive"

So fair, so sweet, withal so sensitive,
Would that the little Flowers were born to live,
Conscious of half the pleasure which they give;

That to this mountain-daisy's self were known
The beauty of its star-shaped shadow, thrown   5
On the smooth surface of this naked stone!

And what if hence a bold desire should mount
High as the Sun, that he could take account
Of all that issues from his glorious fount!

So might he ken how by his sovereign aid   10
These delicate companionships are made;
And how he rules the pomp of light and shade;

And were the Sister-power that shines by night
So privileged, what a countenance of delight
Would through the clouds break forth on human sight!   15

Fond fancies! wheresoe'er shall turn thine eye
On earth, air, ocean, or the starry sky,
Converse with Nature in pure sympathy;

All vain desires, all lawless wishes quelled,
Be Thou to love and praise alike impelled,   20
Whatever boon is granted or withheld.

Sonnet

ON THE PROJECTED KENDAL AND WINDERMERE RAILWAY

Is then no nook of English ground secure
From rash assault? Schemes of retirement sown
In youth, and mid the busy world kept pure
As when their earliest flowers of hope were blown,
Must perish;—how can they this blight endure?   5

And must he too the ruthless change bemoan
Who scorns a false utilitarian lure
Mid his paternal fields at random thrown?
Baffle the threat, bright Scene, from Orrest-head
Given to the pausing traveller's rapturous glance: 10
Plead for thy peace, thou beautiful romance
Of nature; and, if human hearts be dead,
Speak, passing winds; ye torrents, with your strong
And constant voice, protest against the wrong.

WILLIAM WORDSWORTH.

Rydal Mount,
   October 12th, 1844.

"Proud were ye, Mountains, when, in times of old"

Proud were ye, Mountains, when, in times of old,
Your patriot sons, to stem invasive war,
Intrenched your brows; ye gloried in each scar:
Now, for your shame, a Power, the Thirst of Gold,
That rules o'er Britain like a baneful star,   5
Wills that your peace, your beauty, shall be sold,
And clear way made for her triumphal car
Through the beloved retreats your arms enfold!
Heard ye that Whistle? As her long-linked Train
Swept onwards, did the vision cross your view?   10
Yes, ye were startled;—and, in balance true,
Weighing the mischief with the promised gain,
Mountains, and Vales, and Floods, I call on you
To share the passion of a just disdain.

The Westmoreland Girl[1]

TO MY GRANDCHILDREN

PART I

Seek who will delight in fable

---

1 WW described the poem as "truth to the Letter" (WW to Henry Reed, July 31, 1845). Sarah
Mackereth, the Grasmere girl whose story the poem tells, died in 1872 and is buried in
Broughton in Furness churchyard (F. A. Malleson, *Holiday Studies of Wordsworth: By
Rivers, Woods, and Alps* [London, Paris & Melbourne: Cassell & Company, 1890]; he
records Sarah's retelling of the events from which WW framed his poem in chap. 2, pp.
42–46; the chapter is based on an article that Malleson published in 1873 in the magazine
Sunday at Home).

I shall tell you truth. A Lamb
Leapt from this steep bank to follow
'Cross the brook its thoughtless dam.

Far and wide on hill and valley   5
Rain had fallen, unceasing rain,
And the bleating mother's Young-one
Struggled with the flood in vain:

But, as chanced, a Cottage-maiden
(Ten years scarcely had she told)   10
Seeing, plunged into the torrent,
Clasped the Lamb and kept her hold.

Whirled adown the rocky channel,
Sinking, rising, on they go,
Peace and rest, as seems, before them   15
Only in the lake below.

Oh! it was a frightful current
Whose fierce wrath the Girl had braved;
Clap your hands with joy my Hearers,
Shout in triumph, both are saved;   20

Saved by courage that with danger
Grew, by strength the gift of love,
And belike a guardian angel
Came with succour from above.

PART II

Now, to a maturer Audience,   25
Let me speak of this brave Child
Left among her native mountains
With wild Nature to run wild.

So, unwatched by love maternal,
Mother's care no more her guide,   30
Fared this little bright-eyed Orphan
Even while at her father's side.

Spare your blame,—remembrance makes him
Loth to rule by strict command;

Still upon his cheek are living   35
Touches of her infant hand,

Dear caresses given in pity,
Sympathy that soothed his grief,
As the dying mother witnessed
To her thankful mind's relief.   40

Time passed on; the Child was happy,
Like a Spirit of air she moved,
Wayward, yet by all who knew her
For her tender heart beloved.

Scarcely less than sacred passions,   45
Bred in house, in grove, and field,
Link her with the inferior creatures,
Urge her powers their rights to shield.

Anglers, bent on reckless pastime,
Learn how she can feel alike   50
Both for tiny harmless minnow
And the fierce and sharp-toothed pike.

Merciful protectress, kindling
Into anger or disdain;
Many a captive hath she rescued,   55
Others saved from lingering pain.

Listen yet awhile;—with patience
Hear the homely truths I tell,
She in Grasmere's old church-steeple
Tolled this day the passing-bell.   60

Yes, the wild Girl of the mountains
To their echoes gave the sound,
Notice punctual as the minute,
Warning solemn and profound.

She, fulfilling her sire's office,   65
Rang alone the far-heard knell,
Tribute, by her hand, in sorrow,
Paid to One who loved her well.

When his spirit was departed
On that service she went forth;   70
Nor will fail the like to render
When his corse is laid in earth.

What then wants the Child to temper,
In her breast, unruly fire,
To control the froward impulse   75
And restrain the vague desire?

Easily a pious training
And a stedfast outward power
Would supplant the weeds and cherish,
In their stead, each opening flower.   80

Thus the fearless Lamb-deliv'rer,
Woman-grown, meek-hearted, sage,
May become a blest example
For her sex, of every age.

Watchful as a wheeling eagle,   85
Constant as a soaring lark,
Should the country need a heroine,
She might prove our Maid of Arc.

Leave that thought; and here be uttered
Prayer that Grace divine may raise   90
Her humane courageous spirit
Up to heaven, thro' peaceful ways.

"Yes! thou art fair, yet be not moved"

Yes! thou art fair, yet be not moved
    To scorn the declaration,
That sometimes I in thee have loved
    My fancy's own creation.

Imagination needs must stir;   5
    Dear Maid, this truth believe,
Minds that have nothing to confer
    Find little to perceive.

Be pleased that nature made thee fit

To feed my heart's devotion,   10
By laws to which all Forms submit
   In sky, air, earth, and ocean.

"Forth from a jutting ridge, around whose base"

Forth from a jutting ridge, around whose base
Winds our deep Vale, two heath-clad Rocks ascend
In fellowship, the loftiest of the pair
Rising to no ambitious height; yet both,
O'er lake and stream, mountain and flowery mead,   5
Unfolding prospects fair as human eyes
Ever beheld. Up-led with mutual help,
To one or other brow of those twin Peaks
Were two adventurous Sisters wont to climb,
And took no note of the hour while thence they gazed,   10
The blooming heath their couch, gazed, side by side,
In speechless admiration. I, a witness
And frequent sharer of their calm delight
With thankful heart, to either Eminence
Gave the baptismal name each Sister bore.   15
Now are they parted, far as Death's cold hand
Hath power to part the Spirits of those who love
As they did love. Ye kindred Pinnacles—
That, while the generations of mankind
Follow each other to their hiding-place   20
In time's abyss, are privileged to endure
Beautiful in yourselves, and richly graced
With like command of beauty—grant your aid
For Mary's humble, Sarah's silent, claim,
That their pure joy in nature may survive   25
From age to age in blended memory.

At Furness Abbey

Well have yon Railway Labourers to this ground
Withdrawn for noontide rest. They sit, they walk
Among the Ruins, but no idle talk
Is heard; to grave demeanour all are bound;
And from one voice a Hymn with tuneful sound   5
Hallows once more the long-deserted Quire

And thrills the old sepulchral earth, around.
Others look up, and with fixed eyes admire
That wide-spanned arch, wondering how it was raised,
To keep, so high in air, its strength and grace: 10
All seem to feel the spirit of the place,
And by the general reverence God is praised:
Profane Despoilers, stand ye not reproved,
While thus these simple-hearted men are moved!
    June 21st, 1845.

"Why should we weep or mourn, Angelic boy"

Why should we weep or mourn, Angelic boy,
For such thou wert ere from our sight removed,
Holy, and ever dutiful—beloved
From day to day with never-ceasing joy,
And hopes as dear as could the heart employ   5
In aught to earth pertaining? Death has proved
His might, nor less his mercy, as behoved—
Death conscious that he only could destroy
The bodily frame. That beauty is laid low
To moulder in a far-off field of Rome;   10
But Heaven is now, blest Child, thy Spirit's home:
When such divine communion, which we know,
Is felt, thy Roman-burial place will be
Surely a sweet remembrancer of Thee.

"I know an aged Man constrained to dwell"

I know an aged Man constrained to dwell
In a large house of public charity,
Where he abides, as in a Prisoner's cell,
With numbers near, alas! no company.

When he could creep about, at will, though poor   5
And forced to live on alms, this old Man fed
A Redbreast, one that to his cottage door
Came not, but in a lane partook his bread.

There, at the root of one particular tree,
An easy seat this worn-out Labourer found   10
While Robin pecked the crumbs upon his knee

Laid one by one, or scattered on the ground.

Dear intercourse was theirs, day after day;
What signs of mutual gladness when they met!
Think of their common peace, their simple play,   15
The parting moment and its fond regret.

Months passed in love that failed not to fulfil,
In spite of season's change, its own demand,
By fluttering pinions here and busy bill;
There by caresses from a tremulous hand.   20

Thus in the chosen spot a tie so strong
Was formed between the solitary pair,
That when his fate had housed him mid a throng
The Captive shunned all converse proffered there.

Wife, children, kindred, they were dead and gone;   25
But, if no evil hap his wishes crossed,
One living Stay was left, and on that one
Some recompense for all that he had lost.

O that the good old Man had power to prove,
By message sent through air or visible token,   30
That still he loves the Bird, and still must love;
That friendship lasts though fellowship is broken!

To an Octogenarian

Affections lose their objects; Time brings forth
No successors; and, lodged in memory,
If love exist no longer, it must die,—
Wanting accustomed food must pass from earth,
Or never hope to reach a second birth.   5
This sad belief, the happiest that is left
To thousands, share not Thou; howe'er bereft,
Scorned, or neglected, fear not such a dearth.
Though poor and destitute of friends thou art,
Perhaps the sole survivor of thy race,   10
One to whom Heaven assigns that mournful part
The utmost solitude of age to face,
Still shall be left some corner of the heart

Where Love for living Thing can find a place.

Written upon a fly leaf in the Copy of the Author's Poems which was sent
to her Majesty Queen Victoria[1]

Deign Sovereign Mistress! to accept a Lay
No Laureate offering of elaborate Art;
But Salutation taking its glad way
From deep recesses of a Loyal heart.

Queen, Wife, and Mother! may all-judging Heaven   5
Shower with a bounteous hand on Thee and Thine
Felicity, that only can be given
On Earth to goodness, blest by grace divine.

Lady! devoutly honoured and beloved
Thro' every realm confided to thy sway   10
May'st Thou pursue thy course by God approved
And He will teach thy People to obey.

As Thou art wont thy sovereignty adorn
With Woman's gentleness, yet firm and staid;
So shall that earthly Crown thy brows have worn   15
Be changed to one whose glory cannot fade:

And now, by duty urged, I lay this Book
Before thy Majesty, in humble trust
That on its simplest pages Thou wilt look
With a benign indulgence, more than just.   20

Nor wilt Thou blame an aged Poet's prayer
That issuing hence may steal into thy mind
Some solace under weight of Royal care
Or grief, the inheritance of Humankind;

For know we not that from celestial spheres   25
When Time was young an inspiration came
(O were it mine) to hallow saddest tears,
And help life onward in its noblest aim.
                    W.W.
Rydal Mount,
9th Jany 1846

---

1   The volume is in the Royal Library, Windsor Castle. The poem did not appear in print in
    WW's lifetime.

"Who but is pleased to watch the moon on high"

Who but is pleased to watch the moon on high
Travelling where she from time to time enshrouds
Her head, and nothing loth her Majesty
Renounces, till among the scattered clouds
One with its kindling edge declares that soon   5
Will reappear before the uplifted eye
A Form as bright, as beautiful a moon,
To glide in open prospect through clear sky.
Pity that such a promise e'er should prove
False in the issue, that yon seeming space   10
Of sky should be in truth the steadfast face
Of a cloud flat and dense, through which must move
(By transit not unlike man's frequent doom)
The Wanderer lost in more determined gloom!

"How beautiful the Queen of Night, on high"

How beautiful the Queen of Night, on high
Her way pursuing among scattered clouds,
Where, ever and anon, her head she shrouds
Hidden from view in dense obscurity.
But look, and to the watchful eye   5
A brightening edge will indicate that soon
We shall behold the struggling Moon
Break forth,—again to walk the clear blue sky.

"Where lies the truth? has Man, in wisdom's creed"

Where lies the truth? has Man, in wisdom's creed,
A pitiable doom; for respite brief
A care more anxious, or a heavier grief?
Is he ungrateful, and doth little heed
God's bounty, soon forgotten; or indeed,   5
Must Man, with labour born, awake to sorrow
When Flowers rejoice and Larks with rival speed
Spring from their nests to bid the Sun good morrow?
They mount for rapture as their songs proclaim
Warbled in hearing both of earth and sky;   10
But o'er the contrast wherefore heave a sigh?

Like these aspirants let us soar—our aim,
Through life's worst trials, whether shocks or snares,
A happier, brighter, purer Heaven than theirs.

To Lucca Giordano

Giordano, verily thy Pencil's skill
Hath here portrayed with Nature's happiest grace
The fair Endymion couched on Latmos-hill;
And Dian gazing on the Shepherd's face
In rapture,—yet suspending her embrace,   5
As not unconscious with what power the thrill
Of her most timid touch his sleep would chase,
And, with his sleep, that beauty calm and still.
O may this work have found its last retreat
Here in a Mountain-bard's secure abode,   10
One to whom, yet a School-boy, Cynthia showed
A face of love which he in love would greet,
Fixed, by her smile, upon some rocky seat;
Or lured along where green-wood paths he trod.
        Rydal Mount. 1846.

Illustrated Books and Newspapers

Discourse was deemed Man's noblest attribute,
And written words the glory of his hand;
Then followed Printing with enlarged command
For thought—dominion vast and absolute
For spreading truth, and making love expand.   5
Now prose and verse sunk into disrepute
Must lacquey a dumb Art that best can suit
The taste of this once-intellectual Land.
A backward movement surely have we here,
For manhood—back to childhood; for the age—   10
Back towards caverned life's first rude career.
Avaunt this vile abuse of pictured page!
Must eyes be all in all, the tongue and ear
Nothing? Heaven keep us from a lower stage!

On the Banks of a Rocky Stream

Behold an emblem of our human mind
Crowded with thoughts that need a settled home,
Yet, like to eddying balls of foam
Within this whirlpool, they each other chase
Round and round, and neither find   5
An outlet nor a resting-place!
Stranger, if such disquietude be thine,
Fall on thy knees and sue for help divine.

Ode,

PERFORMED IN THE SENATE-HOUSE, CAMBRIDGE, ON THE SIXTH OF JULY,
M.DCCC.XLVII. AT THE FIRST COMMENCEMENT AFTER THE INSTALLATION OF
HIS ROYAL HIGHNESS THE PRINCE ALBERT, CHANCELLOR OF THE UNIVERSITY

Installation Ode

INTRODUCTION AND CHORUS

For thirst of power that Heaven disowns,
For temples, towers, and thrones,
Too long insulted by the Spoiler's shock,
Indignant Europe cast
Her stormy foe at last   5
To reap the whirlwind on a Libyan rock.

SOLO—TENOR

War is passion's basest game
Madly played to win a name;
Up starts some tyrant, Earth and Heaven to dare;
The servile million bow;   10
But will the lightning glance aside to spare
The Despot's laurelled brow?

CHORUS

War is mercy, glory, fame,
Waged in Freedom's holy cause;
Freedom, such as Man may claim   15
Under God's restraining laws.
Such is Albion's fame and glory:
Let rescued Europe tell the story.

RECIT. (Accompanied)—Contralto

But, lo, what sudden cloud has darkened all
    The land as with a funeral pall?   20
The Rose of England suffers blight
The flower has drooped, the Isle's delight,
    Flower and bud together fall—
A Nation's hopes lie crushed in Claremont's desolate hall.

AIR—Soprano

Time a chequered mantle wears;—   25
    Earth awakes from wintry sleep;
Again the Tree a blossom bears,—
    Cease, Britannia, cease to weep!
Hark to the peals on this bright May-morn!
They tell that your future Queen is born!   30

SOPRANO SOLO AND CHORUS

A Guardian Angel fluttered
Above the Babe, unseen;
One word he softly uttered—
It named the future Queen:
And a joyful cry through the Island rang,   35
As clear and bold as the trumpet's clang,
    As bland as the reed of peace—
    "Victoria be her name!"
For righteous triumphs are the base
Whereon Britannia rests her peaceful fame.   40

QUARTETT

Time, in his mantle's sunniest fold,
Uplifted on his arms the child;
And, while the fearless Infant smiled,
Her happier destiny foretold:—
    "Infancy, by Wisdom mild,   45
    "Trained to health and artless beauty;
    "Youth, by Pleasure unbeguiled
    "From the lore of lofty duty;
    "Womanhood in pure renown,
    "Seated on her lineal throne: 50
    "Leaves of myrtle in her Crown,

"Fresh with lustre all their own.
"Love, the treasure worth possessing
"More than all the world beside,
"This shall be her choicest blessing,   55
"Oft to royal hearts denied."

RECIT. (Accompanied)—Bass

That eve, the Star of Brunswick shone
   With stedfast ray benign
On Gotha's ducal roof, and on
   The softly flowing Leine;   60
Nor failed to gild the spires of Bonn,
   And glittered on the Rhine.—
Old Camus too on that prophetic night
   Was conscious of the ray;
And his willows whispered in its light,   65
   Not to the Zephyr's sway,
But with a Delphic life, in sight
   Of this auspicious day:

CHORUS

This day, when Granta hails her chosen Lord,
   And proud of her award,   70
   Confiding in the Star serene
Welcomes the Consort of a happy Queen.

AIR—Contralto

Prince, in these Collegiate bowers,
   Where Science, leagued with holier truth,
   Guards the sacred heart of youth,   75
Solemn monitors are ours.
These reverend aisles, these hallowed towers,
   Raised by many a hand august,
Are haunted by majestic Powers,
   The memories of the Wise and Just,   80
   Who, faithful to a pious trust,
Here, in the Founder's Spirit, sought
To mould and stamp the ore of thought
   In that bold form and impress high
That best betoken patriot loyalty.   85

Not in vain those Sages taught.—
True disciples, good as great,
Have pondered here their country's weal,
Weighed the Future by the Past,
Learnt how social frames may last,   90
And how a Land may rule its fate
By constancy inviolate,
Though worlds to their foundations reel,
The sport of factious Hate or godless Zeal.

AIR—Bass

ALBERT, in thy race we cherish   95
A Nation's strength that will not perish
While England's sceptred Line
True to the King of Kings is found;
Like that Wise[1] Ancestor of thine
Who threw the Saxon shield o'er Luther's life,   100
When first, above the yells of bigot strife,
The trumpet of the Living Word
Assumed a voice of deep portentous sound
From gladdened Elbe to startled Tiber heard.

CHORUS

What shield more sublime   105
E'er was blazoned or sung?
And the PRINCE whom we greet
From its Hero is sprung.
Resound, resound the strain
That hails him for our own!   110
Again, again, and yet again;
For the Church, the State, the Throne!—
And that Presence fair and bright,
Ever blest wherever seen,
Who deigns to grace our festal rite,   115
The pride of the Islands, VICTORIA THE QUEEN!

FINIS

---

1   "Frederick the Wise, Elector of Saxony." WW

Notes

Thanksgiving Ode, January 18, 1816

WW printed an Advertisement to the volume titled *Thanksgiving Ode, January 18, 1816. With Other Short Pieces, Chiefly Referring to Recent Public Events* (1816). The *Ode* occupies the prime place in the volume.

ADVERTISEMENT.

It is not to bespeak favour or indulgence, but to guard against misapprehension, that the author presumes to state that the present publication owes its existence to a patriotism, anxious to exert itself in commemorating that course of action, by which Great Britain has, for some time past, distinguished herself above all other countries.

Wholly unworthy of touching upon so momentous a subject would that Poet be, before whose eyes the present distresses under which this kingdom labours, could interpose a veil sufficiently thick to hide, or even to obscure, the splendor of this great moral triumph. If the author has given way to exultation, unchecked by these distresses, it might be sufficient to protect him from a charge of insensibility, should he state his own belief that these sufferings will be transitory. On the wisdom of a very large majority of the British nation, rested that generosity which poured out the treasures of this country for the deliverance of Europe: and in the same national wisdom, presiding in time of peace over an energy not inferior to that which has been displayed in war, *they* confide, who encourage a firm hope, that the cup of our wealth will be gradually replenished. There will, doubtless, be no few ready to indulge in regrets and repinings; and to feed a morbid satisfaction, by aggravating these burthens in imagination, in order that calamity so confidently prophesied, as it has not taken the shape which their sagacity allotted to it, may appear as grievous as possible under another. But the body of the nation will not quarrel with the gain, because it might have been purchased at a less price: and acknowledging in these sufferings, which they feel to have been in a great degree unavoidable, a consecration of their noble efforts, they will vigorously apply themselves to remedy the evil.

Nor is it at the expense of rational patriotism, or in disregard of sound philosophy, that the author hath given vent to feelings tending to encourage a martial spirit in the bosoms of his countrymen, at a time when there is a general outcry against the prevalence of these dispositions. The British army, both by its skill and valour in the field, and by the discipline which has rendered it much less formidable than the armies of other powers, to the inhabitants of the several countries where its operations were carried on, has performed services for humanity too important and too obvious to allow anyone to recommend, that the language of gratitude and admiration be suppressed, or restrained (whatever be the temper of the public mind) through a scrupulous dread, lest the tribute due to the past, should prove an injurious incentive for the future. Every man, deserving the name of Briton, adds his voice to the chorus which extols the exploits of his countrymen, with a consciousness, at times overpowering the effort, that they transcend all praise.—But this particular sentiment, thus irresistibly excited, is not sufficient. The nation would err grievously, if she suffered the abuse which other states have made of military power, to prevent her from perceiving that no people ever was, or can be, independent, free, or secure, much less great, in any sane application of the word, without martial propensities, and an assiduous cultivation of military virtues. Nor let it be overlooked, that the benefits derivable from these sources, are placed within the reach of Great Britain, under conditions peculiarly favourable. The same insular position which, by rendering territorial incorporation impossible, utterly precludes the desire of conquest under the most seductive shape it can assume, enables her to rely, for her defence against foreign foes, chiefly upon a species of armed force from which her own liberties have nothing to fear. Such are the blessed privileges of her situation; and, by permitting, they invite her to give way to the courageous instincts of human nature, and to strengthen and to refine them by culture. But some have more than insinuated, that a design exists to subvert the civil character of the English people by unconstitutional applications and unnecessary increase of military power. The advisers and abettors of such a design, were it possible that it should exist, would be guilty of the most heinous crime, which, upon this planet, can be committed. The author, trusting that this apprehension arises from the delusive influences of an honourable jealousy, hopes that the martial qualities, which he venerates, will be fostered by adhering to those good old usages which experience has sanctioned; and by availing ourselves of new means of indisputable promise; particularly by applying, in its utmost possible extent, that system of tuition, of which the master-spring is a habit of gradually enlightened subordination;— by imparting knowledge, civil, moral and religious, in such measure that the mind, among all classes of the community, may love, admire, and be prepared and accomplished to defend that country, under whose protection its faculties have been unfolded, and its riches acquired; by just dealing towards all orders of the state, so that no members of it being trampled upon, courage may every where continue to rest immoveably upon its ancient English foundation, personal self-respect;—by adequate rewards, and permanent honours, conferred upon the deserving; by encouraging athletic exercises and manly sports among the peasantry of the country; and by especial care to provide and support sufficient Institutions, in which, during a time of peace, a reasonable proportion

an imperial apologia

of the youth of the country may be instructed in military science.—Bent upon instant savings, a member of the House of Commons lately recommended that the Military College should be suppressed as an unnecessary expense; for, said he, "our best officers have been formed in the field." More unwise advice has rarely been given! Admirable officers, indeed, have been formed in the field, but at how deplorable an expense of the lives of their surrounding brethren in arms, a history of the military operations in Spain, and particularly of the sieges, composed with thorough knowledge, and published without reserve, would irresistibly demonstrate.

The author has only to add that he should feel little satisfaction in giving to the world these limited attempts to celebrate the virtues of his country, if he did not encourage a hope that a subject, which it has fallen within his province to treat only in the mass, will by other poets be illustrated in that detail which its importance calls for, and which will allow opportunities to give the merited applause to PERSONS as well as to THINGS.

W. WORDSWORTH.

Rydal Mount,
March 18, 1816.

The River Duddon
VI, Flowers

10–11   "These two lines are in a great measure taken from 'The Beauties of Spring, a Juvenile Poem,' by the Rev. Joseph Sympson, author of 'The Vision of Alfred,' &c. He was a native of Cumberland, and was educated in the vale of Grasmere, and at Hawkshead school: his poems are little known, but they contain passages of splendid description; and the versification of his "Vision of Alfred" is harmonious and animated. The present severe season, with its amusements, reminds me of some lines which I will transcribe as a favourable specimen. In describing the motions of the Sylphs, that constitute the strange machinery of his 'Vision of Alfred,' he uses the following illustrative simile:—

> 'glancing from their plumes
> A changeful light the azure vault illumes.
> Less varying hues beneath the Pole adorn
> The streamy glories of the Boreal morn,
> That wavering to and fro their radiance shed
> On Bothnia's gulph with glassy ice o'erspread,
> Where the lone native, as he homeward glides,
> On polish'd sandals o'er the imprisoned tides,
> And still the balance of his frame preserves,
> Wheel'd on alternate foot in lengthening curves,
> Sees at a glance, above him and below,

Two rival heav'ns with equal splendour glow.
Sphered in the centre of the world he seems,
For all around with soft effulgence gleams;
Stars, moons, and meteors ray oppose to ray,
And solemn midnight pours the blaze of day.'

He was a man of ardent feeling, and his faculties of mind, particularly his memory, were extraordinary. Brief notices of his life ought to find a place in the History of Westmorland." WW

The River Duddon
XVII Return, XVIII Seathwaite Chapel

THE EAGLE requires a large domain for its support; but several pairs, not many years ago, were constantly resident in this country, building their nests in the steeps of Borrowdale, Wastdale, Ennerdale, and on the eastern side of Helvellyn. Often have I heard anglers speak of the grandeur of their appearance, as they hovered over Red Tarn, in one of the coves of this mountain. The bird frequently returns, but is always destroyed. Not long since one visited Rydal Lake, and remained some hours near its banks; the consternation which it occasioned among the different species of fowl, particularly the herons, was expressed by loud screams. The horse also is naturally afraid of the eagle.—There were several Roman stations among these mountains; the most considerable seems to have been in a meadow at the head of Windermere, established, undoubtedly, as a check over the passes of Kirkstone, Dunmail-raise, and of Hardknot and Wrynose. On the margin of Rydal Lake, a coin of Trajan was discovered very lately.—The ROMAN FORT here alluded to, called by the country people "*Hardknot Castle*," is most impressively situated half way down the hill on the right of the road that descends from Hardknot into Eskdale. It has escaped the notice of most antiquarians, and is but slightly mentioned by Lysons.—The DRUIDICAL CIRCLE is about half a mile to the left of the road ascending Stone-side from the vale of Duddon: the country people call it "*Sunken Church*."

The reader who may have been interested in the foregoing Sonnets, (which together may be considered as a Poem,) will not be displeased to find in this place a prose account of the Duddon, extracted from Green's comprehensive *Guide to the Lakes*, lately published. "The road leading from Coniston to Broughton is over high ground, and commands a view of the river Duddon; which at high water is a grand sight, having the beautiful and fertile lands of Lancashire and Cumberland stretching each way from its margin. In this extensive view, the face of nature is displayed in a wonderful variety of hill and dale; wooded grounds and buildings; amongst the latter, Broughton Tower, seated on the crown of a hill, rising elegantly from the valley, is an object of extraordinary interest. Fertility on each side is gradually diminished, and lost in the superior heights of Blackcomb, in Cumberland, and the high lands between

Kirkby and Ulverstone.

"The road from Broughton to Seathwaite is on the banks of the Duddon, and on its Lancashire side it is of various elevations. The river is an amusing companion, one while brawling and tumbling over rocky precipices, until the agitated water becomes again calm by arriving at a smoother and less precipitous bed, but its course is soon again ruffled, and the current thrown into every variety of form which the rocky channel of a river can give to water." (Vide Green's Guide to the Lakes, vol.i. pp. 98–100.)

After all, the traveller would be most gratified who should approach this beautiful Stream, neither at its source, as is done in the Sonnets, nor from its termination; but from Coniston over Walna Scar; first descending into a little circular valley, a collateral compartment of the long winding vale through which flows the Duddon. This recess, towards the close of September, when the after-grass of the meadows is still of a fresh green, with the leaves of many of the trees faded, but perhaps none fallen, is truly enchanting. At a point elevated enough to shew the various objects in the valley, and not so high as to diminish their importance, the stranger will instinctively halt. On the fore-ground, a little below the most favourable station, a rude foot-bridge is thrown over the bed of the noisy brook, foaming by the way-side. Russet and craggy hills, of bold and varied outline, surround the level valley which is besprinkled with grey rocks plumed with birch trees. A few home-steads are interspersed in some places, peeping out from among the rocks like hermitages, whose scite has been chosen for the benefit of sunshine as well as shelter; in other instances, the dwelling-house, barn, and byer, compose together a cruciform structure, which, with its embowering trees and the ivy clothing part of the walls and roof, like a fleece, call to mind the remains of an ancient abbey. Time, in most cases, and nature every where, have given a sanctity to the humble works of man, that are scattered over this peaceful retirement. Hence a harmony of tone and colour, a perfection and consummation of beauty, which would have been marred had aim or purpose interfered with the course of convenience, utility, or necessity. This unvitiated region stands in no need of the veil of twilight to soften or disguise its features. As it glistens in the morning sunshine, it would fill the spectator's heart with gladsomeness. Looking from our chosen station, he would feel an impatience to rove among its pathways, to be greeted by the milk-maid, to wander from house to house, exchanging "good-morrows" as he passed the open doors; but, at evening, when the sun is set, and a pearly light gleams from the western quarter of the sky, with an answering light from the smooth surface of the meadows; when the trees are dusky, but each kind still distinguishable; when the cool air has condensed the blue smoke rising from the cottage-chimneys; when the dark mossy stones seem to sleep in the bed of the foaming Brook; *then*, he would be unwilling to move forward, not less from a reluctance to relinquish what he beholds, than from an apprehension of disturbing, by his approach, the quietness beneath him. Issuing from the plain of this valley, the Brook descends in a rapid torrent, passing by the church-yard of Seathwaite. The traveller is thus conducted at once into the midst of the wild and beautiful scenery which gave occasion to the Sonnets from the 14th to the 20th inclusive. From the point where the Seathwaite Brook joins the Duddon, is a view upwards, into the pass through which the River makes its way into the Plain of Donnerdale. The perpendicular rock on the right bears the ancient British name of THE PEN; the one opposite is called WALLA-BARROW CRAG, a name that occurs in several places to designate rocks of the same character. The *chaotic* aspect of the scene is well marked by the expression of a stranger, who strolled out while dinner was preparing, and, at his return, being asked by his host, "What way he had been wandering?" replied, "As far as it is *finished!* "

The bed of the Duddon is here strewn with large fragments of rock fallen from aloft; which, as Mr. Green truly says, "are happily adapted to the many-shaped water-falls," (or rather water-breaks, for none of them are high,) "displayed in the short space of half a mile." That there is some hazard in frequenting these desolate places, I myself have had proof; for one night an immense mass of rock fell upon the very spot where, with a friend, I had lingered the day before. "The concussion," says Mr. Green, speaking of the event, (for he also, in the practice of his art, on that day sat exposed for a still longer time to the same peril) "was heard, not without alarm, by the neighbouring shepherds." But to return to Seathwaite Church-yard: it contains the following inscription.

"In memory of the Reverend Robert Walker, who died the 25th of June, 1802, in the 93d year of his age, and 67th of his curacy at Seathwaite.

"Also, of Anne his wife, who died the 28th of January, in the 93d year of her age."

In the parish-register of Seathwaite Chapel, is this notice:

"Buried, June 28th, the Rev. Robert Walker. He was curate of Seathwaite sixty-six years. He was a man singular for his temperance, industry, and integrity."

This individual is the Pastor alluded to, in the eighteenth Sonnet, as a worthy compeer of the Country Parson of Chaucer, &c. An abstract of his character is given in the author's poem of THE EXCURSION . . . .

WW followed this note with a "Memoir of the Rev. Robert Walker" in the first and all later publications in which *The River Duddon* appeared. For this material see *Sonnet Series and Itinerary Poems*, pp. 86–98.

The River Duddon, Conclusion

14   "And feel that I am happier than I know."—Milton.
   The allusion to the Greek Poet will be obvious to the classical reader. (1820)

Postscript to The River Duddon

A Poet, whose works are not yet known as they deserve to be, thus enters upon his description of the "Ruins of Rome,"

> "The rising Sun
> Flames on the ruins in the purer air
> Towering aloft;"

and ends thus,

> "The setting Sun displays
> His visible great round, between yon towers,
> As through two shady cliffs."

Mr. Crowe, in his excellent loco-descriptive Poem, "Lewesdon Hill," is still more expeditious, finishing the whole on a May-morning, before breakfast.

> "To-morrow for severer thought, but now
> To breakfast, and keep festival today."

No one believes, or is desired to believe, that these Poems were actually composed within such limits of time, nor was there any reason why a prose statement should acquaint the Reader with the plain fact, to the disturbance of poetic credibility. But, in the present case, I am compelled to mention, that the above series of Sonnets was the growth of many years;—the one which stands the 14th was the first produced; and others were added upon occasional visits to the Stream, or as recollections of the scenes upon its banks awakened a wish to describe them. In this manner I had proceeded insensibly, without perceiving that I as trespassing upon ground pre-occupied, at least as far as intention went, by Mr. Coleridge; who, more than twenty years ago, used to speak of writing a rural Poem, to be entitled "The Brook," of which he has given a sketch in a recent publication. But a particular subject cannot, I think, much interfere with a general one; and I have been further kept from encroaching upon any right Mr. C. may still wish to exercise, by the restriction which the frame of the Sonnet imposed upon me, narrowing unavoidably the range of thought, and precluding, though not without its advantages, many graces to which a freer movement of verse would naturally have led.

May I not venture, then, to hope, that instead of being a hinderance, by anticipation of any part of the subject, these Sonnets may remind Mr. Coleridge of his own more comprehensive design, and induce him to fulfil it?——There is a sympathy in streams, "one calleth to another;" and, I would gladly believe, that "The Brook" will, ere long, murmur in concert with "The Duddon." But, asking pardon for this fancy, I need not scruple to say, that those verses must indeed be ill-fated which can enter upon such pleasant walks of nature, without receiving and giving inspiration. The power of waters over the minds of Poets has been acknowledged from the earliest ages;—through the "Flumina amem sylvasque inglorius" of Virgil, down to the sublime apostrophe to the great rivers of the earth, by Armstrong, and the simple ejaculation of Burns, (chosen, if I recollect right, by Mr. Coleridge, as a motto for his embryo "Brook")

> "The Muse nae Poet ever fand her,
> Till by himsel' he learned to wander,
> Adown some trotting burn's meander,
> AND NA' THINK LANG."

Ecclesiastical Sketches (1822)

WW printed the "Advertisement" that follows in the first edition of the series.

ADVERTISEMENT.

During the month of December, 1820, I accompanied a much-loved and honoured Friend in a walk through different parts of his Estate, with a view to fix upon the Site of a New Church which he intended to erect. It was one of the most beautiful mornings of a mild season,—our feelings were in harmony with the cherishing influences of the scene; and, such being our purpose, we were naturally led to look back upon past events with wonder and gratitude, and on the future with hope. Not long afterwards, some of the Sonnets which will be found towards the close of this Series, were produced as a private memorial of that morning's occupation.

The Catholic Question, which was agitated in Parliament about that time, kept my thoughts in the same course; and it struck me, that certain points in the Ecclesiastical History of our Country might advantageously be presented to view in Verse. Accordingly I took up the subject, and what I now offer to the Reader, was the result.

When this work was far advanced, I was agreeably surprized to find that my Friend, Mr. Southey, was engaged, with similar views, in writing a concise History of the Church *in* England. If our Productions, thus unintentionally coinciding, shall be found to illustrate each other, it will prove a high gratification to me, which I am sure my Friend will participate.

W. WORDSWORTH.

Rydal Mount, January 24th, 1822.

Ecclesiastical Sketches   II.xxix. Eminent Reformers

" 'On foot they went, and took Salisbury in their way, purposely to see the good Bishop, who made Mr. Hooker sit at his own table; which Mr. Hooker boasted of with much joy and gratitude when he saw his mother and friends: and at the Bishop's parting with him, the Bishop gave him good counsel, and his benediction, but forgot to give him money; which when the Bishop had considered, he sent a Servant in all haste to call Richard back to him, and at Richard's return, the Bishop said to him, "Richard, I sent for you back to lend you a horse which hath carried me many a mile, and I thank God with much ease," and presently delivered into his hand a walking-staff with which he professed he had travelled through many parts of Germany; and he said, "Richard, I do not give, but lend you my horse; be sure you be honest, and bring my horse back to me at your return this way to Oxford. And I do now give you ten groats to bear your charges to Exeter; and here is ten groats more, which I charge you to deliver to your mother, and tell her, I send her a Bishop's benediction with it, and beg the continuance of her prayers for me. And if you bring my horse back to me, I will give you ten groats more to carry you on foot to the college; and so God bless you, good Richard.' *See Walton's Life of Richard Hooker.*" WW

II.xxxv. Laud

"In this age a word cannot be said in praise of Laud, or even in compassion for his fate, without incurring a charge of bigotry; but, fearless of such imputation, I concur with Hume, 'that it is sufficient for his vindication to observe that his errors were the most excusable of all those which prevailed during that zealous period.' A key to the right understanding of those parts of his conduct that brought the most odium upon him in his own time, may be found in the following passage of his speech before the Bar of the House of Peers. 'Ever since I came in place, I have laboured nothing more, than that the external publick worship of God, so much slighted in divers parts of this kingdom, might be preserved, and that with as much decency and uniformity as might be. For I evidently saw, that the publick neglect of God's service in the outward face of it, and the nasty lying of many places dedicated to that service, had almost cast a damp upon the true and inward worship of God, which, while we live in the body, needs external helps, and all little enough to keep it in any vigour.'" WW

III.xi. Pastoral Character

"Among the benefits arising, as Mr. Coleridge has well observed, from a Church Establishment of endowments corresponding with the wealth of the Country to which it belongs, may be reckoned, as eminently important, the examples of civility and refinement which the Clergy, stationed at intervals, afford to the whole people. The established Clergy in many parts of England have long been, as they continue to be, the principal bulwark against barbarism, and the link which unites the sequestered Peasantry with the intellectual advancement of the age. Nor is it below the dignity of the subject to observe that their Taste, as acting upon rural Residences and scenery, often furnishes models which Country Gentlemen, who are more at liberty to follow the caprices of Fashion, might profit by. The precincts of an old residence must be treated by Ecclesiastics with respect, both from prudence and necessity. I remember being much pleased, some years ago, at Rose Castle, the rural Seat of the See of Carlisle, with a style of Garden and Architecture, which, if the Place had belonged to a wealthy Layman, would no doubt have been swept away. A Parsonage-house generally stands not far from the Church; this proximity imposes favourable restraints, and sometimes suggests an affecting union of the accommodations and elegancies of life with the outward signs of piety and mortality. With pleasure I recall to mind a happy instance of this in the Residence of an old and much-valued Friend in Oxfordshire. The House and Church stand parallel to each other, at a small distance; a circular lawn, or rather grass-plot, spreads between them; shrubs and trees curve from each side of the Dwelling, veiling, but not hiding the Church. From the front of this Dwelling, no part of the Burial-ground is seen; but, as you wind by the side of the Shrubs towards the Steeple end of the Church, the eye catches a single, small, low, monumental head-stone, moss-grown, sinking into, and gently inclining towards, the earth. Advance, and the Church-yard, populous and gay with glittering Tombstones, opens upon the view. This humble, and beautiful Parsonage called forth a tribute which will not be out of its place here.

> Where holy ground begins—unhallowed ends,
> Is marked by no distinguishable line;
> The turf unites—the pathways intertwine;
> And, wheresoe'er the stealing footstep tends,
> Garden, and that Domain where Kindred, Friends,
> And Neighbours rest together, here confound
> Their several features—mingled like the sound
> Of many waters, or as evening blends
> With shady night. Soft airs, from shrub and flower,
> Waft fragrant greetings to each silent grave;
> Meanwhile between those Poplars, as they wave
> Their lofty summits, comes and goes a sky
> Bright as the glimpses of Eternity,
> To Saints accorded in their mortal hour." WW

Latimer and Ridley

" 'M. Latimer very quietly suffered his keeper to pull off his hose, and his other aray, which to looke unto was very simple: and being stripped into his shrowd, he seemed as comely a person to them that were present, as one should lightly see: and whereas in his clothes hee appeared a withered and crooked sillie (weak) olde man, he now stood bolt upright, as comely a father as one might lightly behold. * * * * Then they brought a faggotte, kindled with fire, and laid the same downe at doctor Ridley's feete. To whome M. Latimer spake in this manner, 'Bee of good comfort, master Ridley, and play the man: wee shall this day light such a candle by God's grace in England, as I trust shall never bee put out.'—Fox's Acts, &c.

Similar alterations in the outward figure and deportment of persons brought to like trial were not uncommon. See note to the above passage in Dr. Wordsworth's Ecclesiastical Biography, for an example in an humble Welsh fisherman." WW quotes from John Foxe, *Acts and Monuments* (2 vols.; London 1610)

Bruges ("Bruges I saw attired with golden light")

"This is not the first poetical tribute which in our times has been paid to this beautiful City. Mr. [Robert] Southey, in the 'Poet's Pilgrimage,' speaks of it in lines which I cannot deny myself the pleasure of connecting with my own.

> 'Time hath not wronged her, nor hath Ruin sought
> Rudely her splendid Structures to destroy,
> Save in those recent days, with evil fraught,
> When Mutability, in drunken joy
> Triumphant, and from all restraint released,
> Let loose her fierce and many-headed beast.

> "But for the scars in that unhappy rage
> Inflicted, firm she stands and undecayed;
> Like our first Sires, a beautiful old age
> Is hers in venerable years arrayed;
> And yet, to her, benignant stars may bring,
> What fate denies to man,—a second spring.

> "When I may read of tilts in days of old,
> And tourneys graced by Chieftains of renown,
> Fair dames, grave citizens, and warriors bold,
> If fancy would pourtray some stately town,
> Which for such pomp fit theatre should be,
> Fair Bruges, I shall then remember thee.'" WW

The Church of San Salvador, seen from the Lake of Lugano

"This Church was almost destroyed by lightning a few years ago, but the Altar and the Image of the Patron Saint were untouched. The Mount, upon the summit of which the Church is built, stands in the midst of the intricacies of the Lake of Lugano; and is, from a hundred points of view, its principal ornament, rising to the height of 2000 feet, and, on one side, nearly perpendicular. The ascent is toilsome; but the Traveller who performs it will be amply rewarded.—Splendid fertility, rich woods and dazzling waters, seclusion and confinement of view contrasted with sea-like extent of plain fading into the sky; and this again, in an opposite quarter, with an horizon of the loftiest and boldest Alps—unite in composing a prospect more diversified by magnificence, beauty, and sublimity, than perhaps any other point in Europe, of so inconsiderable an elevation, commands." WW

The Eclipse of the Sun, 1820

"The Statues ranged round the Spire and along the roof of the Cathedral of Milan, have been found fault with by Persons whose exclusive taste is unfortunate for themselves. It is true that the same expense and labour judiciously directed to purposes more strictly architectural, might have much heightened the general effect of the building; for, seen from the ground, the Statues appear diminutive. But the *coup d'œil*, from the best point of view, which is half way up the Spire, must strike an unprejudiced Person with admiration; and surely the selection and arrangement of the Figures is exquisitely fitted to support the religion of the Country in the imaginations and feelings of the Spectator. It was with great pleasure that I saw, during the two ascents which we made, several Children, of different ages, tripping up and down the slender spire, and pausing to look around them, with feelings much more animated than could have been derived from these, or the finest works of art, if placed within easy reach.—Remember also that you have the Alps on one side, and on the other the Apennines, with the Plain of Lombardy between!" WW

Desultory Stanzas upon Receiving the Preceding Sheets from the Press

"The Bridges of Lucerne are roofed, and open at the sides, so that the passenger has, at the same time, the benefit of shade, and a view of the magnificent Country. The Pictures are attached to the rafters; those from Scripture History on the Cathedral-bridge, amount, according to my notes. . . . Subjects from the Old Testament face the Passenger as he goes towards the Cathedral, and those from the New as he returns. The pictures on these Bridges, as well as those in most other parts of Switzerland, are not to be spoken of as works of art; but they are instruments admirably answering the purpose for which they were designed.

The following stanzas were suggested by the "TOWER OF TELL," at ALTORF, on the outside walls of which the chief exploits of the Hero are painted: it is said to stand upon the very ground where grew the Lime Tree against which his Son was placed when the Father's archery was put to proof under the circumstances so famous in Swiss History.

[Here follows *Effusion in Presence of the Painted Tower of Tell, at Altorf* (see this poem included above).]

In the 3d of the Desultory Stanzas, I am indebted to M. Ramond, who has written with genuine feeling on these subjects." WW's note refers to Ramond de Charbonnières's *Observations* (see the note to *Aix-la-Chapelle* on p. 778).

XI. Highland Hut

WW's note on this sonnet quotes extensively from his sister Dorothy's journal:

"This sonnet describes the *exterior* of a Highland hut, as often seen under morning or evening sunshine. The reader may not be displeased with the following extract from the journal of a Lady, my fellow-traveller in Scotland, in the autumn of 1803, which accurately describes, under particular circumstances, the beautiful appearance of the *interior* of one of these rude habitations.

'On our return from the Trossachs the evening began to darken, and it rained so heavily that we were completely wet before we had come two miles, and it was dark when we landed with our boatman, at his hut upon the banks of Loch Katrine. I was faint from cold: the good woman had provided, according to her promise, a better fire than we had found in the morning; and, indeed, when I sat down in the chimney corner of her smoky biggin, I thought I had never felt more comfortable in my life: a pan of coffee was boiling for us, and, having put our clothes in the way of drying, we all sat down thankful for a shelter. We could not prevail upon our boatman, the master of the house, to draw near the fire, though he was cold and wet, or to suffer his wife to get him dry clothes till she had served us, which she did most willingly, though not very expeditiously.

'A Cumberland man of the same rank would not have had such a notion of what was fit and right in his own house, or, if he had, one would have accused him of servility; but in the Highlander it only seemed like politeness (however erroneous and painful to us), naturally growing out of the dependence of the inferiors of the clan upon their laird: he did not, however, refuse to let his wife bring out the whisky bottle for his refreshment, at our request. "She keeps a dram," as the phrase is: indeed, I believe there is scarcely a lonely house by the wayside, in Scotland, where travellers may not be accommodated with a dram. We asked for sugar, butter, barley-bread, and milk; and, with a smile and a stare more of kindness than wonder, she replied, "Ye'll get that," bringing each article separately. We caroused our cups of coffee, laughing like children at the strange atmosphere in which we were: the smoke came in gusts, and spread along the walls; and above our heads in the chimney (where the hens were roosting) like clouds in the sky. We laughed and laughed again, in spite of the smarting of our eyes, yet had a quieter pleasure in observing the beauty of the beams and rafters gleaming between the clouds of smoke: they had been crusted over, and varnished by many winters, till, where the firelight fell upon them, they had become as glossy as black rocks, on a sunny day, cased in ice. When we had eaten our supper we sat about half an hour, and I think I never felt so deeply the blessing of a hospitable welcome and a warm fire. The man of the house repeated from time to time that we should often tell of this night when we got to our homes, and interposed praises of his own lake, which he had more than once, when we were returning in the boat, ventured to say was "bonnier than Loch Lomond." Our companion from the Trossachs, who, it appeared, was an Edinburgh drawing master going, during the vacation, on a pedestrian tour to John o'Groat's house, was to sleep in the barn with my fellow-travellers, where the man said he had plenty of dry hay. I do not believe that the hay of the Highlands is every very dry, but this year it had a better chance than usual: wet or dry, however, the next morning they said they had slept comfortably. When I went to bed, the mistress, desiring me to "*go ben*," attended me with a candle, and assured me that the bed was dry, though not "sic as I had been used to." It was of chaff; there were two others in the room, a cupboard and two chests, upon one of which stood milk in wooden vessels, covered over. The walls of the whole house were of stone unplastered: it consisted of three apartments, the cowhouse at one end, the kitchen or house in the middle, and the spence at the other end; the rooms were divided, not up to the rigging, but only to the beginning of the roof, so that there was a free passage for light and smoke from one end of the house to the other. I went to bed some time before the rest of the family: the door was shut between us, and they had a bright fire, which I could not see, but the light it sent up among the varnished rafters and beams, which crossed each other in almost as intricate and fantastic a manner as I have seen the under boughs of a large beech tree withered by the depth of shade above, produced the most beautiful effect that can be conceived. It was like what I should suppose an underground cave or temple to be, with a dripping or moist roof, and the moonlight entering in upon it by some means or other; and yet the colours were more like those of melted gems. I lay looking up till the light of the fire faded away, and the man and his wife and child had crept into their bed at the other end of the room: I did not sleep much, but passed a comfortable night; for my bed, though hard, was warm and clean: the unusualness of my situation prevented me from sleeping. I could hear the waves beat against the shore of the lake; a little rill close to the door made a much louder noise, and, when I sat up in my bed, I could see the lake through an open window-place at the bed's head. Add to this, it rained all night. I was less occupied by remembrance of the Trossachs, beautiful as they were, than the vision of the Highland hut, which I could not get out of my head; I thought of the Fairy-land of Spenser, and what I had read in romance at other times, and then what a feast it would be for a London Pantomine-maker could he but transplant it to Drury Lane, with all its beautiful colours!'—*MS.*" WW

XVII. Bothwell Castle

"The following is from the same MS., and give an account of the visit to Bothwell Castle here alluded to:—

'It was exceedingly delightful to enter thus unexpectedly upon such a beautiful region. The castle stands nobly, overlooking the Clyde. When we came up to it, I was hurt to see that flower-borders had taken place of the natural over-growings of the ruin, the scattered stones and wild plants. It is a large and grand pile of red freestone, harmonising perfectly with the rocks of the river, from which, no doubt, it has been hewn. When I was a little accustomed to the unnaturalness of a modern garden, I could not help admiring the excessive beauty and luxuriance of some of the plants, particularly the purple-flowered clematis, and a broad-leafed creeping plant without flowers, which scrambled up the castle wall, along with the ivy, and spread its vine-like branches so lavishly that it seemed to be in its natural situation, and one could not help thinking that, though not self-planted among the ruins of this country, it must somewhere have its native abode in such places. If Bothwell Castle had not been close to the Douglas mansion, we should have been disgusted with the possessor's miserable conception of *adorning* such a venerable ruin; but it is so very near to the house, that of necessity the pleasure-grounds must have extended beyond it, and perhaps the neatness of a shaven lawn and the complete desolation natural to a ruin might have made an unpleasing contrast; and, besides being within the precincts of the pleasure-grounds, and so very near to the dwelling of a noble family, it has forfeited, in some degree, its independent majesty, and becomes a tributary to the mansion: its solitude being interrupted, it has no longer the command over the mind in sending it back into past times, or excluding the ordinary feelings which we bear about us in daily life. We had then only to regret that the castle and the house were so near to each other; and it was impossible *not* to regret it; for the ruin presides in state over the river, far from city or town, as if it might have a peculiar privilege to preserve its memorials of past ages and maintain its own character for centuries to come. We sat upon a bench under the high trees, and had beautiful views of the different reaches of the river, above and below. On the opposite bank, which is finely wooded with elms and other trees, are the remains of a priory built upon a rock; and rock and ruin are so blended, that it is impossible to separate the one from the other. Nothing can be more beautiful than the little remnant of this holy place: elm trees (for we were near enough to distinguish them by their branches) grow out of the walls, and overshadow a small, but very elegant window. It can scarcely be conceived what a grace the castle and priory impart to each other; and the river Clyde flows on smooth and unruffled below, seeming to my thoughts more in harmony with the sober and stately images of former times, than if it had roared over a rocky channel forcing its sound upon the ear. It blended gently with the warbling of the smaller birds, and the chattering of the larger ones, that had made their nests in the ruins. In this fortress the chief of the English nobility were confined after the battle of Bannockburn. If a man is to be a prisoner, he scarcely could have a more pleasant place to solace his captivity; but I thought that, for close confinement, I should prefer the banks of a lake, or the seaside. The greatest charm of a brook or river is in the liberty to pursue it through its windings; you can then take it in whatever mood you like; silent or noisy, sportive or quiet. The beauties of a brook or river must be sought, and the pleasure is in going in search of them; those of a lake, or of the sea, come to you of themselves. These rude warriors cared little, perhaps, about either; and yet, if one may judge from the writings of Chaucer, and from the old romances, more interesting passions were connected with natural objects in the days of chivalry than now; though going in search of scenery, as it is called, had not then been thought of. I had previously heard nothing of Bothwell Castle, at least nothing that I remembered; therefore, perhaps, my pleasure was greater, compared with what I received elsewhere, than others might feel.'—*MS. Journal.*" WW

XXI. Hart's-horn Tree, near Penrith

" 'In the time of the first Robert de Clifford, in the year 1333 or 1334, Edward Baliol king of Scotland came into Westmorland, and stayed some time with the said Robert at his castles of Appleby, Brougham, and Pendragon. And during that time they ran a stag by a single greyhound out of Whinfell Park to Redkirk, in Scotland, and back again to this place; where, being both spent, the stag leaped over the pales, but died on the other side; and the greyhound, attempting to leap, fell, and died on the contrary side. In memory of this fact the stag's horns were nailed upon a tree just by, and (the dog being named Hercules) this rhyme was made upon them:

"Hercules kill'd Hart a greese

And Hart a greese kill'd Hercules."

The tree to this day bears the name of Hart's-horn Tree. The horns in process of time were almost grown over by the growth of the tree, and another pair was put up in their place.'—*Nicholson and Burns's History of Westmorland and Cumberland.*

The tree has now disappeared, but the author of these poems well remembers its imposing appearance as it stood, in a decayed state, by the side of the high road leading from Penrith to Appleby. This whole neighbourhood abounds in interesting traditions and vestiges of antiquity, viz., Julian's Bower; Brougham and Penrith Castles; Penrith Beacon, and the curious remains in Penrith church-yard; Arthur's Round Table; the excavation, called the Giant's Cave, on the banks of the Eamont; Long Meg and her Daughters, near Eden, &c. &c." WW

IV. To the River Greta

"Many years ago, when the author was at Greta Bridge, in Yorkshire, the hostess of the inn, proud of her skill in etymology, said, that 'the name of the river was taken from the *bridge*, the form of which, as every one must notice, exactly resembled a great A.' But Dr. Whitaker has derived it from the word of common occurrence in the north of England, "*to greet*;" signifying to lament aloud, mostly with weeping: a conjecture rendered more probable from the stony and rocky channel of both the Cumberland and Yorkshire rivers. The Cumberland Greta, though it does not, among the country people, take up *that* name till within three miles of its disappearance in the river Derwent, may be considered as having its source in the mountain cove of Wythburn, and flowing through Thirlmere, the beautiful features of which lake are known only to those who, travelling between Grasmere and Keswick, have quitted the main road in the vale of Wythburn, and, crossing over to the opposite side of the lake, have proceeded with it on the right hand.

The channel of the Greta, immediately above Keswick, has, for the purposes of building, been in a great measure cleared of the immense stones which, by their concussion in high floods, produced the loud and awful noises described in the sonnet.

'The scenery upon this river,' says Mr. Southey in his Colloquies, 'where it passes under the woody side of Latrigg, is of the finest and most rememberable kind:—

—ambiguo lapsu refluitque fluitque,
Occurrensque sibi venturas aspicit undas.'" WW.

The two lines in Latin are by Ovid, in *Metamorphoses*, VIII, ll. 163, 164, where he describes the river Meander ("It flows and flows back in an uncertain course, and confronting itself sees the approach of its own waves").

Stanzas Suggested in a Steam-boat off St. Bees' Heads, on the Coast of Cumberland

75   "The author is aware that he is here treading upon tender ground; but to the intelligent reader he feels that no apology is due. The prayers of survivors, during passionate grief for the recent loss of relatives and friends, as the object of those prayers could no longer be the suffering body of the dying, would naturally be ejaculated for the souls of the departed; the barriers between the two worlds dissolving before the power of love and faith. The ministers of religion, from their habitual attendance upon sick-beds, would be daily witnesses of these benign results; and hence would be strongly tempted to aim at giving to them permanence, by embodying them in rites and ceremonies, recurring at stated periods. All this, as it was in course of nature, so was it blameless, and even praiseworthy; but no reflecting person can view without sorrow the abuses which rose out of thus formalizing sublime instincts, and disinterested movements of passion, and perverting them into means of gratifying the ambition and rapacity of the priesthood. But, while we deplore and are indignant at these abuses, it would be a great mistake if we imputed the origin of the offices to prospective selfishness on the part of the monks and clergy: *they* were at first sincere in their sympathy, and in their degree dupes rather of their own creed, than artful and designing men. Charity is, upon the whole, the safest guide that we can take in judging our fellow-men, whether of past ages, or of the present time." WW

Musings near Aquapendente

"It would be ungenerous not to advert to the religious movement that, since the composition of these verses in 1837, has made itself felt, more or less strongly, throughout the English Church;—a movement that takes, for its first principle, a devout deference to the voice of Christian antiquity. It is not my office to pass judgment on questions of theological detail; but my own repugnance to the spirit and system of Romanism has been so repeatedly and, I trust, feelingly expressed, that I shall not be suspected of a leaning that way, if I do not join in the grave charge, thrown out, perhaps in the heat of controversy, against the learned and pious men to whose labours I allude. I speak apart from controversy; but, with strong faith in the moral temper which would elevate the present by doing reverence to the past, I would draw cheerful auguries for the English Church from this movement, as likely to restore among us a tone of piety more earnest and real, than that produced by the mere formalities of the understanding, refusing, in a degree, which I cannot but lament, that its own temper and judgment shall be controlled by those of antiquity." WW

XIII. At the Convent of Camaldoli

"This famous sanctuary was the original establishment of Saint Romualdo, (or Rumwald, as our ancestors saxonised the name) in the 11th century, the ground (campo) being given by a Count Maldo. The Camaldolensi, however, have spread wide as a branch of Benedictines, and may therefore be classed among the *gentlemen* of the monastic orders. The society comprehends two orders, monks and hermits; symbolised by their arms, two doves drinking out of the same cup. The monastery in which the monks here reside, is beautifully situated, but a large unattractive edifice, not unlike a factory. The hermitage is placed in a loftier and wilder region of the forest. It comprehends between 20 and 30 distinct residences, each including for its single hermit an inclosed piece of ground and three very small apartments. There are days of indulgence when the hermit may quit his cell, and when old age arrives, he descends from the mountain and takes his abode among the monks.

My companion had in the year 1831, fallen in with the monk, the subject of these two Sonnets, who showed him his abode among the hermits. It is from him that I received these particulars. He was then about 40 years of age, but his appearance was that of an older man. He had been a painter by profession, but on taking orders changed his name from Santi to Raffaello, perhaps with an unconscious reference as well to the great Sanzio d'Urbino as to the archangel. He assured my friend that he had been 13 years in the hermitage and had never known melancholy or ennui. In the little recess for study and prayer, there was a small collection of books. "I read only," said he, "books of asceticism and mystical theology." On being asked the names of the most famous Italian mystics, he enumerated *Scaramelli, San Giovanni della Croce, San Dionysia Aeropagitica*, and with peculiar emphasis Ricardo di San Vittori. The works of *Saint Theresa* are among ascetics in high repute, but she was a Spaniard. These names may interest some of my readers.

We heard that Raffaello was then living in the convent; my friend sought in vain to renew his acquaintance with him. It was probably a day of seclusion. The reader will perceive that these sonnets were supposed to be written when he was a young man." WW

At Vallombrosa

The name of Milton is pleasingly connected with Vallombrosa in many ways. The pride with which the Monk, without any previous question from me, pointed out his residence, I shall not readily forget. It may be proper here to defend the Poet from a charge which has been brought against him, in respect to the passage in Paradise Lost, where this place is mentioned. It is said, that he has erred in speaking of the trees there being deciduous, whereas they are, in fact, pines. The fault-finders are themselves mistaken; the natural woods of the region of Vallombrosa are deciduous, and spread to a great extent; those near the convent are, indeed, mostly pines; but they are avenues of trees planted within a few steps of each other, and thus composing large tracts of wood; plots of which are periodically cut down. The appearance of those narrow avenues, upon steep slopes open to the sky, on account of the height which the trees attain by being forced to grow upwards, is often very impressive. My guide, a boy of about fourteen years old, pointed this out to me in several places.

The sun has long been set *and* Thron'd in the Sun's descending car
[*Note placed below the title of the first poem.*]

"The *former* of the two following Pieces appeared, many years ago, among the Author's poems, from which, in subsequent editions, it was excluded. It is here reprinted, at the request of a friend who was present when the lines were thrown off as an impromptu.

For printing the *latter*, some reason should be given, as not a word of it is original: it is simply a fine stanza of Akenside, connected with a still finer from Beattie, by a couplet of Thomson. This practice, in which the author sometimes indulges, of linking together, in his own mind, favourite passages from different authors, seems in itself unobjectionable: but, as the *publishing* such compilations might lead to confusion in literature, he should deem himself inexcusable in giving this specimen, were it not from a hope that it might open to others a harmless source of private gratification." WW

Index of titles, first lines and series titles (Volume 3)

The complete index to all poems in the 3 Volumes appears in
Volume 3 of the Electronic Version
which is available to Librarians from MyiLibrary, EBSCO and Ebrary
and to individual purchasers from

http://www.humanities-ebooks.co.uk

*The complete index is also available in a free Addendum
to this edition which can be downloaded from*

http://www.humanities-ebooks.co.uk/free-ebooks.html

Notable pieces

p 11 ~~first~~ 2 sonnets

p 34 Conclusion 18th sonnet

pp 48-52 death of their two children

pp 127-130 Hermit's Cell - strangely
                    genuine & sincere

p 132 Pilgrim's Dream has life & wit

p 207 Identification of Nature with God

p 208 tribute to his mother, heartfelt

p 323 175-335 'spots of time' in their genesis

p 352 'Stepping Stones' 2 sonnets memorable
                                          & witty

p 359 Sheep Dipping

p 399 Powerful sonnet on Jungfrau & Rhine,
          the indomitable forces they display

p 406 'Catechising' and tribute to his mother

p 411 King's College Chapel sonnet

p 436 The evening song of workers homeward
                          bound entertains,
                          simple & affecting

p 493 Sonnet 12 comes off ...